Ethical Issues in Business
Inquiries, Cases, and Readings

Peg Tittle

Ethical Issues in Business
Inquiries, Cases, and Readings

Peg Tittle

broadview press

Canadian Cataloguing in Publication Data

Main entry under title:
    Ethical issues in business: inquiries, cases, and readings

Includes bibliographical references.
ISBN 1-55111-257-4
1. Business ethics – Canada. 2. Business ethics – Canada – case studies.
I. Title.

HF5387.T57 2000   174'.4'0971   C00-930319-7

Broadview Press Ltd. is an independent, international publishing house, incorporated in 1985.

North America:
P.O. Box 1243, Peterborough, Ontario, Canada K9H 7H5
3576 California Road, Orchard Park, NY, USA 14127
TEL: (705) 743-8990; FAX: (705) 743-8353; E-MAIL: customerservice@broadviewpress.com

United Kingdom:
Turpin Distribution Services Ltd., Blackhorse Rd., Letchworth, Hertfordshire SG6 3HN
TEL: (1462) 672555; FAX (1462) 480947; E-MAIL: turpin@rsc.org

Australia:
St. Clair Press, P.O. Box 287, Rozelle, NSW 2039
TEL: (02) 818 1942; FAX: (02) 418 1923

www.broadviewpress.com

Broadview Press gratefully acknowledges the support of the Book Publishing Development Program, Ministry of Canadian Heritage, Government of Canada.

PRINTED IN CANADA

Contents

Section III - Ethical Issues in Business

Section IV - Institutionalizing Ethics

Thanks

Thanks to my students, past, present, and future - you are the reason for this book.

Thanks to Chris Sarlo, professor of economics at Nipissing University, for his critical commentary on all of the 'original' material in this book and for his work on the case studies, most of which he prepared.

Thanks to Chris Gray, professor of philosophy at Concordia University, for preparing Appendix II.

Thanks to the contributors, most of whom offered their papers for publication free of charge.

Thanks to Nipissing University who provided some assistance: the Faculty and Administrative Support Services staff scanned most of the papers herein, and two research assistants, Maria Chiovetti and John Philippe, did some source-finding while on a few days' loan from Sarlo.

Thanks to John Pliniussen and Wayne Borody for hiring me to teach, respectively, business ethics and critical thinking: both teaching experiences have influenced the writing of this book.

Thanks to Don LePan and Broadview Press for the invitation to publish.

About the Author

Peg Tittle has spent most of her life reading, writing, thinking, composing, choreographing, and teaching. She now teaches applied ethics at Nipissing University; her current interests are stand-up comedy and Riverdance. If you told her twenty years ago that she'd write a philosophy book for business students, she would have said—well, never mind what she would have said. (Special thanks, by the way, to the author's brother who, as a business student, mocked her philosophy studies.) She lives with a dog, chessie, in a cabin on a lake in a forest. Both believe cold pizza to be the perfect breakfast; they also believe that fluorescent green tennis balls should be non-taxable.

Please send suggestions for improvement and papers for consideration, for future editions, to the author/editor at Nipissing University, 100 College Drive, North Bay, Ontario, Canada P1B 8L7 or <ptittle@faculty.unipissing.ca>. Students are included in both parts of this invitation.

Note to the Reader

I happened to read a comment expressing the view that most textbooks seem to be written for other professors rather than for students, and I suddenly realized why I had been procrastinating over the actual writing of this book. The thing is this: I love being in the classroom – I really enjoy talking to students, discussing stuff with them, getting into arguments with them. I can do the other – I can research and write a respectable academic essay that my peers, other professors, will consider publishable (or not) – but to be honest, I don't really like speaking in that rather formal, academic voice. So I decided to use my more informal, classroom voice for this book. Because this is, after all, a book *for students*, not a book for other professors.

But not *just* for students: my hope is that anyone in business who is new to philosophy will find this an exciting book, and that those in philosophy who don't know much about business will find something of value here as well.

A few bits of advice: do go through Section I all at once and do this before you do anything else; don't go through Section II all at once; the chapters in Section III are meant to be done more or less in the order in which they're presented (there's some carefully planned, pedagogically minded progression there).

At one point, I thought of including for each chapter an essay from an academic journal and an article from a business magazine (rather than, as it usually turned out, two essays from academic journals). However, the business magazine articles didn't seem rigorous enough: they seemed to start with assumptions that were not defended (but then that's why we call them assumptions, isn't it?), let alone identified. And they seemed more prescriptive ("do this!") than analytic ("what if we do this?"). Yet, there's no point in theory if it can't be applied, and we as teachers are wrong to assume that our students can, and will, automatically apply the theories we teach. The solution really is a second course, a second book, building on the foundations of the first. Section IV is intended to give you a glimpse of what that next course/book would be like: ethics programs, codes, policies and procedures, best practices, audits, and so on.

But I urge you to check out the business magazines for ethics articles (the *Annual Editions* put out by Dushkin Publishing are full of them – see <http://www.dushkin.com>). See if you can identify the assumptions, then assess them, and figure out if the prescription (the code, the practice, or whatever, being advocated in the article) is soundly based on theory. If it is, great, follow that prescription! If it's not, figure out if the problem is with the foundation (so you can revise or reject it) or with what's built upon it (so you can revise or reject that).

A few bits of caution: don't expect a singular view to be presented here – my intent is to make you aware of the possibilities, to get you to ask the right questions rather than to come up with the (single) right answer. Having said that, don't get discouraged and give up because of all the ifs, ands, and buts – this is complicated stuff, and getting to *better* answers (yes, some answers are better than others) is quite an achievement.

Section I

Introduction to Ethics in Business

INTRODUCTION TO ETHICS IN BUSINESS

Making Ethical Decisions

Suppose someone asks you to help them with their homework? Do you? What about helping with an assignment? What about an exam? Or a résumé? Okay now, how did you decide? That is — and this is **the** question of this whole book — *how do you decide whether something is right or wrong?*

Consider these principles. Circle or check the ones that apply to you. Go ahead, this book is interactive!

1. If it feels right, I do it.
2. I follow my conscience.
3. I do what (my) God says is right.
4. If it's illegal, I don't do it.
5. If it's good for me, I do it.
6. If it's what I'd want others to do, I'd do it.
7. If someone, anyone, will get hurt, I don't do it.
8. If it's unfair, I don't do it.
9. It depends on the circumstances.
10. It depends on the consequences.
11. I follow a set of absolute values such as honesty, justice, and goodness.
12. I toss a coin.
13. I don't know, I just do it, okay?

Now consider the following comments/questions. (Don't put that pen down yet — get ready to talk back to me here!)

1. *If you follow your feelings...* so if in anger you feel like hitting someone, it's okay, it's morally acceptable, to do so?

2. *If you follow your conscience...* what exactly is your conscience? Is it just a collection of moral habits, "the way you were raised"? Is it just a more respectable, sort of religious, name for feelings? Is it something you're born with? (Is everyone born with one? Is it the same for everyone?) Can your conscience ever be wrong? How would you know?

3. *If you do what (your) God says is right...* why your god and not someone else's? And how do you know that God says it's right — does he talk to you? If you follow the Bible, are you sure that what is in the Bible is God's word — every single (translated) word? Why are you so sure? What about contradictions ("Do not kill" — but "Hey, Abraham...")? What about omissions? (I can't find a commandment about patenting DNA.)

4. *If you do only what's legal...* so when the law changes, what was right yesterday is wrong today? Are there no bad laws? Does the law cover everything? (In Canada, it's not illegal to lie to your friend — so is it okay, is it right, to do so?) And anyway, why should you do what's legal, why is it right to obey the law?

5. *If you do whatever's good for you...* no matter what the consequences are for everyone else?

Okay, so where do you draw the line — with certain consequences and/or certain someones? Why there?

6. *If you do to others what you'd like them to do to you...* what if you like pain? (What if you like opera?)

7. *If you don't do something that will hurt someone...* no exceptions? What if they consented to that hurt? (Consider surgery and sports.) What if hurting one person will save a hundred? And by the way, how exactly do you define "hurt"?

8. *If you don't do something that's unfair...* how do you define "fair"? If fair is getting what one deserves, well, how do you determine what someone deserves — according to what they've earned? according to what they need?

9. *If it depends on the circumstances...* exactly what aspects of the circumstances are relevant to whether or not the something is the right thing to do? Is time of day relevant? Is who's involved relevant?

10. *If it depends on the consequences...* so the ends justify the means? Always? And what if you aren't sure about the consequences?

11. *If you follow a set of absolutes...* how did you come up with those absolutes? Why those and not others? And what do you do when they conflict (suppose you can't be both loyal and honest) — which takes priority — and why?

12. *If you toss a coin...* good luck!

13. *If you just do it...* kinda like Nike?

My guess is (my hope is) that you found a lot of these questions not so easy to answer. And if your somewhat hostile response was "Look, everyone can sit here and ask 'what if' questions — I can ask what if to everything, but what's the point?" well, you wouldn't be the first student to respond that way. The point, the reason, for these "what if" questions, is that they help us uncover (or construct, as the case may be) the

foundations of our thought; they help us make distinctions — very important distinctions.

The thing is this: ethically speaking, most of us are quite undeveloped; we haven't updated our childhood. Most of our moral training stopped when we were somewhere around thirteen or fourteen years of age, but as adults, we have to deal with a lot of ethical issues that our childhood morality simply can't handle very well. It doesn't have much in the way of conceptual complexity and subtlety; it doesn't make the fine distinctions that are necessary; it's not as precise as it needs to be. For example, "Do what your parents tell you" is fine — until you realize that parents make mistakes, too. "Don't steal" is adequate as long as you're not starving. Even "Do unto others as you would have them do unto you" must eventually bite the dust: *you* may say "tell me the truth," but some people really may prefer not to know.

Just as someone who is educated about forestry can tell the difference between a sick, five-year-old white pine and a healthy, ten-year-old red pine (to me, they're all trees), and someone educated about colour can distinguish between magenta, scarlet, and burgundy (to you, they might all be red), so someone educated about ethics will be able to distinguish between justified discrimination and unjustified discrimination or between morally acceptable profit and morally unacceptable profit. The educated person can make fine distinctions and use those distinctions to make decisions. To get to that point, we ask "what if" questions — relentlessly. There are several other questions we're relentless about asking as well, and I'll get to them later in this section, but first we have to discuss —

The Role of Ethics in Business

Some of you may be taking a business ethics course because it's mandatory, but you really don't see the need for it. After all, the whole point of business is to make a profit, and as long as you stay within the law, you won't end up doing anything really bad, so why worry about it?

First, consider the questions raised earlier in Item 4 ("do only what's legal"). Then consider: *is* the whole point of business to make a profit? What about non-profit businesses? And even those who think profit-making *is* the main purpose of business (and there are some who don't – see Chapter Seven) usually attach a few strings: the activity has to be profitable, but it can't be illegal; it has to be profitable, but it also has to be fair; it has to be profitable, but it also has to be reasonably safe, or at least it can't kill people (well, at least, not a lot of people); and so on. So what ethical strings will you attach to your business or your employment with a business?

Some of you may recognize the importance of ethics for those in marketing or management, but you're in accounting – there's nothing ethical about 2+2=4. Well true enough, but you *know* you do more than add and subtract numbers: you decide where to put those numbers, and when to put them there. And *that* can be a matter of ethics. But let's not just pick on accountants (despite how much fun that can be): I suggest that everyone in business – just as everyone in life – has to deal with decisions that involve ethics. But we often don't recognize the ethical element even when we trip over it: we make ethical decisions every day without even knowing it. (And that's a two-part problem: one,

unconscious 'decisions' may well be worse than those we think about; two, if we don't even know we're doing something, we won't recognize the need to learn how to do it better.) I list a number of decisions below – which do you think involve ethics?

Management
1) What salary figures should we put into which places on the grid?
2) What benefit package should we offer to our employees?
3) What objectives should we put on the negotiating table?

Human Resources
4) Which applicant should we hire?
5) Should we offer a job to the spouse of our first choice as an added incentive?

Finance
6) What should our interest rate to creditors be?

Accounting
7) Should we take advantage of a particular tax shelter?
8) Should we adopt generally accepted accounting principles?

Operations
9) Where should we locate our next plant?
10) Is our predicted environmental impact acceptable?
11) What paper should we buy for photocopying?

Information Systems
12) Which e-mail messages should have a privacy screen and which should not?
13) Which company should we buy our software from?

Marketing
14) What content should go into our next advertisement campaign?

15) Should we use emotional images to (try to) manipulate people?

Research and Development

16) Should we honour the company's trade secrets policy?

17) Should we use animals for your research?

Which of these are ethical questions? *All of them.* Consider the questions again, this time with a few more questions that expose *some* of the ethical issues, *some* of the implicit assumptions involved:

1) *What salary figures should we put into which places on the grid?* Should there even be different wages for different positions? Why? Should people who have been with the company longer get paid more? Why? Should people doing the same job get paid the same? – even if one person has special needs and requires more money than the other?

2) *What benefit package should we offer to our employees?* Why should a company offer a benefit plan to its employees? Why/Is employee health the company's responsibility? Should it offer such a plan only to its full-time employees? Is there something magical about the number 35 such that those who work 35 hours/week are entitled to medical and pension benefits, but those who work 34 or 24 or 14 hours/week are not?

3) *What objectives should we put on the negotiating table?* Why wouldn't you just put all your objectives on the table? Is it morally acceptable to bluff? Isn't that the same as lying? Do management-union negotiations have to be adversarial?

4) *Which applicant should we hire?* Should you consider race when you hire? Should you consider gender? Should you consider need? Should you consider only merit?

5) *Should we offer a job to the spouse of our first choice as an added incentive?* Isn't that unfair? Shouldn't the spouse have to apply, and compete, for the job? Even if s/he is well-qualified, isn't s/he getting the job because of who s/he sleeps with?

6) *What should our interest rate to creditors be?* Should you accept the "going" market rate? Should the interest rate be the same for everyone? On what basis could you justify different interest rates? Is interest fair? (Why, as Michalos points out, do we call it "Third World debt" instead of "First World usury"?)

7) *Should we take advantage of a particular tax shelter?* Should tax shelters be used only because they're tax shelters – or should the shelter just be a nice consequence to a choice motivated by other reasons?

8) *Should we adopt generally accepted accounting principles?* Are such principles sufficient to keep important stakeholders informed about the firm? What do you do if higher management requests a modest departure from prudent accounting practices in order to exaggerate the actual performance of the company? What if they want you to hide certain damaging information by burying it in the financial statements? Is 'creative accounting' really as harmless as it sounds?

9) *Where should we locate our next plant?* Should you set up your plant where it's most wanted by those living in the area or where it's cheapest? Why should you even set up another plant? (Is more/bigger always better?)

10) *Is our predicted environmental impact acceptable?* Is any environmental damage morally acceptable? Does the nature of the product/service matter?

11) *What paper should we buy for photocopying?* Should you buy the recycled stuff, even

though it's more expensive? (Is it? What are you counting as expense: just the current dollar price?)

12) *Which e-mail messages should have a privacy screen and which should not?* Should supervisors be able to read any of their subordinates' e-mail messages? (Should there even be supervisors and subordinates?) Do employees have a right to any "personal" use of company-owned computers, printers, copiers, etc.?

13) *Which company should we buy our software from?* The one not exploiting its workers? And how do you tell if a company is exploiting its workers – ask the workers? Is that any of your business? (Get it? 'Your *business*'?)

14) *What content should go into our next advertisement campaign?* How do you determine what product information to withhold? Is it okay to advertise any product/service?

15) *Should we use emotional images to (try to) manipulate people?* Is it morally acceptable to manipulate people? Is it less acceptable if a business tries to do it than if it is done in other contexts?

16) *Should we honour the company's trade secrets policy?* Or should you share your knowledge with anyone who could benefit from it? And what if they (those with whom you shared your information) use what they have received from you to earn (more) profit rather than "just" to improve quality of life?

17) *Should we use animals for your research?* Does it depend on what you're researching? Does it depend on whether you hurt them?

Some of you might recognize the importance of ethics but think it's the responsibility of the Executive Directors or the Board – or the Ethics Officer; in any case, it probably won't be *your* responsibility (you figure you'll be happy just to climb the corporate ladder to an office with a window). Well, there are two questions here: (1) *Is* ethics the responsibility of only the higher-ups? (2) *Should* it be?

I would say the answer to both questions is "no." Suppose you've got a run-of-the-mill factory job and you're required to provide a weekly urine sample to confirm that you're not pregnant because your work environment is hazardous to fetal development. That could be considered an unwarranted invasion of privacy; as such, it's an ethical matter that concerns *you*, and perhaps on that basis alone it's *your* responsibility to become involved. Or suppose you're the company's health officer, the one whose job it is to collect and analyze the samples. Are you prepared to agree to do these things in return for a good (or maybe not so good) wage?

To ask the questions from the other side, does that arrangement make for the best business? Are employees who are coerced to act against their own ethical principles going to be good employees? Happy employees? Productive employees? Profitable employees? (Choose whichever is important to you as one of those Executive Directors or Board member.)

Another danger with this view is the potential for creating a chain of passing the buck in which *no one* ends up taking the moral responsibility: the low-level workers figure it's out of their hands; the middle management defers to the executives; the executives say they're obligated to their stockholders; and the stockholders just endorse the view of those involved in the company on a day-to-day basis.

In an excellent article titled "The Moral Muteness of Managers," Frederick B. Bird and James A. Waters observe that "many managers exhibit a reluctance to describe their actions in moral terms even when they are acting for moral reasons. They talk as if their actions were guided exclusively by organization interests, practicality, and economic good sense even when in practice they honour morally defined standards..." (237). They do this, Bird and Waters claim, because moral talk is perceived to be a threat to harmony, efficiency, and effectiveness.

I'd like to add to their analysis: I think there's yet another reason for not talking about whether something is right or wrong – the separation of our personal and work lives. It seems to be a workplace convention that one should leave one's personal "baggage" at home, and many are urged at home to leave their work at the office. Does that foster split selves – and are split selves happy and healthy? (To those who insist I demonstrate the value or importance of ethics to business, let me ask, "How do you justify an ethical dimension at home, in your personal life?" Shouldn't that be sufficient justification for ethics in business – are you not "yourself" at work?)

But would the alternative lead to the following scenario? Your supervisor has several crucifixes on his office walls, and whenever he meets with you, whether to discuss policy and procedure or routine work matters, he tells you about the relevant teachings of Jesus. You might say, wait a minute, what about the separation of church and state? Okay, but what if it's a private business, not a public business (e.g., not a school, hospital, or government office)? Still, you may counter, I am entitled to freedom of (and, equally, freedom from) religion: who is he to impose his religion on me like that? It's not like I can avoid his office. Okay, while his office is not necessarily a public place, you make a good point about not being able to avoid it – meeting with him in his office is part of your job. But you didn't have to accept the job, did you? Were you made aware that it was a Christian business? Were you asked if you were Christian? But, you ask, wouldn't that be discrimination? Good question, but let's back up: even if it *were* a government business, if that supervisor's ethics reside with his religion, and if we're saying ethics should be in business, then isn't it okay?

So maybe bringing ethics into the workplace would be a bad thing. But wait a minute: as we've seen above, *ethics are already in the workplace*, it's part of life. It seems to me that if we fail to recognize that, if we fail to recognize the moral dimension that, whether we like it or not, is present in so many business decisions, then any moral goodness (or badness) we end up with will be merely accidental. Is that what we want? Further, not only must we *recognize* that moral dimension, we must *talk* about it: failure to do so is a good way to ensure "moral totalitarianism" (the absence of plurality and diversity of opinion) – and is *that* what we want? Lastly, although managers, presidents, and directors have no right to impose their morality on others, their decisions affect lots of people in a big way. So one could argue that not only do they have a *right* to become involved with the moral dimensions of their decisions, they have a *responsibility* to do so. So perhaps if the teachings of Jesus are relevant to the matter at hand, and your supervisor is presenting rationale rather than proselytizing – *and* that rationale is open to discussion (and disagreement), then maybe it's okay. And you might begin that discussion by pointing out that ethics discussion can, and perhaps should, occur without reference to religion – see the examination of religionism in Section II. (But what about those crucifixes?)

A Few Words about Terminology

Often the way we use words in everyday speech is a little sloppy, not as precise as the way we use them in academic discussion. This is especially so with ethics. Strictly speaking, *ethics* means "matters of moral right and wrong" – it is a branch of philosophy inquiring into issues that are subject to judgements of right and wrong. So, whether or not to cheat is properly called an ethical issue – it involves right and wrong. However, whether to dry your dishes with a teatowel or let them "air dry" is not an ethical issue (despite the impression your mother might have given you) – while it may involve effective and ineffective, it does not involve moral right and wrong.

To say then, as we do all the time, that a certain person "has ethics" isn't quite right. The word that's wanted in this case is *morality*, which means "a particular system of ethical beliefs or principles" – and no judgement is made about the system (you're not saying the person is good or bad, just that they have some rules about good and bad).

Strictly speaking, *moral* is a synonym for *ethical* – it simply means that the issue has to do with right or wrong. Still, no judgement is being made one way or another. To say "That's a moral thing to do" isn't quite right. The phrase that is wanted in this case, when you *do* want to make a judgement, is *morally right* or *ethically right* – or, simply, *right* (in ethics discussions, "right" is usually understood as a short form of "morally right" – as opposed to, say, factually right or strategically right).

Now *immoral* means "morally wrong" – to say someone is immoral is to say they do wrong. This is probably why people think "moral" means "morally right" – from a semantic point of view, one would think "moral" is the opposite of "immoral," but strictly speaking, it's not.

Rather, "moral" is the opposite of *amoral* – which means the issue does *not* concern matters of right and wrong. The issue of drying one's dishes is an amoral issue. An amoral person would be someone who doesn't have a morality, who doesn't have any morals at all (which is different from saying they're immoral – those people *have* morals, just *bad* ones!).

Which brings us to "moral" as a noun instead of as an adjective: *a moral* is a short form for "a moral belief or principle."

The following chart should clearly summarize things:

Ethics	= the study of right and wrong = the study of morality
Morality	= a system of ethical principles or beliefs = a system of morals
Issues can be	• *moral* (ones that involve right/wrong) • *amoral* (ones that do not involve right/wrong)
Actions can be	• *right* (= ethically right = morally right) • *wrong* (= ethically wrong = morally wrong = immoral)
People can be	• *good* (= ethically good = morally good) • *bad* (= ethically bad = morally bad = immoral)

I am, however, ignoring a great debate about the relation between "right" and "good." I'm suggesting they are the same, but this is not necessarily the case. A lot depends on how you define "right" and "good." Something could be right but bad, or wrong but good. For example, pushing someone away from a full lifeboat would surely be bad because you are essentially ensuring that person's death, but it may well be the right thing to do because otherwise the boat would capsize and everyone in it would die.

So ethics is the study of right and wrong. Clear as that definition may seem, some business students, and even some business professionals, have trouble with ethics courses. Indeed, it's been my experience that for some students, it takes half a semester just to get to an understanding of what the course is all about. Some students will very thoroughly trace a decision-making scenario through several good ifs, ands, and buts, and then say, "Well, it depends on what you think is right and wrong" and stop there. As if there's a stone wall at that point, as if that's the end of it. But *that's* the *beginning* of it — that's exactly where a course in business ethics *starts*: what *do* you think is right and wrong? and why? *That's* what such a course, and this book, is all about. What you think is right and wrong is not written in stone — it is, like all of your ideas, open to discussion: it is subject to examination, justification, and modification.

Sometimes persistently distinguishing between (descriptive) "is" questions (What *do* companies do about trade secrets?) and (prescriptive) "ought" questions (What *should* companies do about trade secrets?) helps — it's the "ought" questions that ethics tries to answer. But sometimes even this is not enough because 'ought' questions can be understood, especially by business students, as questions of effective strategy (What should companies do about trade secrets to maintain a competitive edge?) rather than as questions of ethics (What should companies do

about trade secrets if they are to be morally good companies?). Ethics is not about instrumental value; it's about moral value.

To get a little advance practice at distinguishing moral questions from empirical and strategic questions, let's go back to a few of the decisions listed earlier, all of which I identified as involving ethics. Which of the subquestions listed below get to the ethical aspects? (Keep that pen in hand.)

1. What salary figures should we put into which places on the salary grid?
    (a) How much can we afford to expend on salaries?
    (b) What figures are needed to attract top performers?
    (c) Is it fair to pay our clerical workers less than our maintenance workers?
    (d) Shall we start with equal pay for equal work, then give bonuses for work well done?
    (e) Those with families to support need more money, so should we give them bonuses as well?

2. Where should we locate our next plant?
    (a) Does the area under consideration have a sufficient labour pool?
    (b) Is the area depressed, allowing us to pay lower wages and offer fewer benefits than at our current location?
    (c) Is there sufficient road access?
    (d) Are there environmental bylaws we have to worry about?
    (e) Will the proposed location benefit very many people?
    (f) Will the proposed location require residents to relocate or cause property devaluation because of the nature of our operation?

3. What content should go into our next advertising campaign?
    (a) Do we know what our competitor's next campaign is?
    (b) Can we find out?
    (c) Should we do so covertly?
    (d) What kind of budget do we have?
    (e) Should we withhold information about our product's potential danger?
    (f) Should we use a pop or rock music theme?
    (g) Could we exaggerate the product's merits?
    (h) Should we exaggerate the product's merits?

Okay, let's see how you did. For question 1, (c), (d), and (e) all address the ethical aspect because they all address the question of justice – what's fair? Subquestion (a) is an empirical question in that it inquires about fact; (b) is also an empirical question, directed toward strategy. However, if you scratch the surface of these two questions, you can get to an ethical issue: deciding how much to spend on salaries (whether to attract top performers or not) involves deciding how much to spend on other stuff – it's a question of allocation. And if the other stuff includes, for example, compensating victims of an earlier unsafe product of yours, then by deciding to put more money into salaries than injury compensation, you are making a decision of value, an ethical decision.

For question 2, (b) as it is worded is merely an empirical question: is the area depressed or not? However, there is a strong suggestion that if it *is* depressed, the company will engage in what might be considered exploitation – and this is an ethical issue (addressing rights and fairness). Subquestion (d) is similar in that as worded, it's just an empirical question; but as soon as environmental damage is contemplated, there is a question of ethics involved. Subquestions (e) and (f) consider consequences of benefit and harm, and thus also address ethical aspects. Subquestions (a) and (c) are empirical questions, asking about the facts of the matter.

For question 3, (a) and (b) are empirical questions, asking about what *is* or *could be* the case; (c), however, goes one step further, asking about what *ought to be* the case, and, because it suggests deception, it involves a moral ought. Likewise, (e) and (h), both suggesting deception (and implying some "right to know"), address the ethical aspect.

How to Think about Ethics

Taking an ethics course is a little like taking a math course in that how you get the answer is, in many respects, more important than the answer itself. In fact, my aim throughout this text is not so much to have you arrive at a particular moral judgement (i.e., a particular answer), but to have you develop the skills necessary to do that.

And developing those skills is very much a matter of appreciating both the depth and the breadth of the issues involved. What answer you get depends a lot on what questions you ask (or don't ask). As Mark Twain said, if all you have is a hammer, an awful lot of things are going to look like nails. I want you to have a full toolbox.

Though I am not advocating any particular answer (well, I'm *trying* not to), I *am* advocating a particular way of getting to an answer: one that is conscious, reasoned, and informed by the complexities of the issue – rather than one that is instinctive, intuitive, conditioned, and/or superficial.

When I'm in class trying to facilitate a discussion about ethical issues, I find myself asking the same four questions, over and over, in different versions. So I'll put them here, upfront; if you can, try to get into the habit of asking yourself these questions (and not just when you're examining ethical issues — they're good for almost any situation).

(1) What are your reasons?

You may be surprised at how often answering this question takes more than a little work. Consider yourself forewarned!

Once you have your reasons, make sure they're good ones. Good reasons are, first, *relevant*. For example, thinking that it's wrong to sell unsafe products because people can get hurt is good thinking in that the reason is relevant. Thinking that it's wrong to do so because your company doesn't make unsafe products is not good thinking: whether or not your company *makes* unsafe products is irrelevant to the point of whether or not it's wrong to *sell* unsafe products.

Sometimes what seems irrelevant can be made relevant by filling in a few missing steps. For example, suppose I said that selling unsafe products was wrong because it hurt people (and hurting people is wrong), and you responded by saying that everyone does it. That statement alone is irrelevant because whether everyone does it doesn't affect whether it's wrong — everyone could be wrong for doing it. However, you may have meant that right is determined according to what everyone does. So, since everyone does it, it's right. In that case, "everyone does it" *is* relevant — but you'd have to provide those missing steps.

There are several fallacies — errors in reasoning — that indicate lack of relevance:

(i) To the person (*ad hominem*). When you are making a claim, whether positive or negative, about the person putting forth the position rather than about the position itself (and implying that your claim is a judgement about the position), you are committing the *ad hominem* error. For example, suppose the owner of a funeral parlour refuses to advertise her services, claiming that it's wrong to cash in on people's grief that way. If you dismissed her argument because she's an atheist, a cold-hearted pagan who has no understanding of the religious importance of rituals, you'd be making an *ad hominem* error — you'd be attacking the person instead of the argument. She may well be cold-hearted (though, of course, not all atheists are) and she may well not understand the religious importance of rituals (though, of course, most atheists do), but still, her *argument* that such advertising is wrong may indeed be a good one — what she is (or is not) is not relevant to the strength of the argument.

(ii) Paper tiger. When someone responds to someone else's argument but has turned it into something different (often something far simpler) than it was (perhaps because it's far easier to attack that way), that person is committing the paper tiger fallacy. For example, consider this exchange:

Union representative: We'd like a 5% wage increase effective September 1 of this year, and hereafter, annual increases equal to the cost of living increase.

Management representative: Hey, I'd like a lot more money too, everyone would like to be rich. Gee, it'd be nice to afford dinner out every night, and a new car every year, but this is the real world. We can't afford to give everyone everything they want.

In this case, the management rep has committed the paper tiger fallacy by responding to an exaggerated version of the union rep's argument: the union didn't ask to be rich, they didn't ask management to give *everyone everything* they wanted. The rebuttal may be a very good response to the argument responded to – but it's irrelevant to the argument that was actually presented.

(iii) Red herring. A red herring is a distraction, and as such, it's irrelevant. For example, consider this exchange:

A: I can't accept the plan; we'd be causing too much environmental damage. And given that our product is, in truth, not that essential, such damage is not ethically justified.

B: But if we don't cut down those trees, someone else will, you know that.

It may well be that someone else will – but whether or not they do is irrelevant to whether or not it's morally acceptable for *you* to do it. (Unless you're defining "morally right" as "that which someone else will do," but that's unlikely.)

(iv) Appeal to inappropriate authority. While it is usually acceptable to appeal to experts for support, be careful that you choose not only an expert, but an expert in the relevant field. Certain celebrities may be great actors, but why should their opinion that you should drink milk carry any weight? Also, mere appeal to authority involves a lot of trust, and although that may not be a problem for you, the person you're trying to convince may need more – so try to understand the expert's rationale for the support you claim (and cite the rationale, not just the expert's opinion).

(v) Appeal to popularity. In a way, the appeal to popularity (sometimes called the *bandwagon fallacy*) is a version of the appeal to inappropriate authority: when you support your claim by saying something like "everyone does it" or "everyone agrees," you're implying that the opinion of the majority carries weight. Well, the majority has been known to be wrong – and I'm sure you can think of half a dozen examples

– but even if they're right, the fact that they *are* right isn't a *reason* in support of your point; it's merely an observation – that others agree with your point. You're better off to find out *why* the majority agrees and then use that reason to support your point.

(vi) Appeal to tradition. "The company has always done it this way." So? Maybe we've always taxed food and water, but that's no reason to keep on doing it. As with the appeal to popularity, try to find out *why* the company has always done it that way. And if there is a good reason, use that reason, and not the mere tradition, to support your point.

As well as being relevant, good reasons are *adequate.* This means that they are strong enough to support your claim(s). For instance, to go back to a previous example, suppose that using a certain unsafe product will cause only a very little bit of harm, or suppose that using it will cause harm in only one in a million cases. If that's the case, one might say the reason (it hurts people) is inadequate; it's relevant, yes, but it's not strong enough to support the conclusion that selling the product is therefore wrong. Or maybe it's strong enough for that claim, but not for the next claim, which might be that we should take it completely off the market. Perhaps the product can be sold under restricted circumstances, such as only to adults. Perhaps the manufacture can be slightly modified, such as to incorporate a childproof mechanism. As you can see, adequacy is a matter of degree, and it's sometimes difficult to determine how strong is strong enough.

There are several fallacies that indicate lack of adequacy:

(vii) Slippery slope arguments. Arguing that one thing will lead to another which will lead to another – a slippery slope argument – can be a poor argument. For example, suppose the Human Resources Director says, "First we called

Christmas a holiday, and we give days off if people are sick, we even allow a day off for them to get married; pretty soon they're going to want 'Earth Day' declared a holiday, then they'll ask for a holiday in memory of Louis Riel, and eventually they'll ask for a day off to celebrate their bird's birthday." Although the individual links in the chain may be probable (or not), the connection between the first and the last, which is often the only part of the argument that is made, may not be as probable.

(viii) Post hoc. This error is a case of assuming that because something happens *before* something else, it was the *cause* of that something else. For example, consider this argument: "Last January, we implemented random after-lunch breathalyzer tests for middle management personnel; since then, reports of excessively long lunches and afternoon aggressiveness toward subordinates have decreased. It seems to have worked quite well, and I say we include upper management starting next month." The speaker has assumed that the breathalyzer testing was the cause of fewer "liquid lunches" (actually, if you read closely, the only thing that can be assumed is that the breathalyzer testing was the cause of fewer *reports* of certain activity *presumed to indicate* liquid lunches). But perhaps the only restaurant in town had its liquor licence revoked. Just because X precedes Y, don't assume X caused Y.

Now, in addition to being relevant and adequate, the claims in your reasons, if they involve empirical claims, must be true. An empirical claim is one that can be tested, one that is subject to correspondence (or lack of) with reality – the "is" questions ask about empirical claims. While philosophers typically leave the establishment of truth to others, our arguments are, nevertheless, not good if our premises are false. For example, we might argue that, because

affirmative action programs that require the hiring of members of a certain group just to fill a quota result in feelings of low self-worth on the part of those hired and feelings of resentment on the part of those not, such programs should not be implemented – they cause harm, they do not contribute to the good of society. Now, whether they do, in fact, result in feelings of low self-worth on the part of those hired and feelings of resentment on the part of those not is important to our argument (indeed the truth of that premise is essential to the soundness of the argument), but it's not *our* job to figure that out – we leave that to the social scientists, the psychologists, to establish (or not). If that claim is true, then your argument may well be sound.

However, you should know about appeals to ignorance: that we can't prove something is false is no reason to suppose that it's true. For example, suppose the president of a company is considering whether to extend surveillance from e-mail communications to phone communications, and suppose someone points out that since they had no way of knowing before how many messages were gossip messages, they can't say that the surveillance decreased the number of gossip messages. If the president responds to that claim with "Yes, well, we don't know that it *doesn't* work," and so assumes that it does (and orders the extension of surveillance), s/he'd be making the "appeal to ignorance" mistake.

It's worth drawing your attention to a few other common errors of reasoning so that you can be on the alert for them:

(ix) Circular reasoning. When your reasons assume or require the point they are supposed to support, then your argument is a case of circular reasoning. A classic example is "God exists – because the Bible says so"; since the Bible is supposedly written by God, by accepting it as evidence, you have *assumed* to be true the very thing you were trying to *prove* was true (God's existence). An example from the world of business would be arguing that unjustified discrimination is wrong because it's making judgements unfairly; insofar as "unjustified discrimination" is defined as "making judgements unfairly," the argument is "X is wrong because it's X" – in which case you have assumed ahead of time the very point you were supposed to be proving.

(x) Equivocation. When you use the same word but with different meanings, you are equivocating. For example, consider this argument: "Your supervisor is your superior, and someone who's superior is someone who's better than others, so your supervisor is better than you." "Superior" is used first to mean "organizational superior" or "superior in the hierarchy," but the second time, it's used in a different, general way to mean "better"; because the word "superior" has been equivocated, the argument is not a good one. However, attending to your definitions (see below) will keep you safe from this error.

(xi) False dichotomy. Be careful not to assume that a situation is an either/or (dichotomous) situation; often there will be more than two, especially opposing, options. For example, consider this argument: "If we don't lay off one hundred employees, we will go bankrupt and then everyone will be out of a job." The speaker has falsely assumed that there are only two options: laying off a hundred employees or going out of business. There is, in fact, a third option: all employees could accept a wage decrease, thus reducing payroll expenses and enabling all employees to be retained. No doubt there are more than three options: the profit margin could be reduced (or even eliminated), the stockholders' returns could be decreased, expansion plans could be postponed, etc. However, attending to

alternatives (see below) will keep you safe from this error.

Entire books are written about this field, which is variously called critical thinking, critical reasoning, informal logic, etc. See the list of references at the back of the book if you want to check out a few.

(2) What are your assumptions?

This is the second question I find myself asking over and over. Reconsider the previous argument about it being wrong to sell unsafe products because people can be hurt; the person *assumed* that causing harm is wrong. You may say, "Well, of course." But the value in identifying assumptions is that one can then assess them – one might just as well have *not* agreed that causing harm is wrong; if you don't know what the assumption is, you can't figure out if you agree with it or not. And if it turns out that you *don't* agree with or accept the assumption that was being made, then you don't have to agree with or accept the argument.

Let's consider a few other examples. Selling your product at cost would mean you won't make any profit, so you implement a 10% mark-up. Sounds good. But what have you assumed? You have assumed that it's necessary, or at least important, or perhaps good, to make a profit. But what about not-for-profit business enterprises? If you raise wages, you'll go out of business. So? Why is that a problem? What are you assuming? Maybe going out of business would be a good thing. (Do you make nuclear or biological weapons?)

(3) What do you mean by _____?

In other words, *define your terms.* To continue with the previous example, one may well ask "What do you mean by 'harm'?", "What do you mean by 'unsafe'?", "How 'likely' are you calling 'likely'?" and, of course, "What do you mean by 'wrong'?"

(4) What are the alternatives?

Often the ethical decision seems to be X or not-X, or X or Y. But often there are alternatives – try to find a Z. Referring to our example, selling the product under restricted circumstances might be a good alternative (to selling it or not selling it): it might allow you to keep selling it and at the same time reduce or eliminate the harm caused.

Okay, practice time again! Each of the following, except one, illustrates an error in reasoning. See if you can identify and label them.

1. Martens: Either our company refuses to hire people with AIDS or we put everyone here at risk.

2. MacNabb asks her supervisor for a day off to celebrate her divorce, claiming that since it is company policy to allow wedding leave, it should also be policy to allow divorce leave. MacNamara denies her request, saying that the company can't afford to give employees a day off whenever they request one.

3. Lariviere criticizes Marsh's argument that maximizing profit should be the least important goal of a company by pointing out that he knows nothing, absolutely nothing, about economics.

4. When Milburn suggests that the company should offer pro-rated benefits to all part-time workers regardless of the number of hours worked per week, Madden tells him that it's standard practice across the province to offer benefits only to employees who work 25 hours or more per week.

5. Thorn claims that since she has been hired, sales have doubled; she therefore asks for a raise.

6. Cole claims that failing to advertise steel-toed construction boots to a female target audience is not only unjustified discrimination to women currently working on construction sites, it is also harmful to all the little girls who see in the ads only men working in manual trades – their future job prospects will be limited by their narrowed imaginations. Shortt responds by saying he knows lots of women who work in construction.

7. In response to accusations about cruelty to animals, Purdon's firm's PR person, Charles, visits one of their research labs and then prepares a press release (either denying or affirming the accusation).

8. Roy argues that if we allow people to sell their organs, we will end up with a murder epidemic – people will go on a killing spree, hoping to sell their victims' organs.

9. Didine is an asset to this firm. All assets can be liquidated. Therefore, Didine can be liquidated.

10. Warner and Ducharme question the strip search policy at the detention centre they work at because they think that automatically assigning a same-sex worker to check a resident unjustifiably assumes that everyone is heterosexual. They wonder if homosexual residents and workers might prefer cross-sex arrangements, and suggest that henceforth the resident be asked whether she or he would prefer a male or female worker to conduct the search. The Director of the centre responds with incredulity, and a snicker, and simply says, "Our search policy has been in effect since the centre was opened and I'm not about to change it!"

11. Gonzalez suggests that the company institute flex-time, saying that it doesn't really matter when people put in their 35 hours, as long as they get the job done; being able

to miss rush hour, being at home when the kids get there — these things make for happier employees and happier employees are more productive. Besides, people have a right to a certain amount of autonomy.

12. Eaton, Richmond, and Moulding: We should accept more students because then our tuition revenue would increase. And if we have more money, we could expand. And if we were bigger, we could accept more students.

And the answers are …

1. False dichotomy. An obvious third possibility is that you hire the person with AIDS but restrict his/her duties to those not involving the exchange of bodily fluids. Or perhaps a condition of employment could be disclosure to colleagues so they'll know to glove up before (or refrain from) administering first aid should the occasion arise.

2. Paper tiger. MacNamara responds to what was *not* MacNabb's argument: MacNabb did not just request a day off; she asked for a particular day off, suggesting consistency with current company policy. Had MacNamara responded to her suggestion of consistency, arguing that divorces were somehow different from weddings with respect to needing or deserving a day off, he would have been okay.

3. *Ad hominem.* Lariviere has argued to the person instead of to the position. Marsh may well know nothing about economics (then again, he may be an economics expert) — but that's irrelevant to whether maximizing profit should be the least important goal of a company.

4. Appeal to popularity. Madden's response suggests that "everyone does it this way" (i.e., offers benefits only after 25 hours/week). That may be true but it's irrelevant to whether it's right, and that was Milburn's point (presumably).

5. Post hoc. Thorn has assumed that she is the cause of the increased sales; perhaps the competition shut down.

6. Red herring. Shortt may well know lots of women who work in construction, but what does that have to do with whether or not the proposed advertising campaign would be discriminatory and harmful?

7. Appeal to inappropriate authority. By handling the issue in this way, Purdon's firm has made an erroneous appeal to authority: generally speaking, PR people are not experts about animal welfare and are therefore unqualified to make a judgement on this matter.

8. Slippery slope. Selling one's own organs, probably through carefully regulated channels, *may* lead to selling someone else's organs (though even this step is a leap); but for it to lead to murdering to do so, let alone to an epidemic of such murders, is not that likely.

9. Equivocation. The first "asset" refers to "benefit" but the second "asset" refers to "physical and financial properties" — the meaning of the term has changed throughout the argument. Furthermore, the first "liquidated" refers to "conversion to cash" but the second "liquidated" refers to "killed" — this term has also had its meaning equivocated.

10. Appeal to tradition. The Director may well be right in saying that the policy has been in place since the centre opened, but that's irrelevant to whether it should continue to be in place — the search policy may have been wrong for all those years. (Furthermore, I'd say the snicker is an appeal to immaturity.)

11. This is an instance of good reasoning.
12. Circular reasoning. They have assumed to be good (accepting more students) exactly what they were supposed to be proving was good (accepting more students).

How to Discuss Ethics

One of my biggest challenges when I teach ethics is to shift the classroom discussion from sounding like a bad Jerry Springer show to sounding like a PBS or CBC radio discussion. It's not easy, and students have good reason to be frustrated with a discussion that doesn't go anywhere.

First, yes, everyone's entitled to their opinion. But second, *some opinions are better than others.* You can express your opinion that Santa Claus exists until you're blue in the face, but until you present some reasons for your opinion, the rest of the class is justified in ignoring you (politely, of course). And until you present *good* reasons, the rest of the class is justified in not changing their mind (assuming they disagreed with you).

Second, being rational doesn't exclude being passionate. Indeed, I hope you get excited, I hope you care very deeply about ethical discussions. But in order to avoid hurting each other (which will just lead to people holding back from speaking, which eventually leads to non-discussion), think of yourself and everyone else as putting forth positions. The position you put forth at any given time doesn't necessarily have to be the position you personally subscribe to at the moment. In fact, we don't have to know whether you agree with the position or not. That way, people can disagree *with the position*, not *with you.* You should feel free to play with all sorts of positions. This is a great way to help refine and evaluate your own opinions.

Now, of course, you try to run your life according to your ethical principles. So when someone criticizes your ethical principles, they are criticizing the way you run your life. And that criticism can be hard to take. (Actually, they're probably just defending the way they run theirs — the fact that you run yours differently suggests they might be wrong. Which of course is not necessarily the case: don't forget the false dichotomy fallacy, it doesn't have to be either/or — it could be that *both* ways are okay. Then again, it could be that both ways are wrong.) But you can deal with that criticism on your own. You don't have to defend your *self* in class, just try to defend the *position.* No one has to know which position you most support — in fact, *you* don't even have to know; and anyway, you may change your position, several times, as you think of or become aware of various arguments.

Or you may not change your position. But what's the point of discussion if people don't change? That's the value of disagreement! When someone disagrees with you, they're shining a spotlight on something, and it's to your advantage to take a good look: maybe that particular reason *is* a bad one, maybe you can strengthen it, maybe you should find another reason, maybe you should reject the claim that reason was supposed to have supported. (That's called becoming wise.)

Now, having set the tone for *mature* discussion, there's a method you can follow (until you get the hang of it) that will lead you to *coherent* discussion: noodling. I came up with this one day in class, utterly exhausted by trying to keep the discussion moving, and moving in one direction. That day, I finally articulated what I was valiantly trying to do, and this ad lib response has now become a premeditated component.

Whenever someone said something, I explained, it was as if they just plopped a pile of spaghetti into the middle of the room and expected me to do the hard work of trying to make some order out of their mess — trying to figure out what, if anything, was relevant and how exactly it fit in with what was just said. I want you to try to do some of that work yourself, I said to my students — try to straighten out your noodles before you put them on the table.

I then elaborated on the board, encouraging them to take note of what I was doing. Like this, I said: this is my point (and I drew a horizontal line/noodle) and this is my reason for it (another noodle below it, somewhat indented) and this is another reason for it (another noodle in line with the previous one).

Now when the next person says something, they should try to connect their noodles to the previous person's noodles. You can make a connection in several ways, I continued:

- you can disagree with the point (I draw an X beside that noodle)

    - because you disagree with one or more reasons (I draw an X beside the relevant noodle/s below)

    - because you don't think the point follows from the reasons, even though you agree with the reasons (I draw a line connecting the point with the reason/s and put an X through it)

    - because you have your own reason/s (I draw a separate set of horizontal lines) for your own counter point

- you can agree with the point (a check beside the noodle)

    - but disagree with one or more reasons (Xs wherever)

    - and agree with the reasons (checks beside them)

        - and add another reason (another noodle under the original column)

- you can make an individual noodle thicker (I thicken the line) by adding an example, adding detail, elaborating on the explanation

- you can ask for clarification about a specific noodle (a question mark beside a line)

- you can question a noodle's truth, its relevance, or its adequacy

And so on.

However, if you have something to say but can't figure out if, or how, it fits in, you should say it anyway and the rest of the class can help with the noodling — this method shouldn't become an inhibitor.

Also, it helps if there's a noodle emergency person: someone who doesn't try to participate per se in the discussion, but rather who listens very carefully and jumps in, as necessary, to untangle or straighten out the noodles in order to prevent a real mess from developing. At first, I act as the noodle emergency person, but after a while, I assign the role to individual students. The results are amazing: you'll see for yourself just how challenging it is to facilitate a coherent discussion, but more importantly, by consciously trying to keep the discussion on track, merely by trying to assess every comment for relevance, your own critical skills will really take off.

Lastly, there are a few "discussion fallacies" you should know about, whether you discuss out loud or in writing:

(1) Try not to use loaded language. Consider the difference between "incentive" and "bribe," between "employment opportunity" and "job," between "affirmative action" and "reverse discrimination," between "downsizing" and "mass firing," etc.

(2) Be careful with statistics. Consider "80% of the workers in our Third World plant said they were happy with their wages" – if you asked only a handful, your statistic was not representative and is therefore misleading; if the workers thought they'd be fired if they said they weren't happy, your statistic is not reliable and is therefore misleading.

Closing Comments

Many business students are frustrated with philosophical discussion in general because it doesn't appear to go anywhere. Philosophy must be one of the few disciplines that's still dealing with ideas put forth centuries ago. Law has gotten past lynch mobs, physics has gone beyond Newton, even psychology has outgrown many of its early views. But philosophers are still discussing Plato. Why does philosophy go nowhere? Well, it doesn't go nowhere. Yes, it's still dealing with the same old issues in many cases, but our dealings are far more complicated; we are making much finer distinctions. (Now, philosophers write entire books on the single concept of voluntariness; centuries ago, that issue was exhausted by a mere page or two.)

Also, try not to be overwhelmed by the questions in this chapter (indeed, in this text). "Moral paralysis" can be avoided if you remember that all you need to do is make *better* ethical decisions, more *carefully considered* decisions – you don't have to figure out the single absolutely right answer. (Especially not by the end of just one course/text!) The theories covered in the next chapter will be of value; you can use them to answer those questions, to make those decisions.

And, as I have suggested, asking the right questions is a large part of the way toward getting the right answers. If all you can do at the end of what might be your first attempt to study ethics is know what questions to ask, well, that's a lot – don't underestimate your achievement.

Okay, here's one final exercise.

In threesomes, discuss the following situations. Each of you should take one of the given positions; this will give you practice at seeing yourself and others as trying on positions that are not necessarily in accordance to what you or they really think. Try to get comfortable with the terminology covered in this opening section. Try noodling. And don't forget:

- What are your reasons? (And are they relevant and adequate?)
- What are your assumptions?
- Define your terms.
- Consider alternatives.

Here are the three positions:

- A believes that one should follow the company policies and procedures, the contract, the law.
- B is pretty much a God-abiding person.
- C won't do anything that feels wrong.

And here are a few situations:

1. The three of you work at a video store. Your supervisor has asked you to do the year-end inventory of the video store's collection, but she has also asked you to come up with a (single) list of a dozen or so videos; despite the "Do Not Copy" labels, she wants to dub copies to give to one of the local shelters. She knows that between the three of you, you've watched almost every video in the store and she trusts your judgement as to what might be appropriate. What do you do?

2. You are the team responsible for marketing, including promotion and distribution, of a product. The product is legal; it is also safe if used correctly, but you suspect that some potential buyers may use it incorrectly. What do you do?

3. The three of you would like to start an ethical investment firm, and you are now meeting to decide which stocks to include in your various ethical investment fund portfolios. Proceed.

One more time: What are your reasons? What are your assumptions? Define your terms. Consider alternatives.

References and Further Reading

Beauchamp, Tom L., and Norman E. Bowie, eds. *Ethical Theory and Business.* 5th ed. Upper Saddle River, NJ: Prentice Hall, 1997. (text/anthology)

Bird, Frederick B., and James A. Waters. "The Moral Muteness of Managers." *California Management Review* 32.1 (1989). Rpt. in *Ethi-cal Issues in Business: A Philosophical Approach.* Ed. Thomas Donaldson and Patricia H. Werhane. 5th ed. Upper Saddle River, NJ: Prentice Hall, 1996. 237-250.

Boatright, John R. *Ethics and the Conduct of Business.* 2nd ed. Upper Saddle River, NJ: Prentice Hall, 1997. (good introductions)

De George, Richard T. *Business Ethics.* 5th ed. Upper Saddle River, NJ: Prentice Hall, 1999. (very thorough, comprehensive)

DesJardins, Joseph R., and John J. McCall. *Contemporary Issues in Business Ethics.* 3rd ed. Belmont, CA: Wadsworth, 1996. (text/anthology)

Di Norcia, Vincent. *Hard Like Water: Ethics in Business.* Toronto: Oxford, 1998. (text, Canadian)

Michalos, Alex C. "Issues for Business Ethics in the Nineties and Beyond." *Journal of Business Ethics* 16.3 (February 1997): 219-230.

Newton, Lisa H., and Maureen M. Ford, eds. *Taking Sides: Clashing Views on Controversial Issues in Business Ethics and Society.* 4th ed. Guilford, CT: Dushkin, 1996. (pro/con anthology)

Poff, Deborah C., and Wilfrid J. Waluchow, eds. *Business Ethics in Canada.* 3rd ed. Scarborough: Prentice Hall Allyn and Bacon, 1999. (text/anthology, Canadian, philosophical emphasis)

Richardson, John E., ed. *Annual Editions: Business Ethics.* Guilford, CT: Dushkin, 1999. (anthology of magazine articles) (others listed as anthologies contain journal articles)

Shaw, William H., and Vincent Barry. *Moral Issues in Business.* 7th ed. Belmont, CA: Wadsworth, 1998. (text/anthology)

Stewart, David. *Business Ethics.* NY: McGraw-Hill, 1996. (lots of positive role models in case studies)

Treviño, Linda K., and Katherine A. Nelson. *Managing Business Ethics: Straight Talk About How To Do It Right.* 2nd ed. NY: John Wiley & Sons, 1999. (very practical, very applied, business emphasis)

Velasquez, Manuel G. *Business Ethics: Concepts and Cases.* 4th ed. Upper Saddle River, NJ: Prentice Hall, 1998. (very thorough, comprehensive)

Critical Thinking references

Bickenbach, Jerome E., and Jacqueline M. Davies. *Good Reasons for Better Arguments: An Introduction to the Skills and Values of Critical Thinking.* Peterborough: Broadview Press, 1997.

Browne, M. Neil, and Stuart M. Keeley. *Asking the Right Questions: A Guide to Critical Thinking.* Englewood Cliffs, NJ: Prentice Hall, 1994.

Chaffee, John. *Thinking Critically.* Boston: Houghton Mifflin, 1997.

Damer, T. Edward. *Attacking Faulty Reasoning: A Practical Guide to Fallacy-Free Arguments.* Belmont, CA: Wadsworth, 1995.

Diestler, Sherry. *Becoming a Critical Thinker: A User-Friendly Manual.* New York: Macmillan, 1994.

Dowden, Bradley H. *Logical Reasoning.* Belmont, CA: Wadsworth Publishing Company, 1993.

Engel, S. Morris. *With Good Reason: An Introduction to Informal Fallacies.* New York: St. Martin's Press, 1994.

Feldman, Richard. *Reason and Argument.* Upper Saddle River, NJ: Prentice Hall, 1993.

Groarke, Leo A., Christopher W. Tindale, and Linda Fisher. *Good Reasoning Matters!* Toronto: Oxford University Press, 1997.

Hughes, William. *Critical Thinking: An Introduction to the Basic Skills.* Peterborough: Broadview Press, 1992.

Missimer, C.A. *Good Arguments: An Introduction to Critical Thinking.* Englewood Cliffs, NJ: Prentice Hall, 1995.

Ruggiero, Vincent Ryan. *Beyond Feelings: A Guide to Critical Thinking.* Mountain View, CA: Mayfield, 1995.

Seech, Zachary. *Open Minds and Everyday Reasoning.* Belmont, CA: Wadsworth, 1993.

Thomson, Anne. *Critical Reasoning: A Practical Introduction.* London: Routledge, 1996.

Section II

Introduction to Ethical Theory

INTRODUCTION TO ETHICAL THEORY

Introductory Note

The big question is "How should we determine whether something is right or wrong?" Some people have given this question a lot of thought and have come up with rather coherent and complete answers. These have come to be known as ethical theories, and in this section I'll take you on a brief tour of these theories. For each theory, I'll describe the main principles and suggest some of its strengths and weaknesses; I'll also show that theory in action.

But first, a few comments. One important distinction to make is that between descriptive and prescriptive theories. Simply put, as explained in the previous section, "descriptive" refers to what *is* the case, whereas "prescriptive" refers to what *should be* the case. So, descriptive theories describe what, in fact, we do; prescriptive theories describe what we *should* do. Ethics, and this text, is interested in the latter; science is interested in the former. For example, to say that human beings are selfish and do only what's in their own interest is to be descriptive (and, in fact, this particular theory is called psychological egoism). To say, however, that we *should* do whatever is in our own interest, to say that we should define "right" according to what's in our own interest — that's prescriptive (and, in fact, that particular theory is called ethical egoism).

The distinction is crucial, and failure to grasp it will definitely mess you up with ethical theories (especially egoism and relativism) and ethical discussion in general.

And that takes us to my second point: understand that in this text we're concerned with "should," not "is." Science — whether physical or social — deals with empirical questions: it seeks to discover what is; it seeks to describe. Philosophy — including ethics — deals with conceptual questions. Now that's not to say that the sciences don't deal with concepts; on the contrary, they can be *very* conceptual, very abstract, very theoretical. But they are so in order to explain, to describe what *is*. Ethics uses concepts to explain what *should* be. On the one hand, philosophers don't care about what *is*, we don't care whether something is true. But on the other hand, we do care — in fact, as explained in Section I, our carefully constructed arguments are worthless unless our premises are true — but we leave the job of establishing truth to others, to science.

Third, be on the alert for the "is/ought" fallacy (a.k.a. the fact-value fallacy, Hume's law, the naturalistic fallacy): when one *derives* ought from is, when one says that we *should* do X *because* we *do* do X, one is committing the "is/ought" fallacy. Why is it a fallacy? Well, just because we do something, it doesn't follow that we *should* do it. For example, an angry person may lose his/

her temper and hit someone – but surely we wouldn't conclude that they therefore *should* lose their temper and hit someone. Humans often attempt to settle conflicts with force – but that doesn't mean we *should* attempt to settle conflicts with force.

There are a number of ways to categorize ethical theories: one can divide them into objective and subjective theories; universal and relative; absolute and non-absolute; principle-based and consequence-based; cognitive and non-cognitive; etc. Each of these labels looks at a different aspect, so a theory could be objective and consequence-based; or it could be subjective and non-cognitive. You get the picture. I'm going to steer a little away from categorizing; it's an important and useful skill, to be sure, but it can be confusing unless you spend a lot of time with it. And since this is not a text/course in ethical theories, we're *not* going to spend that much time on it. But if you're interested, by all means check out some of the books on ethical theory (see the list at the end of this section) and know that most universities have entire courses on the subject.

On the same note, please realize that every one of the ethical theories presented has a lot more breadth and depth than I will indicate. In a way, my superficial descriptions are quite unfair to the theories, and indeed many of the questions I will raise, often as weaknesses, already have extensive answers. (I have remedied this a little by including excerpts from the original texts in Appendix I.) However, my purpose here is to give you an introductory tour of the possibilities, and alert you to the important questions.

Egoism

There are two versions of ethical egoism. The first, individual egoism, says, "X is (morally) right if it's in my own interests" – if some action is good for me, it's right. As such, egoism is a consequentialist theory: it determines right and wrong according to the consequences, according to what happens (and, in this case, something is right when what happens is in your own interests).

So, let's say you have to decide whether to create a daycare centre in your company. If you're an egoist, your thinking might go something like this: hey, I'm paying half my salary for private daycare – a company daycare would probably be cheaper; and it would cut out the hassle and expense of dropping the kids off and picking them up; and I could go spend time with them – we could have lunch together every day; I might be criticized for endorsing such a "soft" program – then again, I might be commended as a progressive and innovative manager; it might attract some top performers and that would be to my credit. Yeah. I think I will go ahead with it, it seems like the right thing to do.

Notice how all his (let's assume a 'he' for this one) thoughts focus on the benefits to him. He mentions others – his kids and potential "top performers" – but he does so only insofar as *he* is affected. And he almost gets to "happier employees are better employees," but he really doesn't take that step – he stops at the implication that *he'll* be happier (to be able to spend time with his kids).

Thomas Hobbes, a seventeenth-century thinker and author of *Leviathan*, is often associated with egoism: he argues that our natural condition leads us to a morality of self-interest; he's the one known for the delightful phrase "Life is nasty, brutish, and short" (an attitude revived in the late twentieth century by T-shirts that proclaim "Life's a bitch, then you die"). But actually he went on to say that in the state of nature in which life is so, there is no right and wrong; morality itself doesn't come to be until we become civilized.

Lest you dismiss the selfishness of egoism quickly and easily, consider Ayn Rand's critical but perhaps accurate definition of altruism: "[A]ny action taken for the benefit of others is good, and any action taken for one's own benefit is evil. Thus, the *beneficiary* of an action is the only criterion of moral value — and so long as the beneficiary is anybody other than oneself, anything goes" (vii). And indeed, why should any other person count more than me?

Perhaps the key is to distinguish selfishness from self-interest: the former is self-interest even at the other's expense, to the other's detriment. Thus, while egoists may be self-interested, they might not necessarily be selfish. (Also, don't confuse egoist with egotist: the latter has nothing to do with ethical theory; it merely describes someone who is conceited and brags a lot.)

Also, it may be in our best interests to attend to the interests of others; in this regard, some distinguish between narrow self-interest and wide self-interest. But note that the egoist considers others only if it's in his/her interests to do so; considering others independent of one's own interests is utilitarian (see next subsection).

The second version of egoism, universal egoism, says, "Everyone should consider (morally) right those things that are in their own interests." So the student who answers the question "Is X the right thing to do?" with "It depends on whose point of view you take — as a consumer, you might say yes, but as the business owner, you might say no" is actually presenting the position of a universal egoist. S/he is assuming that everyone will be looking out for their own interests, "voting" for the answer that best suits themselves; s/he is implying, then, that everyone *should* look out for their own interests. (But can't you be a consumer and still say it's wrong to pay the lower price — if, say, the product was manufactured by exploited workers? Can't you be non-egoistic?)

Perhaps with universal egoism, we'd all be better off because, after all, who knows better what's good for us than our own selves? Altruism requires people to figure out, or second guess, what other people would like to happen. (And perhaps altruism is just another word for paternalism.)

Certainly another of egoism's strengths is that it seems to work well. People do seem to be motivated by self-interest (perhaps we are, by nature or nurture, egoists). Certainly Adam Smith, eighteenth-century thinker and author of *Wealth of Nations*, used egoism as a starting point for what has become modern economic theory: he believed that individuals free to pursue their own interests would be led, as if by an 'invisible hand,' to achieve the common good. But so what if egoism works well? Torture works well, too. (The point is that the fact of something working well doesn't make it right.)

And what about people who can't look out for their own interests? For example, children and the elderly? (So maybe it works well under certain conditions.)

Another problem with egoism is that one can't be both an individual and a universal egoist: saying that everyone should look out for their own interests is *not* looking out for your own interests (because what's in someone else's interests may be detrimental to your own interests). Universal egoism violates individual egoism.

Also, unlike utilitarianism (the next theory we'll consider), egoism provides no help for moral conflicts. What if being honest and being dishonest are *both* in your own interest — how do you decide between the two? For example, suppose that reporting a conflict of interest will make your supervisor think very highly of you, and it might lead to a promotion; not reporting the conflict of interest will enable you to get that deal on the side. How do you determine the *greater* self-interest?

Even more problematic, what's in our self-interest isn't always apparent even in the absence of conflict. Sometimes we don't know what we want; sometimes we don't know what's in our own best interest. Is it in our best interest to maximize our own pleasure, to be hedonistic egoists? Or is it in our best interest to do for others, to be altruistic egoists? (And then, how do you determine what to do for others?)

In every business ethics class, there will be at least one student who insists that all of us always act out of self-interest anyway (supporting the theory called psychological egoism — a *descriptive* theory); even altruists do what they do because it makes them feel good. See? They did it for themselves. They appeal to psychology, saying that we always act on our strongest desire.

Well, that may indeed be true. (Then again, it may not; I'm not sure science has established fact in this regard.) So what's the point of having a theory that tells you that you *should* do what you do anyway? Well, remember the is/ought fallacy: just because we *do* do it that way doesn't mean we *should*. So just because we *are* egoists doesn't mean we *should* be. But what if we can't help it? What if we've got no choice? No choice? Well, if you're saying we don't have any free will at all, then, I guess *all* of ethics, not just egoism, is irrelevant. (But I don't believe science has established fact with regard to free will either, and most of us seem to think we have at least some free will. So I *am* going to continue writing this book.)

Before you go on to the next theory, make a few notes: in point form, outline (1) the elements, (2) the strengths, and (3) the weaknesses of this theory. Also, (4) write a short paragraph describing an egoist approach to an ethical decision in a business context (go back and re-read the daycare decision example if you need to).

Utilitarianism

Utilitarianism, like egoism, is a consequence-based theory: it doesn't matter why you did something (intent), nor does it matter exactly what you did (action) — only the end result counts (consequence). In fact, the name *utilitarianism* comes from "utility," the notion that actions have utility — they are useful because of the consequences they bring about. But whereas egoism considers only the one person, the agent (the one performing the action), utilitarianism considers everyone involved. And that is the first important element of utilitarianism, this attention to "all concerned" (the phrase comes from John Stuart Mill, a nineteenth-century thinker and author of *Utilitarianism*).

The second important element of utilitarianism is hedonism, the idea that pleasure is good and pain is bad: "Nature has placed mankind under the governance of two sovereign masters, *pain* and *pleasure*. It is for them alone to point out what we ought to do...." (from Jeremy Bentham, an eighteenth-century thinker and author of *Introduction to the Principles of Morals and Legislation* [p. 1]). More specifically, we ought to maximize good and minimize bad — "the greatest happiness principle" (Mill). Thus, putting the two elements together, utilitarianism is "the greatest good (happiness/pleasure) for the greatest number."

So far so good, but how do you determine which of several possibilities will produce the *greatest* good? The method Bentham suggests is known as the "hedonistic calculus." He identified seven aspects of pleasure and pain, and said that the results of each action should be measured according to these seven aspects; the action with the highest total (of hedons, or units) would be the one resulting in the greatest pleasure – it would be the (morally) right one. These seven aspects are as follows:

1. *Intensity:* How strong will the pain or pleasure be?

2. *Duration:* How long will the pain or pleasure last?

3. *Certainty:* How likely is it that the anticipated pain or pleasure will occur?

4. *Propinquity* (nearness in time): How soon will the pain or pleasure be experienced?

5. *Fecundity* (fruitfulness): Will the pleasure sort of go forth and multiply? Will one be more able to experience other pleasures, having experienced this one?

6. *Purity:* How much pain is mixed in with the pleasure (or vice versa)?

7. *Extent:* How many sentient beings will be affected by the pain or pleasure?

One does the calculus, subtracting the pain from the pleasure for a net total, and voilà, you have the right answer!

Go ahead and try to apply Bentham's hedonistic calculus to a simple ethical decision: What's the right thing to do – read that great sci-fi novel or do your business ethics homework? (Don't forget to consider everyone who would be affected by your decision.)

	Sci-fi novel		Business ethics homework	
	Pleasure	Pain	Pleasure	Pain
1. Intensity				
2. Duration				
3. Certainty				
4. Propinquity				
5. Fecundity				
6. Purity				
7. Extent				
Subtotals	minus		minus	
Totals (in hedons)				

Which action resulted in the greatest total (the greatest pleasure for the greatest number)? *That's* the (morally) right thing to do!

Now, if one of the main weaknesses of this theory didn't become evident, try it with a more complicated decision: Should you hire the more qualified woman, knowing the men won't want to take orders from her, or should you hire the less qualified man?

	More qualified woman		Less qualified man	
	Pleasure	Pain	Pleasure	Pain
1. Intensity				
2. Duration				
3. Certainty				
4. Propinquity				
5. Fecundity				
6. Purity				
7. Extent				
Subtotals	minus		minus	
Totals (in hedons)				

Though the method promises a high degree of precision, it's almost impossible to make good on that promise: how do you quantify the qualities of pleasure? (How many hedons is a chocolate bar worth? And is a chocolate bar worth the same number of hedons to you as it is to me?) Even *identifying* the pleasures (and pains) is problematic, especially if they're not immediately evident.

And not only is "the greatest good" difficult to determine, "the greatest number" is equally problematic: how do we know, how can we determine, exactly who will be affected by the proposed action – how do we identify "all concerned"? In some cases, surely that would be society as a whole, perhaps even every person on Earth (why stop at people? why not every*thing* on Earth? as Bentham says, "The question

is not, Can they *reason*? nor Can they *talk?*, but Can they *suffer*?" [chap.XVIII, sec.1]): where do we draw the line? Well, we can't foresee the future, but surely we can make educated predictions – perhaps that's sufficient. (Perhaps not.)

Another criticism of Bentham's utilitarianism is directed toward its hedonism: many think pleasure is too shallow a measure of morality. "Correcting" this "flaw," Mill expanded the definition of pleasure to include not just the so-called base, physical pleasures, but also the so-called higher, aesthetic, and intellectual pleasures. Furthermore, Mill distinguished between various pleasures, not just in quantity, but also in quality: he argued, for example, that intellectual pleasures are *better than* physical pleasures: "It is better to be a human being dissatisfied than a pig satisfied; better to be a Socrates dissatisfied than a fool satisfied. And if the fool, or the pig, are of a different opinion, it is because they know only their side of the question" (10). Mill's version is known as qualitative hedonism; Bentham's view as quantitative hedonism. But with purity, fruitfulness, and intensity in Bentham's calculus, I'm not sure this is a fair description (or criticism). Most people equate hedonism with a sort of selfish self-indulgence, but it certainly can be more refined than that.

There are two kinds of utilitarianism: *act utilitarianism* and *rule utilitarianism*. Act utilitarianism judges just a single, one-time act: for example, is this lie in this advertisement morally acceptable? Rule utilitarianism judges the rule, the action in general: for example, is lying morally acceptable? (To this extent, however, rule utilitarianism may be more properly considered a separate principle-based theory than a species of utilitarianism – and yet, it does consider consequences.) Although rule utilitarianism may seem easier (you have to figure it out just once and for all), act utilitarianism allows fine differences in context to be taken into account: for example, maybe lying generally speaking is immoral, but in advertisements, for some reason, it's okay. (Hm. And the reason is?)

Some people consider one of utilitarianism's strengths to be the fact that it takes everyone into account; not only that, it considers everyone equally, you can't play favourites. However, this is exactly what others see as a weakness: if you, as an organ peddler, have only one liver to sell, you can't choose your daughter over some stranger (well, you can, but not because she's your daughter – you can if and only if it works out that choosing her results in the greatest good for the greatest number – maybe she's on the edge of discovering a cure for AIDS and the stranger is not.)

Somewhat related to this "no favourites" aspect of utilitarianism is the criticism that it doesn't take into account any rights. Suppose the stranger had a greater right to the liver for some reason (you'd have to be clear about what right that was and how it was determined – maybe your daughter, an alcoholic, already used up two livers). That doesn't matter, says utilitarianism. And so, in addition, the decision may be called unfair – which is another criticism of utilitarianism: it ignores the matter of justice.

Now of course you could consider relationships, rights, and justice in your calculation: maybe not selling it to your daughter (wait a minute – it's your *daughter*, wouldn't you just *give* it to her? Hey, this is a *business* example – we don't just give stuff away!) would cause great pain to you, so much so that it outweighs the good created by selling it to the stranger; maybe violating rights, maybe doing an injustice, is not for the good of society at large. But these concerns (of relationships, rights, and justice) are relevant only insofar as they're relevant to "the greatest good for the greatest number."

Another strength of utilitarianism might be that because it involves comparison of potential actions, it encourages the consideration of alternatives. Many other theories involve consideration of just a single action – is *this* action right? Utilitarianism, on the other hand, involves a sort of competition between actions – *which* action is right? One might, then, become more innovative with utilitarianism.

Cost-benefit analysis is sometimes considered an example of utilitarianism. It does, after all, involve a calculation of net good (benefits minus costs). However, it seems a little more like egoism in that often the issue is not the greatest good *for the greatest number* but the greatest good *for our company* (there's that self-interest characteristic of egoism). Second, it measures in dollars, not hedons; attaching *monetary* (market) value is different than just attaching value (see the Kel-man article). Third, it usually emphasizes short-term consequences. Fourth, cost-benefit analysts don't usually claim to be seeking the *morally* right answer as much as the *strategically* right answer.

Perhaps the greatest strength of utilitarianism is that, unlike most other ethical theories, it does provide – at least in theory – a solution to moral conflicts. You just do your calculus for whatever options are in conflict, and the one that wins, wins. (Though I suppose you could end up with a tie.)

Let's go back now to the decision about whether to create a daycare centre in your company. The utilitarian would certainly consider the benefits to self that the egoist considered, but she would also consider the benefits to the kids involved (they could see their parents at lunch every day), the benefits to other (current and potential) employees who are parents (they'd also save money and time, and get to see their kids), probably the benefits to society as a whole (the improved parent-child relationships may decrease a number of social ills). Then the utilitarian would figure in the negative side: the daycare would cost the company, so something (profits? wages?) would have to be cut – how much of a "pain" this would be would probably depend on the size of the company; perhaps a local daycare would be put out of business (though maybe it would just be able to take more of the kids on its waiting list); employees without kids may resent the special program – would they, could they, call it discrimination? If the good stuff outweighs, by hedons, the bad stuff, then the greatest good for the greatest number results if the daycare is, rather than is not, created – so that

would be the (morally) right thing to do. (But did you consider alternatives to is/is not?)

That would be an act-utilitarian analysis of the situation. A rule-utilitarian might generalize the question "Should I create a daycare centre in this company?" to "Should companies establish programs to meet employees' external needs?" – and then similarly, systematically, work through the pleasures and pains for all concerned. (And, conceptualized in this broader fashion, one might then consider also the impact of the decision on the role of government, and its need to tax, should companies take on the responsibility for such programs.)

Now before you go on, again do your short summary – what are (1) the elements, (2) the strengths, and (3) the weaknesses of utilitarianism? And, (4) try using this theory to make an ethical decision in a business context.

Kantian Ethics

Unlike consequence-based theories, the end cannot justify the means in principle-based theories. Principle-based theories consider not the consequences, but the intent. And intents are guided by certain principles (or perhaps, virtues – see the next subsection on virtue ethics). However, don't assume that the principles in a principle-based ethical theory are necessarily absolutes; exceptions may be permissible.

The ethical theory of Immanuel Kant, an eighteenth-century thinker and author of *Grounding for the Metaphysics of Morals*, is perhaps the most famous (the most lionized?) principle-based ethical theory. Acts done with the right intent (the "good will") are right acts. So what's the right intent? Kant's answer is "that which accords with duty." And what's our duty? "That which is rational" – rationality is what makes us human. (It's interesting to note that Kant is not the first, or the last, to suggest that reason – rationality – plays a central role in morality; see Aristotle and Rawls.)

So, how do we know what's rational? Enter Kant's categorical imperative: "Act only according to that maxim whereby you can at the same time will that it should become a universal law" (30). Now be careful that you understand him not to be appealing to bad consequences as the test, but to non-contradictoriness as the test; Kant considers rationality to be the essence of being human – and rationality is intolerant of contradictions. So his imperative is not just a "do unto others as you would have them do unto you" thing; rather, he's saying that whatever principle we can imagine everyone following *without ending up with some sort of logical impossibility or inconsistency* is a principle we should follow.

For example, if everyone cheated on tests, tests would lose their value, their meaning, and then so too would cheating: if everyone cheated, what would be the point of cheating? Actually, if everyone cheated, it couldn't even be called cheating: you're cheating in order to gain some sort of unfair advantage over other test-takers, but if everyone's allowed to cheat, then no longer is what you're doing unfair, nor will it give you any special advantage. So in future when you cheated, you'd be acting for a purpose that would not, could not, be achieved; one couldn't "cheat" if everyone did. So cheating is *not* something you can make into a universal law (without it logically falling apart) – so it's not rational. So it's not (morally) right.

Now, as Mill pointed out, Kant *is* actually considering consequences, albeit the logical consequences, when determining the morality of an action, so it's *not* really a non-consequentialist

theory. However, one could distinguish between considering the consequences for logic and the consequences for good/happiness/pleasure.

The other important element of Kantian ethics is respect for persons, which is expressed by Kant through his practical imperative: "Act in such a way that you treat humanity, whether in your own person or in the person of another, always at the same time as an end and never simply as a means" (36). And, since Kant understands persons to be essentially rational beings with free will, respect for persons means respect for their autonomy.

As with all principle-based theories, one must ask why these principles and not others? What's the justification for these principles? Do we agree that rationality is the essence of being human? And even if we do, why should that also be the essence of being moral?

One strength of Kant's theory is the attention to motive, the attention to one's reason for behaviour – regardless of the consequences. So if you meant well, if you intended to do good, but unfortunately injury still occurred, your action is still judged favourably, it is still judged to have been the right thing to do. Like all non-consequentialists, Kant recognizes that consequences are not necessarily within our control.

Another strength of this theory is its universality: there is no "it depends" involved in Kant's theory. However, there is a bit of grey area here similar to the rule-act distinction in utilitarianism: when we ask about universalizing the act, does Kant mean us, for example, to consider cheating in general or cheating in this situation, by a person in these specific circumstances?

Yet another strength is its impartiality: everyone is considered equally, there's no playing favourites. One must apply the imperatives consistently; this would seem to lead to fairness.

What are its weaknesses? Well, it's certainly not as precise as, say, utilitarianism. What exactly does it mean to say one should respect another's autonomy? How far must we go to ensure that one can choose, can act freely and rationally?

Also, Kant is an absolutist: he allows no exceptions. For example, if a psychopath with a gun comes to your door and asks if anyone else is in the house, you must not lie – you must say "Yes, my kids are asleep upstairs: would you like to meet them?" For many, that's a problem – and one might argue, as Mill does, that a rational person would *not* universalize a moral rule that would result in harm (they *would* lie to the psychopath).

Lastly, as in many ethical theories, conflicts are a problem. What if actions X and Y both respect the other's autonomy and are both universalizable – what do you do?

Let's see how this theory can be applied to ethical decision-making in a business context. Suppose you've got Kant on your marketing team – what do you do? Well, you prepare yourself for some major changes in the advertising industry: no deception, full disclosure, enabling the rational consumer, who is not a means to your end, to make his/her own free choices. (You say Kant's on your negotiating team as well?)

Don't forget to do your summary – elements, strengths, and weaknesses. And, for application practice, how would a Kantian ethicist handle this one: should you send your openly gay employee on an international mission to a country that considers homosexuality abnormal and sinful?

Virtue Ethics

Although most of the other ethical theories ask "What's the right thing to do?", virtue ethics asks "What's the right kind of person to be?" The answer is "a virtuous person." So far, so good. But you must define your terms: what's virtuous? You'll need to make a list of virtues (those things a virtuous person has). Then you'll have to justify that list.

Aristotle, a thinker who lived around 350 B.C.E. and author of *The Nicomachean Ethics*, is considered a virtue ethicist. His list of virtues includes the standard four of the ancient Greeks – justice, temperance, courage, and wisdom – and adds a few others such as pride, magnanimity, proper ambition, veracity, modesty, gentleness, sincerity, and frankness. The big thing for Aristotle is that all virtues are at the midpoint between two extremes, the extreme of deficiency and the extreme of excess – this is his theory of "the golden mean." For example, be courageous, not cowardly nor foolhardy. He justifies his list by saying that these are the qualities that enable us to experience *eudamonia* (loosely translated as happiness, but a broad, well-being kind of happiness rather than a narrow pleasure kind of happiness), which is achieved by developing our unique human function, that of rationality. However, Aristotle also emphasizes that moral virtue is the result of habit and training – one is taught to become a virtuous person. This notion of habit seems, at least to me, to contradict his emphasis on rationality.

William David Ross, a twentieth-century thinker and author of *The Right and the Good*, suggests the following list, phrased in terms of obligations rather than virtues (and therefore his theory is perhaps more an example of principle-based ethics than of virtue ethics – however, one can simply regard virtues as deriving from principles): fidelity, reparation, gratitude, justice, beneficence, self-improvement, and non-maleficence. As for justification for this list, Ross says we intuitively know these are our duties. But there's one problem: if these virtues are indeed intuitively known, or self-evident, then there would be no disagreement about them. And, of course, there is. So if my intuition is different from yours, where does that leave us? (Check out the subsection on intuitionism.)

Alasdair MacIntyre, another contemporary virtue ethicist and author of *After Virtue*, says that virtues are dependent on the culture involved, more specifically on the practice involved: virtues are whatever traits are needed to do whatever it is one is doing with excellence, according to the tradition of the endeavour. For example, a virtuous soldier has the virtues of loyalty, physical courage, and physical resilience. And perhaps a virtuous businessperson would have the virtues of innovativeness and persistence?

Whatever your list, and whatever your justification, eventually you'll have to decide on priorities: for example, what do you do when honesty and loyalty collide? That is one of the weaknesses of virtue ethics: it doesn't help us with moral conflict.

Let's try virtue ethics with the situation I left with you for Kantian ethics: should you send your openly gay employee on that mission to a country that considers homosexuality abnormal and sinful? Well, an Aristotelian virtue ethicist would ask if doing so would be just and wise. (These seem to be the most applicable virtues on Aristotle's list; the question doesn't seem to be a matter of temperance, pride, magnanimity, etc.) And it seems to me that if that employee was indeed competent and deserving, sending him would indeed be just – but would it be wise? The employee may well be injured, and the company may lose the deal and possibly the client. Ross would encounter a similar conflict: sending him would be just, but it would surely

do some harm (so it violates the virtue of non-maleficence). Perhaps MacIntyre, who might identify as a necessary trait for a businessperson that of catering to the client, would say don't send that particular employee – it could be an offense to the client. But *would* MacIntyre identify that as a necessary trait, a virtue? And would, should, a virtue be adopted at any expense, possibly at the expense of other virtues? (I can as easily suggest that MacIntyre would identify competence as a virtue.)

Okay, you know the summary routine: elements, strengths, weaknesses, application. (I know this is getting boring, but, do it anyway. It's the right thing to do!)

Feminist Ethics

Many textbooks cover feminist ethics as a separate ethical theory, but I'm not sure this is warranted. It seems to me that what's called feminist ethics is a kind of virtue ethics in which the virtue of caring is most important, along with things like compassion and sensitivity – i.e., those qualities stereotypically associated with women (and I emphasize "stereotypically").

Nel Noddings, a contemporary thinker and author of *Caring: A Feminine Approach to Ethics and Moral Education*, advocates such an ethics of care: actions done out of care for others are (morally) right actions. This theory emphasizes responsibility, especially responsibility arising from relationships. However, reciprocity is also important: Noddings claims that caring-for is morally right when cared-for is also in the picture.

Given care as a determinant of rightness, one would need to decide whether intent or consequence mattered more. What if you do something because you care, but it turns out to have not-so-good results? Some parents hit their kids because they care about them. Further, how do we determine who we should care about? No doubt, there will be competition – how do we rank those we (are to) care about?

This ethic of care developed, perhaps, as a reaction to the Kantian ethic of duty; to some, and perhaps more often to women than to men, duty seemed too bereft of emotion. Further, the emphasis on relationships is thought to be a re-action to the Kantian ethic which emphasizes autonomy, often as if people existed completely independent of any social context.

Indeed this rejection of the autonomous person, as either possible or preferable, is the basis of communitarianism (see Michael Walzer and Amitai Etzioni) which, like communism/Marxism (see Karl Marx, co-author of *The Communist Manifesto*), rejects this primacy of the in-dividual – both claim that we are, and should be, presumably, *social* beings. African and Na-tive ethical systems also give a dominant posi-tion to the community over the individual.

The Noddings/communitarian view would, I think, yield a "go ahead" about the company daycare decision presented in the subsection on egoism – care, responsibility, and relationships are all endorsed by such a decision and so cre-ating the daycare would be the right thing to do. (Though whether *the company* should do it might be arguable.) What about the gay employee and the international mission discussed in "Kantian Ethics" and "Virtue Ethics"?

However, it is important to note that not all feminists advocate this particular ethic. Alison Jaggar, another contemporary thinker and femi-nist, argues that for something to be called femi-nist ethics, it must in some way correct male bias and subvert women's subordination; it must ad-dress both public and private domains; and it must take women's experiences seriously.

One of the basic tenets of feminism – equal-ity of the sexes – is not incompatible with other ethical theories, especially justice theories and utilitarianism. Given this, it may be difficult to identify the main elements, strengths, and weak-nesses of feminist ethics, but give it a try any-way with respect to Noddings and Jaggar.

Naturalistic Theories

Aristotle is the person associated with natural law theory (as well as virtue ethics), which states that whatever is true to nature is right (so note that by "natural law," "nature" is meant, not "the laws of nature" or "science"). Recall that Aris-totle claimed, as did Kant much later, that what made humans (well, male humans – Aristotle considered women to be "mutilated male[s]", clearly inferior, and without rational capability) different from (other) animals was "our" capac-ity to be rational: "It is the life which accords with reason then that will be best and pleasantest for Man, as a man's reason is in his highest sense himself" (346). It would follow that Aristotle saw as morally right anything that accorded with this essence, this true nature of humans. So rational action is right action.

We might ask, of course, as we did with Kant, whether he should have focused on that attribute – *is* rationality the unique nature of humans? Many would say that other animals are capable of rational behaviour. Many would say that the capacity to deceive or the capacity to laugh is a better candidate for what defines us as human beings. (Though these latter at-tributes have been observed in other animals as well.)

Also, many consider Aristotle's natural law theory to be the quintessential case of the is/ought fallacy: so what if we *are* by nature rational? It doesn't necessarily follow that we *should* be rational.

Thomas Aquinas, a medieval thinker and author of *Summa Theologica*, is another advocate of natural law, but his version of natural law is really divine law: everything – nature – was created by God, so of course that which is natural is good, and that which is unnatural is bad. Therefore, we should follow our inclinations, we should follow what nature – by God's command – leads us to do; interestingly, Aquinas identified our inclinations as staying alive, reproducing, doing no harm, and seeking knowledge of God.

But not only does this have the problem of all religionist ethics (see the subsection on religionism), it seems that Aquinas forgot to notice that among our inclinations are a few "bad" ones, such as seeking revenge (*doing* harm). In fact, the classic problem (for religionists) of evil becomes especially applicable: if God created everything, he also created people who do evil; in fact, when an evil person does something "unnatural," well, aren't they just doing what comes naturally to them? So isn't it good? One of the classic counters to this problem of evil is the notion of free will; one might ask, however, whether free will is compatible with inclinations.

This brings us to a more central problem with naturalistic theories: what exactly do "nature" and "natural" mean? If they are opposed to artificial, well, aren't artificial things just things created by humans, using natural substances but in combinations not occurring without our intervention? Eventually, it all comes down to a hundred or so elements, doesn't it? Why should something *we* create using our natural intelligence be less good? (Are bricks then unnatural, and evil?)

Or does "natural" mean "instinctive"? Well, doesn't "instinctive" really mean "unthinking" or "not learned"? Why should something with*out* thought be better than something *with* thought, something learned?

A sort of contemporary version of natural law theory is evolutionary ethics. As the name suggests, this theory adds an ethical dimension to evolution: that which evolves as it does is (morally) good/right as it is. However, survival superiority doesn't necessarily mean moral superiority. Otherwise we should consult the cockroach about what's right and wrong.

Let's look at a new scenario: Is it right, according to a natural law ethicist, to sell your product/service to countries that are violating human rights? You might respond first by saying "That depends on what my product/service is." Fair enough. So let's suppose two possibilities: (a) your product is weaponry; (b) your service is conflict resolution and mediation. I'll do the first one and you can do the second one.

Aristotle might argue that it's irrational to use weapons; communication and negotiation are more reasonable approaches to problems. So, by selling weapons to such countries, perhaps to *any* countries (if only because *all* countries, including our own, probably violate *some* human rights), you are endorsing, supporting, even encouraging, the irrational, the unnatural – so it's wrong.

Aquinas, however, might say that selling weapons violates our inclination to do no harm. But it might very well support our inclination to stay alive. Well, no, it might support *the client's* inclination to stay alive. (*Might.* What are they really going to use the weapons for?) As for the godliness issue, a close reading of the Bible shows that the Judaeo-Christian gods can be strong advocates of weaponry (for example, "He that hath no sword, let him sell his garment, and buy one" – Luke 22:36).

And what about evolutionary ethics? Some might say we are evolving beyond "might is right," but others might say weapons simply take "survival of the fittest" to a higher level of technological sophistication. In any case, your decision is whether to *sell* weapons, not whether to *use* them. There's a difference, right? (A *moral* difference?)

Okay, your turn: what do naturalistic theories say about selling conflict resolution services to countries involved in human rights violations? Is it the right thing to do?

Summary time – elements? strengths? weaknesses? (Yes, I *am* being less explicit about these as we go on – so it *is* getting harder to pick them out. I'm trying to develop your critical reading skills. Put some thought between the lines and you'll be fine.)

Intuitionism

Intuitionism as an ethical theory says that you should act according to your intuition (recall Ross's suggestions in the subsection on virtue ethics). I have seen some business ethics accounts refer to this as the "gut test." Another quick ethical check touted in business ethics circles, the "media test," is also basically intuitionism: you are asked to imagine that the media got wind of your contemplated action – how would that make you feel?

I am also going to put into the intuitionism category the "follow your conscience" theory. It seems to me that what we call our conscience is often no more than our feelings: "conscience" seems to refer to what we "deep down" (what-

ever that means) think is right. Yet despite the word "think," there doesn't seem to be any rational element involved – we never suggest that one critically examine one's conscience, develop it, or reconsider it. Some people may believe that conscience is something we're born with, but there's no scientific evidence of this. Rather, conscience seems to be nothing more than the moral habits we're conditioned to follow as we are raised (recall Aristotle), and as with many childhood acquisitions, it simply feels wrong to violate any of them.

There are a few problems with intuitionism. The most significant, I think, is the unreliability of our feelings. Emotion often seems to be a less evolved aspect of our existence: many times you feel a certain way because of some information, but after you realize the information is incorrect, it takes a while for your feelings to "catch up" – you still feel angry or sad or whatever, even though you know you have no reason to.

Second, one might do well to ask whether we should always act on our feelings. Certainly anger is one feeling it is best not to act on – at least not right away. Sometimes even feelings of love (or am I confusing that with lust?) are better not acted upon.

A third problem with intuitionism is that it offers no solution for moral conflicts: what if your feelings tell you to do two mutually exclusive things – say, save employees' jobs and save shareholders' returns – how do you decide between the two?

Lastly, the very subjective nature of intuitionism may be problematic: it can never be wrong; others may not be able to predict or understand how you'll behave; certainly your behaviour will not be open to discussion. And what if you don't know? What if your intuition doesn't give you a strong nudge one way or the other?

So, how would an intuitionist decide what to do about creating a company daycare? If it feels right, do it! And sending the gay employee on that international mission? If it feels right, do it! Okay, you try one. Is it right for your company to sell weapons to those countries involved in human rights violations? How about selling mediation services?

When you've completed your summary for intuitionism, take a few moments to do a bit of comparison among the seven ethical theories we've covered so far. Are any similar in any way? What are the main differences? Which theory is the best so far? (Define your terms — what do you mean by "best"?)

Rights Theories

Rights theories say that it is wrong to violate someone's rights. So the big questions for rights theorists are: (1) What rights do we have? (2) Why those and not others? (i.e., what's the basis for those rights?), and (3) In the event of conflict, which rights can override which others?

Some people, natural rights theorists, argue that we have certain rights just because we are human — we don't have to do anything in particular to earn them. Such theorists would have to define "human" — does a fetus have those "human rights"? Some would like to extend natural rights to all *sentient* life forms or to all life forms *with interests*; others propose extending natural rights to *all* life forms, period.

Natural rights are usually considered inalienable; that means that they can't be given or taken away (neither forfeited, nor waived, nor traded). Certainly proponents of capital punishment would disagree in this regard: they would claim that one forfeits one's own right to life when one violates another's.

Unlike natural rights theorists, social contract theorists argue that certain rights are ours because we *have* done something to acquire those rights. Locke, for example, argued that when we enter society, we enter into a social contract, an agreement to respect each other's rights — and indeed, the purpose of government is to protect those rights; he considered foremost the rights to life, liberty, and property.

Kant seems to be in both groups: he speaks of innate rights, those we have by nature, and acquired rights, those which depend on human society. However — no surprise — all rights must be universalizable and respectful of autonomy.

Ronald Dworkin, a contemporary advocate of rights theories and author of *Taking Rights Seriously*, argues that rights, when they are applicable, should count more than social well-being. He values respect for individuals and believes that violating people's rights is always an injustice. Unlike the utilitarian view, which holds the social good supreme, Dworkin's view is that it would be wrong to violate people's rights in order to achieve a social good.

It is important to distinguish rights from obligations: having a right to property doesn't mean someone (perhaps the state) is obligated to provide you with property; it just means they can't take away any property you have. At least so say natural rights theorists. Duty-based rights theorists, however, would disagree; they would say that any right implies a corresponding duty or obligation — if I have a right to X, you have a duty to honour that right. Such rights were identified as "claim rights" by Wesley Hohfeld and Joel Feinberg, two contemporary rights theorists, and such rights can be held against specific individuals or society at large.

Claim rights can be divided into positive rights and negative rights: when someone else has a duty to do something to/for you, you have a positive right – for example, Canadians have a right to unemployment insurance (the state has a duty to make payments, if applicable); when someone else has a duty *not* to do something to/for you, you have a negative right – for example, we have a right to privacy (others have a duty *not* to intrude).

Let's consider a new ethical decision using a rights-based approach: you would like to conduct your business in the language of your choice – should you? Now remember, we're asking about the morally right thing to do, not the legally right thing – so it doesn't necessarily matter if we're talking about French or Cree or Japanese. I say "not necessarily" – if you define moral right by legal right, then it *would* matter (see the subsection on relativism): since French is one of Canada's official languages, you would have more of a legal right to conduct business in French than in Japanese. As for conducting business in Cree, well, depending who and where you are, you may argue that Canada's laws are not binding on First Nations' business.

But as for *moral* rightness, independent of legal rightness, well, which rights and whose rights are you exercising or violating by conducting business in the language of your choice? Do you have language rights? Do you have a right to freedom of speech? Does that include language of speech or just, as is the usual interpretation, content of speech? Do you have a right to preserve your culture? Is using your language, in business, a way of doing that? A necessary way? Do your customers/clients have the same rights that may be supported or violated by your decision (depending on what *their* language of choice is)? What about your employees, current and potential – do you have a right to require

them to speak (and learn?) the language you choose? Would it matter whether or not your customers and employees were unilingual? These are some of the questions that would need to be asked, from a rights-based point of view, before making a decision.

Don't forget to do your summary – and then try using the rights-based approach with an ethical decision in a business context of your choice.

Justice Theories

Justice theories say that whatever's fair is right. But what's fair? Well, there are a number of possibilities. One is egalitarianism: everyone gets an equal portion of whatever and that's that.

However, another possibility considers desert: every gets what they deserve. But how do you determine what people deserve? Usually, it's what they've earned. But what if you can't do much, what if you'd like to "earn" what you get, but you just can't? Even if you can, how do we connect doing with deserving? By time? So an hour's work is worth so much, no matter what you do in that hour? By effort? So the more you sweat in that hour, the more you deserve? (And what if you're unlucky enough to find most things easy, what if you never sweat?) By skill? So the better nurse gets paid more than the other one? By contribution? So an hour of literacy teaching is worth more than an hour of playing hockey? By risk to self? So an hour of playing hockey is worth more than an hour of literacy teaching? By "finder's keepers"? By inheritance?

Perhaps fair is getting what one needs rather than what one deserves. Then how shall we define "need" – food, water, shelter? So when people say they need at least $30,000/year, what are *they* calling "need"? Maybe the truth is they *want* $30,000/year.

Note that in both of these cases, determining by desert and determining by need, treating everyone justly would *not* mean treating everyone the same. To look only at the last example, people with greater needs would receive a greater share of the goods.

Two big names in justice theory are Aristotle and Rawls. Aristotle divided justice into three kinds: distributive justice (how the goods are divided up), retributive justice (punishing transgressors), and compensatory justice (compensating those transgressed). He also distinguished between just procedures and just outcomes.

With respect to distributive justice, with which business is perhaps most concerned, Aristotle said to treat like cases alike; one has to identify relevant similarities and differences in order to determine whether or not cases *are* alike. For example, with respect to the opening discussion, A gets more X (for example, pay) than B if A has more Y (effort, value, need, etc.) than B, and the 'more' is exactly proportionate – twice the pay for twice the effort, for example.

Of course, one might wonder whether one can calculate X and Y with as much precision as is necessary. And of course, Aristotle never says what the X, or especially what the Y, should be (though Aristotelians tend toward contribution) – he just identifies the procedures to be used; it's all form, then, and no content. But it does seem to many to be a very fair form(ula).

The utilitarian version of justice is simply that whatever provides the greatest utility is the most just – so it doesn't really matter who gets how much of what, just that the final total is as high as possible. So two societies with equal income per capita might be considered equally fair, despite that in Society A, the wealth is spread out among everyone, and in Society B, there are a few very, very rich people and everyone else is poor.

It may well be, however, that those few rich people, through judicious use of their wealth, achieve a higher level of happiness for everyone than would result if everyone had the same amount of money. Or it may be that such unequal distribution has not violated anyone's rights: Mill argues that justice involves respect for rights, especially the right to equal treatment, *unless* utility says otherwise. However, it may also be that distribution among individuals that is perceived to be unfair causes unhappiness within the society, thus decreasing the overall utility.

John Rawls, a contemporary thinker and author of *A Theory of Justice*, emphasizes, like Kant, human rationality. And like Aristotle, Rawls takes a procedural justice approach: if the procedure is fair, the result of the procedure will be fair. The decision-making procedure that Rawls argues best ensures social justice and fairness is described with a thought experiment: imagine, Rawls says, a group of self-interested and rational people whose responsibility is to divide up the social goods – and they don't know their race, sex, socio-economic status, abilities, etc. A group in this 'original position' under that 'veil of ignorance' would, says Rawls, establish the following two principles: (1) "Each person is to have an equal right to the most extensive total system of basic liberties compatible with a similar system of liberty for all," and (2) "Social and economic inequalities are to be arranged so that they are both: (a) to the greatest benefit of the least advantaged ..., and (b) attached to offices and positions open to all under conditions of fair equality of opportunity" (302) – in other words, equal shares unless in a certain arrangement of unequal shares, even the worst off is better off than in another arrangement. Rawls believes that this approach makes sure that certain biases do not taint the decision-making process: since no one knows whether they'll turn out to be wealthy or poor, able-bodied or disabled, or even elderly or young, Rawls argues that the rational person will always choose to divide up goods in a way that always benefits the least advantaged.

One criticism of Rawls is that he doesn't rank the basic liberties – so what happens if they come into conflict? And his list of primary goods – the stuff any rational person is supposed to want – has been criticized as incomplete or not satisfactorily justified. Another criticism of Rawls is that even with the veil of ignorance, rational people would not necessarily choose the two principles he says they would – Rawls seems to have in mind people who aren't great risk-takers.

Robert Nozick, another contemporary thinker and author of *Anarchy, State, and Utopia*, presents a view of justice that incorporates very strongly a right to liberty – but he seems to assume everyone is equally able to exercise that right. His view also incorporates an entitlement theory: things are just if what we have is what we're entitled to; and we're entitled to whatever is ours by history – by transfer, purchase, gift – as long as each step in the history is fair. And it is this last "as long as" that is a little problematic: what exactly is a just transfer?

All right, you've just opened up your very own business and you need to decide how much to charge for your service. What price is (morally) right? Well, you may have been taught some handy-dandy formula – total expenses divided by anticipated sales plus 10% profit margin. Well, why is that morally right? Is it fair? Are you entitled to 10% profit? Why not 5%? Why not 15%? What do you deserve? Do you deserve *any* profit? So are not-for-profit businesses *un*fair?

And when you say expenses, are you including everything it took to make your service available – for example, long-term environmental degradation? Who pays for that if not your customers? Who *should* pay for that? For example, your heating bill, besides being heavily subsidized, doesn't reflect the real cost of the energy; I suspect your garbage disposal is also very much underpriced. Will you incorporate these less obvious costs?

And are you going to charge everyone the same or will you have a sliding scale? What if someone can't afford your standard fee? Yeah, but what if they can't afford it because they just bought a new car (and they could've used public transit) – is that different than if they can't afford it because their McJob pays only minimum wage?

Summary? Application?

Religionism

Religionism isn't typically considered an ethical theory, but since many people connect religion with morality, it deserves some examination. And although reference to religionism isn't very standard, reference to the divine command theory is; however, although I will deal with that, it's just part of what I want to address.

Some people connect religion with morality so much so that atheists (people who don't believe in gods) are automatically considered immoral. There are a few errors and a few difficulties with this position. First, one can have a morality without a religion, so one could be a morally good person without adhering to a religion. Keep in mind that religion involves much more than morality: mainly, it involves belief in a god (or gods); it also, usually, involves the practice of specific rituals. Not believing in a god and not practicing certain rituals does not mean you can't establish some list of values or ethical principles. And in fact we've just covered nine ways to do just that, to establish right and wrong, and none of them involved gods or rituals.

Religionists may counter by asking what those values or principles would be based on. Their assumption is that their values and principles are based on belief in a god, so without that god, there can be no value(s). And that's the error. One can say honesty is good because God says so (the divine command theory), but one could also say that honesty is good because that makes for a happy society (utilitarianism) or because that shows respect for others (Kantian ethics).

Indeed, my guess is that many religionists adhere to their value system not so much because God says so but because of those other reasons. While this eliminates the difficulties of establishing the existence and moral expertise of God (see below), it invites the difficulties of principle-based theories: what is the basis (if not "because God says so") for that value system, for those principles? That is to ask, why those principles (for example, the Ten Commandments) and not others? Further, what do you do when principles conflict? Some religions may provide answers to these questions, but some may not, and you would need to do further work.

However, let's grant that religious people *do* consider what their God says to be the basis of ethics. This is what's called the "divine command" theory, and there are actually two versions of it. One argues that God, being the all-loving and benevolent being that he is, will command us to do only that which is good and right. The problem with this version is that it suggests some standard of good and right (the standard God bases his commands on) that is independent of, and presumably prior to, God

– so suddenly God is not the Creator of All, God is not "always was and always will be."

The other version of the divine command theory argues that whatever God says to do is what's right – his command *defines* (rather than is based on) right. This is a kind of ethical relativism (see the next subsection): right/wrong is relative to one's God. But basically, it's an appeal to authority – the authority of God. And although appeals to authority can be valid, recall that they aren't necessarily so. There are actually two problems with appealing to God as an authority on moral matters. First, one needs to establish that he does, in fact, exist. And there are a considerable number of very good arguments *against* his existence (not the least of which is simply the absence of sufficient evidence), especially against his existence as a *god*. (See, for example, B.C. Johnson, *The Atheist Debater's Handbook*.)

Second, even if we did have proof of his existence, we would need to establish his moral authority. For example, that the Judaeo-Christian God killed almost everyone on earth (see the story of Noah's ark) and that he condones animal torture (see the story about Samson and what he did to a few hundred foxes) seems to suggest he may not be the one to consult about right and wrong.

There are also problems with the appeal itself. If one appeals by prayer, well, how can you be sure it's *God* who's telling you what to do and not just your own mind? And how can you convince others that it's God's voice you heard? (And without proof, how can you expect others to believe you?) Another question: what if two people claim that God spoke to them and, apparently, he told each of them a different thing – which person do you believe? How do you prove which one is telling the truth?

Well, religionists might counter, you could use the Bible (or the Torah or the Qur'an) instead of personal divine revelation. After all, it's the word of God. But appeals through some record of God's word are similarly problematic. First, there is the matter of validity: one would need to be sure the Bible is indeed God's word. And even Biblical scholars are in disagreement about that. For example, the story of Jesus' birth is very similar to many pre-Christian tales, suggesting that the Bible may be a book of myths instead of the word of a god.

Second, there is the matter of reliability: which version is the authoritative one? And then, what about errors of translation and errors of editing? Consider the Apocrypha, a collection of books edited out of the Bible by various popes and scholars. And what about the contradictions, even within the chosen version — for example, God said do not kill (Exodus 20:13) and he said do kill (Exodus 22:18–20).

Third, there is the matter of adequacy: many moral issues are not dealt with in the Bible — quite simply, there are a lot of ethical issues that the Judaeo-Christian God hasn't said anything about. For example, is it morally acceptable to patent DNA? For the answer to questions like this, religionists often depend on Biblical scholars to pull the answer from relevant values and principles, but what if the scholars disagree?

I have put Judaeo-Christianity front and centre in my discussion, because that's the dominant religion in Canada at the time of writing, but other religions argue in similar fashion and have similar difficulties. For example, Islamic ethics are also very much an instance of the divine command theory. During the Iran-Iraq war, many Shiite Muslims went willingly to their deaths, believing they were doing the (morally) right thing, acting according to their god's will.

On the other hand, Hindu ethics, while religionist, do not exemplify the divine command theory. Rather, "right" is defined as that which fulfils your particular role, that which fulfils your *dharma*, your duty, according to the cosmic scheme of things. The questionable premise is that each person *has* a particular role, that people are born with a certain nature, fitting to certain responsibilities. Indeed, it's questionable that there *is* a "cosmic scheme of things."

Now of course many religionists would dismiss this whole discussion as irrelevant because, they would argue, religion is not a matter of reason but a matter of faith: one must simply *believe*, without reasons, without evidence. Well, if that's the case, then I can simply believe in the Great Big Purple Platypus, who tells me to kidnap and eat your kids, and that's that. (I don't need to tell you why, I don't need to give you any proof.)

Let's reconsider the pricing decision: how would a religionist decide what price to charge? Given Jesus' treatment of the money-changers in the temple, maybe you shouldn't be in business in the first place! Or maybe — charity being a Christian virtue — you should just give it away.

Main elements? Strengths? Weaknesses? Application of your own?

Relativism

I've left relativism for last because it's the most slippery, but if you keep clearly in mind the descriptive/prescriptive distinction, you should be okay. Many people think moral relativism means "all people have their own opinions about right and wrong" or "right and wrong depend on the person." Well, first, those two statements are not quite saying the same thing, and second, neither is quite right as an expression of ethical relativism.

The first, "all people have their own opinions about right and wrong," is just descriptive: it's simply expressing an observation. And the observation is implying that there are different ways to determine right and wrong. And this is certainly true. (As you are now, perhaps painfully, aware.)

The second statement, that "right and wrong *depend* on the person," verges on prescription, and recall that's what we're interested in. But "depend" needs a little clarification. If by "depend" we mean that different people will give different answers — the answer depends on the person giving it — then, again, we're just being descriptive, we're just recognizing moral plurality or moral diversity.

But if by "depend" we mean "is determined by" or "is defined by," then we have what we're after: individual relativism — X is right *if* I think it's right (or whatever I think is right *is* right).

This may seem to be an almost useless theory, however, because it says nothing about *how* you should come to think X is right (in fact, it verges on being descriptive when you look at it closely). Any answer to that question is bound to simply take you to another theory: X is right if I think it's right, and I think it's right if it's good for me (egoism); or X is right if I think it's right, and I think it's right if it's fair (justice theory).

More interesting is social/cultural relativism: X is right if the society or the culture thinks it's right. A longer definition is provided by John Ladd: "Ethical relativism is the doctrine that the moral rightness and wrongness of actions varies from society to society and that there are no absolute universal moral standards binding on all men at all times. Accordingly, it holds that whether or not it is right for an individual to act in a certain way depends on or is relative to the society to which he belongs" (1). Now you still

have to respond, "Okay, but on what basis does the society/culture make *its* decisions?" – which, as was the case for individual relativism, may just take you to another ethical theory. But at least the question is answered for the individual: if the society I live in thinks it's right, then okay, I'll accept its terms and definitions, it's right. (Remember to make the descriptive/prescriptive distinction, though: it's not merely that what people *think* is right/wrong that varies according to the society in which they live, but that what actually *is* right/wrong varies according to the society in which a person lives.)

However, there are a number of problems even to this point. First, what group do you choose? There are cultures coexisting with other cultures, and cultures within cultures. The Canadian culture? The black subculture? (And what *is* the Canadian culture? Or the black subculture, for that matter ...)

Second, what do you do when the answers from the various groups conflict? As you surely can imagine, there are ethical issues over which the abovementioned two groups disagree — policing standards and practices, for example.

Third, how do you determine what the morality of the group is? By its customs? By its laws? So are there no bad customs? No bad laws? Apparently a lot of people thought it was wrong to deny women the vote even though it was legal; and a lot of people today don't think it's wrong to smoke marijuana, but it is illegal. And when laws change, does that mean that yesterday X was wrong but today it's okay? On such and such a date it was not wrong to hire children for fourteen-hour shifts, but the next day, it was? What about ethical matters not covered by law? It's not illegal to refuse to lend your friend, who has just had her wallet stolen, some lunch money – so is it morally okay?

Speaking of the law, I find it interesting (distressing, actually) that many business ethics texts give the law a fairly prominent place (it's often right next to economics — another distressing observation about many business ethics texts). Doing so seems to presume an ethical relativist stance, one sometimes called "legal moralism" or "legalism." In addition to the problems mentioned above, legalism would be very problematic for international business: which society's laws does one follow? Those of the society in which the investors/owners live? Those of the society in which the workers live? Those of the society in which the consumers live?

Given this, you might be surprised to find Appendix II at the back of this book which briefly describes Canadian law and landmark cases relevant to each of the issues we'll explore. First, well, let's say it's for the relativists among you — enjoy! Second, the judgements described *do* cover some arguments well worth considering.

Back to moral relativism in general: one might suggest that one of its strengths is that it accords with reality, and theories that fit reality are good theories — after all, it is a poor theory that says sunny skies cause rain because that's just not what happens. However, ethical theories are different from scientific theories — we're back again to the prescriptive/descriptive distinction. Ethical theories say not what *does* occur but what *should* occur, so correspondence with reality is not as crucial. To remind you of the example at the beginning of this section, it may be the case that angry men get violent, but that's not necessarily what we want to say *should* be the case. We may say that angry men should control their tempers, that although they may indeed get violent, doing so is morally *wrong*.

Perhaps the most interesting thing about relativism is the implications: if what is right is

relative to one's group, then there is no objective or universal right or wrong. This caution might be laudable. But if there is no objective right or wrong, then all views are equally "correct" — because how could one judge the view? That is, by what measure, what standard, would one judge?

It seems to me that many people who subscribe to relativism believe they're being tolerant and open-minded. Indeed, that may be *why* they subscribe to it: they think being tolerant and open-minded is good. But first, if you are an individual relativist, there'd be no reason to discuss morality with anyone because there's no way disagreement can be reconciled: A thinks X is right and B thinks Y is right and that's the end of it — there are no reasons to examine and assess, there is no discussion and no resolution of conflicts. Doesn't sound very open-minded to me.

And second, be careful: while open-minded is good at the consideration stage, it may not be at the acceptance stage. What I mean is, it may be good to have an open mind when you're considering things — consider everything. But when it comes to accepting things — do you want to accept everything? Do you want to accept, do you want to tolerate, torture? Just because "it's their way"? Child sacrifice, too? And yet as soon as you draw a line, any line, then you're not really a relativist — you're saying there *are* some things that are wrong, anywhere, anytime, for anyone (which makes you a universalist, but not necessarily an absolutist — you could allow exceptions to your universals).

Furthermore, let's back up a bit: why do you think tolerance is good? If you *are* a (social) relativist, then you think tolerance is good because your society thinks it's good. And that gets you into circular reasoning: you value tolerance and therefore you're a relativist, and because you're a relativist, you value tolerance — something can't be both the cause and effect, both the reason for and the result of.

Lastly, the relativist assumes that the majority is right; s/he is thus uncritically conforming to social customs. But surely just because most (or even a lot) (or even one) person thinks X is right, it isn't necessarily wise to agree. Hopefully, you'll want to know *why* they think X is right (consider the reasons, identify the assumptions, define the terms, explore the alternatives).

So how would a relativist approach this ethical decision: you are part of an interviewing team for your company's new recruitment officer and at the end of the interviews, discussion seems to focus less on the applicants' expertise and experience than on their appearance — it seems a given that lean and male bodies are preferable to large and female bodies. What do you do? Well, you might notice that there are very few large people in the company, and the few there are do not hold frontline positions. So the company culture seems clear. Then you might note that there are laws against sex discrimination, but not against size discrimination, so that's half and half. And despite the realities of our bodies, our social culture seems to prefer those who are small (or at least not large); indeed, we seem to condemn, even in moral terms, those who are large (they're not very ambitious or industrious, they're certainly not hard-working, they have no self-control, etc.). And, we do seem to attend more to the authority of men than of women, of male bodies than of female bodies. So, choosing the lean male would be the right thing to do.

Summary time: Consider the main elements, strengths, weaknesses, and an application of ethical relativism to an ethical decision in a business context.

Closing Note

A really good review assignment for this whole section would be to list the questions one would ask, for each theoretical approach, in order to make an ethical decision. (I know, that's a big task. But trust me — you'll be glad you did it!)

Some parting comments. Sometimes ethical theories will be mutually exclusive: two different theories will lead you to two different answers, so you obviously can't use them both — you'll have to choose. But sometimes, as R.M. Hare argues, the theories operate at different levels of moral thinking (rather like Newtonian and Einsteinian theories of physics), and sometimes, as W.D. Ross and others have suggested, it may be the case that different theories apply better in different situations.

One important point is that you use the theories to get to your answer — your decision about what to do — rather than using them 'after the fact' merely to justify what you've already decided to do. Another important point is that you critically examine not only your decisions (what is right and wrong) but your approaches to your decisions (how you determine what is right and wrong) — both should be open to evaluation and perhaps modification or rejection. The rest of the book, I hope, gives you practice doing this.

References and Further Reading

ETHICAL THEORIES — THE ORIGINAL STUFF

Aquinas, Thomas. *Summa Theologica* and *Treatise on the Virtues.* 1265-1273. (many translations around)

Aristotle. *The Nicomachean Ethics.* 384-322 B.C.E. (many translations around; I used the one by J.E.C.Welldon, NY: Prometheus, 1987)

Bentham, Jeremy. *Introduction to the Principles of Morals and Legislation.* 1789. London: Clarendon Press, 1907.

Dworkin, Ronald. *Taking Rights Seriously.* Cambridge, MA: Harvard University Press, 1977.

Epicurus. See Diogenes Laertius. *Lives of Eminent Philosophers.* 230. Trans. R.D.Hicks. Cambridge, MA: Harvard University Press, 1972.

Etzioni, Amitai. *The Moral Dimension: Towards a New Economics.* NY: Free Press, 1988.

Feinberg, Joel. *Rights, Justice, and the Bounds of Liberty.* Princeton: Princeton University Press, 1980.

Hobbes, Thomas. *Leviathan.* 1651. NY: The Liberal Arts Press, 1958.

Hohfeld, Wesley. *Fundamental Legal Concepts.* New Haven: Yale University Press, 1964.

Hume, David. *An Enquiry Concerning the Principles of Morals.* 1751. NY: Oxford University Press, 1976.

Jaggar, Alison. "Feminist Ethics: Some Issues for the Nineties." *Journal of Social Philosophy* 20.1-2 (Spring/Fall 1989): 91-107.

Johnson, B.C. *The Atheist Debater's Handbook.* NY: Prometheus, 1983.

Kant, Immanuel. *Grounding for the Metaphysics of Morals.* 1785. Trans. James W. Ellington. Indianapolis, IN: Hackett, 1993.

Ladd, John. ed. *Ethical Relativism.* Belmont, CA: Wadsworth, 1973.

Locke, John. *Second Treatise on Civil Government.* 1690. Cambridge: Cambridge University Press, 1960.

MacIntyre, Alasdair. *After Virtue.* Notre Dame, IN: Notre Dame University Press, 1981.

Marx, Karl, and Friedrich Engels. *The Communist Manifesto.* 1848. NY: Washington Square Press, 1965.

Mill, John Stuart. *Utilitarianism.* 1861. Indianapolis, IN: Hackett, 1979.

Mill, John Stuart, and Harriet Taylor. *On Liberty.* London: J.W.Parker, 1859.

Nielsen, Kai. *Ethics Without God.* London: Pemberton, 1973.

Noddings, Nel. *Caring: A Feminine Approach to Ethics and Moral Education.* Berkeley: University of California Press, 1984.

Nozick, Robert. *Anarchy, State, and Utopia.* NY: Basic Books, 1974.

Rand, Ayn. *The Virtue of Selfishness.* NY: New American Library, 1964.

Rawls, John. *A Theory of Justice.* Cambridge: Harvard University Press, 1971.

Ross, William David. *The Right and the Good.* Oxford: Clarendon, 1930.

Smith, Adam. *An Inquiry into the Nature and Causes of the Wealth of Nations.* 1776. NY: Modern Library, 1937.

Spencer, Herbert. *The Principles of Ethics.* London: Williams & Norgate, 1892. (This is about evolutionary ethics. See Anthony Flew, *Evolutionary Ethics* NY: Macmillan, 1967, for a critique.)

Tong, Rosemarie. *Feminine and Feminist Ethics.* Belmont, CA: Wadsworth, 1995.

Walzer, Michael. "The Communitarian Critique of Liberalism." *Political Theory,* 18.1 (February 1990): 6-23.

ETHICAL THEORIES — GOOD SECOND-HAND STUFF

Art, Brad. *Ethics and the Good Life: A Text with Readings.* Belmont, CA: Wadsworth, 1994. (This book is delightful — Brad Art has an attitude I love!)

Beck, Clive. *Ethics: An Introduction.* Toronto: McGraw-Hill Ryerson, 1972.

Boss, Judith A. *Ethics for Life: An Interdisciplinary and Multicultural Introduction.* Mountain View, CA: Mayfield, 1998.

Ellin, Joseph. *Morality and the Meaning of Life: An Introduction to Ethical Theory.* Fort Worth: Harcourt Brace, 1995. (This book includes a very thorough discussion of egoism, and a sophisticated discussion of religion and naturalism.)

Holmes, Robert L. *Basic Moral Philosophy.* Belmont, CA: Wadsworth, 1993. (This book includes a good discussion of the divine command theory.)

MacKinnon, Barbara. *Ethics: Theory and Contemporary Issues.* Belmont, CA: Wadsworth, 1995. (This book includes clear, careful, and brief explanations of many of the ethical theories.)

Pojman, Louis P. *Ethics: Discovering Right and Wrong.* Belmont, CA: Wadsworth, 1995.

Section III

Ethical Issues in Business

Introductory Note

Section III is divided into 12 chapters, each devoted to one important ethical issues in business. Each of these chapters will have four components.

First, you'll be presented with a hypothetical decision-making scenario (called a "What to Do!"), created to get you thinking about that particular issue. You may be tempted to just read these and then carry on, but I urge you to stop and really think about what you would do and why. One, you'll get good practice in critical thinking about ethical issues – and that *is* the point of this text: to develop the ability to think deeply and clearly about such issues. Two, you might surprise yourself and discover on your own some of the major problems, and solutions, within these issues.

Second, you will be presented with an introduction outlining those major problems and (some of) the solutions. To get the (morally) right answer, you need to know which questions to ask; I hope these introductions will lead you to that knowledge.

Third, you will find two essays, each with a set of questions. (Note that in the questions "P" refers to "paragraph," e.g., "P4" refers to the fourth paragraph in the essay.) Some of the essays are comprehensive, seeming to repeat the introductory material; some take one single aspect of the issue and examine it in detail; and

some argue for one particular view of the issue (or of one aspect of the issue).

For many of you, this will be your first experience reading essays of this nature, essays that are fairly abstract and that make an argument of some kind. *Merely reading the essays will not be enough.* You are advised also to do the following:

1. Write an outline of the points made in the essay, along with the support (reason, evidence) given for each point. (That is, what values, principles, and/or concepts does the author argue for?) Do not make the mistake of writing a paragraph-by-paragraph summary: authors don't always present one point per paragraph – several paragraphs may be background, there may be a point made in one paragraph while its support may be found in another, or perhaps a point and its support may be in the same paragraph, or maybe the support is quite extensive and spread over several paragraphs, etc.; you will need to *pick out* the author's points (sometimes the author may not even *say* what his/her point is), and then recognize what supports those points. (And if you're really up for it, you will try to distinguish between major and minor points, and try to understand which points, if any, depend on other points.) However, many au-

thors do summarize their argument in one of the introductory paragraphs (and/or a concluding paragraph) – look for that!

2. Think about those arguments (the points with their support) and decide whether or not you agree: if you do, know why; if you don't, figure out why not. (That is, are the reasons that are given *good* ones? Why or why not? Are there any unacceptable assumptions? Has the author neglected to consider anything? Are there exceptions or distinctions the author has failed to make? Reread the subsection, "How to Think About Ethics" in Section I.) You might even want to prepare a "reading guide" – a list in point form of things to do, to look for, or to ask, as you read. Then if you follow your list, consciously and systematically, for each of the ten or twenty essays you'll read, you will become a better reader/thinker by the end of the course – the training you will have put yourself through will, I promise, make such a difference not only in your studies, but in your life!)

3. Prepare a list of questions raised by the essay that you're interested in discussing (and, I hope, writing about: how can you add to the academic discourse? – how can you solve the remaining problems?).

Nor will merely reading the essays once be enough. In fact, you will probably spend more time per page with philosophical work than with readings in other disciplines. This is (hopefully) not because such material is so poorly written, but rather, as mentioned above, because (1) it deals with (abstract) concepts, rather than with facts (to use Bloom's taxonomy, it deals with the higher cognitive skills of analysis, synthesis, and evaluation, rather than knowledge, comprehen-

sion, and application: you're not just reading for information, to know and understand; you're reading for argument, to follow and assess); and (2) such content is simply more difficult to understand – partly because of its nature and partly because most students (indeed, most people) have had so little practice with it.

Keep in mind that reading is writing in reverse: when you write, you come up with a skeleton or plan for your essay, then flesh it out – you have an outline of points and then you write the paragraphs with detail, explanation, example, etc., to "make" those points; when you read, you're trying to extract that skeleton, that plan – you need to separate the detail, explanation, and example from the points they serve.

The questions accompanying the essays are multi-purpose. Partly, they are designed to highlight the argument of the essay (so use them as guides *as* you read, not *after* you read – even though they're at the end), to develop your ability to read essays like these with critical understanding; you will note that there are more questions accompanying the essays at the beginning of the text than at the end (my assumptions are that you will need less guidance as you go on, and that you will go through the chapters pretty much in the order in which they're presented). And partly the questions are designed to provoke you to consider alternatives to the positions presented by the authors.

Lastly, you will be presented with a case study, a description of a real situation in Canadian business that illustrates the ethical issue of the chapter. In some cases, you may find action worth imitating – many Canadian companies are trying to do the right thing. In other cases, you may be challenged to figure out what should have been done differently to avoid what happened.

CHAPTER 1
WHISTLEBLOWING

What to Do? – Rivertree's Grocery

You have a summer job as stockperson for your local grocery store, Rivertree's Grocery. One day, as you're unpacking and shelving produce, you notice that many of the crates are marked "U.S.A. Produce" and some are labelled "Product of Mexico." However, the refrigerated shelves on which you're placing the produce have tag labels indicating "Produce of Canada, No. 1." You search in the stockroom for tag labels indicating U.S.A. and Mexico, but you can't find any. When you explain this to your manager, he says, "Don't worry about it."

You think that probably fruits and vegetables from the States are okay – but still there's the principle of the matter. However, you're aware that some countries, perhaps especially poorer countries like Mexico, don't have the same environmental/agricultural standards as Canada and the U.S. It's possible, you think, that produce from Mexico has been grown or sprayed with pesticides that are illegal in Canada, possibly even hazardous to one's health. In fact, you recall that a few years ago, grapes from somewhere had to be pulled off the shelves because of some chemical health risk.

But, of course, you don't know about this particular produce – it could be fine. And yet, better safe than sorry – people should know.

You consider telling someone – the local paper? They'd probably print some sort of story – they're usually desperate for news. Then again, the manager might be friends with the paper's editor – you're not sure.

There is another grocery store and the town is barely large enough to support both. So unfortunately, it wouldn't take much for Rivertree's Grocery to go out of business.

And in any case, you don't want to get fired: you've worked here for three summers in a row, and you're going into your last year of university; while your parents have agreed to cover your food and shelter expenses, the rest is up to you – if you get fired now, you probably won't be able to get another summer job because by this time, mid-July, they're all gone, and then you won't be able to pay for tuition and books come September. Still – apart from the blatant lying, people could get very sick …

What do you decide to do? Why?

Introduction

Simply defined, whistleblowing refers to *the re-lease of information to the public, by an employee, of his/her employer's wrongdoing*. To many, a whistleblower is a "tattle-tale." But, as is often the case, the ethics that got us through childhood may be inadequate for our adult life. (Indeed, they may have been inadequate for childhood too – what exactly is wrong with being a tattle-tale?) Perhaps a better label, an adult label, is "ethical resister" (suggested by Glazer and Glazer) or simply "person of principle" (suggested by Aldergrove).

Like most ethical decisions, deciding whether to blow the whistle is difficult because there are *conflicting interests* involved. Specifically, one must consider three parties – *the public, the company or organization, and the individual* – and somehow measure and compare their interests.

One way to determine whose interests are greater, or whose interests have greater moral priority, is to consider the *consequences*. Very often, consequences are measured in terms of *harm and benefit*. So one important question is "How much harm to the public would result if you did *not* blow the whistle?" Another is "How much harm to the company and to yourself would result if you *did* blow the whistle?"

However, you must first define 'harm," and further, you need to be able to measure harm. Perhaps some sort of utilitarian calculus could be used. *How many* people would be harmed? (Is "the public" the community, the country, or the entire planet?) *How severe* would the harm be? (Are we talking about inconvenience or injury? A slight decrease in profits or bankruptcy? A little ostracism or loss of job?) *How long* would it last? *How likely* is it to occur? Sure, saving the entire planet is worth losing your job – but is preventing short-term, somewhat severe, harm to a hundred people worth causing a company to go bankrupt and lay off three times that many?

For such a consequentialist approach, Sissela Bok's comments in the essay that follows about the conditions necessary for *successful* whistleblowing may be relevant: if the whistleblowing under consideration is unlikely to succeed, then the harm to the public is unlikely to be avoided, and that changes things.

Further, if a consequentialist approach is used, perhaps Bok's comments about immediacy and specificity are relevant because both are variables which define the exact nature of the harm.

Bok's comments about considering *alternatives* are also relevant: is whistleblowing the best way to achieve the consequences? (Did you try other things first – such as internal reporting – to minimize the negative consequences?)

Consequences are not the only worthy consideration, however. You could determine whether whistleblowing is morally justified solely on the basis of *intent*: if your intentions are good, then whistleblowing is the right thing to do (whether or not it succeeds). In this case, you'd have to define "good." Perhaps "good" corresponds to some list of virtues, and insofar as whistleblowing is telling the truth, for example, it is good; on the other hand, as Bok suggests, motives rising from malice may qualify the whistleblowing as unjustified.

Another area of consideration is that of *rights, duties,* and *obligations*. Whistleblowing is seen by many, including Bok but excluding Duska (in the second essay in this chapter), to be a violation of *loyalty* to the company or organization. (Consider that if you were not an employee, informing the public of a company's wrongdoing would be, without question, praiseworthy.) To accept this claim, you must first accept the premise that employees *have* an obligation of loyalty to the company. Upon what basis might this obligation rest? That is, why could an employer demand, or why should an employer expect, its employees to be loyal? And what exactly does "loyalty" mean? Does it include obedience? What are the limits of that loyalty? Does it extend forever or just while you are employed by the company? Does it extend over all company behaviour or just legal behaviour? Whatever the limits, are they absolute or can there be exceptions? What might these exceptions be? What happens when loyalty conflicts with honesty?

Even if you agree that there *is* an obligation of loyalty, you must then determine whether whistleblowing violates that loyalty. This will probably take you back to defining clearly the nature of that loyalty.

Another duty or obligation to consider is that of *confidentiality*. Again, one must determine whether one has a duty to maintain confidentiality, what the limits of that duty are, and whether whistleblowing does in fact violate that duty.

Both loyalty and confidentiality are in the company's interests; what about duties and obligations to yourself and to others? Do you have an obligation to be loyal to your family? Which obligation comes first? Do you have any duties to society-at-large that might supersede duties to the company?

And what about the rights of others? Does society have a right to freedom of information?

Does it have a right to freedom from harm? Perhaps, in light of these rights, one has *a duty, an obligation,* to *blow the whistle.* (Duska argues in this direction at the end of his essay.) Consider Ralph Nader's comments:

> Corporate employees are among the first to know about industrial dumping of mercury or fluoride sludge into waterways, defectively designed automobiles, or undisclosed adverse effects of prescription drugs and pesticides. They are the first to grasp the technical capabilities to prevent existing product or pollution hazards. But they are very often the last to speak out, much less to refuse to be recruited for acts of corporate or governmental negligence or predation. Staying silent in the face of a professional duty has direct impact on the level of consumer and environmental hazards. (Nader, Petakas, and Blackwell, p. 4)

Indeed, perhaps companies and organizations have a duty to allow, rather than a right to prohibit, whistleblowing. And not "just" a duty, but perhaps also an interest, in doing so: Burton and Near found that "a large number of business undergraduates admitted cheating while only a small percentage reported peers' cheating when they observed it" (abstract). They add, "these results should be sobering for managers...." Indeed. A company committed to high ethical standards – not to mention high quality products and services and a good public reputation – will *value* its potential whistleblowers: it will have an effective internal program (an ethics office or an ombudsperson, for example) that genuinely supports reports of wrongdoing and truly protects those employees who make such reports – and, of course, corrects the situation quickly and completely.

And certainly individuals considering whistleblowing have a duty to verify the facts. You may see or hear something that you consider unacceptable and that, if true, could result in harm to others. However, if it's not true, your whistleblowing could put the company in financial jeopardy due to the bad publicity which, in turn, could have negative consequences for the employees, and perhaps even the community at large. Further, mistaken whistleblowing could make it harder for future whistleblowers – they may be dismissed as misguided alarmists. So you want to have your facts straight. However, verification may not always be easy. Perhaps the degree of certainty that wrongdoing is happening bears on the moral rightness of the whistleblowing.

In any case, prevention is the best cure. Walters suggests that organizations can reduce the need for whistleblowing in the first place by ensuring that they don't interfere with employees' basic political freedoms and that they are truly socially responsible companies. Davis suggests several internal procedures, such as space on evaluation forms specifically for negative comments, review meetings specifically for problem identification, and changing the "chain" of command to a "lattice" of command.

The very nature of whistleblowing is such that media coverage may be quite limited: the company involved may want to squelch the story as soon as possible, and the whistleblower may not want publicity that invades privacy and disrupts life, not to mention future livelihood. It's my guess, then, that there are many more people out there than we know about who have stood up and done the right thing, who have made personal sacrifices for principles – not to mention the prevention of harm. Do not underestimate your capacity for small-scale heroism.

Kernaghan says "the number of whistleblowing incidents involving government employees has increased significantly" (35), and he lists several examples: a forester in the Ontario Ministry of Natural Resources reported that it was granting timber cutting rights where volumes were insufficient, an employee of the Ontario Ministry of Correctional Services reported overcrowding in two Toronto jails, an employee in the Canadian Department of Indian and Northern Affairs reported that it routinely broke financial agreements with Indian bands, and an employee of the Department of Immigration reported that it allowed people with criminal records to stay in Canada illegally. There you go!

Having said that, let me also say: do not underestimate the politics. Note that despite restricting his whistleblowing to internal channels, Boisjoly (one of the engineers aware of and very concerned about the O-rings whose failure resulted in the death of the space shuttle *Challenger*'s crew) was, after his testimony to the government investigation, essentially demoted and reportedly harassed, and he eventually left his job at Morton Thiokol. If, after checking your facts, you *do* decide to blow the whistle, do so after careful planning (see the material by James and Raven-Hansen for advice) – you want to make it count!

REFERENCES AND FURTHER READING

Aldergrove, John Romney. *Enemies: The Rationalist View of Human Nature.* Burnaby, BC: Stentorian, 1998.

Burton, Brian K., and Janet P. Near. "Estimating the Incidence of Wrongdoing and Whistle-blowing." *Journal of Business Ethics* 14.1 (January 1995): 17-31.

Callahan, Elleta Sangrey, and Terry Morehead Dworkin. "Internal Whistleblowing: Protecting the Interests of the Employee, the Organization, and Society." *American Business Law Journal* 37 (1991): 267-308.

Davis, Michael. "Avoid the Tragedy of Whistleblowing." *Business and Professional Ethics Journal* 8.4 (Winter 1989): 3-19.

De George, Richard T. ed. *Business Ethics.* 4th ed. Englewood Cliffs, NJ: Prentice Hall, 1995. 240-262.

Elliston, Frederick A. "Anonymity and Whistleblowing." *Journal of Business Ethics* 3.1 (1982): 167-177.

Glazer, Myron. "Ten Whistleblowers and How They Fared." *The Hastings Center Report* 13 (December 1983): 33-41.

Glazer, Myron Peretz, and Penina Migdal Glazer. *The Whistleblowers: Exposing Corruption in Government and Industry.* New York: Basic Books, 1989.

James, Gene G. "Whistle Blowing: Its Moral Justification." In *Business Ethics: Readings and Cases in Corporate Morality.* Ed. W. Michael Hoffman and Robert E. Frederick. 3rd ed. New York: McGraw-Hill, 1995. 290-301.

Kernaghan, Kenneth. "Whistle-Blowing in Canadian Governments: Ethical, Political and Managerial Considerations." *Optimum* 22.1 (1991-2): 34-43.

Larmer, Robert A. "Whistleblowing and Employee Loyalty." *Journal of Business Ethics* 11.2 (February 1992): 125-128.

Nader, Ralph, Peter J. Petakas, and Kate Blackwell. *Whistle Blowing: The Report of the Conference on Professional Responsibility.* New York: Grossman, 1972.

Nielsen, Richard P. "Changing Unethical Organizational Behaviour." *The Executive* (May 1989): 123-130.

Peters, Charles, and Taylor Branch. *Blowing the Whistle: Dissent in the Public Interest.* New York: Praeger, 1972.

Raven-Hansen, Peter. "Dos and Don'ts for Whistleblowers: Planning for Trouble." *Technology Review* 83 (May 1980): 34-44.

Walters, Kenneth. "Your Employees' Right to Blow the Whistle." *Harvard Business Review* (July/August 1975): 160-162.

Westin, Alan F. *Whistle Blowing! Loyalty and Dissent in the Corporation.* New York: McGraw-Hill, 1981.

Whistleblowing and Professional Responsibility

Sissela Bok[1]

1 "Whistleblowing" is a new label generated by our increased awareness of the ethical conflicts encountered at work. Whistleblowers sound an alarm from within the very organization in which they work, aiming to spotlight neglect or abuses that threaten the public interest.

2 The stakes in whistleblowing are high. Take the nurse who alleges that physicians enrich themselves in her hospital through unnecessary surgery; the engineer who discloses safety defects in the braking systems of a fleet of new rapid-transit vehicles; the Defense Department official who alerts Congress to military graft and overspending: all know that they pose a threat to those whom they denounce and that their own careers may be at risk.

Moral Conflicts

3 Moral conflicts on several levels confront anyone who is wondering whether to speak out about abuses or risks or serious neglect. In the first place, he must try to decide whether, other things being equal, speaking out is in fact in the public interest. This choice is often made more complicated by factual uncertainties: Who is responsible for the abuse or neglect? How great is the threat? And how likely is it that speaking out will precipitate changes for the better?

Sissela Bok, "Whistleblowing and Professional Responsibility," *New York University Education Quarterly* 11 (Summer 1980): 2-7. © 1980 by Sissela Bok. Reprinted with permission of the author.

4 In the second place, a would-be whistleblower must weigh his responsibility to serve the public interest against the responsibility he owes to his colleagues and the institution in which he works. While the professional ethic requires collegial loyalty, the codes of ethics often stress responsibility to the public over and above duties to colleagues and clients. Thus the United States Code of Ethics for Government Servants asks them to "expose corruption wherever uncovered" and to "put loyalty to the highest moral principles and to country above loyalty to persons, party, or government."[2] Similarly, the largest professional engineering association requires members to speak out against abuses threatening the safety, health, and welfare of the public.[3]

5 A third conflict for would-be whistleblowers is personal in nature and cuts across the first two: even in cases where they have concluded that the facts warrant speaking out, and that their duty to do so overrides loyalties to colleagues and institutions, they often have reason to fear the results of carrying out such a duty. However strong this duty may seem in theory, they know that, in practice, retaliation is likely. As a result, their careers and their ability to support themselves and their families may be unjustly impaired.[4] A government handbook issued during the Nixon era recommends reassigning "undesirables" to places so remote that they would prefer to resign. Whistleblowers may also be downgraded or given work without responsibility or work for which they are not qualified; or

else they may be given many more tasks than they can possibly perform. Another risk is that an outspoken civil servant may be ordered to undergo a psychiatric fitness-for-duty examination,[5] declared unfit for service, and "separated" as well as discredited from the point of view of any allegations he may be making. Outright firing, finally, is the most direct institutional response to whistleblowers.

6   Add to the conflicts confronting individual whistleblowers the claim to self-policing that many professions make, and professional responsibility is at issue in still another way. For an appeal to the public goes against everything that "self-policing" stands for. The question for the different professions, then, is how to resolve, insofar as it is possible, the conflict between professional loyalty and professional responsibility toward the outside world. The same conflicts arise to some extent in all groups, but professional groups often have special cohesion and claim special dignity and privileges.

7   The plight of whistleblowers has come to be documented by the press and described in a number of books. Evidence of the hardships imposed on those who chose to act in the public interest has combined with a heightened awareness of professional malfeasance and corruption to produce a shift toward greater public support of whistleblowers. Public service law firms and consumer groups have taken up their cause; institutional reforms and legislation have been proposed to combat illegitimate reprisals.[6]

8   Given the indispensable services performed by so many whistleblowers, strong support is often merited. But the new climate of acceptance makes it easy to overlook the dangers of whistleblowing: of uses in error or in malice; of work and reputations unjustly lost for those falsely accused; of privacy invaded and trust undermined. There comes a level of internal prying and mutual suspicion at which no institution can function. And it is a fact that the disappointed, the incompetent, the malicious, and the paranoid all too often leap to accusations in public. Worst of all, ideological persecution throughout the world traditionally relies on insiders willing to inform on their colleagues or even on their family members, often through staged public denunciations or press campaigns.

9   No society can count itself immune from such dangers. But neither can it risk silencing those with a legitimate reason to blow the whistle. How then can we distinguish between different instances of whistleblowing? A society that fails to protect the right to speak out even on the part of those whose warnings turn out to be spurious obviously opens the door to political repression. But from the moral point of view there are important differences between the aims, messages, and methods of dissenters from within.

Nature of Whistleblowing

10   Three elements, each jarring, and triply jarring when conjoined, lend acts of whistleblowing special urgency and bitterness: dissent, breach of loyalty, and accusation.

11   Like all dissent, whistleblowing makes public a disagreement with an authority or a majority view. But whereas dissent can concern all forms of disagreement with, for instance, religious dogma or government policy or court decisions, whistleblowing has the narrower aim of shedding light on negligence or abuse, or alerting to a risk, and of assigning responsibility for this risk.

12   Would-be whistleblowers confront the conflict inherent in all dissent: between conforming and sticking their necks out. The more repressive the authority they challenge, the greater the personal risk they take in speaking out. At exceptional times, as in times of war, even ordinarily tolerant authorities may come to regard dissent as unacceptable and even disloyal.[7]

13   Furthermore, the whistleblower hopes to stop the game; but since he is neither referee nor coach, and since he blows the whistle on his own team, his act is seen as a violation of loyalty. In holding his position, he has assumed certain obligations to his colleagues and clients. He may even have subscribed to a loyalty oath or a promise of confidentiality. Loyalty to colleagues and to clients comes to be pitted against loyalty to the public interest, to those who may be injured unless the revelation is made.

14   Not only is loyalty violated in whistleblowing, hierarchy as well is often opposed, since the whistleblower is not only a colleague but a subordinate. Though aware of the risks inherent in such disobedience, he often hopes to keep his job.[8] At times, however, he plans his alarm to coincide with leaving the institution. If he is highly placed, or joined by others, resigning in protest may effectively direct public attention to the wrongdoing at issue.[9] Still another alternative, often chosen by those who wish to be safe from retaliation, is to leave the institution quietly, to secure another post, and then to blow the whistle. In this way, it is possible to speak with the authority and knowledge of an insider without having the vulnerability of that position.

15   It is the element of accusation, of calling a "foul," that arouses the strongest reactions on the part of the hierarchy. The accusation may be of neglect, of willfully concealed dangers, or of outright abuse on the part of the colleagues or superiors. It singles out specific persons or groups as responsible for threats to the public interest. If no one could be held responsible – as in the case of an impending avalanche – the warning would not constitute whistleblowing.

16   The accusation of the whistleblower, moreover, concerns a present or an imminent threat. Past errors or misdeeds occasion such an alarm only if they still affect current practices. And risks far in the future lack the immediacy needed to make the alarm a compelling one, as well as the close connection to particular individuals that would justify actual accusations. Thus an alarm can be sounded about safety defects in a rapid-transit system that threaten or will shortly threaten passengers, but the revelation of safety defects in a system no longer in use, while of historical interest, would not constitute whistleblowing. Nor would the revelation of potential problems in a system not yet fully designed and far from implemented.[10]

17   Not only immediacy, but also specificity, is needed for there to be an alarm capable of pinpointing responsibility. A concrete risk must be at issue rather than a vague foreboding or a somber prediction. The act of whistleblowing differs in this respect from the lamentation or the dire prophecy. An immediate and specific threat would normally be acted upon by those at risk. The whistleblower assumes that his message will alert listeners to something they do not know, or whose significance they have not grasped because it has been kept secret.

18   The desire for openness inheres in the temptation to reveal any secret, sometimes joined to an urge for self-aggrandizement and publicity and the hope for revenge for past slights or injustices. There can be pleasure, too – righteous or malicious – in laying bare the secrets of co-

workers and in setting the record straight at last. Colleagues of the whistleblower often suspect his motives: they may regard him as a crank, as publicity-hungry, wrong about the facts, eager for scandal and discord, and driven to indiscretion by his personal biases and shortcomings.

19   For whistleblowing to be effective, it must arouse its audience. Inarticulate whistleblowers are likely to fail from the outset. When they are greeted by apathy, their message dissipates. When they are greeted by disbelief, they elicit no response at all. And when the audience is not free to receive or to act on the information — when censorship or fear of retribution stifles response — then the message rebounds to injure the whistleblower. Whistleblowing also requires the possibility of concerted public response: the idea of whistleblowing in an anarchy is therefore merely quixotic.

20   Such characteristics of whistleblowing and strategic considerations for achieving an impact are common to the noblest warnings, the most vicious personal attacks, and the delusions of the paranoid. How can one distinguish the many acts of sounding an alarm that are genuinely in the public interest from all the petty, biased, or lurid revelations that pervade our querulous and gossip-ridden society? Can we draw distinctions between different whistleblowers, different messages, different methods?

21   We clearly can, in a number of cases. Whistleblowing may be starkly inappropriate when in malice or error, or when it lays bare legitimately private matters having to do, for instance, with political belief or sexual life. It can, just as clearly, be the only way to shed light on an ongoing unjust practice such as drugging political prisoners or subjecting them to electroshock treatment. It can be the last resort for alerting the public to an impending disaster. Tak-

ing such clear-cut cases as benchmarks, and reflecting on what it is about them that weighs so heavily for or against speaking out, we can work our way toward the admittedly more complex cases in which whistleblowing is not so clearly the right or wrong choice, or where different points of view exist regarding its legitimacy — cases where there are moral reasons both for concealment and for disclosure and where judgments conflict. Consider the following cases:[11]

A. As a construction inspector for a federal agency, John Samuels (not his real name) had personal knowledge of shoddy and deficient construction practices by private contractors. He knew his superiors received free vacations and entertainment, had their homes remodeled and found jobs for their relatives — all courtesy of a private contractor. These superiors later approved a multimillion no-bid contract with the same "generous" firm.

Samuels also had evidence that other firms were hiring nonunion laborers at a low wage while receiving substantially higher payments from the government for labor costs. A former superior, unaware of an office dictaphone, had incautiously instructed Samuels on how to accept bribes for overlooking sub-par performance.

As he prepared to volunteer this information to various members of Congress, he became tense and uneasy. His family was scared and the fears were valid. It might cost Samuels thousands of dollars to protect his job. Those who had freely provided Samuels with information would probably recant or withdraw their friendship. A number of people might object to his using a dictaphone to gather information. His agency would start covering up and vent its collective wrath upon him. As for reporters and writers, they would gather for a few days, then move on to the next story. He would be left without a job, with fewer friends, with massive battles looming, and without the financial means of fighting them. Samuels decided to remain silent.

B. Engineers of Company "A" prepared plans and specifications for machinery to be used in a manufacturing process and Company "A" turned them over to Company "B" for production. The engineers of Company "B," in reviewing the plans and specifications, came to the conclusion that they included certain miscalculations and technical deficiencies of a nature that the final product might be unsuitable for the purposes of the ultimate users, and that the equipment, if built according to the original plans and specifications, might endanger the lives of persons in proximity to it. The engineers of Company "B" called the matter to the attention of appropriate officials of their employer who, in turn, advised Company "A." Company "A" replied that its engineers felt that the design and specifications for the equipment were adequate and safe and that Company "B" should proceed to build the equipment as designed and specified. The officials of Company "B" instructed its engineers to proceed with the work.

C. A recently hired assistant director of admissions in a state university begins to wonder whether transcripts of some applicants accurately reflect their accomplishments. He knows that it matters to many in the university community, including alumni, that the football team continue its winning tradition. He has heard rumors that surrogates may be available to take tests for a fee, signing the names of designated applicants for admission, and that some of the transcripts may have been altered. But he has no hard facts. When he brings the question up with the director of admissions, he is told that the rumors are unfounded and asked not to inquire further into the matter.

Individual Moral Choice

22 What questions might those who consider sounding an alarm in public ask themselves? How might they articulate the problem they see and weigh its injustice before deciding whether or not to reveal it? How can they best try to make sure their choice is the right one? In thinking about these questions it helps to keep in mind the three elements mentioned earlier: dissent, breach of loyalty, and accusation. They impose certain requirements – of accuracy and judgment in dissent; of exploring alternative ways to cope with improprieties that minimize the breach of loyalty; and of fairness in accusation. For each, careful articulation and testing of arguments are needed to limit error and bias.

23   Dissent by whistleblowers, first of all, is expressly claimed to be intended to benefit the public. It carries with it, as a result, an obligation to consider the nature of this benefit and to consider also the possible harm that may come from speaking out: harm to persons or institutions and, ultimately, to the public interest itself. Whistleblowers must, therefore, begin by making every effort to consider the effects of speaking out versus those of remaining silent. They must assure themselves of the accuracy of their reports, checking and rechecking the facts before speaking out; specify the degree to which there is genuine impropriety; consider how imminent is the threat they see, how serious, and how closely linked to those accused of neglect and abuse.

24   If the facts warrant whistleblowing, how can the second element – breach of loyalty – be minimized? The most important question here is whether the existing avenues for change within the organization have been explored. It is a waste of time for the public as well as harm-

ful to the institution to sound the loudest alarm first. Whistleblowing has to remain a last alternative because of its destructive side effects: it must be chosen only when other alternatives have been considered and rejected. They may be rejected if they simply do not apply to the problem at hand, or when there is not time to go through routine channels, or when the institution is so corrupt or coercive that steps will be taken to silence the whistleblower should he try the regular channels first.

25 What weight should an oath or a promise of silence have in the conflict of loyalties? One sworn to silence is doubtless under a stronger obligation because of the oath he has taken. He has bound himself, assumed specific obligations beyond those assumed in merely taking a new position. But even such promises can be overridden when the public interest at issue is strong enough. They can be overridden if they were obtained under duress or through deceit. They can be overridden, too, if they promise something that is in itself wrong or unlawful. The fact that one has promised silence is no excuse for complicity in covering up a crime or a violation of the public's trust.

26 The third element in whistleblowing – accusation – raises equally serious ethical concerns. They are concerns of fairness to the persons accused of impropriety. Is the message one to which the public is entitled in the first place? Or does it infringe on personal and private matters that one has no right to invade? Here, the very notion of what is in the public's best "interest" is at issue: "accusations" regarding an official's unusual sexual or religious experiences may well appeal to the public's interest without being information relevant to "the public interest."

27 Great conflicts arise here. We have witnessed excessive claims to executive privilege and to secrecy by government officials during the Watergate scandal in order to cover up for abuses the public had every right to discover. Conversely, those hoping to profit from prying into private matters have become adept at invoking "the public's right to know." Some even regard such private matters as threats to the public: they voice their own religious and political prejudices in the language of accusation. Such a danger is never stronger than when the accusation is delivered surreptitiously. The anonymous accusations made during the McCarthy period regarding political beliefs and associations often injured persons who did not even know their accusers or the exact nature of the accusations.

28 From the public's point of view, accusations that are openly made by identifiable individuals are more likely to be taken seriously. And in fairness to those criticized, openly accepted responsibility for blowing the whistle should be preferred to the denunciation or the leaked rumor. What is openly stated can more easily be checked, its source's motives challenged, and the underlying information examined. Those under attack may otherwise be hard put to defend themselves against nameless adversaries. Often they do not even know that they are threatened until it is too late to respond. The anonymous denunciation, moreover, common to so many regimes, places the burden of investigation on government agencies that may thereby gain the power of a secret police.

29 From the point of view of the whistleblower, on the other hand, the anonymous message is safer in situations where retaliation is likely. But it is also often less likely to be taken seriously. Unless the message is accompanied by indications of

how the evidence can be checked, its anonymity, however safe for the source, speaks against it.

30   During this process of weighing the legitimacy of speaking out, the method used, and the degree of fairness needed, whistleblowers must try to compensate for the strong possibility of bias on their part. They should be scrupulously aware of any motive that might skew their message: a desire for self-defense in a difficult bureaucratic situation, perhaps, or the urge to seek revenge, or inflated expectations regarding the effect their message will have on the situation. (Needless to say, bias affects the silent as well as the outspoken. The motive for holding back important information about abuses and injustice ought to give similar cause for soul-searching.)

31   Likewise, the possibility of personal gain from sounding the alarm ought to give pause. Once again there is then greater risk of a biased message. Even if the whistleblower regards himself as incorruptible, his profiting from revelations of neglect or abuse will lead others to question his motives and to put less credence in his charges. If, for example, a government employee stands to make large profits from a book exposing the iniquities in his agency, there is danger that he will, perhaps even unconsciously, slant his report in order to cause more of a sensation.

32   A special problem arises when there is a high risk that the civil servant who speaks out will have to go through costly litigation. Might he not justifiably try to make enough money on his public revelations – say, through books or public speaking – to offset his losses? In so doing he will not strictly speaking have *profited* from his revelations: he merely avoids being financially crushed by their sequels. He will nevertheless still be suspected at the time of revelation, and his message will therefore seem more questionable.

33   Reducing bias and error in moral choice often requires consultation, even open debate:[12] methods that force articulation of the moral arguments at stake and challenge privately held assumptions. But acts of whistleblowing present special problems when it comes to open consultation. On the one hand, once the whistleblower sounds his alarm publicly, his arguments will be subjected to open scrutiny; he will have to articulate his reasons for speaking out and substantiate his charges. On the other hand, it will then be too late to retract the alarm or to combat its harmful effects, should his choice to speak out have been ill-advised.

34   For this reason, the whistleblower owes it to all involved to make sure of two things: that he has sought as much and as objective advice regarding his choice as he can *before* going public; and that he is aware of the arguments for and against the practice of whistleblowing in general, so that he can see his own choice against as richly detailed and coherently structured a background as possible. Satisfying these two requirements once again has special problems because of the very nature of whistleblowing: the more corrupt the circumstances, the more dangerous it may be to seek consultation before speaking out. And yet, since the whistleblower himself may have a biased view of the state of affairs, he may choose not to consult others when in fact it would be not only safe but advantageous to do so; he may see corruption and conspiracy where none exists.

NOTES

1. A more complete discussion of whistleblowing can be found in Sissela Bok, *Secrets: On the Ethics of Concealment and Revelation* (NY: Vintage, 1989).
2. Code of Ethics for Government Service passed by the U.S. House of Representatives in the 85th

Congress (1958) and applying to all government employees and office holders.

3. Code of Ethics of the Institute of Electrical and Electronics Engineers, Article IV.

4. For case histories and descriptions of what befalls whistleblowers, see Rosemary Chalk and Frank von Hippel, "Due Process for Dissenting Whistle-Blowers," *Technology Review* 81 (June-July 1979): pp. 48-55; Alan S. Westin and Stephen Salisbury, eds., *Individual Rights in the Corporation* (New York: Pantheon, 1980); Helen Dudar, "The Price of Blowing the Whistle," *New York Times Magazine*, 30 October 1979, pp. 41-54; John Edsall, *Scientific Freedom and Responsibility* (Washington, D.C.: American Association for the Advancement of Science, 1975), p. 5; David Ewing, *Freedom Inside the Organization* (New York: Dutton, 1979); Ralph Nader, Peter Petkas, and Kate Blackwell, *Whistle Blowing* (New York: Grossman, 1972); Charles Peter and Taylor Branch, *Blowing the Whistle* (New York: Praeger, 1972).

5. Congressional hearings uncovered a growing resort to mandatory psychiatric examinations. See U.S. Congress, House Committee on Post Office and Civil Service, Subcommittee on Compensation and Employee Benefits *Forced Retirement/Psychiatric Fitness for Duty Exams*, 95th Cong., 2nd sess., 3 November 1978, pp. 2-4. See also the Subcommittee hearings of 28 February 1978. Psychiatric referral for whistleblowers has become institutionalized in government service, but it is not uncommon in private employment. Even persons who make accusations without being "employed" in the organization they accuse have been classified as unstable and thus as unreliable witnesses. See, e.g., Jonas Robitscher, "Stigmatization and Stone-Walling: The Ordeal of Martha Mitchell," *Journal of Psychohistory*, 6, 1979, pp. 393-407.

6. For an account of strategies and proposals to support government whistleblowers, see Government Accountability Project, *A Whistleblowers' Guide to the Federal Bureaucracy* (Washington, D.C.: Institute for Policy Studies, 1977).

7. See, e.g., Samuel Eliot Morison, Frederick Merk, and Frank Friedel, *Dissent in Three American Wars* (Cambridge: Harvard University Press, 1970).

8. In the scheme worked out by Albert Hirschman in *Exit, Voice and Loyalty* (Cambridge: Harvard University Press, 1970), whistleblowing represents "voice" accompanied by a preference not to "exit," though forced "exit" is clearly a possibility and "voice" after or during "exit" may be chosen for strategic reasons.

9. Edward Weisband and Thomas N. Franck, *Resignation in Protest* (New York: Grossman, 1975).

10. Future developments can, however, be the cause for whistleblowing if they are seen as resulting from steps being taken or about to be taken that render them inevitable.

11. Case A is adapted from Louis Clark, "The Sound of Professional Suicide," *Barrister*, Summer 1978, p. 10; Case B is Case 5 in Robert J. Baum and Albert Flores, eds., *Ethical Problems of Engineering* (Troy, N.Y.: Rensselaer Polytechnic Institute, 1978), p. 186.

12. I discuss these questions of consultation and publicity with respect to moral choice in chapter 7 of Sissela Bok, *Lying* (New York: Pantheon, 1978); and in *Secrets* (New York: Pantheon Books, 1982) Ch. IX and XV.

Questions

1. After a brief introduction, Bok describes three important areas of concern for whistleblowers (P3, 4, 5). For each area, what is the central question to be asked?

2. She describes these as "moral conflicts," but the word 'conflict' usually refers to the clashing of two or more interests. Which of the three areas of concern truly involve a conflict and which involve simply a difficult decision?

3. Give an example of when one's responsibility to the public would outweigh one's responsibility to one's employer.

4. In what way does whistleblowing call into question "self-policing" (P6)?

5. While noting increasing support for whistleblowing, Bok also notes that there are dangers involved (P8). List these.

6. Before attempting to distinguish between justified and unjustified whistleblowing, Bok defines whistleblowing. According to her definition, whistleblowing is composed of three major elements. What are they?

7. How is whistleblowing different from other cases of dissent?

8. In what way is whistleblowing seen by Bok to be a breach of loyalty? Do you agree that "in holding [a] position, [one] has assumed certain obligations to [one's] colleagues and clients" (P13) which include loyalty and confidentiality?

9. How does organizational hierarchy make the issue more complicated?

10. To qualify as whistleblowing, Bok claims that the accusation must concern a threat that satisfies two criteria (P16, 17). What are they? Do you agree that these two criteria must be met in order for the public dissent to count as whistleblowing?

11. Bok claims that certain conditions must apply for whistleblowing to be effective (P19). What are they?

12. In order to distinguish between justified and unjustified whistleblowing, Bok suggests that one must examine the aim, message, and method. To this end, she revisits the three elements of whistleblowing, specifying the qualities that must accompany each in order for the whistleblowing to be justified (P22). Explain these qualities.

13. How could the director in Bok's Case C fulfil the requirement of accuracy?

14. With respect to alternatives, does Bok insist that they be tried before opting for whistleblowing?

15. Suppose you are an engineer at Company "B" (see Bok's Case B) – what alternatives to whistleblowing could you consider?

16. Does Bok claim that loyalty and confidentiality are absolute obligations? If not, under what conditions can they be overridden (P25)?

17. Accusation can be an invasion of privacy. When do you think the public has a "right to know"?

18. What are the advantages and disadvantages of anonymous whistleblowing (P28, 29)?

19. Summarize Bok's comments about bias (P30–33).

Whistleblowing and Employee Loyalty

Ronald Duska

Three Mile Island. In early 1983, almost four years after the near meltdown at Unit 2, two officials in the Site Operations Office of General Public Utilities reported a reckless company effort to clean up the contaminated reactor. Under threat of physical retaliation from superiors, the GPU insiders released evidence alleging that the company had rushed the TMI cleanup without testing key maintenance systems. Since then, the Three Mile Island mop-up has been stalled pending a review of GPU's management.[1]

1   The releasing of evidence of the rushed cleanup at Three Mile Island is an example of whistleblowing. Norman Bowie defines whistleblowing as "the act by an employee of informing the public on the immoral or illegal behavior of an employer or supervisor."[2] Ever since Daniel Ellsberg's release of the Pentagon Papers, the question of whether an employee should blow the whistle on his company or organization has become a hotly contested issue. Was Ellsberg right? Is it right to report the shady or suspect practices of the organization one works for? Is one a stool pigeon or a dedicated citizen? Does a person have an obligation to the public which overrides his obligation to his employer or does he simply betray a loyalty and become a traitor if he reports his company?

2   There are proponents on both sides of the issue — those who praise whistleblowers as civic heroes and those who condemn them as "finks." Glen and Shearer who wrote about the whistleblowers at Three Mile Island say, "Without the *courageous* breed of assorted company insiders known as whistleblowers — workers who often risk their livelihoods to disclose information about construction and design flaws — the Nuclear Regulatory Commission itself would be nearly as idle as Three Mile Island … That whistleblowers deserve both gratitude and protection is beyond disagreement."[3]

3   Still, while Glen and Shearer praise whistleblowers, others vociferously condemn them. For example, in a now-infamous quote, James Roche, the former president of General Motors said:

> Some critics are now busy eroding another support of free enterprise — the loyalty of a management team, with its unifying values and cooperative work. Some of the enemies of business now encourage an employee to be *disloyal* to the enterprise. They want to create suspicion and disharmony, and pry into the proprietary interests of the business. However this is labelled — industrial espionage, whistle blowing, or professional responsibility — it is another tactic for spreading disunity and creating conflict.[4]

4   From Roche's point of view, whistleblowing is not only not "courageous" and deserving of "gratitude and protection" as Glen and Shearer would have it, it is corrosive and not even permissible.

5   Discussions of whistleblowing generally revolve around four topics: (1) attempts to define

whistleblowing more precisely; (2) debates about whether and when whistleblowing is permissible; (3) debates about whether and when one has an obligation to blow the whistle; and (4) appropriate mechanisms for institutionalizing whistleblowing.

6   In this paper I want to focus on the second problem, because I find it somewhat disconcerting that there is a problem at all. When I first looked into the ethics of whistleblowing, it seemed to me that whistleblowing was a good thing, and yet I found in the literature claim after claim that it was in need of defense, that there was something wrong with it, namely that it was an act of disloyalty.

7   If whistleblowing was a disloyal act, it deserved disapproval, and ultimately any action of whistleblowing needed justification. This disturbed me. It was as if the act of a good Samaritan was being condemned as an act of interference, as if the prevention of a suicide needed to be justified. My moral position in favor of whistleblowing was being challenged. The tables were turned and the burden of proof had shifted. My position was the one in question. Suddenly instead of the company being the bad guy and the whistleblower the good guy, which is what I thought, the whistleblower was the bad guy. Why? Because he was disloyal. What I discovered was that in most of the literature it was taken as axiomatic that whistleblowing was an act of disloyalty. My moral intuitions told me that axiom was mistaken. Nevertheless, since it is accepted by a large segment of the ethical community it deserves investigation.

8   In his book *Business Ethics*, Norman Bowie, who presents what I think is one of the finest presentations of the ethics of whistleblowing, claims that "whistleblowing ... violate[s] a *prima facie* duty of loyalty to one's employer." According to Bowie, there is a duty of loyalty which prohibits one from reporting his employer or company. Bowie, of course, recognizes that this is only a *prima facie* duty, i.e., one that can be overridden by a higher duty to the public good. Nevertheless, the axiom that whistleblowing is disloyal is Bowie's starting point.

9   Bowie is not alone. Sissela Bok, another fine ethicist, sees whistleblowing as an instance of disloyalty:

> The whistleblower hopes to stop the game; but since he is neither referee nor coach, and since he blows the whistle on his own team, his act is seen as a *violation of loyalty* [italics mine]. In holding his position, he has assumed certain obligations to his colleagues and clients. He may even have subscribed to a loyalty oath or a promise of confidentiality ... Loyalty to colleagues and to clients comes to be pitted against loyalty to the public interest, to those who may be injured unless the revelation is made.[5]

10   Bowie and Bok end up defending whistleblowing in certain contexts, so I don't necessarily disagree with their conclusions. However, I fail to see how one has an obligation of loyalty to one's company, so I disagree with their perception of the problem, and their starting point. The difference in perception is important because those who think employees have an obligation of loyalty to a company fail to take into account a relevant moral difference between persons and corporations and between corporations and other kinds of groups where loyalty is appropriate. I want to argue that one does not have an obligation of loyalty to a company, even a *prima facie* one, because companies are not the kind of things which are proper objects of loyalty. I then want to show that to make them objects of loyalty gives them a moral status they do not deserve and in raising their sta-

tus, one lowers the status of the individuals who work for the companies.

11 But why aren't corporations the kind of things which can be objects of loyalty? ...

12 Loyalty is ordinarily construed as a state of being constant and faithful in a relation implying trust or confidence. And according to John Ladd, "The ties that bind the persons together provide the basis of loyalty."[6] But all sorts of ties bind people together to make groups. I am a member of a group of fans if I go to a ball game. I am a member of a group if I merely walk down the street. I am in a sense tied to them, but don't owe them loyalty. I don't owe loyalty to just anyone I encounter. Rather I owe loyalty to persons with whom I have special relationships. I owe it to my children, my spouse, my parents, my friends and certain groups, those groups which are formed for the mutual enrichment of the members. It is important to recognize that in any relationship which demands loyalty, the relationship works both ways and involves mutual enrichment. Loyalty is incompatible with self-interest, because it is something that necessarily requires we go beyond self-interest. My loyalty to my friend, for example, requires I put aside my interests some of the time. It is because of this reciprocal requirement which demands surrendering self-interest that a corporation is not a proper object of loyalty.

13 A business or corporation does two things in the free enterprise system. It produces a good or service and makes a profit. The making of a profit, however, is the primary function of a business as a business. For if the production of the good or service was not profitable, the business would be out of business. Since non-profitable goods or services are discontinued, the providing of a service or the making of a product is not done for its own sake, but from a business perspective is a means to an end, the making of profit. People bound together in a business are not bound together for mutual fulfillment and support, but to divide labor so the business makes a profit. Since profit is paramount, if you do not produce in a company or if there are cheaper laborers around, a company feels justified in firing you for the sake of better production. Throughout history, companies in a pinch feel no obligation of loyalty. Compare that to a family. While we can jokingly refer to a family as "somewhere they have to take you in no matter what," you cannot refer to a company in that way. "You can't buy loyalty" is true. Loyalty depends on ties that demand self-sacrifice with no expectation of reward, e.g., the ties of loyalty that bind a family together. Business functions on the basis of enlightened self-interest. I am devoted to a company not because it is like a parent to me. It is not, and attempts of some companies to create "one big happy family" ought to be looked on with suspicion. I am not "devoted" to it at all, or should not be. I *work* for it because it pays me. I am not in a family to get paid, but I am in a company to get paid.

14 Since loyalty is a kind of devotion, one can confuse devotion to one's job (or the ends of one's work) with devotion to a company.

15 I may have a job I find fulfilling, but that is accidental to my relation to the company. For example, I might go to work for a company as a carpenter and love the job and get satisfaction out of doing good work. But if the company can increase profit by cutting back to an adequate but inferior type of material or procedure, it can make it impossible for me to take pride in my work as a carpenter while making it possible for me to make more money. The company does not exist to subsidize my quality work as a carpenter. As a carpenter, my goal may be good

houses, but as an employee my goal is to contribute to making a profit. "That's just business!"

16   This fact that profit determines the quality of work allowed leads to a phenomenon called the commercialization of work. The primary end of an act of building is to make something, and to build well is to make it well. A carpenter is defined by the end of his work, but if the quality interferes with profit, the business side of the venture supercedes the artisan side. Thus profit forces a craftsman to suspend his devotion to his work and commercializes his venture. The more professions subject themselves to the forces of the marketplace, the more they get commercialized; e.g., research for the sake of a more profitable product rather than for the sake of knowledge jeopardizes the integrity of academic research facilities.

17   The cold hard truth is that the goal of profit is what gives birth to a company and forms that particular group. Money is what ties the group together. But in such a commercialized venture, with such a goal there is no loyalty, or at least none need be expected. An employer will release an employee and an employee will walk away from an employer when it is profitable for either one to do so. That's business. It is perfectly permissible.

18   Loyalty to a corporation, then, is not required. But even more it is probably misguided. There is nothing as pathetic as the story of the loyal employee who, having given above and beyond the call of duty, is let go in the restructuring of the company. He feels betrayed because he mistakenly viewed the company as an object of his loyalty. To get rid of such foolish romanticism and to come to grips with this hard but accurate assessment should ultimately benefit everyone.

19   One need hardly be an enemy of business to be suspicious of a demand of loyalty to some-

thing whose primary reason for existence is the making of profit. It is simply the case that I have no duty of loyalty to the business or organization. Rather I have a duty to return responsible work for fair wages. The commercialization of work dissolves the type of relationship that requires loyalty. It sets up merely contractual relationships. One sells one's labor but not one's self to a company or an institution.

20   To think we owe a company or corporation loyalty requires us to think of that company as a person or as a group with a goal of human enrichment. If we think of it in this way we can be loyal. But this is just the wrong way to think. A company is not a person. A company is an instrument, and an instrument with a specific purpose, the making of profit. To treat an instrument as an end in itself, like a person, may not be as bad as treating an end as an instrument, but it does give the instrument a moral status it does not deserve, and by elevating the instrument we lower the end. All things, instruments and ends, become alike.

21   To treat a company as a person is analogous to treating a machine as a person or treating a system as a person. The system, company, or instrument gets as much respect and care as the persons for whom they were invented. If we remember that the primary purpose of business is to make profit, it can be seen clearly as merely an instrument. If so, it needs to be used and regulated accordingly, and I owe it no more loyalty than I owe a word processor.

22   Of course if everyone would view business as a commercial instrument, things might become more difficult for the smooth functioning of the organization, since businesses could not count on the "loyalty" of their employees. Business itself is well served, at least in the short run, if it can keep the notion of a duty to loyalty alive. It does this by

comparing itself to a paradigm case of an organization one shows loyalty to, the team.

23   Remember that Roche refers to the "management team" and Bok sees the name "whistleblowing" coming from the instance of a referee blowing a whistle in the presence of a foul. What is perceived as bad about whistleblowing in business from this perspective is that one blows the whistle on one's own team, thereby violating team loyalty. If the company can get its employees to view it as a team they belong to, it is easier to demand loyalty. The rules governing teamwork and team loyalty will apply. One reason the appeal to a team and team loyalty works so well in business is that businesses are in competition with one another. If an executive could get his employees to be loyal, a loyalty without thought to himself or his fellow man, but to the will of the company, the manager would have the ideal kind of corporation from an organizational standpoint. As Paul R. Lawrence, the organizational theorist says, "Ideally, we would want one sentiment to be dominant in all employees from top to bottom, namely a complete loyalty to the organizational purpose."[7] Effective motivation turns business practices into a game and instills teamwork.

24   But businesses differ from teams in very important respects, which makes the analogy between business and a team dangerous. Loyalty to a team is loyalty within the context of sport, a competition. Teamwork and team loyalty require that in the circumscribed activity of the game I cooperate with my fellow players so that pulling all together, we can win. The object of (most) sports is victory. But the winning in sports is a social convention, divorced from the usual goings on of society. Such a winning is most times a harmless, morally neutral diversion.

25   But the fact that this victory in sports, within the rules enforced by a referee (whistleblower), is a socially developed convention taking place within a larger social context makes it quite different from competition in business, which, rather than being defined by a context, permeates the whole of society in its influence. Competition leads not only to winners but to losers. One can lose at sport with precious few serious consequences. The consequences of losing at business are much more serious. Further, the losers in sport are there voluntarily, while the losers in business can be those who are not in the game voluntarily (we are all forced to participate) but are still affected by business decisions. People cannot choose to participate in business, since it permeates everyone's life.

26   The team model fits very well with the model of the free-market system because there competition is said to be the name of the game. Rival companies compete and their object is to win. To call a foul on one's own teammate is to jeopardize one's chances of winning and is viewed as disloyalty.

27   But isn't it time to stop viewing the corporate machinations as games? These games are not controlled and not over after a specific time. The activities of business affect the lives of everyone, not just the game players. The analogy of the corporation to a team and the consequent appeal to team loyalty, although understandable, is seriously misleading at least in the moral sphere, where competition is not the prevailing virtue.

28   If my analysis is correct, the issue of the permissibility of whistleblowing is not a real issue, since there is no obligation of loyalty to a company. Whistleblowing is not only permissible but expected when a company is harming society. The issue is not one of disloyalty to the company, but the question of whether the

whistleblower has an obligation to society if blowing the whistle will bring him retaliation. I will not argue that issue, but merely suggest the lines I would pursue.

29   I tend to be a minimalist in ethics, and depend heavily on a distinction between obligations and acts of supererogation. We have, it seems to me, an obligation to avoid harming anyone, but not an obligation to do good. Doing good is above the call of duty. In-between we may under certain conditions have an obligation to prevent harm. If whistleblowing can prevent harm, then it is required under certain conditions.

30   Simon, Powers and Gunnemann set forth four conditions:[8] need, proximity, capability, and last resort. Applying these, we get the following:

1. There must be a clear harm to society that can be avoided by whistleblowing. We don't blow the whistle over everything.

2. It is the "proximity" to the whistleblower that puts him in the position to report his company in the first place.

3. "Capability" means that he needs to have some chance of success. No one has an obligation to jeopardize himself to perform futile gestures. The whistleblower needs to have access to the press, be believable, etc.

4. "Last resort" means just that. If there are others more capable of reporting and more proximate, and if they will report, then one does not have the responsibility.

31   Before concluding, there is one aspect of the loyalty issue that ought to be disposed of. My position could be challenged in the case of organizations who are employers in non-profit areas, such as the government, educational institutions, etc. In this case, my commercialization argument is irrelevant. However, I would maintain that any activity which merits the blowing of the whistle in the case of non-profit and service organizations is probably counter to the purpose of the institution in the first place. Thus, if there were loyalty required, in that case, whoever justifiably blew the whistle would be blowing it on a colleague who perverted the end or purpose of the organization. The loyalty to the group would remain intact. Ellsberg's whistleblowing on the government is a way of keeping the government faithful to its obligations. But that is another issue.

NOTES

1. Maxwell Glen and Cody Shearer, "Going after the Whistle-blowers," *The Philadelphia Inquirer*, Tuesday, Aug. 2, 1983, Op-ed Page, p. 11a.

2. Norman Bowie, *Business Ethics* (Englewood Cliffs, N.J.: Prentice-Hall, 1982), 140. For Bowie, this is just a preliminary definition. His fuller definition reads, "A whistle blower is an employee or officer of any institution, profit or non-profit, private or public, who believes either that he/she has been ordered to perform some act or he/she has obtained knowledge that the institution is engaged in activities which a) are believed to cause unnecessary harm to third parties, b) are in violation of human rights or c) run counter to the defined purpose of the institution and who inform the public of this fact." Bowie then lists six conditions under which the act is justified. 142–143.

3. Glen and Shearer, "Going after the Whistleblowers," 11a.

4. James M. Roche, "The Competitive System, to Work, to Preserve, and to Protect," *Vital Speeches of the Day* (May 1971), 445. This is quoted in Bowie, 141, and also in Kenneth D. Walters, "Your Employee's Right to Blow the Whistle," *Harvard Business Review*, 53, no. 4.

5. Sissela Bok, "Whistleblowing and Professional Responsibilities," *New York University Education Quarterly*, vol. II, 4 (1980), 3.

6. John Ladd, "Loyalty," *The Encyclopedia of Philosophy*, vol. 5, 97.

7. Paul R. Lawrence, *The Changing of Organizational Behavior Patterns: A Case Study of Decentralization* (Boston: Division of Research, Harvard Business School, 1958), 208, as quoted in Kenneth D. Walters, op. cit.

8. John G. Simon, Charles W. Powers, and Jon P. Gunnemann, *The Ethical Investor: Universities and Corporate Responsibility* (New Haven: Yale University Press, 1972).

Questions

1. Duska says that accusing a whistleblower of disloyalty is like accusing a Samaritan (who saves a would-be suicide) of interference (P7). Do you think this is a good analogy?

2. On what major point do Bok and Duska differ?

3. What is Duska's main reason for claiming that one does not have an obligation of loyalty to a company (P10)?

4. What reason does he give to support his view that a corporation can't be an object of loyalty (P12)?

5. As evidence of the inability to be in a mutually-enriching, i.e., reciprocal, relationship, Duska cites the self-interested motive of profit-making that is, he says, the primary function of business (P13). Do you agree that profit-making is the primary function of business?

6. Larmer (see the References and Further Reading list at the end of the introduction to this chapter) disagrees with Duska, arguing that loyalty *can* be a one-way thing, and he gives as an example the loyalty of a parent to an erring and disloyal teenager. Which do you think is the stronger position, that of Duska or that of Larmer?

7. Duska might concede that loyalty can be one-way, but he would probably still maintain that feeling loyalty toward a company is misguided. Why? (Read carefully P20–21.)

8. Why is the appeal to a team and team loyalty in a company's best interests (P23)?

9. Explain Duska's criticisms of the team analogy (P24–27).

10. Duska concludes that whistleblowing is permissible. In fact, his conclusion is even stronger than that – how so?

11. Anticipating the objection that his position is not applicable to non-profit organizations (such organizations do not have as their primary function the self-interested pursuit of profit and therefore may be appropriate objects of loyalty), Duska provides a response.

    (a) Explain what it is.

    (b) Could this response also be applied to profit-making organizations? That is, could one argue that the activity meriting whistleblowing is also counter to the purpose of the for-profit business?

Case Study – Dr. Olivieri vs. Apotex

Dr. Nancy Olivieri is a medical researcher with the University of Toronto and head of a blood disorder research program at the Hospital for Sick Children. In April 1993, she signed a contract with Apotex Research Inc., a Canadian pharmaceutical company, to conduct a study of the effects of a new drug, deferiprone, which treats a deadly blood disorder, thalassemia.

In September 1995, she and an expert in iron metabolism discovered dangerously high levels of iron in some of the liver biopsies taken from her patients who were on the drug; heart disease and early death could result from such a condition. She contacted Apotex, hoping to put an end to the study.

Apotex, however, maintained that the drug was safe, claiming that other researchers disagreed with her conclusions; they wanted her to continue the study. They also reminded Olivieri of the confidentiality agreement she had signed and threatened to sue her if she made her opinions public.

Olivieri then contacted the hospital's Research Ethics Board: they told her to change the consent forms so that patients would be informed of the risk; they also told her to report her discovery to the Health Protection Branch in Ottawa, which is responsible for granting drug approvals. She did both.

In May 1996, Apotex terminated the trials at the Hospital for Sick Children and removed Olivieri as lead investigator on the international study she was also conducting for them.

The executive of the Hospital for Sick Children did not support Olivieri in her dispute with Apotex. Publicly, they maintained that it was a scientific controversy which was best settled within the scientific community. (In August 1998, the *New England Journal of Medicine* published Olivieri's article, which concluded that deferiprone was ineffective and may be toxic to the liver.) Privately, in e-mail messages sent to many scientists across Canada, the hospital executive stated that "both Apotex and other scientists involved in the [deferiprone] trials disagreed with Olivieri's interpretation of the data." Olivieri and her supporters within the medical and university community felt betrayed by a prominent public institution they viewed as having "sold out" to commercial interests.

The comments of Dr. Allan Detsky, Physician-in-chief at Mount Sinai Hospital in Toronto, go to the heart of the ethical issue in the case, at least from one perspective. He stated, "Forget about the confidentiality agreement, forget about the hospital's financial interests [in drug company research funding], forget about the pharmaceutical companies' interest. What was the right thing to do in the case? How could somebody whose motivation is to protect children from harm ever be wrong?"

In early January 1999, reportedly for personnel issues that happened before the Apotex study, Olivieri was demoted by the hospital: though retaining hospital privileges, she was no longer head of the blood research program and could not conduct any clinical trials. However, just a few weeks later, in late January, University of Toronto President Rob Prichard gathered all the parties together and managed to broker a deal that reinstated Olivieri as head of the program and cleared her reputation. As well, the University of Toronto resolved to develop for its teaching hospitals "a seamless policy environment reflecting our commitment to academic freedom and ethical research."

REFERENCES

Boyle, Theresa, and Rita Daly. "Olivieri Pledges to Battle 'Bias'." *The Toronto Star* 11 Dec. 1998: A1+.

Foss, Krista, and Paul Taylor. "Sick Kids demotes controversial MD." *The Globe and Mail* 8 Jan. 1999: A12.

O'Hara, Jane. "Whistleblower." *Maclean's* 16 Nov. 1998: 65-69.

Quinn, Jennifer and Tanya Talaga. "Blood Research, Hospital Agree to End 2 1/2-year Battle." *The Toronto Star* 27 Jan. 1999: A1+.

Questions:

1. We aren't told if there is an existing treatment for thalassemia. Is this information relevant to the moral rightness of Olivieri's decision/action?

2. Do you agree with Detsky – can somebody whose motivation is to protect children from harm ever be wrong?

3. If you were the ethics consultant hired by the University of Toronto, what specific recommendations would you make for the policies they intend to develop?

CHAPTER 2
ADVERTISING

What to Do? – AdNet

You have just been offered a job by AdNet, a new and exciting firm specializing in full-screen, non-closeable website advertising. The creative potential of working with a full screen is very attractive – all that space! The non-closeable feature is also a plus – thirty seconds' viewing guaranteed! It's like the difference between designing a stamp and choreographing a poster. However, not only are users unable to close the ads, opening them is also out of their control – AdNet's intent, their marketing strategy, is to make the web like television: every ten minutes or so, users' access would be interrupted with a jump to an advertisement.

As a heavy Internet user, you know you'd be irritated by such interruptions. No doubt ad-free versions of the sites would also be available for a fee, but you figure that until your student loan is paid off, you would never be able to afford the ad-free versions. And you're not thrilled with the net becoming two-tiered: one version for the haves, another for have-nots. And yet *someone* has to pay for the net – why shouldn't it be the users, either directly through the price of access or indirectly through watching ads?

It's not that the ads themselves are problematic – in fact, yours would be works of art: why wouldn't someone want to watch them? It's the coercive and persistent nature of their presentation that bothers you. (Which would be compounded if there *was* a problem with the ads themselves – i.e., if they were deceptive, for example, or violent. or just plain ugly.) True, people *choose* to use the net. But is it right for such strings to be attached? Do you want to work for a company that supports, indeed encourages, those kinds of strings? Then again, if this direction is inevitable, isn't better to have people like you designing the ads – so they *won't* be deceptive or violent?

What do you decide to do?

Introduction

One might suppose that the main ethical question with regard to advertising is whether it's morally acceptable to *lie* in advertisements. Certainly that's an important question, but perhaps it's too easy. Consider instead whether it's morally acceptable to *deceive*. Aha. And what exactly is deception? Is it more or less than *misleading*?

It is reasonably certain that you will never be able to include in an advertisement everything there is to know about your product or service (supposing you wanted to). So you'll have to be selective. And there's part of the issue: what do you leave out – and why?

As for what you put *in*, perhaps the question becomes whether or not it's morally acceptable to *manipulate*. And actually, *that* question depends on whether or not advertisements are, in fact, capable of manipulating people. (See Packard for an argument that they do; see Arrington for an argument that they don't.) And if they *are* capable of manipulation, perhaps next we must ask why. Really, can we hold a company morally responsible if the consumer is too lazy to think clearly and critically about the claims being made and too insecure to resist even the most ludicrous of suggestions? Isn't that consumer the one who's morally at fault?

Another question is whether it's morally acceptable to *try to* manipulate (whether or not one *can*). Whereas the previous question required establishing cause and effect, this one requires establishing intentions.

Either way, we need to define our terms: What exactly is manipulation? Is/how is it different from persuasion? From influence? From coercion? When does influence become control?

Or at least controlling enough to be immoral? Does the context matter? The presence of attractive alternatives? How much resistance is it reasonable to expect? In addition to lies and omissions, we need to consider ambiguities, exaggerations, and implications.

Surely it's a matter of degree: manipulating by intentionally withholding information may be worse than manipulating by merely associating two things (your product with certain qualities, usually wealth and sexual attractiveness). Or maybe both of those are equally reprehensible because of their subtlety, whereas manipulating by making explicit but outlandish claims is less reprehensible (because only an idiot would accept your claims). (By the way, see the magazine *Adbusters* for some heavy and often hilarious critique of manipulative advertisements.)

But perhaps even explicit and outlandish claim-making entails subtlety – advertisers know the power of repetition: it leads to familiarity, which leads to consumer choice (humans choose what's familiar, what's recognizable – science has established that). Even content-free ads – i.e., the mere presentation of the brand name (I think of the tab on jeans, the animated television station logo in the corner of the screen, etc.) – can be manipulative.

Does it matter whether the method of persuasion is rational (evidence, reason) or non-rational (emotional, subliminal)? If you argue that advertising fails to respect people's autonomy, then yes, it does matter: rational argument (unaccompanied by intellectual intimidation) would be morally acceptable; only other means of persuasion could be morally unacceptable.

Also, does the medium make a difference? Are we more susceptible to images, especially moving images (frogs are like that — they can see something only if it moves), and if so, then should television advertising have higher standards?

Now arguments *against* lying, deceiving, misleading, manipulating, coercing usually involve several concepts we've already covered: respect for persons, which includes respect for their autonomy (recall Kant in Section II; see the article by Crisp); people's rights, such as freedom of choice; fairness; and the social good (recall utilitarianism).

Concerning respect to persons, one can ask whether or not the consumer is being treated as a means to the company's end or as an end in him/herself.

Concerning autonomy issues, it's not just the autonomy of the targeted person that one can consider; the person being used as "bait" is also exploited. Thus, every ad that shows women in child-like or sexual-object roles, and *only* in those roles (and there's the "lie"), restricts the freedom of all women because people, men and women alike, see so often, get used to seeing, expect to see, women in that role and that role only (even though they know it's "just" an ad).

But undermining autonomy and therefore restricting freedom of choice is not the only harm that deception can incur. Very real physical injury can occur. Perhaps one of the classic cases of ethically questionable advertising is that of Nestlé's infant formula: it has been argued that its advertising campaign to mothers in developing countries "failed to consider" (intentionally ignored?) the need for clean water (mothers mixed it with polluted water, the only kind available) and the ability to afford enough of the formula (they couldn't, so they diluted the formula) — as a result, babies died.

With respect to fairness, expecting the consumer to make a choice based on incomplete or slanted information isn't fair. But nor is expecting a business to thrive if it can't let people know about its products and services. Ah, but "let people know" isn't the same as "suggest they're inadequate without your product/service."

As for the social good argument, many claim that advertising doesn't just "make" people *buy*; many argue that it makes them *want* (see Galbraith on this point). In this way, it encourages unhappiness and dissatisfaction; in fact, advertisers *count* on people being unhappy (and they therefore try to create such a state): after all, if people were happy with what they had, they wouldn't need (to buy) more.

The standard rebuttal to this is a denial: business merely supplies what the people demand — consider the notion of consumer sovereignty. But one might ask, then, if the people genuinely want to buy X, why does a company need to advertise X? I don't recall ever seeing an advertisement for mittens and yet many people buy them every winter. Well, the response goes, a company needs to advertise X because it needs to inform the consumer of the product's existence. But then the ad should simply say, "X is available at this store." And we all know it says more than that.

Another part of the social good argument is that advertising, perhaps especially manipulative advertising, creates the consumer culture, a culture in which "going shopping" is a bona fide activity, just like "going bowling." According to Waide, advertising fosters "the ideology of acquisitiveness." Barbara J. Phillips disagrees, however, blaming not advertising but capitalism for our increasing materialism.

Kant's universality principle can also be used to argue against deceptive advertising: if everyone deceived in advertising, it would eventually fail to achieve its goal, that of persuading to purchase.

A virtue ethicist might measure advertising against honesty, respect, and integrity. Or cleverness and gainfulness.

Now, arguments *for* such advertising also include people's rights, such as to the pursuit of profit and freedom of speech, as well as the social good (it fosters competition, which improves quality).

As for the rights, as always, surely they are not absolute. For example, we may have the right to say whatever we want, but still, if we lie or cause harm, it's morally reprehensible – whether we're advertising, proselytizing, campaigning, or "just" talking. (And in fact, maybe deception in the last three instances is more harmful than in the first, because at least with advertising we *expect* the bias of a vested interest.)

And why is it the responsibility of the buyer to beware? Why should Person A have to be vigilant against deception instead of Person B having to refrain from deceiving? Shouldn't the right thing be the default mode? (Isn't the other just blaming the victim?)

As for the social good, in addition to fostering competition, advertisements simply do the public service of informing people about what's available. If this argument is valid, then companies would present an objective "advantages and disadvantages" advertisement of their products. And why not? If a product is good, if it has more (or more important) advantages than disadvantages, won't people choose it? (And if it doesn't have more advantages than disadvantages, why are you making it?) Don't you have faith in people's rationality? (If not, could it be that in a world bereft of rational argument, a world characterized by mindless and emotional ads, most people haven't had the chance to develop that

rationality? Lippke ventures into this area, arguing that "advertising, in concert with other social conditions, deprives individuals of the ability and willingness to critically reflect on their beliefs, desires, aims, and interests" [103].)

One might respond, well, if my competition had to do that too, it'd be okay, but if I'm the only one to do it, it'd be unfair. Okay, so if it is the right thing to do, then should government make such a regulation? (Assuming that business owners won't do the right thing unless they have to – unless everyone else does. Are you going to be that kind of business owner?)

Another social good to consider is the sponsorship aspect of advertising. Without advertising, we'd have no television shows. (Does advertising support TV or does TV support the advertisers – read Joyce Nelson's book!) We'd also have no arts centres, no sports competitions, etc. Well, couldn't you just pass the expenses on to the consumer? But already, many can't afford the ticket. Well, how do our libraries exist? At the expense of authors who do not get paid, or get paid very little, per loan? Should governments cover the costs? ("This kids' show is brought to you by … the incumbent government"?)

As mentioned earlier, many deny that ads influence, let alone manipulate – but if they *don't* influence, then why do businesses spend so much money on them? This leads us to another argument, that advertising is wasteful. Just think about what advertising's billions of dollars per year could do to quality of life if spent otherwise. Or, just think how much lower the cost of living would be if we didn't have to pay for that advertising when we buy whatever it is we buy. One could argue that advertising increases profit and that profit could be directed toward improvements in product and service quality, or workplace conditions. Could be. And much advertising is intended to maintain, not increase, profit.

Another aspect of ethics in advertising focuses on the target of the ad rather than the content of the ad. Lynn Sharp Paine argues that because young children are not autonomous consumers (they have no sense of self as an independent human being, a prerequisite for self-control and rational choice, nor do they have a sense of time), advertising to them is morally wrong. Perhaps, given the relative absence of even *potential* autonomy, *any* advertising to children is especially manipulative, and especially morally wrong. If adults have trouble resisting the slick emotional messages, what hope do children have? (*Not* advertising to a certain group could also be morally wrong – see the Krohn and Milner paper.)

It was this concern about target group that led Umbro Canada to turn down a profitable cross-promotion marketing campaign for the World Cup of Soccer: the partnership would have been with a beer company, but Umbro's target market is primarily youth under the legal drinking age. "Instead of compromising its integrity and commitment to its target market, Umbro let the cross promotion go, choosing not to promote an image associating alcohol and youth" (Ethics in Action) – because of this, they won Ethics in Action's 1998 Award for Ethical Decision Making.

And how did you determine that target group? Consider "data mining" – "the latest technique in information gathering and exchange" whereby one uses a data discriminator program on databases (existing courtesy of your handy-dandy plastic cards) to identify people by all sorts of factors (they know how much you make, how much you spend, and when, and where, and on what, how much you owe ... they

know where you live). Is it a legitimate marketing research method or an illegitimate invasion of privacy? (See Pulfer's article.)

Not only "what" and "to whom" are issues. Consider "where" – is there something morally unacceptable about advertising on billboards along a highway? One, people really can't help but see them (closing one's eyes while driving is not really an option), so it's a touch coercive. Two, they can be quite distracting (indeed, many are designed to blink, move, and otherwise divert one's attention away from the road) and, therefore, can increase the chance of accidents. Yeah, but protestors along the side of the road can also be distracting. (That's a red herring – you may be quite right, but that's irrelevant to whether billboards are distracting and therefore immoral: protestors at the side of the road, especially those who are persistent, and have blinking lights, may *also* be morally unacceptable.) Advertising on buses and subways similarly involve captive audiences, though without the possibility of real physical injury.

"How much" might also be an issue. Should the extent of advertising – whether on highways, in magazines, on television, or on the net – be limited? Why/not? (And are we talking self-regulation by the industry – or government regulation?)

"By whom" is another issue. Some argue that it's morally wrong for some businesses to advertise at all; traditionally, "the professions," such as doctors and lawyers, have been under this prohibition. But why? Why is it okay for a car mechanic to advertise her services but not for a surgeon to do so? Is the assumption that advertising *does* manipulate, and it's particularly immoral to manipulate when serious things (your health, not your car) are at stake? Well, a bad brake job can certainly affect one's health!

Or is it that advertising implies varying degrees of quality, of competence, and some professions don't want that thought to even cross our minds (no doctor wants people to wonder whether they were at the bottom of their class) ... in which case, though, wouldn't the *failure* to advertise be deceptive?

Does it matter *what* you're advertising – are the moral standards different for baby cribs than for books? (Or politicians' positions?) Some have suggested no advertising at all for harmful products, such as tobacco and alcohol. But why? If the product is so bad we shouldn't advertise it, why is it okay to make it? And who's making the decisions here about badness – if I want to hurt myself, knowingly and voluntarily, that's nobody's business but my own, don't patronize me, don't decide for me what's good for me! (Do you agree?)

De George (288) identifies another ethical aspect of advertising: who is morally responsible for the advertising? The company that paid for it? The agency that created it? The media that aired/printed it? The consumer that responds to it with a purchase? The government that allowed it? Some combination of the above? Are they *all*, in their own way, endorsing, supporting, it? (So as the agency, do you refuse to create it, on moral grounds? As the TV station, do you refuse to air it?)

Advertising is only one marketing tool, and the others are as subject to concern about truth and autonomy. Product promotion is another area with many ethical questions (or assumptions!) – from the ethics of free samples (are expectations attached?) to the ethics of the packaging (consider the shape of the bottle, the composition of the label). But PR departments are also marketing tools: media releases and even annual reports can be used to attract consumers, customers, clients. They, too, are subject to ethical standards regarding influence and manipulation. Surely a report full of distorted data is as deceptive as the advertisement claiming X can do the unlikely.

FURTHER READING AND REFERENCES

Arrington, Robert L. "Advertising and Behavior Control." *Journal of Business Ethics* 1 (1982): 3-12.

Banker, Steve. "The Ethics of Political Marketing Practices, the Rhetorical Perspective." *Journal of Business Ethics* 11.11 (November 1992): 843-848.

Crisp, Roger. "Persuasive Advertising, Autonomy, and the Creation of Desire." *Journal of Business Ethics* 6.5 (July 1987): 413-418.

De George, Richard T. *Business Ethics* 5th ed. NJ: Prentice Hall, 1999.

Ethics in Action. <http://www.ethicsinaction.com>

Galbraith, John Kenneth. *The Affluent Society.* London: Houghton Mifflin, 1958.

Krohn, Franklin B. and Laura M. Milner. "The AIDS Crisis: Unethical Marketing Leads to Negligent Homicide". *Journal of Business Ethics* 8.10 (October 1989): 773-780.

Laczniak, Gene R. and Patrick E. Murphy. *Ethical Marketing Decisions: The Higher Road.* Boston, MA: Allyn & Bacon, 1993.

Lippke, Richard. *Radical Business Ethics.* Lanham, MD: Rowman and Barry, 1995. (Chapter 5, "Advertising and the Social Conditions of Autonomy")

Nelson, Joyce. *The Perfect Machine: TV in the Nuclear Age.* Toronto: Between the Lines, 1987.

Packard, Vance. *The Hidden Persuaders.* NY: Pocket Books, 1958.

Paine, Lynn Sharp. "Children as Consumers: An Ethical Evaluation of Children's Television

Advertising." *Business & Professional Ethics Journal* 3.3-4 (1983): 119-125, 135-145.

Phillips, Barbara J. "In Defense of Advertising: A Social Perspective." *Journal of Business Ethics* 16.2 (February 1997) 109-118.

Pulfer, Rachel. "Mining your Business." *This Magazine* 32.5 (March/April 1999): 13-15.

Waide, John. "The Making of Self and World in Advertising." *Journal of Business Ethics* 6.2 (February 1987) 73-79.

The Inconclusive Ethical Case Against Manipulative Advertising

Michael J. Phillips

Introduction

1   Back in 1982, the *Business and Society Review* sponsored an exchange on advertising (Colloquy, 1982). The occasion was a statement by Robert Heilbroner in the June 11, 1981 *New York Review of Books*:

> If I were asked to name the deadliest subversive force within capitalism – the single greatest source of its waning morality – I would without hesitation name advertising. How else should one identify a force that debases language, drains thought, and undoes dignity? If the barrage of advertising, unchanged in its tone and texture, were devoted to some other purpose – say the exaltation of the public sector – it would be recognized in a moment for the corrosive element that it is. But as the voice of the private sector it escapes this startled notice. (p. 64)

The colloquy's business and advertising participants made several predictable responses to Heilbroner's statement. Advertising, they said, stimulates technological advance by enabling innovative firms to inform consumers about their products. By thus enhancing competition, it also helps prevent market concentration and the stagnation that frequently accompanies it. Because advertising provides the media with financial support, moreover, it helps keep them free from government control. And since people approach advertising more or less rationally, there are limits on its ability to manipulate consumers.

2   However, William Winpisinger, then president of the International Association of Machinists and Aerospace Workers, saw things differently.

> I am in wholehearted agreement with Professor Heilbroner's view of advertising as a corrosive element in our society. Its major function and purpose has been to feed already bloated corporate beasts. They've discovered that the only way they can keep their revenues up is by paying

Michael J. Phillips, "The Inconclusive Ethical Case Against Manipulative Advertising" *Business and Professional Ethics Journal* 13.4 (Winter 1994): 31-64. © 1994 by Michael J. Phillips. Reprinted with permission of the author.

exorbitant sums to advertising professionals who combine art and psychology to exploit and manipulate the vast range of human fears and needs. (p. 65)

He concluded his remarks with the ritual demand the corporate influence on public policy be neutralized.

3   This article explores the ethical implications of Winpisinger's perception that advertisers successfully "exploit and manipulate the vast range of human fears and needs." It begins by defining its sense of the term "manipulative advertising." Then the article asserts for purposes of argument that manipulative advertising actually works. Specifically, I make two controversial assumptions about such advertising: (1) that it plays a major role in increasing the general propensity to consume, and (2) that it powerfully influences individual consumer purchase decisions. With the deck thus stacked against manipulative advertising, the article goes on to inquire whether either assumption justifies its condemnation, by considering four ethical criticisms of manipulative advertising. Ethically, I conclude, manipulative advertising is a most problematic practice. If probabilistic assertions are valid in ethics, that is, the odds strongly favor the conclusion that manipulative advertising is wrong. Nevertheless, there still is room for doubt about its badness. Like the apparently easy kill that continually slips out of the hunter's sights, manipulative advertising evades the clean strike that would justify its condemnation for once and all.

What Is Manipulative Advertising?

4   Some ethical evaluations of advertising (e.g., Crisp, 1987, p. 413) use the label "persuasive advertising" to name the phenomenon discussed in this article. However, because there is such a thing as rational persuasion and because such persuasion seems unobjectionable (Benn, 1967, pp. 265-66), this usage is questionable. Thus, following Tom Beauchamp (1984), I employ the term "manipulative advertising." According to Beauchamp, manipulation occupies a position about midway along a continuum of influences ranging from coercion, at one end, to rational persuasion, at the other (pp. 3-6). He defines it as including "any deliberate attempt by a person P to elicit a response desired by P from another person Q by noncoercively altering the structure of actual choices available to Q or by nonpersuasively altering Q's perceptions of those choices" (p. 8). Virtually all of Beauchamp's examples, however, involve what lawyers call deceptive advertising. Deceptive advertising involves false or misleading assertions or omissions that cause reasonable consumers to form erroneous judgments about the nature of a product.

5   What, then, is manipulative advertising? As used here, the term relates mainly to the "nonpersuasively altering Q's perceptions" portion of Beauchamp's definition. Building on that language, I define "manipulative advertising" as advertising that tries to favorably alter consumers' perceptions of the advertised product by appeals to factors other than the product's physical attributes and functional performance. There is no sharp line between such advertising and advertising that is nonmanipulative; even purely informative ads are unlikely to feature unattractive people and depressing surroundings. Nor is it clear what proportion of American advertising can fairly be classed as manipulative. Suffice it to say that that proportion almost certainly is significant. As we will see, advertising's critics sometimes seem to think that all of it is manipulative.

6   Perhaps the most common example of manipulative advertising is a technique John

Waide (1987, pp. 73-74) calls "associative advertising."[1] Advertisers using this technique try to favorably influence consumer perceptions of a product by associating it with a nonmarket good (e.g., contentment, sex, vigor, power, status, friendship, or family) that the product ordinarily cannot supply on its own. By purchasing the product, their ads suggest, the consumer somehow will get the nonmarket good. Michael Schudson describes this familiar form of advertising as follows: "The ads say, typically, 'buy me and you will overcome the anxieties I have just reminded you about' or 'buy me and you will enjoy life' or 'buy me and be recognized as a successful person' or 'buy me and everything will be easier for you' or 'come spend a few dollars and share in this society of freedom, choice, novelty, and abundance'" (1986, p. 6). Through such linkages between product and nonmarket good, associative advertising seeks to increase the product's perceived value and thus to induce its purchase. Because these linkages (e.g., the connection between beer and attractive women) generally make little sense, such advertising is far removed from rational persuasion.

The Effects of Manipulative Advertising: What the Critics Think

7   In the previous section, I tried to describe manipulative advertising in terms of sellers' *efforts*, rather than their actual accomplishments. But does manipulative advertising successfully influence consumers? As might be expected, advertising's critics generally answer this question in the affirmative. Perhaps the best-known example is chapter XI of John Kenneth Galbraith's *The Affluent Society*, where he described his well-known dependence effect.

8   Galbraith's dependence effect might be described as the way the process of consumer goods production creates and satisfies consumer wants (1958, p. 158). "That wants are, in fact, the fruit of production," he intoned, "will now be denied by few serious scholars" (p. 154). In part, these wants result from emulation, as increased production means increased consumption for some, followed by even more consumption as others follow suit (pp. 154-55). But advertising and salesmanship provide an even more direct link between production and consumer wants. Those practices, Galbraith says:

> [C]annot be reconciled with the notion of independently determined desires, for their central function is to create desires.... This is accomplished by the producer of goods or at his behest. A broad empirical relationship exists between what is spent on production of consumers' goods and what is spent in synthesizing the desires for that production. A new consumer product must be introduced with a suitable advertising campaign to arouse an interest in it. The path for an expansion of output must be paved by a suitable expansion in the advertising budget. Outlays for the manufacturing of a product are not more important in the strategy of modern business enterprise than outlays for the manufacturing of demand for the product. (pp. 155-56)

All these propositions, Galbraith concluded, "would be regarded as elementary by the most retarded student in the nation's most primitive school of business administration" (p. 156).

9   To Galbraith, therefore, advertising in general is manipulative. In *The Affluent Society*, it apparently worked mainly to promote aggregate demand, rather than to shift demand from one brand to another. Many of advertising's critics follow Galbraith's lead by stressing how it socializes people to embrace consumerist values (e.g.,

Held, 1984, pp. 62-63; Lasch, 1978, p. 72; Lippke, 1990, pp. 38-39, 41-48; Waide, 1987, p.75). Some of these accounts flesh out the causal links between advertising and the consumer mentality. To Richard Lippke, for instance, certain background factors – authoritarian management structures, unequal access to quality higher education, the media's insipid program content, and the dependence of political power on economic power – pave the way for advertising's success by depriving people of autonomy (1990, pp. 41-43). With the path thus cleared, advertising's consumerist message triumphs because it is pervasive, is not effectively challenged, and is implanted early in life (pp. 43-44).

10   From all this, it is a short step to the notion that advertising plays a major role in shaping and sustaining the modern society of material abundance. Implicitly, at least, some accounts of this kind (e.g., Krutch, 1959, ch. II) liken society to a huge machine whose aim is the conversion of natural resources into consumer products. For the machine to work properly, its human components must be motivated to play their role in producing those products. This can be accomplished by (1) implanting in people an intense desire for consumer goods, and (2) requiring that they do productive work to get the money to buy those goods. If this metaphorical picture is at all accurate, advertising obviously plays a major role in sustaining the system. As Joseph Wood Krutch once argued:

> If we could convincingly accuse the advertisers of greed..., we might reasonably ask why they should be allowed to invade our homes, destroy the beauty of the countryside, and deface the sky. But if "prosperity" as currently defined is the only reasonable meaning or measure of the good life, then a strong case can be made ... that when I am urged to trade in my car, buy a new wash-

ing machine, or try some new gadget, the profit motive of the seller is of less than secondary importance. Primarily, as he will eagerly explain, he is performing a public service by explaining to me my duty to support prosperity by behaving in the only manner in which this prosperity can be maintained. (1959, pp. 28-29)

Galbraith suggested that these social imperatives of production and consumption make the worker/consumer resemble a squirrel who races full-tilt to keep abreast of a wheel propelled by his own efforts (1958, pp. 154, 159).

11   Although they naturally evaluate the matter differently, business leaders often second Krutch's argument that advertising is essential to prosperity. In another *Business and Society Review* colloquy, this one a 1985 exchange on advertising expenditures by the fast-food industry, William H. Genge, the chairman of Ketchum Communications' board, wrote:

> I regard the many millions of dollars spent by fast-food companies (and other retailers as well) as healthy and necessary stimulation of the consumption that makes our economy the most dynamic and productive in the world.
>
> Some people talk as though large advertising budgets are wasteful and nonproductive. It just takes one simple question to put that down. The question is: Where does the money go? The answer is: It provides jobs and livelihoods for hundreds of thousands of people – not only in the advertising and communications sector but for all the people employed by fast-food companies and, indeed, all marketing organizations. (1985, pp. 58-59)

"So," Genge concluded, "large advertising expenditures are not a misallocation of economic resources. They are, in fact, an essential allocation and the driving force behind consumption, job creation, and prosperity" (p. 59).

12   Advertising that is sufficiently manipulative to create a consumer society also might be able to determine consumers' individual purchase decisions. Most often, I suppose, these would be brand choices within a particular product category, although advertising might also steer people toward certain products and away from others. Although advertising's critics often do not mention this particular form of manipulation,[2] some stress it (e.g., Crisp, 1987, *passim*).

Assumptions and Plan of Attack

13   As we have just seen, many critics of advertising say that it socializes people to a life of consumption. And some regard it as a strong influence on individual brand or product decisions. However, these beliefs are not universally shared. Some students of advertising doubt that ads do much to dictate individual brand choices (e.g., Schudson, 1986, pp. xiv, 85-89). And even if advertising strongly influences consumer decisions, it does not follow that any specific ad invariably compels the purchase of the product it touts. The reason is that a particular product advertisement is only one of many factors – especially competing advertisements – influencing consumers (Hayek, 1961, p. 347). For the same general reason, it is difficult to assess advertising's role in making people lifetime consumers. As Geoffrey Lantos has observed, this question "involves an almost impossible problem of causal inference" due to "the wide variety of institutional influences on our values and lifestyles" (1987, p. 106). "[T]here is," he adds, "no well-developed sociology of consumption" (p. 106).

14   Despite such difficulties, this article assumes for the sake of argument that manipulative advertising really works. Thus, I assume that such advertising strongly influences individual purchase decisions, and that it plays a major role in producing consumerist attitudes among the populace. In neither case, however, do I wish to specify all the links in the causal chain through which manipulative advertising does its work. In particular, I make no assumptions about the personal traits that render consumers responsive to manipulative advertising. Later in the article, for example, I consider the possibility that manipulative advertising succeeds because consumers want and need it.

15   Operating under the assumptions just stated, I now consider four possible ethical attacks on manipulative advertising. These are the claims that such advertising: (1) has negative consequences for utility, (2) undermines personal autonomy, (3) violates Kant's categorical imperative, and (4) weakens the personal virtue of its practitioners and its victims. I also consider one qualified defense of manipulative advertising: that even though no moral person would choose it were he writing on a clean slate, by now its elimination would be worse than its continuance.[3]

16   For each attack on manipulative advertising, I assume the validity of the relevant moral value or ethical theory, thus precluding defenses of manipulative advertising which attack the value or theory itself. A defender of manipulative advertising, for example, might argue that its inability to satisfy the categorical imperative does not matter because Kant was a fool and his moral philosophy is nonsense; but I do not consider such claims. This agnosticism about the validity of my four values or theories creates difficulties, for it is unlikely that all four could be fully valid simultaneously. To meet this difficulty while preserving as much scope as possible for each value or theory, I treat them as *prima facie* valid; and I assume that their claims must somehow be balanced against one another when conflicts arise.

Utilitarianism

17 As just stated, this article assumes that advertising can manipulate people in two distinct ways: (1) by socializing them to embrace consumerist values, and (2) by dictating individual purchase decisions. One important utilitarian criticism of manipulative advertising seems mainly to involve the first of these effects. Another implicates the second effect. A third criticism probably involves both.[4] I now discuss each of these utilitarian attacks in turn. Throughout, I explicitly or implicitly compare my assumed world in which manipulative advertising exists and is effective with a world in which all advertising is merely informative.

The Implications of the Dependence Effect

18 *The Affluent Society* marked Galbraith's arrival as a critic of consumer society and its works. For his critique to be persuasive, he had to counter the argument that America's enormous production of consumer goods is justified because people want, enjoy, and demand them. This required that he undermine at least two widespread beliefs: (1) that consumer desires are genuinely autonomous, and (2) that they produce significant satisfactions. As we saw earlier, he attacked the first assumption by maintaining that consumer wants are created by the productive process through which they are satisfied, with advertising serving as the main generator of those wants. This argument would have enabled Galbraith to contend that advertising is bad because it denies autonomy, but he seemed not to emphasize that point. Instead, he maintained that the satisfaction of advertising-induced desires generates little additional utility. His argument was that if advertising is needed to arouse consumer wants, they cannot be too strong. "The fact that wants can be synthesized by advertising, catalyzed by salesmanship, and shaped by the discreet manipulations of the persuaders shows that they are not very urgent. A man who is hungry need never be told of his need for food" (1958, p. 158).

19 As a result, Galbraith continued, one cannot assume that the increased production characterizing the modern affluent society generates corresponding increases in utility. Instead, as he summarizes the matter:

> [O]ur concern for goods ... does not arise in spontaneous consumer need. Rather, the dependence effect means that it grows out of the process of production itself. If production is to increase, the wants must be effectively contrived. In the absence of the contrivance the increase would not occur. This is not true of all goods, but that it is true of a substantial part is sufficient. It means that since the demand for this part would not exist, were it not contrived, its utility or urgency, ex contrivance, is zero. If we regard this production as marginal, we may say that the marginal utility of present aggregate output, ex advertising and salesmanship, is zero. (p. 160)

Because wants must be contrived for production to increase, on Galbraith's assumptions production would be lower were advertising completely informative. Since on those assumptions that contrived production generates little additional utility, however, the loss would not be much felt. Indeed, with resources shifted away from advertising and consumption and toward activities that improve the quality of our lives, overall utility might well grow in manipulative advertising's absence.

20 Galbraith's basic argument was that because consumer wants are contrived, they are not urgent; and that because they are not ur-

gent, their satisfaction does not generate much utility. One way to attack his argument is to maintain that consumer desires really do arise from within the individual, but my two assumptions foreclose that possibility here. Another is to follow the lead established by Friedrich Hayek's 1961 critique of Galbraith's dependence effect. To Hayek, Galbraith's argument involves a massive *non sequitur*: the attempt to reason from a desire's origin outside the individual to its unimportance (1961, pp. 346-47). If that assertion were valid, he thought, it would follow that "the whole cultural achievement of man is not important" (p. 346).

> Surely an individual's want for literature is not original with himself in the sense that he would experience it if literature were not produced. Does this mean that the production of literature cannot be defended as satisfying a want because it is only the production which provokes the demand? In this, as in the case of all cultural needs, it is unquestionably, in Professor Galbraith's words, "the process of satisfying the wants that creates the wants." (p. 347)

Presumably, the same general point applies to utility-maximization. Just because product desire A originated within Cal Consumer while product desire B came his way through manipulative advertising, it does not follow that satisfying desire A would give him more utility than satisfying desire B. Indeed, as we will see presently, the opposite may be true.

The Frustration of Rational Interbrand Choices

21 The second major utilitarian objection to manipulative advertising concerns its power to distort consumer choices among brands and products. As R.M. Hare once observed:

> [T]he market economy is only defensible if it really does ... lead to the maximum satisfaction of the preferences of the public. And it will not do this if it is distorted by various well-known undesirable practices.... By bringing it about that people decide on their purchases ... after being deceived or in other ways manipulated, fraudulent advertisers impair the wisdom of the choices that the public makes and so distort the market in such a way that it does not function to maximize preference-satisfactions. (Hare, 1984, pp. 27-28)

For example, now suppose that Cal Consumer's preferences would find their optimum satisfaction in Product A. Intoxicated by Product B's manipulative advertising, Cal instead buys that product, which satisfies his original preferences less well than Product A. If Cal would have bought Product A in a regime where advertising is purely informative, presumably B's manipulative advertising cost him some utility.

22 The previous argument, however, might fail if manipulative advertising gives consumers satisfactions that they would not otherwise obtain from their purchases. In that event, the utility lost when manipulative advertising causes consumers to choose the wrong product for their needs must be weighed against the utility consumers gain from such advertising. Due to the inherent uncertainty of utility calculations, it may be unclear which effect would predominate. Sometimes, though, the gains could outweigh the losses: that is, manipulative advertising could generate more utility than purely informative advertising.

23 But how can "manipulated" desires and purchases generate more utility than their "rational" counterparts? One answer emerges from the dark masterpiece of the literature on manipulative advertising – Theodore Levitt's 1970 con-

tribution to the *Harvard Business Review.* Levitt's main thesis is that "embellishment and distortion are among advertising's legitimate and socially desirable purposes" (Levitt, 1970, p. 85).[5] His determinedly nonlinear argument for that conclusion may be regarded as proceeding through several steps. The first is his assertion that when seen without illusions, human life is a poor thing. Natural reality, Levitt insists, is "crudely fashioned"; "crude, drab, and generally oppressive"; and "drab, dull, [and] anguished" (pp. 86, 90). For this reason, people try to transcend it whenever they can. "Everybody everywhere wants to modify, transform, embellish, enrich, and reconstruct the world around him – to introduce into an otherwise harsh or bland existence some sort of purposeful and distorting alleviation" (p. 87). People do so mainly though artistic endeavor, but also through advertising. "[W]e use art, architecture, literature, and the rest, and advertising as well, to shield ourselves, in advance of experience, from the stark and plain reality in which we are fated to live" (p. 90). Thus, "[m]any of the so-called distortions of advertising, product design, and packaging may be viewed as a paradigm of the many responses that man makes to the conditions of survival in the environment" (p. 90).

24   From all this, it follows that consumers demand more than "pure operating functionality" from the products they buy (p. 89). As Charles Revson of Revlon, Inc. once said: "'In the factory we make cosmetics; in the store we sell hope'" (p. 85). Thus "[i]t is not cosmetic chemicals women want, but the seductive charm promised by the alluring symbols with which these chemicals have been surrounded – hence the rich and exotic packages in which they are sold, and the suggestive advertising with which they are promoted" (p. 85). In other words, con-

sumers demand an expanded notion of functionality which includes "'non-mechanical' utilities," and do so to "help ... solve a problem of life" (p. 89). Therefore, "the product" they buy includes not only narrowly functional attributes, but also the emotional or affective content produced by its packaging and advertising. "The promises and images which imaginative ads and sculptured packages induce in us are as much the product as the physical materials themselves.... [T]hese ads and packagings describe the product's fullness for us; in our minds, the product becomes a complex abstraction which is ... the conception of a perfection which has not yet been experienced" (pp. 89-90).

25   For all these reasons, advertisements are not *supposed* to be literal representations of the products they tout (p. 90). "[D]eep down inside," moreover, "the consumer understands this perfectly well" (p.90). Indeed, Levitt maintains, consumers give industry a "fiat ... to 'distort' its messages" (p. 89). Thus, while the consumer wants "'truth,'" "he also wants and needs the alleviating imagery and tantalizing promises of the advertiser and designer" (p. 92). As a result, ethical firms with "rational" advertising imperil their survival. "There is hardly a company that would not go down in ruin if it refused to provide fluff, because nobody will buy pure functionality" (p. 92).

26   To Levitt, therefore, we do not merely buy a physical product, but also a set of positive feelings connected with it by advertising. If his argument is sound, those feelings give us extra utility above and beyond the utility we get from the product's performance of its functions. This extra utility might well outweigh the utility we lose because manipulative advertising has made us buy a product that is suboptimum in purely functional terms and that we would not have bought were advertising only informative.

27   Is Levitt's argument sound? Although his description may not apply to all people, or even to most, it hardly seems ridiculous. People who object to Levitt's contention that human life is crude, drab, and dull should recall that he is speaking of a human life we infrequently experience – human life absent the embellishments all civilizations try to give it. If his contention is correct, the need to transcend our natural condition is an obvious motive for those embellishments. John Waide, however, insists that our need for embellishment can be satisfied without manipulative advertising – through, for example, ideals, fantasies, heroes, and dreams (Waide, 1987, p. 76). But why assume this? If the need for comforting illusions is strong and pervasive, why should embellishment not extend to the products people buy?

28   Bigger problems, however, arise from Levitt's assumption that consumers are aware of advertising's illusions.[6] If people know that advertising lies, how can they derive much psychic benefit – i.e., much utility – from its embellishments? Worse yet, products tend not to deliver on manipulative advertising's promises of sex, status, security, and the like. When this is so, how can such advertising deliver much utility to the consumers it controls (cf. Waide, 1987, p. 75)? Indeed, the gap between manipulative advertising's implicit promises and its actual performance may lead to frustrated expectations and significant *disutility*.

29   Recall, however, that for Levitt consumers want and need to be manipulated because life without advertising's illusions is too much to bear. If so, it is unlikely that everyone would be *continuously* aware of advertising's illusions and the low chance of their realization. Only intermittently, in other words, would people assume a tough-minded, rational-actor mentality toward

advertising. On other occasions, some would effectively suspend disbelief in advertising's embellishments. Although they might retain latent knowledge of those illusions, that knowledge would not be constantly present to their consciousness. And when the illusions rule, they could generate real satisfactions.

30   Are these assumptions about consumers realistic ones? To me, they are plausible as applied to some people some of the time. If everyone were consistently able to approach manipulative advertising rationally, how often would it succeed? As Waide correctly maintains, moreover, manipulative advertising is easy to spot if people bother to look (1987, p. 74). But as Waide's observation implicitly suggests, people often do not bother. To think otherwise requires one to believe that people are without mood swings and contradictory impulses, and that they consistently prefer undiluted reality to pleasant illusions. Both of these assumptions, I submit, simply are ridiculous. For that reason, there also is nothing ridiculous in assuming that people gain utility by accepting advertising's illusions, while retaining some latent and/or intermittent knowledge of their condition.

Long-Run Harm

31 Even if manipulative advertising generates utility by associating products with pleasant feelings, and even if this additional utility outweighs the utility lost when consumers buy suboptimum products, manipulative advertising may still produce a negative utility balance in the end. The reason is the long-run harm that certain "manipulated" purchases may cause. As Alan Goldman asserted while discussing Galbraith's critique of advertising:

One weak criterion [of advertising] that can be adopted from a want-regarding or utilitarian moral theory relates to whether satisfaction of the desires in question increases overall satisfaction in the long run, whether it contributes to fulfilled or worthwhile lives. Desires are irrational when their satisfaction is incompatible with more fundamental or long-range preferences.... Alcoholism is an example of such irrational desire, the satisfaction of which is harmful overall. Desires for junk food, tobacco and certain kinds of conspicuous consumption are other examples, at least for certain consumers. Processes that create and feed such desires are not utility maximizing, since even the satisfaction of these desires lowers the subject's general level of utility in the long run. (Goldman, 1982, pp. 254-55)[7]

Here, Goldman appears to embrace a kind of virtue ethics ("fulfilled or worthwhile lives"), and seems to feel that a life of virtue and moderation will produce the greatest happiness in the long run. But while this may be true, the "happiness" in question probably cannot be equated with utility – or at least with utility in its Benthamite form. Judged solely in pleasure-pain terms, that is, Goldman's argument is questionable.

32   From such a standpoint, Goldman's biggest errors are his tendency to overrate the probability and the severity of manipulative advertising's long-run harms, and his complete failure to consider the pleasure generated by it and the products it touts. This is true even assuming (as I have assumed) that manipulative advertising actually can make people drink, smoke, eat junk food, and so forth. On the probability and severity questions, it is initially worth noting that most manipulative advertising tries to make people buy material things, not the harmful items that Goldman's analysis suggests. Even where alcohol, tobacco, and junk food are at issue, how many people actually suffer severe health or other consequences from such items, as compared with those who suffer lesser consequences or none at all? Even if harmful consequences eventually do occur, moreover, they must be balanced against the utility people accumulate during their years of smoking, drinking, and eating unwisely. In my experience, at least, these are pleasurable activities. Furthermore, if Levitt is correct, manipulative advertising could surround those activities with pleasing associations that generate still more utility.

33   To illustrate some of the previous points, suppose that Joe Camel, a young stockbroker, is induced to smoke, drink, and eat high-fat foods because a series of ads depict these activities as manly and sophisticated. In addition to the pleasure Joe derives from the activities, Joe also gets satisfaction from the advertising-induced perception that he is tougher and cooler than the (to him) growing tribe of health-conscious sissies. After years of dissipation finally take their toll, Joe dies in his sleep of a heart attack at age 55. In this admittedly loaded example, I cannot help but think that manipulative advertising had positive long-term consequences for utility. Nor would this conclusion necessarily change if Joe instead dies an excruciatingly painful death from lung or colon cancer. Even here, Joe's utility account would be positive if the pleasure accumulated during years of unhealthy living outscores the pain associated with the final reckoning. More importantly, Joe might still have faced a painful death even if all advertising were informative and he had lived a life of sanity and moderation. And while it is true that such a life would probably give Joe more time on earth, it is debatable whether those "Golden Years" are a high-utility experience.

Autonomy

34   All things considered, the utilitarian arguments against manipulative advertising are unimpressive. Indeed, utilitarianism might even support that practice. Galbraith claimed that little utility is generated when we satisfy contrived wants. But the connection between a desire's origin outside the individual and the low utility resulting from its satisfaction is unclear. At first glance, it appears that manipulative advertising robs consumers of utility by inducing them to buy functionally suboptimal products. But while this may be true, the resulting utility losses arguably are counterbalanced by the utility people gain from manipulative advertising. Finally, although manipulative advertising can induce behavior with harmful long-term consequences, those consequences do not always occur and, even when they do occur, do not invariably outweigh the pleasure accumulated during years of unhealthy living.

The Autonomy-Related Objection to Manipulative Advertising

35   To some people, however, the preceding points may say more about utilitarianism's deficiencies than about manipulative advertising's worth. One standard criticism of utilitarianism emphasizes its indifference to the moral quality of the means by which utility is maximized. Thus, even if manipulative advertising increases consumers' utility, it is bad because it does so by suppressing their ability to make intelligent, self-directed product choices on the basis of their own values and interests. In a word, manipulative advertising now seems objectionable because it denies personal *autonomy*.

36   Among the many strands within the notion of autonomy, one of the most common equates it with self-government or self-determination (see Christman, 1988, p. 110). According to Steven Lukes, for example, autonomy is "self-direction"; the autonomous person's "thought and action is his own, and [is] not determined by agencies or causes outside his control" (Lukes, 1973, p. 52). At the social level, Lukes adds, an individual is autonomous "to the degree to which he subjects the pressures and norms with which he is confronted to conscious and critical evaluation, and forms intentions and reaches practical decisions as the result of independent and rational reflection" (p. 52).

37   If manipulative advertising has the effects this article assumes, it apparently denies autonomy to the individuals it successfully controls. On this article's assumptions, people become consumers and make product choices precisely through "agencies and causes outside [their] control," and not through "conscious and critical evaluation" or "independent and rational reflection." To Lippke, moreover, advertising also has an "implicit content" that further suppresses autonomy. Among other things, this implicit content causes people to accept emotionalized, superficial, and oversimplified claims; desire ease and gratification rather than austerity and self-restraint; let advertisers dictate the meaning of the good life; defer to their peers; and think that consumer products are a means for acquiring life's nonmaterial goods (pp. 44-47). People so constituted are unlikely to be independent, self-governing agents who subject all social pressures to an internal critique. Nor is it likely that they would have much resistance to manipulative appeals to buy particular products.

Are Consumers Autonomous on Levitt's Assumptions?

38 On Levitt's assumptions, however, perhaps consumers do act autonomously when they submit to manipulative advertising. If Levitt is correct: (1) manipulative advertising works much as its critics say that it works; because (2) consumers suspend disbelief in its claims and embrace its illusions; because (3) they want, need, and demand those illusions to cope with human existence; while (4) nonetheless knowing on some level that those illusions indeed are illusions. In sum, one might say, advertising manipulates consumers because they knowingly and rationally want to be manipulated. That is, they half-consciously sacrifice their autonomy for reasons that make some sense on Levitt's assumptions about human life. In still other words, they more or less autonomously relinquish their autonomy. This might be thought inconsistent with autonomy itself, but on Levitt's bleak assumptions even a "self-directed" person who exercises "independent and rational reflection" (Lukes, 1973, p. 52) might well do the same. Unless autonomy is an inalienable right,[8] it seems difficult to object to such a decision if Levitt's factual argument is sound.

39 Levitt's argument, however, appears to concern only individual purchase decisions, and not advertising's assumed ability to socialize people to accept consumerism and reject autonomy. But his argument is broad enough to explain this second process. On Levitt's assumptions, people would more or less knowingly embrace consumerism because unfiltered reality is too much to bear, and would reject autonomy in favor of Lippke's "implicit content" because autonomy offers too little payoff at too much cost. If those assumptions are accurate, moreover, people arguably have sound reasons for behaving in these ways.

Arrington's Attempt to Reconcile Manipulation and Autonomy

40 In the previous section, I argued that Levitt's assumptions at least are plausible. Demonstrating their truth, however, obviously would be a difficult endeavor. For this reason, at least, they are not a decisive objection to the claim that manipulative advertising undermines autonomy. Another way to attack that claim, however, is to adopt a conception of autonomy that is consistent with advertising's manipulations. Robert Arrington attempts just such a reconciliation.

41 Arrington begins his attempt by asking whether advertising creates desires which are not the consumer's own. His answer is: "Not necessarily, and indeed not often" (p. 7). In reaching this conclusion, Arrington does not deny that advertising frequently manipulates consumers. Instead, he maintains that this manipulation is consistent with autonomous choice. "[T]here is something wrong," Arrington asserts, "in setting up the issue over advertising and behavior control as a question whether our desires are truly ours *or* are created in us by advertisements. Induced and autonomous desires do not separate into two mutually exclusive classes" (p. 7).

42 How can manipulation and autonomy coexist? As I just suggested, the key to their reconciliation is a particular conception of autonomy. Although Arrington does not explicitly define the term "autonomy,"[9] he does provide a practical test for distinguishing autonomous and non-autonomous desires. He does so by utilizing a distinction between first-order and second-order desires that apparently originated with Harry Frankfurt (1989).

To obtain a better understanding of autonomous and nonautonomous desires, let us consider some cases of a desire which a person does not *acknowledge* to be his own even though he *feels* it. The kleptomaniac has a desire to steal which in many instances he repudiates.... And if I were suddenly overtaken by a desire to attend an REO concert, I would immediately disown this desire.... These are examples of desires which one might have but with which one would not identify. They are experienced as foreign to one's character or personality. Often a person will have ... a second-order desire ... *not* to have another desire. In such cases, the first-order desire [the other desire] is thought of as being nonautonomous, imposed on one. When on the contrary a person has a second-order desire to maintain and fulfill a first-order desire, then the first-order desire is truly his own, autonomous, original to him. So there is in fact a distinction between desires which are the agent's own and those which are not, but this is not the same as the distinction between desires which are innate to the agent and those which are externally induced. (p. 7)

Arrington then asserts that because people generally do not disown or repudiate the products they purchase, those purchase decisions usually are autonomous. "[M]ost of the desires induced by advertising I fully accept, and hence most of these desires are autonomous. The most vivid demonstration of this is that I often return to purchase the same product over and over again, without regret or remorse" (p.7). In fact, Arrington concludes, even purchase decisions induced by subliminally implanted advertising could be autonomous if the consumer's implanted subconscious desires are consistent with her conscious ones (p. 7).

43   For Arrington, then, the autonomy of one's desires and one's subsequent actions is determined by after-the-fact, second-order reflection on their congruence with one's nature, and not by their genesis inside the individual. Because it allows for external manipulation, autonomy so conceived may be inconsistent with the notions of self-direction, self-governance, and self-rule described earlier. The problem, however, may rest more with these notions than with Arrington's conception of autonomy. In other words, because so much of our behavior seems to result from external influences, we may need a conception of autonomy, like Arrington's, which reflects that fact. Indeed, such a conception has been the "received model" of autonomy in recent years (Christman, 1991, p. 4). In Gerald Dworkin's statement of this model, "[i]t is only when a person identifies with the influences that motivate him, assimilates them to himself, views himself as the kind of person who wishes to be moved in particular ways, that these influences are to be identified as 'his'" (Dworkin, 1989, p. 60; see also Frankfurt, pp. 69-72). But, Dworkin continues, if "a person resents being motivated in certain ways, is alienated from these influences, would prefer to be the kind of person who is motivated in different ways, then these influences, which may be causally effective, are not viewed by him as 'his'" (Dworkin, 1989, p. 60).

44   Lippke attempts to dismiss Arrington's argument by claiming that while it may hold for particular choices consumers make (my second assumption about advertising's powers) Arrington has nothing to say about advertising's general tendency to promote a consumer consciousness (my first assumption). "If advertising induces uncritical acceptance of the consumer lifestyle as a whole, then Arrington's vindication of it with respect to the formation of particular desires or the making of particular choices *within* that lifestyle is hardly comforting" (1990, p. 39). But Arrington's conception of autonomy prob-

ably is broad enough to include the adoption of a consumer lifestyle as well as specific product decisions. Just as a person can engage in second-order reflection on her product choices, she also could ask herself whether she identifies with her consumer lifestyle.

45   But if people have been thoroughly socialized to accept consumerism, can second-order reflection on that fact be genuinely autonomous? Even if such people could step back and ask "Is this consumer-person really me?", would not the answer invariably be "Yes"? The same argument probably applies to individual purchase decisions. If I bought product X because its advertising successfully associated the product with my strong desires for power, status, and sexual conquest, how likely am I to reject it upon second-order reflection?

46   To deal with such problems, Dworkin has a second criterion for autonomy – one that Arrington's article apparently does not mention. This is the *procedural independence* of the second-order identification process. Procedural independence means that the identification "is not itself influenced in ways which make ... [it] in some way alien to the individual" – for example, by being "influenced by others in such a fashion that we do not view it as being his own" (Dworkin, 1989, p. 61). For a person's individual purchases and her acceptance of consumerism to be autonomous, therefore, her second-order reflection on each must be uninfluenced in the sense just described. But can this be the case if advertising is as strong a force as its critics claim? On that assumption, how can our consumer be sure that her second-order reflection is sufficiently free from advertising's influence? To be certain, she may have to make a third-level identification with her second-level judgment. But for the reasons just stated, one also can doubt the genuineness of the third-level identification, which means that a fourth level of reflection is necessary. Because the same doubt can be raised about the fourth level, however, we seem to be forced into an infinite regress (e.g., Christman, 1991, pp. 7-8; Thalberg, 1989, p. 130).

47   To summarize, Arrington's claim that most advertising-induced purchases are autonomous apparently can be valid only if: (1) his conception of autonomy is sound, and (2) people actually exhibit procedural independence when they identify with their purchase decisions. Both of these assumptions are questionable. It is difficult not to suspect a conception of autonomy so capacious as to include purchases induced by subliminal advertising. On almost any notion of the self, such purchases are not self-determined at the time they occur; the most that can be said for them is that they meet the approval of some later self. Perhaps for this reason, the "received model" of autonomy has not gone unchallenged. For example, one recent competing account of the concept focuses on the conditions under which desires are formed and actions take place, rather than the actor's after-the-fact identification with a desire or an action (e.g., Christman, 1991, pp. 10-18).

48   As for the second assumption required by Arrington's account, it seems difficult to determine whether a person's subsequent approval of his consumerist orientation or his individual purchases was genuine, or was wholly or partially produced by the advertising that by hypothesis caused each. The question is the procedural independence of the identification process, and determining this may require an infinite series of identifications with one's previous identification.

The Categorical Imperative

49 One problem with some of the claims discussed thus far is that they present difficult empirical issues. This is plainly true of Levitt's claims. It also is true of Galbraith's assertion that because advertising-induced wants originate outside the individual, they have low urgency and therefore generate little utility when they are satisfied. The same can be said of Hayek's response to Galbraith. Given these problems, maybe manipulative advertising is best addressed by ethical theories whose conclusions do not depend on empirical matters like consumer psychology, or on manipulation's consequences for utility. Kant's categorical imperative is an obvious candidate.

50 R.M. Hare made two Kantian arguments against manipulative advertising. "Kantians will say ... that to manipulate people is not to treat them as ends – certainly not as autonomous legislating members of a kingdom of ends.... But even apart from that it is something that we prefer not to happen to us and therefore shall not will it as a universal maxim" (Hare, 1984, p. 28; see also Beauchamp, 1984, p. 17). His reference, of course, was to the two major formulations of Kant's categorical imperative. The first, which comes in several versions, underlies Hare's second argument. The version employed here goes as follows: "Act only on that maxim through which you can at the same time will that it should become a universal law" (Kant, 1964, p. 88). According to the second major formulation of the imperative, one must "[a]ct in such a way that you always treat humanity, whether in your own person or in the person of any other, never simply as a means, but always at the same time as an end" (p. 96).

51 Under either formulation of the imperative, it seems, manipulative advertising stands condemned. Under the first formulation, it seems difficult to identify a maxim that would: (1) clearly justify manipulative advertising, and (2) be universalized by any advertiser. Consider, for example, the following possibility: "In order to induce purchases and make money, business people can use advertising tactics that undermine the rational evaluation and choice of products by associating them with desired states to which they have little or no real relation." Presumably, no one would will the maxim's universalization, because to do so is to waive any moral objection to manipulative advertising aimed at oneself. Manipulative advertising apparently fares even worse under the second statement of the categorical imperative. As James Rachels has noted, under this formulation "we may never *manipulate* people, or *use* people, to achieve our purposes" (Rachels, 1993, p. 129). Instead, we should respect their rational nature by giving them the information that will enable them to make informed, autonomous decisions (Rachels, 1993, pp. 129-30; see also MacIntyre, 1984, p. 44). As the term "manipulative advertising" suggests, businesses that employ it to generate sales obviously try to use people as means to their own ends, and do so precisely by undermining their rationality and their ability to make informed, autonomous decisions.

52 Even in the Kantian realm, however, empirical concerns intrude. Suppose again that Levitt is right in claiming that people want and need manipulative advertising. Given this assumption, the relevant maxim becomes something like the following: "In order to induce purchases and make money, people can use manipulative advertising tactics that undermine the rational evaluation and choice of products and services, but only when such advertising tactics liberate consumers from their dark, stark,

and depressing natural existence." Although I cannot speak for everyone (or for Kant), I might will this maxim's universalization if I found Levitt's conception of the human condition at all plausible. This illustrates a common criticism of the first formulation of the categorical imperative: that one can manipulate the imperative to get the results one wishes by framing the maxim appropriately (cf. MacIntyre, 1966, pp. 197-98).

53   Even if Levitt's account is perfectly accurate, however, the second major statement of the imperative still creates problems for manipulative advertising. Here, the question seems to boil down to the following: are firms that employ manipulative advertising using a consumer merely as a means to their own ends and therefore violating the imperative if the consumer, in effect, needs and wants to be manipulated? If, as I suggested earlier, the suspension of disbelief required for one to accept manipulative advertising may be more or less reasonable, then advertisers conceivably *are* respecting consumers' rationality by providing them with product-related illusions. Kant, however, thought that "[r]ational nature exists as an end in itself" (1964, p. 96). For this reason, he probably would not have acceded to any diminution of human rationality, even one arguably justified on rational grounds. This is suggested by his conclusion that committing suicide to avoid a painful situation – an arguably rational termination of rational nature – violates the second major formulation of the imperative (pp. 96-97).

54   In this article, however, I am assuming that each of my four ethical perspectives is *prima facie* valid, and that their claims should somehow be balanced against each other when conflicts occur. On this assumption, other moral duties may sometimes compete with those established by the categorical imperative, and the conflicting

obligations must be reconciled in some fashion. Thus, if Levitt's view of our condition is correct, if we have a *prima facie* duty to maximize utility, and if manipulative advertising in fact makes human life more bearable, *perhaps* that duty might outweigh the duty to respect the rational element of human nature. If so, we have yet another ethical escape hatch through which manipulative advertising might slip.

Virtue Ethics

55   Earlier I depicted Galbraith as a utilitarian, but other moral aspirations probably were at work within *The Affluent Society*. The book opened with the following quotation from Alfred Marshall: "The economist, like everyone else, must concern himself with the ultimate aims of man." Galbraith's conviction that consumerism does not rank high among those aims pervades much of his writing, and almost certainly informed his critique of advertising. However, the ethical values and theories previously considered in this article do not state and enjoin the desirable substantive conditions of human life. It seems foreign to the notion of autonomy to dictate the choices the autonomous person should make.[10] As Waide (1987, p. 77) accurately notes, for example, Arrington offers "no standard to which we can appeal to judge whether a desire enhances a life." Although utilitarianism obviously has a substantive criterion for actions, utility can be acquired in innumerable ways, some of them ethically questionable. Waide suggests as much when he correctly remarks of Levitt that he "appears to assume that in a satisfying life one has many satisfied desires – *which* desires is not important" (p. 77). As for Kant's categorical imperative, we have already seen that its first major formulation is notoriously manipulable. And

while the second major formulation has some content, all it commands is that we treat other people as rational agents when we propose a course of action to them.

56   Waide's alternative to such approaches is to examine "the virtues and vices at stake" in manipulative advertising (1987, p. 73), and to see "what kinds of lives are sustained" by it (p. 77). Stanley Benn sounds the same note when he suggests that the key question about advertising is whether it promotes "a valuable kind of life," with this determination depending on "some objective assessment of what constitutes excellence in human beings" (1967, p. 273). Because manipulative advertising encourages advertisers to ignore the well-being of their targets and encourages those targets to neglect the cultivation of nonmarket goods, Waide concludes that it makes us less virtuous persons and therefore is morally objectionable (1987, pp. 74-75). Many other critics of advertising make the same general point. The Heilbroner quotation that opened this article is an example. On another occasion Heilbroner called advertising "perhaps the single most value-destroying activity of a business civilization," due to the "subversive influence of the relentless effort to persuade people to change their lifeways, not out of any knowledge of, or deeply held convictions about the 'good life,' but merely to sell whatever article or service is being pandered" (1976, pp. 113-14). His main specific complaint is that by offering a constant stream of half-truths and deceptions, advertising makes "cynics of us all" (p. 114). Virginia Held makes a related point when she criticizes advertising for undermining intellectual and artistic integrity (1984, pp. 64-66).

57   To Christopher Lasch, on the other hand, advertising's greatest evil may be its tendency to leave consumers "perpetually unsatisfied, restless, anxious, and bored" (1978, p. 72). In a passage which echoes Levitt, he adds that advertising:

> [U]pholds consumption as the answer to the age-old discontents of loneliness, sickness, weariness, lack of sexual satisfaction.... It plays seductively on the malaise of industrial civilization. Is your job boring and meaningless? Does it leave you with feelings of futility and fatigue? Is your life empty? Consumption promises to fill the aching void; hence the attempt to surround commodities with an aura of romance, with allusions to exotic places and vivid experiences; and with images of female breasts from which all blessings flow. (pp. 72-73)

From Levitt's basically utilitarian perspective, this condition is defensible because the alternative-our everyday natural existence – is even less satisfying, and there is no other criterion by which to judge the worth of social practices. But one suspects that Lasch might reject advertising's consequences as inherently bad even if they did mark an increase in utility. The same probably holds for most of advertising's cultural critics. As a group, Michael Schudson remarks, they see "the emergence of a consumer culture as a devolution of manners, morals and even manhood, from a work-oriented production ethic of the past to the consumption, 'lifestyle'-obsessed, ethic-less pursuits of the present" (1984, pp. 6-7).

58   Uniting all these varied criticisms of advertising is the notion that it promotes substantive behaviors, experiences, and states of character which are inherently undesirable, and that it is morally objectionable for this reason. Ordinarily, however, those denunciations are not accompanied by any systematic development of the virtues advertising undermines, let alone any effort to justify those virtues. For the philosophers among advertising's critics, the most likely

explanation for these omissions is the difficulty of stating and justifying a convincing account of the virtues – especially today. (Heilbroner's putting "the good life" in quotations while attacking advertising on just that presupposition is suggestive here.) In this section's introduction, however, I waived this difficulty when I assumed that each ethical basis for attacking manipulative advertising is *prima facie* valid.

59   This still leaves open the question whether any existing scheme of virtue ethics would condemn manipulative advertising, but I hope I can dismiss this problem without much discussion. This article assumes that manipulative advertising both creates a consumer culture and strongly influences individual purchase decisions. Its main means for accomplishing the second aim (and perhaps the first) is to associate the product with such nonmarket goods as sex, status, and power. On those assumptions, manipulative advertising almost certainly undermines such standard virtues as honesty and benevolence in its practitioners, and arguably dilutes its targets' moderation, reasonableness, self-control, self-discipline, and self-reliance (Rachels, 1993, p. 163 (listing these virtues)). Only with difficulty can one imagine Aristotle's proud man succumbing to such advertising or using it to escape reality.

Manipulative Advertising's Last Defense

60 All things considered, virtue ethics appears to be the best basis for attacking manipulative advertising. In particular, it seems to dispose of a defense that has plagued our other three attacks on such advertising: Levitt's claim that people want and need advertising's illusions and therefore more or less knowingly and willingly embrace it. Like our

other bases for attacking manipulative advertising, however, virtue ethics is not assumed to be an absolute. This might mean that the claims of virtue would have to give way if human beings simply could not endure without advertising's illusions or if its psychic satisfactions give people enormous amounts of utility.

61   In any event, there is yet another possible defense of manipulative advertising. This defense is mainly utilitarian, but it also implicates my other three ethical criteria to some degree. It arises because by hypothesis all my criteria must be weighed against competing moral claims. The defense does not so much challenge the assertion that manipulative advertising is bad, as argue that it is the lesser of two evils.

62   Throughout this article, I have assumed for the sake of argument that manipulative advertising's critics are correct in their assessment of its effects. As we have seen, these people usually maintain that manipulative advertising plays an important role in socializing people to consume. This means that on the critics' view of things, manipulative advertising is central to the functioning of modern consumer society. But if manipulative advertising is central to the system's operation, how safely can it be condemned? Assuming that the condemnation is effective, manipulative advertising disappears, and all advertising becomes informative, people gradually would be weaned from their consumerist ways. This is likely to create social instability, with a more authoritarian form of government the likely end result. That, in turn, could well mean an environment in which aggregate utility is lower than it is today, human autonomy and rational nature are less respected, and/or the virtues less recognized.

63   One set of reasons for these conclusions is largely economic. If people become less con-

sumerist as manipulative advertising leaves the scene, aggregate demand and economic output should decline. At first glance, this would seem to be of little consequence because by hypothesis people would value material things less. The problem is that the economic losses probably will be unevenly distributed: for example, some businesses will fail and some will not, and some people will lose their jobs while others stay employed. These inequalities are a potential source of social instability. Both to redress them and to preserve order, government is likely to intervene. This may involve a significant increase in outright governmental coercion.

64   One obvious objection to the previous scenario is the claim that once people are liberated from manipulative advertising, they will become less egoistic, more cooperative, and more self-sacrificing. As a result, the necessary economic readjustments could be accomplished with very little coercion. But while this conceivably may be true, there is no reason to believe that these traits dominate human nature, and this article has made no such assumption. Earlier, I assumed for purposes of argument that manipulative advertising actually works, but nowhere did I say that people would be predominantly cooperative and caring in its absence. In fact, it is questionable whether manipulative advertising would be effective if these traits are strongly implanted in human nature. To reverse Galbraith's earlier argument, if people are naturally disposed toward his version of the good life, why does manipulative advertising work so well? Indeed, manipulative advertising's success may be most compatible with the assumption that people are highly malleable because they lack strongly-rooted traits. On this assumption, manipulative advertising's departure creates a void that probably will be filled with *something*,

maybe different somethings for different people. Some may settle down to a "sane" lifestyle that respects nature and tolerates diversity while fulfilling our "real needs." Others, however, may develop strong ethnic, racial, or religious loyalties. Some of these loyalties may be antagonistic to others. The likely result is either a degree of social disintegration, or its prevention through a more authoritarian government.

65   To my knowledge, Waide is the only business ethicist to raise these kinds of problems, and he finds himself without a solution to them. Because "[i]t seems unlikely that [manipulative] advertising will end suddenly," however, Waide is "confident that we will have the time and the imagination to adapt our economy to do without it" (1987, p. 77). Although I suspect that Waide is too optimistic, I have no solution to the dilemma either. Thus, I am left with the unsatisfactory conclusion that while various moral arguments may provide sound bases for attacking manipulative advertising, prudential considerations dictate that none of them be pressed too vigorously. Manipulative advertising's ultimate justification, in other words, may be its status as a necessary evil.

Concluding Remarks

66   For all the preceding reasons, it seems that there is no completely definitive basis for condemning manipulative advertising. But this obviously is not to say that the practice is morally unproblematic. Of my four suggested attacks on the practice, virtue ethics seems the strongest, with Kantianism a close second, autonomy third, and utilitarianism last. Indeed, utilitarianism may even support manipulative advertising. The main reason is that the practice's three most important defenses – Levitt's argument, the as-

sertion that there is little connection between a want's origin outside the individual and the benefit resulting from its satisfaction, and manipulative advertising's centrality to our economic system – are more or less utilitarian in nature.

67 Except perhaps for hard-core utilitarians, therefore, manipulative advertising is a morally dubious practice. However, this conclusion may depend heavily on a critical assumption made earlier: that manipulative advertising actually works. Specifically, I assumed that such advertising: (1) socializes people to adopt a consumerist lifestyle, and (2) strongly influences individual purchase decisions. But what happens if, by and large, each assumption is untrue?

68 On first impressions, at least, it appears that if manipulative advertising is inefficacious, utilitarianism, autonomy, and virtue ethics largely cease to be bases for criticizing it. (On the other hand, manipulative advertising's "last defense" also bites the dust on this assumption. How can manipulative advertising's elimination threaten economic stability if such advertising does not stimulate consumption in the first place?) Manipulative advertising's ineffectiveness, for example, dooms Galbraith's argument that little utility results from the satisfaction of contrived wants, because now the relevant wants are not contrived. If manipulative advertising does not control individual purchase decisions, moreover, it cannot be blamed for the utility consumers lose when they choose the wrong product for their needs. On the other hand, because Levitt's arguments also seem to fail if manipulative advertising is inefficacious, it probably could not *generate* utility either. In addition, the dollars expended on the practice presumably would produce more utility if deployed elsewhere.

69 If manipulative advertising neither determines people's values nor directs their purchases, it is also hard to see how the practice denies their autonomy. On the same assumption, it likewise seems improbable that manipulative advertising significantly undermines virtues such as moderation, reasonableness, self-control, self-discipline, and self-reliance in its targets. However, because advertisers still would be trying to manipulate consumers, their honesty and benevolence would continue to be compromised by such behavior. This is especially true since by hypothesis they now would be peddling an ineffective marketing technique to the businesses they profess to serve.

70 However, Kantian objections to manipulative advertising might well remain even if it is inefficacious. On that assumption, admittedly, perhaps one would will the universalization of a maxim permitting such advertising. If manipulative advertising simply fails to work, moreover, maybe it does not treat consumers merely as means to advertiser's ends. But such arguments ignore the strong anticonsequentialism of Kant's ethics, which arguably renders advertising's ineffectiveness irrelevant. More importantly, those arguments ignore Kant's stress on the motives with which people should act. The only thing that is unqualifiedly good, Kant says, is a good will; and the good will is good not because of what it accomplishes, but simply because it wills the good (Kant, 1964, pp. 61-62). Even if manipulative advertising is unsuccessful, advertisers presumably try to make it work. Unless they believe that their efforts would benefit consumers in the end, it is unlikely that they are acting with a good will when they devise and employ their stratagems.

71 At a first cut, therefore, it seems that if manipulative advertising is ineffective, the only significant ethical objections to it are Kantian. (To these we might add the money wasted on the

practice, as well as its effect on the virtue of its practitioners.) For those inclined to ignore Kantian objections, therefore, it seems that manipulative advertising's rightness or wrongness depends less on ethical theory than on empirical questions within the purview of the social sciences. To people who regard ethical theory as hopelessly soft and subjective, and who think that the social sciences are producing genuine knowledge, this might mean that a definite evaluation of manipulative advertising is within reach.

72   This line of argument, however, ignores the intractability of the factual issues relevant to any ethical evaluation of manipulative advertising. As the preceding discussion suggests, the most important such question is the extent to which manipulative advertising actually affects purchase decisions and socializes people to consume. Even if manipulative advertising actually has those effects, other more or less empirical issues would remain. These include the validity of Levitt's arguments, Galbraith's asserted connection between a desire's origin outside the individual and the low utility resulting from its satisfaction, and manipulative advertising's contribution to gross domestic product. All these questions, I submit, are unlikely to be answered any time soon. Readers who think otherwise are invited to suggest research programs for resolving them. Viewed against that task, ethical theory's interminable debates seem less hopeless. But while this conclusion may give business ethicists some comfort, it further clouds the inconclusive ethical case against manipulative advertising.

NOTES

1. In addition to associative advertising, other manipulative techniques mentioned by business ethicists include subliminal suggestion (in which the implanted message is not consciously perceptible at the time of its implantation) and simple repetition (which tries to establish the product in consumers' minds) (Arrington, 1982, pp. 4-5; Crisp, 1987, p. 413). However, although I say so with my fingers crossed, there is little to suggest that the former is, or has been, much used.

2. In fact, some (e.g., Lippke, 1990, p. 38) reject it.

3. However, I do not consider the "everyone's doing it" defense. On this subject, see Ronald M. Green, "When Is 'Everyone's Doing It' a Moral Justification?" *Business Ethics Quarterly* 1(1): 75-93.

4. Another possible utilitarian argument involves the voluminous scholarly literature on the economic impact of advertising. To oversimplify considerably, one school of thought on this subject regards advertising as primarily manipulative, and sees it as a means by which oligopolists preserve their market position (through, for example, advertising-created brand identification). The result is decreased competition, somewhat lower output, and somewhat higher prices than otherwise would be the case. This means that consumers get somewhat less value per dollar and somewhat less utility. A newer, more laissez-faire, school of thought contends that advertising increases competition by (among other things) providing more information. This probably means that it increases utility by giving consumers a maximum return on their dollars. The many studies on the issues created by this debate apparently are inconclusive. See Mark S. Albion & Paul W. Faris, *The Advertising Controversy: Evidence on the Economic Effects of Advertising* (Boston, MA, Auburn House, 1981); Robert B. Ekelund, Jr. & David S. Saurman, *Advertising and the Market Process: A Modern Economic View* (San Francisco, CA, Pacific Institute for Public Policy, 1988); Julian L. Simon, *Issues in the Economics of Advertising* (Urbana, IL, U. of Illinois P., 1970).

5. However, Levitt did condemn "falsification with larcenous intent" (1970, p. 85) – that is, the *deceptive* advertising described earlier.

6. Some poll data support this assumption. According to Michael Schudson (1986, p. 10), a 1976 survey found that 46% of the public regard all or most television advertising as "seriously misleading," while 83% regard at least "some" television advertising as seriously misleading. Also, those polled in a 1981 *Newsweek* survey rated advertising executives lowest in honesty and ethical standards among several listed professions (including members of Congress).

7. Goldman also raised the possibility that advertising creates desires that will never be satisfied, thus generating even more long-run disutility. In the interest of brevity, I will not consider that argument here.

8. Much recent literature on inalienable rights argues that few, if any, rights are inalienable. See, e.g., J. Nelson, "Are There Inalienable Rights?" *Philosophy* 64: 519-24 (1989); L. Stell, "Dueling and the Right to Life," *Ethics* 90(1): 7-26 (1979); D. Van De Veer, "Are Human Rights Inalienable?" *Philosophical Studies* 37(2): 165-76 (1980).

9. Instead, Arrington said that autonomy is a "complex, multifaceted concept" which must be approached "through the more determinate notions of (a) autonomous desire, (b) rational desire and choice, (c) free choice, and (d) control or manipulation" (Arrington, 1982, p. 6). Here I only consider Arrington's discussion of autonomous desire.

10. However, Benn (1967, p. 274) suggests that within the liberal tradition, the ability to make responsible choices among competing ways of life *is* a human excellence.

REFERENCES

Arrington, R.: 1982, "Advertising and Behavior Control," *Journal of Business Ethics*, 1(1): 3-12.

Beauchamp, T.: 1984, "Manipulative Advertising," *Business and Professional Ethics Journal*, 3(3 & 4): 1-22.

Benn, S.: 1967, "Freedom and Persuasion," *The Australasian Journal of Philosophy*, 45: 259-75.

Christman, J.: 1988, "Constructing the Inner Citadel: Recent Work on the Concept of Autonomy," *Ethics*, 99(1): 109-24.

Christman, J.. 1991, "Autonomy and Personal History," *Canadian Journal of Philosophy*, 21(1): 1-24.

Colloquy: 1982, "Advertising and the Corrupting of America," *Business and Society Review*, 1(41): 64-69.

Crisp, R.: 1987, "Persuasive Advertising, Autonomy, and the Creation of Desire," *Journal of Business Ethics*, 6: 413-18.

Dworkin, G.: 1989, "The Concept of Autonomy," in Christman, J. (ed.), *The Inner Citadel: Essays on Individual Autonomy* (New York: Oxford U.P.), pp. 54-62.

Frankfurt, H.: 1989, "Freedom of the Will and the Concept of a Person," in J. Christman, (ed.), *The Inner Citadel: Essays on Individual Autonomy* (New York: Oxford U.P.), pp. 63-76.

Frankena, W.: 1973, *Ethics* (Englewood Cliffs: Prentice-Hall, 2nd ed.).

Galbraith, J.K.: 1958, *The Affluent Society* (Boston: Houghton Mifflin).

Genge, W.: 1985, "Ads Stimulate the Economy," *Business and Society Review*, 1(55): 58-59.

Goldman, A.: 1982, *The Moral Foundations of Professional Ethics* (Totowa: Rowman & Littlefield).

Hare, R.M.: 1984, "Commentary," *Business & Professional Ethics Journal*, 3(3 & 4): 23-28.

Hayek, F.A.: 1961, "The *Non Sequitur* of the 'Dependence Effect,'" *Southern Economic Journal*, 27: 346-48.

Heilbroner, R.: 1976, *Business Civilization in Decline* (New York: W.W. Norton).

Held, V.: 1984, "Advertising and Program Content," *Business and Professional Ethics Journal,* 3(3 & 4): 61-76.

Kant, I.: 1964, *Groundwork of the Metaphysic of Morals* (New York: Harper Torchbook, H.J. Paton tr.).

Krutch, J.W.: 1959, *Human Nature and the Human Condition* (New York: Random House).

Lantos, G.: 1987, "Advertising; Looking Glass or Molder of the Masses?" *Journal of Public Policy and Marketing,* 6: 104-128.

Lasch, C.: 1978, *The Culture of Narcissism; American Life in An Age of Diminishing Expectations* (New York: W.W. Norton).

Levitt, T.: 1970, "The Morality (?) of Advertising," *Harvard Business Review,* (July-August): 84-92.

Lippke, R.: 1990, "Advertising and the Social Conditions of Autonomy," *Business and Professional Ethics Journal,* 8(4): 35-58.

Lukes, S.: 1973, *Individualism* (Oxford: Basil Blackwell).

MacIntyre, A.: 1966, *A Short History of Ethics* (New York: Collier).

MacIntyre, A.: 1981, *After Virtue: A Study in Moral Theory* (Notre Dame: U. of Notre Dame P.).

Rachels, J.: 1993, *The Elements of Moral Philosophy* (New York: McGraw-Hill, 2nd ed.).

Schudson, M.: 1986, *Advertising, The Uneasy Persuasion: Its Dubious Impact on American Society* (New York: Basic Books, 2nd ed.).

Thalberg, I.: 1989, "Hierarchical Analyses of Unfree Action," in Christman, J. (ed.), *The Inner Citadel: Essays on Individual Autonomy* (New York: Oxford U.P.), pp. 123-36.

Waide, J.: 1987, "The Making of Self and World in Advertising," *Journal of Business Ethics,* 6(2): 73-79.

Questions

1. Give an example, if you can, of a current ad that:

   (a) "debases language"

   (b) "drains thought"

   (c) "undoes dignity"

2. Defenders of advertising claim that:

   (a) it *informs* consumers about their products, which enhances *competition*, which prevents market *concentration* and *stagnation*. Do the ads you described in question one inform consumers about products, and does informing by advertising enhance competition? (Could non-informative ads also enhance competition? Is competition the only way to prevent market concentration and stagnation?)

   (b) it provides the media with financial support, which keeps it free from *governmental* control. Is governmental control better or worse than sponsor control?

   (c) people approach advertising *rationally* and *therefore* it can't be too manipulative. *Do* people approach advertising rationally, and would a rational approach necessarily limit an ad's manipulativeness?

3. What is Phillips' overall point, his thesis, his conclusion (in one sentence)?

4. Phillips makes two assumptions, accepts as "givens" two claims.

   (a) What are they?

   (b) Do you accept those claims?

5. (a) How does Phillips define "manipulative advertising"?

(b) Is it a good definition – will it include everything you want to include and will it exclude everything you want to exclude?

6. (a) What is the first ethical attack against manipulative advertising that Phillips examines (in one sentence)?

(b) Phillips presents three arguments for this first claim:

(i) The first argument is that made by Galbraith. Outline the argument (summarize P18-19; check your work with P20), then explain the two objections to it that Phillips presents (pay special attention to the second one, that by Hayek).

(ii) Referring to Hare, state the second argument. Phillips presents Levitt's argument as an objection – how exactly does Levitt argue that manipulated desires and purchases can provide *more* utility than rational desires and purchases? (Summarize P23-24; check your work with P26.)

(iii) The third argument seems to be grounded in virtue ethics – explain. Does Phillips think that manipulative advertising will necessarily cause long-term harm, regardless of Goldman's virtues? And does he think any long-term harm will necessarily outweigh the attendant pleasures?

7. (a) What is the second ethical attack against manipulative advertising that Phillips examines (in one sentence)?

(b) Arrington says that one can be manipulated and at the same time be autonomous – how so? (Look carefully at how he determines whether a desire is autonomous.) Does Phillips accept Arrington's conception of autonomy (P47)?

(c) What is Lippke's objection to Arrington? Does Phillips accept Lippke's objection (P44)?

8. (a) What is the third ethical attack against manipulative advertising that Phillips examines (in one sentence)?

(b) Both of Kant's imperatives can be used to condemn manipulative advertising. However, if Levitt's view that people want to be manipulated is correct, the support of which imperative is seriously weakened?

9. (a) What is the fourth ethical attack against manipulative advertising that Phillips examines (in one sentence)?

(b) Be sure to highlight the statements against manipulative advertising made by Waide, Heilbroner, and Held (P55) – all argue from a virtue ethics point of view.

(c) Which virtue does Phillips consider manipulative advertising to most undermine?

10. Phillips argues that a non-consumerist society would be unstable and "a more authoritarian form of government the likely end result" (P62). Do you agree? (Before you answer, be sure you understand the economic reasons Phillips gives in P63 and the social reasons he gives in P64.)

The AIDS Crisis:
Unethical Marketing Leads to Negligent Homicide

Franklin B. Krohn and Laura M. Milner

ABSTRACT. The purpose of this paper is to demonstrate how condom manufacturers and their marketers have failed to adequately promote their product to the male homosexual population (gays). Inasmuch as the AIDS syndrome constitutes a major life-threatening danger and that gays appear to be particularly vulnerable, failure to aggressively promote a known preventive such as condoms to gays constitutes negligent homicide.

The method used here defines what is traditionally viewed as a viable "target market," analyzes the major elements of marketing with regard to gays, and examines the neglect of condom promotion by their manufacturers.

It is concluded that condom marketers have failed to promote a known protection against AIDS to a highly susceptible group. That group would normally be seen as a highly attractive market for condoms and were it not for homophobia, marketers would zealously pursue more aggressive promotion of condoms to gays.

Franklin B. Krohn and Laura M. Milner, "The AIDS Crisis: Unethical Marketing Leads to Negligent Homicide." *Journal of Business Ethics* 8.10 (October 1989): 773-780. © 1989 by Kluwer Academic Publishers. Reprinted with permission of the publisher and the authors.

Introduction

1 This paper employs the traditional organizational approach of marketers in analyzing their subject matter where the development of a marketing strategy requires the selection of a target market and the development of a marketing "mix." The target market is defined as a portion of the total market consisting of buyers with similar traits that the organization wants to attract (Lusch and Lusch, 1987). The target market is usually analyzed in terms of numbers, demographics, and psychographics (lifestyle indices). The marketing mix consists of four essential and controllable marketing variables: (1) product (goods and services); (2) place (physical distribution, store outlets); (3) price; and (4) promotion. The successful manipulation of these variables to achieve the maximum response from the target market normally is the goal of the marketing strategy.

2 Marketing strategy does not exist in a vacuum free of ethical considerations any more than other facets of business endeavor. In fact, it is likely that marketers face more ethical dilemmas than other businesspeople (Krohn, 1984). Resolving ethical dilemmas is especially problematic for marketers in that much of their activity is involved in persuasion. Laczniak (1983) suggests three ethical frameworks that appear especially appropriate for determining ethical behavior among marketers: (1) The

Prima Facie Duties Framework developed by Ross (1930); (2) The Proportionality Framework Model articulated by Garrett (1966); and (3) The Social Justice Framework proposed by Rawls (1971).

3   All three of the ethical frameworks differ with one another in varying ways but are in agreement on one point: failing to engage in customary behavior that will prevent serious harm to innocent others is unquestionably unethical.

4   It will be suggested that condom marketers have been reluctant to aggressively promote their product to what should be a highly desirable and potentially profitable target market because of homophobia. If true, marketers of condoms would be guilty of negligent homicide for failing to effectively promote a product that is a known preventive for the AIDS syndrome to a highly vulnerable population.

The target market

Numbers

5   Establishing a truly accurate number concerning the population of gays in the United States is particularly problematic. Unlike other highly obvious groups such as men, women, Caucasians, Blacks, and Hispanics, gays are considered an invisible target group who are very capable of being unidentified. Admission of homosexuality still involves risks, the effects of which are reflected in sampling. For example, CBS conducted an exit poll after a recent election in West Village, a well known gay area of New York City. Only 4% of those interviewed admitted to being homosexual (DiSabato, 1987b). Part of the problem lies in the definition. In a classic example of the "attitude vs. behavior" puzzle, conclusions reached by Griffitt and Hatfield (1985) based on a number of studies indicate that exclusive behaviorally heterosexual history pertains to 70% of men and 85% of women. That means that 30% of the males and 15% of the females have engaged in homosexual behaviors at some time; however, many of these people do not have self-identities as homosexual. Therefore, the index of whether people are considered homosexual is often their self-identity as exclusively homosexual with perhaps incidental heterosexualism. Griffitt and Hatfield (1985) suggest that, conservatively, six to seven percent of the male population, or at least three to five million American men, are homosexual. They also suggest that two to four percent of the female population, or at least one to three million women, are homosexual. Another commonly cited statistic, based on research by Kinsey and his colleagues, is that ten percent of the population are gay and lesbian (Kinsey *et al.*, 1948, 1953). One common characteristic of these studies is that their figures are probably underestimates, suggesting that the percentages may be even higher.

Demographics and psychographics

6   Griffitt and Hatfield (1985) note that

in order to accurately describe the characteristics of any population it is necessary to draw a sample that is representative of that population in terms of all the characteristics of interest. In the study of homosexuals, or any other socially stigmatized group of people, it is probably impossible to obtain representative samples (p. 333).

Acknowledging one's own homosexuality ranges on a continuum from individuals privately recognizing their homosexuality to admitting it to the public at large. However, Griffitt and Hatfield (1985) conclude that the available data (e.g., Bell and Weinberg, 1978; Kinsey *et al.*, 1948) suggest that homosexuals differ little from heterosexual men and women in terms of education, occupation, social class, religion, age, and race. However, they do tend to be less religious, more politically and socially liberal, and more likely to live in urban areas. Lest anyone erroneously conclude that gay men and lesbian women are identical because they are homosexual, it should be recalled that the previous research compared gay men against heterosexual men and lesbians against heterosexual women. Just as heterosexual men and heterosexual women are different from each other, so too are gays and lesbians. For instance, lesbians have fewer sex partners and more stable, committed relationships than gays (Griffitt and Hatfield, 1985).

7   Despite some difficulties in identifying specific individuals as homosexual, there can be little question that they share an interest in homosexual topics and consequently can be inferred to be the prime patrons of homosexually oriented publications, resorts, clubs, and services. Mailing lists from businesses catering to homosexuals are as readily available as any other special interest group.

8   Thus it would appear that homosexuals in general and gays in particular can be identified as a target market because of their numbers, identifiable demographic characteristics, and special interests and needs (life-style).

The marketing mix

Products

9 Gays are considered innovators and early adopters in many product categories, particularly those products and services that are associated with high style and high technology. Indeed, they are the epitome of conspicuous consumption. Seagram's research of the psychographics of gay publication readers identified gay men "... as fashion-conscious and trend-setting ..." (Urbanski, 1983). Seagram's Product Manager Marsha Clay says, "They party a lot, spend a lot of money on themselves and buy premium products.... They are also more willing than straights to try something new" (Urbanski, 1983, p. 46-47). Gays are considered responsible for the wide-spread use of hair dryers and hair spray among men in general, running shoes and painter's pants for casual attire, as well as the rise of disco (Berling-Manuel, 1984; *Business Week*, 1979; *The Economist*, 1982). Gay males are also very likely, however, to drop a trend once it "catches on." For instance, Berling–Manuel (1984) notes, "... once the blow–dry hair styles were accepted in the mainstream, many gays turned to short hair" (p. M-5).

10   The gay market is considered an excellent target for different products including concerts, theatre, movies, VCR's, CD's, records, books and magazines as well as the latest technologies such as microwaves, telephone answering machines, and home computers (Bell and Weinberg, 1978; Gold, 1986; Hummler, 1985; Myrick, 1978; Simmons Market Research Bureau, 1987). Media events with gay themes are obviously especially popular with this market. For instance, Hunt (1985) notes that video companies have capitalized on the gay home market with pornographic cassettes and recently, Peter Frisch, former editor of *The Advocate*, started Humanus, a video production company specializing in non-sexual cassettes for the homosexual market. Topics range from massage to relationships and even include a video for parents who have discovered that their child is homosexual. Recent movies such as "Maurice," "My Beautiful Laundrette," "Parting

Glances," "Desert Hearts," and "Dona Herlinda and Her Son," plays such as "Torch Song Trilogy," "La Cage aux Folles," "The Normal Heart" and "As Is," and even the cable television show "Brothers" are very successful and perhaps even more successful because of the increasing popularity of gay themes with heterosexuals (Gold, 1986; Hummler, 1985).

11   Going beyond the home market, however, travel and tourism seems to be a growing area in the gay and lesbian market. There are several resort areas which cater to gays, such as those in Palm Springs and Key West in Florida and Fire Island in New York, as well as gay cruises and travel clubs (Myrick, 1978; Taylor, 1977). Applying the term "gentrification," both *Business Week* (1979) and *The Economist* (1982) note that gays are associated with the return of the white middle class to the inner city where families with children and women fear to tread. Although often provoking an ethnic group backlash, this group emphasizes home restoration. Indeed, in the San Francisco area, landlords welcome gays as tenants with expectations of improving their property. The gay market seems to be an excellent market for realtors, landlords, and home-related products and services.

12   However, simply targeting the homosexual market is not a key to success. One notable failure was Azygos, a line of men's toiletries (Berling-Manuel, 1984). Azygos, meaning "single" or "unpaired," was marketed openly and exclusively to the gay market. However,

> being gay oriented was not the problem .... 'It was a case of being severely under–capitalized.... They put all their money into the products launch, but then had none to back it up with.' (Berling-Manuel, p. M-58).

As indicated above, the gay market is a wealthy, trend-setting market. By virtue of their "innovator-early adopter" approach to buying, they are a viable market for products that utilize the skimming pricing strategy during the introduction stage. By demanding the best and being known for a desire for quality, gays are an excellent market for prestige-priced products and services.

Place

13   Retail establishments, both store and non-store outlets, are increasingly accessible to the homosexual community. For instance, there are 1,000 bars and restaurants in the U.S. catering to homosexual clientele (Berling–Manuel, 1984). Banks, as well as savings and loans, established specifically to serve homosexual clientele are also doing well (Berling-Manuel, 1984; Drew, 1986).

14   A variety of outlets for literature exists. There are 60 book stores in the United States, carrying a wide variety of book and non-book items of interest to lesbians (Frey, 1987). Lambda Rising, a book store in Washington, D.C., has a catalog business with over 186,000 names on the mailing list. Joseph DiSabato, president of Rivendell Marketing Company, a company specializing in marketing to gay newspapers and magazines, notes that magazines have a high secondary readership (three or more people), since many homosexuals prefer not to purchase outright (*Advertising Age*, 1980). One might assume that a high secondary readership also exists for catalogs. Indeed, an option that exists for homosexuals, one which is perhaps envied by heterosexuals, is the ability not to have one's name from a mailing list made available to other organizations, as well as the policy of many companies catering to homosexual clientele to not sell their lists (Berling-Manuel, 1984).

Price

15 *Business Week* (1979) cites research indicating that gays control 19% of the spendable income in the U.S. In addition, a recent marketing study of the readership of *The Advocate*, a gay newsmagazine, found the average household income to be $47,800, with 25% of the households reporting incomes of over $60,000 (Simmons Market Research Bureau, 1987). If accurate, these studies would suggest that the buying power of gays is far above what one would expect given their purported percentage of the population. Consequently, coupled with the knowledge that gays are likely to be an excellent market for prestige-priced products and services, their incomes would support the contention that they are likely prospects for up-scale and quality products and services.

Promotion

16 As with any other group, homosexuals prefer those businesses that direct their promotions to them. For instance, Drew (1986) notes one study which revealed that four out of five gays said they would be more likely to purchase the products and services of national businesses that maintained a presence in the gay media or community. However, as Berling-Manuel (1984) points out "... marketing by sexual preference remains one of the most uncomfortable—and least discussed—advertising topics since blacks insisted on being represented in consumer advertising" (p. M-4). As an example, Joseph DiSabato "...recalls one potential client suggesting gay ads to his boss, to which the boss replied, 'John, I think you should spend more time with your wife'" (Berry, 1987, p. 16). And, Baltera (1975) notes that advertisers are not expected to become involved in the homosexual rights movement.

17 Companies that have specifically targeted homosexuals through such media as *The Advocate* or service directories such as the *Gayellow Pages* out of New York include Bank of America and Chartered Bank of London, and car rental companies such as Hertz and Budget. Alcohol, beer, and non-alcoholic drink manufacturers/distributors include Carillon, Seagram's, Anheuser-Busch, Coors, Miller, Schlitz, and Stroh's as well as Calistoga and Perrier. Major motion picture studios, publishers, and record companies listed include Paramount, Universal, Twentieth Century Fox, Harper & Row, St. Martin's, RCA, Capitol, and CBS. It would seem that these large multi-national corporations promote their products and services directly to gays without homophobic apprehension or fear of heterosexual backlash.

Marketing strategies

18 Contrary to the preceding information, marketing to homosexuals is problematic. The gay market has all the ingredients that make it attractive to marketers, but the controversy and paradox for marketers is that it is still legal to discriminate against homosexuals in a variety of ways. Homophobia also exists to a large extent, and sadly no conversation about gay men is complete without reference to AIDS. Despite the denials of some, AIDS is likely to become an "epidemic unlike any other in our history" (Dhooper, Royse, and Tran, 1987-88, p. 109). The reasons which make that epidemic likely are threefold: (1) the projections of 1 to 1.5 million cases of AIDS-infected persons may be unrealistically low (Contact Center, 1986); (2) it is estimated that 20–30% of those infected may develop the disease by 1991 (*Newsweek*, 1986); and (3) that those already infected are infected

for life with little prospect for early development of a preventative vaccine (Bayer, 1986). Worldwide, the number of officially reported AIDS cases rose by 7% in one year (*Reuters News Service*, 1989).

19   Some scholars believe that as severe as the AIDS epidemic may become, a secondary epidemic of fear and irrationality against homosexual men, drug users, and minorities will occur (Fettner and Check, 1985). Recent calls for the quarantine of AIDS victims and their ostracism in schools and workplaces may be a precursor to just such a secondary epidemic (McLeod and Miller, 1985). Unfortunately, much media commentary on AIDS has been neither helpful nor accurate and has been referred to as "garrulous babble" (Watney, 1987, p. 8). The only resolution in sight appears to be more responsible information and education about the AIDS syndrome (Dhooper *et al.*, 1987-88). One of the most effective and prevalent forms of communication and education is advertising (Berkman and Gilson, 1987).

20   Recent articles on marketing to homosexuals have not been as sympathetic to this market as earlier ones. For instance, Berry (1987) noted that

> overall ... the number of national advertisers targeting gays have levelled off or declined in recent years ... the great expectations of national advertisers courting the gay market were far from realized ... which contrasts sharply with five years ago (p. 16).

Many companies suggest their recent lack of interest in the gay market is due to general budget cuts, but DiSabato says economics have little to do with it; rather AIDS has "added another stigma" (Berry, 1987, p. 16).

21   Marketers, however, have responded to the complexities of this segment using combinations of strategies and tactics. One response was to produce a product or service exclusively for gays as with the Azygos toiletries or *The Advocate*. With products that have crossover appeal, two approaches have been used. For instance, the manufacturer of RID, a treatment for body lice, used different advertisements for the heterosexual and homosexual segments (Urbanski, 1983). An undifferentiated strategy is often followed as well by using the same advertisement for both gay and heterosexual audiences. Carillon, makers of Absolut vodka, has followed this approach (Berling-Manuel, 1984). Seagram's uses a similar approach with Boodles Gin that is subtly gay oriented to the extent that it plays on heterosexual ignorance about the gay lifestyle:

> It sold a $19.95 bar mirror that features 'Six Famous Men of History' etched on it. The six were Oscar Wilde, Lawrence of Arabia, Walt Whitman, Edgar Allen Poe, Ludwig van Beethoven and Edgar Degas, and although neither the ad nor the mirror made any reference to it, all six are well known in the gay community as being purportedly homosexual (Berling-Manuel, 1984, p. M-58).

Furthermore, Pendleton (1980) notes:

> the belief that gays are on the cutting edge of fashion and other trends ... can provide a powerful launch. Casablanca Records, for instance, positioned its group, 'The Village People' to gays almost exclusively in the beginning. The strategy was that general public acceptance would follow, and evidently it was right (p. 84).

Companies using these preceding approaches are not overly concerned with offending heterosexuals (straight backlash). Indeed, Berling-Manuel (1984) notes,

> ... the companies that have done advertising in the gay market are relatively frank about it—the dollars do seem to be there, and the risk of of-

fending 'straights' has surfaced more in the planning stages than in reality (p. M-4).

Many base their decisions on the low probability of heterosexuals being exposed to gay media. Others, however, do not care:

> For Remy Martin, gay marketing is a 'long-term philosophy,' D'Amico [marketing manager] says. The company has extended its effort by supporting gay causes. I have seen no repercussions from heterosexuals.... The issues facing gays ... will increase their loyalty to companies sympathetic to them (Berry, 1987, p. 16).

The last approach used is to not advertise to the gay community at all, certainly a prerogative of any company. However, this approach has been followed, controversially and perhaps with dire effects for gays, by most condom manufacturers.

The condom controversy

22 Paradoxically, AIDS is responsible for the recovery of the condom market after the decline in sales in the 1960s and 1970s with the advent of the birth control pill (DiSabato, 1987b). O'Leary (1987) notes "condom marketers broke into mainstream media by crusading on an AIDS public-service soapbox. But these same manufacturers, ironically, have yet to spend one dime in the highest risk group's own media" (p. 2). Even when dealing with the AIDS crisis, "invariably there is a stereotypical heterosexual face—such as the blond in the current 'I Enjoy Sex But I'm Not Ready to Die for It' pitch from Lifestyles condoms" (O'Leary, 1987, p. 2).

23 There are a number of rationales advanced by the condom companies for pursuing the heterosexual market exclusively. The president of Ansell, Inc., manufacturer of Lifestyles condoms, was quoted in a February, 1987 *Time* magazine article that AIDS is a "condom marketer's dream" (Smilgis, 1987). Conversely, another representative of that company was reported as saying, "The danger, the threat, is in the heterosexual population. Very simply, there are more heterosexuals than homosexuals" (O'Leary, 1987, p. 2). Such an assertion ignores the research suggesting that risk of AIDS from heterosexual transmission is exceedingly slight for most Americans (Associated Press, 1987). Suggestions by the condom companies that gays are pre-sold on condom usage can be contrasted against research by *The Advocate* suggesting that only 59.5% of the gay population use condoms, a low figure considering the high risk as well as the indications that gays, similar to heterosexuals, need to be educated on the proper use of condoms (O'Leary, 1987). Additionally, many companies perceive that gays will get the message from being exposed to ads directed toward heterosexuals (O'Leary, 1987). Such thinking would probably preclude advertising to minorities those products that majorities use. Of even greater importance to marketers, such thinking would contradict the commonly accepted marketing theory that more precise target marketing is less costly because it focuses the persuasive message more directly to a more receptive audience.

24 Eventually, however, Ansell, Inc. did take up the challenge with their Lifestyles Extra Strength condom promotion begun October 31, 1987 in gay newspapers around the country. However, both Carter-Wallace (maker of Trojan with 55% of the market share) and Schmid (maker of Ramses and Sheik with 39% of the market share) have emphatically declined to market to gays. Obviously then, the condom manufacturers with 94% of the market share, through homophobia and/or fear of straight backlash, were not marketing to the gay seg-

ment. Certainly ethical questions arise when a possible prevention for a deadly disease exists but is not marketed to the high risk group. However, assuming it is fear of straight backlash that poses the dilemma for the condom manufacturers, there are a variety of "safe" approaches that could be used to minimize risk. For instance, DiSabato suggests, "if mainstream media wanted to avoid obvious gay references in ads, using a man in the Lifestyles ad could have cut across sexual preferences" (O'Leary, 1987, p. 2). Another possibility is for condom manufacturers to band together as the dairy industry has to produce advertisements and educational segments aimed at the gay population. No one manufacturer could then be singled out for retribution.

Summary and conclusions

25 This paper has attempted to demonstrate that the gay population is a viable target market—in numbers, demographics, and life style—for the marketing of a variety of products. The four traditional facets of the marketing mix (product, place, price, and promotion) were examined in respect to marketing to gays illustrating a wide diversity of products, means of distribution, pricing strategies, and promotional endeavors. It was observed that as a target market, gays are an excellent market for prestige products and services. In addition, they can be readily segmented and thereby addressed with persuasive messages in media to which they are particularly exposed.

26 It was suggested that the threat of AIDS adds a grave dimension to the marketing of condoms because they are a known preventive that should be vigorously promoted to a highly vulnerable group such as gays. With condom manufacturers representing 94% of the market share declining to energetically promote their product

to gays, it is likely that many will contract the AIDS syndrome and probably suffer a long debilitating illness before dying. Failing to advertise to a viable target market in need of their product is negligent marketing, but to contribute to the death of human beings by failing to take preventive action is analogous to negligent homicide.

27 Whether the condom manufacturers refuse to promote their product to gays because of homophobia or fear of straight backlash, they are failing their ethical responsibilities. Pressure should be applied to them through professional publications, educational programming, and public outrage. When some condom advertising can be clearly identified as directed toward gays, only then will condom manufacturers be able to plead "not guilty" to the charge of negligent homicide.

REFERENCES

Advertising Age: 1980, 'New Media Buying Service Will Concentrate on Gay Magazines', Jan. 28, 66.

Associated Press: 1987, 'Heterosexual AIDS risk said low', *Fairbanks Daily News Miner* September 29, 1, 5.

Baltera, Lorraine: 1975, 'Marketers Still in Closet Over Gays as "Them and Us" Attitude Lingers', *Advertising Age* July 7, 2, 38.

Bayer, R.: 1986, Review essay, *Journal of Health Politics, Policy and Law* 11(1), 171–177.

Bell, A. and Weinberg, S.: 1978, *Homosexualities: A Study of Diversity Among Men and Women* (Simon and Schuster, New York).

Berkman, Harold W. and Gilson, Christopher: 1987, *Advertising: Concepts and Strategies* (Random House, New York) pp. 4–6.

Berling-Manuel, L.: 1984, 'Reaching the Gay Market', *Advertising Age* March 26, M-4, M-5, M-58.

Berry, J.: 1987, 'U.S. Marketers are Rediscovering Homophobia: Only Recently a Market Everybody Wanted, Gays are Now Largely Ignored', *Adweek* October 26, 16.

Business Week: 1979, 'Gays: A Major Force in the Marketplace', September 3, 118–120.

Contact Center Information Updated: 1986 Jan., *Acquired Immune Deficiency Syndrome (AIDS)* (contact Center, Lincoln, Nebraska).

Dhooper, S. S., Royse, D. D., and Tran, T. V.: 1987–88, 'Social Work Practitioners' Attitudes Toward AIDS Victims', *Journal of Applied Social Sciences* 12(1), 108–123.

DiSabato, J.: 1987a, Personal communication with Joseph DiSabato, President of Rivendell Marketing Company, November 24.

DiSabato, J.: 1987b, 'Can Anyone Stop the Homophobia in the Condom Industry?' *The Lavendar Letter* (March) 7(3), 13–14.

Drew, P.: 1986, 'Alternate Markets: Low Ratings, High Profits', *Billboard* June 7, 19.

The Economist: 1982, 'The Homosexual Economy', Jan. 23, 71–72.

Fettner, A. G. and Check, W. A.: 1985, *The Truth about AIDS: Evolution of an Epidemic* (Holt, Rinehart and Winston, New York).

Frey, L: 1987, Personal communication with Dr. Lucille Frey, past owner of the Alaska Women's Bookstore, December 16.

Garrett, T.: 1966, *Business Ethics* (Prentice–Hall, Inc., Englewood Cliffs, NJ).

Gold, R: 1986, 'Gay-Themed Features Hot B.O. Stuff: Mainstream Auds More Accepting', *Variety* April 9, 5, 26.

Griffitt, W. and Hatfield, E.: 1985, *Human Sexual Behavior* (Scott, Foresman & Co., Glenview, IL).

Hummler, R: 1985, 'Mainstream Visibility for Gay Legit: Hit 'Torch Song' Cues New Wave', *Variety* July 17, 111.

Hunt, D.: 1985, 'Original Non-Sexual Programs for Gay Market', *Los Angeles Times* Aug. 16, 22.

Kinsey, A., Pomeroy, W., and Martin, C.: 1948, *Sexual behavior in the human male* (Saunders, Philadelphia).

Kinsey, A., Pomeroy, W., Martin, C., and Gebhard, P.: 1953, *Sexual behavior in the human female* (Saunders, Philadelphia).

Krohn, F.: 1984, 'Four Difficult Ethical Problems and Ways for Professors to Overcome Them', *Marketing Educator* Winter, 3.

Laczniak, G.: 1983, 'Frameworks for Analyzing Marketing Ethics', *Journal of Macromarketing* Spring, 7–18.

Lusch, R and Lusch, V.: 1987, *Principles of Marketing* (Kent Publishing Co., Boston, MA).

McLeod, D. W. and Miller, A. W. 1985, *Medical, Social and Political Aspects of the Acquired Immune Deficiency Syndrome (AIDS) Crisis: A Bibliography*, Toronto, Canada: Canadian Gay Archives.

Myrick. F.: 1987, 'Consumption Differences between Heterosexually and Homosexually Oriented Males', Southern Marketing Association *Proceedings* 493–496.

Newsweek: 1986, Department of Health and Human Services Report. June 23, 68.

O'Leary, N.: 1987, 'Condom Marketers Missing the Mark? Gay Media Have Yet to See a Dime Spent on Advertising', *Adweek* March 23, 2.

Pendleton, J.: 1980, 'National Marketers Beginning to Recognize Gays', *Advertising Age* October 6, 84–85.

Pennington, L.: 1981, 'But Will It Play in West Hollywood', *Los Angeles* May, 118–126.

Playboy Magazine: 1989, 'Advertisement by Adam and Eve', 36(4), 153.

Rawls, J.: 1971, *A Theory of Justice* (Harvard University Press, Cambridge, MA).

Reuters News Service: 1989, 'World AIDS Cases Rise by Nearly 7%', *Buffalo News* March 2, A-6.

Ross, W.: 1930, *The Right and the Good* (Clarendon Press, Oxford).

Royse, D., Dhooper, S. S., and Hatch, L. R: 1987, 'Undergraduate and Graduate students' Attitudes towards AIDS', *Psychological Reports* 60, 1185–1186.

Simmons Market Research Bureau: 1987, 'The Advocate Reader. Summary of "Profile of Readers"', January.

Smilgis, Martha: 1987, 'The Big Chill: Fear of AIDS', *Time* Feb. 16, 50–59.

Taylor, C.: 1977, 'Gay Power', *New York* Aug. 29, 10, 45–47.

Urbanski, A.: 1983, 'Marketers Get a Foot in the Closet Door', *Sales and Marketing Management* Oct. 10, 46–48.

Watney, S.: 1987, *Pornography, AIDS, and the Media* (Methuen, London).

Questions

1. Appealing to three ethical perspectives for support (which three?), Krohn and Milner make what claim about right and wrong (P3)? Do you agree?

2. What "customary behaviour" are they dealing with in this paper?

3. Much of the paper (P5–21) focuses on proving that gays are an identifiable, viable, and accessible market. Why do Krohn and Milner do this?

4. Not only do Krohn and Milner call failure to market condoms to gays "unethical," they call it "negligent homicide." Do you agree that this is so?

5. Krohn and Milner examine three reasons given by condom companies for *not* marketing to the gay sector. Which, if any, do they accept as valid?

6. What two solutions do Krohn and Milner offer to condom companies for minimizing, or even avoiding, the feared "straight backlash"?

Case Study - Youth News Network (YNN)

Early in 1999, a pilot project called Youth News Network (YNN) got underway at Meadowvale Secondary School in Mississauga, Ontario. The private interests behind YNN agreed to provide the school with free TVs, computers, a satellite dish, and software in return for which students would be shown a daily newscast about issues relevant to youth. The daily newscast would be about 10 to 12 minutes in length and would have advertising.

Opponents of the YNN project were quick off the mark. Concern has been expressed about the potential for manipulation of impressionable young minds who are a captive audience for the YNN broadcasts. One critic, Michele Landsberg, a *Toronto Star* columnist and social activist, claims that students have difficulty distinguishing between what is news and what is advertising, given the slick, hip nature of the programming. She points to a U.S. study (similar projects have been going on in America for some time under the education-corporate banner "Channel One") which shows that students remember the ads, not the news, and have "reinforced materialistic values." Another concern is over the loss of teaching time. YNN broadcasts would eat up about one hour per week and over 40 hours over the school year at a time when there is concern that our schools are not rigorous enough.

Further concerns have been expressed about the teachers' loss of control over the curriculum and about the growing commercialization of our educational institutions. As one teacher, Bob Fisher, in York Region expressed it, "Its sole objective is to make a profit from a captive audience, our students." The Canadian Teachers' Federation, a major teachers' union, has denounced the project and does not want it in other schools.

Advocates of the YNN project argue that it is intended to support teachers. The video programs, software, and the newscasts themselves are valuable resources for the school. They maintain that teachers and students are encouraged to develop and produce their own programming for exposure on YNN. Further, they dispute claims that the newscasts are not valuable. They refer to a University of Michigan study that shows a direct benefit to students. They also point to Channel One programs on such social issues as violence in schools, conflict resolution, and drug awareness that have been highly praised and have won awards including the prestigious Peabody Award.

The parent company of YNN, Athena Educational Partners, has maintained that the project will receive independent evaluation from OISE (the Ontario Institute for Studies in Education), school boards, teachers, parents, and others with an interest in education. The Canadian Teachers' Federation has been invited to participate but has declined. Athena clearly sees YNN as a win-win situation in which the schools get equipment and educational programming, and they receive commercial revenues. Their president, Rod MacDonald, makes the following point about the natural link between the corporate and education sectors: "Technology is already changing the way in which students learn and the way teachers teach. To deny that the private sector must play a role in managing this change is tantamount to sticking one's head in the sand."

REFERENCES

Landsberg, Michele. "Let's Signal 'No' to TV Network in Schools." *The Toronto Star* 14 Mar. 1999: A2.

MacDonald, Rod. "Students Profit from Classroom TV." *The Toronto Star* 26 Mar. 1999: A20.

"Parents and Educators Warned about Proposed YNN Launch." *SchoolNet Weekly*. February 15-19/99. <http://www.newswire.ca/releases/February1999/11/c5348.html>

Questions

1. Is there any difference between advertisements (that may "reinforce materialism") that children see after school on "regular" television and those they would see at school on the YNN network?

2. Is there any difference between YNN being a mandatory part of the school day and either "the prayer" or "the anthem" being a mandatory part of the school day?

3. Does the moral rightness or wrongness depend on whether YNN would be in an elementary school or a high school? Or a university/college?

4. As a principal or school board member, make a list of three or four questions you would like answered before deciding to sign a contract with YNN.

CHAPTER 3
PRODUCT SAFETY

What to Do? – Back to Basics

You run a tape duplication service and you've been approached by a very large and well-financed group called *Back to Basics*. They want you to dub a million copies of their founder's "keystone speech" for wide distribution.

The thing is, the speech is such that it's very manipulative: the tone is very emotional, there is a lot of "loaded" language, it's full of mere assertions, with no reasons, let alone solid arguments, for any of its positions, most of which are racist, sexist, and homophobic, and there are appeals throughout to various gods and feel-good guardian angels as authorities.

The tape could be "used correctly" – it is an audio tape of the speech: for the illiterate, blind, and others who cannot read the printed text version, it's surely valuable. And it would probably be of interest to researchers.

But you suspect that many people will use the tape "incorrectly": repeated playing of the tape, most probably (as is recommended in the speech itself) while driving, will amount to almost hypnotic indoctrination. The repetition of platitudes without a context of critical analysis (which can hardly occur when one is driving, even if it was encouraged) is common in cults. But maybe that's not your problem, not your responsibility.

Nevertheless, you're concerned about product safety: not physical harm, but mental harm is at issue. You consider, therefore, refusing to be a part of the production process. You know that if you refuse, they'll find someone else. But that's not the point.

What do you decide to do?

Introduction

One might think that it's morally wrong to manufacture or market an unsafe product, a product that causes harm – and that's that. What else need one say about it?

Well, first one might ask "How unsafe?" Surely for many products, safety is a matter of degree. How likely is the harm? How severe? How permanent? And what, exactly, counts as harm? Are we talking about just physical injury or should we talk about psychological injury as well? High school shootings by "disturbed adolescents" have been blamed on violent movies, TV shows, video games, and Internet sites – are these, therefore, "unsafe products"?

Second (or rather first, since this question must precede the other), one might ask "Is it okay to make a product that's less than perfectly safe?" Especially if, for some reason, you *can't* make a perfectly safe one? (Is there even such a thing as a "perfectly safe" product?)

And if it is okay, is it okay not to advertise the risk associated with the product because of its less-than-perfectly-safe nature? Perhaps informing the potential consumer of the risks makes the so-so safe product morally acceptable to make because it puts the moral responsibility for its use on the consumer (respecting their autonomy, their ability to think, and their freedom to choose). Certainly the warnings about content and intended audience which are placed at the beginning of the aforementioned movies seem to have this intent.

But what if the "especially" doesn't apply – is it okay to manufacture a less-than-perfectly-safe product even when you *can* make a perfectly safe one? Maybe there'd be less, or no, profit in

the perfectly safe one. But by not making the less-safe product, you're depriving consumers of the product altogether. And again, the marketing question must also be asked: is it okay not to advertise the low quality?

What about totally unsafe products, such as land mines? Is it okay to make them? I mean, what possible warning could you put on the label that would inform potential users of the risk: "This product is unsafe, anywhere, anytime"? That may inform of the risk, but in doing so, it does nothing to reduce the likelihood of harm (which was the moral point of such warnings); since it's *always* harmful, only refusing to make the product would achieve that.

And do all weapons fit into that category, from nuclear bombs to hand guns? Can you make a moral argument for their manufacture despite their obvious lack of safety/risk of harm? (Such an argument would probably be utilitarian – harm outweighed by good. Or principled-based – distinguishing between defensive use and offensive use.)

Not only may carefully considered advertising make a so-so safe product morally acceptable; carefully considered sales may achieve the same thing. For example, one could refuse to sell land mines (and nuclear weapons) to psychopaths. (Might be a good idea to include the hand guns here, too.)

The standard response to these questions (i.e., those involving products that are potentially harmful) has been "let the buyer beware" (i.e., it's the buyer's responsibility to find out, not the seller's responsibility to tell). Perhaps if such information were easily accessible, this would be a reasonable distribution of responsibility. (Though maybe not – why *should* the buyer have to find out? If *you* want the sale, *you* should have to tell – tell me what I need to know.) (Well, but, if *you* want the product, you should have to find out!) But such information is often not easily accessible. And it seems to me that placing the responsibility on the buyer suggests that the default mode is deceit rather than honesty – what's there to "find out" in the first place? If one were honest, why wouldn't one "tell"? (And well, does honesty rank higher than profit?)

Another answer to these questions is the "due care" response: the manufacturer has the responsibility of taking due care, reasonable precautions, to prevent harm. (How reasonable is reasonable?)

Yet another answer, contract theory, says that the manufacturer is bound only by the terms of the contract – which ideally is explicit and precise, and freely entered into by all parties. (How often is there such a contract?)

And according to the strict liability answer, the manufacturer is "responsible for all harm resulting from a dangerously defective product even when due care has been exercised and all contracts observed" (Boatright 305) – seller beware? This answer is often justified by appealing to affordability: who better can afford to compensate for injuries than the company (i.e., its insurance company, meaning its premium-paying policyholders), and to incentive: it will motivate companies to be extra safe (do you need *that* kind of motivation?). On the other hand, such complete denial of any responsibility on the consumer/user's part seems unfair, not to mention insulting. (See Velasquez for a discussion of the strengths and weaknesses of these views.)

One element of product safety and moral responsibility running through these various views is foreknowledge: Did the company know of the risk? And does that make a difference? How much can we expect the company to know about its product? That is, how thoroughly must it test the product? Sometimes side effects don't show up for 30 or 40 years (consider asbestos; even now that we know asbestos is carcinogenic, Canada is the world's second largest exporter of it, mostly to developing countries); sometimes not until the next generation (consider DES and thalidomide). Does the product sit on the shelf until then? What if it's really important to some people and they're willing to take the risk?

And how will the company know about these side effects? That is, is it okay to test the product on living animals? Only on those that can give informed consent? (So, not non-human animals?) Only when there are no alternatives? (Colgate has developed an "artificial mouth" which simulates the conditions of the human mouth for testing their oral health products.) Only when the benefits of the product outweigh any pain and suffering caused by the testing? (Do we really need another kind of mascara so badly we have to torture rabbits to get it?) And do these benefits include financial benefits?

In addition to asking "How safe?", we should ask "Safe for what?" Really, is it the company's fault the consumer stuck his fingers in the snowblower while trying to fix it? Just how many warnings must one put on the label? (Indeed, Bucciarelli argues that "idiotproofing" may actually work against safety: "With the user 'out of the loop,' shielded from the details of the device, there is less possibility he or she will act rationally, judiciously, if the unaccounted-for weighs in" [55]. Economists call this situation "moral hazard.") Often the answer to this question is something like "whatever the reasonable person might require." But, again, what's "reasonable"? Who decides?

And "safe for whom?" Just people? Or other animals too? Just for the people who use the products or for others who may be affected by that use? (Consider the victims of a drunk driver.) Affected only in the short-term or also in the long-term? (Consider the victims of environmental degradation.)

Given that many products will be in households with children, are you obligated to childproof everything you make or sell? Or is that the parent's moral responsibility?

The phrase "product safety" can be narrowly interpreted to refer only to the finished product or broadly interpreted to refer to the full process of its manufacture – from getting the raw materials to disposing of the waste. The finished product might be harmless, but what if a great deal of harm was done in order to make it? This broad interpretation gives rise to questions that overlap with those in Chapter Ten on the environment and Chapter Four on workers' rights (most specifically, the right to a safe workplace). Nuclear energy is a good example of this aspect of product safety.

Attention to harm is characteristic of a utilitarian analysis, but one can examine the issue of product safety from other perspectives. A rights-based analysis would consider buyers' rights – for example, the right to be adequately informed and to be protected from harmful products; the right to choice (between degrees of safety, of quality, of price) might also be considered. These would be measured against sellers' rights – for example, the right to decide what to make and sell, as well as how to market it. Obviously, there are conflicts. Which rights take priority? Why?

Safety may become an even more difficult issue if you're the distributor, not the manufacturer. Consider grocery stores: pesticides and additives can make a product harmful – how morally responsible is the grocer for ensuring that the produce sold is safe for consumption? Will merely labelling a product "BGH" be sufficient to inform potential consumers that the product came from cows injected with the controversial Bovine Growth Hormone? Perhaps. After all, isn't making the decision for them (deciding not to carry any BGH products) patronizing? Perhaps many people would rather eat an apple that is really red and perfectly round (i.e., grown with pesticides) than one that perhaps has a worm in it.

And after all, a consumer can simply shop at "organic produce only" stores. Well, what if s/he can't – what if there are no such stores in the area? Does that change the only grocer's moral responsibility? Does any of this depend on government regulations? That is, are you morally bound only to conform to safety regulations? Is that a moral minimum or a moral maximum?

Canada's "tainted blood scandal" is an example of just how complicated this issue can get. In the 1980s, an estimated 1,200 recipients of Red Cross blood were infected with HIV and 60,000 with Hepatitis C. Part of the problem, according to the *Report of the Commission of Inquiry on the Blood System in Canada* (the Krever Report), was that adequate measures were not taken to track down infected individuals, some of whom unknowingly infected their partners or children. Risks were downplayed and the information eventually provided to the public was vague and confusing. A test for Hepatitis C in blood products, available after 1986, may have saved almost 24,000 people, but Canada did not adopt it for reasons of cost and efficiency. Talk about a bottom line. How much financial compensation is enough in this case?

Certainly a classic case of product safety involves the Ford Pinto. Some argue that Ford knowingly put an unsafe car on the road, causing pain and suffering, and Ford executives are therefore morally at fault (see Dowie). Ford argued that others caused the accidents that resulted in that pain and suffering (i.e., someone had to rear-end a Pinto for it to explode) and so Ford was not at fault – the Pinto was intended for driving, not colliding (see the Ford Motor Company article).

But isn't colliding part of driving, or at least a regular sort of risk involved in driving? If so, then Ford should have foreseen and eliminated (reduced?) the risk of harm. But what chance of happening makes it a reasonable expectation – one in a hundred or one in a million? And does it matter at all how cheap or how expensive the remedy was? (The Pinto could've been fixed for $11/car.) Dow Corning's silicone breast implants (see Boatright) is another classic case in product safety – or lack of. Ditto for A.H. Robins' Dalkon shield (see Buchholz and Rosenthal).

But then don't forget that J.C. Penney recalled an entire line of radios when it discovered that some – fewer than one percent – had defective resistors that caused them to catch fire. And Johnson Wax withdrew all its CFC products when the connection was made between CFCs and the ozone layer. And more recently, Johnson and Johnson recalled all its Tylenol when seven people in Chicago died as a result of cyanide in tampered-with capsules.

REFERENCES AND FURTHER READING

Boatright, John R. *Ethics and the Conduct of Business.* 2nd ed. NJ: Prentice Hall, 1997. 284-286.

Bucciarelli, Louis. "Is Idiot Proof Safe Enough?" *International Journal of Applied Philosophy* 2 (Fall 1985): 49-57.

Buchholz, Rogene A., and Sandra B. Rosenthal. *Business Ethics: The Pragmatic Path Beyond Principles to Process.* NJ: Prentice Hall, 1998. 511-529.

Curtis, Gary L. "What Cosmetic Companies Can Learn from Pharmaceutical Testing." *DCI* 157.2 (August 1995): 48-53.

Dowie, Mark. "Pinto Madness." *Mother Jones* 2.8 (September/October 1977).

Fern, Richard L. "Human Uniqueness as a Guide to Resolving Conflicts Between Animal and Human Interests." *Ethics and Animals* 2.1 (March 1981): 7-21.

Ford Motor Company. "Closing Argument by Mr. James Neal" (Brief for the Defense, State of Indiana v. Ford Motor Company, U.S. District Court, South Bend, Indiana, January 15, 1980). Ed. Lisa H. Newton and Maureen M. Ford. *Taking Sides: Clashing Views on Controversial Issues in Business Ethics and Society.* 4th ed. CT: Dushkin Publishing Group, 1996. 263-271.

Frey, R.G. *Interests and Rights: The Case Against Animals.* NY: Oxford University Press, 1980.

Krever, Horace. *The Final Report of the Commission of Inquiry on the Blood System in Canada.* Ottawa: Public Works and Government Services Canada, 1997.

Smyth, D. H. *Alternatives to Animal Experimentation.* London: Scholars' Press, 1978.

VanDeVeer, Donald. "Interspecific Justice." *Inquiry* 22 (Summer 1979): 55-79.

Velasquez, Manuel G. *Business Ethics: Concepts and Cases.* 3rd ed. NJ: Prentice Hall, 1992. 277-292.

On the Ethics of the Use of Animals in Science

Dale Jamieson and Tom Regan[1]

1 As you read this, animals are being killed, burned, radiated, blinded, immobilized and shocked. They are being locked and strapped into the Noble-Collip Drum, tossed about at the rate of 40 revolutions per minute and thrust against the iron projections that line the drum. This procedure crushes bones, destroys tissues, smashes teeth and ruptures internal organs. Right now, somewhere, animals are in isolation, deprived of all social contact, while others are in alien environments, manipulated into cannibalizing members of their own species. It is not just a few animals at issue. In the year 1978 alone, about 200 million animals were used for scientific purposes, about 64 million of these in the United States. This number includes 400,000 dogs, 200,000 cats and 30,000 apes and monkeys.[2] From anyone's point of view, these are disagreeable facts, but some will say they are the concern of scientists only. We who are not scientists cannot get off the hook so easily, however. The use made of animals in science frequently is carried out in the name of improving the quality of human life: to find cures for cancer, heart disease and a thousand other ailments; to develop safe new products for our consumption; and to instruct others in, and to advance our knowledge of, the world in which

we live. Because these things are done in our name, ostensibly to help us live better lives, and because these activities frequently are financed by public monies (approximately $5 billion dollars in federal support in the United States for 1980) we cannot in good faith or with good sense avoid confronting the facts about the use of animals in science, and assessing its morality.

2 In the past this debate has usually been put in terms of being for or against vivisection. But this term, "vivisection," is ill-suited for our purposes. To vivisect an animal is to dissect it, to cut it, while it is alive. Not all practices that demand our attention involve vivisection. Animals placed in the Noble-Collip drum or those that are radiated or shocked, for example, are not dissected while they are alive. For this reason it would be misleading at best to pose our central question in terms of whether one is for or against vivisection. Our interest lies in assessing the use made of animals in science in general, not just in those cases where they are vivisected.

3 There are three major areas of science in which animals are routinely used. These are (1) biological and medical education; (2) toxicology testing; where the potential harmful affects for human beings of various chemicals and commercial products are first tested on animals; and (3) original and applied research, including not only research into the causes and treatment of various diseases but also into the basic biochemical nature and behavior of living organisms.[3] All of us are familiar with the use of animals in education from our time spent in laboratory sections

Dale Jamieson and Tom Regan, "On the Ethics of the Use of Animals in Science" from *And Justice for All: New Introductory Essays in Ethics and Public Policy.* Ed. Tom Regan and Donald Van De Veer. NJ: Rowman and Allanheld, 1982. 169-196. Reprinted with permission of the editors and the authors.

in biology, for example, and most of us have an outsider's inkling of what goes on in original and applied research from what we read in the newspapers and are exposed to by the other media. As for the use of animals in toxicity testing, that will become clearer as we proceed, when we discuss various toxicity tests, including the so-called Draize test and the LD-50 test.

4   It is possible that some people might object to our including all three uses of animals under the general heading of the use of animals in science. In particular, some scientists might have a narrower view of science, according to which only original and applied research counts as "genuine science"; the use of animals in educational contexts or in toxicological testing isn't science, on this view, or not "real" science at any rate. This narrower conception of science is understandable, if science is viewed exclusively in terms of the devising and testing of original hypotheses. The fact remains, however, that it is not by witchcraft or astrology, say, that the acute or chronic toxicity of pesticides, food additives, hair sprays and oven cleaners are determined; it is a matter of applied science. And it is not to turn out persons educated in, say, philology or accounting that lab sections are held in connection with standard courses in biology; it is to educate persons in biological science. So, while there may be a sense in which neither toxicity tests nor instructional labs are "science," there is certainly another sense in which they are a recognized part of those activities carried on by scientists, in their capacity as scientists or as teachers of science, and it is this more general but still proper sense of 'science' that we shall have in mind throughout the pages that follow. Thus, when we inquire into the morality of how animals are used in science or for scientific purposes, we intend to include their use in all three

areas – in biological and medical education, in toxicology testing, and in original and applied research – though we shall feel free occasionally to emphasize their use in one area over their use in the others.

5   Before setting forth our own view regarding the ethics of the use of animals in science, two extreme positions will be characterized and debated. By subjecting their supporting arguments to criticism, we hope to show the need for a more reasonable, less extreme position. We shall call the two positions "The Unlimited Use Position" and "The No Use Position." The former holds that it is permissible to use any animal for any scientific purpose, so long as no human being is wronged. The latter holds that no use of any animal for any scientific purpose is morally permissible. We shall first examine the leading arguments for the Unlimited Use Position.

I.

6   The first argument that we shall consider is the Cartesian Argument. It is named after the seventeenth century philosopher, René Descartes, who held that animals are mindless machines. Here is the argument.

1. If a practice does not cause pain, then it is morally permissible.
2. Unlimited use of animals for scientific purposes would not cause them any pain.
3. Therefore, the use of any animal for any scientific purpose is morally permissible.

So simple an argument is not without far reaching consequences. The tacit assumption of the Cartesian Argument by the scientists of Descartes' day helped pave the way for the rapid growth of animal experimentation in the seventeenth and eighteenth centuries. The following passage, written by an unknown contemporary of Descartes, gives a vivid and unsettling picture of science at that time.

> They [i.e., scientists] administered beatings to dogs with perfect indifference; and made fun of those who pitied the creatures as if they felt pain. They said the animals were clocks; that the cries they emitted when struck, were only the noise of a little spring that had been touched, but that the whole body was without feeling. They nailed poor animals up on boards by their four paws to vivisect them and see the circulation of the blood which was a great subject of controversy.[4]

It is well to remember this passage whenever we doubt that ideas can make a difference. Clearly Descartes' idea that animals are mindless machines profoundly influenced the course of science. The influence of an idea, however, is not a reliable measure of its truth, and we need to ask how reasonable the Cartesian Argument is.

7   A moment's reflection is enough to show that some crucial qualifications must be added if the Cartesian Argument is to have any plausibility at all. Inflicting pain is not the only way to harm an individual. Suppose, for example, that we were to kill humans painlessly while they are asleep. No one would infer that because such killing would be painless it would therefore be quite all right. But even if the necessary qualifications were introduced, the Cartesian Argument would still remain implausible. The evidence for believing that at least some animals feel pain (and it is only those animals with which we shall be concerned) is virtually the same as the evidence for believing that humans feel pain. Both humans and animals behave in ways that are simply, coherently and consistently explained by supposing that they feel pain. From a physiological point of view, there is no reason to suppose that there are features that are unique to humans that are involved in pain sensations. Veterinary medicine, the law and common-sense all presuppose that some animals feel pain. Though some seem to accept the Cartesian Argument implicitly, it is doubtful that many would try to defend it when it is clearly stated.

8   The failure of the Cartesian Argument has important implications regarding the moral status of animals. Once we acknowledge the reality of animal consciousness and pain we will be hard pressed indeed to exclude animals from membership in the moral community. Membership in the moral community might be thought of as in some ways analogous to membership in a club, with both qualifications and possible benefits. The key potential benefit of membership is that limits are placed on how others may treat you. For example, as a member, your life and property are protected by moral sanctions. Who belongs to the moral community? Evidently all those individuals who can themselves be treated wrongly qualify as members. But which individuals are these? A variety of answers have been proposed, including the following:

– all and only rational beings;
– all and only autonomous beings (individuals having free will).

It will not be possible to discuss these views in detail.[5] It is sufficient to note their common failing: Infants and severely enfeebled human beings, for example, are neither rational nor autonomous, and yet we treat them wrongly if we cause them significant pain for no good reason. Thus, since we can treat these individuals wrongly, they qualify as members of the moral community; and since they qualify as members of this community despite the fact that they are neither rational nor autonomous, neither rationality nor autonomy are requirements for membership in the moral community.

9   Still, infants and the enfeebled are human beings, and it might be suggested that membership in the moral community is determined by species membership. In other words, it might be suggested that all and only human beings are members of the moral community. This requirement for membership is also unsatisfactory. To restrict membership in the moral community to those who belong to the "right" species is analogous to the racist's attempt to restrict membership to those who belong to the "right" race, and to the sexist's effort to exclude those of the "wrong" gender.[6] Racism and sexism are today recognized as unacceptable prejudices. Rationally, we recognize that we cannot mark moral boundaries on the basis of such biological differences. Yet this is precisely what those who attempt to restrict membership in the moral community to all and only *Homo Sapiens* are guilty of. They assume that membership in a particular species is the only basis for deciding who does and who does not belong to the moral community. To avoid this prejudice of "speciesism," we must reject this way of setting the boundaries of the moral community, and recognize that when needless pain and suffering are inflicted on infants and enfeebled humans, it is wrong, not because they are members of our species, but because they experience needless pain and suffering. Once this is acknowledged we may then come to see that it must be wrong to cause any individual, human or otherwise, needless pain or suffering. Thus, since many animals are conscious beings who can experience pain, as was argued in response to the Cartesian Argument, we must recognize that we can wrong them by causing them needless pain or suffering. Since they themselves can be wronged, they themselves must be members of the moral community.

10   The failure of the Cartesian Argument, therefore, does indeed have important implications regarding the moral status of animals. We shall have occasion to remind ourselves later of these implications.

11   But now let us consider a second argument that might be urged on behalf of the Unlimited Use Position. We shall call this the "Might Makes Right Argument."

1. If a practice is in the interests of the stronger, then it is morally permissible.
2. Humans are stronger than animals.
3. Unlimited use of animals in science would be in the interests of humans.
4. Therefore, the use of any animal for any scientific purpose is morally permissible.

Even if we accept the view that only human interests determine how animals ought to be treated, what premise 3 asserts is false. Sometimes it is not in our interests to allow the use of just any animal for just any scientific purpose. Some animals are members of species that many people care about. Our reasons for caring are sometimes romantic or sentimental. Sometimes they are educational or aesthetic. Increasingly they are prudential. The more we learn about the interrelatedness of life on this planet, the more we recognize that the quality of our lives is inextricably linked to the welfare of other species. Because we care about some animals, we have an interest in how they are treated, and therefore their unlimited use cannot be said to be in the interests of humans. Consider, too, that the first premise, that what is permissible is determined by what is in the interest of the stronger, implies that strong humans do nothing wrong when they pursue their ends by using weaker humans, however badly they might treat them. Thus the Might Makes Right Argument would permit, not just unlimited use of animals, but unlimited use of weak and defenseless humans as well. If we are unwilling to swallow this repugnant conclusion, we must reject this argument. If, on the other hand, we are willing to accept unlimited use of weak and defenseless humans, then most and possibly all animal experimentation and toxicity testing performed in the name of human welfare is unnecessary. However useful animal experimentation or toxicity tests might be in improving the quality of the lives of stronger humans, surely the use of weaker humans would be even more useful. When animals are used, the problem of "extrapolating the data," that is, applying the results to humans, inevitably arises. (We shall have occasion to return to this problem in the pages that follow.) The problem of extrapolation could be overcome, however, if weaker humans instead of animals were used. After all, what could be a better experimental model of a human than another human? But no one, presumably, will seriously argue that weak humans should be exploited in this way. Thus no one will seriously espouse the Might Makes Right Argument.

12   A third argument, the Soul Argument, overcomes some of these difficulties.

1. Moral constraints only apply to beings who have souls.
2. All humans have souls.
3. No animals have souls.
4. Therefore, moral constraints apply to what may be done to humans but not to what may be done to animals.
5. Therefore, unlimited use of animals for scientific purposes is morally permissible.

One who accepts this argument can use it to avoid the unsavory implications for weaker humans of the Might Makes Right Argument. Since premise 2 states that all humans have souls, it follows that even weak humans have souls; thus the Soul Argument would not permit unlimited use of weak humans by stronger humans. Animals, however, are not protected by morality since they allegedly lack souls. Thus, according to the Soul Argument, morality permits us to use any animal for any scientific reason.

13   This argument is open to numerous objections. To begin with, the claim that all humans have souls is both vague and difficult to support. What is a soul? How do we know that humans have them but animals don't? On any account, these are not easy questions to answer. Moreover, although the dominant religions of the Western world typically deny that animals have souls, other religions, for example Hinduism and some Native American religions, do attribute souls to animals. Just as there is great controversy concerning the nature of the soul and the very coherence of the concept, so there is controversy about what individuals have souls.

14   Suppose however, that we were to accept the view that all and only humans have souls. Now, having a soul clearly would make an important difference to an individual's chances for a life beyond the grave. Those lacking a soul will have no chance for a future life. Thus the bodily death of an animal, assuming all animals lack souls, would mark its complete annihilation as a conscious individual. The influential Christian writer, C. S. Lewis, argues that this fact would have the opposite implication from the one drawn in the Soul Argument.[7] If animals have no souls and no possible life beyond the grave, then the pain and suffering that they are made to endure in this life cannot possibly be balanced or overcome by the pleasures and enjoyments of an afterlife. In other words, if animals have no souls there is no possibility that the travails of their earthly existence can be recompensed

in a world beyond. Thus the obligation to minimize the pain and suffering of animals during this their only life would seem to be, if anything, increased rather than diminished by their lack of a soul. If this is true, then we shall certainly fail to discharge that obligation if we permit the use of any animal for any scientific purpose. The Soul Argument, rather than providing grounds for the Unlimited Use Position, actually contains the seeds of an argument that can be used to criticize that Position.

15   A fourth argument for Unlimited Use is the Knowledge Argument.

1. If a practice produces knowledge, then it is morally permissible.

2. Unlimited use of animals for scientific purposes would produce knowledge.

3. Therefore, unlimited use of animals for scientific purposes is morally permissible.

Here we should balk at the first premise. Torturing suspects, spying on citizens, vivisecting cousins, all could produce knowledge, but surely that alone would not make these activities morally all right. Some knowledge is simply not worth the price in pain required to get it, whether those who suffer the pain are humans, as in the activities just listed, or animals, as in the case about to be described.

16   The Draize Test is a procedure employed by many manufacturers to determine whether proposed new products, most notably new cosmetics, would irritate the eyes of humans.[8] The most recent Federal guidelines for the administration of the Draize Test recommend that a single large volume dose of the test substance be placed in the conjunctival sac in one eye of each of six albino rabbits. The test substance is to remain in the eyes of the rabbits for a week, and observations are to be periodically recorded. The guidelines recommend that in most cases anesthetics

should not be used. The rabbits are often immobilized in restraining devices in order to prevent them from clawing at their eyes. At the completion of a week, the irritancy of the test substance is graded on the basis of the degree and severity of the damage in the cornea and iris.

17   The Draize Test is not a very good test by anyone's standards. It is unreliable and crude. In fact, a 1971 survey of twenty-five laboratories employing the Draize Test concluded that the Draize Test is so unreliable that it "... should not be recommended as standard procedures in any new regulation."[9] But even if the Draize Test were a reliable test, the most that we would gain is some knowledge about the properties of some inessential new products. Can anyone really believe that there is a scarcity of cosmetics already on the market? The value of whatever knowledge is provided by the Draize Test is insignificant compared to the cost in animal pain required to obtain it. Indeed, no less a figure than Harold Feinberg, the chairperson of the American Accreditation For the Care of Laboratory Animals Committee, has stated that "the testing of cosmetics is frivolous and should be abolished."[10]

18   A fifth argument seeks to remedy this deficiency of the Knowledge Argument. Here is the Important Knowledge Argument.

1. If a practice produces important knowledge, then it is morally permissible.

2. Unlimited use of animals for scientific purposes would produce important knowledge.

3. Therefore, unlimited use of animals for scientific purposes is morally permissible.

The Important Knowledge Argument fares no better than the Knowledge Argument. Consider an example. Surely it cannot be denied that it is important to know what substances are carcinogenic in humans. But animal tests for carcinogenicity in humans are often inconclusive. For example, in recent years there has been great controversy over whether one can infer that saccharin or oral contraceptives are carcinogenic in humans on the basis of data collected in animal tests. Some have argued that because of the methods used in such research, such an inference cannot be made.[11] Massive doses are administered to rats and mice in these studies over short periods of time; there is no reason to believe that human cancers develop in response to similar conditions. Moreover, unlike humans, rats and mice tend spontaneously to develop a high incidence of tumors. One prominent medical journal remarked with respect to the oral contraceptive controversy:

> It is difficult to see how experiments on strains of animals so exceedingly liable to develop tumors of these various kinds can throw useful light on the carcinogenicity of a compound for man.[12]

If, however, we were to adopt the policy of unlimited use of *humans*, we could conclusively determine which substances are carcinogenic in humans. Moreover, such a policy would be sanctioned by the Important Knowledge Argument, since unlimited toxicology testing and experimentation on humans would unquestionably produce important knowledge. If the production of important knowledge makes a practice permissible, then unlimited testing and experimenting on humans is permissible. But again, this is a repugnant conclusion. If we are unwilling to accept it, we must give up the Important Knowledge Argument. If, on the other hand, we are willing to accept it, then most and possibly all toxicology tests and experiments carried out on animals in the name of human interests are unnecessary, since better models, namely humans, are available.

19   Finally there is the Freedom Argument. The Freedom Argument does not seek to show directly that unlimited use of animals is permissible. Rather it seeks to show that limitations on a researcher's freedom to use animals are wrong. Here is the argument.

1. Outside limits placed on the scientist's right to freedom of inquiry or academic freedom are not permissible.
2. Any outside restriction placed on the use of animals for scientific purposes would place limits on the scientist's right to freedom of inquiry or academic freedom.
3. Therefore, no outside restrictions on how animals may be used for scientific purposes are morally permissible.

This argument focuses attention away from the value of the goal of science (knowledge or important knowledge) to the value of the freedom to inquire. But though this change is noteworthy, and though this freedom is important and ought to be one among a number of factors considered in the course of examining the ethics of the use of animals in science, it is clear that freedom of inquiry is not the only morally relevant consideration. The right to freedom of inquiry is no more absolute than, say, the right to freedom of speech. There are limits on what can be done by individuals in exercising their rights. To say precisely just what these limits are is difficult; but limits there are. Almost no one would say that the right to freedom of inquiry would sanction some of the things that have been done to humans in the name of science. For example, in the eighteenth century "charity children" were infected with smallpox in experiments conducted by Princess Caroline. Early in the twentieth century condemned criminals in the Philippines were injected with plague bacillus. And as recently as the 1960's, black prisoners in

Alabama were left untreated to suffer from syphilis after having been intentionally infected. That there are limitations on what can be done in the name of science is a principle that is enshrined in international agreements, including the Nuremberg Code of 1947 and the World Medical Association's Declaration of Helsinki drafted in 1961. Since some limits on the right to freedom of inquiry clearly are justified, the unlimited use of animals cannot be defended by appealing to some supposed absolute right to freedom of inquiry. For this reason the Freedom Argument, like the others before it, fails to provide a rational defense of the Unlimited Use Position.[13]

20 Although we haven't canvassed all possible arguments that might be given in support of the Unlimited Use Position, we have examined those that seem most common. None of these arguments provides any rational support for this Position. It is now time to examine an alternative view.

II.

21 The No Use Position holds that no use of any animal for any scientific purpose is ever permissible. Is this position rationally defensible? We think not. We propose to argue for this conclusion in ways analogous to the case made against the Unlimited Use Position. We shall characterize some representative arguments for this position, indicating where and why these arguments go wrong.

22 Before addressing these arguments, it is worth noting that the reasonableness of the No Use Position does not follow from the inadequacy of the Unlimited Use Position, any more than it follows, say, that no men are bald because it is false that all men are. Those who accept the No Use Position may take some comfort in our critique of the Unlimited Use Position, but they cannot infer from that critique that their own position is on the side of the truth.

23 We shall discuss four arguments for the No Use Position. Here is the Pain Argument.
1. If an action causes pain to another being, then it is not morally permissible.
2. The use of animals for scientific purposes causes animals pain.
3. Therefore, no use of any animal for any scientific purpose is morally permissible.

We should note first that not all scientific uses made of animals cause them pain. For example, some experimental uses of animals involve operant conditioning techniques, and most of these do not cause pain at all. Other experiments call for minor modifications in animals' diets or environments. Still others require killing anesthetized animals. The Pain Argument does not provide a basis for objecting to any of these uses of animals. Because the Pain Argument cites no morally relevant consideration in addition to pain, it cannot provide a thorough-going defense of the No Use Position.

24 More importantly, the Pain Argument is defective from the outset. Contrary to what the first premise states, it is sometimes permissible to cause pain to others. Dentists cause pain. Surgeons cause pain. Wrestlers, football players, boxers cause pain. But it does not follow that these individuals do something that is not permissible. Granted, the presumption is always against someone's causing pain; nevertheless, causing pain is not itself sufficient for judging an act impermissible.

25 Suppose, however, that, unlike the case of dentists, pain is caused against one's will or without one's informed consent. Does it follow that what we've done is wrong? This is what the In-

formed Consent Argument alleges. Here is the argument.

1. If an action causes pain to another being without that being's informed consent, then it is not morally permissible.
2. The use of animals for scientific purposes causes animals pain without their informed consent.
3. Therefore, no use of any animal for any scientific purpose is morally permissible.

The second premise is open to the same objections raised against the corresponding premise in the Pain Argument: Not all scientific uses made of animals cause them pain. Thus, one cannot object to every use made of animals on this ground. Besides, animals are not the sort of beings who *can* give or withhold their informed consent. Explanations of what will be done to them in an experiment or test cannot be understood by them, so there is no possibility of "informing" them. Thus, there is no coherent possibility of causing them pain "without their informed consent."

26   The first premise also falls short of the truth. Suppose that a small child has appendicitis. If not operated on, the condition will worsen and she will die. Scary details omitted, the situation is explained to the child. She will have none of it: "No operation for me," we are told. The operation is performed without the child's consent and causes some amount of pain. Was it wrong to perform the operation? It is preposterous to answer affirmatively. Thus, we have a counterexample to the basic assumption of the Informed Consent Argument, the assumption that it is not permissible to cause others pain without their informed consent.

27   Still, one might say that there is a difference between hurting others (causing them pain) and harming them (doing something that is detri-

mental to their welfare). Moreover, it might be suggested that in the example of the child and appendicitis, what we've stumbled upon is the fact that something that hurts might not harm. Accordingly, it might be held that what is always wrong is not causing pain, or causing others pain without their informed consent; rather, what is always wrong is harming others. This suggestion gains additional credence when we observe that even a painless death can be a great harm to a given individual. These considerations suggest another argument. Here is the Harm argument.

1. If an action harms another being, then it is not morally permissible.
2. The use of animals for scientific purposes harms animals.
3. Therefore, no use of any animal for any scientific purpose is morally permissible.

This argument, like the ones before it, has gaping holes in it. First, it is clear that it will not even serve as a basis for opposing all animal experimentation, since not all animal experimentation harms animals. More fundamentally, it is simply not true that it is always wrong to harm another. Suppose that while walking alone at night, you are attacked and that through luck or skill you repel your assailant who falls beneath your defensive blows, breaks his neck, and is confined to bed from that day forth, completely paralyzed from the neck down. We mince words if we deny that what you did harmed your assailant. Yet we do not say that what you did is therefore wrong. After all, you were innocent; you were just minding your own business. Your assailant, on the other hand, hardly qualifies as innocent. He attacked you. It would surely be an unsatisfactory morality that failed to discriminate between what you as an innocent victim may do in self-defense, and what your attacker can do in offense against your person or your property.

Thus despite the initial plausibility of the first premise of the Harm Argument, not all cases of harming another are impermissible.

28   The difficulties with the Harm Argument suggest a fourth argument, the Innocence Argument.

1. If an action causes harm to an innocent individual, then it is not permissible, no matter what the circumstances.

2. Animals are innocent.

3. The use of animals for scientific purposes harms them.

4. Therefore, no use of any animal for any scientific purpose is morally permissible.

This argument, unlike the Harm Argument, can account for the case of the assailant, since by attacking you the assailant ceases to be innocent, and therefore in harming him you have not wronged him. In this respect if in no other, the Innocence Argument marks a genuine improvement over the Harm Argument. Nevertheless, problems remain. Again, since animals are not always harmed when used for scientific purposes, the Innocence Argument does not provide a foundation for the No Use Position. It could also be argued that animals cannot be viewed as innocent. We shall return to this issue in the following section. The more fundamental question, however, is whether the basic assumption of this argument is correct: Is it always wrong to harm an innocent individual, no matter what the circumstances?

29   Here we reach a point where philosophical opinion is sharply divided. Some philosophers evidently are prepared to answer this question affirmatively.[14] Others, ourselves included, are not. One way to argue against an affirmative answer to this question is to highlight, by means of more or less far-fetched hypothetical examples, what the implications of an affirmative answer would be. The use of such "thought-experiments" is intended to shed light on the gray areas of our thought by asking how alternative positions would view far-fetched hypothetical cases. The hope is that we may then return to the more complex situations of everyday life with a better understanding of how to reach the best judgment in these cases. So let us construct a thought-experiment, and indicate how it can be used to contest the view that it is always wrong to harm an innocent individual, no matter what the circumstances. (A second thought-experiment will be undertaken near the beginning of Section III.)

30   Imagine this case.[15] Together with four other friends, you have gone caving (spelunking) along the Pacific coast. The incoming tide catches your group by surprise and you are faced with the necessity of making a quick escape through the last remaining accessible opening to the cave or else all will drown. Unfortunately, the first person to attempt the escape gets wedged in the opening. All efforts to dislodge him, including his own frantic attempts, are unsuccessful. It so happens that one member of your party has brought dynamite along, so that the means exist to widen the opening. However to use the explosive to enlarge the escape route is certain to kill your trapped friend. The situation, then, is this: If the explosive is used, then it is certain that one will die and likely that four will escape unharmed. If the explosive is not used, it is certain that all five will die. All the persons involved are innocent. What ought to be done? Morally speaking, is it permissible to use the dynamite despite the fact that doing so is certain to harm an innocent person?

31   Those who think it is always wrong to harm an innocent individual, no matter what the circumstances, must say that using the dynamite

would be wrong. But how can this be? If the death of one innocent individual is a bad thing, then the death of considerably more than one innocent individual must be that much worse. Accordingly, if it is claimed that you would be doing wrong if you performed an act that brought about the death of one innocent individual *because it is wrong to act in ways that harm an innocent individual,* then it must be a more grievous wrong for you to act in ways that will bring equivalent harm to a greater number of innocent individuals. But if this is so, then we have reason to deny that it is always wrong to harm an innocent individual, *no matter what the circumstances.* What our thought experiment suggests is that it is possible that some circumstances might be so potentially bad that morality will permit us to harm an innocent individual. In the thought-experiment it would be permissible to use the dynamite.

32   Those who incline toward viewing the prohibition against harming the innocent as absolute, admitting of no exceptions whatever, are not likely to be persuaded to give up this view just by the weight of the argument of the previous paragraphs. The debate will — and should — continue. One point worth making, however, is that those who like ourselves do not view this prohibition as absolute can nevertheless regard it as very serious, just as, for example, one can view the obligation to keep one's promises as a very serious moral requirement without viewing it as absolute. Imagine that you have borrowed a chain saw from a friend, promising to return it whenever he asks for it. Imagine he turns up at your door in a visibly drunken state, accompanied by a bound and gagged companion who has already been severely beaten and is in a state of terror. "I'll have my chainsaw now," he intones. Ought you to return it, under *those* circum-

stances? The obligation to keep one's promises can be regarded as quite serious without our having to say, yes, by all means, you ought to fetch the chain saw! There are other considerations that bear on the morality of what you ought to do in addition to the fact that you have made a promise. Similarly, the fact that some action will harm an innocent individual is not the only consideration that is relevant to assessing the morality of that action. In saying this we do not mean to suggest that this consideration is not an important one. It is, and we shall attempt to develop its importance more fully in the following section. All that we mean to say is that it is not the only morally relevant consideration.

33   There would appear to be cases, then, whether they be far-fetched hypothetical ones or ones that might arise in the real world, in which morality permits us to harm an innocent individual. Thus, even in those cases in which animals used for scientific purposes are harmed, and even assuming that they are innocent, it does not follow that how they are used is morally wrong. Like the other arguments reviewed in this section, the Innocence Argument fails to provide an acceptable basis for the No Use Position. Assuming, as we do, that these arguments provide a fair representation of those available to advocates of this position, we conclude that the No Use Position lacks a rationally compelling foundation, either in fact, or in logic, or in morality.

III.

34 The previous two sections criticized two extreme positions, one favoring, the other opposing, all uses of animals for scientific purposes. In the present section, and in the one that follows, two different arguments will be developed for less extreme positions, positions which though they

place severe limitations on when animals may be used in science, do allow for the possibility that some animals may sometimes be used for some purposes, even some that harm them. The argument of the present section takes up where the argument of the last one ended: with the wrongness of harming the innocent. The argument of the next section is based on the different idea of maximizing the balance of good over evil. The differences between the two arguments will be sketched in Section V.

35   The prohibition against harming innocent individuals is a very serious, but not an absolute, prohibition. Because it is not absolute, it has justified exceptions. The problem is to say under what circumstances an exception is permitted. Perhaps the best way to begin formulating an answer is to again consider the spelunking example. Notice first that in that case we assumed that other alternatives had been exhausted; for example, every effort had been made to find an alternative route of escape and to dislodge your trapped friend. Second, we assumed that you had very good reason to believe that all would be drowned if the only remaining exit was not widened. Very dreadful consequences – death – would obtain, therefore, for five as compared with one person, if the dynamite was not used. These considerations suggest a modified principle concerning the harming of those who are innocent. We shall call this principle the "Modified Innocence Principle" (MIP), and formulate it in the following way.

> (MIP) It is wrong to harm an innocent individual unless it is reasonable to believe that doing so is the only realistic way of avoiding equal harm for many other innocents.[16]

The role of this principle can be illustrated by means of another regrettably not too far-fetched thought-experiment.

36   Imagine that a terrorist has possession of a well-armed tank and is systematically slaughtering forty-five innocent hostages who he has fastened to a wall.[17] Attempts to negotiate a compromise fail. The man will kill all the hostages if we do nothing. Under the circumstances, there is only one reasonable alternative: Blow up the tank. But there is this complication: The terrorist has strapped a young girl to the tank, and any weapon sufficient to blow up the tank will kill the child. The girl is innocent. Thus to blow up the tank is to harm an innocent, one who herself stands no chance of benefiting from the attack. Ought we to blow up the tank?

37   MIP would sanction doing so. If, as we argued in the previous section, it is worse that harm befalls many innocent individuals than that an equal harm befall one, then surely it would be worse if all the hostages were killed rather than just the one innocent child. Moreover, we have assumed that other alternatives to the attack have been tried, that they have failed, and that the only realistic way to prevent the slaughter of the remaining hostages is to blow up the tank. Thus MIP should not be understood as sanctioning a policy of "shooting first and asking questions later." It is only *after* other non-violent or less violent alternatives have been exhausted that we are permitted to do what will harm an innocent individual.

38   Problems remain however. Consider the notion of "equal harm." MIP will not permit harming an innocent just so that others might avoid some minor inconvenience. We cannot, for example, confine innocent vagrants to concentration camps just because we find their appearance aesthetically displeasing. Still, not all harms are equal. It is a matter of degree how much a given harm will detract from an individual's well-being, and problems will arise con-

cerning just how serious a given harm is, or whether two or more different harms are "equal." Moreover, there is also certain to be a problem concerning the number of innocents involved. The thought-experiment involving the terrorist and the tank was a clear case of harming one innocent in order to prevent equal harm to many other innocents. But how many is many? If the only way to avoid the death of two innocents is to kill one, ought we to do this? This question, and others like it, would have to be explored in a comprehensive examination of MIP. We by-pass them now, not because they are unimportant, but because they are less important than another question which cannot be passed over. This concerns the very intelligibility of viewing animals as innocent. The fundamental nature of this issue is clear. If no sense can be made of the idea of the "innocence of animals," then whatever else may be said of MIP, at least this much could be: It simply would be inapplicable to our relations with animals. So let us ask whether sense can be made of the view that animals are innocent.

39 One argument against the intelligibility of animal innocence is The Moral Agent Argument.

1. Only moral agents can be innocent.
2. Animals are not moral agents.
3. Therefore, animals cannot be innocent.

By "moral agents" is meant individuals who can act from a sense of right and wrong, who can deliberate about what they ought to do, who can act and not merely react, and who thus can be held accountable or responsible for what they do or fail to do. Normal adult human beings are the clearest examples of individuals having the status of moral agents.

40 The first premise states that only moral agents can be innocent. Why might this be claimed? The most likely explanation is the following. Because moral agents are responsible for their actions, they can be accused of acting wrongly. Individuals who are not moral agents, however, can do no wrong. If a tree falls on someone causing death or injury, it makes no sense to condemn the tree. Since the tree "had no choice," it cannot be faulted. Moral agents can be faulted, however. If a moral agent commits murder, then he has done what is wrong; he is guilty of an offense. Suppose, however, that a moral agent is falsely accused of committing murder; he is not guilty; he is (and here is the crucial word) innocent. Thus it makes perfectly good sense to say that a moral agent is innocent because moral agents can be guilty. It makes no sense to say that a tree is innocent because trees cannot be guilty.

41 The second premise denies that animals are moral agents. This *seems* true. Granted, we reward and punish animals for their behavior, hoping to incline them towards behaving in ways we prefer and away from those we do not; but it is doubtful that many, if any, animals meet the requirements of moral agency.[18] Thus, if the first premise of the Moral Agent Argument is accepted, and assuming as we shall that the second premise is true, then there would seem to be no way to avoid the conclusion that animals cannot be innocent. If, like trees, they cannot be guilty, then they cannot be innocent either. And if this conclusion cannot be avoided, a conclusive case would have been made against viewing MIP as bearing on the morality of how animals may be treated. Since MIP is concerned with how *innocent* individuals may be treated, it has no bearing on how animals may be treated, if animals cannot be innocent.

42 But is it true that animals cannot be innocent? The preceding argument at most estab-

lishes only that they cannot be innocent in the sense that moral agents can be said to be innocent. Is this the only intelligible sense of "innocence" that plays a role in our moral thought? The answer is definitely no, if we take our actual practice as our guide. Much of the debate over the morality of abortion, for example, centers on the alleged "innocence of the fetus." If only moral agents can be innocent, then referring to the fetus as "innocent" cannot make sense. The same is true when very young children who are killed or maimed are referred to as "innocent victims." Since they are not moral agents, it ought to be senseless to refer to them in this way. But in actual practice we do speak this way, which suggests that the concept of innocence is not restricted in its application to moral agents only, but can be meaningfully applied to those individuals who are *moral patients.*[19] These are those individuals who, though they are not moral agents and thus can do no wrong, can be the *undeserving recipients* of wrongs done to them by others. That is, they can *be* wronged, even though they can *do* no wrong. Children *are* the innocent victims of war, in this sense, not because they can be falsely accused of some wrongdoing, but because they can be made to suffer undeserved harm, in this case, undeserved harm done to them by those who make war.

43   A question arises regarding what individuals qualify as moral patients. Our answer harkens back to our earlier discussion of the moral community. An individual qualifies as a member of that community, we claimed, if it is possible for others to wrong her directly. Thus moral agents qualify, but so do moral patients. Young children, the aged and helpless, the mentally enfeebled and the emotionally deranged of all ages, qualify as members of the moral community if it is possible to wrong them. In order

to avoid the prejudice of speciesism we must also recognize that all those *animals* who can be harmed must likewise be recognized as members of the moral community, not because they can do what is wrong, but because, as moral patients, they can suffer wrongs.

44   An argument has been offered for the intelligibility of the idea of animal innocence. This is a controversial subject, and we shall return to it again at the beginning of the following section. If we assume for the moment that animals can be innocent in a morally relevant way, then we may also assume that MIP does apply to how we may treat them, and thus develop the implications of its applicability to the use of animals in science by means of the following argument, the Modified Innocence Argument.

1. It is wrong to harm the innocent unless we have very good reason to believe that this is the only realistic way to prevent equal harm for many other innocents.
2. Animals are innocent.
3. Therefore, it is not permissible to harm them unless the conditions set forth in premise (1) are satisfied.
4. At least a great deal of the use of animals in science harmful to them fails to meet the conditions set forth in premise (1).
5. Therefore, at least a great deal of this use is wrong.

The first and second premises already have been addressed. The conclusion drawn in step three follows from steps one and two. The step that remains to be examined is the fourth one, and it is to the task of defending it that we shall now turn.

45   As a minimal condition, MIP requires that it be reasonable to believe that the harming of an innocent will prevent equal harm to many other innocents. Apart from the issue of experi-

mentation, it is clear that not all uses of animals in science harmful to them satisfy this requirement. For example, very many animals are harmed for instructional purposes in school and laboratory settings and in science fairs. The fulfilment of these purposes cannot reasonably be viewed as an essential step leading to the prevention of equal harms for many other innocents.[20] As for experimentation, it is clear that there are many cases in which animals are harmed to obtain trivial bits of knowledge. For example, recently the Canadian Department of Indian Affairs and Northern Development spent $80,000 to determine the effect of oil spills on polar bears.[21] The procedure involved immersing three polar bears in a container of crude oil and water. One polar bear died after licking oil from her fur for 12 hours. A second polar bear was killed for "humane reasons" after suffering intense pain from kidney failure. The third survived after suffering from severe infection that was caused by injections that the bear was given through her oil-stained skin by veterinarians who were attempting to treat her for the kidney and liver damage that was caused by her immersion in oil. The Canadian government, with the cooperation of the American government, is now planning to conduct similar experiments on dolphins.

46   The polar bear experiment is not an isolated incident. There is a growing body of literature that documents the triviality of much that routinely passes for "original scientific research."[22] The situation in toxicology testing is regrettably similar, as the following test illustrates.

47   The standard measure of the toxicity of a substance (i.e., the accepted measure of the degree to which a given substance is poisonous to humans) is its median lethal dose. The median lethal dose, or the LD_{50} as it is called, is defined as the amount of a substance needed to kill 50% of the test animals to which it is administered. The United States Government requires that the LD_{50} be determined for each new substance bound for the market. The substances in question are not just exotic life-saving drugs, but include such ordinary products as the latest household detergent, shoe polish, oven cleaner, deodorants and soda pop. There are at least two reasons for believing that these tests, which cause great harm to the test animals, will not prevent equal harm to many other innocents. First, many of the substances for which the LD_{50} is obtained already are known to be relatively non-toxic. As a result, enormous quantities of these substances must be forcibly fed or otherwise administered to the test animals in order to cause 50% fatalities. In such cases it is often very clear long before 50% of the test animals have died, that the substance poses no serious threat to human beings. To put the point baldly: Determining the toxicity of substances which are never likely to harm anyone except the test animals to whom they are initially administered, is blatantly impermissible, given MIP. There is no good reason to believe that these tests *will* prevent equal harm to many other innocents.

48   But secondly, the data obtained in LD_{50} tests often are just not reliable. There are a number of reasons why. (1) It is not always possible to extrapolate toxicity data from animals to humans. As an expert in the field has noted, "(t)here are countless known examples of ... species differences."[23] Penicillin is highly toxic to guinea pigs but not to humans, while strychnine is highly poisonous to humans but not to guinea pigs. Dinitrophonol will not cause cataracts in most laboratory animals but will in humans, and morphine, which is an effective sedative for humans, has the exact opposite effect on cats.

(More will be said about the problem of extrapolation in the next section.) (2) LD_{50} tests are not performed in a uniform way. Differences in the test animals' strain, sex, age, ambient and nutritional condition, and so forth, often result in the reporting of different LD_{50} for the same substance. Studies of four household chemicals conducted in six different laboratories produced toxicity data that were inconsistent, not just with respect to the absolute toxicity of the four substances but with respect to their relative toxicity as well.[24] Though this is perhaps an extreme case, the phenomenon is not uncommon, and serves to illustrate why a test like the LD_{50} fails to comply with MIP: We simply do not have good reason to believe that the harm done to the test animals will prevent equal harm to many other innocents.

49   MIP also requires that other realistic alternatives be exhausted before it is permissible to harm an innocent individual. This requirement does make a difference. If, prior to attempted negotiations with the terrorist, for example, we blew up the tank, we would be morally culpable. We would have resorted to violence, knowing this would harm the innocent child, without having first determined whether we could have acted to prevent harm being done to *all* the innocents. So let us ask whether all scientific uses of animals harmful to them is undertaken only after other realistic alternatives have been tried.

50   Unfortunately, the answer is no: a great deal of the use made of animals in science clearly fails to satisfy this requirement, though of course we cannot say exactly how much, anymore than we can say exactly how much water there is in the Pacific. What we can say is that the amount in each case is *a lot.* "But there are no alternatives," it is often said. This is an answer that we shall

examine more fully shortly. Sometimes, however, there *are* well established alternatives to the use of animals. These alternatives include tissue and cell cultures, mathematical modelling, chemical analysis, mechanical models, clinical examination and epidemological surveys.[25] In cases where there are established, scientifically viable alternatives to using animals and other innocent individuals who can be hurt or harmed (e.g., humans), MIP requires that these alternatives be employed and not the innocents.

51   However, it remains true that sometimes, in some cases, there are no known alternatives that have been proven to be scientifically reliable. What does MIP imply about these cases? Here we must take note of an important disanalogy between the scientific enterprise and our thought-experiments. Those experiments presented us with crisis situations in which the alternatives are clearly defined, in which neither time nor circumstances allow for the investigation of new options, and in which we could not reasonably be expected to have done anything before the crisis developed so that we might have another realistic option at our disposal. (There is nothing we could reasonably be expected to do today, for example, to increase the options that would be available to us in the extremely unlikely event that we should find ourselves in the predicament we imagined in the spelunking example). There is, however, a great deal that science can begin to do today and could have done in the past in an effort to explore alternatives to the use of animals for scientific purposes. Time and circumstances *do* allow for the scientific investigation of such alternatives; indeed, it is part of the very essence of the scientific enterprise to search for new ways to approach old (and emerging) problems. The longer the life-sciences, including psychology,[26]

are delayed in making a conscientious effort to search for alternatives, the greater the wrong, given MIP, since an insufficient commitment in this regard itself offends against the spirit of MIP. To harm the innocent is so *serious* a moral matter that we must do all that we can reasonably be expected to do so that we can avoid causing this harm. If the life-sciences, through lack of will, funding, or both, fail to do all that can reasonably be expected of them in this regard, then we have no reason to assume that the use made of animals in science is justified "because there are no available alternatives." On the contrary, we have reason to deny the moral propriety of such use. To put this same point differently: Since we are justified in believing that it is wrong to harm the innocent unless we can be shown that it isn't, we are justified in regarding the harm caused to animals in science as unjustified unless we can be shown that all that reasonably could be done has been done to avoid causing it. If we cannot be shown that these efforts have been made, then we are right to regard their use as wrong, given MIP.

52   Viewed from this perspective, *at least most* harmful use of animals in science ought to be regarded as morally unjustified. The "search for alternatives" has been a largely token effort, one that has not been given a priority anywhere approaching that required by MIP. But this is not the fault only of those involved in the life-sciences. As a society we have not seriously thought about the moral status of animals. We have failed to recognize that animals are members of the moral community, or we have minimized the importance of their membership. As a result, we have not funded the search for alternatives sufficiently. Since (as it is well said) "research goes where the money is," the investigation of alternatives has not prospered.

53   Those involved in the life-sciences are not entirely free of responsibility however. Though they do not control the flow of money from public and private sources, their voice is not without its influence. Moreover, the voices of scientists carry more weight in determining what research finds funding than do the voices of ordinary citizens, or even the voices of those active in the humane movement. A demand on the part of scientists that the search for alternatives be given the priority MIP requires is essential, if this search is to have any chance of receiving the funding that acceptance of MIP would require.

54   We may conclude the present section, then, as follows. About much use of animals in science that harms them, it is false to suppose that it will prevent equal harm befalling many other innocents. About some harmful use that might prevent such harm, it is false to suppose that these uses are known to be the only realistic way to achieve such results. And about most use of animals that causes them harm, it is false to suppose that as a society we have made the conscientious effort to search for alternatives that the MIP requires. Thus, if MIP should guide our behavior with respect to animals, we cannot avoid concluding that *at least most* of the uses made of animals in science that harms them is not morally permissible – is morally wrong.

IV.

55 The argument of the previous section relied heavily on the idea that animals are innocent. The attempt to undermine this idea by means of the Moral Agent Argument was considered and found wanting. There are other ways to contest this idea, however. The Rights Argument is one.

1. Only those individuals who have rights can be innocent.
2. Animals cannot have rights.
3. Therefore, animals cannot be innocent.

A defense of the first premise might proceed along the following lines. To speak of individuals as innocent assumes that they can suffer *undeserved* harm. But undeserved harm must be harm that is unjust or unfair, and what is unjust or unfair is what violates an individual's rights. Thus, only those individuals who have rights can be the recipients of undeserved harm. As for the second premise, not very long ago it was assumed to be so obvious as not to require any supporting argument at all. Recently, however, the idea of animal rights has been debated, and there is a steadily growing body of literature, in an expanding number of prestigious professional journals from scientific and humanistic disciplines, devoted to the reflective assessment of this idea.[27] It will not be possible to review this debate on the present occasion. We mention it only in order to indicate how the idea of the innocence of animals is relevant to the more widely discussed idea of animal rights. A thorough examination of the former idea would have to include a thorough examination of the latter one as well.

56 It is possible to approach the question of the ethics of animal use in science from a perspective that does not place fundamental importance on innocence and the allied idea of rights. Utilitarianism is one such perspective. It is a view that has attracted many able thinkers, and represents today, in the English speaking world at least, the primary alternative to views of morality that place central importance on individual rights. Moreover, utilitarianism's most influential advocates, from Jeremy Bentham (1748-1832) and John Stuart Mill (1806-1873) to the contemporary Australian philosopher Peter Singer, have explicitly recognized the membership of animals in the moral community. It will be instructive, therefore, to sketch the utilitarian position in general and to mark its implications for the use of animals for scientific purposes in particular.

57 Utilitarianism is the view that we ought to act so as to bring about the greatest possible balance of good over evil for everyone affected. Utilitarianism is thus not a selfish doctrine; it does not prescribe that each individual is to act so as to maximize his or her own self-interest. For the utilitarian, your neighbor's good counts the same as yours; in Bentham's words, "Each to count for one, no one for more than one." In trying to decide what ought to be done, therefore, we must consider the interests of everyone involved, being certain to count equal interests equally. The point of view required by utilitarianism is uncompromisingly impartial; we are not allowed to favor our own interests, or those of our friends, or say, White-Anglo-Saxon-Protestant's, over the like interests of others. It is, in the words of the nineteenth century utilitarian Henry Sidgwick, "the point of view of the universe." For the utilitarian, the ideas of the innocence and the rights of individuals are not independent considerations to be used in determining what ought to be done. They have a role only if they bear on the determination of what the best consequences would be. Utilitarianism recommends a "forward-looking" morality. Results are the only things that matter in the determination of right and wrong.

58 Utilitarians have disagreed over many points, including the nature of the good consequences they seek and the evil ones they seek to avoid. Classical utilitarians, including Bentham and Mill, viewed goodness as pleasure and evil as

pain. Some recent utilitarians understand goodness as the satisfaction of an individual's preferences.[28] On either view, many animals must find a place in the utilitarian calculation of the best consequences, if, following these thinkers, we agree that many animals can experience what is pleasant or painful, or have preferences. For the sake of simplicity, in what follows we shall think of good consequences (utility) as pleasure, and bad consequences (disutility) as pain.

59   Bentham, in an oft-quoted and justly famous passage, declares the relevance of the pain of animals in the following way.

> The French have already discovered that the blackness of the skin is no reason why a human being should be abandoned without redress to the caprice of a tormentor. It may come one day to be recognized, that the number of the legs, the villosity of the skin, or the termination of the *os sacrum*, are reasons equally insufficient for abandoning a sensitive being to the same fate.... (T)he question is not, Can they *reason?* nor, Can they *talk?* but, Can they *suffer?*[29]

If we assume, as we have throughout, that the animals of which we speak can suffer, how might a utilitarian such as Bentham argue against their use for scientific purposes? Clearly no utilitarian would accept the principal assumption of the Pain Argument; the assumption that it is *always* wrong to cause another pain. The permissibility of causing pain, like the permissibility of performing any other act, must depend for the utilitarian on the utility of doing it, and since it could be true in any given case that we will bring about the best consequences for everyone involved by an act that causes pain to some individual(s), the utilitarian will not accept the prohibition against causing pain as absolute (as impermissible at all times, no matter what the consequences).

60   It remains true, nevertheless, that utilitarians will regard causing pain as a negative feature of an act. Any action which causes pain and fails to bring about a greater amount of pleasure will be ruled out by the utilitarian as morally wrong, except when every other alternative action would bring about an even greater balance of pain over pleasure. Thus one way of formulating the Utilitarian Argument against the use of animals in science is the following.

1. Acts are not morally permissible if they cause pain to some individuals and yet fail to bring about the best possible consequences for everyone involved.

2. A great deal of the scientific use of animals causes them pain and fails to bring about the best possible consequences.

3. Therefore, a great deal of this use is not morally permissible.

61   There are many reasons for accepting the second premise of this argument. Even in the case of animal based experimentation or research, much is redundant, and is carried on well beyond the threshold needed for replication. Experimental studies of shock are a good example. As early as 1946 a survey of the literature indicated that over 800 papers had been published on experimental studies of shock. These studies induced shock by various means, including: tourniquets, hammer-blows, rotations in the Noble-Collip drum, gunshot wounds, strangulation, intestinal loops, burning and freezing. By 1954 a survey article reported that although "animal investigations in the field of traumatic shock have yielded diversified and often contradictory results," the investigators looked forward to "future experimentation in this field."[30] In 1974 researchers still described their work as "preliminary." Presumably such work will continue as long as someone is willing to fund it.

62   There is no question but that much animal experimentation, like the research on shock described in the previous paragraph, continues from habit, convenience, desire for professional advancement and so forth. Dr. Roger Ulrich, one of the leading researchers in aggression studies, has performed experiments on rats that involve blinding, mutilation and castration, as well as the administration of electric shock and bursts of intense noise. Recently, in a letter to the American Psychological Association's *Monitor*, he wrote:

> Initially my research was prompted by the desire to understand and help solve the problem of human aggression but I later discovered that the results of my work did not seem to justify its continuance. Instead I began to wonder if perhaps financial rewards, professional prestige, the opportunity to travel, etc., were the maintaining factors.[31]

63   Other experiments are performed in order to confirm hypotheses that almost everyone already knows are true. The experiments on polar bears discussed in the previous section are an obvious example. As one Vancouver newspaper editorialized:

> The experts wanted to determine the effects of oil spills on the polar bears. Apparently no children of, say, 12 years of age were on hand to give them a pretty good idea.[32]

Moreover, similar experiments had been conducted in Canada on seals only five years before. To the surprise of no one except possibly the researchers, most of the seals died after being immersed in oil.

64   Other experiments are performed in order to falsify hypotheses that almost everyone knows are false. Here is the voice of David Hubel of Harvard Medical School reporting one such case.

A few years ago the notion was advanced that memories might be recorded in the form of large molecules, with the information encoded in a sequence of smaller molecules, as genetic information is encoded in DNA. Few people familiar with the highly patterned specificity of connections in the brain took the idea seriously, and yet much time was consumed in many laboratories teaching animals tasks, grinding up their brains and either finding differences in the brain chemistry of the trained animals or finding "statistically significant" improvement in the ability of other animals, into which extracts of the trained animals' brains were injected, to learn the same tasks. The fad has died out....[33]

65   Many animal experiments are rendered useless by the unreliability of the data obtained. Experimental results have been found to vary depending on the time of day that the experiment was performed, the appearance of the researcher, the temperature of the room and other equally subtle factors. It is almost impossible to control such complex background variables.[34] Moreover, even when the data are reliable with respect to the test animals, the problem of extrapolating the results to humans remains severe. As two prominent researchers from the Institute of Experimental Pathology and Toxicology of the Albany Medical College have written:

> At the present time ... the legitimate question can still be asked, for we do not have the answer: "How can we be sure that the extrapolation of animal data to man is accurate?"[35]

After noting substantive difficulties in extrapolating data, the authors conclude:

> To be sure, these data may have little or no relevance to man, but they are the best basis for prediction of hazard to man that we have at the present time.... Unfortunately, Alexander Pope's remark of many years ago, "The proper study of

mankind is man" is still true. Various committees of the World Health Organization find of the National Academy of Sciences are in general agreement with this statement.[36]

In another paper, one of the co-authors goes so far as to advance the proposal that routinely using animals as test or experimental models is premature at best.

> Species differences in metabolism is one of the primary reasons why projection of animal data to man is not always possible. Differences in the metabolic pathways and the rate of detoxification are observed among the animal species and between animals and man. That is why early trial in man, to learn something of the metabolic rate and pathway in man, as compared to animals, is recommended before long-term animal studies are initiated.[37]

The extrapolation problem is so severe, then, that at least one prominent toxicologist has advocated human studies *before* long-term animal studies! This suggestion, of course, raises ethical issues of its own. But one must certainly wonder why and how animal tests would be necessary at all in a situation in which a substance had already been administered to humans.

66   The utilitarian argument could go even further. John Cairns, Director of the Imperial Cancer Research Fund's Mill Hill Laboratory in London, has pointed out that during the last 150 years in the Western world, there has been an enormous increase in life expectancy.[38] He notes that this increase in life expectancy began before the advent of "what we would call medical science" and argues that it is primarily due to better nutrition and hygiene rather than to the development of exotic new drugs and surgical procedures. He goes on to say that the chance of dying of cancer in the United States has not altered appreciably in the last 35 years, in spite

of intense research activity. Claims to the contrary are based on statistical gimmicks: Since "cure" is defined as survival five years after diagnosis, the earlier a cancer is diagnosed the greater the likelihood of cure, even if the course of the disease and the time of death are unaffected in any way. In commenting on the eradication of infectious diseases, Cairns claims:

> It is significant, however, that what is often thought of as one of the accomplishments of sophisticated medical science was, in large part, the product of some fairly simple improvements in public health. In the end, history may well repeat itself and the same prove to be true for cancer.[39]

Cairns is not the only prominent figure in the scientific establishment to have made such an argument. Perhaps it goes too far, but it does suggest how thorough-going a utilitarian critique of animal experimentation, or the use of animals in toxicology experiments or in education, can be. If most of our use of animals in these activities are largely irrelevant to producing longer and pleasanter lives, then there is no justification for using animals in ways that cause them pain.

67   But it is not just the unreliability and redundancy of the data that utilitarians will contest. They can also object to the *kind* of animal used for scientific purposes. Rocks cannot feel pleasure or pain. Only conscious beings can. Nevertheless, there are great differences among conscious beings regarding the degree or level of their consciousness. Some conscious beings have a conception of their own identity, a self-concept: they can make plans for the future, regret the past, and envision their own bodily death. Beings that lack a concept of self might experience something like pleasure, but they cannot anticipate future pleasure, nor regret those pleasures they have missed in the past. It is for this reason that we think of some beings

as having more complex, richer and "higher" states of consciousness than other conscious beings. Beings with a sense of self are utility "hot spots," so to speak. Because they have the kind of consciousness they do, they can experience richer, fuller pleasures and pains, and because of this we should take special care to maximize their pleasures and minimize their pains. That would seem to be a winning strategy for bringing about the best consequences.

68   Where, precisely, we draw the line between animals who do, and those who do not, have a concept of self is unclear. Probably there is no *precise* line to be drawn. That problem is not what demands our attention just now. The point to notice is that utilitarianism will not allow the use of animals having higher levels of consciousness, even if their use would bring about a net balance of good over evil, if these same (or better) results could be obtained by using animals of less highly developed consciousness. Wherever possible, that is, utilitarianism requires that science deal with the most rudimentary forms of conscious life *and* as few of these as possible, or, most preferable by far, with non-conscious beings, living or otherwise. Since there is ample evidence that most chimpanzees, for example, have a sense of self,[40] and growing evidence that some species of Cetaceans do,[41] the case for regarding these animals as having higher consciousness is increasingly reinforced and the utilitarian grounds for cautioning against the use of these animals for scientific purposes is correspondingly strengthened. It is exceedingly doubtful that the 30,000 primates used for scientific purposes in America in 1978 were used justifiably, given the Utilitarian Argument.

69   There is welcome evidence that contemporary scientists, unlike Descartes' contemporaries, are becoming increasingly sensitive to the issues discussed in the previous paragraph. Talk of "the Three R's" is in the air. The goal of research, it is said, is replacement, reduction and refinement. Commenting on these ideas, D. H. Smyth writes that "Replacement (means) the substitution of insentient material for conscious living higher animals. Reduction (means) reduction in the number of animals used to obtain information of given amount and precision. Refinement (means) any decrease in the incidence or severity of inhumane procedure (i.e., pain or suffering) applied to those animals which still have to be used."[42] These are goals that both utilitarians and supporters of the Modified Innocence Principle can endorse. But both positions can be used to press the case for justification of the use of animals in science at a deeper level. The question is, how can any use of any animal for any scientific purpose be justified? To be told that, whenever possible, we ought to replace, reduce or refine, does not address this question. Built into the Three R's is the assumption that the use of animals in science sometimes *is* justified, and it is precisely this question that must be addressed rather than begged. Utilitarianism provides us with one way of answering it, the Modified Innocence Principle provides us with another; but the Three R's provides us with no answer at all.

70   Perhaps it will be replied that the goal of refinement gets at the heart of the matter. "Only that suffering that is absolutely necessary for the scientific integrity of an experiment or test is allowed," it may be said. Suppose this is true. Does it follow that, judged on utilitarian grounds, the animal's use is permissible? It does not. The larger question is whether *the experiment, test, or other use of the animal is itself justified.* Only if it is can the pain involved be justified. Until the issue of the moral justifiability of the animal's use

is addressed, therefore, the justification of the animal's pain, even if the pain is "kept to a minimum," remains in doubt.[43]

71   In summary, the principle of utility demands that stringent requirements be met before we can be justified in using any animal for any scientific purpose that causes it pain. It must be shown that a proposed use will promote the utilitarian objective of bringing about the greatest possible balance of good over evil for everyone involved. If it does not, then, as premise 2 of the Utilitarian Argument asserts, the procedure is morally wrong. There is ample reason to believe that at least a great deal of the use of animals in science does not satisfy this requirement. Thus, if utility be our guide, there is strong reason to condemn much of the current use made of animals in science.

V.

72 In the two preceding sections we sketched two moral perspectives that converge on the same general conclusion: At least much of the scientific use made of animals is morally wrong and ought to be stopped. Despite their agreement in a broad range of cases however, the Principle of Utility and the Modified Innocence Principle (MIP) support conflicting judgments in some cases.

73   Recall that MIP will allow harming an innocent only if we have very good reason to believe that this is the only realistic way to prevent equivalent harm to many other innocents. MIP does not sanction harming innocents so that others may reap positive goods (e.g., pleasures); it is limited to the prevention or elimination of harms or evils (e.g., pain). Thus, in principle, MIP will not allow, say, contests between a few innocent Christians and hungry lions so that great amounts of otherwise unobtainable pleasure might be enjoyed by large numbers of Roman spectators. MIP does not permit evil (the harming of innocents) so that good may come. In principle, utilitarianism could allow this. Classical utilitarianism is aggregative in nature: it is the *total* of goods and evils, for *all* the individuals involved, that matters. Theoretically, then, it is possible that achieving the optimal balance of good over evil in any given case will necessitate harming the innocent. The point can be illustrated abstractly by imagining that we face a choice between two alternatives, A_1 which will harm an innocent individual and A_2 which will not. A utilitarian, we may assume, will assign some disutility, some minus-score, to the harm caused in A_1. Suppose this is -20. Suppose further, however, that A_1 would bring about much better consequences for others than A_2; suppose that the difference is a magnitude of 100 to 1, A_1 yielding benefits that total +1000, A_2 yielding only +10. A greater balance of good over evil would result if we did A_1 than if we did A_2. Utilitarians, therefore, must choose the former alternative, but not those who accept MIP: they must favor the latter alternative (A_2).

74   The Principles of Utility and that of Modified Innocence do differ in theory, therefore, despite their agreement in many practical cases. Which principle ought we to accept? That is far too large an issue to be decided here, but it is pursued in considerable depth in some of the other essays in the present volume.[44] It is enough to realize that utilitarianism theoretically could allow more use of animals in science that harms the animals than MIP allows. Whether or not this difference is a sign of the moral superiority or inferiority of utilitarianism in comparison to MIP, at least this much is clear: there is a difference.

VI.

75 Some general points should be kept in mind as we conclude. First, given either the Principle of Utility or MIP, to harm an animal is in need of moral defense; both principles view the harming of an individual as *presumptively* wrong, as something that is wrong unless it can be shown that it isn't. Given either principle, therefore, the burden of proof must always be on those who cause harm to animals in scientific settings. Unless these persons can show that what they do is morally permissible, we are entitled to believe that it is not. This burden, obvious as it may seem, has not always been recognized. Too often it has been "those who speak for the animals" who have been called upon to shoulder the burden of proof. But it is not the critics, it is the advocates of animal use in science who should bear it. This fundamental point must never be lost sight of in the debate over the ethics of the use of animals in science.

76 Second, the kind of knowledge (one might better say "wisdom") sometimes required to determine the permissibility of using an animal, especially in experiments in basic research, clearly is not the exclusive property of any particular profession, let alone any particular branch of science. For that reason we should draw upon the expertise of many people, from many fields, to review experimental proposals before they are funded. It is very important that these decisions not be left just to those who have a professional interest in their outcome. Not very long ago in this country experiments were performed on humans with impunity. Today we have recognized the merits of the idea that decisions about the permissibility of research that might harm human subjects must be made on a case by case basis, involving the best judgment of persons from diverse areas of expertise; we wouldn't dream of leaving these decisions entirely in the hands of those doing the research. Because animals cannot, except by prejudice, be excluded from the moral community, it is reason, not "mere sentiment," that calls for similar procedural safeguards for their use in science generally and in scientific experimentation in particular. It is not enough, even if it is a salutary development, that principles for the care and maintenance of laboratory animals are in place,[45] though even here one should raise questions about how conscientiously these principles are enforced. How often, for example, has a scientific establishment been found in violation of these principles? And how impartial are those in whose hands the business of enforcement rests? One need not prejudge the answers to these questions by insisting upon the propriety of asking them.

77 At this point someone will accuse us of being "anti-scientific" or, more soberly, perhaps it will be argued that instituting procedural safeguards of the kind we recommend, in which research proposals are considered case by case by a panel of experts from diverse fields, would "rein in science," thus having a chilling effect on important research. The "anti-science" accusation will be answered in this essay's final paragraph. As for the "chilling effect" argument, it is true that adopting the kind of procedural safeguards we recommend *would* place limits on what scientists would be permitted to do. These safeguards would thus restrict the scientists's "freedom to inquire." The right to inquire, however, as was argued earlier, is not absolute; one may not do anything one pleases in the name of this right; it can and should be limited by other, weightier moral concerns. It is no longer possible in this country, for example, to infect

poor Black males in Alabama with syphilis and to record the development of the disease when left untreated. This *is* a restriction on science, but one which ought to be viewed as welcome and appropriate. An unfortunate consequence of instituting and effectively enforcing procedural safeguards for the use of animals in science, it is true, is that research proposals would have to be screened by another, interdisciplinary committee, requiring that yet another set of forms be filled out and so forth. Both the bureaucracy and the red tape are almost certain to increase if our call for safeguards is heeded. Researchers may see "Big Brother" at work, and descry, in the words of a leader in brain transplant research, Robert J. White, "the ever-present danger of government control of biological research through the limitation of animal availability and experimental design."[46] But the inconvenience "red-tape" causes would seem to be a comparatively small price to pay to insure that scientific practice meets the demands of morality. The life-sciences are not physics, and the costs that must be borne in the conduct of biological and psychological research cannot be measured merely in dollars and cents.

78   In reply it may be objected that the kind of safeguards we propose would be impracticable, and, in any event, would cost too much to implement. Neither objection is well-founded. In July of 1977 some initial procedural safeguards for experimental animals were put into place in Sweden. It has been noted that simply by establishing ethics committees to review research proposals, research designs have been improved; and these designs often require the use of fewer animals than was formerly the rule.[47] In addition, greater use is being made of animals with less highly developed conscious lives, animals which, not surprisingly, are cheaper to procure

and maintain; and the employment of less harmful procedures is growing. It has been reported that the Swedish approach has proven satisfactory to many, both in the scientific and in the animal welfare communities. The "Swedish experiment" suggests that it is possible to develop a framework that is practical and financially sound, a framework which, though not a panacea, does go some way toward protecting the interests of animals while at the same time nurturing our interest in the growth and maintenance of science.

79   Two final points. First, nothing that we have said should be taken as condemning the motives, intentions or character of those engaged in scientific research. We are not saying that these people are nasty, vicious, cruel, dehumanized, heartless, depraved, pitiless, evil people. No one who uses animals in science has been accused of being, in White's terminology, a "monster-scientist, perpetrator of abominable crimes."[48] Neither are we saying that "all scientists" are on an ego-trip, motivated to do their work only to pump out another publication, to be used to secure yet another grant, to be parlayed into yet a bigger name, yet another promotion, yet another raise, and so forth and so forth. These accusations may have powerful rhetorical force in some quarters, but they have no place, and have found none, here, in a reflective assessment of the ethics of the use of animals in science. Our concern throughout has been to assess the ethics of *what* scientists do, not *why* they do it. The point that must be recognized is that people can do what is wrong even though they have the best motives, the best intentions, even though they are "the nicest people." The question of the moral status of animal use in science thus is not to be decided by discovering the motives or intentions of those who do it *or* of those who criti-

cize it. The sooner all the parties to the debate realize this, the better.[49]

80   Lastly, there is the idea of alternatives again. The search for alternatives to using animals in science is only in its infancy. Many scientists tend to scorn the idea and to believe that the number and utility of alternatives are very limited. One would have thought that recent developments would have put this attitude to rest. To cite just one encouraging example, a promising new bacterial test for carcinogens has been developed by Professor Bruce Ames at the University of California. Whereas animal tests for carcinogenicity typically take two to three years and cost in excess of $150,000, the Ames' test takes two to three days, uses no animals, and costs just a few hundred dollars.[50] Ames himself stops short of claiming that his test is 100% accurate, and he does not rule out the present need to use animals as an ancillary part of research into carcinogens. Yet his test does much to suggest the potential benefits to be realized from the search for alternatives, both in terms of the savings in animal pain and in dollars and cents. Those skeptical of "alternatives" ("impossible" it may be said) may hold their ground, but we should not be discouraged. Yesterday's "impossibilities" are today's commonplaces. We must press on despite the skeptics, acting to insure that adequate funds become available to those qualified to search for alternatives. The call to intensify the search is not "anti-scientific." In fact, it is just the opposite. It is a call to scientists to use their skill, knowledge and ingenuity to progress toward our common aspirations: a more humane approach to the practice of science. It is a call to *do* science, not to abandon it. The commitment to search for alternatives should be viewed as an index both of our moral *and* our scientific progress.[51]

NOTES

1 Readers are referred to Tom Regan's *The Case for Animal Rights* (CA: University of California Press, 1983) for a sustained presentation of his current views, which differ in important ways from what they will find in the following paper.

2 For documentation and additional information see J. Diner, *Physical and Mental Suffering of Experimental Animals* (Washington: Animal Welfare Institute, 1979); and R. Ryder, *Victims of Science* (London: Davis-Poynter, 1975).

3 These three areas are identified and discussed more fully by Andrew N. Rowan in his *Alternatives to Laboratory Animals: Definition and Discussion* (Washington: The Institute for the Study of Animal Problems, 1980).

4 As quoted in L. Rosenfield, *From Animal Machine to Beast Machine* (New York: Octagon Books, 1968) p. 54.

5 These views are discussed more fully in Tom Regan, "The Moral Basis of Vegetarianism," *Canadian Journal of Philosophy* (1975), pp. 181-214. Reprinted in Tom Regan, *All That Dwell Therein: Animal Rights and Environmental Ethics* (Berkeley: University of California Press, 1982).

6 Richard Ryder was the first to argue in this way in *op. cit.*

7 C. S. Lewis, "Vivisection" in *Undeceptions* (London: Geoffrey Blass, 1971).

8 In January 1981 Revlon, Inc. the world's largest cosmetics manufacturer, announced that it had awarded Rockefeller University $750,000 to research and develop an alternative to the Draize test. The company also granted $25,000 to establish a trust, the purpose of which is to fund further research into alternatives. Thus other cosmetic companies can join Revlon's pioneering move — (this is the first time a commercial firm has funded the search for alternatives to the use of live animals for testing) — by the simple expe-

dient of contributing to the trust. The political realities being what they are, chances are good that Revlon's efforts will soon be imitated by other firms in the cosmetics industry. Revlon's actions were prompted by an uncommonly well organized campaign, involving more than four hundred separate animal welfare related organizations, conducted over a two year period. Through meetings with representatives of Revlon, through the media, through petitions to the Congress, through letter writing campaigns, and through protest marches and rallies, the Coalition to Stop the Draize Rabbit Blinding Tests, Inc. helped to persuade Revlon to take its revolutionary step. The Coalition's success gives a clear demonstration of what can be done on behalf of animals and what must be done to succeed. When the money required to seek alternatives is on hand, there will be no lack of persons willing to do it.

9 M. Weil and R. Scala, "A Study of Intra- and Inter-Laboratory Variability in the Results of Rabbit Eye and Skin and Irritation Tests," *Toxicology and Applied Pharmacology* 19 (1971), pp. 271-360.

10 Dr. Feinberg made this claim while serving on a panel discussion on animal experimentation, sponsored by the Anti-Cruelty Society of Chicago, in October 1980.

11 Some of these issues are explored in a rather extreme way in S. Epstein, *The Politics of Cancer* (Garden City: Anchor Press/Doubleday, 1979).

12 *British Medical Journal,* October 28, 1972, p. 190. We have taken this example as well as several others from Deborah Mayo's unpublished paper, "Against a Scientific Justification of Animal Experiments."

13 Recently even many scientists have become concerned about the possibilities inherent in certain kinds of research. The interested reader should see the essays collected in the following volumes: G. Holton and R. Morison (eds.), *Limits of Scien-*

tific Inquiry (New York: W. W. Norton and Co., 1978); K. Wulff (ed.), *Regulation of Scientific Inquiry: Social Concerns with Research,* American Association for the Advancement of Science Selected Symposium no. 37 (Boulder, CO: Westview Press, 1979); J. Richards (ed.), *Recombinant DNA: Science, Ethics and Politics* (New York: Academic Press, 1978); and D. Jackson and S. Stich (eds.), *The Recombinant DNA Debate* (Englewood Cliffs, NJ: Prentice-Hall 1979).

14 Baruch Brody is apparently one such philosopher. See his *Abortion and the Sanctity of Life: A Philosophical View* (Cambridge: The MIT Press, 1974).

15 The example is given by the contemporary American philosopher, Richard Brandt in his essay "A Moral Principle About Killing," in Marvin Kohl, ed., *Beneficent Euthanasia* (Buffalo: Prometheus Books, 1972). The philosophical propriety of using more or less unusual hypothetical examples in assessing moral principles is critically discussed by the contemporary English philosopher G.E.M. Anscombe in her "Modern Moral Philosophy," *Philosophy,* 33 (1958), reprinted in Judith J. Thomson and Gerald Dworkin, eds., *Ethics* (New York: Harper & Row, 1968).

16 MIP would probably have to be reformulated to account for a range of cases (e.g., "innocent threats") with which we are not primarily concerned in this paper. Insane persons can kill just as surely as sane ones and, though they are innocent, morality surely allows us to defend ourselves against their threatening attacks.

17 Here we develop an example introduced by Robert Nozick in Chapter 3 of his *Anarchy, State and Utopia* (New York: Basic Books, 1979).

18 The possibility that certain species of animals have a morality of their own, based on mutual sympathy, is explored and defended by James Rachels in "Do Animals Have a Right to Liberty?", Tom Regan and Peter Singer. eds., *Animal*

Rights and Human Obligations (Englewood Cliffs: Prentice-Hall, 1976).

19 For further comments on this term, see G. J. Warnock in his *The Object of Morality* (New York: Methuen, 1971).

20 For a fuller discussion of these issues, see Heather McGiffin and Nancie Brownley, eds., *Animals in Education: The Use of Animals in High School Biology Classes and Science Fairs* (Washington: Institute for the Study of Animal Problems, 1980).

21 The results have not been published in a professional journal. But see the reports published in the Vancouver, B.C. newspapers (*The Province* and *The Vancouver Sun*) on March 28, 1980 and April 8, 1980. This case and the relevant documentation were brought to our attention by David Rinehart of the *Greenpeace Examiner*.

22 See again, the works by Diner and Ryder referred to in Endnote 2, as well as Peter Singer, *Animal Liberation* (New York: Avon Books, 1975).

23 R. Levine, *Pharmacology: Drug Actions and Reactions* (New York: Little, Brown, 1978).

24 These studies are reported in R. Loosli, "Duplicate Testing and Reproducibility," in Regamey, Hennessen, Ikic and Ungar, *International Symposium on Laboratory Medicine* (Basel: S. Karger, 1967).

25 These methods are reviewed in, for example, Rowan, *op. cit.*, and Ryder, *op. cit.*

26 For a critical assessment of the use made of animals in psychological research, see Alan Bowd, "Ethical Reservations About Psychological Research with Animals," *The Psychological Record.*

27 See "A Select Bibliography on Animal Rights and Human Obligations," *Inquiry*, Vol. 21, Nos. 1-2, 1978.

28 For example, R. M. Hare in "Ethical Theory and Utilitarianism," in H. D. Lewis (ed.), *Contemporary British Philosophy* 4 (London: Allen and Unwin,

1976); and P. Singer, *Practical Ethics* (Cambridge: Cambridge University Press, 1980).

29 Jeremy Bentham, *The Principles of Moral and Legislation* (1789) Chapter 17, Section 1; reprinted in T. Regan and P. Singer (eds.), *Animal Rights and Human Obligations, op. cit.*

30 S. Rosenthal and R. Milliean, *Pharmacological Review* 6 (1954), p. 489. See also Peter Singer, *Animal Liberation, op. cit.*

31 *Monitor*, March, 1978, p. 16. The view that science develops mainly through habit, convenience, desire for prestige and so forth is one that has gained currency in contemporary philosophy of science. See, for example, T. Kuhn, *The Structure of Scientific Revolutions*, second edition (Chicago: University of Chicago Press, 1970); Paul Feyerabend, *Against Method* (London: New Left Books, 1975); and L. Laudan, *Progress and Its Problems* (Berkeley: University of California Press, 1977).

32 *The Vancouver Sun*, March 28. 1978.

33 David Hubel, "The Brain," *Scientific American* 241 (1979), p. 53.

34 The literature concerning such difficulties has been proliferating. See, for example, H. Magalhaes (ed.), *Environmental Variables in Animal Experimentation* (New Jersey: Associated University Presses, Inc., 1974).

35 F. Coulston and D. Serrone, "The Comparative Approach to the Role of Nonhuman Primates in Evaluation of Drug Toxicity in Man: A Review," *Annals of the New York Academy of Sciences* 162 (1969), p. 682.

36 *Ibid.*, pp. 682-683.

37 F. Coulston, "Benefits and Risks Involved in the Development of Modern Pharmaceutical Products," presented in Bonn and in Luxemburg in September, 1980.

38 J. Cairns. *Cancer: Science and Society* (San Francisco: W. H. Freeman and Co., 1978).

39 *Ibid.*, p. 7.

40 On chimpanzees, see G. Gallup, "Self-Recognition in Primates," *American Psychologist* 32 (1977), 329-338.

41 On Cetaceans, see the essays collected in K. Norris (ed.), *Whales, Dolphins, and Porpoises* (Berkeley: University of California Press, 1966) and J. McIntyre (ed.), *Mind in the Waters* (New York: Charles Scribners' Son, 1974).

42 D. H. Smyth, *Alternatives to Animal Experiments* (London: Scholar Press, 1978) p. 14.

43 For further comments on the ambiguity of "unnecessary suffering," see Tom Regan, "Cruelty, Kindness and Unnecessary Suffering," *Philosophy*, Vol. 55, No. 214, 1980.

44 See, in particular, the essays "Utilitarianism," "Justice and Equality," and "Rights."

45 These federal regulations are part of The Animal Welfare Act. The physical facilities in which animals used in science are housed and the attention given to some of their basic needs (food, water) have improved as a result of these regulations. Not all animals are covered by the Act, however, rats and mice being notable exceptions; and the regulations apply to, and thus are enforceable only in the case of, federally supported programs.

46 R. J. White, "Antivivisection: The Reluctant Hydra," *The American Scholar*, Vol. 40, No. 3 (Summer 1971); reprinted in Tom Regan and Peter Singer (eds.), *Animal Rights and Human Obligations*, *op. cit.*

47 For a discussion of the Swedish experiment, see M. Ross, "The Ethics of Animal Experimentation: Control in Practice," *Australian Psychologist* 13 (1978).

48 *op. cit.*, p. 166.

49 Some of these matters are discussed in Tom Regan, "Cruelty, Kindness, and Unnecessary Suffering," *op. cit.*

50 See "Bacterial Tests for Potential Carcinogens," *Scientific American* 241 (1979).

51 We wish to thank Barbara Orlans and Andrew Rowan for helpful comments on an earlier draft of this essay. Professor Jamieson's work on this project was assisted by a grant from the University Awards Committee of the State University of New York, while Professor Regan's was assisted by a grant from the National Endowment for the Humanities. It is a pleasure to express our gratitude in a public way to these respective agencies.

SUGGESTED READINGS

J. Diner, *Physical and Mental Suffering of Experimental Animals* (Washington: The Animal Welfare Institute, 1978).

G. Holton and R. Morrison, eds., *The Limits of Scientific Inquiry* (New York: W. W. Norton and Co., 1978).

T. Regan and P. Singer, eds., *Animal Rights and Human Obligations* (Englewood Cliffs: Prentice-Hall, 1976).

A. Rowan, *Alternatives to Laboratory Animals: Definition and Discussion* (Washington: The Institute for the Study of Animal Problems, 1980).

R. Ryder, *Victims of Science* (London: Davis-Poynter, 1975).

H. Salt, *Animals' Rights in Relation to Social Progress* (Clark's Summit, Pa.: Society for Animal Rights, 1980).

P. Singer, *Animal Liberation* (New York: Avon Books, 1975).

D. Smyth, *Alternatives to Animal Experiments* (London: The Scholar Press, 1978).

J. Vyvyan. *The Dark Face of Science* (Levittown, NY: Transatlantic Arts, 1972).

Questions

1. (a) Of the products you generally buy, do you know which ones have been tested on animals?

   (b) Of the companies you may seek employment with, do you know which ones use animals to test the safety of their products?

   (c) Do you know how you can find out these things? (See Section IV.)

2. What two objections do Jamieson and Regan present to the LD50 test? (Are they the same as their objections to the Draize test?)

3. (a) Of the six arguments supporting *unlimited* use of animals,

      (i) which has been rendered unsound because one of its premises is now known to be false?

      (ii) which might certain religionists find convincing?

      (iii) which might appeal to natural law theorists?

   (b) Do Jamieson and Regan make the same objection to both the Knowledge Argument and the Important Knowledge Argument?

   (c) (i) The Freedom Argument focuses on rights and science. Think of an argument similar to this one that focuses on rights and business.

      (ii) Would the objection raised by Jamieson and Regan apply as well to this new argument?

4. With regard to the four arguments supporting *no* use of animals...

   (a) Enrich Jamieson and Regan's objection by articulating the conditions necessary for permissible pain-causing (i.e., *when* is causing pain morally acceptable?).

   (b) (i) Jamieson and Regan say that "animals are not the sort of beings who can give or withhold their informed consent" (P25). Do you agree — for all (nonhuman) animals?

      (ii) Enrich the authors' objection by articulating the conditions necessary for permissible pain-causing that is without consent (i.e., *when* is it morally acceptable to cause pain even though you don't have consent?).

   (c) The authors' example to refute the Harm Argument involves pain and self-defence as a motive/intent. Can you think of an example of morally permissible harm that does not involve pain (but is nevertheless harmful) and uses a different motive/intent?

   (d) Would you use the dynamite?

5. (a) In what way can animals be innocent?

   (b) In what way can they be said to have rights?

6. Of the products and companies you listed in question one, are any morally justifiable by either the Modified Innocence argument or the Utilitarian argument put forth by the authors?

7. What alternatives to animal testing do Jamieson and Regan list?

8. What is the authors' purpose in describing the Swedish situation and the Ames test?

Nuclear Power —
Some Ethical and Social Dimensions

Richard and Val Routley[1]

One hardly needs initiation into the dark mysteries of nuclear physics to contribute usefully to the debate now widely raging over nuclear power. While many important empirical questions are still unresolved, these do not really lie at the centre of the controversy. Instead, it is a debate about values ... many of the questions which arise are social and ethical ones.[2]

I. The Train Parable and the Nuclear Waste Problem

1 A long distance country train has just pulled out. The train, which is crowded, carries both passengers and freight. At an early stop in the journey, someone consigns as freight, to a far distant destination, a package which contains a highly toxic and explosive gas. This is packed in a very thin container which, as the consigner is aware, may well not contain the gas for the full distance for which it is consigned, and certainly will not do so if the train should strike any real trouble, for example, if the train should be derailed or involved in a collision, or if some passenger should inter-

fere inadvertently or deliberately with the freight, perhaps trying to steal some of it. All of these sorts of things have happened on some previous journeys. If the container should break, the resulting disaster would probably kill at least some of the people on the train in adjacent carriages, while others could be maimed or poisoned or sooner or later incur serious diseases.

2 Most of us would roundly condemn such an action. What might the consigner of the parcel say to try to justify it? He might say that it is *not certain* that the gas will escape, or that the world needs his product and it is his duty to supply it, or that in any case he is not responsible for the train or the people on it. These sorts of excuses, however, would normally be seen as ludicrous when set in this context. Unfortunately, similar excuses are often not so seen when the consigner, again a (responsible) businessman, puts his workers' health or other peoples' welfare at risk.

3 Suppose he says that it is his own and others' pressing needs which justify his action. The company he controls, which produces the material as a by-product, is in bad financial straits, and could not afford to produce a better container even if it knew how to make one. If the company fails, he and his family will suffer, his employees will lose their jobs and have to look for others, and the whole company town, through loss of spending, will be worse off. The poor and unemployed of the town, whom he would otherwise have been

Richard and Val Routley, "Nuclear Power–Some Ethical and Social Dimensions" from *And Justice for All: New Introductory Essays in Ethics and Public Policy*. Ed. Tom Regan and Donald Van De Veer. NJ: Rowman and Allanheld, 1982. 116–138. Reprinted with permission of the editors and Val Plumwood (formerly Routley).

able to help, will suffer especially. Few people would accept such grounds as justification. Even where there are serious risks and costs to oneself or some group for whom one is concerned, one is usually considered not to be entitled to simply transfer the heavy burden of those risks and costs onto other uninvolved parties, especially where they arise from one's own, or one's group's chosen life-style.

4   The matter of nuclear waste has many moral features which resemble the train case. How fitting the analogy is will become apparent as the argument progresses. There is no known proven safe way to package the highly toxic wastes generated by the nuclear plants that will be spread around the world as large-scale nuclear development goes ahead. The waste problem will be much more serious than that generated by the 50 or so reactors in use at present, with each one of the 2000 or so reactors envisaged by the end of the century producing, on average, annual wastes containing 1000 times the radioactivity of the Hiroshima bomb. Much of this waste is extremely toxic. For example, a millionth of a gramme of plutonium is enough to induce a lung cancer. A leak of even a part of the waste material could involve much loss of life, widespread disease and genetic damage, and contamination of immense areas of land. Wastes will include the reactors themselves, which will have to be abandoned after their expected life times of perhaps 40 years, and which, some have estimated, may require 1½ million years to reach safe levels of radioactivity.

5   Nuclear wastes must be kept suitably isolated from the environment for their entire active lifetime. For fission products, the required storage period averages a thousand years or so, and for transuranic elements, which include plutonium, there is a half million to a million year storage problem. Serious problems have arisen with both short-term and proposed long-term methods of storage, even with the comparatively small quantities of waste produced over the last twenty years. Short-term methods of storage require continued human intervention, while proposed longer term methods are subject to both human interference and risk of leakage through non-human factors.

6   No one with even a slight knowledge of the geological and climatic history of the earth over the last million years, a period whose fluctuations in climate we are only just beginning to gauge and which has seen four Ice Ages, could be confident that a rigorous guarantee of safe storage could be provided for the vast period of time involved. Nor does the history of human affairs over the last 3000 years give ground for confidence in safe storage by methods requiring human intervention over perhaps a million years. Proposed long-term storage methods such as storage in granite formations or in salt mines, are largely speculative and relatively untested, and have already proved to involve difficulties with attempts made to put them into practice. Even as regards expensive recent proposals for first embedding concentrated wastes in glass and encapsulating the result in multilayered metal containers before rock deposit, simulation models reveal that radioactive material may not remain suitably isolated from human environments. In short, the best present storage proposals carry very real possibilities of irradiating future people and damaging their environment.[3]

7   Given the heavy costs which could be involved for the future, and given the known limits of technology, it is methodologically unsound to bet, as nuclear nations have, on the discovery of safe procedures for storage of wastes. Any new procedures (required before 2000) will

probably be but variations on present proposals, and subject to the same inadequacies. For instance, not only have none of the proposed methods for safe storage been properly tested, but they may well prove to involve unforeseen difficulties and risks when an attempt is made to put them into practice on a *commercial scale*. Only a method that could provide a rigorous guarantee of safety over the storage period, that placed safety beyond reasonable doubt, would be acceptable. It is difficult to see how such rigorous guarantees could be given concerning either the geological or future human factors. But even if an economically viable, rigorously safe long term storage method *could* be devised, there is the problem of guaranteeing that it would be universally and invariably *used*. The assumption that it would be (especially if, as appears likely, such a method proved expensive economically and politically) seems to presuppose a level of efficiency, perfection, and concern for the future which has not previously been encountered in human affairs, and has certainly not been conspicuous in the nuclear industry.

8   The risks imposed on the future by proceeding with nuclear development are, then, *significant*. Perhaps 40,000 generations of future people could be forced to bear significant risks resulting from the provision of the (extravagant) energy use of only a small proportion of the people of 10 generations.

9   Nor is the risk of direct harm from the escape or misuse of radioactive materials the only burden the nuclear solution imposes on the future. Because the energy provided by nuclear fission is merely a stop gap, it seems probable that in due course the same problem, that of making a transition to renewable sources of energy, will have to be faced again by a future population which will probably, again as a result of our actions be very much worse placed to cope with it. Their world will most likely be a world which is seriously depleted of non-renewable resources, and in which such renewable resources as forests and soils as remain, resources which inevitably form an important part of the basis of life, are run-down or destroyed. Such points tell against the idea that future people must be, if not direct beneficiaries of energy from nuclear fission, at least indirect beneficiaries.

10   The "solution" then is to buy time for contemporary society at a price which not only creates serious problems for future people but which reduces their ability to cope with these problems. Like the consigner in the train parable, contemporary industrial society proposes, in order to get itself out of a mess arising from its own life-style – the creation of economies dependent on an abundance of non-renewable energy, which is limited in supply – to pass on costs and risks of serious harm to others who will obtain no corresponding benefits. The "solution" may enable the avoidance of some uncomfortable changes in the lifetime of those now living and their immediate descendants, just as the consigner's action avoids uncomfortable changes for him and those in his immediate surroundings, but at the expense of passing heavy burdens to other uninvolved parties whose opportunity to lead decent lives may be seriously jeopardised.

11   If we apply to the nuclear situation the standards of behaviour and moral principles generally acknowledged (in principle, if not so often in fact) in the contemporary world, it is not easy to avoid the conclusion that nuclear development involves *injustice with respect to the future* on a grand scale. There appear to be only two plausible ways of trying to avoid such a conclusion. First, it might be argued that the moral principles and obligations which we acknowl-

edge for the contemporary world and perhaps the immediate future do not apply to those in the non-immediate future. Secondly, an attempt might be made to appeal to overriding circumstances; for to reject the consigner's action in the circumstances outlined is not to imply that there are *no* circumstances in which such an action might be justifiable. As in the case of the consigner of the package, there is a need to consider what these justifying circumstances might be, and whether they apply in the present case. We consider these possible escape routes for the proponent of nuclear development in turn.

II. Obligations to the (Distant) Future

12 The especially problematic area is that of the distant (i.e. non-immediate) future, the future with which people alive today will have no direct contact; by comparison, the immediate future gives fewer problems for most ethical theories. In fact the question of obligations to future people presents tests which a number of ethical theories fail to pass, and also has serious repercussions in political philosophy as regards the adequacy of accepted (democratic and other) institutions which do not take due account of the interests of future creatures.

13   Moral philosophers have, predictably, differed on questions of obligations to distant future creatures. A good many of the philosophers who have explicitly considered the question have come down in favour of the same consideration being given to the rights and interests of future people as to those of contemporary or immediately future people. Others fall into three categories: those who acknowledge obligations to the future but who do not take them seriously or who assign them a lesser weight, those who

deny, or who are committed by their general moral position to denying, that there are moral obligations beyond the immediate future, and those who come down, with admirable philosophical caution, on both sides of the issue, but with the weight of the argument favouring the view underlying prevailing economic and political institutions, that there are no moral obligations to the future beyond those perhaps to the next generation.

14   According to the most extreme of these positions against moral obligations to the future, our behaviour with respect to the future is morally unconstrained; there are no moral restrictions on acting or failing to act deriving from the effect of our actions on future people. Of those philosophers who say, or whose views imply, that we do not have obligations to the (non-immediate) future, many have based this view on accounts of moral obligation which are built on relations which presuppose some degree of temporal or spatial contiguity. Thus, moral obligation is seen as presupposing various relations which could not hold between people widely separated in time (or sometimes in space). Let us call the position that we have no obligations to (distant) future people the *No-constraints position.*

15   Among suggested bases or grounds of moral obligation for the position, which would rule out obligations to the non-immediate future, are these. Firstly, there are those accounts which require that someone to whom a moral obligation is held be able to *claim* his rights or entitlement. People in the distant future will not be able to claim rights and entitlements against us, and of course they can do nothing to enforce any claims they might have against us. Secondly, there are those accounts which base moral obligations on social or legal *convention*, for example a convention which would require

punishment of offenders or at least some kind of social enforcement. But plainly these and other conventions will not be invariant over change in society and amendment of legal conventions; hence they will not be invariant over time. Also future people have no way of enforcing their interests or punishing offending predecessors.

16   The No-constraints view is a very difficult one to sustain. Consider, for example, a scientific group which, for no particular reason other than to test a particular piece of technology, places in orbit a cobalt bomb set off by a triggering device designed to go off several hundred years from the time of its despatch. No presently living person and none of their immediate descendants would be affected, but the population of the earth in the distant future would be wiped out as a direct and predictable result of the action. The No-constraints position clearly implies that this is an acceptable moral enterprise, that whatever else we might legitimately criticize in the scientists' experiment (perhaps its being over-expensive or badly designed), we cannot lodge a moral protest about the damage it will do to future people. The No-constraints position also endorses as morally acceptable the following sorts of policy: A firm discovers it can make a handsome profit from mining, processing and manufacturing a new type of material which, although it causes no problem for present people or their immediate descendants, will over a period of hundreds of years decay into a substance which will cause an enormous epidemic of cancer among the inhabitants of the earth at that time. According to the No-constraints view, the firm is free to act in its own interests, without any consideration for the harm it does remote future people.

17   Such counterexamples to the No-constraints position which are easily varied and multiplied, might seem childishly obvious. Yet this view is far from being a straw man; not only have several philosophers endorsed this position, but it is a clear implication of many currently popular views of the basis of moral obligation, as well as of prevailing economic theory. It seems that those who opt for the No-constraints position have not considered such examples, despite their being clearly implied by their position. We suspect that (we certainly hope that) when it is brought out that their position admits such counterexamples, that without any constraints we are free to cause pointless harm for example, most of those who opted for this position would want to assert that it was not what they intended. What many of those who have put forward the No-constraints position *seem* to have had in mind (in denying moral obligation) is rather that future people can look after themselves, that we are not responsible for their lives. The popular view that the future can take care of itself also seems to assume a future causally independent of the present. But it is not. It is not as if, in the counterexample cases or in the nuclear case, the future is simply being left *alone* to take care of itself. Present people are *influencing* it, and in doing so thereby acquire many of the same sorts of moral responsibilities as they do in causally affecting the present and immediate future, most notably the obligation to take account in what they do of people affected and their interests, to be careful in their actions, to take account of the genuine probability of their actions causing harm, and to see that they do not act so as to rob future people of the chance of a good life.

18   Furthermore, to say that we are *not responsible* for the lives of future people does not amount to the same thing as saying that we are free to do as we like with respect to them. In just

the same way, the fact that one does not have or has not acquired an obligation to some stranger with whom one has never been involved does not imply that one is free to do what one likes with respect to him, for example to rob him or to seriously harm him when this could be avoided.

19 These difficulties for the No-constraints position result in part because of a failure to make an important distinction. Some of our obligations to others arise because we have voluntarily entered into some agreement with them – for example, we have made a promise. Other obligations, however, such as our duty not to damage or harm someone, do not assume that an agreement has been struck between us. Let us call obligations of the former kind *acquired obligations* and those of the latter *unacquired obligations*. There is a considerable difference in the type of responsibility associated with each. In the case of acquired obligations, responsibility arises because one should do something which one can fail to do, e.g., keep a promise. In the case of unacquired duties, responsibility arises as a result of being a causal agent who is aware of the consequences or probable consequences of his action, a responsibility that is not dependent on one's having performed some act in the past (e.g., made a promise). Our obligations to future people clearly are unacquired, not acquired, obligations, a fact the No-constraints position simply fails to take into account. These obligations arise as a result of our ability to produce causal effects of a reasonably predictable nature, whether on our contemporaries *or* on those in the distant future. Thus, to return to the train parable, the consigner cannot argue in justification of his action that he has, for example, never assumed or acquired responsibility for the passengers, that he does not know them and there-

fore has no love or sympathy for them and that they are not part of his moral community; in short, that he has acquired no obligation, and has no special obligations to help them. All that one needs to argue concerning the train, and in the nuclear case, is that there are moral obligations against imposing harm which are not specially acquired. Nor can this claim be rebutted by the pretence that all obligations to the distant future involve heroic self sacrifice, something "above and beyond" what is normally required. One is no more engaging in heroic self sacrifice by not forcing future people into an unviable life position or by refraining from causing them direct harm than the consigner is resorting to heroic self sacrifice in refraining from shipping the dangerous package on the train.

III. Attempts to Reduce Obligations to the Future

20 In evading these difficulties, the No-constraints position may be qualified rather than wholly abandoned. According to the *Qualified position*, we are not entirely unconstrained with respect to the distant future. There are obligations, even to distant future people, but these are not so important as those to the present, and the interests of distant future people cannot weigh very much in the scale against those of the present and immediate future. The interests of future people then, except in unusual cases, count for very much less than the interests of present people. Hence such things as nuclear development and various exploitative activities which benefit present people should proceed, even if people of the distant future are (somewhat) disadvantaged by them.

21 The Qualified position appears to be widely held and is implicit in prevailing economic theo-

ries, where the position of a decrease in weight of future costs and benefits (and so of future interests) is obtained by application over time of a discount rate, so discounting costs and risks to future people. The attempt to apply economics as a moral theory, an approach that is becoming increasingly common, can lead then to the Qualified position. What is objectionable in such an approach is that economics must operate within the bounds of acknowledged non-acquired moral constraints, just as in practice it operates within legal constraints. What economics cannot legitimately do is determine what these constraints are. There are, moreover, alternative economic theories and simply to adopt, without further ado, one which discounts the future, giving much less importance to the interests of future people, is to beg all the questions at issue.

22   Among the arguments that economists offer for generally discounting the future, the most threadbare is based on the *Rosy-future assumption*, that future generations will be better off than present ones (and so better placed to handle the waste problem). Since there is mounting evidence that future generations may well *not* be better off than present ones, especially in things that matter, no argument for discounting the interests of future generations on this basis can carry much weight. For the waste problem to be handed down to the future generations, it would have to be shown, what recent economic progress hardly justifies, that future generations will be not just better off but so much better off that they can (easily) carry and control the nuclear freight.

23   A more plausible argument for discounting, the *Opportunity-cost argument*, builds directly on the notion of opportunity cost. It is argued from the fact that a dollar gained now is worth much

more than a dollar received in the nonimmediate future (because the first dollar could meanwhile be invested at compound interest), that discounting is required to obtain equivalent monetary values. This same line of reasoning is then applied to the allocation of resources. Thus, compensation – which is what the waste problem is taken to come to economically – costs much less now than later; for example, a few pennies set aside (e.g. in a trust fund) for the future, if need be, will suffice to compensate eventually for any victims of remote radioactive waste leakage. Two problems beset this approach.[4] First, there are, presently at least, insurmountable practical difficulties about applying such discounting. We simply do not know how to determine appropriate future discount rates. A more serious objection is that the argument depends on a false assumption. It is not true that value, or damages, can always be converted into monetary equivalents. There is no clear "monetary compensation" for a variety of damages, including cancer, loss of life, a lost species.

24   The discounting theme, however argued for, is inadequate, because it leads back in practice to the No-constraints position. The reason is that discounting imposes an "economic horizon" beyond which nothing need be considered, since any costs or benefits which might arise are, when discounted back to the present, negligible.

25   A different argument for the Qualified position, the *Probabilities argument*, avoids the objections from cases of certain damage through appeal to *probability considerations*. The distant future, it is argued, is much more uncertain than the present and immediate future, so that probabilities are consequently lower, perhaps even approaching or coinciding with zero, for any hypothesis concerning the distant future. Thus, the argument continues, the interests of future

people must (apart from exceptional cases where there is an unusually high degree of certainty) count for (very much) less than those of present and neighbouring people where (much) higher probabilities are attached. So in the case of conflict between the present and the future, where it is a question of weighing certain benefits to the people of the present and the immediate future against a much lower probability of indeterminate costs to an indeterminate number of distant future people, the issue would normally be decided in favour of the present assuming anything like similar costs and benefits were involved. The argument is, however, badly flawed. Firstly, probabilities involving distant future situations are not always less than those concerning the immediate future in the way the argument supposes. Though we do not know what kind of cars the denizens of earth will drive in the twenty-second century, for example, or even if they will drive cars, we do know that they will have a need for food, clothing, and shelter. Moreover, the outcomes of some moral problems often do not depend on a high level of probability. In many cases it is enough, as the train parable reveals, that a significant risk is created; such cases do not depend critically on high probability assignments. Nor, of course, can it be assumed that anything like similarly weighted costs and benefits are involved in the nuclear case, especially if it is a question of risking poisoning some of the earth for half a million or so years, with consequent risk of serious harm to thousands of generations of future people, in order to obtain quite doubtful, or even trivial, benefits for some present people in the shape of the opportunity to continue (unnecessarily) high energy use. And *even if* the costs and benefits were comparable or evenly weighted, such an argument would be defective, since an analogous argument would show that

the consigner's action in the train parable is acceptable provided the benefit (e.g. the profit the company stood to gain from imposing significant risks on other people) was sufficiently large.

26   Such a cost-benefit approach to moral and decision problems, with or without the probability frills, is quite inadequate when different parties are involved or when cases of conflict of interest involving moral obligations are at issue.[5] For example, such a cost-benefit approach would imply that it is *permissible* for a company to injure, or very likely injure, some innocent party provided only that the company stands to make a sufficiently large gain from it, that costs to some group are more than morally compensated for by larger benefits to another group. But costs or benefits are not legitimately transferred in any simple way from one group to another. The often appealed to maxim "If you (or your group) want the benefits you have to accept the costs" is one thing, but the maxim "If I (or my group) want the benefits then *you* have to accept the costs (or some of them at least)" is another and very different thing. It is a widely accepted moral principle that one is not, in general, entitled to simply transfer costs of a significant kind arising from an activity which benefits oneself onto other parties who are not involved in the activity and are not beneficiaries.[6] This *Transfer-limiting principle* is especially clear in cases where the significant costs include an effect on life or health or a risk thereof, and where the benefit to the benefitting party is of a noncrucial or dispensable nature – e.g., the manufacture and sale of thalidomide. The principle is of fundamental importance in the nuclear debate, and appears again and again: it applies not merely to the waste problem but also to several other liabilities of nuclear development, e.g. the risk of nuclear war, the matter of reactor meltdown. In particular, the principle invalidates the compari-

son, heavily relied on in building a case for the acceptability of the nuclear risks, between nuclear risks and those from such activities as airplane travel or cigarette smoking. In the latter case, those who supposedly benefit from the activity are also, to an overwhelming extent, those who bear the serious health costs and risks involved. In contrast, the users and supposed beneficiaries of nuclear energy will be risking not only, or even primarily, *their own* lives and health, but also that of others who may not be beneficiaries at all – who may be just the opposite!

27   More generally, the distribution of costs and damage in such a fashion, i.e. on to non-beneficiaries, is a characteristic of certain serious forms of pollution, and is among its morally objectionable features. Large-scale energy production, from nuclear or fossil fuel sources, can cause or lead to serious pollution. Thus from the Transfer-limiting principle emerges an important necessary condition for energy options: *To be morally acceptable, an energy option should not involve the transfer of significant costs or risks of harm onto parties who are not involved, who do not use or do not benefit correspondingly from the energy source.* Included in the scope of this condition, which nuclear development violates, are future people, i.e. not merely people living at the present time but also future generations (those of the next towns). A further corollary of the principle is the *Transmission Principle*, that we should not hand the world we have so exploited on to our successors in substantially worse shape than we "received" it. For if we did then that would be a significant transfer of costs.

28   The Transfer-limiting principle can be derived from certain ethical theories (e.g. those of a deontic cast such as Kant's and Rawls') and from common precepts (such as the Golden Rule), where one seriously considers putting oneself in another's position. But the principle is perhaps best defended, on a broader basis, inductively, by way of examples. Suppose, to embroider the train parable, the company town decides to solve its disposal problem by shipping its noxious waste to another town down the line, which (like future towns) lacks the means to ship it back or to register due protest. The inhabitants of this town are then forced to face the problem either of undertaking the expensive and difficult disposal process or of sustaining risks to their own lives and health. Most of us would regard this kind of transfer of costs as morally unacceptable, however much the consigner's company town flourishes.

IV. Uncertainty and Indeterminacy Arguments for Reduced Responsibility

29 Many of the arguments designed to show that we cannot be expected to take too much account of the effects of our actions on the distant future appeal to uncertainty. There are two main components to the General Uncertainty argument, capable of separation, but frequently tangled up. Both arguments are mistaken, the first, an argument from ignorance, on *a priori* grounds, the second on *a posteriori* grounds. The *Argument from ignorance* concerned runs as follows: In contrast to the exact information we can obtain about the present, the information we can obtain about the effects of our actions on the distant future is unreliable, woolly and highly speculative. But we cannot base assessments of how we should act on information of this kind, especially when accurate information is obtainable about the present which would indicate different action. Therefore we must regretfully ignore the uncertain effects of our actions on the distant future.

A striking example of the argument from ignorance at work is afforded by official US analyses favouring nuclear development, which ignore (the extensive) costs of waste control on the grounds of uncertainty.[7] More formally and crudely the argument concerned is this: One only has obligations to the future if these obligations are based on reliable information. There is no reliable information at present as regards the distant future. Therefore one has no obligations to the distant future.

30   This argument is essentially a variant on a sceptical argument concerning our knowledge of the future (formally, replace 'obligations' by 'knowledge' in the crude statement of the argument above). The main ploy is to considerably overestimate and overstate the degree of certainty available with respect to the present and immediate future, and the degree of certainty which is *required* as the basis for moral consideration both with respect to the present and with respect to the future. Associated with this is the attempt to suggest a sharp division as regards certainty between the present and immediate future on the one hand and the distant future on the other. We shall not find, we suggest, that there is any such sharp or simple division between the distant future and the adjacent future and the present, at least with respect to those things in the present which are normally subject to moral constraints. We can and constantly do act on the basis of such "unreliable" information, which the sceptic as regards the future conveniently labels "uncertain". In moral situations in the present, assessments of what to do often take account of risk and probability, even quite low probabilities. Consider again the train parable. We do not need to know for certain that the container will break and the lethal gas escape. In fact it does not even have to be probable, in the rel-

evant sense of more probable than not, in order for us to condemn the consigner's action. *It is enough that there is a significant risk of harm* in this sort of case. It does not matter if the decreased well-being of the consigner is certain and that the prospects of the passengers quite uncertain. It is wrong to ship the gas. But if we do not require certainty of action to apply moral constraints in contemporary affairs, why should we require a much higher standard of certainty in the future? The unwarranted insistence on certainty as a necessary condition before moral consideration can be given to the distant future, then, amounts to a flagrant double standard.

31   According to the second argument, the *Practical-uncertainty* argument, even if *in theory* we have obligations to the future, we cannot *in practice* take the interests of future people into account because uncertainty about the distant future is so gross that we cannot determine what the likely consequences of actions on it will be. Therefore, however good our intentions to the people of the distant future are, in practice we have no choice but to ignore their interests. Given that moral principles are characteristically of universal implicational form, e.g. of forms such as "if x has character h then x is wrong, for every (action) x", the argument may be stated more sharply thus: We can never obtain the information about future actions which would enable us to affirm the antecedent of the implication (x has character h). Therefore, even if in theory moral principles do extend to future people, in practice they cannot be applied to obtain clear conclusions.

32   It is true that if the distant future really were so grossly uncertain that in every case it was impossible to determine in any way better than chance what the effects of present action would be, and whether any given action would help or

hinder future people, then moral principles, although applicable in theory to the future, would not in practice yield any clear conclusions about how to act. In this event, the distant future would impose no practical moral constraints on action. However, the argument is factually incorrect in assuming that the future always is so grossly uncertain or indeterminate. Admittedly there is often a high degree of uncertainty concerning the distant future, but as a matter of (contingent) fact it is not always so gross or sweeping as the argument has to assume. There are some areas where uncertainty is not so great as to exclude constraints on action. For example, we may have little idea what the fashions will be in a hundred years or, to take another morally-irrelevant factor, what brands of ice cream people will be eating, if any, but we do have excellent reason to believe, especially if we consider 3000 years of history, that what people there are in a hundred years are likely to have material and psychic needs not entirely unlike our own, that they will need a healthy biosphere for a good life; that like us they will not be immune to radiation; that their welfare will not be enhanced by a high incidence of cancer or genetic defects, by the destruction of resources, or the elimination from the face of the earth of that wonderful variety of non-human life which at present makes it such a rich and interesting place. The case of nuclear waste storage, and of uncertainty of the effects of it on future people, is one area where uncertainty in morally relevant respects is not so great as to preclude moral constraints on action. For this sort of reason, the Practical uncertainty argument should be rejected.

33 Through the defects of the preceding arguments, we can see the defects in a number of widely employed uncertainty arguments used to write off probable harm to future people as out-side the scope of proper consideration. Most of these popular moves employ both of the uncertainty arguments as suits the case, switching from one to the other. For example, we may be told that we cannot really take account of future people because we cannot be sure that they will exist or that their tastes and wants will not be completely different from our own, to the point where they will not suffer from our exhaustion of resources or from the things that would affect us. But this is to insist upon complete certainty of a sort beyond what is required for the present and immediate future, where there is also commonly no guarantee that some disaster will not overtake those to whom we are morally committed. Again we may be told that there is no guarantee that future people will be worthy of any efforts on our part, because they may be morons or forever plugged into machines for their enjoyment. Even if one is prepared to accept the elitist approach presupposed – according to which only those who meet certain properly civilized or intellectual standards are eligible for moral consideration – what we are being handed in such arguments is again a mere outside possibility. Neither the contemporary nor the historical situation gives any positive reason for supposing that a lapse into universal moronity or universal-pleasure-machine escapism is a serious possibility. We can contrast with these mere logical possibilities the very real historically supportable risks of escape of nuclear waste or decline of a civilisation through destruction of its resource base.

34 Closely related to uncertainty arguments are arguments premised on the indeterminacy of the future. For example, according to the *Indeterminacy argument*, the indeterminacy of the number and exact character of people at future times will prevent the interest of future people

being taken into account where there is a conflict with the present. Since their numbers are indeterminate and their interests unknown how, it is asked, can we weigh their competing claims against those of the present and immediate future, where this information is available in a more or less accurate form? The question is raised particularly by problems of sharing fixed quantities of resources, for example oil, among present and future people when the numbers of the latter are indeterminate. Such problems are indeed difficult, but they are not resolved by *ignoring* the claims of the future. Nor are distributional problems involving non-renewable resources as large and representative a class of moral problems concerning the future as the tendency to focus on them would suggest. It can be freely admitted that there will be cases where the indeterminacy of aspects of the future will make conflicts very difficult to resolve or indeed irresoluble – no realistic ethical theory can give a precise answer to *every* ethical question. But, as the train parable again illustrates, there are cases where such difficulties do not hinder resolution, and cases of conflict which are not properly approached by weighing numbers, numbers of interests, or whatever, cases for which one needs to know only the most general probable characteristics of future people. The case of nuclear power is like that.

35   The failure of these various arguments reveals, what can be independently argued from the universalisability features of moral principles,[8] that their placement does not disqualify future people from full moral consideration or reduce their claims below the claims of present people. That is, *we have the same general unacquired obligations to future people as to the present*, thus there is the same obligation to take account of them and their interests in what we do, to be careful in our actions, to take account of the probability (and not just the certainty) of our actions causing harm or damage, and to see, other things being equal, that we do not act so as to rob them of what is necessary for the chance of a good life. Uncertainty and indeterminacy do not relieve us of these obligations.

V. Problems of Safe Nuclear Operation: Reactor Emissions and Core Meltdown

36 The ethical problems with nuclear power are by no means confined to waste storage and future creatures. Just as remoteness in time does not erode obligations or entitlement to just treatment, neither does location in space, or a particular geographical position. Hence several further problems arise, to which principles and arguments like those already arrived at in considering the waste problem apply. For example, if one group (social unit, or state) decides to dump its radioactive wastes in the territory or region of another group, or not to prevent its (radioactive) pollution entering the territory of another group, then it imposes risks and costs on presently existing people of the second group, in much the way that present nuclear developments impose costs and risks on future people. There are differences however: spatially distant people cannot be discounted in quite the way that future people can be, though the interests and objectives of the former often get ignored or overridden.

37   People living in the vicinity of a nuclear reactor are subject to special costs and risks. One is radioactive pollution, because reactors routinely discharge radioactive materials into the air and water near the plant: hence the *Emission problem*. Such "normal" emission during plant

operation of low level radiation carries carcinogenic and mutagenic costs. While there are undoubtedly costs, the number of cancers and the precise extent of genetic damage induced by exposure to such radiation are both uncertain. If our ethical principles permitted free transfer of costs and risks from one person to another, the ethical issue directly raised by nuclear emissions would be: what extent of cancer and genetic damage, if any, is permissibly traded for the advantages of nuclear power, and under what conditions? Since, however, risks and benefits are NOT (morally) transferable in this way – recall the Transfer-limiting principle – such a cost-benefit approach to the risks nuclear emission poses for those who live near a reactor cannot with justice be approached in this fashion. And these risks *are* real! In the USA, people who live within 50 miles of a nuclear power plant bear a risk of cancer and genetic damage as much as 50 times that borne by the population at large. And children living in this region are even more vulnerable, since they are several times more likely to contract cancer through exposure than normal adults. The serious costs to these people cannot be justified by the alleged benefits for others, especially when these benefits could be obtained without these costs. Thus it is not just complacent to say 'It's a pity about Aunt Ethel dying of cancer, but the new airconditioners make life comfortable'. For such benefits to some as airconditioners provide, benefits which can be alternatively obtained, for example by modification of buildings, can in no way compensate for what *others* suffer.

38   Among the other strategies used in trying to persuade us that the imposition of radiation on those who live close to nuclear plants – most of whom have no genuine voice in the location of reactors in their environment and cannot move

away without serious losses – is really quite all right is the *Doubling argument*. According to the US Atomic Energy Commission, it is permissible to double, through nuclear technology, the level of (natural) radiation that a population has received with apparently negligible consequences, the argument being that the additional amount (being *equivalent* to the "natural" level) is also likely to have negligible consequences. The increased amounts of radiation – with their large man-made component – are then accounted *normal*, and, it is claimed, what is normal is morally acceptable. This argument is not sound. Drinking one bottle of wine a day may have no ill-effects, whereas drinking two a day certainly may affect a person's well-being; and while the smaller intake may have become normal for the person, the larger one will, under such conditions, not be. Finally, what is or has become normal, e.g. two murders or twenty cancers a day in a given city, may be far from acceptable.

39   In fact, even the USA, which has very strict standards by comparison with most other countries with planned nuclear reactors, permits radiation emissions very substantially in excess of the standards laid down; so the emission situation is much worse than what consideration of the standards would disclose. Furthermore, the monitoring of the standards "imposed" is entrusted to the nuclear operators themselves, scarcely disinterested parties. Thus public policy is determined not so as to guarantee public health, but rather to serve as a "public pacifier" while publicly-subsidized private nuclear operations proceed relatively unhampered.[9]

40   While radioactive emissions are an ordinary feature of reactor operation, reactor breakdown is, hopefully, not: official reports even try to make an accident of magnitude, as a matter of *definition*, an 'extraordinary nuclear occurrence'.

But "definitions" notwithstanding, such accidents can happen, and almost have on several occasions (the most notorious being Three Mile Island): hence the *Core-meltdown problem.*

41   If the cooling and emergency core cooling systems fail in American (light water) reactors, then the core melts and 'containment failure' is likely, with the result that an area of 40,000 square miles could be radioactively contaminated.[10] In the event of the worst type of accident in a very small reactor, a steam explosion in the reactor vessel, about 45,000 people would be killed instantly and at least 100,000 would die as a result of the accident, property damages would exceed $17 billion and an area the size of Pennsylvania would be destroyed. Modern nuclear reactors are about five times the size of the reactor for which these conservative US figures (still the best available from official sources) are given[11]: the consequences of a similar accident with a modern reactor would accordingly be much greater.

42   The consigner who risks the lives and well-being of passengers on the train acts inadmissibly. A government or government-endorsed utility appears to act in a way that does not differ in morally significant respects in siting a nuclear reactor in a community, in planting such a dangerous package on the "community train". More directly, the location of a nuclear reactor in a community, even if it should happen to receive a favourable benefit-cost analysis and other economic appraisal, would violate such ethical requirements as the Transfer-limiting principle.

43   The advocates of nuclear power have, in effect, endeavoured to avoid questions of cost-transfer and equity, by shifting the dispute out of the ethical arena and into a technological dispute about the extraordinary improbability of reactor malfunction. They have argued, in particular, what contrasts with the train parable, that there is no real possibility of a catastrophic nuclear accident. Indeed in the influential Rassmussen report – which was extensively used to support public confidence in US nuclear fission technology – an even stronger, an incredibly strong, improbability claim was stated: namely, the likelihood of a catastrophic nuclear accident is so remote as to be (almost) impossible. However, the mathematical models relied upon in this report, variously called "fault tree analysis" and "reliability estimating techniques", are unsound, because, among other things, they exclude as "not credible" possibilities that may well happen in the real world. It is not surprising, then, that the methodology and data of the report have been soundly and decisively criticised, or that official support for the report has now been withdrawn.[12] Moreover, use of alternative methods and data indicates that there is a real possibility, a non-negligible probability of a serious accident.

44   In response it is contended that, even if there is a non-negligible probability of a reactor accident, still that is acceptable, being of no greater order than risks of accidents that are already socially accepted. Here we encounter again that insidious engineering approach to morality built into decision models of an economic cast, e.g. benefit-cost balance sheets, risk-assessment models, etc. *Risk assessment*, a sophistication of transaction or trade-off models, purports to provide a comparison between the relative risks attached to different options, e.g. energy options, which settles their ethical status. The following assumptions are encountered in risk assessment as applied to energy options:

Ai. If option A imposes (comparable) costs on fewer people than option B then option A is preferable to option B;

Aii. Option A involves a total net cost in terms of cost to people (e.g. deaths, injuries, etc.) which is less than that of option B, which is already accepted; therefore option A is acceptable.[13]

These assumptions are then applied as follows. Since the number likely to be killed by nuclear power station catastrophe is less than the likely number eventually killed by cigarette smoking, and since the risks of cigarette smoking are accepted, it follows that the risks of nuclear power are acceptable. A little reflection reveals that this sort of risk assessment argument grossly violates the Transfer-limiting principle. In order to obtain a proper ethical assessment we need a much fuller picture, and we need to know at least these things: Do the costs and benefits go to the same parties; and is the person who *voluntarily undertakes* the risks also the person who primarily receives the benefits, as in driving or cigarette smoking, or are the costs *imposed* on other parties who do not benefit? It is only if the parties are the same in the case of the options compared, and there are no distributional problems, that this sort of a comparison would be soundly based. This is rarely the case, and it is not so in the case of risk assessments of energy options.

VI. Other Social and Environmental Risks and Costs of Nuclear Development, Especially Nuclear War

45 The problems already discussed by no means exhaust the environmental, health and safety risks and costs in, or arising from, the nuclear fuel cycle. The full fuel cycle includes many stages both before and after reactor operation, apart from waste disposal, namely, mining, milling, conversion, enrichment and preparation, reprocessing spent fuel, and transportation of materials. Several of these stages involve hazards. *Unlike the special risks in the nuclear cycle* – of sabotage of plants, of theft of fissionable material, and of the further proliferation of nuclear armaments – *these* hazards have parallels, if not exact equivalents, in other highly polluting methods of generating power, e.g. 'workers in the uranium mining industry sustain "the same risk" of fatal and nonfatal injury as workers in the coal industry.'[14] The problems are not unique to nuclear development.

46 Other social and environmental problems – though endemic where dangerous large-scale industry operates in societies that are highly inegalitarian and include sectors that are far from affluent – are more intimately linked with the nuclear power cycle. Though pollution is a common and generally undesirable component of large-scale industrial operation, radioactive pollution, such as uranium mining for instance produces, is especially a legacy of nuclear development, and a specially undesirable one, as rectification costs for dead radioactive lands and waterways reveal. Though sabotage is a threat to many large industries, sabotage of a nuclear reactor can have dire consequences, of a different order of magnitude from most industrial sabotage (where core meltdown is not a possibility). Though theft of material from more dubious enterprises such as munitions works can pose threats to populations at large and can assist terrorism, no thefts for allegedly peaceful enterprises pose problems of the same order as theft of fissionable material. No other industry produces materials which so readily permit fabrication into such massive explosives. No other industry is, to sum it up, so vulnerable on so many fronts.

47 In part to reduce its vulnerability, in part because of its long and continuing association

with military activities, the nuclear industry is subject to, and encourages, several practices which (given their scale) run counter to basic features of free and open societies, crucial features such as personal liberty, freedom of association and of expression, and free access to information. These practices include secrecy, restriction of information, formation of special police and guard forces, espionage, curtailment of civil liberties.

> Already operators of nuclear installations are given extraordinary powers, in vetting employees, to investigate the background and activities not only of employees but also of their families and sometimes even of their friends. The installations themselves become armed camps, which especially offends British sensibilities. The U.K. Atomic Energy (Special Constables) Act of 1976 created a special armed force to guard nuclear installations and made it answerable ... to the U.K. Atomic Energy Authority.[15]

These developments, and worse ones in West Germany and elsewhere, presage along with nuclear development increasingly authoritarian and anti-democratic societies. That nuclear development appears to force such political consequences tells heavily against it. Nuclear development is further contra-indicated politically by the direct connection of nuclear power with nuclear war. It is true that ethical questions concerning nuclear war – for example, whether a nuclear war is justified, or just, under any circumstances, and if so what circumstances – are distinguishable from those concerning nuclear power. Undoubtedly, however, the spread of nuclear power is substantially increasing the technical means for engaging in nuclear war and so, to that extent, the opportunity for, and chances of, nuclear engagement. Since nuclear wars are never accounted positive goods, but are at best the lesser of major evils, nuclear wars are always highly ethically undesirable. The spread of nuclear power accordingly expands the opportunity for, and chances of, highly undesirable consequences. Therefore, what leads to it – nuclear development – is undesirable. This is, in outline, *the argument from nuclear war against large-scale nuclear development.*[16]

VII. Beneath Conflict Arguments: The Ideological Bases of Nuclear Development

48 Much as with nuclear war, so given the cumulative case against nuclear development, only one justificatory route remains open, that of appeal to overriding circumstances. That appeal, to be ethically acceptable, must go beyond merely economic considerations. For, as observed, the consigner's action, in the train parable, cannot be justified by purely economistic arguments, such as that his profits would rise, the company or the town would be more prosperous, or by appealing to the fact that some possibly uncomfortable changes would otherwise be needed. So it is also in the nuclear case: the Transfer-limiting principle applies. But suppose now the consigner argues that his action is justified because unless it is taken the town will die. It is by no means clear that even such a justification as this would be sufficient, especially where the risks to the passengers is high, since the case still amounts to one of transfer of costs and risks onto others. But such a conflict situation, where a given course of action, though normally undesirable, is alleged to be the lesser of two evils in a given case, is morally more problematical than cases where the Transfer-limiting principle is clearly violated. Nuclear development is often defended in this

way, through *Conflict arguments*, to the effect that even though nuclear development does have undesirable features, nevertheless the alternatives are worse.

49 Some of the arguments advanced to demonstrate conflict are based on competing commitments to present people, and others on competing obligations to future people, both of which are taken to override the obligations not to impose on the future significant risk of serious harm. The success of such conflict arguments requires the presentation of a genuine and exhaustive set of alternatives (or at least practical alternatives) and showing that the only alternatives to admittedly morally undesirable actions are even more undesirable ones. If some practical alternative which is not morally worse than the action to be justified is overlooked, suppressed, or neglected in the argument (for example, if in the train parable it turns out that the town has another option to starving or to shipping the parcel, namely earning a living in some other way), then the argument is defective and cannot readily be patched. Just such a suppression of practicable alternatives, we shall argue, has occurred in the argument designed to show that the alternatives to the nuclear option are even worse than the option itself.

50 A first argument, the *Poverty argument*, is that there is an overriding obligation to the poor, both the poor of the third world and the poor of industrialised countries. Failure to develop nuclear energy, it is often claimed, would amount to denying them the opportunity to reach the standard of affluence we currently enjoy and would create unemployment and poverty in the industrialised nations. And this would be worse – a greater evil – than such things as violating the Transfer-limiting principle through nuclear development.

51 The Poverty argument does not stand up to examination, either for the poor of the industrial countries or for those of the third world. There is good evidence that large-scale nuclear energy will help *increase unemployment and poverty* in the industrial world, through the diversion of very much available capital into an industry which is not only an exceptionally poor provider of direct employment, but also tends to reduce available jobs through encouraging substitution of energy use for labour use. The argument that nuclear energy is needed for the third world is even less convincing. Nuclear energy is both politically and economically inappropriate for the third world, since it requires massive amounts of capital, requires numbers of imported scientists and engineers, creates negligible local employment, and depends for its feasibility upon largely non-existent utility systems – e.g. established electricity transmission systems and back-up facilities, and sufficient electrical appliances to plug into the system. Politically it increases foreign dependence, adds to centralised entrenched power, and reduces the chance for change in the oppressive political structures which are a large part of the problem. The fact that nuclear energy is not in the interests of the people of the third world does not of course mean that it is not in the interests of, and wanted (often for military purposes) by, their rulers, the westernised and often military elites in whose interests the economies of these countries are usually organised. But that does not make the poverty argument anything other than what it is: a fraud. There are well-known energy-conserving alternatives and the practical option of developing further alternative energy sources, alternatives some of which offer far better prospects for helping the poor, both in the third world and in industrial countries: coal and

other fossil fuels, geothermal, and a range of solar options (including as well as narrowly solar sources, wind, water and tidal power).

52   Another major argument advanced to show conflict, the *Lights-going-out argument*, appeals to a set of supposedly overriding and competing obligations to future people. We have, it is said, a duty to pass on the immensely valuable things and institutions which our culture has developed. Unless our high-technology, high-energy industrial society is continued and fostered, our valuable institutions and traditions will fall into decay or be swept away. The argument is essentially that without nuclear power, without the continued level of material wealth it alone is assumed to make possible, the lights of our civilization will go out. Future people will be the losers.

53   The argument does raise important questions about what is valuable in our society and what characteristics are necessary for a good society. But for the most part these large questions can be by-passed. The reason is that the argument adopts an extremely uncritical attitude to present high-technology societies, apparently assuming that they are uniformly and uniquely valuable. It assumes that technological society is unmodifiable, that it cannot be changed in the direction of energy conservation or alternative (perhaps high technology) energy sources without collapse.

54   These assumptions are all hard to accept. The assumption that technological society's energy patterns are unmodifiable is especially so; after all, it has survived events such as world wars which required major social and technological restructuring and consumption modification. If western society's demands for energy were (contrary to the evidence) totally unmodifiable without collapse, not only would it be committed to a program of increasing destruction, but much of its culture would be of dubious value to future people, who would very likely, as a consequence of this destruction, lack the resource base which the argument assumes to be essential in the case of contemporary society.

55   The uniformity assumption should certainly be challenged. Since high-technology societies appear not to be uniformly valuable, the central question is, what is necessary to maintain what is *valuable* in such a society? While it may be easy to argue that high energy consumption centrally controlled is necessary to maintain the political and economic status quo of such a society, it is not so easy to argue that it is essential to maintain what is valuable, and it is what is valuable, presumably, that we have a duty to pass on to the future.

56   The evidence from history is that no very high level of material affluence or energy consumption is needed to maintain what is valuable. There is good reason in fact to believe that a society with much lower energy and resource consumption would better foster what is valuable than our own. But even if a radical change in these directions is independently desirable, it is unnecessary to presuppose such a change in order to see that the assumptions of the Lights-going-out argument are wrong. The consumption of less energy than at present need involve no reduction of well-being; and certainly a large increase over present levels of consumption, assumed in the usual economic case for nuclear energy, is quite unnecessary. What the nuclear strategy is really designed to do then is not to prevent the lights going out in western civilisation, but to enable the lights to go on burning all the time – to maintain and even increase the wattage output of the Energy Extravaganza.

57   In fact there is good reason to think that, far from a high energy consumption society fostering what is valuable, it will, especially if energy is obtained by means of nuclear fission, be positively inimical to it. A society which has become heavily dependent upon a highly centralised, controlled and garrisoned, capital- and expertise-intensive energy source, must be one which is highly susceptible to entrenchment of power, and one in which the forces which control this energy source, whether capitalist or bureaucratic, can exert enormous power over the political system and over people's lives, even more than they do at present. Such a society would almost inevitably tend to become authoritarian and increasingly anti-democratic, as an outcome, among other things, of its response to the threat posed by dissident groups in the nuclear situation.

58   Nuclear development may thus help in passing on to future generations some of the *worst* aspects of our society – the consumerism, alienation, destruction of nature, and latent authoritarianism – while many valuable aspects, such as the degree of political freedom and those opportunities for personal and collective autonomy which exist, would be lost or diminished: political freedom, for example, is a high price to pay for consumerism and energy extravagance.

59   Again, as in the case of the poverty arguments, clear alternatives, alternative social and political choices, which do not involve such unacceptable consequences, are available. The alternative to the high technology-nuclear option is not a return to the cave, the loss of all that is valuable, but either the adoption of an available alternative such as coal for power or, better, the development of alternative technologies and lifestyles which offer far greater scope for the maintenance and further development of what is

valuable in our society than the highly centralised nuclear option. The Lights-going-out argument, as a moral conflict argument, accordingly fails.

60   Thus this remaining escape route, the appeal to conflict, is, like the appeal to futurity, closed. If we apply, as we have argued we should, the same moral standards to the future that we ought to acknowledge for the present, the conclusion that large-scale nuclear development is a crime against the future is inevitable. Closed also, in the much same way, are the escape routes to other arguments (from reactor meltdown, radiation emissions, etc.) for concluding that nuclear development is unacceptable. In sum, nuclear development is morally unacceptable on *several* grounds.

VIII. Social Options: Shallow and Deep Alternatives

61   The future energy option that is most often contrasted with nuclear power, namely coal power, while no doubt preferable to nuclear power, is hardly acceptable. For it carries with it the likelihood of serious (air) pollution, and associated phenomena such as acid rain and atmospheric heating, not to mention the despoliation caused by extensive strip mining, all of which will result from its use in meeting very high projected consumption figures. Such an option would, moreover, also violate the Transfer-limiting principle: it would impose widespread costs on non-beneficiaries for some concentrated benefits to some profit takers and to some users who do not pay the full costs of production and replacement.

62   To these main conventional options a third is often added which emphasizes softer and more benign technologies, such as those of solar energy and hydroelectricity. Such softer options – if suitably combined with energy

conservation measures (for there are solar ways, as well as nuclear ways, of energy extravagance and of producing unnecessary trivia which answer to no genuine needs) – can avoid the ethical objections to nuclear power. The deeper choice is not however technological, nor merely an individual matter, but social, and involves the restructuring of production away from energy intensive uses and, at a more basic level, a change to nonconsumeristic, less consumptive life-styles and social arrangements.[17] These more fundamental choices between social alternatives, tend to be observed by conventional technologically-oriented discussion of energy options. It is not just a matter of deciding in which way to meet the unexamined goals nuclear development aspires to meet, but also a matter of examining the goals themselves. That is, we are not merely faced with the question of comparing different technologies for meeting some fixed or given demand or level of consumption, and of trying to see how best to meet these; we are also, and primarily, faced with the matter of examining those alleged needs and the cost of a society that creates them.

63   It is doubtful that any technology, however benign in principle, will be likely to leave a tolerable world for the future if it is expected to meet unbounded and uncontrolled energy consumption and demands. Even more benign technologies may well be used in a way which creates costs for future people and which are likely to result in a deteriorated world being handed on to them. In short, even more benign technologies may lead to violation of the Transmission requirement. Consider, to illustrate, the effect on the world's forests, commonly counted as a solar resource, should they be extensively used for production of methanol or of electricity by woodchipping. While few would object to

the use of genuine waste material for energy production, the unrestricted exploitation of forests – whether it goes under the name of "solar energy" or not – to meet ever increasing energy demands could well be the final indignity for the world's already hard-pressed natural forests.

64   The effects of such additional demands on the maintenance of the forests are often dismissed by the simple expedient of waving around the label "renewable resources". Many forests are in principle renewable, it is true, given a certain (low) rate and kind of exploitation, but in fact there are now very few forestry operations anywhere in the world where the forests are treated as completely renewable in the sense of the renewal of all their values. In many regions too the rate of exploitation which would enable renewal has already been exceeded, so that a total decline is widely thought to be imminent. It certainly has begun in many regions, and many forest types, especially rain-forest types, are now, and rapidly, being lost for the future.[18] The addition of a major further and not readily limitable demand pressure for energy *on top of* the present demands is one which anyone with both a realistic appreciation of the conduct of forestry operations and a concern for the long-term conservation of the forests and remaining natural communities must regard with alarm. The result of massive deforestation for energy purposes, resembling the deforestation of much of Europe at the beginning of the Industrial Revolution, again for energy purposes, could be extensive and devastating erosion in steeper lands and tropical areas, desertification in more arid regions, possible climatic change, and massive impoverishment of natural ecosystems, including enormous loss of natural species. Some of us do not want to pass on, and by the Transmission principles we are not entitled to pass on,

a deforested world to the future, any more than we want to pass on one poisoned by nuclear products or polluted by coal products. In short, as the forest situation illustrates, a mere switch to more benign technologies – important though this is – without any more basic structural and social change, is inadequate.

65   The deeper social option involves challenging and beginning to alter a social structure which promotes consumerism, consumption far beyond genuine needs and an economic structure which encourages increasing use of highly energy-intensive modes of production. The *social change option* tends to be obscured in most discussions of energy options and of how to meet energy needs, in part because it does question underlying values of current social arrangements. The conventional discussion proceeds by taking alleged demand (often conflated with reasonable wants or needs) as unchallengeable, and the issue to be one of which technology can be most profitably employed to meet them. This effectively presents a false choice, and is the result of taking needs and demand as lacking a *social context*, so that the social structure which produces the needs is similarly taken as unchallengeable and unchangeable. The point is readily illustrated. It is commonly argued by representatives of such industries as transportation and petroleum, as for example by Mc-Growth of the XS Consumption Co., that people want deep freezers, air conditioners, power gadgets.... It would be authoritarian to prevent them from satisfying these wants. Such an *argument from created wants* conveniently ignores the social framework in which such needs and wants arise or are produced. To point to the determination of many such wants at the framework level is *not* however to assume that they are entirely determined at the framework level (e.g. by

industrial organisation) or that there is no such thing as individual choice or determination at all. It is to see the social framework as a major factor in determining certain kinds of choices [such as those for jet set travel] and kinds of infrastructure [the priority given to highway construction over mass transit], and to see apparently individual choices made in such matters as being *channelled and directed by a social framework determined largely in the interests of corporate and private profit and advantage.*

66   The social change option is a hard option, insofar as it will be difficult to implement politically; but it is ultimately the only way of avoiding the passing on of serious costs to future people. And there are other sorts of reasons than *such* ethical ones for taking it: it is the main, indeed the only sort of option, open to those who adopt what is now called a *deep ecological* perspective, as contrasted with a *shallow ecological* outlook which regards the natural world and its nonhuman denizens as not worthwhile in themselves but only of value in as much as they answer back to human interests. The deep ecological perspective is an integral part of the *Alternative Ecological Paradigm* and is incompatible with central theses of the *Dominant Social Paradigm* (which is essentially the ideology of classical and neoclassical economics) and its variants (roughly, what are called State Socialism and Democratic Socialism).[19] It is incompatible with viewing the natural environment as having value only as a resource, as by and large hostile and wild, calling for humans to tame, control, and manage it, and with the other human-domination-over-nature themes which characterize the Dominant Paradigm and its variants.

67   The conflict between Alternative and Dominant Paradigms, which is fast increasing, extends

of course far beyond attitudes to the natural world, since core values of the Dominant Paradigm such as the merits of unimpeded economic growth and material progress are at stake; the conflict involves fundamental differences over the whole front of economical, political and social arrangements. The conflict underlies much of the nuclear debate, insofar as it is not specifically limited to questions of technological fixes, but takes up the basic ethical issues and the social questions to which they lead.[20] The ethical requirements already defended and applied bring us out, when followed through, on the Alternative side of the paradigm conflict, and accordingly lead to the difficult social change option.

68   The social changes that the deep alternative requires will be strongly resisted because they mean changes in current social organisation and power structure. To the extent that the option represents some kind of threat to parts of present political and economic arrangements, it is not surprising that official energy option discussion proceeds by misrepresenting and often obscuring it. But difficult as it is to suitably alter "the system," especially one with such far-reaching effects on the prevailing power structure, it is imperative to try: we are all on the nuclear train.

NOTES

1 This paper is a condensation of an early version of our 'Nuclear power — ethical, social, and political dimensions' (ESP for short, available from the authors), which in turn grew out of Routley (i.e. the work so referred to in the reference list). For help with the condensation we are very considerably indebted to the editors.

   In the condensation, we simplify the structure of the argument and suppress underlying political and ideological dimensions (for example, the large measure of responsibility of the USA for spreading nuclear reactors around the world, and thereby in enhancing the chances of nuclear disasters, including nuclear war). We also considerably reduce a heavy load of footnotes and references designed and needed to help make good many of our claims. Further, in order to contain references to a modest length, reference to primary sources has often been replaced by reference through secondary sources. Little difficulty should be encountered however in tracing fuller references through secondary sources or in filling out much important background material from work cited herein. For example, virtually all the data cited in sections I and VII is referenced in Routley. At worst ESP can always be consulted.

2 All but the last line of the quote is drawn from Goodin, p. 417; the last line is from the Fox Report, p. 6.

   While it is unnecessary to know much about the nuclear fuel cycle in order to consider ethical and social dimensions of nuclear power, it helps to know a little. The basics are presented in many texts, e.g. Nader & Abbotts, Gyorgy. Of course in order to assess fully reports as to such important background and stage-setting matters as the likelihood of a core meltdown of (lightwater) reactors, much more information is required. For many assessment purposes however, some knowledge of economic fallacies and decision theory is at least as important as knowledge of nuclear technology.

3 Naturally the effect on humans is not the only factor that has to be taken into account in arriving at moral assessments. Nuclear radiation, unlike most ethical theories, does not confine its scope to human life and welfare. But since the harm nuclear development may *afflict* on nonhuman life, for example, can hardly *improve* its case, it

suffices if the case against it can be made out solely in terms of its effects on human life in the conventional way.

For reference to and a brief discussion of (human-oriented) simulation models see Goodin, p. 428.

4 The Opportunity-cost argument is also defective in other respects. It presupposes not merely the (mistaken) reductions involved in the contraction of the ethical domain to the economic; it also presupposes that the proper methods for decision which affect the future, such as that of energy choice, apply discounting. But, as Goodin argues, more appropriate decision rules do not allow discounting.

5 This is *one* of the reasons why expected utility theory, roughly cost-benefit analysis with probability frills, is inadequate as a decision method in such contexts.

6 Apparent exceptions to the principle such as taxation (and redistribution of income generally) vanish when wealth is construed (as it has to be if taxation is to be properly justified) as at least partly a social asset unfairly monopolised by a minority of the population. Examples such as that of motoring dangerously do not constitute counterexamples to the principle: for one is not morally entitled to so motor.

7 For details and as to how the official analyses become arguments against nuclear development when some attempt is made to take the ignored costs into account, see Shrader-Frechette. p.55 ff.

8 See Routley. p. 160.

9 For much further discussion of the points of the preceding two paragraphs, see Shrader-Frechette, p. 35 ff., and also Nader & Abbotts.

10 Most of the reactors in the world are of this type: see Gyorgy.

11 See Shrader-Frechette, chapter 4.

12 See Shrader-Frechette. A worthwhile initial view of the shortcomings of the Rassmussen report may be reached by combining the critique in Shrader-Frechette with that in Nader & Abbotts.

13 There are variations on Ai and Aii which multiply costs against numbers such as probabilities. In this way risks, construed as probable costs, can be taken into account in the assessment. (Alternatively, risks may be assessed through such familiar methods as insurance.)

A principle varying Aii and formulated as follows

Aii'. A is ethically acceptable if (for some B) a includes no more risks than b and b is socially accepted.

was the basic ethical principle in terms of which the Cluff Lake Board of Inquiry recently decided that nuclear power development in Saskatchewan is ethically acceptable: see *Cluff Lake Board of Inquiry Final Report*, Department of Environment, Government of Saskatchewan, 1978, p. 305 and p. 288. In this report, A is nuclear power and B is other activities clearly accepted by society as alternative power sources. In other applications, B has been taken as cigarette smoking, motoring, mining and even the Vietnam war(!).

The points made in the text do not exhaust the objections to principles Ai – Aii'. The principles are certainly ethically substantive, since an *ethical* consequence cannot be deduced from nonethical premises, but they have an inadmissible *conventional* character. For look at the origin of B: B may be socially accepted though it is no longer socially acceptable, or though its social acceptability is no longer so clearcut and it would not have been socially accepted if as much as is now known had been known when it was introduced. What is required in Aii', for instance, for the argument to begin to look convincing is that B is 'ethically accept*able*' rather than 'socially accept*ed*. But even with the amendments the principles are invalid, for the reasons given in the text, and others.

It is not disconcerting that principles of this type do not work. It would be sad to see yet another area lost to the experts, ethics to actuaries.

14 See Shrader-Frechette, p. 15.

15 Goodin p. 433.

16 The argument is elaborated in ESP.

17 For some of the more philosophically important material on alternative nonconsumeristic social arrangements and lifestyles, see work cited in V. and R. Routley, 'Social theories, self management and environmental problems' in Mannison et al., where a beginning is made on working out *one* set of alternatives, those of a pluralistic anarchism.

18 The imperilled situation of the world's tropical rainforests is explained in Barney and Myers, though the real reasons for this elude them: the reasons are untangled in R. and V. Routley 'World rainforest destruction – the social causes' (available from the authors). See also G.O. Barney, *The Global 2000 Report to the President of the U.S. Entering the 21st Century*, Volume I and Volume II (New York: Pergamon Press, 1980).

19 For a fuller account of the Dominant Social Paradigm and its rival, the Alternative Environmental Paradigm, see Cotgrove and Duff, especially the table on p. 341 which encapsulates the main assumptions of the respective paradigms; compare also Catton and Dunlap, especially p. 33. Contemporary variants on the Dominant Social Paradigm are considered in ESP.

The shallow/deep contrast as applied to ecological positions, which is an important component of the paradigm conflict, was introduced by Naess. For further explanation of the contrast and of the larger array of ecological positions into which it fits, see R. and V. Routley, 'Human chauvinism and environmental ethics' in Mannison et

al. and the references there cited, especially to Rodman's work.

20 The more elaborate argument of ESP sets the nuclear debate in the context of paradigm conflict. But it is also argued that, even within the assumptions framework of the Dominant Social Paradigm and its variants,

(1) Nuclear development is not the rational choice among energy options. The main argument put up for nuclear development within the framework of the dominant paradigm is an *Economic growth argument*. It is the following version of the Lights-going-out argument (with economic growth duly standing in for material wealth, and for what is valuable!): Nuclear power is necessary to sustain economic growth; economic growth is desirable (for all the usual reasons, e.g. to increase the size of the pie, to postpone redistribution problems, etc.); therefore nuclear power is desirable. The first premiss is part of US energy policy (see Shrader-Frechette, p. 111) and the second premiss is supplied by standard economics textbooks. But both premisses are defective, the second because what is valuable in economic growth can be achieved (not without growth but) by *selective* economic growth, which jettisons the heavy social and environmental costs carried by unqualified economic growth. More to the point, since the second premiss is an assumption of the Dominant Paradigm, the first premiss (or rather an appropriate and less vulnerable restatement of it) fails even by Dominant Paradigm standards. For of course nuclear power is not *necessary*, given that there are other, perhaps costlier alternatives. The premiss usually defended is some elaboration of the premiss: Nuclear power is the economically best way to sustain economic growth, 'economically best' being filled out as 'most efficient', 'cheapest' as 'having the most favourable benefit-cost ratio', etc. Unfortunately for the argument,

and for nuclear development schemes, nuclear power is none of these things *decisively* (unless a good deal of economic cheating – easy to do – is done).

(2) On proper Dominant Paradigm accounting, nuclear choices should generally be rejected, both as private utility investments and as public choices. Nuclear development is not economically viable but has been kept going, not by clear economic viability, but by massive subsidization of several types (discussed in Shrader-Frechette, Gyorgy, and Nader & Abbotts).

Even on variants of the Dominant Paradigm, nuclear development is not justified, as consideration of decision theory methods will reveal:

(3) Whatever reasonable decision rule is adopted, the nuclear choice is rejected, as the arguments of Goodin on alternative decision rules help to show.

What sustains the nuclear juggernaut is not the Dominant Paradigm or its variants, but contemporary corporate capitalism (or its state enterprise image) and associated third world imperialism, as the historical details of nuclear development both in developed countries and in less developed countries makes plain (for main details, see Gyorgy p. 307 ff.). And the practices of contemporary corporate capitalism and associated imperialism are not acceptable by the standards of either of the Paradigms or their variants: they are certainly not ethically acceptable.

SUGGESTED READINGS

Works especially useful for further investigation of the ethical issues raised by nuclear development are indicated with an asterisk (*).

W. R. Catton, Jr. and R. E. Dunlap, 'A new ecological paradigm for post exuberant sociology' *American Behavioral Scientist* 24 (1980), 15 – 47.

S. Cotgrove and A. Duff, "Environmentalism, middle-class radicalism and politics' *Sociological Review* 28(2) (1980), 333 – 51.

Fox Report: *Ranger Uranium Environmental Inquiry First Report* Australian Government Publishing Service, Canberra, 1977.

*R. E. Goodin, 'No moral nukes' *Ethics* 90 (1980), 417-49.

*A. Gyorgy and friends, *No Nukes: everyone's guide to nuclear power*, South End Press, Boston, Mass., 1979.

*D. Mannison, M. McRobbie and R. Routley (editors), *Environmental Philosophy*, RSSS, Australian National University, 1980.

N. Myers, *The Sinking Ark*, Pergamon Press, Oxford, 1979.

R. Nader and J. Abbotts, *The Menace of Atomic Energy*, Outback Press, Melbourne, 1977.

*K. S. Shrader-Frechette, *Nuclear Power and Public Policy*. Reidel, Dordrecht, 1980.

R. and V. Routley, 'Nuclear energy and obligations to the future' *Inquiry* 21 (1978), 133 – 79.

Questions

1. How do the Routleys respond to the consequence-based justification offered in P3? (Be sure to understand both parts.)

2. "[C]ontemporary industrial society proposes, in order to get itself out of a mess arising from its own life-style – the creation of economies dependent on an abundance of non-renewable energy, which is limited in supply – to pass on costs and risks of serious harm to others who will obtain no corresponding benefits" (P10).

   (a) Is this an accurate description of the situation?

   (b) What two possibilities do the authors see as moral justifications for such a situation?

   (c) Can you think of a third?

3. With respect to the "No-Constraints Position," the authors seem at first, with the counterexamples presented in P16, to call on intuitionism to arrive at their conclusion that this position is untenable. However, at the end of P17 and in P19, a clear argument is articulated: even in the absence of contractual agreement, we have obligations – why?

4. (a) What is the "Qualified Position"?

   (b) Explain the three arguments the authors present in support of this position.

   (c) Explain their objections to each of these arguments.

   (d) (i) What is the "Transfer-Limiting Principle" (P26)?

   (ii) Which ethical theories support this principle?

5. Explain the General Uncertainty argument and the objections presented by the authors.

6. What is the most interesting point, to you, in Section V?

7. What problem do the authors see with risk-assessment models?

8. Both technical and political connections are made between nuclear power and nuclear war. Explain.

9. Can you think of any overriding circumstances not considered by the authors that would ethically justify nuclear development? (Keep in mind that "Ontario is one of the most nuclear-dependent areas in the world," "there are enough hazardous 'low level' uranium tailings in Ontario to fill 60,000 hockey rinks up to the top of the boards," and "in the five-year period from 1989 to 1993, there were over 900 'reportable significant events' at Ontario Hydro's nuclear stations – an average of about ten per reactor per year" [from *Nuclear Hazards in Ontario*, Nuclear Awareness Project, Oshawa].)

10. (a) Identify other industries in which the safety concerns of production and disposal involve future people and/or uncertainty.

    (b) To what extent could the Routleys' arguments be applied to your answers in (a)? (Or, are there significant differences that would render the authors' arguments inapplicable to those industries?)

Case Study – DINP in PVC Teethers

In November 1998, Health Canada advised parents that "products designed for sucking or teething (soft teethers, soft rattles) which are made of soft vinyl (PVC) pose a potential health risk to very young children (weighing less than eight kilograms) when sucked or chewed for prolonged periods (three hours or more a day on a daily basis)." The health risk, damage to liver or kidneys ultimately leading to cancer, comes from a substance called di-isononyl phthalate (DINP), a "plasticizer" added to PVC to make it soft; the lead and cadmium released by DINP can also affect the brain and nervous system. Included in the list of things to throw out are toys made of soft vinyl (not all soft vinyl contains DINP, but you can't tell by looking, feeling, or smelling); pacifiers and feeding bottle nipples, which are made from silicone and latex, are considered safe.

One of the manufacturers of DINP, Aristech Chemical Corporation, denies the risk. They claim that extensive testing of phthalates for 25 years indicates that they "do not pose a health hazard to children and adults when used properly in vinyl products." In particular, their six-year study of DINP led to the following conclusions: "First, adverse liver effects occurred in rats and mice only at very high doses of DINP. The dose levels necessary to show adverse effects in rodents far exceed any realistic exposure that people may receive by using vinyl products. Second, the research confirms – in conjunction with a large body of other scientific research –

that these effects are specific to rats and mice and do not occur in humans."

The Canadian Toy Association supports these claims of safety, but nevertheless they recommend – "in order to maintain parents' confidence that [their] industry is committed to Canada's children" – that companies begin to temporarily use alternative plasticizers (such as polyethelyene).

However, as reported in *Herizons*, "a Greenpeace study found 18% of the 131 toys tested contained levels of lead and cadmium that exceeded Health Canada's draft limits for PVC mini-blinds. Most soft PVC toys tested contain DINP in quantities between 10 and 40 percent by weight". Greenpeace also claims that DINP is a developmental and reproductive toxin. Furthermore, PVC manufacture and incineration is a main source of dioxin, one of the most toxic substances known.

Despite Health Canada's belief that these teethers and toys can be harmful to children, they cannot be recalled – phthalates don't appear in Canada's Hazardous Products Act. Environmentalists are calling for an amendment to the act; mandatory labelling on PVC toys has also been requested (but a private member's bill to that effect was defeated).

Nevertheless, some manufacturers (Nike, The Body Shop, Lego, Mattell, Little Tikes) are phasing out or reducing soft PVC products, and some retailers (The Bay, Zellers, Best Value, Fields) have pulled stock off their shelves.

REFERENCES

Adam, Betty Ann. "Parents Told to Keep Track of Time Child Chews Vinyl Toys." *The Saskatoon StarPhoenix.* 19 Nov. 1998: A9.

Aristech Chemical Corporation. "Information on DINP in Children's Toys." <http://www.aristechchem.com/dinpinfo.htm>

"Business: Chewing on the Issue." *The Economist.* 11 July 1998: 65-66.

"Canada's Toy Industry Takes Action on Soft Teethers and Rattles." Canada NewsWire. <http://www.newswire.ca/releases/November1998/16/c4882.html>

Foster, Andrea. "Health Canada Move Against Soft PVC Toys." *Chemical Week.* 25 Nov. 1998: 16.

"Getting the Lead out of Toys." *Herizons* 12.4 (Winter 1999): 10-11.

Health Canada. "Information for Parents and Caregivers of Very Young Children: Soft Vinyl (PVC) Teethers and Soft Vinyl (PVC) Rattles." November 1998.
<http://www.hc-sc.gc.ca/advisory/par.htm>

Health Canada. "Advisory: Health Canada Advises Parents and Caregivers of Very Young Children to Dispose of Soft Vinyl (PVC) Teethers and Soft Vinyl (PVC) Rattles." November 16/98. <http://www.hc-sc.gc.ca/advisory/index.htm>

Lee-Shanok, Philip. "Beware Toxin in Rattles, Teethers." *The Toronto Sun* 17 Nov. 1998: 7.

Wald, Matthew. "Chemical Element of Vinyl Toys Causes Liver Damage in Lab Rats." *New York Times.* 13 Nov. 1998. <http://www.junkscience.com/nov98/greentoy.htm>

Questions

1. What might account for the discrepancy between Aristech's findings and Greenpeace's findings?

2. (a) It would seem that many animals were given DINP in sufficient quantities to cause cancer. Was that (morally) right?

   (b) In order to determine the risk for humans, scientists in the Netherlands are testing the saliva of humans who have volunteered to chew on soft PVC (*The Economist* article). Is that more or less (morally) right?

3. Consider, in particular, the nature of the harms, risks, and alternatives involved; consider also the rights of the various parties that are involved.

   (a) Should Health Canada or some other government office recall existing PVC products (with or without DINP?) and ban their future manufacture? Why/not?

   (b) Would you, as a manufacturer or retailer, regardless of legislation, stop making and selling PVC with DINP products? Why/not?

CHAPTER 4
EMPLOYEE RIGHTS

What to Do? - Caregivers' Overload

Caregivers' Overload is an international agency that provides short-term (and often short-notice) temporary replacement for caregivers – whether a single parent of a colicky baby and two toddlers or someone looking after an elderly parent – who need a break! Among the quality control mechanisms suggested, in a recent memo to management, is monitoring employees' e-mail. The purpose is not to discover personal details of employees' correspondence but to determine when and how much time is spent in communication unrelated to company business. The reason for this determination is not to monitor (and perhaps reprimand) any individual employee, but to determine whether or not a formal company policy regarding the use of e-mail is warranted (until now, employees have been trusted to use their own judgement).

All of the employees under your supervision are getting their jobs done in a satisfactory manner (done by deadline and done well). You believe you have a good relationship with them; you respect them and are reluctant to read their e-mail messages – especially "behind their backs." You suspect some messages are personal, and you have no problem with this: one, you yourself make personal use of the e-mail system; two, it may be a good thing to allow the whole person to flourish a bit at the workplace. But given your suspicion, monitoring your department's e-mail would clearly be an invasion of personal privacy – and you *do* have a problem with that.

However, you understand and support the motives expressed in the memo. Invasion of privacy is not intended. Your department may be working well, but others may not – perhaps a company policy is necessary. And if you refrain and other managers go ahead, well, is that fair? At the very least, you'll be the cause of company inconsistency.

What do you decide to do?

Introduction

If you've read the subsection on rights theories in Section II, you'll know that "*what* rights?" and "on what *basis*?" are two of the first questions that need to be answered if we are to discuss employee rights.

But even before that, you should wonder "why *employee* rights?" – or at least "why not also *employer* rights?" Good question. I suppose that attention tends to focus more on the rights of the employ*ee* because the employ*er* tends to have more power – including the power to ignore others' rights. And traditionally, it seems that employ*ers* have violated employ*ee* rights more often than the other way around. But that's a lame excuse, isn't it, for ignoring a whole half of an issue. (Is it?)

Another point you should wonder about is why *rights* and not *responsibilities*? Well, one could say that rights entail responsibilities: if I have a right to X, you have a responsibility to provide X, or at least to not stand in the way of my acquiring X. Don't skip over that "or" too quickly – which is it? And is it definitely one of the two?

If we were to call this chapter, then, "Employee/Employer Rights and Responsibilities," well, that would pretty much cover the whole text: whistleblowing falls under employee responsibilities; product safety falls under employer responsibilities; profit falls under employer rights *and* responsibilities, as does the chapter on the environment, and the one on advertising, and so on. And certainly this chapter also overlaps with the chapter on international issues to the extent that employee rights are the same *wherever* you set up business. Actually, this chapter developed as a sort of "miscel-laneous" chapter – for employee rights issues not big enough to warrant chapters on their own. So perhaps it's best for you to consider this conceptual arrangement more of an arbitrary organization thing than a significant logic/value statement thing.

Now, to go back to our two opening questions, as to *what* rights employees might have, well, that may depend on what *basis* you establish. Some argue that the only rights an employee has, or should have, are those stipulated by the employment contract (which would, we hope, stipulate the employer's rights as well, and also both parties' responsibilities).

However, such a contract theory is open to a few criticisms. First, contract theory seems to ignore the reality that many contracts are not entered into freely. Sure, the employee signed it, voluntarily and with full knowledge of its contents, but if there were no other alternatives, no other income-providing jobs, how "free" was that person to *not* sign it? Some argue that for consent to be *truly* voluntary, not only must there *be* alternatives, but there must be *attractive* alternatives – did the person have another just-as-good job offer?

Second, the contract may allow parties to abuse each other: if the contract doesn't include, say, so-called "human rights," then the employer is under no obligation to respect those rights. An employer could, theoretically, be morally in the clear to hit employees, as long as the contract didn't specify that "employers shall not hit employees."

A modified contract theory might say that rights and responsibilities accord to the contract *as long as* no human rights are violated. And, in the absence of a contract, one might simply say that employees are entitled to the basic human rights; in fact, one might ask what's so different about being an employee – how are employee rights any different than ordinary human and civil rights? That is to say, why should we have more, or fewer, or different, rights at work than we do before or after work? (And why should an employer have any more, or less, or different, responsibility than any other person?)

Well, perhaps they're not any different; perhaps there are just special applications to the business sphere of standard rights. For example, the right to security of person (Article 3 of the United Nations' Declaration of Human Rights includes the right to life, liberty, and security of person) may translate into the right to a safe workplace. The right to marry and to found a family (Article 16) may translate into the right to parental leave and on-site childcare facilities. The right to rest and leisure (Article 24) might translate into the right to breaks and holidays. And so on.

What about the right to freedom of thought and belief, freedom of opinion and expression (Articles 18 and 19) – does that mean you should be able to pray all day long? Or just on your breaks? Does it mean you should have your holy days off? With pay? (Why? Why not?) Maybe the employer can't do anything to stop you from being religious (for example, forbid you to go to church after work), but that doesn't mean he or she has to let you be religious at work (for example, let you go to church on company time).

Can the company reprimand you for freely expressing your opinion if it's against the company? Why/not? Does it matter whether you do so on company time or on your own time? (Can't employees talk and work at the same time? And if they *can* talk, why can't they speak the truth as they understand it?) How far can a company go to project/protect its image? (Shouldn't image, appearance, pretence, be irrelevant – isn't reality, substance, the point? Why should I censor myself or dress a certain way to maintain a facade? And if it's not a facade, you won't need me to censor myself or dress a certain way; I'll *be* a certain way.)

Article 23 of the Declaration is especially relevant to our focus, as it claims that all people have the right to work, to free choice of employment, to just and favourable conditions of work, and to protection against unemployment; the right to equal pay for equal work; and the right to just and favourable remuneration.

I'm not suggesting, however, that the United Nations' Declaration is the definitive statement on human rights, let alone employee rights. There are other perspectives. Werhane describes a bill of rights for employees and employers, listing among others, for employees, the right to due process in the workplace, the right to engage in outside activities of their choice, and the right to participate in the decision-making processes entailed in his or her job. (See Ewing's "An Employee's Bill of Rights" for something similar.)

In addition to asking *what* rights, and on what *basis*, of course, we have to ask what do we do when rights collide? My right to freedom of speech steps on your right to freedom from a hostile environment – so now what? Well, if you can rank the principles or virtues involved, perhaps that will provide a solution. So will a utilitarian approach.

So much for rights in general: let's get specific.

The Right to Equal Treatment

– or the right not to be discriminated against. This one *does* have a separate chapter all to itself (it's next).

The Right to a Job

The right to a job? Is there such a thing? On what basis? One might say that it's a prerequisite for the pursuit of life, liberty, and happiness. Wait a minute – I have a *right* to happiness? How much happiness? (I can imagine that if an employer has to pay Person A $X for A to be happy, then s/he can't hire Persons B, C, or D, which causes them unhappiness, or then the employer will have to raise prices, so neither E nor F will be able to buy the product, which will make them unhappy, not to mention the employer him/herself – perhaps we're confusing the right to X with the right to *pursue* X, or even the right to pursue, *on equal grounds*, X.)

De George argues that the right to employment derives from the right to work, which can be derived from the right to life, to development, and to respect. He examines assumptions and conditions involved in this position, one of which is that the supply of labour exceeds the demand (359–365). Weiss argues that we have the right to a job because a job equals social status and self-esteem. (But do we have a *right* to those things?)

And once you have a job, is the employer under any obligation to let you keep it? Can he or she take the job away? For any reason or only for some certain specified reason? Why must s/he have a reason? There are a few essays about plant closings that address the obligation of the employer not to take away your job – they're well worth the read. (See, for example, Singer's article.)

As for the reasons for firing or dismissal, the common view is that this may be done only for "just cause." But what's "just"? De George suggests several possibilities: economic recession, inefficiency, immorality on the job, chronic late-ness or absenteeism, lack of ability to perform at the level expected, incompatibility with management or with other workers, lack of respect or deference to superiors, poor attitude toward work, the voicing of dissent, an employer's belief that he or she can find someone who can do the job better, the employer's dislike of the employee for personal reasons (394) – are all of these *just* cause? Where do you draw the line (and why)? See Boatright's chapter on unjust dismissal for a good discussion of this very question.

For example, why is lack of deference just cause? Why should I be deferential to another human being, my equal (and quite possibly my "junior," and less or at least differently experienced than me, and less or differently qualified than me)? And why is voicing dissent just cause? If you want your employees to be thinking, morally responsible, adults, then how can you also demand deference and acquiescence?

In the case of lay-offs, certainly the current prevalence of downsizing brings this ethical issue into the spotlight: Who do you lay off? How do you lay off? And what about the "survivors"? (See the Ridler article for a few suggestions.) Di Norcia suggests that downsizing is often reactive and usually not at all the best of the options available to management:

> Not only does it worsen employee morale, it also results in productivity declines, loss of competitiveness and other costs. Nor does cost-cutting itself improve sales or increase market share. Layoffs have costs too: severance payouts, the loss of employees with valuable corporate knowledge, poor morale, and lower productivity. (146)

Alternatives to this "pathological management syndrome" (146) include "cutting overtime, reducing/rearranging the work week; reducing benefits and wages; days off without pay; redeploying and retraining employees" (148). He goes on to say that

> [w]here personnel cuts are necessary they should be distributed equitably across the organization, beginning in the executive suite and moving down, not the other way around. Where employees must be let go, attrition is preferable to layoffs or resignations as a means of workforce reduction. (148)

Lay-offs are often done according to seniority – but should this be the case? Is that morally right? Some associate seniority with loyalty, but are we sure that length of employment at any one company is a measure of the employee's loyalty to that company? Might it be, instead, as is more likely the case today, a measure of the paucity of other employment opportunities for that employee? Or perhaps it is just a measure of the employee's reluctance to take risks, to change directions. Seniority *per se* is merely longevity; it is a measure of quantity, not quality. Quantity *may* affect quality, longevity *may* increase ability and accomplishment, but then again, they may not. (Many mediocre employees are given raises year after year just because they've been there one more year. Is it any wonder then that so many employees develop a clock-punching mentality, thinking that just being there, just putting in time, is enough? After all, it is: if they put in enough time, they get that wage increase, those extra holidays – and a stronger guarantee that they'll continue to just be there.)

And of course not just *whether* you dismiss or lay-off, but *how* you do so can be an ethical issue: Do you provide notice and a reason? Do you provide the right to appeal, due process? (Why not – are management decisions infallible? But then again, why – just whose company is this?)

The Right to a Fair Wage

The right to a fair wage – what's fair? Recall the justice theories discussed in Section II of this text – do we determine according to need, value, time, effort....

Shaw (217–218) suggests seven questions worth asking to determine what's fair in this case: what's the law, what's the prevailing wage in the industry, what's the community wage level, what's the nature of the job itself, is the job secure and what are its prospects, what are the employer's financial capabilities, and what are other employees inside the organization earning for comparable work? De George also discusses this right to a just wage (366–370).

Here's another question for you: Does setting a minimum wage, a wage that ensures some minimum standard of living, some minimum justice, imply that you should also set a maximum wage? Why/not? Or perhaps, in the interests of justice, you should set a maximum ratio of maximum to minimum wage – are the upper-level managers *really* entitled to fifty times what your front-line workers earn?

The Right to Privacy

This is an issue that is becoming increasingly important, given the development of informational technology: there are many more ways to invade, and perhaps many more reasons for invading, employees' privacy. Both Boatright and De George devote an entire chapter to this issue.

What exactly is privacy? Garrett and Klonoski (47–49) distinguish between psychological privacy (one's thoughts, feelings, desires, etc.) and physical privacy (one's physical activities). A starting point for a definition of psychological privacy might be that the right to privacy is the right to control access by others to personal knowledge. Next, we'd have to define "personal" – and determine when, if ever, the company has a right to personal knowledge.

A manager or company may be justifiably interested in whatever affects job performance (a narrow view) or whatever affects the company (a broader view), but how far can they go in acting on that interest? Are they entitled to acquiring the information? Anytime, anywhere, anyhow?

One potential invasion of privacy involves monitoring job performance. After all, how else can you be sure you have a quality workforce? Certainly first-hand evidence is preferable to rumour. But what, exactly, should this evidence include? Logging the number of calls, the length of calls, or the content of calls? Reading the employee's e-mail messages? (Is it reasonable, is it healthy, to demand, to expect, that all e-mail messages be bereft of anything personal, any personality? If not, then is it fair, is it right, to read e-mail? And if so, why exactly would you need to do so?) Observing the employee's actions – time away from the desk, trips to the washroom, etc.? (Won't respecting privacy, and trusting, ensure quality performance? Treat someone like an irresponsible, cheating kid and soon enough they'll act like one, no?) And should any of this be done without the employee's knowledge?

Privacy invasion may include more than just monitoring performance at work; in fact, it can start even before you get the job – interview questions, background checks, and reference contacts may also be unjustified invasions of privacy.

And gathering information is one issue – whether to gather, how to gather (overtly or covertly), what to gather (information about sex, age, race, religion, health, performance, income, interests, personality, etc.). But the use of it is another – whether to give it to other employees, to other companies (database trading), to governments, to landlords, to banks, etc.

Privacy invasion can continue even after you go home from work – can a company tell you not to smoke, even at home? Well, maybe if they're going to be the ones to pay for your lung cancer treatments.

So exactly what is justified invasion? Only that which is relevant to job performance? So if your employees are professional athletes – then is drug testing justified? And would those found *not* to be using performance-enhancing steroids be required to do so? See Caste for an interesting article along these lines. What if they're bank employees? Toronto Dominion Bank's drug-testing policy to screen new hires was deemed discriminatory against the disabled, which was taken to include those with a previous or existing dependence on a drug. DesJardins and Duska explore the job-relevant criterion, considering both job performance (which affects productivity and profits) and harm to individuals (employees, consumers); they find the first inadequate justification for the invasive testing, the second *conditionally* adequate. (Moore would disagree, arguing that "responsibility for the actions of others does not entitle us to do anything at all to control their behavior" [abstract].)

What about invasions that are relevant to the cost of employee benefits? (Is this employee likely to cost us a lot – because of illness? because of pregnancy? because she is a bungee-jumping freak likely to become a paraplegic? But so what – will you not hire that person then? Or will you just demand that she stop bungee jumping – and smoking? Or will you demand she change her genes, if she's predisposed to develop Parkinson's disease?) See Kupfer for an essay about genetic screening – does a company have a right to do that? See also Gunderson et al., Ladd et al., and Simms – all address testing, hiring (or not), and healthcare costs.

Utilitarian arguments in favour of respecting privacy and in favour of violating privacy weigh the consequences for all involved: maybe it's for the good of the company, for the good of the customers, to monitor a pilot's off-time alcohol consumption. But maybe covert surveillance of the office floor will just result in distrust, lower morale, and paranoia.

Kantian ethics seem to favour respect for privacy – invasions of privacy not only fail to respect persons, but they hinder their autonomy. See Lippke about the relationship between privacy and autonomy: "[p]rivacy conveys to individuals the sense that they are capable of acting autonomously, that they are worthy of doing so, and that they are entitled to do so" (83).

Is it a question of ownership? Then how much does the owner of the company own – physical stuff, workers' time, workers' ability, workers? And anyway, the owner doesn't own, not in a large business; the stockholders own, don't they? But ownership alone might not justify control; recall the stakeholder theory.

One might also consider whether invasion of privacy is the best, the only, way to acquire the information needed or desired. (Consider your alternatives!)

The Right to a Safe Workplace

A first important question is "Is an employer obligated to provide a healthy and safe workplace?" Yes, because we have a right to survival? (Why, just because we happened to be born?) Or yes, because an employer who has an unsafe, unhealthy workplace is obviously treating its workers as the means to his/her end and is therefore morally in the wrong (an appeal to Kantian ethics rather than to rights theories)?

A second important question regarding workplace safety is, as with product safety, "How safe is safe enough?" Lowrance presents a valuable insight when he distinguishes between, and then connects, safety and risk: "Safety is not measured. *Risks* are measured. Only when those risks are weighed on the balance of social values can safety be judged: *a thing is safe if its attendant risks are judged to be acceptable*" (224). He goes on to determine acceptability according to custom of usage, prevailing of professional practice, best available practice, detectable adverse effects, and the threshold principle.

But is it necessarily and completely the employer's decision to make? What if your employees are *willing* to work in a dangerous workplace? (Don't I have the right to be a crash test dummy if that's what I want to be when I grow up?) Especially if it's for more pay? Shouldn't people have the right to choose? (Perhaps a theory of rights can be *too* robust – and can thereby infringe on people's autonomy, their freedom of choice.)

But should a company influence that choice by offering danger pay? (Should it expect dangerous jobs to be done at regular pay?) Is that influence or manipulation? Do your employees have alternatives – *attractive* alternatives? (Is that necessary before we call their willingness a free choice?)

Asking whether employees have the right to choose to accept the danger is separate from asking whether the employee has the right to be *told* about the danger. And then can they refuse any dangerous part without losing their job?

Peskin and McGrath note that "accidents do not happen randomly; they are caused" (66) — by inadequate worker training, lack of understanding of the job, improper tools and equipment, hazardous work environments, poor equipment maintenance, and overly tight scheduling (and hotshot workers who show off or who partied the night before?), suggesting that one's moral responsibility may be not just to passively do no harm but to actively prevent harm. One might add that prevention is important not only with industrial injuries: carpal tunnel syndrome from keyboarding and chronic lower back pain from cashiering are both preventable (why *do* they have to *stand* for eight hours, lifting stuff across the checkout with the upper body only?) (and at a checkout that's about 6" too high — I swear the engineers neglected to consider that the average cashier would be 5'4", not 5'10"). See Boatright, who has an entire chapter on occupational health and safety.

In the matter of prevention, does foreknowledge matter? A classic case of worker safety is the Johns Manville company, which became aware of the adverse health effects of asbestos exposure in the 1930s but, nevertheless, did nothing to inform its workers. Are they therefore more at fault? With respect to foreknowledge, how much must the employer do to determine long-term ill effects of the work environment? Is it fair to require over ten years of testing before you even open your business?

Also, with respect to prevention, does the availability of alternatives matter? (Well, one alternative is *always* available — shut down the business. ... Yes, that *is* an option.)

Frances Early, focusing on the Canadian nuclear industry, makes an interesting point about discrimination and the right to a safe workplace: traditionally, women of reproductive age, whether pregnant or not, have been kept out of jobs that pose reproductive health hazards; but men, whose sperm may be damaged by the same conditions, have not been so restricted, not so protected. How can this be justified?

The Right to Parental Leave

Before focusing on this particular benefit, we may well ask about benefits in general: Is it the employer's obligation to provide benefits? Why/ not? What benefits should be provided? Why those and not others? And should benefits be available only to full-time workers or to all workers, on a pro-rated basis?

Now, as for parental leave, why should that be a right — with or without pay? I mean if Person A gets a year off to have a child, why shouldn't B get a year off to write a symphony? Is there something special about children? (Let's face it — almost anyone can make a baby, but few people can write music; some children grow up to be real nasty, but I've seldom heard of music doing any real damage — well, okay, except for country.) Is there something special about children that obligates an employer to provide some benefit to employees? If anything, shouldn't society as a whole bear the burden of maintaining the species? (And I'm not suggesting for a minute that maintaining the species is necessarily a good thing.)

Shaw supports parental leave, suggesting that we shouldn't have to choose between a meaningful career and meaningful parenthood (though the latter *is* the former):

> Enhanced opportunities for part-time employment and job sharing, along with generous parental leave arrangements and flexible, affordable, and accessible firm-sponsored child-care facilities, could enable both fathers and mothers to achieve a more personally desirable balance between paid work and family relations. (255)

But again, why is that a *company's* responsibility?

Right to Participation

A right that has recently entered the forum of discussion is the right to democratic participation in the company's decision-making. McCall argues that there *is* an ethical basis for such participation in corporate decision-making. Shaw supports this view, pointing out that worker dissatisfaction results from the company's "preoccupation with quantity, not quality; the rigidity of rules and regulations; ...the lack of opportunities to be one's own boss..." (255, referring to a 1970s study by the U.S. Secretary of Health, Education, and Welfare).

But input into company policies and procedures? This is not a co-op! You didn't help start the company, it's not *your* company, *I* started it, *I* funded it (did you? 100%?), *I* own it (do you? 100%?), *I'll* run it! (all by yourself?)

Right to Respect

Harassment often gets categorized with discrimination, but the one doesn't necessarily involve the other; for example, a bisexual person could harass *everyone* s/he was sexually interested in. It is also important to distinguish between sex-*ist* harassment (discriminatory) and sex*ual* harassment (discriminatory or non-discriminatory). And harassment may not be sex-based at all – employees may be harassed for holding certain "unpopular" opinions, for example, or they may be harassed just because they're very annoying.

There are generally two kinds of harassment. "Quid pro quo" ("this for that") cases, in which an employee is promised something (a promotion or a pay increase, for example) in return for sexual interaction (or threatened with loss of job or demotion unless such interaction is provided), are easily understood as morally unacceptable.

But "hostile work environment" cases, in which certain employees work in an environment that is intimidating, offensive, or demeaning to them because of comments, gestures, decorations, dress codes, and so on, are a little more difficult.

One big question is "how offensive is offensive?" One way to decide this is according to the "reasonable person" standard. But one of the problems with this is that a reasonable man may react quite differently than a reasonable woman: for example, suppose there is someone walking behind you at night who changes sides of the street every time you do – if you're a woman, you might reasonably fear attack, but if you're a man, you might reasonably just think that some idiot can't make up his mind about which side of the road to walk on. (See Abrams, as well as Paetzold and Shaw, for a discussion of this issue.)

Another way to decide offense is according to the subjective standard: if the person involved considers the action offensive, it's offensive. Period. But how would you know that your action is going to be offensive, or unwelcome, to that particular person until you do whatever it is?

Well, one might suggest that you could just play it safe and wait until after work to ask for that date. But why does asking for a date, which may be harassment if it's done during the workday, suddenly become *not* harassment when it's done after work?

A more fundamental question is "why is it wrong to offend?" Do we have a right not to be offended? Anywhere, anytime? Is it wrong because it causes psychological harm? Does psychological harm count as much as physical harm? Some argue that when the offensive behaviour involves touching, it is wrong because it violates one's privacy, one's physical integrity. (What exactly is that?) It may also be wrong because it violates one's rights to freedom – harassment restricts one's choices in very subtle ways.

But what about offensive behaviour that "just" involves speech? It may be wrong to insult, but some people are offended merely by an opposing point of view. Do we really want to limit freedom of speech to that which is agreeable to others?

In addition to these rights arguments, one can make a Kantian argument that certain behaviour often identified as harassment does not show respect for persons as persons. Furthermore, a hostile work environment keeps individuals from the offices and positions for which Rawls argues all must have equal opportunity in a just society. One can also make a utilitarian argument: the low morale, let alone the lower productivity, of harassed employees is certainly not good for the company (or society as a whole).

Another question is "how interfering is interfering enough?" Is a one-time occurrence considered harassment or must the behaviour be persistent?

Lastly, one should consider the power relationship. An interaction between a so-called superior and a subordinate may have different value than the same interaction between equals, simply because of the ability, in the first case, of the one party to bring about specific consequences (such as promotion or pay increase).

Another interesting issue related to the right to respect, and one that Velasquez looks at in his discussion of the political organization of the company, is the ethics of political tactics, the things one does to "get ahead" (467–474).

But one might do well to look at the ethics of the political organization itself. The traditional corporate structure – hierarchy – seems to leave little room for respect for the person. The very words 'subordinate' and 'insubordination' (the latter basically means criticizing one's superiors – one's *organizational* superiors – and is usually considered just cause for dismissal) suggest this. So too do the starting and quitting time buzzer, that sounds like the school bell; the regimented morning and afternoon 15-minute coffee breaks, reminiscent of recess; performance reviews treated like report cards; disciplinary hearings that feel like being called in to the principal's office; dress codes like school uniforms. Really, is all this necessary? Excuse me, but I'm an adult, I can dress myself! (Safety helmets, okay; hospital whites for quick emergency identification, okay; cleanliness, okay – but beyond that?)

Isn't this organization structure founded on a very insulting view of people, people who are adults (and often have been for quite some time)? See the essay by Maguire in this chapter for a more academic discussion of this issue.

Consider the standard corporate view of responsibility: the subordinate actually *does* X, but the superordinate (I will not say 'superior') is *responsible for* X. If there's a problem, s/he's the one who'll be held accountable. This conception of responsibility infantilizes the subordinate. A sign of maturity is that one takes responsibility for one's actions. Only with children (and the mentally incompetent) is someone else held responsible. Denying the subordinate that responsibility, then, is insisting on juvenile (or incompetent) status. (It also puts a great deal of strain on the superordinate. It is very stressful to be responsible for someone else's behaviour. One has the responsibility, but not the power, not the control. No wonder superordinates develop ulcers. And no wonder they can develop into control freaks: if one is responsible for something, one is surely going to try to have some control over that something. Which of course will be resented by any truly mature and autonomous 'subordinate'...)

Perhaps virtue ethics can play a valuable role here in deciding what's right: trust, respect, honesty, integrity, dignity, self-development, well-being, security, respect, dignity, pride, choice, freedom...are these fostered in such an environment?

REFERENCES AND FURTHER READING

Abrams, Kathryn. "The Reasonable Woman: Sense and Sensibility in Sexual Harassment Law." *Dissent* (Winter 1995): 48-55.

Boatright, John R. *Ethics and the Conduct of Business.* 2nd ed. NJ: Prentice Hall, 1997.

Brenkert, George G. "Privacy, Polygraphs and Work." *Business and Professional Ethics Journal* 1.1 (Fall 1981): 19-35.

Caste, Nicholas J. "Drug Testing and Productivity." *Journal of Business Ethics.* 11.4 (April 1992): 301-306.

De George, Richard T. *Business Ethics.* 5th ed. NJ: Prentice Hall, 1999.

DesJardins, Joseph and Ronald Duska. "Drug Testing in Employment." *Business and Professional Ethics Journal* 6 (1987): 3-21.

Di Norcia, Vincent. "Downsizing, Change and Ownership." Rpt. in *The Ethics of the New Economy: Restructuring and Beyond.* Ed. Leo Groarke. Waterloo: WLU Press, 1998. 143-154.

Dodds, Susan M., Lucy Frost, Robert Pargetter, and Elizabeth W. Prior. "Sexual Harassment." *Social Theory and Practice* 14.2 (Summer 1988): 111-130.

Early, Frances H. "Reproductive Health Hazards at Work: The Canadian Atomic Industry." *Business Ethics in Canada.* Ed. Deborah C. Poff and Wilfrid J. Waluchow. 2nd ed. Scarborough: Prentice Hall, 1991. 216-221.

Ewing, David. W. "An Employees' Bill of Rights." *Moral Issues in Business.* 7th ed. Ed. William H. Shaw and Vincent Barry. Belmont, CA: Wadsworth, 1998. 278–289.

Ewing, David W. *Freedom Inside the Organization.* NY: Dutton, 1977.

Garrett, Thomas M., and Richard J. Klonoski. *Business Ethics.* 2nd ed. NJ: Prentice Hall, 1986.

Gunderson, Martin, David Mayo, and Frank Rhame. "AIDS Testing Mandated by Insurers and Employers." *AIDS: Testing and Privacy.* Ed. Martin Gunderson, David Mayo, and Frank Rhame. Salt Lake City: University of Utah Press, 1989. 165-188.

Kupfer, Joseph. "The Ethics of Genetic Screening in the Workplace." *Business Ethics Quarterly* 3.1 (January 1993): 17-25.

Ladd, Rosalind, Lynn Pasquerella, and Sheri Smith. "Liability-driven Ethics: The Impact on Hiring Practices." *Business Ethics Quarterly* 4.3 (July 1994): 321-333.

Lippke, Richard. *Radical Business Ethics.* Lanham, MD: Rowman & Littlefield, 1995. (Chapter 4, "Privacy, Work, and Autonomy")

Lowrance, William W. "Of Acceptable Risk." *Ethical Issues in Business.* Ed. Michael Boylan. Fort Worth, TX: Harcourt Brace College Publishers, 1995. 223–231.

Manning, Rita C. "Liberal and Communitarian Defenses of Workplace Privacy." *Journal of Business Ethics* 16.8 (June 1997): 817-823.

McCall, John J. "An Ethical Basis for Employee Participation." *Contemporary Issues in Business Ethics.* Ed. Joseph R. Desjardins and John J. McCall. 3rd ed. Belmont, CA: Wadsworth, 1996: 199-206.

Moore, Jennifer. "Drug Testing and Corporate Responsibility: The 'Ought Implies Can' Argument." *Journal of Business Ethics* 8.4 (April 1989): 279-287.

Ottensmeyer, Edward J., and Mark A. Heroux. "Ethics, Public Policy, and Managing Advanced Technologies: The Case of Electronic Surveillance." *Journal of Business Ethics* 10.7 (July 1991): 519-526.

Paetzold, Ramona L., and Bill Shaw. "A Postmodern Feminist View of 'Reasonableness' in Hostile Environment Sexual Harassment." *Journal of Business Ethics* 13.9 (September 1994): 681-691.

Peskin, Myron I., and Francis J. McGrath. "Industrial Safety: Who Is Responsible and Who Benefits?" *Business Horizons* 35.3 (May-June 1992): 66-70.

Ridler, Jim. "Ethical Downsizing: How to Walk the Talk." *Engineering Dimension* (July/August 1997): 40-41.

Schwoerer, Catherine E., Douglas R. May, and Benson Rosen. "Organizational Characteristics and HRM Policies on Rights: Exploring the Patterns of Connections." *Journal of Business Ethics* 14.7 (July 1995): 531-549.

Shaw, William H. *Business Ethics.* 2nd ed. CA: Wadsworth, 1996.

Simms, Michele. "Defining Privacy in Employee Health Screening Cases: Ethical Ramifications Concerning the Employee/Employer Relationship." *Journal of Business Ethics* 13.5 (May 1994): 315-325.

Singer, Joseph William. "The Reliance Interest in Property." *Stanford Law Review* 40/611 (February 1988): 614-733.

Stewart, Wayne H., Donna E. Ledgerwood, and Ruth C. May. "Educating Business Schools about Safety & Health is No Accident." *Journal of Business Ethics* 15.8 (August 1996): 919-926.

Velasquez, Manuel G. *Business Ethics: Concepts and Cases.* 4th ed. NJ: Prentice Hall, 1998.

Weiss, Joseph W. *Business Ethics: A Managerial, Stakeholder Approach.* CA: Wadsworth, 1994. 188-196.

Wells, Deborah L., and Beverly J. Kracher. "Justice, Sexual Harassment, and the Reasonable Victim Standard." *Journal of Business Ethics* 12.6 (June 1993): 423-431.

Werhane, Patricia H. *Persons, Rights and Corporations.* NJ: Prentice Hall, 1985. 168-170.

Ethical Outsourcing in UK Financial Services: Employee Rights

Mike J. Henderson

[Introductory material about outsourcing (definitions − "outsourcing is taken to mean buying a service which forms part of the value chain of the business from an outside supplier where previously that service was provided through an in-house operation", descriptions, decisional factors) and ethics in business (duties, rights) has been omitted.]

The Ethical Dimension to Employee Rights

1   As an approach to the analysis of the rights of employees, it is useful to begin by considering the possible argument that the only rights which employees have are those specifically created by statute or by a contract of employment (De George, 1982). Although few people today would take this view of the ethical position, it does, at least, have the merit of logical clarity, and some of the arguments around the moral responsibilities of business do come close to rejecting employee rights grounded in morality. For instance, Barry (1991, pp. 70-71) argues that efficiency is moral, thus giving a moral justification for actions such as lay-offs and plant clo-

sures which other writers have seen as posing moral problems. In one sense, the employment contract must be seen as a matter for management judgement alone, but as Selekman and Selekman (1956) comment,

> In terms of technical considerations, man's labor must be viewed impersonally, as an item of cost, an objective matter-of-fact element in the task of turning out wealth for the community. But the human being, as an acting part of any job content and as the ultimate recipient of the products of the enterprise, inevitably introduces ethical criteria. (p. 60)

Buono and Bowditch (1989) similarly reject the view that employees only have rights which they have negotiated, and, therefore, similarly distance themselves from the suggestion that in mergers and acquisitions the moral dilemmas arise from conflict between different groups of shareholders. They see the issues as much broader than this, taking the employees' interests into account too.

2   Werhane (1985) makes a particularly strong case for the rights of employees, in a careful analysis of the distinction between employee rights and property rights to a job.

> Rights to jobs are not property rights because ... persons are not property, nor do we want to think of them as such since this opens up the opportunity to defend voluntary slavery. Because persons are *not* forms of property, violations of

Mike J. Henderson, "Ethical Outsourcing in UK Financial Services: Employee Rights" *Business Ethics* 6.2 (1997): 110-124. © 1997 by Blackwell Publishers Ltd. Reprinted with permission of the publisher and the author.

the rights of persons are more serious, much more serious, than violations of property rights. (p. 150)

If it is accepted that employee rights exist at the moral level, independently of any legislation on employment, the question of the ethical impact of outsourcing then depends on the nature and extent of the moral rights of the employee. One way to look at this is in fairly strict utilitarian terms, based on a calculation of the benefits and costs as Hosner (1987) suggests, though he does go on to argue that how the benefits are distributed may also matter. However, in general terms, the weakness of the utilitarian argument is that it is based on calculations which are impossible to complete; no one can know the full range of consequences of any action. Moore's attempts to get round some of the difficulties bring in such factors as motivation for the action and the relationship between actual and probable outcomes. All of these elements suggest that guidelines for moral behaviour cannot be derived from the application of utilitarianism, and may leave an ethical vacuum which allows any behaviour regardless of moral considerations.

3   As already discussed, an alternative to a general approach to the treatment of employees is to develop a checklist of specific rights which arise from the concept of the ethical context of the employment relationship. Although there is clearly a certain arbitrariness about this approach, it does seem worthwhile as a practical means of setting criteria to apply to decisions. The decision to outsource can then be assessed like any other policy change, such as a takeover or merger (considered in Malachowski, 1992) or a closure of a plant (Carroll, 1989), both of which have important similarities to outsourcing. Werhane (1985) is again helpful in suggesting a range of possible items for inclusion in a list of rights, and from her list a number of issues seem particularly pertinent in examining the question of outsourcing. Two of these issues she sees as basic rights, the right to employee information and the right to fair pay. She also goes on to discuss the right not to be fired, which she argues is not a basic right, but one which, nevertheless, should be recognised. This is, of course, separate from the question of unfair dismissal, considered, for example, in Green (1994) which seems much less of an ethical issue since the rights and wrongs are more obvious.

4   Although the question of where these rights derive from is clearly an important one to consider, it is part of a far deeper analysis of the whole idea that rights can exist, which it is not the purpose of this paper to explore. Even if there can be no certainty that people, and specifically people as employees, have any rights, the assumption that there are such rights is a viable basis for discussion, and the following sections take that assumption as a starting point. Linked to this assumption that rights exist, there is probably a corresponding implication that managers dealing with their staff have a duty to respect those rights, but the following discussion focusses only on rights, as the issue of duties does not alter the basic argument.

The Right to Employee Information

5   In the event of a management decision to outsource certain operations, access to information is clearly important, but as with other management decisions, for example, about products or about pricing, it could be argued that employees have no specific right to know what is under consideration. The claim that such a right does exist may be based largely on the belief that people are entitled to respect as human beings.

Respect for the employee also entails keeping the employee well-informed about his or her job, the quality of his or her work, and the stability of the company. This information is required because employees are persons and persons should retain control of their lives. Only with accurate information about the place of employment can an employee make informed decisions about the future. One cannot be expected to be committed to an employer if one is ill-informed about one's job, the status of one's position, or the economic situation of the employer. This is not to say that an employer is a welfare agency responsible for every aspect of his or her employees' lives, but the employer is responsible for the decency and the safety of the work situation and should enable the employee to improve, if possible, those aspects of her life that are under the employer's control. (Werhane, 1985, p. 103)

The latter part of this paragraph also hints at the possibility of a moral duty on employers to help their employees to develop, and this idea is taken further in Drew and Smith (1995). If a firm wants to outsource, then it might be ethically more acceptable if staff who were likely to be transferred to a new employer, or made redundant, received adequate preparation for the change in their circumstances, including such matters as skills training suitable for the needs of local industry.

The Right to Fair Pay

6 I accept the argument put forward by Werhane for a right to fair pay whilst recognising that there are enormous practical difficulties about establishing what constitutes a fair rate. Given that there are potential difficulties of definition, if there is assumed to be a right to fair pay, this right may be threatened by a decision to outsource, because the employee may have chosen to work for a particular organisation on the grounds that the policies of the company towards staff and their remuneration are fair. If a management decision deprives the employee of that relationship, and substitutes for it a relationship with a different employer, not of the employee's choosing, there is potential for decisions on pay to be made on a different basis, which could be an unfair basis.

7 It would be simplistic to suggest that current pay for all employees is fair and that any reduction in pay is inherently unfair, but the argument about fair pay could be seen as broader than that. Fair pay must take into account the whole remuneration package and working conditions, so that extra benefits in one respect might make up for lower rewards in some other sense. Fair must also mean something different from the current level, since otherwise everyone, by definition, would be getting fair pay. A working definition might be that pay (in the very broadest sense, adjusted for other elements of the total reward to employees) is fair if it comes within a range typical for work of that type in the society within which the analysis is being carried out. This too has its drawbacks as a definition since it rules out an important possibility, which logically it might be preferable to allow, i.e., that a whole sector of the economy suffers from unfair pay (either too low, to the detriment of those working in the sector or too high, to the detriment of everyone else).

8 Even within the limits of the suggested definition, issues relating to outsourcing seem significant. As discussed, one of the reasons for outsourcing is to get to the point where an area of work is being done more cheaply than before, and lower pay could be one of the ways by which this is achieved. Shifting staff to a new

employer who cuts pay, or at the very least, freezes it while others get pay rises, could mean unfairly low pay for those affected. This is not to say that staying with the same employer would have prevented a similar outcome; on the contrary, if a particular operation has become overpriced in comparison to competing operations, the original employer might feel compelled to cut the pay offered to staff as an alternative to outsourcing, in which case outsourcing would seem to be ethically neutral. If job security is taken to be one of the broad components which make up the overall package an employer offers, staff with a long period of service in the financial services sector have already suffered a substantial reduction in what their own employers have offered to them, since job security has clearly been dramatically reduced, with the sense of having a job for life now long gone.

9   Another important point to make is that the likelihood of a pay cut for the staff affected by outsourcing may be a way of achieving greater fairness if the previous level of pay was too high, according to the earlier definition.

The Right Not to be Fired

10 Accepting again that Werhane's analysis has some validity, the right not to be fired is linked to the sense that human beings should be treated with respect, as something more than just resources to be manipulated in the interests of the business for which they work. The argument that such a right exists does not mean that an employer would never be justified in getting rid of staff, but firing people without the kind of valid reasons recognised by workers themselves and incorporated into legislation is seen as being of doubtful morality, partly because it does have

the kind of harmful influence on people which no human being should lightly exert on another. If this is true for the actual process of firing staff, it has similar force where job losses are threatened. As McDonald and Doyle (1981) argue:

> The anxiety caused by the constant threat of unemployment is very real — and the actual effect of being made redundant is often traumatic.
>
> How severe the effects of unemployment are depends on a number of things, like how unexpected the job loss was and how long the person is without a job. Often the initial reaction to job loss is optimistic — about getting another job, and treating the time off as a holiday. However, as the money runs short and no job is forthcoming this soon gives rise to anxiety and depression. Once in a state of depression a person feels lacking in energy, will spend a good deal of time lying in bed, which in turn leads to an acceptance of being unemployed; accompanied with feelings of apathy, inferiority and submissiveness. (p. 22)

The picture provided here is, if anything, over-optimistic, given the high levels of unemployment and the widespread awareness that long-term unemployment is not unusual; the initial optimism which McDonald and Doyle refer to is surely rarer now than it was in the early eighties.

11   The decision to outsource tends to have implications of reduced job security, and is, therefore, one which an employer should only make if it is possible to show that the criteria needed to make a firing decision are being met.

12   Generally speaking, factors specific to an individual apart, this would mean that the employer would be faced with declaring jobs redundant. If this is the position, then outsourcing as a means of dealing with the problem might be seen as an appropriate way of giving staff a good opportunity to adapt to a different work-

ing environment rather than simply leaving each of them individually to evaluate other employment possibilities. Such a convenient arrangement seems hardly likely, however, because the nature of outsourcing implies that the work does still need to be done; the process or operation remains part of the value chain. There is no redundancy involved, except perhaps at the margin, and therefore a move equivalent to firing does not seem ethically justified without some further rationale. Possible examples of adequate rationales, like those associated with the concept of fair pay, might be based on the needs of other interest groups such as the customers or investors, for whom some ethical priority might be established, as discussed later.

The Right to be Free from Discrimination

13 One of the issues for employers dealing with outsourcing (and with other changes in employment such as redundancies or promotion policy) is the need to ensure that staff who are affected are not treated in a discriminatory way. To some extent the legislative protections against discrimination (Sex Discrimination Act 1975, Race Relations Act 1976 and Equal Pay Act 1970) take this out of the moral arena and make it a matter of compliance with the law. However, it remains true that the staff who are most likely to be adversely affected by outsourcing in financial services are those working in back-office processing where women outnumber men.

14   Issues of discrimination against women in work practices have been extensively reported (for example, Huws, 1982), and some of the specific issues arising from the restructuring of the banking industry are discussed in Halford and Savage (1995). Although this does not directly address outsourcing as an approach to restructuring, the arguments put forward about a newly emerging culture are significant because the power struggle to establish a culture arises from similar conflicts to those which mean that decisions about outsourcing are ethical dilemmas: different parties to the decision have different needs. Women in low status jobs are among those most directly affected. It can, of course, be argued that the general failure to promote women (or members of other identifiable groups) within our society is most appropriately criticised on the grounds that such waste of talents is economically inefficient in the long-term. To accept this view is not to reject the view that discriminatory structures are also ethically unacceptable. On the contrary, the ethical dimension gives added force to the criticism. If outsourcing increases the extent to which women suffer from reduced opportunities to use their abilities, this can be seen as evidence of both long-term inefficiency and unethical decision-making. As Miller (1996) argues, ethical human resource management goes hand-in-hand with a long-term strategic perspective.

The Treatment of Staff Left Behind

15 Apart from the need to treat outsourced staff in a fair, non-discriminatory way, it would be ethically desirable to ensure that staff remaining within an organisation that has outsourced operations are also treated in a way which recognises their moral rights, and again, in particular, the rights to information and to fair pay. As far as information is concerned, remaining staff are likely to anticipate that further upheaval will occur, and the evidence suggests (Brockner et al, 1993) that this will lead to stress and anxiety unless clear and positive measures are taken to counteract such responses.

Ethical Aspects of the Impact of Outsourcing on Customers

16 Although this paper concentrates on the position of employees when outsourcing takes place, there is some effect too on customers, quite apart from the extent to which the importance of their stake in the business has a bearing on the treatment of staff. A customer of a financial services business is likely to make a choice about the use of the organisation on the basis of trust and confidence. The fiduciary nature of the relationship between, for example a bank and a customer, and the importance of security and secrecy about the customer's private affairs means that the disclosure of information and the handing over of control of particular operational matters to a third party significantly changes the position. In general, customers are not clearly informed about outsourcing, are certainly not consulted about it and tend to remain in ignorance of it, unless or until something goes seriously wrong. With most manufactured goods, the fact that a seller is not the manufacturer is unlikely to matter to the customer (although issues about sources of supply and their acceptability do arise – for example, imported goods made by child labour sold as UK made), but with financial services, the consumer does not expect to buy something which could be considered to be misleadingly labelled.

17 More significantly, the change which takes place as a result of outsourcing may, in some circumstances, change price and/or quality without the consumer intending that this should happen. Where a house purchase loan provided by one institution is sold to another institution as a means of outsourcing the funding or the processing stage of the value chain, the borrower may find that the attitude to late payment of instalments is tougher than before or that the interest rate charged is higher than that of competitors. Clearly outsourcing could also work to the customer's benefit (though, for reasons of cost discussed earlier, this is unlikely), so the ethical issue is not that conditions may get worse, but that the change has taken place in a way which treats the customer as having no say. In any economic system, information has a cost, so there is no inherent right to knowledge. However, a buyer in a market choosing a particular seller on the basis of information obtained would consider it unethical if the seller had deliberately provided false information. A transfer of part of what a seller does to some other organisation is a way of changing the information without revealing that this is happening, and could certainly be considered to be "economical with the truth".

Ethical Expectations of Investors

18 The interests of investors in a business which outsources are also not central to this paper, but ethical questions tend to occur where there are conflicting objectives. For investors, a primary goal is to obtain a return on the investment, and the higher the return, the better this objective is met, but investors may also have their own ethical stance to take into account (which leads to the work of EIRIS [EIRIS, 1989] and other analysts assessing organisations in terms of their suitability for investors with specific preferences). Outsourcing may be a means of increasing the return earned by the investors, but it may be at a cost to those investors who do not believe the decision to be ethical.

19 In general, the views of investors present less of a problem for the managers who make the decision to outsource because the shareholder, at least in a quoted company, is freely

able to re-invest elsewhere and does not have the commitment to a long-term relationship that a customer or an employee has (Institute of Business Ethics, 1990). Concern for the shareholder might also be less of an ethical issue because the likelihood of gain when outsourcing occurs is greater than for other stakeholders, since the primary rationale for the decision is improved performance of the business.

The Ethical Context of Outsourcing

20 Outsourcing, as one of the many ways in which an organisation can restructure some of its activities, is a change which can have a major impact on the lives of many people. The managers who decide to implement such a change can do so without regard to the needs and interests of those people or can attempt to take those needs and interests into account. An ethical approach to the decision is based on the latter perspective.

Decision Making in Financial Services Organisations

21 In practice, the difficulty of weighing up and quantifying the wide range of general factors identified as influencing the outsourcing decision leaves little scope for a separate, superimposed evaluation based on ethical guidelines. However, each element brought into the decision process will be influenced, consciously or unconsciously, by the personal values of those who put together or analyse the information on which the final decision is to be based. For financial services organisations in particular, the importance of reputation is unlikely to be overlooked, but this may have its influence partly in terms of a choice of partner if outsourcing is under consideration. Ultimately, for a major strategic step

such as the outsourcing of a substantial part of an institution's processing work, an individual manager is unlikely to be the final decision-maker. A committee at or near to board level will probably determine the policy to be adopted, and take part in the short-listing and interviewing process by which the outsourcer eventually wins a contract. This implies that certain shared values will be more influential than any one individual set of moral values, and the source of these shared values may be a matter of agreed policy across the organisation.

The Ethical Firm

22 There has been strong growth over the last few years in the emphasis on explicit statements of values in business (Adams et al., 1991; Carmichael, 1995), and the idea of the mission statement is perhaps being superseded by the ethical mission statement. There is, of course, a danger that fashion leads only to superficial application of principles and that ethical claims are not taken seriously, but the growth in ethical funds does give some indication of a shift in investor attitudes which is likely to be advantageous to those firms which can put across the image of behaving ethically. The anti-ethical argument, attributed to Jensen (*Economist*, 1996), that any attempt to pursue some form of social good will impoverish society because it will lead to bad, i.e., inefficient, decisions, seems to ignore the fact that business decisions are made by human beings. This suggests either that no human activity should be expected to have an ethical basis, in case that is inefficient, or that whenever a decision comes within the definition of business, normal human standards should not apply. I would not accept the more general argument (although it could be sustained as a valid basis

for the emphasis on self-interest and the denial of society associated with Thatcherism). The specific argument seems untenable because of the difficulties of distinguishing between business decisions and those in other categories.

23   Although promoting an ethical image may be good for business, I would argue that motivation does matter. To act in a way which is perceived as good, but for reasons of self-interest, cannot be the same as a good action with no underlying calculation of advantage (although without a religious framework this is a weak argument because it suggests that what is ethical cannot be judged from outside, but only by having inside knowledge of another human being's thoughts). However, to act on the basis of a clear ethical position is not incompatible with attracting customers and staff who approve of the stance the organisation is taking, as in the case of Co-operative Bank (see, for example, the discussion by Harvey, 1995 and the assessment by Kitson, 1996).

24   Stating that a firm has an ethical policy is only one small step towards being an ethical firm. To go further than this might entail ensuring high level management support for continuous monitoring of the ethical considerations of decisions made within the organisation. Such an approach is not common in the financial services industry, where many firms are struggling to comply fully with legal constraints on their behaviour without going beyond what is strictly required by law. However, a fully implemented ethical policy could provide some measure of protection for employees from violations of their rights.

Stakeholders and the Ethical Use of Power

25 The kind of monitoring which an ethical firm would need to put in place to ensure that all decisions complied with agreed values would have to ensure that managers in positions of power do not exploit that power. Essentially, where a decision is made under such constraints that no alternatives are available or where outcomes are largely determined by the response of others to the initial decision, the decision maker is not in a position to choose to harm the interests of others. However, where a decision will affect stakeholders in a business, leaving them with little option but to put up with the effects of the decision, the decision maker is exercising power. An ethical policy would seek to ensure that the outcomes of such decisions are fair, defined in this sense as complying with the agreed ethical policy (and therefore also likely to be seen as being fair by employees or other stakeholders).

26   As discussed, in the case of outsourcing it is most likely to be employees who will be faced with an exercise of power over them by a manager's decision, and, although outsourcing may affect other groups the impact on them is less likely to be severe.

Conclusions

27 In making the assertion that it is possible to act unethically towards specific groups of stakeholders, this paper does not put forward a surprising or self-evidently unreasonable claim, though it may be an unprovable one. Assuming that the assertion is valid, outsourcing seems to present a particular threat to employees, to a much greater degree than to customers or shareholders. The paper argues that this threat arises because of the factors which have led to outsourcing and the way in which outsourcing tends to work. Given the current environment of the financial services industry, outsourcing has the potential to jeopardise

some of the basic rights of employees. The existence of these rights is, of course, debatable, but even if employees do not have such specifically defined rights as those considered here, the right to employee information, the right to fair pay, the right not to be fired, and the right not to be discriminated against, it would still be valid to argue that treating people as though they have rights is ethically preferable to taking advantage of their lack of rights.

28   The broad question of the balance between objectivity and subjectivity in values may not be critical to the debate about the ethics of outsourcing, though clearly a thorough-going subjectivist approach would leave little to say about the ethical aspects of anything so specific. Accepting that values can be treated as essentially fixed, even if only within a narrowly defined sociological context, it is possible to posit the existence of the rights outlined above and to examine the aspects of outsourcing which might give rise to ethical judgements.

Issues for Further Consideration

29 In putting the main emphasis on employees, this paper pays little attention to other stakeholder groups or to the broader issue of whether business has an ethical obligation to meet some form of social responsibility.

30   ... Because examples in this paper are taken from the UK financial services environment, questions of comparative standards in ethics and cross-cultural differences in approaches to ethics, as discussed in Evans (1981) are not of major relevance, though the extent to which outsourcing has been adopted elsewhere is certainly of interest. The experience in the USA, such as the major pioneering project by Continental Bank (Huber, 1993 and Kiely, 1991) sug-

gests that there may well be much further to go down the outsourcing road in the UK. The comparative work of O'Reilly (1992) also indicates that further change may well occur as lessons can be learned from approaches elsewhere.

31   Similarly, much of the specific work on ethics in financial services is only marginally applicable here, because it deals broadly with issues of professional standards in dealing with clients (as, for example, in Bayles, 1981 and Bennion, 1969), with the related question of fiduciary responsibility (discussed in Lynch (1991) and others), or with unethical practices in charging interest or marketing credit (as in Mahoney, 1991).

BIBLIOGRAPHY

Adams, R., Carruthers, J. and Hamil, S. (1991) *Changing corporate values: a guide to social and environmental practice in Britain's top companies*, London, Kogan Page.

Alexander, M. and Young, D. (1996) "Strategic outsourcing", *Long Range Planning*, Vol 29, No 1, pp. 116-119.

Argyle, M. (1967) *The psychology of interpersonal behaviour*, London, Penguin.

Aristotle (tr. Thomson, J. A. K.) (1955) *Ethics*, London, Penguin.

Ayer, A. J. (1946) (2nd edition) *Language, truth and logic*, London, Gollancz.

Barry, N. (1991) *The morality of business enterprise*, Aberdeen, Aberdeen University.

Bayles, M. D. (1981) *Professional ethics*, Belmont CA, Wadsworth.

Bennion, F. A. R. (1969) *Professional ethics: the consult ant professions and their code*, London, Charles Knight.

Bowie, N. E. and Duska, R. F. (1990) (2nd edition) *Business ethics*, Englewood Cliffs, Prentice Hall.

Brockner, J., Grover, S., O'Malley, M. N., Reed, T. F. and Glynn, M. A. (1993) "Threats of future layoffs, self-esteem, and survivors' reactions: evidence from the laboratory and the field", *Strategic Management Journal*, Vol 14, pp. 153-166.

Buono, A. F. and Bowditch, J. L. (1989) "Ethics and transformation tactics: human resource considerations in mergers and acquisitions", pp. 125-145 in Hoffman, W. M., Frederick, R. and Petry, E. S. Jr. (eds) *The ethics of organizational transformation: mergers, takeovers and corporate restructuring*, London, Quorum.

Carmichael, S. (1995) *Business ethics: the new bottom line*, London, Demos.

Carroll, A. B. (1989) "Managing public affairs. When business closes down: social responsibilities and management actions", pp. 230-240 in Iannone, A. P. (ed) *Contemporary moral controversies in business*, Oxford, Oxford University.

Caudron, S. (1994) "Contingent work force spurs HR planning", *Personnel Journal*, July, pp. 52-60.

Coase, R. H. (1937) "The nature of the firm", *Economica*, Vol IV, pp. 386-405.

Cressey, P. and Scott, P. (1992) "Employment, technology and industrial relations in UK clearing banks: is the honeymoon over?" *New Technology, Work and Employment*, Vol 7, No 2, pp. 83-96.

De George, R. T. (1982) *Business ethics*, London, Macmillan.

Donaldson, J. (1989) *Key issues in business ethics*, London, Academic Press.

Drew, S. A. W. and Smith, P. A. C. (1995) "The learning organization: 'change proofing' and strategy", *The learning organization*, Vol 2, No 1, pp. 4-14.

Economist (1996), "Management focus: Civics 101", *Economist*, 11 May, p. 85.

EIRIS – Ethical Investment Research Service (1989), *The attitudes of ethical investors: an EIRIS survey*, London, EIRIS.

Evans, W. A. (1981) *Management ethics: an intercultural perspective*, The Hague, Martinus Nijhoff.

Freeman, R. E. (1984) *Strategic management: a stakeholder approach*, London, Pitman.

Goodwin, B. (1996) *Ethics and responsibility in a bank: Henley research centre working paper 9613*, Henley on Thames, Henley Management College.

Green, R. M. (1994) *The ethical manager*, New York, Macmillan College.

Halford, S. and Savage, M. (1995) "Restructuring organisations, changing people: gender and restructuring in banking and local government", *Work, Employment and Society*, Vol 9, No 1, March, pp. 97-122.

Harrison, B. and Kelley, M. R. (1993) "Outsourcing and the search for 'flexibility'", *Work, Employment and Society*, Vol 7, No 2, June, pp. 213-235.

Harvey, B. (1995) "Ethical banking: the case of the Co-operative Bank", *Journal of Business Ethics*, Vol 14, No 12, pp. 1005-1013.

Hendry, J. (1995) "Culture, community and networks: the hidden cost of outsourcing", *European Management Journal*, Vol 13, No 2, pp. 193-200.

Hoffman, W. M., Frederick, R. and Petry, E. S. Jr. (eds) (1989) *The ethics of organizational transformation: mergers, takeovers and corporate restructuring*, London, Quorum.

Hosner, L. T. (1987) *The ethics of management*, Homewood IL, Irwin.

Huber, R. L. (1993) "How Continental Bank outsourced its 'Crown Jewels'", *Harvard Business Review*, Jan-Feb, pp. 121-129.

Huws, U. (1982) *New technology and women's employment: case studies from West Yorkshire*, Leeds, Leeds Trade Union and Community Resource and Information Centre.

Institute of Business Ethics (1990) *Takeovers – what ethical considerations should apply? – conference papers 24 November 1989*, London, IBE.

Institute of Management/Manpower PLC (1994) *Survey of long-term employment strategies*, London, IOM/Manpower.

Jennings, D. (1996) "Outsourcing opportunities for financial services", *Long Range Planning*, Vol 29, June, pp. 393-404.

Kiely, T. (1991) "Finding a new niche", *CIO*, November 15, pp. 40-42.

Kitson, A. (1996) "Taking the pulse: ethics and the British Co-operative Bank", *Journal of Business Ethics*, Vol 15, No 9, September, pp. 1021-1031.

Labour Research Department (1994) *Contracts of employment*, London, LRD.

Labour Research Department (1995) *Human resource management: a trade unionist's guide*, London, LRD.

Lax, D. A. and Sebenius, J. K. (1986) *The manager as negotiator*, New York, Free Press.

Lynch, J. L. (1991) *Ethical banking: surviving in an age of default*, London, Macmillan.

Mahoney, J. (1991) "Ethical aspects of banking" pp. 43-59 in *The banks and society: Gilbart lectures 1990*, London, Chartered Institute of Bankers.

Malachowski, A. (1992) "Ethical considerations on corporate restructuring" pp. 243-251 in *Business ethics – contributing to business success: conference proceedings*, Sheffield, Sheffield Business School.

McDonald, N. and Doyle, M. (1981) *The stresses of work*, London, Nelson.

Miller, P. (1996) "Strategy and the ethical management of human resources", *Human Resources Management Journal*, Vol 6, No 1, pp. 5-18.

Mitroff, I. (1983) *Stakeholders of the organizational mind*, London, Jossey-Bass.

Moore, G. E. (undated) *Ethics*, London, Williams and Norgate.

O'Reilly, J. (1992) "Subcontracting in banking: some evidence from Britain and France", *New Technology, Work and Employment*, Vol 7, No 2, Autumn, pp. 107-115.

Quinn, J. B. and Hilmer, F. G. (1994) "Strategic outsourcing", *Sloan Management Review*, Summer, pp. 43-55.

Reich, R. B. (1991) *The work of nations*, New York, Alfred Knopf.

Rodgers, C. S. (1993) "The flexible workforce: what have we learned?", *Human Resource Management*, Fall, Vol 31, No 3, pp. 183-199.

Russell, B. (1961) (2nd edition) *History of western philosophy*, London, George Allen and Unwin.

Selekman, S. K. and Selekman, B. M. (1956) *Power and morality in a business society*, London, McGraw Hill.

Vincent-Jones, P. (1996) "Contract, governance and accountability in the provision of local authority services", unpublished paper presented at ESRC seminar on Contracts and Competition, University of Essex, 3rd June.

Werhane, P. H. (1985) *Person, rights, and corporations*, Englewood Cliffs NJ, Prentice Hall.

Williamson, O. E. (1975) *Markets and hierarchies: analysis and antitrust implications – a study in the economics of internal organization*, New York, Free Press.

Williamson, O. E. (1985) *The economic institutions of capitalism: firms, markets, relational contracting*, New York, Free Press.

Wright, D. (1971) *The psychology of moral behaviour*, London, Penguin.

Questions

1. What exactly is Henderson's point about outsourcing and ethics?

2. Summarize, in one sentence for each, the view of rights held by De George, Buono and Bowditch, and Werhane (as presented by Henderson). Which of the three adopts a Kantian view?

3. Why does Henderson reject a utilitarian approach?

4. What rights of employees does Henderson consider to be relevant to a decision regarding outsourcing?

5. What potential wrongdoing toward customers does Henderson identify with respect to outsourcing? (P17)

6. Henderson notes (in a part of his article not included here) that outsourcing custodial and catering services is common. Is it (how could it be), by the standards he proposes, morally acceptable?

The Discourse of Control[1]

Stephen Maguire

1 Organizational control is deeply embedded in the discourse of management. Most management texts agree that control, the process of setting performance standards, monitoring performance, and taking corrective action to achieve organizational goals, is one of the four major management functions (Daft & Fitzgerald, 1992; Donnelly et al., 1995; Gatewood et al., 1995; Schermerhorn et al., 1995). These texts describe a variety of control systems such as strategic planning, financial forecasting, budgeting, operations management systems, performance evaluations, and management information systems. There are also much broader forms of organizational control, and three have emerged as the most relevant to large contemporary organizations: bureaucratic, clan, and concertive (Barker, 1993; Ouchi, 1980). These three forms of organizational control describe ways to control employees through technical and social control (Graham, 1993). Each form of control describes different ways in which employees are told what to do, how to do it, and how long to take. They also describe ways to manipulate employee attitudes to their work so that organizational goals may be more effectively and efficiently accomplished.

2 Bureaucratic control structures work activities through a hierarchical division of positions assigning to each specific tasks, responsibilities, and a level of authority. Bureaucratic control is usually recommended in circumstances where tasks are routine and the external environment is relatively stable (Perrow, 1995). Clan control regulates employee behavior through a system

Stephen Maguire, "The Discourse of Control" *Journal of Business Ethics* 19.3 (March 1999): 109-114. © 1999 by Kluwer Academic Publishers. Reprinted with permission of the publisher and the author.

of shared goals, values, and traditions and is usually recommended when non-routine tasks are situated in unstable environments (Ouchi, 1980). Recently a new form of control called "concertive control" has been described in the literature (Barker, 1993). Concertive control is achieved by the pressure of peers in self-managed teams and has been successfully adopted for routine and non-routine tasks and in stable and unstable environments (Barker, 1993; Stayer, 1990).

3   It is too early to tell whether concertive control will become another recommended form of control, but it is clear that bureaucratic and clan control already are. Couched in the scientific discourse of organizational behavior and organizational theory, the recommendations to match appropriate forms of control to specific environments appear to be the logical consequence of a synthesis of organizational strategy and environmental dynamics. The problem here, however, is not which form of control is appropriate to specific situations. The problem is whether we should be talking about controlling people at all. The problem is essentially a moral one which has been given a scientific hearing.

4   Organizational control was first legitimated by Max Weber's theory of bureaucracy (1947) and Frederick Taylor's theory of scientific management (1916). Taylor in particular formalized the shift in the knowledge of production from worker to manager (Braverman, 1974). Taylor's concern with management control and with doing more with less workers continues to influence the contemporary discourse of control. Recent management trends including management by objectives, total quality control, delayering, restructuring, re-engineering, downsizing, just in time workers, outsourcing staff functions, and the new employment contract have all been interpreted as ways of increasing organizational control over workers. Team talk, in which business is compared to sport, is also a means of legitimating unquestioned loyalty, fragmentation of labor, the sacrifice of self-interest to organizational interests, and acquiescence to hierarchical authority (Jackall, 1988). Sometimes control talk is legitimated by humanistic discourse which we find in discussions of management's manipulation of cultural rituals, symbols, and stories (Ray, 1986) or in the use of such terms as mentoring, teamwork, and empowerment (Simons, 1995). So successful has our immersion been in the paradigm of control that we are now beginning to talk about controlling for ethical behavior (Johnson, 1996; Lindsay, 1996; Treviño, 1995; Weaver, et. al., 1999). In this paper I will argue that the use of such morally problematic discourse is indicative of a much deeper problem, a failure to understand the fundamental conditions which sustain moral practices.

5   I will also argue that the discourse of control objectifies workers, denies their moral agency, and violates the principle of moral equality. Control talk also undermines our notion of reciprocity which is a fundamental condition of moral communities and organizations. Finally, I will suggest an alternative discourse, a discourse of accountability which appropriately highlights the reciprocity necessary to build ethical organizations.

Is "control" an apt description?

6   Before I can begin, however, I first need to consider an argument which suggests that organizational control of employees is pervasive and hence unavoidable. If employees are always subject to subtle and pervasive means of organiza-

tional control, then doing away with the discourse of control as a description of organizational life amounts to undermining the integrity of science and submitting to the worst elements of political correctness. I do not propose, however, to dispense with the discourse of control in general. Instead I suggest that we (1) separate its descriptive and normative components, (2) more carefully examine the range of its descriptive scope, and (3) do away with the normative component of the discourse of control.

7 The normative discourse of control is legitimated if we believe that every conceivable work environment is subject to organizational control. If organizational control is impossible to avoid, then there is some justification for discussing appropriate ways to control employee behaviour. Pessimism about achieving freedom from organizational control is supported by two findings. First, employee behavior is controlled through the internalization of organizational culture which is impossible to avoid (Treviño, 1995). If organizational culture is inescapable, then so too is organizational control. Second, self-managed work teams, the exemplars of employee autonomy in the workplace, have been found to be stronger than traditional forms of organizational control (Barker, 1993; Graham, 1993). If, therefore, the best autonomy supportive conditions in the workplace ultimately result in stronger organizational control, then it seems that whatever employees do in the workplace is a result of organizational control.

8 Let us first examine the issue of controlling employee behaviour through organizational culture. And let us concede that organizational culture is internalized by employees. It does not follow, however, that if we concede that organizational culture is internalized, organizational culture is pervasive in controlling employee behaviour. If we accept that internalization of knowledge, beliefs, and values is tantamount to being controlled, we would no longer be able to specify conditions in which we are free from control. We always act from an internal source. All of our actions must be accompanied by a desire to act (Bond, 1983). What we desire to do will be based on a synthesis of our knowledge, beliefs, values, and situational contingencies. Some of those situational contingencies, such as close supervisory control, may be coercive. Many other situations, such as new responsibilities or promotions, may be construed as opportunities. Hence we need to distinguish those conditions under which desires are coerced from those in which they are not.

9 Similarly it would be a mistake to argue from the fact that all human experience is situated within an historical context of knowledge, values, and interests, that all human social behavior is controlled by historical and cultural forces. It is impossible to conceive of persons independent of cultural and historical conditions. Nonetheless the struggle for freedom and self-determination takes place within such a context of social constraints. Just because we are never entirely free of such constraints does not mean that autonomy is illusory. If autonomy is "the capacity of persons to make rationally reflective choices about their ends and activities" (Lippke, 1997, p. 331), then freedom is the exercise of our rationally reflective choices made within the context of a given cultural and historical situation.

10 How does this discussion bear on organizational culture? Precisely because some organizational cultural values which are readily internalized are consistent with our rationally reflective choices. Organizational cultural values which support living a meaningful life are more

likely to be willingly adopted and sustained in workplace practices. These are instances of self-determined behavior. Values which are inconsistent with living a meaningful life are likely to be resisted or experienced as controlling. Supportive organizational cultures, on the other hand, will value openness, dialogue, and collaboration, values which promote self-determination and self-fulfilment. Whether a culture is supportive of self-determination or is instead controlling will be determined by the relationship between organizational cultural values and the living of a meaningful life.

11   Nor does it follow from specific studies which highlight organizational attempts to control the values of self-managed teams (Graham, 1993) or from studies which emphasize the pressure of peers in controlling behavior (Barker, 1993) that self-managed teams are inevitably controlling. What these studies implicitly provide are fascinating accounts of the ways in which ostensibly autonomy enhancing conditions are undermined. Other research also supports the view that autonomy supportive conditions may be jeopardized if a threshold of such conditions is breached. Research into the contextual factors which facilitate internalization of regulations supports the view that a threshold of supportive conditions must exist to facilitate integration of external regulations in a self-determining style (Deci, et al., 1994). Once this threshold is undermined, individuals experience external regulation as controlling rather than supporting (Deci, et al., 1994). The studies which have concluded that self-managed teams are inevitably controlling have failed to differentiate between autonomy supportive conditions and controlling conditions. With this difference in mind, we will be in a better position to explain how autonomy supportive conditions are undermined.

Controlling conditions versus autonomy enhancing conditions

12 On the basis of established research by Deci and colleagues, we can distinguish between controlling conditions and those which enhance autonomy. Controlling conditions are experienced as compulsion, of having to do what one has to do. They are characterized by an absence of choice, a lack of opportunity to provide meaningful input, and an obligation to perform work which is not valued for its own sake or for the ends it provides (Deci & Ryan, 1987; Deci, Connell, & Ryan, 1989; Deci et al., 1994). In general, routine work which is highly specialized, standardized, and formalized is experienced as controlling. Close supervision whether by persons or technology, is also controlling. So too is corrective action issued as commands, or as one ought to do "x", or one should do "x" (Deci & Ryan, 1987). Even positive feedback can be experienced as controlling according to the context of evaluation; if you are told that you have done well *as expected*, the experience is one of control (Deci, Connell, & Ryan, 1989). To summarize, if one does work which one does not value, and does what one is told to do under close supervision or because of rewards, threats, and externally imposed deadlines, and is peremptorily corrected for making mistakes, the experience is one of external control.

13   Autonomy enhancing conditions contrast with controlling conditions. If individuals are able to exercise choice among meaningful options in the absence of pressure, if they are able to initiate action and take responsibility for their actions, if they have opportunities to provide meaningful input, if their perspective is acknowledged, if rationales are provided with requests, if the work they are able to perform is inherently

meaningful or helps to achieve meaningful ends, and if individuals are allowed to develop their competencies through the exercise of their judgment and skill, then organizations which sustain such conditions have a supportive rather than a controlling culture (Deci & Ryan, 1987; Deci, Connell, & Ryan, 1989; Deci et al., 1994).

14   We should reasonably expect self-managed teams, decentralized organizations, and learning organizations to foster such autonomy supportive conditions. Nevertheless even within such organizational structures, conditions may develop which undermine the threshold of autonomy supportive conditions. I claim that in general such organizational structures are more likely to be supportive of employee autonomy in the workplace. Bureaucratic rule bound organizational cultures, autocratic cultures, and high risk cultures are much more likely to foster controlling conditions. Responsive cultures, cultures which value their employees, are much more likely to support conditions which enhance the autonomy of their employees (Di Norcia, 1998). In summary, control is an apt description of how some organizational cultures do attempt to determine employee behaviour. The range of its descriptive application, however, ought to be limited only to those cultures which can be observed as exhibiting controlling conditions.

How ethical is control talk?

15 It ought to be clear that, at least in some organizations, control will not be an apt description of the ways in which employees are encouraged to go about their work. Nevertheless, if control talk remains an appropriate way to describe how many organizations structure employee behaviour, we still need to determine whether the normative discourse of control is also appropriate.

Suppose we concede, for the sake of argument, that controlling organizations are more efficient and effective for routine tasks and stable environments. Is this not a powerful utilitarian justification of control? Does not the good which society enjoys as a result of tightly controlled organizations justify arguably immoral methods? I will argue that the assumptions underlying the discourse of control are sufficiently disturbing to give us cause to consider this question more deeply than we presently do. In particular, we need to consider whether control talk presupposes a denial of individual autonomy, moral agency, and the possibility of moral community.

16   One of the underlying assumptions of control is that those who command are more knowledgeable and capable, and those who serve need direction. Hence management does the thinking and employees do what they are told to do. Compliance with externally imposed standards, however, undermines an individual's autonomous self-concept. To be autonomous, one must be able to conceive of oneself as being able to act autonomously (Kupfer, 1987; Lippke, 1997). To act autonomously, one must be able to deliberate about one's actions by examining the relationship of those actions to values which contribute to the living of a meaningful life. In the workplace, this suggests that workers ought to be given reasons to act and the power to criticize, modify, reject or accept those reasons. They ought to be given the opportunity to engage in dialogue about the way things are done, or could be done. They ought to be able to "buy in" to organizational goals. Control talk, on the other hand, presupposes that individuals will not rationally accept organizational goals and as a consequence obviates opportunities for employees to develop and exercise autonomy and to voluntarily commit to organizational goals. Instead,

control talk perpetuates the view that people are objects to be manipulated in accordance with organizational goals.

17   Insofar as one's self-esteem is dependent on the successful exercise of one's abilities and insofar as control minimizes the need for employees to exercise their rational abilities, their self-esteem will at best be modest, at worst constantly undermined. The perception of worthlessness is directly related to one's being valued only as a means to an end. Control talk, particularly that which emphasizes ethical compliance, ignores a human need to experience self-worth. Programs which are meant to control for ethical compliance stress obedience. Self-worth is dependent upon the exercise of virtue, particularly moral virtue. Self-worth grows from valuing one's judgments about doing what is right and good. One values these judgments because one has become engaged with others in determining and acting on shared moral beliefs. Compliance denies opportunities to exercise judgment and discursively engage in the determination of what is right. In doing so, compliance programs eliminate the conditions upon which self worth and moral agency depend.

18   The same conditions which preempt moral agency also preempt the formation of a moral community. One encourages autonomy by providing choice, by providing a rationale for requests, by acknowledging the perspective of the other, and by engaging in collaborative reflection. These are also conditions which support dialogue with others. Dialogue is further supported by the values of trust, openness, and a willingness to learn, conditions which are also necessary for the development of a moral community. Kant (1959) also recognized that the conditions which support autonomy are necessarily linked to the supporting conditions of moral community. Autonomous agents are able to recognize the role which reciprocity plays in developing a community of autonomous moral agents. Agents who recognize and value the development of rationality will be motivated to foster its development in others. Through such reciprocal action friendship, fraternity, and solidarity may blossom.

19   If we are interested in building ethical organizations, then we need to give up the normative discourse of control, particularly the more recent discourse which is committed to "controlling" for ethical behavior. The relationship between discourse and reality is now so much more apparent to us all. There is no need to review why racist language is offensive or why feminists advocate non-sexist language. There is no need to explore the deeper philosophical underpinnings of language and world expressed in the Greek concept of *logos* (Gadamer, 1976). It is clear that language expresses and creates our reality. If we continue to use the discourse of control, the reality we will create will be organizations bereft of the fundamental conditions for the exercise of autonomy, self-worth, and moral community. We will continue to objectify workers and legitimate an instrumental view of employees as another resource to exploit.

Accountability as an alternative discourse

20 Where does this leave us? How ought we to describe the way in which organizations coordinate individuals to pursue organizational ends? How do we ensure that workers responsibly pursue those ends? How do we reframe managers' control orientations and practices (Winter et al., 1997)? If we concede the importance of reciprocity in fostering moral community, then why not

adopt a discourse of accountability? To be accountable means to be responsible for one's actions and to be willing to engage in dialogue to explain and defend them. It means a willingness to be questioned, to ask for, or to provide clarification. It involves a willingness to share in the construction of explanations. Dialogical rationality presupposed by accountability in turn presupposes a collaborative and reciprocal spirit of inquiry. It both presupposes and strives to achieve mutual understanding (Gadamer, 1989).

21   Accountability cuts both ways. Status and authority do not provide immunity from accountability to subordinates. To hold others accountable is to be subject to reciprocal action, to be accountable for asking the right questions, and for contributing in a spirit of inquiry to a collaborative partnership in resolving issues at hand. Accountability presupposes autonomous agents willing to discursively settle their differences and agree on common worthwhile goals. The practice of being accountable and demanding accountability helps to build and sustain moral organizations.

22   Accountability encourages self-responsibility, self-monitoring, and self-management. It encourages the kind of autonomous reflection necessary for recognizing moral issues and voicing moral doubt, disagreement, or protest (Bird, 1996). By voicing one's concern, one invites a dialogical analysis and resolution of moral problems. If building and sustaining moral organizations is our goal, then dialogue which grows from accountability is the kind of talk we need. And the first thing we ought to be accountable for is the way we talk about the people with whom we work.

NOTE

1   Please note that this is a slightly revised version of the paper that appeared in *Journal of Business Ethics*.

REFERENCES

Barker, J. R.: 1993, "Tightening the Iron Cage: Concertive Control in Self-managing Teams", *Administrative Science Quarterly* 38, 408-437.

Bird, F. B.: 1996, *The Muted Conscience: Moral Silence and the Practice of Ethics in Business* (Quorum Books, Westport, Connecticut).

Bond, E. J.: 1983, *Reason and Value* (Cambridge: Cambridge University Press).

Braverman, H.: 1974, *Labor and Monopoly Capital: The Degradation of Work in the Twentieth Century* (Monthly Review Press, New York).

Daft, R. L., and P. A. Fitzgerald: 1992, *Management* (Dryden, Toronto).

Deci, E. L., J. P. Connell, and R. M. Ryan: 1989, "Self-determination in a Work Organization", *Journal of Applied Psychology* 74, 580-590.

Deci, E. L., and R. M. Ryan: 1987, "The Support of Autonomy and the Control of Behavior", *Journal of Personality and Social Psychology* 53, 1024-1037.

Deci, E. L., H. Eghrari, B. C. Patrick, and D. R. Leone: 1994, "Facilitating Internalization: The Self-Determination Theory Perspective", *Journal of Personality* 62, 119-142.

Di Norcia, V.: 1998, *Hard Like Water: Ethics in Business* (Oxford, Toronto).

Donnelly, J. H. Jr., J. L. Gibson, and J. M. Ivancevich: 1995, *Fundamentals of Management* (Irwin, Chicago).

Gadamer, H. G.: 1976, "Man and Language" in *Philosophical Hermeneutics* (University of California Press, Berkeley) 59-68.

Gadamer, H. G.: 1989, *Truth and Method* (Crossroad, NY).

Gatewood, R. D., R. R. Taylor, and O. C. Ferrell: 1995, *Management: Comprehension, Analysis, and Application* (Irwin, Chicago).

Graham, L.: 1993, "Inside a Japanese Transplant: A Critical Perspective", *Work and Occupations* 20, 147-173.

Jackall, R.: 1988, *Moral Mazes: The World of Corporate Managers* (Oxford University Press, Oxford).

Johnson, P., C. Cassell, and K. Smith: 1996, "The Management Control of Ethics: The Case of Corporate Codes", *Business Ethics and Business Behaviour* (International Thomson Business Press, London), 163-181.

Kant, I.: 1959, *Foundations of the Metaphysics of Morals* trans. by Lewis White Beck (Bobbs-Merrill, Indianapolis).

Kupfer, J.: 1987, "Privacy, autonomy, and self-concept", *American Philosophical Quarterly* 24, 81-89.

Lindsay, R. M., L. M. Lindsay, and V. B. Irvine: 1996, "Instilling Ethical Behavior in Organizations: A Survey of Canadian Companies", *Journal of Business Ethics* 15, 393-407.

Lippke, R. L.: 1995, "The Importance of Being Autonomous", *Radical Business Ethics* (Rowman and Littlefield, Lanham), 27-48.

Lippke, R. L.: 1997, "Work, Privacy, and Autonomy", *Moral Issues in Business* 7th ed., eds. W. H. Shaw and V. Barry (Wadsworth, Belmont, CA).

Ouchi, W. G.: 1980, "Markets, Bureaucracies, and Clans", *Administrative Science Quarterly* 25, 129-141.

Perrow, C.: 1995, "Why Bureaucracy?" *Foundations of Organizational Communication: A Reader* (Longman, White Plains, NY), 28-50.

Ray, C. A.: 1986, "Corporate Culture: The Last Frontier of Control", *Journal of Management Studies* 23, 287-297.

Schermerhorn, J. R. Jr., R. J. Cattaneo, and A. Templer: 1995, *Management* (John Wiley & Sons, Toronto).

Simons, R., 1995, "Control in an Age of Empowerment", *Harvard Business Review* March-April, 80-88.

Stayer, R.: 1990, "How I Learned to Let My Workers Lead", *Harvard Business Review* Nov-Dec, 66-83.

Taylor, F. W.: 1995, "The Principles of Scientific Management", *Foundations of Organizational Communication: A Reader* (Longman, White Plains, NY), 65-75.

Treviño, L. K., and K. A. Nelson: 1995, *Managing Business Ethics: Straight Talk About How To Do It Right* (John Wiley and Sons, New York).

Weaver, G. R., L. K. Treviño, and P. L. Cochran: 1999, "Corporate Ethics Programs as Control Systems: Influences of Executive Commitment and Environmental Factors", *The Academy of Management Journal* Feb., 41-57.

Weber, M.: 1947, *The Theory of Social and Economic Organizations*, eds. and trans. A. M. Henderson and T. Parsons (Free Press, New York).

Winter, R. P., J. C. Sarros, and G. A. Tanewski: 1997, "Reframing Managers' Control Orientations and Practices: A Proposed Organizational Learning Framework", *The International Journal of Organizational Analysis* Vol. 5, No. 1, 9-24.

Questions

1. (a) Do you think it is necessary for managers to be in control? Of what? Why?

   (b) Do you think such control can be morally acceptable?

   (c) Does the contractual nature of employment bear on this at all?

2. (a) What is "the discourse of control"? Give some examples, if you can, from your own employment experience (as employee or employer).

   (b) "It is clear that language expresses and creates our reality" (P19) – do you agree?

3. Maguire claims that "control talk" does four things.

   (a) What are they? (P5)

   (b) How does it do these things? (P16–18)

4. Kantian ethics and virtue ethics seem to provide the strongest basis for Maguire's argument.

   (a) Would a rights-based approach strengthen or weaken his argument?

   (b) What about a justice-based approach?

5. Maguire disagrees with the opinion that it is impossible to avoid organizational control, presenting and refuting two arguments in support of that opinion. What are the arguments and how does he respond to each? (P7–11)

6. (a) Explain and assess Maguire's alternative to the discourse of control.

   (b) Could his alternative enable managers to meet the three functions of setting performance standards, monitoring performance, and taking corrective action to achieve organizational goals (see P1)? How?

Case Study – The Westray Mine Disaster

The report of the public inquiry into the coal mine disaster at the Westray mine in Nova Scotia called the mine "an accident waiting to happen". On May 9, 1992, the accident happened. On that day, a methane gas explosion in a 300-foot-deep seam of the mine killed 26 miners.

While the proximate cause of the explosion was a spark coming from a mining machine, the public inquiry found that the mine had an inadequate ventilation system, inadequate treatment of coal dust, and inadequately trained workers. A proper ventilation system would have diluted the potentially flammable methane gas, eliminating the risk of an explosion; stone dusting (which makes coal dust non-explosive) should have been done on a regular basis; and properly trained workers would have been more familiar with the equipment and safe work methods.

The testimony of witnesses at the public inquiry reveals the virtual absence of a "safety mentality" at the mine. In the months leading up to the explosion, Westray management, according to the inquiry, had "ignored or encouraged a series of hazardous or illegal practices" – despite a history of rock falls, cave-ins, and even roof collapses. Managers hired by Westray were unqualified (a senior engineer had no experience in underground coal mines and a surveyor failed to obtain provincial certification), and miners could not follow safety methods because of the pressure to keep production levels high.

Many of the workers were certainly aware of the dangers. For example, one of the mine mechanics noticed one of the mine supervisors recalibrating a monitor so that excessive levels of methane would not cause an automatic shut-off. But when he said he would report the tampering, he was threatened with losing his job. Others reported high methane gas and coal dust levels to visiting mine inspectors on more than one occasion.

The public inquiry was particularly harsh in criticizing government regulators for their role in the tragedy. The Nova Scotia Department of Natural Resources was responsible for ensuring, before permits were granted, that mining plans were not only efficient, but safe. However, "the department did not insist that the company submit sufficient information to support its application. Furthermore, it did not insist that the company submit any changes to approved plans. Consequently, for a critical period, the department was not aware that Westray was working an unapproved section of the mine." The Department of Labour, the report points out, also "failed to carry out its mandated responsibilities to the workers at Westray and to the people of Nova Scotia": there were repeated violations of regulations governing mine operations, and the report insists that "the Department of Labour's mine inspectorate should have detected these violations and ensured compliance."

An expert in mine ventilation, Andrew Liney, testified that it would have been relatively easy to eliminate the dangerous gases in the mine, which would also have increased worker productivity. There were so many violations of Department of Labour regulations that he doubted the competence and commitment of the provincial mine inspectors. Overall, Liney viewed the situation at Westray to be "an absolutely unbelievable disgrace." Two of the Westray managers were charged with criminal negligence causing death and manslaughter, but the charges were stayed.

REFERENCES

Di Norcia, Vincent. *Hard Like Water: Ethics in Business.* Toronto: Oxford University Press, 1998. 79-81.

Richard, Peter. *Report of the Westray Mine Public Inquiry.* Province of Nova Scotia, 1997. <www.gov.ns.ca/legi/inquiry/westray/>

Questions

1. If you had to apportion blame for the Westray disaster, how much would you say should go to the Westray management, how much to the provincial regulators (Natural Resources and Labour), and how much to the workers who were aware of the hazards? Would you also include shareholders and consumers who demand the high returns and low prices that can only come from high production levels?

2. By accepting and keeping a job as a miner (indeed some Westray miners quit in the months preceding the disaster), isn't one also accepting the risk that goes along with that occupational choice?

3. If, as Liney claimed, the improvements in safety would have also improved productivity, why do you think Westray management failed to make those improvements?

4. What if improvements in safety do *not* also improve productivity – how obligated (morally speaking) would management be to nevertheless make those improvements?

CHAPTER 5
DISCRIMINATION

What to Do? –
Woodworking at the Education Centre

You are on the Selection Committee at one of the new Education Centres in B.C. (used to be called schools, before education was privatized – I'm trying to prepare you for the future in this text!), and you're in the process of hiring a new woodworking instructor. The 'best' applicant is an Asian-appearing person who currently teaches your art courses: he has all the requisite teaching credentials and he's been teaching for 15 years. His woodworking skills are excellent (you have purchased some of his work – it's beautiful). He also does some metal sculpture, so he's handy with quite a range of tools – in short, he knows his way around a shop.

The "problem" is that the Woodworking class he is to teach will almost certainly consist of boys – 14-year-old boys – 14-year-old white boys. You are quite sure they will not pay atten-

tion to him: they will no doubt consider him effeminate because of his soft manner and small size; some will claim that "they" are taking over the province and resent his authority (except, of course, in math and engineering, "they're" good at that); others will simply make jokes about "slant-eyes." So, in fact, he will not be a very good teacher: to some degree, teachers need students to cooperate; when your students don't listen to you and don't follow your instructions, they will not learn from you; how can it be said, then, that you're a good teacher? This is of particular concern for this position, for this course, because students are liable to be seriously injured if they *don't* pay attention to their woodworking teacher.

What do you decide to do?

Introduction

When considering the issue of discrimination, there are several questions to be asked. First, what *is* discrimination? (Define your terms.) Second, is discrimination *wrong*? Discrimination in general? This kind of discrimination? This particular instance of discrimination? And if so, *why* is it wrong?

All right, let's try some answers. Strictly speaking, the word 'discrimination' refers to distinguishing one thing from another, to making a distinction, to noting a difference between things. So we discriminate when we choose ripe fruit over rotten fruit, we discriminate when we say this music has more rhythmic complexity than that music. And we certainly discriminate when we run "discriminator" programs through a database using specific search parameters ("data mining is in essence a kind of automated discrimination," says Pulfer [13]).

However, commonly speaking, the word 'discrimination' is a short form for '*unjustified* discrimination' – distinguishing between two (or more) things on some basis that's *not justified.* Recall that Aristotle's view of distributive justice says that like cases should be treated alike, so if you have similar merit, you get similar consideration, and irrelevant aspects such as sex and colour are, well, irrelevant. (The trick is in determining what's relevant and what's irrelevant – we'll get to that.) Because of this element of injustice, such discrimination is considered morally wrong.

One can appeal to rights instead of justice (though, of course, the two can be related) to explain the moral wrongness of discrimination. Consider Abella's definition: "practices or attitudes that have, whether by design or impact, the effect of limiting an individual's or a group's right to the opportunities generally available because of attributed rather than actual characteristics" (253). Recall that Rawls argues that we should have an equal right to opportunities, and, presumably, such discrimination makes that impossible; see Narveson, however, for an argument that we don't have the right to non-discrimination.

Note, however, that Abella's definition is different not only in its attention to rights rather than justice, but in its mention of attributed and actual characteristics rather than irrelevant and relevant characteristics. I believe Abella's point, however, is not that it would not be unjustified discrimination to distinguish according to religion, for example, as long as the subject actually was of the religion at issue, but that it would be discrimination to judge a person, for example, dishonest (an attribute) because of his/her religion rather than because he/she was actually dishonest.

Thus discrimination is defined in relation to membership in a group: what supposedly happens when people discriminate is that they stereotype the individual, they prejudge the individual, attributing certain characteristics, according to their view of the group to which that individual belongs. However, perhaps one could be guilty of unjust discrimination without stereotyping: one simply need judge according to an irrelevant standard. Nevertheless, insofar as discrimination *does* involve this group thing, then surely Kantian ethics would argue against it: if we were to universalize the practice of judging an individual according to the characteristics of the group, the very notion of 'individual' would come to be meaningless.

Furthermore, discrimination is typically defined as a negative judgement. No doubt, that is what has moved us to identify, and attempt to rectify, this injustice, but I think we should be as vigilant against positive discrimination: is it not as wrong to assume the distinguished-looking man before us is wise and capable? (I know many distinguished-looking men who are complete idiots.)

People often think of unjustified discrimination in the workplace in relation to hiring (and firing) decisions and promotion (and demotion) decisions. However, discrimination can also show up in recruitment methods, benefits plans and salaries (compare Bell Canada's outsourcing of its construction workers, 100% male, with its plan to outsource its operators, 98% female: the men got to keep their union, their seniority, and their wage – the women won't [Rebick, 44]), as well as purchasing and contracts decisions, and even product lines. (Are your "flesh-tone" cosmetics and crayons beige or black? And take a look at your toys with race, ethnic, age, and ability in mind.)

The questionable criteria, the bases used for distinguishing that usually result in a claim of unjustified discrimination, are often those listed in the Canadian Charter of Rights and Freedoms: race, national or ethnic origin, colour, religion, sex, age, or mental or physical disability.

Let's consider religious discrimination for a moment. Why is it morally wrong, for example, to refuse to hire people who believe in a certain religion? Is belief in *any* ideology unjust grounds for discrimination, or just belief in religious systems of thought? (Just dominant religious systems or any supernaturalist cult?) And if you must hire them, must you also accommodate their beliefs in the workplace? How far? And when does "accommodate" become "im-pose" become "harass"? Is beginning a staff meeting with a prayer accommodating Xs or harassing non-Xs? Or both? So how do you solve this conflict?

Let's also consider that noticeably absent from the Charter's list is sexual orientation. (Do your benefits plans extend only to other-sex partners?) Many are trying to rectify this, and most provincial human rights codes *do* include sexual orientation.

While we're thinking about benefits, why are they extended only to same-species dependents?

A more common basis for discrimination that's not on the human rights list is discrimination on the basis of health conditions. Consider AIDS. Is it right to limit people with AIDS to certain jobs? Is it right not to hire them in the first place because of medical costs? (See the Häyry and Häyry article.)

Discrimination can also occur because of body type or other aspects of physical appearance (see Willard's paper). Certainly airline attendants have a history dealing with this: it has been the case that not only a certain weight must be maintained (though this might be justified on the basis of airplane carrying capacity and aisle size), but female attendants must wear make-up (what does eyeliner have to do with flight attendant skills?). Consider dress codes in this light.

What about class discrimination: do your well-to-do clients and customers get better service? (Do the others even *get* service – are you a bank?) Is that justified or unjustified discrimination? It may well be justified from an egoistic perspective (well-to-do clients are more valuable to the company), but what about the other moral perspectives?

And what about discrimination against pregnant employees? When exactly is non-pregnancy a bona fide job requirement? And do fetal protection policies, such as those excluding pregnant women, and even potentially-pregnant (i.e., non-sterile) women, from certain jobs discriminate against women? (See Quinn, as well as Andiappan, Reavley, and Silver.)

Age discrimination is another possible injustice, and certainly as the baby boomers age, one might expect this to become a 'popular' issue. Some jobs have a minimum age requirement, some a maximum, and many enforce mandatory retirement (see the Wedeking paper in this chapter) – could any of that be fair? See also Ferris and King, who examine the differences between subjective and objective performance evaluations of older workers and conclude that to some extent age discrimination is actually intentional.

Consider, too, genetic discrimination, another issue bound to become more prevalent. Brockett and Tankersley thoroughly examine the implications of genetic knowledge for the insurance business (and employers) – individual rights to privacy and employment vs. insurance companies' desire for better informed decisions (fairer decisions? discriminatory decisions?). See Murray as well, who takes a distributive justice approach to the issue; see also Hubbard and Wald.

What makes the many criteria mentioned above questionable is their irrelevance to the decision (to hire, to promote, or whatever). For example, whether you are male or female would seem to be irrelevant to whether you can be an architect, so if only male architects are hired, perhaps some (unjustified) discrimination is going on. That is to say, sex is not a *bona fide occupation qualification (BFOQ)* for the occupation of architect. However, hiring only women to be surrogate mothers would be okay, because the possession of a uterus is most definitely required for the job, it is a BFOQ, and only women have uteruses.

The implication is that only ability or capacity is relevant (and note that I say "ability or capacity," not "degree or diploma" – it seems to me that in many cases having a university degree is listed as a job requirement, but in fact, those skills represented by the degree are *not* required on the job). However, some have argued that our society is not a meritocracy (despite the belief of the "haves" that they got what they have by merit, and not luck or discrimination – we all like to think we got the job because we were the best candidate, not because we were lucky, or because we look okay, or because we were the last interviewed and the freshest in their minds...). Nor should it be a meritocracy, say some (see Wasserstrom). What then should be the criterion for hiring? Need? Desire?

Why not simply the preferences of the company's owners? Why shouldn't they be able to hire whomever they want? After all, it's their company. And if they happen to believe, for example, that Asians are more intelligent, well, why shouldn't they hire the applicant they believe to be most competent, the Asian? One might be tempted to suggest to the owners a psychology lesson in emotional bias and/or an epistemology lesson in validity of evidence, but still, why should they not do as they see best? People are allowed to be ignorant every day; why should company owners be any different, why should they be held to a different, higher standard? One, the company owners' decisions affect others in a far greater way than most individual personal decisions – maybe *that's* why they should be held to a higher standard. (Well, but one can certainly argue with the first part of that – many personal decisions shatter lives in a way no business decision ever will.) Two, people are "allowed" to be ignorant every day, yes, but we may call such people immoral (and we may do so every day) – and *that's* our focus (deciding what's immoral, what's ethically wrong).

To return to the implication behind most claims of unjustified discrimination: *is* ability sufficient? The decision-making scenario that opened this chapter is, unfortunately, applicable beyond the situation described; many adults are as immature as those 14-year-old boys and refuse to accept people of certain ethnic origins as authorities in any way. Does this mean that people of those origins should not be promoted to positions of authority? But what if the attending surgeon doesn't take direction from the German chief surgeon during an operation? What if television viewers don't believe the Jamaican anchor when she reads the news? In these situations, *can ethnic origin be said to be a bona fide occupational qualification?* After all, it seems that being "non-ethnic" (whatever that means!) is *required* for the job – or at least, for doing the job with any degree of success.

Now, recognizing that discrimination on the basis of irrelevant aspects isn't morally right, we could just stop it. Unfortunately, it's not that easy for two reasons. The first is that it's so subtle, so unconscious. Even the most vigilant of people find themselves "automatically" making unfair assumptions. Let's consider sex: literally from the moment of birth, we identify, we discriminate, according to sex: "It's a girl!" "It's a boy!" Room decor, toys, and clothes are different according to sex (and not just for babies and kids); even our language is sexist – "he," "she," "Ms.," "Mr." (why do we need different words?!) It's not surprising, then – indeed it may be realistic – to assume that of the two people before you, the woman will be the teacher, the man, the manager. (And neither of them will be a First Nations person in a wheelchair.)

And it's not just a nurture thing. It could be a very built-in nature thing: men choose other men, whites choose other whites – we choose what's familiar, what's similar, rather than what's different. So as long as white men are doing the choosing....

Even with rigorous interview and performance appraisal techniques, which require that all applicants be asked and scored on the same questions, multiple standards may still interfere with merit as the sole criterion for hiring and promotion. Consider: women are expected to smile more than men, so even though both a male and a female applicant may actually smile the same number of times during an interview, the woman may be considered less friendly than the man – the friendliness bar was set higher for her. On the other hand, men are expected to be more aggressive than women, so even though both may wait patiently, without interrupting, before speaking, the man may be considered "lacking in initiative" whereas the women is simply "polite."

Lest you think this is just speculation, take a look at Purdy's essay, which includes mention of research findings such as these: male students rated identical course syllabi higher when the instructor was known to be male; male students rated articles higher when the author was thought to be male; when a woman is recognized as having done a good job, her success is attributed to factors other than her ability.

Velasquez reports similar findings of discrimination:

> In 1993, for example, ABC sent a male and female, Chris and Julie, on an "experiment" to apply in person for jobs several companies were advertising. Chris and Julie were both blonde, trim, neatly dressed college graduates in their 20s, with identical

resumes indicating management experience.... [W]hen the company recruiter spoke with Julie, the only job he brought up was a job answering phones. A few minutes later, the same recruiter spoke with Chris. He was offered a management job. (370)

Velasquez notes that similar experiments have shown that racial discrimination is happening in much the same way (371).

Besides this subtlety, the other obstacle to just putting an end to discrimination is that it's often systemic; that means that it's not due to any individual's decisions, conscious or otherwise, but it's built right into the system. For example, a fire department may swear up and down that it does not discriminate on the basis of sex: if a woman is able to pass the tests, she will be considered alongside the men. Sounds fair enough. Even the tests have been revamped to eliminate any sex bias (for example, push-ups, which give the male body an advantage because of its higher centre of gravity, have been replaced with bicep curls and shoulder rolls as tests of upper body strength), and all the skills and standards are demonstrably required for firefighting. However, the department may store its hoses at a height that makes it much more difficult for a 5'4" person to get them off the wall than for a 5'10" person. So women invariably do worse than men on any test that involves getting the hoses. So they score worse on the physical part of the testing. So they have less of a chance of getting hired. Because they were female.

The same kind of systemic discrimination may apply to a position for which staying late at the office is seen as evidence of the preferred "teamwork," "drive," and "dedication." Anyone responsible for children is unlikely to meet those requirements. And if that is indeed the only

demonstration of teamwork, drive, and dedication, being able to work late may be a BFOQ. But my guess is that one could have, and could exhibit, those qualities in other ways – such as taking work home, having shorter lunches, being sensitive to one's colleagues' work, etc.

Because discrimination has been so hard to root out, many companies institute affirmative action or employment equity programs; in Canada, these are, by law, focused on women, natives, visible minorities, and the employable handicapped. First, it's important to note that there are different kinds of affirmative actions programs, from tie-breaking (if two candidates are judged to be equally well qualified you hire the one from the "disadvantaged" group) to quotas (a certain number of positions are for members of those groups only). Each has its problems.

For example, seldom are candidates "equally qualified." And, given that people in the identified groups may have had to work twice as hard and overcome twice as many obstacles to get where they are, getting where they are probably means they're twice as good as the others, so choosing them over the other candidates may well mean you are choosing the *better* qualified. Say you've got two runners: Jane starts a few seconds after John (John was told the starting time by his coach, but Jane has no coach, and no one she asked seemed to know); Jane hasn't got her running clothes on (she spent half an hour looking for the women's changeroom – there were signs everywhere directing runners to the men's changerooms, but none pointed to the women's changerooms); and even if she did have her running stuff on, she wouldn't be wearing spikes like her competitor (they don't make them in women's size 6); she hasn't warmed up (she spent that time looking for the changeroom); and her lane is strewn with holes and rocks (the holes are there because her lane hasn't been maintained by the field operators; the rocks were thrown there by angry spectators who don't think she should be allowed in the race). Now if Jane finishes at the same time as John, she's actually the better runner, right? Even if she finishes a little behind, she's better (though you'd have to be able to measure just how much all that stuff affected her time – how could you do that?).

Second, one should understand and assess the various justifications for affirmative actions programs (see the Dimock and Tucker paper in this chapter for a much fuller examination). Achieving a representative workforce is one aim; if 10% of the population is gay, then 10% of your workforce should be gay. But why? Why should every workplace, or every career field, *be* representative of the population at large? (At the very least, one would think the workforce-at-large should be representative of the society-at-large; however, "In Canada, native people account for 2.1% of the workforce, but have only 1% of the jobs...5.4% of available workers are disabled, but only 1.7% are employed" [Southerst 67].) To some extent, a representative workforce ensures diversity, and diversity in the workplace is a good thing because more perspectives are available, leading to better solutions (more alternatives will be considered).

And to some extent, such representation ensures role modelling: unless First Nations kids see First Nations lawyers, for example, they might not even consider that career. How many boys thought of being a nurse when they grew up? Diversity helps get rid of the stereotypes; it changes the expectations of both those in the group and those outside the group. It thus increases the freedom of choice for future generations (at the expense of freedom of choice for some of the present generation?) and moves us closer to a meritocracy. Such justifications seem to fit with many of the ethical approaches we've covered: utilitarianism – the consequence is a good society (is it? see Groarke 1996, Ferris and King, and Dimock and Tucker); Kantian ethics – the individual gains respect and autonomy (which individual?); justice theories – a meritocracy is fair (but in the meantime, the merits of some are ignored); rights theories – one's right to one's deserts is upheld (depends on which "one" you're talking about).

Compensation for past injuries (to well-being and prospects) is another aim of employment equity programs (recall Aristotle). (See Thomson for a discussion of the compensation argument, and Fullinwider for a critique of Thomson's argument; see also Groarke 1990.) One problem with this justification is that you're not compensating the individuals who were actually injured. However, insofar as people identify themselves not as individuals – and more importantly, insofar as others identify them not as individuals – but as members of a group, maybe today's individuals, the ones being compensated, *are* (also the ones) being injured; inheritance (of attitude, of opportunity) should not be lightly dismissed. But how do you measure the extent of injury? And how much compensation is enough?

Also, the ones bearing the burden of compensation may not be the ones guilty of injuring. But again, consider group identity: whether they like/want/accept it or not, white males have benefited and perhaps continue to benefit from that past discrimination. (Does that include the corporate coronary?) Too, often these individuals are not asked to give up something they already have; they are merely asked not to take something they have yet to get.

Then again, if it's a case of group injury, it should be a case of group compensation – not individual compensation. Maybe affirmative action programs are unfair on an individual basis, and thus justifiably called reverse discrimination, but fair on a group basis. This may be especially convincing if one considers the group to be society as a whole.

In addition to the claim that affirmative action programs are wrong because they are simply reverse discrimination, they could be wrong because they cause harm to the target groups themselves, members of which are made to feel that they need special help (the equal start often looks like a head start). However, as Boatright points out, "Success in life is often unearned, but there is little evidence that the beneficiaries of good fortune are psychologically damaged by it" (204) – if white men have not suffered for it, why should now non-whites and women have a problem with it? (Because they *know* they're getting it unearned – white men have deluded themselves.)

Furthermore, affirmative action programs may perpetuate rather than get rid of the problem of stereotypes (see Heilman's paper for this argument), if only by continually drawing attention to such irrelevant differences.

Also, if such programs do lead to hiring and promoting genuinely less qualified/capable people, well, the work just won't be as good (assuming both the more and the less qualified work to their potential), and this could have a negative effect on the society as a whole.

Rooting out discrimination doesn't necessarily stop at affirmative action hiring strategies; to be fair, to do the right thing, one must also provide equal pay for work of equal value. But how do we define "equal value"? Value to who? To the company? To society? To the worker? And

how is that value determined? By effort, skill, productivity, qualifications/training, experience, responsibility, risk, stress? To consider more deeply the factor of responsibility, consider Simon's questions: "Is responsibility related to the number of people one supervises, the level of decision making one holds within a firm, the costs of misjudgment, or what?" (400). And how are these assessed, and by whom? The person who currently holds the position or some middle-manager?

Jennifer Quinn presents an interesting analysis of the role job evaluations play in determining pay equity: she argues that what usually gets the points on a job evaluation are those skills primarily associated with "men's jobs" (for example, secretaries, usually women, are usually required to do several things at once, with a smile, while being constantly interrupted – that skill is seldom on the list for points); that jobs that are traditionally the same as those women do at home (for free) go unrecognized ("So while men, for example, typically receive points for dirt and grease that they encounter on the job under a factor designated 'working conditions,' nurses, who deal with vomit, blood, and excrement on a daily basis, receive no such points" [396]); that men's jobs such as those in the trades requiring a lot of visible and on-the-job training get credit, but women's jobs such as those in the clerical category requiring the same level of training, but invisible and off-the-job, don't get credit.

Righting our wrongs may not even stop with pay equity; Kavka argues, on the grounds of distributive justice and self-respect, that handicapped people's right to work includes not only a right to nondiscrimination in employment and promotion, but also a right to compensatory training and education and a right to reasonable investments by society and employers to make jobs accessible.

FURTHER READING AND REFERENCES

Abella, Judge Rosalie. *Equality in Employment, A Royal Commission Report.* Government of Canada: Minister of Supply and Services, 1984.

Andiappan, P., M. Reavley, and S. Silver. "Discrimination Against Pregnant Employees: An Analysis of Arbitration and Human Rights Tribunal Decisions in Canada." *Journal of Business Ethics* 9.2 (February 1990): 143-149.

Boatright, John R. *Ethics and the Conduct of Business.* 2nd ed. NJ: Prentice Hall, 1997.

Brockett, Patrick L., and E. Susan Tankersley. "The Genetics Revolution, Economics, Ethics and Insurance." *Journal of Business Ethics* 16.15 (November 1997): 1661-1676.

Falkenberg, L.E., and L. Boland. "Eliminating the Barriers to Employment Equity in the Canadian Workplace." *Journal of Business Ethics* 16.9 (June 1997): 963-975.

Ferris, Gerald R., and Thomas R. King. "The Politics of Age Discrimination in Organizations." *Journal of Business Ethics* 11.5-6 (May 1992): 341-350.

Fullinwider, Robert K. "Preferential Hiring and Compensation" *Social Theory and Practice* 3.3 (Spring 1975): 307-320.

Groarke, Leo. "Affirmative Action as a Form of Restitution." *Journal of Business Ethics* 9.3 (March 1990): 207-213.

Groarke, Leo. "What's in a Number? Consequentialism and Employment Equity in Hall, Hurka, Sumner and Baker et al." *Dialogue* XXXV (1996): 359-373.

Häyry, Heta, and Matti Häyry. "AIDS Now." *Bioethics* 1.4 (1987): 339-356.

Heilman, Madeline E. "Sex Discrimination and the Affirmative Action Remedy: The Role of Sex Stereotypes." *Journal of Business Ethics* 16.9 (June 1997): 877-889.

Hubbard, Ruth, and Elijah Wald. *Exploding the Gene Myth.* Boston: Beacon Press, 1993: 133-144.

Hurka, Thomas. *Principles: Short Essays on Ethics.* Toronto: Harcourt Brace, 1994.

Kavka, Gregory S. "Disability and the Right to Work." *Contemporary Issues in Business Ethics.* Ed. Joseph R. DesJardins and John J. McCall. 3rd ed. Belmont, CA: Wadsworth, 1996. 486–492.

Murray, Thomas H. "Genetics and the Moral Mission of Health Insurance." *Hastings Center Report* 22.6 (November/December 1992): 12-17.

Nagel, Thomas. "A Defense of Affirmative Action." Testimony before the Subcommittee on the Constitution of the Senate Judiciary Committee, June 18, 1981. *Ethical Theory and Business.* Ed. Tom L. Beauchamp and Norman E. Bowie. 5th ed. NJ: Prentice Hall, 1997. 370-374.

Narveson, Jan. "Have We a Right to Non-Discrimination?" *Business Ethics in Canada.* Ed. Deborah C. Poff and Wilfrid J. Waluchow. 3rd ed. Scarborough: Prentice Hall, 1999. 270-287.

Pojman, Louis P. "The Moral Status of Affirmative Action." *Public Affairs Quarterly* 6.2 (April 1992): 181-206.

Pulfer, Rachel. "Mining Your Business." *This Magazine* 32.5 (March/April 1999): 13-15.

Purdy, Laura M. "In Defense of Hiring Apparently Less Qualified Women." *Journal of Social Philosophy* 15 (Summer 1984): 26-33.

Quinn, Jennifer M. "Visibility and Value: The Role of Job Evaluation in Assuring Equal

Pay for Women." *Law & Policy in International Business* 25 (1994): 1403-1444. Rpt. in *Ethical Theory and Business*, Ed. Tom L. Beauchamp and Norman E. Bowie. 5th ed. NJ: Prentice Hall, 1997. 393-398.

Quinn, John F. "Business Ethics, Fetal Protection Policies, and Discrimination Against Women in the Workplace." *Business & Professional Ethics Journal* 7.3-4 (Fall/Winter 1988): 3-27.

Rebick, Judy. "Collect Call to Ma Bell." *This Magazine* 32.5 (March/April 1999): 44.

Shaw, Bill. "Affirmative Action: An Ethical Evaluation." *Journal of Business Ethics* 7.10 (October 1988) 763-770.

Simon, Robert L. "Comparable Pay for Comparable Work?" *Ethical Theory and Business.* Ed.

Tom L. Beauchamp and Norman E. Bowie. 5th ed. NJ: Prentice Hall, 1997. 398-409.

Southerst, John. "What Price Fairness?" *Canadian Business* 64.12 (December 1991): 67-72.

Thomson, Judith Jarvis. "Preferential Hiring" *Philosophy and Public Affairs* 2 (Summer 1973): 364-384.

Velasquez, Manuel G. *Business Ethics: Concepts and Cases.* 4th ed. NJ: Prentice Hall, 1998.

Wasserstrom, Richard. "A Defense of Programs of Preferential Treatment." *National Forum (The Phi Beta Kappa Journal)* LVIII.1 (Winter 1978): 15-18.

Willard, L. Duane. "Aesthetic Discrimination Against Persons." *Dialogue* XVI.4 (1977): 676-692.

Affirmative Action and Employment Equity in Canada

Susan Dimock and Christopher Tucker[1]

I. Introduction

1   Canada is a country committed to the principle of legal equality amongst its citizenry. This principle is enshrined, among other places, in the fundamental law of the land: the Canadian Constitution. In particular, the *Canadian Charter of Rights and Freedoms* (1982) lays down in s.15 (1) that "Every individual is equal before and under the law and has the right to the equal protection and equal benefit of the law without

Susan Dimock and Christopher Tucker, "Affirmative Action and Employment Equity in Canada" © 1999 by Susan Dimock and Christopher Tucker. Printed with permission of the authors.

discrimination and, in particular, without discrimination based on race, national or ethnic origin, colour, religion, sex, age or mental or physical disability." Notwithstanding this commitment to equality, the subsection of the *Charter* immediately following this allows for the implementation of affirmative action programs. Thus s.15 (2) states that "Subsection (1) does not preclude any law, program or activity that has as its object the amelioration of conditions of disadvantaged individuals or groups including those that are disadvantaged because of race, national or ethnic origin, colour, religion, sex, age or mental or physical disability."

2   The affirmative action programs which s.15(2) permits may take a number of forms.

They may be adopted by educational institutions, employers, financial institutions, landlords, insurance companies and many other institutions that are in a position to award benefits within society; depending upon the benefit in question, the specific details of the affirmative action plan will vary, of course. Moreover, even within a single sector there is considerable variation as to the steps that an institution might take by way of adopting affirmative action policies. Take, for example, affirmative action programs within the area of employment. It may be decided that the best way to ameliorate the disadvantages of those discriminated against in the past is to adopt a tie-breaking mechanism: if two candidates are otherwise equally qualified for a job, but one is from a disadvantaged group, then the company will hire that person. Or the company may decide that, because of past discrimination, persons from disadvantaged groups cannot compete on a fair footing with those from more privileged groups, and so it may adopt a policy of ranking applicants which gives minority candidates extra credit, as it were, just for being members of the minority group. Alternatively, a company might decide that more aggressive measures are needed to attract persons from previously disadvantaged groups into their workforce. Thus it might adopt a policy whereby certain positions are set aside for members of minority groups, or it might adopt a quota system which sets hiring targets for specific groups. Though many people think that the exact nature of the program adopted matters to its justification (typically people tend to think that tie-breaking measures are easier to justify than quota systems, for example), we shall not be concerned with the differences between these approaches in what follows. For we believe that all affirmative action programs stand or fall together.

3 Our concern in this paper is with the justification of affirmative action programs. That they stand in need of justification can be seen from a number of different perspectives. First, the allowance (and in some cases requirement) that educational institutions, employers and others adopt affirmative action programs seems problematic in a society committed to equality. For such programs clearly privilege some over others; they treat people unequally. Secondly, it would seem that affirmative action policies must be inefficient in a certain way. For such programs allow that a candidate may or must be admitted to the institution or hired even though he or she is not the most qualified for the position, because he or she belongs to an historically disadvantaged group. Finally, for every person who is benefited by an affirmative action plan, there is another person who is disadvantaged by it. Those who would have received the benefit on the basis of merit in the absence of affirmative action seem to have some legitimate grievance: they have been adversely discriminated against. Those who view affirmative action programs in this light tend to refer to them as policies of "reverse discrimination". Whatever we call it, though, it is clear that affirmative action stands in need of justification for these reasons.

4 We shall concentrate on affirmative action as it applies only to employment in what follows. Our concern will be to examine the arguments that are offered in favour of affirmative action policies in hiring, particularly those which have played an important role in setting Canadian policy and law on matters of affirmative action and employment equity. We shall conclude that the reasons typically offered in defence of affirmative action are inadequate.

5 The basic argument will proceed as follows. Those who wish to defend the use of affirmative

action programs typically do so on one of two importantly different grounds. The first general approach to justifying affirmative action programs is to argue that they are required by justice. The second approach is to argue that they produce good consequences for society. We shall argue that the arguments from justice are problematic, and that only consequentialist reasons seem capable of providing a defensible justification of affirmative action. But whether a particular policy like affirmative action actually produces good consequences is an empirical matter. So while we can agree with those consequentially-minded philosophers and legal theorists that *if* affirmative action programs produced significant goods for society then they could be justified, we shall question whether they actually do produce such goods. And we shall find that most of the goods which it is suggested are made available by affirmative action programs not only are not produced by such programs, but are actually retarded by them. Thus the second approach to defending affirmative action policies is also unsuccessful.

II. Justice-Based Defenses of Affirmative Action

6   Those who wish to argue that affirmative action programs are justified because they are required by justice have two routes available to them, and both have had numerous followers. They each correspond to the kind of justice that affirmative action is supposed to serve: compensatory justice or distributive justice.

II.1 Compensatory Justice

7   The first argument from justice has it that affirmative action is required as a matter of *com-*

pensatory justice. The idea is this: members of the groups that are now to be favoured by affirmative action have in the past been adversely discriminated against. As a result of that discrimination, they now occupy a significantly disadvantaged position relative to those who were not discriminated against in the past. Because the past discrimination was unjustified, based on attributed rather than actual characteristics, it was unfair. Therefore, the resulting advantages for some and disadvantages for others were equally unfair; some benefited unjustly at the expense of others. As a matter of justice, then, we must right this wrong.

8   Now this argument has been subject to considerable attack. Most important, we think, is that it is incompatible with the actual way in which affirmative action programs must work. For affirmative action programs identify those who are to be favoured by group membership. Thus, for example, the Canadian Employment Equity Act which was passed in 1986 identified four designated groups whose members were to be advantaged via affirmative action programs: women, aboriginal peoples, persons with disabilities, and persons who are, because of their race or colour, in a visible minority in Canada. If we adopted the compensatory justice model for defending such legislation, we should have to say that every member of these groups has been disadvantaged relative to others who are not members of these groups, such that those who were not disadvantaged gained benefits unfairly at the expense of those who were disadvantaged. And this is precisely the position that the courts have in fact taken in Canada. Group membership alone is taken as sufficient evidence that a person has been discriminated against or is entitled to affirmative action assistance. Under s.15(2) of the Charter, "The court

would be spared assessing the situation of every individual covered by an ameliorative program to determine whether he or she were entitled to be included in the class of *disadvantaged* persons. Every member of the disadvantaged group would be assumed to have been disadvantaged and thereby entitled to the benefit of the program...."[2]

9   But of course the presumption that every member of a disadvantaged group has thereby been disadvantaged is highly implausible! We cannot assume that just because an individual belongs to an historically disadvantaged group, that that individual has been disadvantaged and so deserves compensation. It may be true, for example, that women as a group have been discriminated against to their detriment in employment, but that surely does not alone entitle someone like Princess Diana or Jackie Kennedy-Onassis to compensatory benefits. For they simply have not suffered from adverse discrimination and so have no claim to compensation. The point of all this is a general one, though: because we cannot identify individual victims of past discrimination on the basis of group membership alone, affirmative action programs which make entitlements to compensatory benefits available just on that basis cannot be justified. They will extend benefits to those who do not deserve them. Furthermore, they are unlikely to benefit those who are most entitled to compensation on this model because, even with affirmative action programs that grant them extra points or that reserve positions for members of their group, those individuals who have been most severely disadvantaged by past discrimination will not be able to compete for valuable employment positions; they will lack the skills needed to compete even for an affirmative action position.

10   A similar problem arises if we concentrate, not on the beneficiaries of affirmative action, but on those who lose out as a result of such programs. According to the compensatory justice approach, we may disadvantage those who belong to groups that have benefited from past discriminatory practices (white, abled, non-aboriginal males, in particular). The reason given for this is that they have gained unfair benefits at the expense of others, and so must now provide compensation for their ill-gotten gains. But the group problem re-emerges here: not every white, abled, non-aboriginal man has participated in discriminatory practices or benefited from them. Just as we cannot identify the victims of discrimination by group membership alone, nor can we identify the beneficiaries of discrimination in that way.

11   Consideration of those who are to be relatively disadvantaged by affirmative action programs on compensatory grounds raises a further concern. The discrimination at issue is an historical event, which has produced significant disadvantages for those in the designated groups. But the people who have participated in that discrimination are long since dead; they are certainly not the same people who are now told that they must suffer loses in order to compensate those who have been historically disadvantaged. But is this not a case of "the sins of the father being visited upon his sons"? In other words, is this not a clear case of holding the descendants of those who have committed past wrongs responsible for those wrongs, even though they in no way participated in them or had control over them? And do not societies committed to justice abhor such practices?

12   Whatever the deficiencies of the compensatory justice argument for affirmative action may be and whether its advocates can meet the chal-

lenges raised here need not concern us any longer, however, for this argument has not been particularly important in Canada (unlike the United States). It certainly has not been a significant influence in the development of our legislative programs, at least, and since we are concerned with assessing the reasons that have actually been given in support of our affirmative action policies and laws, we can safely move along.

II.2 Distributive Justice

13 A second argument founded on justice is offered by those in favour of affirmative action as well. In this approach affirmative action is defended as a matter of distributive justice. Those in the designated groups have been unjustly deprived of opportunities and benefits in the past, which make them unable to compete now on the same terms with others who have not been similarly disadvantaged. The result is distributively unjust, because some have a vastly greater share of the goods which society makes available than others do, through no fault of their own. This injustice in the distribution of society's benefits has to be rectified, and affirmative action is one way to do that.

14   It is frequently taken as evidence of past discrimination, on this view, that different groups are under-represented in various positions in society relative to their percentage of the population at large. Thus, for example, the fact that only 7% of upper management positions in the private sector are held by women, despite the fact that women make up just over 50% of the total population, is taken as evidence of discrimination against women in employment and career advancement. Not surprisingly, then, the goal of affirmative action which defenders of this

view usually adopt is that of having in all sectors of employment a level of representation for each group which is equal to their proportion of the general population.

15   As with the previous argument from justice, however, this approach faces some very serious challenges. Problems of identifying individuals solely by group membership arise again here, for example, though in a different form. For individuals are not typically identifiable as members of a single group. Is a disabled woman who occupies a managerial position to count as increasing the representation of one group or two?

16   More importantly, this argument rests upon two very dubious assumptions. The first is that, in the absence of past discrimination, there would in fact be participation in all sectors of the economy equal to representation in the population. This is very unlikely. Given that some differences are genetic, some are a contingent feature of such circumstances as geography, and others are cultural without being based on discrimination, it is unlikely that people will be drawn to or excel at different occupations proportionately with their share of the general population.

17   The second problem is that this approach assumes that the just distribution of economic positions in society will be equal across groups. This is a controversial moral judgement; those who wish to defend it must shown that a distribution of the economic rewards of society which maintains an equality between a group's percentage of the population and their participation in all sectors of society is better than (more just than) alternative principles of distributive justice. Such alternatives include principles which hold that economic rewards should be distributed according to merit, need, virtue, contribution, etc. Though we cannot enter into the debate

concerning the proper conception of distributive justice here, we need not; for again, such arguments have not played a central role in the development of Canadian public policy and law.

18   Though these arguments from justice have occupied much of the attention of philosophers and other theorists in thinking about affirmative action, they are at best highly contentious and they have failed to generate any consensus concerning the permissibility of such programs. Indeed, for every defender of affirmative action on the grounds that it is required by justice (compensatory or distributive), one can find opponents who insist that it is a subversion of justice. It subverts justice, moreover, in exactly the same way that discrimination of the type to be resisted does, because it makes benefits available to people on such arbitrary grounds as skin colour or gender, rather than on relevant grounds such as merit.

19   Those who think that affirmative action is in fact discriminatory against those who have been privileged in the past may nonetheless think that it is justified, as a necessary means to eliminating the gross inequality that characterises our society and as a way of providing those who have been previously disadvantaged with a fair opportunity of bettering their fortunes. To take this kind of line, however, is to adopt a very different approach to the justification of affirmative action, one which looks not to its justice but to its good social consequences.

III. Consequentialist Justifications of Affirmative Action

20   Those who argue that affirmative action is justified because it will lead to significant social benefits are offering a consequentialist position. Consequentialism is the view that an action, policy, law or what have you is justified when it produces good consequences. The best action is that which, of the alternatives available, produces the best consequences. The most common consequentialist position is typically some form of utilitarianism, which holds that the consequences that matter are those affecting the welfare, happiness, well-being or utility of all those affected by the action, policy or law in question. Utilitarianism then says that the right thing to do, or the morally justified thing to do, is whatever, among the alternatives, will maximise the welfare, happiness, well-being or utility of all those affected by the choice. This has been the route adopted by most Canadian philosophers who have sought to defend affirmative action, as well as by our legislators in setting public policy and developing laws designed to achieve employment equity and eliminate discrimination in the work-place.

21   Now those who wish to defend affirmative action on the grounds that it will produce good social consequences (and that nothing less invasive of freedom will do so) must explain what good consequences are to be expected from such policies. A number of good consequences have been proposed in this regard.

III.1 To Better Serve the Needs of Minority Cultures

22   It is frequently claimed in support of affirmative action that the needs of minority cultures are unique in important ways, and that the best way of ensuring that those needs are met in a way that is sensitive to their differences is to have representatives from the minority cultures themselves providing the services. This is typically taken to require affirmative action programs specifically designed to increase the spaces available to members of the minority cultures in advanced educa-

tional and training programs, rather than affirmative action designed to achieve employment equity in all sectors of the economy.

23   This argument may be able to provide a limited defence of affirmative action programs, particularly in relation to fields such as medicine in which cultural differences are often very significant and dictate a different approach to the physician/patient/family relationship, death, medical procedures, consent and patient autonomy, etc. A similar case may be made with respect to the legal profession. In such cases it may be plausible to conclude that medical and legal services provided by members of one's own community would be better than those provided by others from outside of one's cultural group.

24   This argument faces some serious challenges, however. First, it is simply not possible to ensure that members of the various ethnic, racial, linguistic and cultural groups that constitute Canada's diverse population be served by professionals drawn from their own communities exclusively or even primarily. The resources that would be required to implement such a system are simply not available. Most communities can only support a small number of specialised professionals, whether they be medical, legal or financial specialists, for example. Furthermore, if one were to attempt to increase the participation of various minority cultures' members in the different professions as a means of providing better service to those groups, one would not only have to adopt affirmative action policies to ensure that training was available to these individuals, but one would then also have to ensure that they practised their professions in centres whose population is made up of a sufficient number of the minority group's members. This would be a significant invasion into the freedom of those who are to be the beneficiaries of such programs, and it is certainly not a policy that has received political support or expression in Canada. Finally, such an argument seems to run a serious risk of isolating minority communities, of maintaining their distinctiveness and homogeneity at the price of cutting them off from other communities and their members. This model seems ill-suited to achieve the Canadian vision of a multi-cultural society, in which distinct and diverse peoples come together, not into a melting pot which eliminates their differences, but into a mosaic where each piece of the pattern is unique but related to all the rest in a way that renders the result unified and beautiful. The Canadian vision of multi-culturalism depends upon interaction between peoples, which will give rise to knowledge and tolerance of differences. Any policy which presupposes that individuals in minority cultures can only receive adequate service from members of their own group flies in the face of our national ideal.

25   Thus while increasing the participation of various minority groups within such professions as medicine and law would, perhaps, improve the quality of service available to members of those groups, this approach provides only a very limited defence of affirmative action programs at best. For the good that such a policy would make available can be provided to only a few groups, likely in large urban centres, and even there members of minority groups would still have to receive a considerable amount of service from non-member specialists. Furthermore, this good cannot be achieved by affirmative action programs alone but must be conjoined with restrictive requirements designed to ensure that those who receive the professional training use their skills in the service of their minority group; this is a serious cost which may offset any good that such a policy might make possible. Finally, this approach runs the risk of isolating and

marginalizing the groups it is designed to assist. For these reasons, this consideration is not sufficient to justify the wide-spread use of affirmative action programs in society at large.

26   This case does, however, raise an issue that permeates our discussion of the various consequentialist defences that are offered in favour of affirmative action programs: those who wish to employ consequentialist arguments must consider *all* of the consequences a policy is likely to achieve. For it is not enough to establish that a policy would have some good consequences, if those are vastly outweighed by bad consequences that would also attend it. Furthermore, this case, like those to follow, should serve as a warning. In particular, philosophers are notorious for speculating about the likely consequences of various proposals, without much empirical investigation. Thus while a good consequence of affirmative action might on first glance seem plausible in the abstract, the details often belie the suggested benefit. When discussing empirical matters, it is best to get out of our armchairs and consult the experts in the field, as we shall see.

III.2 To Promote Diversity

27 Affirmative action policies are often advocated on the grounds that they will promote diversity in employment situations. Philosophers and other academics are often among those who advance diversity as a reason for adopting affirmative action programs. It is likely that this is a case in which a specific good for a very unique profession has been inappropriately applied to others where it fits less well. For there may indeed be good reason to think that universities and other centres of research and learning benefit from a diversity of views, cultural influences, histories,

etc. It is not surprising, therefore, that professional philosophers and other academics should promote diversity as a value in its own right; within their professions diversity is a significant good. But it would be problematic to conclude from this that affirmative action as a general program in society is justified, for it is not at all clear that diversity is a value in its own right. Rather, it seems vastly more likely that diversity is promoted as a good because people believe that it will be instrumental in achieving other goods: tolerance, understanding, an undermining of the racist/sexist/ablist attitudes that produce the invidious discrimination in the first place, different groups will then have role models available upon which their members can draw, etc. These goods, which diversity in the population of various employment sectors is supposed to generate, all depend on diversity itself leading to some fundamental changes in attitudes, both by those who are to be the beneficiaries of affirmative action and those who are thereby forced not to discriminate against those whom they otherwise would discriminate against. Since the effect on attitudes has occupied a central place in Canadian justifications of affirmative action, both in the political and academic arena, we shall examine this claim closely in what follows.

III.3 Attitudinal Changes and the Reduction of Prejudice

28 Those who adopt a consequentialist approach to affirmative action typically relate the good consequences that they anticipate from affirmative action programs ultimately to a change of attitudes among the members of society. This is not surprising, of course, since the discrimination that affirmative action policies is supposed to ameliorate ultimately stems from prejudicial at-

titudes based on arbitrary characteristics of persons such as race, ethnicity, gender, physical disabilities, etc. If these attitudes are fundamentally responsible for discriminatory practices, then policies aimed at eliminating these attitudes seem the best approach to eliminating discrimination. It would seem, furthermore, that changing attitudes is really behind the more specific consequentialist arguments that are advanced in favour of affirmative action: that it will promote diversity, lead to better service for minority groups, provide role models for members of groups which have been previously disadvantaged because of prejudice and the like are all held out as good because they will lead to greater tolerance and understanding between groups. Those who have been prejudiced against in the past will come to be seen as competent and contributing members of their professions, both by those who previously undervalued them and by themselves. Through participation, previously disadvantaged groups will gain not only the esteem they deserve from others, but self-respect as well. As prejudicial attitudes are eroded, people from previously disadvantaged groups will be increasingly able to simply compete on a fair basis with others, for they will no longer have to overcome the arbitrary biases against them that racism, sexism, etc. put in their way in the past. The end result of this process, consequentialists hope, is a society in which people are judged and rewarded purely on the basis of merit. When such a state is reached, affirmative action programs will no longer be needed; affirmative action is at best a temporary means to overcoming the prejudice that denies some people the opportunities they deserve, and once those prejudicial attitudes have been overcome affirmative action commitments can simply whither away.

29   Now these are some very sweeping generalisations about what all or most consequentialists think on the matter of affirmative action. They are borne out, however, by an examination both of the writings of our most prominent philosophers and of our legislators and policy makers. Take, for example, the work of L.W. Sumner. Sumner argues that affirmative action, or positive discrimination as he calls it, cannot be defended on grounds of corrective or compensatory justice. He does think that it can be defended on consequentialist grounds, however, and he rests his argument on using affirmative action as a means of overcoming certain prejudicial attitudes. Concentrating just on the use of affirmative action policies that favour women in employment, Sumner argues that affirmative action programs are needed principally to combat the effects of sexism, and ultimately to eliminate sexist attitudes themselves. He identifies two forms of sexism: primary (direct or overt) sexism and, more importantly, what he calls "secondary sexism", which consists in a host of attitudes by which the abilities or commitment of female candidates for employment or promotion are undervalued because of prejudicial attitudes about women. Secondary sexist attitudes include such things as the belief that women will be less committed to their jobs because of family responsibilities, that a female candidate will not be able to fit into a male dominated work environment, etc. Now Sumner thinks that secondary sexism is "one of the main mechanisms whereby employment practices continue to discriminate against women"[3] and that affirmative action programs must discriminate in favour of women in order to neutralise the immediate effects of such sexist attitudes and thereby ultimately eliminate those attitudes: "The centrepiece of the consequentialist argu-

ment is the claim that introducing a measure of discrimination against men will be the most effective means of eliminating discrimination against women, and thus of minimising discrimination in the long run."[4]

30   Likewise, Thomas Hurka believes not only that sexist attitudes lead to discrimination against women in employment, but that changing those attitudes is one of the principal benefits of affirmative action. Indeed, he thinks that affirmative action will produce positive changes not only in men's attitudes toward women but also in women's attitudes towards themselves:

> If the belief that women are inferior persists in Canada, either consciously or sub-consciously, it's partly because women aren't sufficiently prominent in Canadian life. Moving them quickly into important jobs can help dispel that belief and the many harms it does.
>
> Equally important are the changes in women's attitudes. What you aspire to in life depends on what you think you can do, which depends on what people like you have done before. Women in prominent jobs can be role models, encouraging young women to work for similar success. If the young women achieve success this will benefit both them and society, which now wastes much of their potential.[5]

In this quotation we find Hurka appealing to two of the consequentialist reasons discussed above – increasing the representation of a given group in a particular field and the role model argument – though his reason for doing so is not that these benefits alone are sufficient to justify affirmative action, but that they will lead to the change in attitudes that will ultimately eliminate discrimination based on the prejudicial belief that women are inferior to men.

31   Let us turn now to an examination of the legal literature supporting affirmative action, and

particularly employment equity. The Supreme Court of Canada, for example, has made it clear in a number of rulings that the purpose of s.15 of the Charter, as well as the various Provincial Human Rights Codes, is to prevent the deleterious effects of discrimination. In so doing, they have adopted a consequentialist position at two levels. First, whether a particular law, labour practice, insurance provision or what have you is discriminatory depends upon its effects, not the intent of those who have adopted it. No intent to discriminate or other foul motive is necessary in order to establish that discrimination has occurred. Secondly, they have attributed to anti-discrimination and equity legislation a consequentialist justification or purpose: to remove the negative effects of prejudice.[6]

32   The Supreme Court's position is not unique in this respect. Indeed, as we shall see, the approach taken by the members of our legal community has been thoroughly consequentialist, with the goal of changing prejudicial attitudes as a means of reducing discrimination occupying a prominent position in their deliberations about the justification of affirmative action policies. This concentration on creating a climate in which attitudes of fellow-feeling, respect, inclusivity and mutual understanding replace those of prejudice, ascriptions of inferiority upon whole groups and exclusion of those who are different than oneself, as a means of effecting greater equality within society, is reflected in virtually all of the Provincial and Territorial Human Rights Codes. Thus we read in the Preamble to the Human Rights Code of Ontario, for example, that "WHEREAS it is public policy in Ontario to recognise the dignity and worth of every person and to provide for equal rights and opportunities without discrimination that is contrary to law, and having as its aim the creation

of a climate of understanding and mutual respect for the dignity and worth of each person so that each person feels a part of the community and able to contribute fully to the development and well-being of the community and the Province..."[7] The Canadian commitment to affirmative action and employment equity must be understood against the backdrop of this more sweeping commitment to equality and the goal of creating a society free of invidious prejudice.

33   In 1986 the federal Government of Canada passed the Employment Equity Act. In that Act four groups of persons were identified as victims of prejudicial discrimination in employment and designated as groups for whom employment equity was immediately needed: women, aboriginal peoples, persons with disabilities, and persons who are, because of their race or colour, in a visible minority in Canada. It is clear from writings related to this Act that its framers intended it to have the effect of increasing the participation of members of the designated groups in employment situations from which they had traditionally been excluded on grounds that they belonged to one of the designated groups: "Employment Equity is a result-oriented program which seeks evidence that employment situations for the designated groups are improving, indicated by their greater numerical representation in the workforce, improvement in their employment status, occupations, and salary levels in jobs for which they are available and qualified."[8]

34   Now the government of Canada clearly recognises that the factors contributing to the relative employment disadvantage of persons in the designated groups are diverse. Many which they identified in discussing the Employment Equity Act might be categorised as structural, involving the way employment activity is structured: thus lack of day-care facilities for women, lack of ramps and elevators for disabled persons, the organisation of the work-day into standard eight-hour shifts and the like present barriers to certain groups. These can be easily remedied, however, and the Supreme Court of Canada has made it clear that the equality guaranteed to all Canadians under the law requires that employers take reasonable steps to accommodate workers with special needs.[9] Much more important for our purposes are the attitudinal causes which the government identified as leading to the under-representation of the designated groups in the workforce, particularly at the managerial or professional levels. For these attitudes are not only a barrier in and of themselves, but they retard the willingness or ability of employers to see the value of making the needed structural changes. Among those attitudes, identified in the Government of Canada Background Paper to the proposed Employment Equity Act, are the following: "Foremost is the attitude of many non-disabled persons: there is a widespread misunderstanding and under-rating of the abilities of disabled persons." And in relation to aboriginal peoples, "Native people face attitudinal and cultural barriers to their equitable participation in the economy. Racial intolerance and misunderstanding" are chief amongst them. Likewise, "Research attests to the existence both of prejudicial attitudes to non-whites and systemic discrimination based on racial factors."[10] It is clear from these and similar claims that the authors of the Background Paper believe that prejudicial attitudes play a crucial role in the perpetuation of discrimination against the designated groups, and insofar as they adopted employment equity (affirmative action) as their response to such discrimination, they believe that affirmative action policies can (help to) eliminate those pernicious attitudes.

35   The perceived relation between prejudicial attitudes and discrimination in employment was perhaps nowhere more clearly articulated than in the report of the Royal Commission on Equality in Employment, headed by Judge Rosalie Abella. In their report the members of the Royal Commission made it clear that they understood both discrimination and equity to essentially involve certain attitudes. Thus "the goal of equality is more than an evolutionary intolerance to adverse discrimination. It is to ensure, too, that the vestiges of these arbitrarily restrictive assumptions do not continue to play a role in our society."[11] And as to their understanding of discrimination, they characterised it this way: "Discrimination in this context means practices or attitudes that have, whether by design or impact, the effect of limiting an individual's or a group's right to the opportunities generally available because of attributed rather than actual characteristics."[12]

36   Group membership and prejudicial attitudes based on group membership are central in the approach adopted by the Royal Commission on Equality in Employment:

> Remedial measures of a systemic and systematic kind are the object of employment equity and affirmative action. They are meant to improve the situation for individuals who, by virtue of belonging to and being identified with a particular group, find themselves unfairly and adversely affected by certain systems or practices. System remedies are a response to patterns of discrimination that have two basic antecedents:
>
> a) a disparate negative impact that flows from the structure of systems designed for a homogeneous constituency; and
>
> b) a disparately negative impact that flows from practices based on stereotypical characteristics ascribed to an individual because of the characteristics ascribed to the group of which he or she is a member.[13]

37   Judge Abella does not believe that voluntary programs can effect a significant reduction in employment discrimination; mandatory programs are necessary. "Given the seriousness and apparent intractability of employment discrimination, it is unrealistic and somewhat ingenuous to rely on there being sufficient public goodwill to fuel a voluntary program."[14] Apparently coercion will effect an end of discrimination even in the absence of a change of attitude (increase of goodwill), contrary to everything else that we have seen!

IV. The Real Consequences of Affirmative Action

38 In the introductory paragraph of the last section, we suggested that if it is believed that prejudiced attitudes are responsible for discriminatory practices then any policy designed to eliminate these attitudes seems to be the best way to eliminate discrimination. We then went on to make clear that affirmative action policies, at least in Canada, have been traditionally defended on the grounds that the increased representation of target groups in the workforce would eliminate these prejudiced attitudes, as well as arrest (or at least retard) the discriminatory hiring practices which result from them. The appropriateness of these policies, then, must be evaluated by how effectively they serve their ends. In other words, these affirmative action policies may only be deemed appropriate responses to discriminatory acts and prejudiced attitudes if they serve to eliminate these acts and attitudes; insofar as the former largely stem from the latter, moreover, the efficiency with which affirmative action eliminates those prejudiced attitudes will deter-

mine whether it can be justified on consequentialist grounds.

39   As we have argued above, that the elimination of prejudiced attitudes is of paramount import to the Canadian philosophical and legal communities is clear: Sumner focuses primarily on the importance of changing sexist attitudes, while Hurka believes that the overcoming of prejudiced attitudes is one of the principal benefits of affirmative action. The Ontario Human Rights Code states explicitly that creating a prejudice free environment in which its citizens can live is one of its principal aims. Canada's Employment Equity Act, likewise, must be understood as an attempt to overcome prejudicial attitudes.

40   So, then, affirmative action policies may be viewed as appropriate responses to discriminatory hiring practices only insofar as they can be thought to aid the overcoming of prejudiced beliefs. Unfortunately, as we shall see, there is no good reason to believe that these policies serve this end. The psychological literature on the subject indicates that affirmative action policies would actually frustrate efforts geared towards the elimination of prejudiced attitudes held by persons against others because of their membership in historically disadvantaged groups, building resentment in prejudiced individuals, and further entrenching their previous discriminatory behaviours. This literature also fails to indicate that the 'role model' approach to overcoming negative attitudes that disadvantaged persons hold regarding their own social group is served by affirmative action.

IV.1 The Alteration of Other's Attitudes

41 It is easy to understand why someone would suppose that a workforce which well represents minorities at large would be one in which prejudiced attitudes dwindle off and die. A bigot, prejudiced against each and every type of person who is different than himself, when at work would first be forced to get to know people of type X, Y, and Z, and, through continued interaction with these persons, would then come to respect them, or at least tolerate them. After watching presentation after presentation by persons of groups X, Y and Z, the bigot would have to reason to the conclusion that he was wrong after all, and that these groups are not lazy and stupid (to take common prejudiced beliefs). After sharing a change room with them, the bigot would be forced to conclude that they did not smell. And after a very long time, it may even be the case that the bigot is forced to reason to the conclusion that all the members of these groups are not out to get him, and do not even hate him *en masse*. This is a fairly persuasive presentation, and no reasonable person would ignore its power. Unfortunately, there is data available to justify supposing that the bigot is not appropriately described as being 'reasonable'.

42   Persons with no prejudice imagine themselves in the situation just described, and come to the conclusion that they would end up as unprejudiced persons. They then hastily conclude that anyone in that situation, whether previously prejudiced or not, would likewise come to judge people from minority groups fairly upon getting to know them better. But the results of imposing affirmative action programs upon non-prejudiced people is not particularly telling, since all it amounts to is this: those who are not already prejudiced will not become so if they are forced through affirmative action to interact in the workplace with members of previously disadvantaged groups. But this is not the group that affirmative action must reform

in order to eliminate discrimination. What reaction can we expect to our scenario from those who are prejudiced?

43 People with prejudice need not find the evidence undermining their prejudiced beliefs compelling, and it is far from clear that the imagined scenario would have the desired effects. Persons with prejudiced attitudes have incentive to reason to entirely different conclusions than non-prejudiced persons when confronted with a workplace enhanced by affirmative action policies. In fact, there is ample evidence to suggest that workplaces affected by affirmative action policies would have negative, rather than positive or even negligible, consequences on the bigot's opinions. There is evidence that suggests that affirmative action policies, and indeed "politically correct" (PC) environments more generally, lead to the entrenching of a bigot's disposition, and lead to more radical, but perhaps less obvious, discriminatory behaviours.

44 For the last several decades, it has been recognised by several psychologists that transgressing a personal standard or conviction creates mental costs for the transgressor. If you maintained throughout your life that John Denver's songs were all a bit cheesy, and then actually heard a song which you said you quite liked, and were then informed that it was by John Denver, you would experience some mental discomfort (and some razzing). It is also recognised quite generally (indeed, it is sometimes treated as a tautology) that one avoids discomfort when one can. To tie this together to the point at hand: if a racist was forced to admit that race X was not so bad after all, then he would experience some psychological costs. Further, if a racist was going to experience some psychological harm, then he would have reason to avoid it if it were possible.

45 It turns out that in the case in question – the discomfort associated with coming to the conclusion that being a racist is wrong – it is possible to avoid the harm. Ziva Kunda has presented us with a compelling argument which suggests that a person's choice of rules of inference to reason with depends upon the conclusion desired.[15] While there are limits to how wild the reasoning may be, if there is a seemingly plausible argument which may be constructed that allows for the conclusion desired to continue to be endorsed, then it will continue to be endorsed. Bigots, then, are able to construct an argument which allows them to maintain that their racist attitude is warranted, and thus avoid the psychological discomfort which would result from coming to the conclusion that their racist attitudes are incorrect, and must be changed. We certainly recognise these types of rationalisations: "I have to work with an X, but *he's not like the others, he ...*", or "You're O.K., for a skirt", or the somewhat more disturbing, "I wonder who she's getting assistance from, and why?" It is worth noting that the stronger one's racism is, the more discomfort may be expected to obtain after realising that one's personal opinions regarding race X are incorrect. Deeply racist persons would have stronger motivation to avoid coming to the conclusion that their attitudes are inappropriate.

46 Interestingly enough, it was likely the recognition of the desire to minimise the discomfort associated with an action that contravened one's ideology which led people to the conclusion that affirmative action policies were a good idea to begin with. It was previously thought that by forcing one to say that something was the case, one would then modify one's previous position with regard to the opinion in question. To turn back to our previous example, upon being

told that the song was played by John Denver, one may then modify one's previous position and say "Well, at least *that* wasn't cheesy, like his earlier material" or something similar which allows you to maintain some form of consistency. In the case of affirmative action, then, once forced to the conclusion that the co-workers from group X aren't lazy/stupid/smelly, etc., the bigot would then be motivated to conclude that X's, overall, aren't that bad, really. Unfortunately, this is not how cognitive dissonance is believed to actually work. The discomfort associated with expressing something that is inconsistent with one's personal values only arises when one freely chooses to engage in the expression.[16] Forced expressions of non-prejudiced sentiments do not result in a bigot being motivated to become less bigoted.

47   Being forced to publicly endorse non-racist/sexist sentiments, and to recognise that one is apt to react in a way that society at large prohibits, leads to stress of quite another type, as well. Bigots who recognise that they are living in a PC environment are likely to alter their public behaviours to appear to conform to PC standards, and feel threatened and fearful. E. Ashby Plant and Patricia Devine have recently run several tests which measure the degrees to which people have adopted anti-racist attitudes due to personal endorsement of non-prejudiced beliefs, compared with others who have adopted anti-racist behaviours due to external pressure.[17] Their findings indicate that people who 'cave in' and conform to anti-racist behaviours in response to external pressure do not thereby internalise anti-racist sentiments. Racists can retain their racist sentiments, and feel threatened and fearful, in proportion to how deep the racism runs – the more racist, the more threatened they feel.

48   Plant and Devine write:

We are much less sanguine about the likelihood that threat-related feelings, in the absence of guilt, will lead to prejudice reduction ... simply avoiding situations in which non-prejudiced social pressure is experienced and/or situations involving contact with outgroup members would be effective strategies to remove the anticipated threat....[18]

When possible, then, it is likely that these racist individuals would engage in anti-social behaviour, or band together in closed communities. It is not always possible to avoid members of a given group, or a PC society, especially when in the workforce, and especially in a workforce in which affirmative action policies are implemented. What then of the results of the tension created by a racist's fear?

It seems plausible that such resentment could ultimately culminate in these people lashing out against the ... norms ... or even outgroup members ... under anonymous conditions....[19]

Incidents of a group of masked individuals gathering and beating members of minority cultures/lifestyles are certainly not rare enough to make this chilling speculation as implausible as one may desire.

49   To summarise, then: If one consults the psychological literature of the day, affirmative action policies cannot be thought to result in a change of attitude of the racist/sexist/ablist. All that they can reasonably be thought to result in is increased hostility towards already disadvantaged groups. This is not a result to be applauded, nor even tolerated. And insofar as the purpose of affirmative action policies is to change the dispositions of the racists/sexists/ablest at large, these policies must be thought to utterly fail.

IV.2 Changing Attitudes about Oneself

50 Even if affirmative action cannot change the attitudes of racists/sexists/ablists, does it not still have value insofar as it provides role models for members of disadvantaged groups and raises their self-esteem? Certainly changing the attitudes of members of previously disadvantaged groups about themselves has been seen as integral to the purpose of affirmative action in Canada. Hurka, for example, explicitly mentions the inspiring of individuals to achieve as one of the goals of such programs. So, while failing to justify affirmative action policies on the grounds that they would lead to the eradication of racist attitudes, advocates may still find grounds to justify affirmative action because of the positive effects a role model could have to the members of the relevant group.

51 Members of disadvantaged groups, having been raised in a culture that inculcates the belief that they cannot achieve success in a given field, do not attempt to do so, even if they have the desire. To this extent we can agree with Hurka. In order to overcome this belief, and realize their dreams, it is thought that a role model would allow disadvantaged persons to come to the conclusion that they, too, could achieve such success. A successful group member in the field of figure-skating could, for example, provide the necessary example for a member of a disadvantaged group to say to himself, "That person is an X, and he is a good figure skater. Therefore people who are from group X can succeed. I am an X, and therefore, despite what I previously thought, I can probably succeed at what I wish to do."

52 Unfortunately, it turns out that this is a simplistic expectation. It is generally accepted in the literature that *relevant* others are necessary to inspire. An aspiring academic is not inspired by a successful football player of the same group, for example; to be relevant, the role model must have achieved success in the same particular field as the person to be inspired desires success in. By hypothesis of affirmative action supporters, it is also necessary that the role model be relevant in another respect, namely, be of the same group membership. This is also supported by the literature on the subject of how relevance is determined.

53 The existence of even relevant role models may nonetheless fail to inspire others or boost their self-esteem. Penelope Lockwood and Ziva Kunda have presented strong evidence that suggests that when another person is perceived as relevant, that person will only inspire if his or her success is seen as achievable by the person engaging in the comparison.[20] An aspiring football-player from group X, seeing a quite successful football-player of the same group membership, will not be inspired if the star player's success is due to the fact that he weighs 325 pounds, and the football-player-to-be weighs only 165 pounds, and has little chance at gaining the weight necessary to achieve the success of the role model in question. In fact, if the role model's success is seen as unattainable, the person whom one hopes would be inspired is likely to be discouraged, insofar as the comparison is seen to be relevant. Whatever the profession, the message is the same: only perceivably attainable success will inspire, while perceivably unattainable success will deflate.

54 This has disastrous consequences for the advocate of affirmative action. Each role model must be successful in order for him or her to inspire anyone at all. This success will be seen as attainable by some, unattainable by others, according to how highly they value their own po-

tential. For those who do not think that they can achieve the same level of success, this example will deflate, leaving them worse off than before. For affirmative action to have as a goal the raising of certain people's self-esteem, it must be thought that these people have low self-esteem. If they have low self-esteem, it is then more likely that they will perceive the role model's success as unattainable, which would then deflate their feelings of self-worth. We are not claiming that all members of group X will find the success of any relevant role model unattainable; we are merely claiming that it is likely that *most* of the members of this group X, interested in achieving success at activity Y, will find that success unachievable because of their low self-esteem. If this is the case, overall affirmative action policies would be causing more harm than good on their supporters' own terms.

55   It may be argued that people's self-esteem is not *so* low, and that overall they feel that they can achieve the success showcased by the relevant role model. But that being the case, the need for affirmative action policies to raise the self-esteem of the members of these groups is puzzling, to say the least.

56   Lastly, to consider the middle ground, it could be suggested that the group's self-esteem is low enough to warrant an attempt to have it raised, yet high enough to make it the case that a typical role model will, overall, have a positive effect on the group in question. In this case, we would have to weigh the relative success of affirmative action in achieving both of its stated objectives – changing the opinions of bigots, sexists, and ablists on the one hand, and inspiring members of the disadvantaged groups to reach for their dreams on the other. We would then have to suggest that it fails to achieve the first objective, indeed it achieves quite the opposite ef-

fect, and would only marginally achieve the second. When looked at in this light, then, it seems to us that the conclusion to draw is that affirmative action programs are not justified on their stated grounds, and ought to be rescinded.

V. Conclusion

57 We have argued that none of the common defenses of affirmative action programs are successful. Employment equity policies are not required by justice, and they fail to significantly reduce the prejudice that produces invidious discrimination against the members of identifiable groups within society. Given that such policies have the significant costs outlined in the introduction of this paper, their failure to provide significant counter-balancing benefits requires that we declared them unjustified. This is not to say, of course, that racism/sexism/ablism must be countenanced nor that those who are committed to eradicating prejudice and the discrimination it inspires should relax their efforts. But to those who suggest that, while not perfect, affirmative action is the only solution we have, we suggest turning instead to focus their efforts on education, paying particular attention to the young, in order to ensure that racist/sexist/ablist attitudes fail to obtain in our society.

NOTES

1. I wish to thank SSHRC for its support of my research – Christopher Tucker.

2. Report of the Commission on Equality in Employment, *Employment and Immigration Canada* 1984 (Supply and Services, Canada); reprinted in Wesley Cragg, ed., *Contemporary Moral Issues* 3rd edition (Toronto: McGraw-Hill Ryerson Ltd, 1992). Hereafter cited as Abella, for its chief au-

thor, Judge Rosalie Abella; page numbers refer to
Cragg, p. 191.

3. L.W. Sumner, "Positive Sexism", *Contemporary Moral Issues* 3rd edition, ed. Wesley Cragg (Toronto: McGraw-Hill Ryerson Ltd., 1992), p. 221; originally published in *Social Philosophy and Policy* 15:1. He takes the term "secondary sexism" from Mary Anne Warren, "Secondary Sexism and Quota Hiring", *Philosophy and Public Affairs* 6:3 (1977).

4. *Ibid.*, p.223.

5. Thomas Hurka, "Affirmative Action: How Far Should We Go?", *Contemporary Moral Issues* 3rd ed. Cragg *op. cit.*, p. 209; originally published in *The Globe and Mail.*

6. *Cf.* Law Society of B.C. et al *v* Andrews et al, Supreme Court of Canada (1989) 1 S.C.R. 143; Ontario Human Rights Commission et al and Simpson-Sears Ltd., Supreme Court of Canada (1985) 2 S.C.R. 536; Brooks *v* Canada Safeway Ltd., Supreme Court of Canada (1989) 1 S.C.R. 1219.

7. Preamble to the Human Rights Code of Ontario 1990, Chapter H.19.

8. Government of Canada Paper, "Outline of the Employment Equity Act", reproduced in *Ethical Issues: Perspectives for Canadians*, ed. Eldon Soifer (Toronto: Broadview Press, 1992), p. 418.

8. *Cf.* Ontario Human Rights Commission et al and Simpson-Sears Ltd., Supreme Court of Canada (1985) 2 S.C.R. 536.

10. Government of Canada Background Paper, "Employment Equity and Economic Growth", reproduced in *Ethical Issues*, ed. Soifer *op. cit.*, p. 420.

11. Abella *op cit.* p. 185.

12. *Ibid.*

13. *Ibid.*, p. 189.

14. *Ibid.*, p. 192.

15. Ziva Kunda, "The Case for Motivated Reasoning", *Psychological Bulletin*, 1990, Vol. 108, No. 3, p. 480-498.

16. *Ibid.*, p. 484.

17. E. Ashby Plant and Patricia G. Devine, "Internal and External Motivation to Respond without Prejudice, In Press: *Journal of Personality and Social Psychology.*

18. *Ibid.*, p. 44.

19. *Ibid.*, p. 45.

20. Penelope Lockwood and Ziva Kunda, "Superstars and Me: Predicting the Impact of Role Models on the Self," *Journal of Personality and Social Psychology*, 73:1, p. 91-103.

Questions

1. With respect to justification, do Dimock and Tucker believe it matters what *kind* of affirmative action program is being judged?

2. What three reasons do Dimock and Tucker give in support of their claim that affirmative action programs need justification? (P3)

3. In P4, Dimock and Tucker state, "We shall conclude that the reasons typically offered in defence of affirmative action are inadequate." Does it necessarily follow that affirmative action programs are indefensible or unjustified?

4. Dimock and Tucker first examine justice-based arguments for affirmative action.

   (a) With respect to the compensatory justice argument, they identify and reject its key assumption – what is it? (P9)

   (b) However, even if they accepted that assumption, affirmative action programs, they argue, would fail to provide compensatory justice to those disadvantaged in the past – why?

(c) With respect to distributive justice, under-representation of some groups in various positions relative to their percentage of the population-at-large is taken to be due to discrimination; Dimock and Tucker offer three alternative explanations – what are they? (P16)

(d) Explain Dimock and Tucker's second objection (to distributive justice arguments for affirmative action programs).

5. Dimock and Tucker next examine consequence-based arguments for affirmative action.

(a) What is the first good consequence said to result from affirmative action programs? For such a consequence to result, Dimock and Tucker argue, freedoms must be violated – explain.

(b) Dimock and Tucker claim the argument for diversity depends on what other argument?

(c) Dimock and Tucker proceed to show that "increased representation of target groups in the workforce" (diversity) does *not* "eliminate...prejudiced attitudes" – why not? (Be sure to include the main points of P44 and P46.)

(d) Do you agree with Dimock and Tucker's analysis of the role model argument as failing to result in attitude change (consider the effect of the presence or absence of role models in your own life) and/or as failing to justify affirmative programs?

6. What, if *not* adopt affirmative action programs, can business do to eradicate discrimination?

Is Mandatory Retirement Unfair Age Discrimination?

Gary A. Wedeking

I. Discrimination

1   In this paper I will deal with two questions. One is the relatively specific issue of whether mandatory retirement is unjust discrimination against the aged. The position taken is that it is not. But in the development of this argument, a principle is advanced which appears to have the consequence that nothing, or at least very few of the practices that we are intuitively inclined to regard as unfair discrimination, are discriminatory with respect to *age*. The second question is thus what, if anything, is to count as unjust age discrimination.

2   In any discussion of discrimination, one needs to bear in mind that not all forms of discrimination raise problems of justice or possible violation of human rights. Some principles of discrimination are obviously benign (teachers rewarding gifted and diligent students), others are clearly unfair (preferential hiring of members of an already privileged group), and still others (preferential hiring of members of a disadvantaged group) are policies reasonable people may differ about. Age discrimination in particular is not a practice any society could dispense with. No one would suggest that minimum ages for voting and driving as such raise questions of fundamental justice. But of course such questions do arise about certain practices, and rightly so. Think of the issue concerning the equity of military conscription at the age of 18 combined with a minimum voting age of 21.

3   Whether a policy or form of discrimination is ceteris paribus[1] unjust or inequitable is distinct from whether it is desirable as a social policy. And policies found not to be unjust are not for that reason necessarily wise policies. In general, we expect social policy to be decided by ordinary political means (acts of Parliament, etc.). But if a policy involves treating some people unjustly, then questions of its social utility seem largely beside the point.[2] Thus we regard it as appropriate for unjust forms of discrimination to be proscribed absolutely, as enshrined in constitutional principles, and prohibited by the courts. Where, as in Canada, age discrimination is specifically prohibited constitutionally, there is thus a presumption that the application of the proscription applies *only* to *unjust* forms of discrimination. A constitutional challenge to the minimum driving age, for example, would rightly be regarded as frivolous.

4   One requirement for an adequate theory of discrimination is that it should specify a means for deciding whether a kind of discrimination is unjust. A theory must have some principled way of discriminating between forms of discrimination. Many discussions, including virtually all informal discussions I have seen, in both the press and in legal decisions and commentary,

Gary A. Wedeking, "Is Mandatory Retirement Unfair Age Discrimination?" *Canadian Journal of Philosophy* 20.3 (September 1990): 321-334. © 1990 by Gary A. Wedeking. Reprinted with permission of the publisher and the author.

fail in this respect. And even in the rather scant philosophical literature on the topic, one finds writings which offer little guidance here. The principle which informs the argument of this paper, supported through some intuitive considerations below in this introductory section, is that discrimination is unjust only if it allocates harm and benefit unjustly.[3]

5   Age discrimination as such cannot be conceptually assimilated to the usual models of unjust discrimination, such as race or sex discrimination.[4] In the latter, someone's preference is defeated in a given case on the irrelevant grounds of race or sex.[5] In such a case, we shall say that the discriminatory policy 'decides against' that person. In this defined usage, a 'contrary' decision is a decision contrary to one's *preference* in a particular case. But there is usually in such cases the additional circumstance that the decision causes harm or denies a benefit to the person it decides against. There are of course occasional cases, e.g. a black person denied passage on the Titanic for racial reasons, where the person thus discriminated against is actually benefitted. So the harmfulness to a person of a decision should be understood as harm that is antecedently and reasonably to be anticipated from the decision – in short, 'expected harm.' This harm or denial of benefit (henceforth simply 'harm') may consist simply in the frustration of the present desire, including our standing desire to avoid gratuitous insult, or it may involve harm to one's long-term interests, as when a woman is denied employment in high paying 'man's work.' The injustice of such discrimination consists in the fact that the affected person is unfairly harmed. Here there is a straightforward denial of social equity.

6   In many cases of age discrimination, on the other hand, the person the policy *decides against* may not, either as the intended effect or the actual result in the vast majority of cases, be *harmed* by the discriminatory policy. Paternalistic treatment of children includes a large class of cases where no harm results from age discrimination. Compulsory schooling, medical care, and so on, may run contrary to the child's preferences, but they do not, at least when the practices have their intended effects, thereby harm the child. Clearly discrimination of this sort, though based on age, cannot be considered *unfair*, since the child is not harmed, there is not even a prima facie case that equity is denied.

7   The connection between unjust discrimination and a presumption of harm (or denial of benefit) might be challenged along the following lines. Paternalistic practices concerning children are often justified by the benefits to the child. The same practices regarding a group of adults, even where the benefits are precisely the same, would amount to unjust discrimination. Thus we consider it reasonable and fair to restrict smoking, for example, to adults, but unfair to restrict it to adult males. Yet the intention and the actual effect of the latter may be to keep women from harming themselves. So, it is argued, the presumption of harm is irrelevant to the unfairness of this restriction.

8   An adequate treatment of why paternalism in the treatment of a group of responsible adults is unjust would take us beyond the scope of this paper. But how an account would be developed is fairly clear; it is the importance of individual autonomy, the role of agency in our conception of the good life, on which such an account should be centred. In short, what is denied to women in the above example is their right to make their own decisions in a matter which society leaves open to individual decision. But this is rightly to be viewed as the denial of a benefit,

and it is on this that our analysis of discrimination insists.

9   The difference between paternalism regarding children and paternalism regarding women consists in the far greater capacity of the latter for the benefit in question.[6] There is thus a different trade-off between the benefit conferred and the one denied (choice). And rather than being an insult to children, the implied lesser capacity is simply an acknowledgement of fact. (There may, of course, also be somewhat greater harm which children are protected from, greater health risks, probability of addiction, etc., in smoking at an earlier age. This might reinforce, but is not central to, the present argument.) Women as a group do not differ from men in this capacity. Thus there is no relevant difference between these groups to justify dissimilar treatment. Relevance, here, should be taken to mean relevance to the (legitimate) purpose of the law or policy. Included in the standard of relevance would be differences in the impact the policy has on the interests of the members of the various groups affected.

II. Is the Presumption of Continuing Employment Unfair to The Unemployed?

10   We are all vigilant against certain forms of discrimination, those based on race, sex and religion in particular, because historically many of the most flagrant violations of human rights have involved selection by these characteristics. It is important to see, however, that almost any characteristic could conceivably be the basis for unjust discrimination. For certain purposes, it is appropriate to recognize and reward athletic ability. But if there were a kind of athletic fascism which made athletic achievement a crite-

rion for all high paying jobs, including the most sedentary, and viciously persecuted those whose performance in the decathlon fell below a certain level, all civilized people would condemn it as discrimination of the most pernicious sort.

11   Being poor and/or unemployed is a condition that inevitably brings with it a disproportionately small share in the advantages of social life. To the extent that we see the distribution of those advantages as subject to deliberate social policy, many of us see this disproportion as already inherently unjust. Any social policy that deliberately inflicted additional harm on this already disadvantaged group would rightly be seen as flagrantly so. Thus an attempt to solve our problem of homelessness after the fashion of Henry VIII's vagrancy laws, by simply hanging the victims, would be unjust persecution of the worst sort. In the following, I want to consider a policy that, while hardly as draconian as that of Henry VIII, might nevertheless appear to be an instance of unfairly inflicting harm on the unemployed.

12   The policy I have in mind is one entrenched in virtually all collective agreements between employers and labour organizations that gives workers a presumption in favour of continuing employment unless either redundancy or inadequate performance (cause for firing) can be demonstrated. It is of course no mystery why this policy is traditionally a minimum demand for organized labour; it places limits on the traditional prerogatives of employers that can easily be used to defeat any attempts of employees to organize and press for collective gains. To a certain extent, however, it might be possible to limit the power of employers in this respect by instituting objective methods for the measurement of performance and limiting the employer's prerogative to hiring and firing on the basis

of the results of these measurements. Thus an employee would enjoy no presumption in favor of continuing employment if there were someone available in the labour market who could perform the work better. Let us say that a policy regulating continuing employment of this latter sort is governed by the Best Performance Principle (BPP). The principle underlying those policies restricting employers along the former lines, we call the Adequate Performance Principle (APP).

13 Now it cannot be denied that there is a kind of systematic bias in the APP. Hiring decisions and non-decisions (cases where decisions are not made under the APP but *would* be made if unrestricted employer's prerogative or the BPP were in force) in many cases will favour the employed and go against the unemployed job seeker. It might therefore be argued – indeed it *has* often been argued – that the APP is unfair discrimination against the unemployed.

14 A defense of the APP might go as follows. So long as the unemployed person who loses in a particular decision under the APP will sooner or later become employed, that person may gain in the long run by the fact that the APP is in force. Once the qualified job-seeker finds employment she will herself benefit from security of employment as well as from the better working conditions which might be expected to result from limited competition. The argument assumes, of course, that the presently unemployed can look forward to employment in the future. Where there is a pool of permanently unemployed people who would stand some chance of at least occasional employment under the BPP, it seems clear that the APP *would* be unfair to those people. But in a society that meets the *minimum condition* that all qualified people can look forward to employment at some time,

the APP appears to be *generally* beneficial and therefore not inequitable.

15 Suppose, then, that this condition is met. Now some people will nevertheless complain that the APP denies them the fruits of their diligence and abilities. And some of the particularly well-qualified would have a case. These are the people who are sufficiently well-qualified that *their* jobs will never be threatened under the BPP. Certainly there are many people who are that confident of their abilities, and it is reasonable to suppose that some of them are rationally so. Suppose that Jones is such a person. Unemployed, she notes that the APP denies her opportunities for employment that would exist for her under the BPP. And she correctly complains that *she* does not benefit from the APP, since she is so well qualified that her job, once she has one, will never be jeopardized by the existence of a more competent competitor.

16 Is Jones therefore unfairly discriminated against by the APP? A follower of John Rawls might argue that she is not. For if we impose an appropriate constraint on Jones' self-interested assessment of the two principles, it may turn out that she must rationally decide in favor of the APP after all. The constraint is that Jones' approval or disapproval must not be based upon information about her particular place in the society governed by the principle. The question is whether Jones would (rationally and in her own interest) approve the APP if she lacked the knowledge that her merits are so outstanding, or conversely, since this is a relative matter, that the population includes so many less able than herself. But given this constraint, Jones has precisely the same reason to approve the APP that everyone else has. If it is *generally* beneficial, then our idealized, dispassionate (but not disinterested) Jones must *rationally* approve it.

17   But there are some who will reject this Rawlsian defense of the APP against Jones' complaints. It is the real Jones, competent, well-qualified and perspicacious in her self-assessment, who is treated unfairly. The approval of an ideal *ignorant* Jones is irrelevant. In support of this response, consider a social system which imposes great burdens on a very small racial minority but derives great benefits for the majority thereby. Smith, a member of the minority, will of course feel hard done by. But we might console Smith with the thought that if he were unaware of the peculiarities of his situation (namely his membership in the minority) he would rationally approve the policy of discrimination. (The benefits are so great that it is worth the small risk that he might turn out to be a member of the minority.) Certainly this kind of argument could not show that no injustice is done to the actual Smith. And so, one might argue, an injustice is done *Jones* regardless of how our idealized Jones might decide.

18   Let us accept the point and agree that at least prima facie an injustice is done to Jones. What I want to challenge is the claim that Jones is discriminated against *by virtue of* her being unemployed. Recall that the situation is this: the highly qualified Jones is seeking employment at a firm where the competent but unexceptional Adams works. Adams keeps his job according to the APP, and Jones loses *in this case* because she is the one who is unemployed. But the fact that Jones does not benefit from the APP does not depend on the fact that she is unemployed. For most of the unemployed, as we have seen, actually *benefit* from the APP. And since (given the minimum condition for the fairness of the APP) everyone qualified is employed at some time, some of the *employed* are also harmed by the APP. This is clear where we regard, as we

should, the harm or benefit incurred by an individual as aggregated over that individual's life. But the argument can in fact be made in the present case even without invoking this aggregative principle. For in general, income lost at an earlier period of one's life is generally reflected in one's present wealth. And those in the position of Jones at an earlier time have indisputably lost income, as well as opportunities for promotion, etc., because of the APP. It follows that harm from the APP is incurred regardless of present employment. Therefore the APP does not selectively harm the unemployed.

19   The principle that underlies this perhaps rather surprising conclusion is this:

> If a policy P distributes harm and benefits in roughly equal proportions between the members of groups f and g, then P does not discriminate unfairly against the members of f *relative to* g or conversely, i.e. membership in f as opposed to g is not the basis for unfair discrimination due to P.

Call this the *Selection Principle*.

20   It should be noted that the Selection Principle does not presuppose what I would regard as the metaphysically suspect notion of justice to (and hence the interests of) collectivities *as opposed to* individuals.[7] Discrimination is unfair treatment of *individuals*; but whether treatment is unfair is a matter of the *reason why* a person is selected for such treatment. The Selection Principle can be thought of as a criterion of adequacy that a charge of discrimination against a person – for a reason, i.e. qua member of some group – must satisfy. It states a *necessary* (but not sufficient) condition that must be satisfied for a member of f to be unfairly discriminated against *qua* f relative to the members of some other group.

21   Now in light of the above principle, I think it is clear that *if* Jones is treated unfairly, it is not

by virtue of her membership in the class of un-employed people, but rather by virtue of her membership in the class of people so able as not to benefit under the APP. If the APP discriminates unfairly, it is unfair to the exceptionally able. And of course for this very reason, the APP will appear to many to be causing no injustice at all, but rather to be effecting greater equity between the members of an advantaged and those of a relatively less advantaged group.

III. Mandatory Retirement

22 What is objectionable about mandatory retirement is apparently that it treats differently individuals who differ with respect to age, but are in other respects similar. For this discrimination to raise the question of fairness, it must distribute harm differently. And apparently it does so, since members of the younger age group (x) receive a benefit (the option of continued employment) that those reaching retirement age (y) are denied.

23   But appearances to the contrary, this cannot be the injustice that the policy perpetrates. For workers in the younger age group will normally receive no advantage at all from the practice of mandatory retirement. The only way the policy impinges on their interests, given that they are employed, is negatively. For in the long or short term future they are all faced with mandatory retirement themselves.

24   But of course that is not the whole story. The benefits to be reaped from the policy are incurred by the unemployed who are qualified for the jobs opened up through retirements. To evaluate the precise effects on this class would require considerable empirical input and would reasonably include calculation of the extent to which these effects might be mitigated by com-bining the abolition of mandatory retirement with other policies (e.g. attractive early retirement) which would increase job openings. But this sort of calculation is just the kind of essentially political issue we must avoid here. The distribution of benefits and harm are sufficiently clear to allow us to assess the fairness of the policy as it affects the members of different groups, and that is what is relevant to the question of the fundamental justice of the kind of discrimination it involves.

25   The people most obviously and directly affected in one way or the other by the policy of mandatory retirement in a given kind of work are those who are qualified or *nearly* qualified for that work. By 'nearly qualified' I mean to include those who would and could relatively easily become qualified for that line of work but might be deterred from acquiring the qualifications through a rational assessment of the lack of job opportunities in the field. We can divide this group into three sub-groups:

(A) The presently unemployed,

(B) The employed who are below retirement age,

(C) The employed or once employed who are at or above retirement age.

26   Now any application of the mandatory retirement rule will be 'against' (in the sense we have defined) members of group C. But those who stand to gain directly from an application of the rule are not, as we have seen, members of B, but rather of A. But this in itself is not an adequate basis for assessing how the policy distributes benefits and harm among these groups. For of course a member of B may have benefitted from a *previous* application of the rule, and thus (as we have observed in connection with our discussion of the policies regulating continuing employment) they *still* benefit. And

so may a member of C. And those who benefit in this way (gaining employment in their chosen fields, or earlier employment with greater opportunities for advancement, higher life-time incomes, etc.) are in fact likely to be as frequent in either of these groups. And both groups contain some individuals, like Jones, who are sufficiently qualified that their job aspirations would have been so quickly realized, their promotions so speedy, etc., even in the absence of a mandatory retirement policy, that they must be regarded as overall losers by the policy. It follows, of course, from the Selection Principle that the policy does not unfairly discriminate between members of B and C.

27   What then of group A? It can scarcely be denied that there are many who stand to gain from the policy in this group. Furthermore, the overall losers by the policy will tend to be underrepresented here; the unemployed who are so well qualified that the policy does not aid them in their job search obviously gain employment readily once they are qualified, so they quickly move out of group A. This group therefore contains a greater proportion of the beneficiaries of the policy than B and C. It may appear, then, that any bias of the policy is in favour of group A, as against B and C. Since B and C *combined* contain a wide range of ages, this bias is not *strongly* age sensitive. But of course since unemployment tends to be higher among the young, there will be some age bias due to the policy, just as a graduated income tax policy is age sensitive in that the young tend to have lower incomes. If this is indeed the distributional bias of the policy, then some serious argument needs to be brought forward to show that it is unfair. After all, members of B and C are (on average) already privileged relative to members of A, so it may be more reasonable to regard the policy as actually *increasing* equity between these groups.

28   But the gainers and losers from the policy can, of course, be pinned down much more precisely than this. Since there are many beneficiaries of the policy in groups B and C – perhaps the overwhelming majority of the members of those groups – it seems unreasonable to say that as a group they lose from the policy vis-à-vis group A. The losers from the policies are precisely the class we have specified, those so well-qualified that the policy is no advantage to them in their earlier job search, their promotions and so on. *If* the policy is unfair, it is unfair to *them.* And of course many will find no unfairness *here* at all.

IV. Is unfair age discrimination possible?

29 It may appear from the above argument that the very concept of age discrimination is a confusion, one based in part on the common confusion between unjust discrimination and other more or less benign sorts of discrimination.[8] The question of whether a person is harmed by an act or policy cannot be decided simply by a narrow consideration of how one is treated at a particular time.[9] This way of deciding the question, in the first place, runs contrary to the indisputable empirical truth invoked above, that for many people past economic gain is reflected in present well-being. So present treatment under a policy cannot be equated with how one's present welfare is affected by the policy.

30   In addition to conflicting with empirical fact, the idea that a policy that applies to one differently in different periods of one's life is thereby unfairly discriminatory ceteris paribus is not consistent with our view of persons as temporal con-

tinuants who have projects and interests extending over a lifespan, not temporally restricted to a person *at a certain age.* This is obvious to everyone but the most short-sighted when the object of concern is one's own future. Indeed, the very concept of self interest is tied to one's future well being and ability to satisfy future desires.[10] It is less obvious, perhaps, when the object is one's past. But I think that unrestricted aggregation over one's entire life is the only intuitively satisfactory basis for assessments of the distributive justice of a policy. It does not seem plausible to suppose that the question of the *justice* of a policy must ignore how one fared in the past under that policy.[11] Mary may perhaps reasonably complain about the unfairness of a situation in which Johnny accumulates more Halloween treats than she; but if she consumes her treats in the first week of November, she has no valid complaint against the more prudent boy who still has some left. If there is a plausible principle stopping short of unrestricted aggregation, which can still accommodate the intuitions we have about such cases as this, it certainly needs to be advanced explicitly for consideration. The proponents of a conception of age discrimination which rejects the aggregative principle are shouldering a large burden of proof on this point, of which most seem quite unaware.

31   In light of these considerations, it may seem reasonable to think that no policy which treated people the same at the corresponding periods of their lives, no matter how oppressive to the members of a particular age group, could logically be unfair age discrimination. And if we are careful to distinguish the issues of whether a policy is *discriminatory* (and therefore harmful to members of some group relative to others) from whether it is *generally* harmful, this appearance may be

strengthened. For a generally harmful policy, such as conscription at age 18 when not required by the national interest, or the absence of a national medical plan, from which most people will incur harm when older, are harmful to nearly everyone even though the harm is experienced at a certain age. Why should such harmful policies be considered any more discriminatory than the various generally beneficial policies (free or subsidized schooling, pensions, etc.) which are directed toward people at certain ages?

32   Justice Brennen of the U.S. Supreme court once described age as an 'immutable characteristic determined solely by accident of birth.'[12] If this were correct, then it would be easy to find examples of unfair age discrimination; any policy selecting those with the characteristic in question for burdens not borne by those without the characteristic would be a candidate. But of course age is in reality the most mutable of characteristics; even the Haracleitean river might *logically* be frozen in time, but age cannot be. What *is* an unchanging feature of a person is the characteristic of having been born at a specific time (not, *pace* Brennen, of having been born at a specific age). Now policies selecting for *this* characteristic, differentially harming those born at or (say) after a given date may well be unfairly discriminatory. Such discrimination could not by its very nature be a long term policy of any society, but it is a conceivable short term one. And of course the short term could be quite long for a person subject to such a policy.

33   But of course that is not the sort of thing one usually has in mind in speaking of age discrimination. Perhaps the paradigm of what we do have in mind is the policy of firms to avoid hiring new workers over (say) 45. Surely, this is unfair. But the selection principle appears to entail that it is not *age* discrimination since it af-

fects the members of various age groups equally. But of course it does not affect *everyone* equally; many suffer serious harm by the policy, while others suffer not at all. Now the characteristics delineating the group of persons harmed by the policy are relatively clear; those harmed are those who have not obtained secure employment by the age of 45 or who become unemployed near or above that age. Those characteristics, while not precisely accidents of birth, are often enough contingencies over which people have very little control. And a policy discriminating against such people will strike most of us as egregiously unfair.

34   The feature that makes it plausible to regard the above unfairness as a kind of age discrimination is not, as we have seen, that it is an injustice to members of a certain age group, or to individuals by virtue of their membership in such a group. Rather, it is the fact that the group treated unfairly is defined by the age at which members have a certain characteristic. Age is an essential *aspect* of the definition of the group in question. When age is in this way essential to the definition of an unfairly treated group, we have age discrimination in a *real* sense.

35   Now it is of course *possible* for mandatory retirement to be age discrimination in the above sense. But the argument will be hard to make for a retirement age that is widely accepted in a society and from which people often benefit when in search of employment. (It will of course be much easier to make the case against special earlier retirement ages in selected occupations.) For even if the policy were harmful, it would not be age discrimination if it harmed everyone alike. And those like Jones, who we concede *may* be unfairly harmed by the policy, are not harmed by virtue of age or any age-related characteristics, as we have seen.

36   But consider the group of people who for reasons beyond their control, say war and military conscription or economic depression in their youth, are not able to take up employment in the job they are qualified for until relatively late in life. They suffer relative to others by lower lifetime incomes and so on. It is certainly arguable that such individuals are treated unfairly if they are forced to retire at the same age as others. Here the unfairness would be caused by a person's membership in an age-defined group. It would, therefore, be age discrimination in the above sense, although, somewhat paradoxically, the *age* in the age-relative characteristic would be (roughly) young adulthood, not the age of retirement.

37   Clearly, if the argument of this paper is correct, any case for the discriminatory effect of mandatory retirement will need to be made in terms much more specific to the individual case than is suggested by current litigation and discussions of the issue. It seems unlikely that such arguments could be the basis for a reasonable proscription of the general policy.

V. A Cautionary Note

38 The abolition of mandatory retirement threatens to create an obvious and possibly great inequity. If a policy of mandatory retirement is in force prior to some time T, and it is abolished at T, there will be a very large group, those employed prior to T and particularly those nearing retirement age at T or shortly after T who will be beneficiaries of the policy, but will incur no losses from the policy whatever. The losses from the policy of mandatory retirement will be borne by those who retire prior to T, while the losses due to the new policy will be borne exclusively by the unemployed and perhaps some younger em-

ployees who will lose opportunities for advancement. This, while a happy situation for the gainers, is unfair. The unfairness will not be eliminated, but it might be mitigated if the policy is abolished gradually, by raising the retirement age, perhaps a year at a time, at five year intervals. In any case, the alleged unfairness of mandatory retirement must be weighed against this demonstrable unfairness in any reasonable evaluation of the justice of abolishing it.[13]

NOTES

1. The qualification is to allow for the possibility that in certain exceptional cases *all things considered* the upshot of a just principle might turn out to be unjust. This would be due to a competing justice claim from some other source or sources which outweighs the claim stemming from the principle. So a principle that is ceteris paribus just in my sense is one that creates a justice claim, but one which may be defeated by conflicting claims. Thus its violation in such a case might reasonably be regarded as effecting no injustice.

2. I would not maintain, of course, that a relatively minor injustice could *never* be outweighed morally by some great social utility. But the utility would have to be great relative to the injustice indeed. The normal presumption is that the requirements of justice should be met before the claims of utility are heard.

3. Janet Radcliffe Richards argues against the connection between discrimination and harm by reference to cases of sexual discrimination which (a) benefit women rather than men, (b) 'work against women without apparently benefiting men' or (c) are neutral with respect to harm and benefit ('Discrimination,' *Aristotelian Society*, suppl. vol. 59 [1985] 70). But her case (b) is consistent with the harm thesis and those she cites for (a) appear to be straightforward cases of discrimination against

males, thus serving in fact to substantiate the connection between discrimination and harm. As for 'neutral' treatment (different but equal distribution of harm and benefit), my intuition is that bona fide cases (perhaps a Mars Bar for Johnny, an O'Henry for Mary) would be non-discriminatory because not unfair. But intuitions here may be clouded by the obvious ideological use of the 'separate but equal' formula to try to pass off discrimination as non-discriminatory.

4. See Nathan Brett, 'Equality Rights in Retirement,' in Poff and Waluchow, *Business Ethics in Canada* (Scarborough, ON: Prentice Hall 1987), 230.

5. Perhaps the best treatment of the relevance of a classification to a (legitimate) legal purpose is still that of Joseph Tussman and Jacobus TenBroek, 'The Equal Protection of the Laws' (*California Law Review* 37 [1949]), esp. section 6, 344ff. It is not part of my argument here that race or sex could *never* be relevant to such a purpose.

6. See Gerald Dworkin, 'Paternalism,' in Rolf Sartorius, ed., *Paternalism* (Minneapolis: University of Minnesota Press 1983) 28ff. (Reprinted from *The Monist* 56 [1972].)

7. See Samuel V. LaSelva, 'Mandatory Retirement: Inter-generational Justice and the Canadian Charter of Rights and Freedoms,' *Canadian Journal of Political Science* 20 (1987) 149-62, for an argument based on this idea.

8. See Tussman and TenBroek, 358, n. 35.

9. An especially strong version of this assumption has been stated by Robert J. Drummond ('Comment on "Mandatory Retirement: Integenerational Justice and the Canadian Charter of Rights and Freedoms" by Samuel La Selva,' *Canadian Journal of Political Science* 21 [1988] 588). Drummond asserts that the problem of intergenerational justice should be assessed by the treatment of individuals at a 'single time point.' His criterion is that 'access to [scarce] jobs should

be no more varied between generations than within generations at any one time.' This principle appears to have the counterintuitive result that discrimination *within* a generation (say because it includes a despised racial minority) would show an otherwise unjust pattern of discrimination *between* generations to be fair. But not only is the criterion flawed in this obvious way, Drummond's underlying assumption is undefended and in my view indefensible. *Why* should the justice of a policy be assessed by the way it treats individuals at a single time, rather than by its over-all impact on their well-being?

10. Brian Barry, *Political Arguments* (London: Routledge and Kegan Paul 1965) 184-6.

11. We should note that our argument against the theory that mandatory retirement is unfair age discrimination did not depend on this backward looking feature of our concept of fair treatment. For in this case, one's past employment results in a straightforward way in present material well-being. The argument could of course be strengthened by making it independent of this contingent circumstance, if we accept the relevance of past consummations to the question of fairness at a later time.

12. Frontiero V. Richardson, 411 U.S. 677 (1973), plurality opinion.. Quoted in Leslie W. Abramson, 'Compulsory Retirement,' *Missouri Law Review* 44 (1977) 48.

13. I would like to thank the participants in the UBC Law Seminar and Philosophy Colloquium, and in particular to Earl Winkler, Kurt Preinsperg and Michael Philips, for helpful comments on earlier drafts of this paper.

Questions

1. One might argue that a certain policy is "unjust discrimination" because members of one group are harmed more than members of another. Or one might argue that a certain policy is "unjust discrimination" because the selection principle used to discriminate, or differentiate, is unjust. The first might be called "unfairly distributed discrimination"; the second, "unfair discrimination." Which approach does Wedeking take in his examination of the policy of mandatory retirement?

2. "If human beings underwent an inevitable and natural sex change at, say, thirty years of age, policies that discriminate on the basis of sex could not be called unjust discrimination since everyone would, at one point or another, be harmed (or benefitted)." Is this an accurate transformation of Wedeking's main argument? (Consider Wedeking's statement in P35: "It would not be age discrimination if it harmed everyone alike.")

3. Wedeking claims that retiring people who are, say, over 65 (mandatory retirement) is *not* unfair discrimination, but refusing to hire people who are, say, over 45 *is* unfair discrimination − because "age is an essential aspect of the definition of the group in question" (P34) in the second, but not the first case. Do you accept his distinction? (You may have to re-read P22–26.)

4. According to Wedeking, the Adequate Performance Principle (APP) discriminates against the hypothetical well-qualified Jones, not because of her unemployed status, but

because of her competence. Could one argue that mandatory retirement is unfair because, like APP, it doesn't select according to competence? (This would be taking the second approach described in question one.) If so, what is being assumed about jobs and justice?

5. If there were an unlimited number of jobs, or at least more jobs than people, would that

affect Wedeking's argument? That is, does Wedeking's argument depend on there being a greater demand than supply in the job market? Would justice be easier to attain in that case?

6. Are there any occupational fields in which you could justify a policy of mandatory retirement at, say, 40 years of age? (That is, is age *ever* a BFOQ?)

Case Study – Safeway's Jewelry Policy

On July 12, 1996, a part-time cashier at a Safeway store in Winnipeg was told by her manager that she could not work until she removed her nose stud. The company's Jewelry Policy stated that jewelry worn at work must be "conservative in appearance and size." Facial jewelry in particular was prohibited unless it was worn for religious reasons. The employee refused to remove the stud and filed a grievance.

Safeway said the purpose of the Jewelry Policy, and indeed of a number of Personal Appearance Policies (one of which prohibits beards), was to ensure that Safeway "present a conservative business-like image to the customers it serves" in order to attract (and maintain) business. According to a Customer Opinion Survey conducted by the Angus Reid Group (hired by Safeway after they set the policy),

certain types of facial jewelry such as nose rings, nose studs, and eyebrow rings are not acceptable to a large proportion of Winnipeg grocery shoppers. Further, this type of facial jewelry will adversely affect Canada

Safeway Limited since a significant proportion of shoppers indicated that they would discontinue shopping at a store which permits employees to wear nose rings, nose studs or eyebrow rings.

The United Food and Commercial Workers' Union argued, however, that the policy was unreasonable, unjust, and unnecessary. They pointed out that there had been no complaints from customers about the nose stud worn by the grievor or those worn by other employees. Furthermore, they argued, the policy was an "unwarranted intrusion into [the employee's] private life."

Arbitration decided in favour of Safeway and dismissed the grievance: agreeing with previous and similar decisions, Teskey noted that "an employer's legitimate concerns for its business image and operations" justifies rules about appearance and that community standards are valid guidelines, as long as employees' personal rights are not unduly infringed upon (which in this case they were not, as the employee could wear the nose stud outside of work). Citing Silbert, he concluded "both [employer and employee] are entitled to their preferences, on their own time."

In a similar case, a Calgary Co-Op employee was told to stop wearing an eyebrow ring. The store claimed that "visible piercings suggest unsanitary standards" and "make customers feel uncomfortable." The union responded, "employees who wear facial jewelry provide friendly, helpful service ... physical appearances are no barrier to good service." Nevertheless, the Alberta Human Rights and Citizenship Commission supported the store: "Unless the body piercing is part of a religious or cultural tradition, an employer can create a dress and appearance code ... employers have the right to establish appearance, grooming and dress standards that they think are necessary for the safe and effective conduct of a business."

REFERENCES

Drohan, Paul, and Mario Toneguzzi. "Co-Op Issues Ban on Facial Jewelry." *Calgary Herald* 21 Aug. 1998: B4.

"Employer Justified in Protecting its Image." *Focus on Canadian Employment and Equality Rights* 4.31 (July 1997).

Slattery-Aisling, Cross-Val. "Minimum Wage Hell." *Spank!* November 1998.

Teskey, P. S. "Canada Safeway Ltd. and United Food and Commercial Workers' Union, Local 832." *Labour Arbitration Cases* 63 L.A.C.(4th): 256-278.

Questions

1. Safeway seems to assume that "business-like" and "conservative" are synonyms.

    (a) Why do you think that is?

    (b) Do you agree?

    (c) What does "business-like" mean and what's so good about it?

    (d) What does "conservative" mean and what's so good about it?

2. Safeway also seems to emphasize image. Their "Guide to Providing Superior Customer Service" tells employees to "Always present a professional image. Creating a good first impression is essential. It helps give our customers confidence in us and our ability to give them superior service."

    (a) Define "professional" and explain why eyebrow-rings are *not* professional, but ear-rings *are*.

    (b) How important do you think appearance should be? Consider these comments about the Calgary Co-Op case: "Last time we looked, we were pretty sure nose rings did not alter the art of bagging groceries ... [and] this is MINIMUM WAGE, after all" (Slattery-Aisling).

    (c) How far should an employer go to ensure "effective conduct of a business"?

        (i) When is personal appearance *really* related to job performance and not just a reflection of the employer's personal preferences?

    (ii) When are appearance standards an *undue* infringement on the employees' rights?

3. Safeway seems to be appealing to community standards to determine what's acceptable and what's not. Is that morally acceptable? (Recall the subsection on relativism in Section II of this text. And consider retailers' refusal to serve black people because it might offend the white customers, and their insistence that women cover themselves top to bottom because the sight of a female forehead or elbow might offend the male customers....)

4. (a) What argument can be offered to justify exemption on religious grounds (belief in a certain supernatural standard) but not on aesthetic grounds (belief in a certain beauty standard)?

     (b) And what counts as a "cultural tradition" (the other exemption mentioned by the Alberta Human Rights and Citizenship Commission)?

CHAPTER 6
MANAGEMENT/UNION MATTERS

What to Do? – The Grievance

The Grievance Officer has brought to you, the manager responsible for such things, a grievance you believe to be very legitimate. However, the time lines as specified in the Collective Agreement have not been adhered to – presentation of the grievance is two days late.

You'd like to accept the grievance, but you don't want to set a precedent for late grievances, nor do you want to set a precedent for ignoring the stipulations of the Agreement. If you refuse to accept the grievance, however, you may lose a very good worker, and the general morale of the workplace will probably suffer, at least a bit and at least temporarily.

What do you do?

Introduction

Insofar as the purpose of a union is to define and protect employees' rights through the collective agreement, management/union issues overlap with employee rights issues. However, many issues are unique to the management/union relationship.

Let's start with whether or not there should even *be* unions. As Shaw explains, the formation of unions is

> based on the indisputable premise that employers have tremendous power over individual workers. They can hire and fire, relocate and reassign, set work hours and wages, create rules and work conditions. Acting individually, a worker rarely is an employer's equal in negotiating any of these items. The position of most workers acting independently is further weakened by their lack of capital, occupational limitations, and personal and family needs. (222)

To the extent that this initial inequality exists — and to the extent such an inequality is morally unacceptable (on what grounds?) — the existence of unions seems legitimate.

De George argues that the right to form unions derives from the right to pursue one's own ends and the right to associate with others to achieve common ends. (De George, like Shaw, is one of the few business ethics text authors to address union matters — both are worth checking out.)

However, is *collective* action necessarily morally good? Could it be coercive? Does it appeal to "majority rule"? That might be okay if the majority is right, but even then, what about "the tyranny of the majority"? Does it appeal to

"might (and intimidation) is right"? Or does it just recognize, as Shaw suggests, that "united we stand, divided we fall" — especially if the employer tries to divide and conquer? As a collective, a union may well restrict rather than enhance individual rights: one is no longer free to negotiate one's terms of employment (not that most workers ever really were).

If a unionized company is more expensive to run than a non-unionized company (because of wages and benefits), how can a unionized company compete? So perhaps unions are not in the best interests of the company (at least in the short term). But if being unionized may eventually lead to poor sales, layoffs, and even closure, well, such consequences suggest unions may not be in the best interests of the employees either (at least in the long term?).

But while wages and benefits may cost, do all union "demands" cost? Not necessarily. Maybe workers want to go from one shift arrangement (rotating days and nights, for example) to another (steady days or nights, for example), or from rigid hours to flextime, or from regular sick days only to sick kid days in lieu of regular sick days (which means, for many parents, just not having to lie about it, which is, for some people, a big thing — most people don't like lying and may resent having to do so just to be with their sick kid) — these changes need not cost the company.

What about recruiting members? How and when and where may be ethical questions. And should management intervene (interfere)? When does a "goodwill visit" become "union-busting"? For example, what moral justification can you as a manager give for asking for the names of those employees who attend a union information meeting, off-hours and off-site? And what moral justification can you as an employee give for using the company list of employee names and phone numbers for the invitations to such a meeting? Are both unjustified invasions of privacy? Is the latter just cause for dismissal? Do you keep a union out this way (and by refusing to hire people who have previously worked at unionized workplaces) or by paying a fair wage and providing good working conditions? (See the article by Patricia D'Souza, which focuses on unions and Canada's grocery stores, especially Sobeys.)

Should the union be a closed or open shop? That is, should membership be compulsory or not? If it's an open shop, then management can hire non-unionized workers at lower wages, so it won't be hiring unionized workers (which defeats the union's purposes); and if management hires non-unionized workers at the same wages, then non-unionized workers benefit from the union's efforts without paying the dues (which isn't fair). Both of these points support a closed shop. However, freedom of choice and freedom of association both support an open shop. And yet, as Gibson observes, "There is no way the 'independents' can avoid benefiting from the presence of the union, and no way they can, acting as independents, avoid weakening the union" (104). Is that true? Would independents always benefit from a union? What if the presence of a union makes management grudging in all interactions with all its employees? A middle way may be that dues deduction is mandatory, but actual membership is not; this addresses the second point in favour of a closed shop, but not the first. And again, consider Gibson: "We don't allow individuals to avoid paying their share of the police or national defense or air pollution control budget on the grounds that they prefer

to go it alone. Why should this case be different?" (104). But why compare a union with the state; why not compare it to a business and ask that it operate in that manner, showing the workers what it can do and in that way persuading them to "buy in"? (See Gibson [98-105] for a fuller discussion of these issues.)

Collective bargaining is another area of ethical concern. (See the paper by Reitz, Wall, and Love in this chapter.) In particular, the ethics of bluffing should be considered. During negotiation (and not just collective agreement bargaining, but any negotiation – contract bids, for example), some may think it's morally acceptable, if only because it's the convention, the "understanding," to overstate one's wants, to conflate wants and needs, in order to achieve one's ends (see Carr). Carson suggests that deception in negotiation is morally acceptable self-defence against the harmful actions of the other side. Strudler also argues that it is acceptable, but on the grounds that it is a "mutually beneficial solution to a problem confronted by negotiators who, for morally benign reasons, cannot trust each other" (806). Others disagree: negotiation is supposed to be in good faith – how can it be when one side deceives? It's hard enough to reach an agreement when two parties have different objectives; to lie about those objectives makes it harder, not easier. Certainly Kantian ethics would say tell the truth; recall the categorical imperative (if everyone lied, the very notions of 'truth' and 'lie' would logically fall apart into meaningless). But a utilitarian analysis might yield another prescription.

Let's back up one step to recognize that the bluffing, the deception, presumes in the first place an adversarial relationship – and that's another issue: is the adversarial model of management/union right? Is it true? Is it in everyone's best interests? Consider this excerpt from a piece written by yours truly after attending a leadership workshop held by a major union:

> "Negotiations is a game." One seminar leader said it. And another illustrated it. The ice breaker in her seminar was a game called "Diverse Points." Basically the game went like this: the Leisure Area was for single players to form pairs in preparation for negotiation; the Negotiations Area was for negotiation – people met in pairs and tried to reach agreement on how to divide 100 points between them in any of four proportions, 90/10, 80/20, 70/30, 60/40 (a division of 50/50 was not permitted); the object of the game was to accumulate as many points as possible and the player with the highest total score wins.
>
> Well. First of all, trying to get as many points as possible is not negotiating, it's competing.
>
> Second, why isn't a split of 50/50 permitted? In the absence of significance (the points have no meaning) and therefore rationale, a split of 50/50 is, to my mind, most fair. Why structure a game that excludes fairness as a possibility? Could it be that achieving fair agreement is not the point?
>
> Third – the Leisure Area! I suppose it simulates the golf course, the tennis court, the cocktail lounge – you butter up your associate, pretending to be friends, doing the leisure thing together, and then you saunter over to the Negotiations Area. Talk about mixing business with pleasure! "How To Use Your Friends" couldn't be written more clearly over the entrance. Instead, why not just show up at the Negotiations Area when you want to negotiate?
>
> I played the game, with great reluctance and after considerable thought, trying to average 50 points per negotiation. It was the best I could do in terms of fairness (I believe a split of 90/10 could also be fair – it depends on context, which was absent). To my pleasant surprise, many of the people I interacted with were quite happy with this approach, and we easily and peacefully decided who would get 40 and who would get 60, based on each of our totals so far; sometimes we agreed on 70/30, or even 80/20, if one was quite a bit over an average of 50 and the other quite a bit under.
>
> However, at least one person lied to me about her point average. This was not surprising, given the preceding instruction. She may have been the winner, I'm not sure; to be honest, I didn't care much who won. But, of course, the winner was applauded for her high point total.
>
> The last thing I remember was this statement: "Collective bargaining has nothing to do with logic or reason." Apparently it has nothing to do with ethics either.

Consider also Bowie who rejects the adversarial model because it "undermines trust and ignores the cooperative features of business" (abstract); he argues that the values of dignity and fairness should characterize labour/management negotiation. (See also Koehn's commentary on Bowie's paper.) Also, check out Post, who proposes, in lieu of the adversarial collective bargaining process, a five-stage collaborative collective bargaining process (commitment, explanation, validation, prioritization, and negotiation) which insists on honesty and teamwork.

To strike or not – this one is always a big question. Does the right to bargain necessarily entail the right to strike? Should it depend on what you do – for example, on whether you're providing essential or non-essential services? Does a strike involving essential services give the union an unfair advantage (unfair, that is, if the company is at all sensitive to the pain and death that may be caused by a lack of medical or firefighting personnel)? But if essential service providers don't have that right to strike, is the company at an unfair advantage? Are there no satisfactory alternatives in between? (See Gibson's piece in this chapter; Burton also addresses public sector strikes but the ethical standard he uses is jurisdictional law; also see Gotbaum, for something rather provocative.)

But even if you're providing *non*-essential services, do you have the right to inconvenience or to use others (clients, customers) for your ends? According to Gonsalves (see Fagothey and Gonsalves; also in Shaw), strikes are justified when they are with just cause, with proper authorization, and as a last resort. (And what is "just cause"?) De George argues that if one has the right to refuse employment and the right to refuse or accept employment only on certain conditions, then one does have the right to strike (379); but *does* one have those rights? And just because we may have a right to do something, it doesn't mean it's morally good to do that something: maybe overall good trumps rights – consider a utilitarian analysis of the consequences if you go on strike; maybe intent trumps rights – consider whether one is going on strike just for vengeance at the current management. (See Liesch's paper for an analysis of teachers' strikes.)

Are sympathetic strikes also justifiable? Shaw defines a sympathetic strike as one in which "workers who have no particular grievance of their own and who may or may not have the same employer decide to strike in support of others" (224). One might argue in favour of such strikes on the basis of obligations of loyalty; however, in the case of different employers, the consequences would be suffered by innocent people, the owners. (And, as with any strike, the clients and customers are also innocent victims – though some may be perfectly happy to be so!)

Now, what about "scabs" – workers who cross a picket line to accept work, who are hired by the employer to fill the positions left vacant by the striking workers. What's wrong with someone who's unemployed taking over a union member's job while that person is on strike? They're unemployed! Don't they have the right to look out for themselves – as the union members are doing? And why shouldn't a company hire such workers? If the company can safely operate with workers who may (*or may not*) be untrained, well, why not? Keeping them on *after* the strike, however, and firing the strikers is another matter. Management backlash actions – benefits reductions, pay cuts, dismissals – how are these justified? (Well, how were the poor conditions which prompted the strike, perhaps even the union formation in the first place, justified?)

Let's take a look at this tendency, this unquestioned mandate, of unions to look out for themselves at the expense of others. Fully employed union members often get first chance at extra work (for example, at many universities, spring and summer courses are offered first to full-time faculty members) – shouldn't extra work go to the un/underemployed (for example, the part-time faculty)? Is it right for a union to limit the numbers of people working in a certain occupation so supply doesn't exceed demand, thus ensuring the value of each individual in the occupation? Doesn't that infringe on people's freedom of choice? In short, if corporations have social responsibilities, responsibilities for those outside the corporation, why don't unions have the same social responsibilities?

REFERENCES AND FURTHER READING

Adler, Robert S., and William J. Bigoness. "Contemporary Ethical Issues in Labor-Management Relations." *Journal of Business Ethics* 11.5-6 (May 1992): 351-360.

Bowie, Norman E. "Should Collective Bargaining and Labor Relations Be Less Adversarial?" *Journal of Business Ethics* 4 (1985): 283-291.

Burton, Jr. John F. "Public Sector Strikes: Legal, Ethical, and Practical Considerations." *Ethics, Free Enterprise, and Public Policy: Original Essays on Moral Issues in Business.* Ed. Richard T. De George and Joseph A. Pichler. NY: Oxford University Press, 1978. 127-154.

Carr, Albert Z. "Is Business Bluffing Ethical?" *Harvard Business Review* 46.1 (January/February 1968): 143-153.

Carson, Thomas. "Second Thoughts About Bluffing." *Business Ethics Quarterly* 3.4 (1993): 317-341.

Cohen-Rosenthal, Edward. "Should Unions Participate in Quality of Working Life Activities?" *Quality of Working Life: The Canadian Scene* 3.4 (January 1980).

De George, Richard T. *Business Ethics.* 5th ed. NJ: Prentice Hall, 1999. 375-385.

D'Souza, Patricia. "Food Fights." *This Magazine* 32.5 (March/April 1999): 30-35.

Fagothey, Austin and Milton A. Gonsalves. *Right and Reason: Ethics in Theory and Practice.* St. Louis: Mosby, 1981. 428-429.

Gibson, Mary. *Workers' Rights.* Totowa, NJ: Rowman & Allanheld, 1983.

Gotbaum, Victor. "Public Service Strikes: Where Prevention is Worse than the Cure." *Ethics, Free Enterprise, and Public Policy: Original Essays on Moral Issues in Business.* Ed. Richard T. De George and Joseph A. Pichler. NY: Oxford University Press, 1978. 155-169.

Koehn, Donald R. "Commentary upon 'Should Collective Bargaining and Labor Relations Be Less Adversarial?'" *Journal of Business Ethics* 4 (1985): 293-295.

Liesch, James R. "Strikes and Sanctions: A Moral Inquiry." *Educational Theory* (1968): 253–261.

Post, Frederick R. "Collaborative Collective Bargaining: Toward an Ethically Defensible Approach to Labor Negotiations." *Journal of Business Ethics* 9.6 (June 1990): 495-508.

Shaw, William H. *Business Ethics.* 2nd ed. Belmont, CA: Wadsworth, 1996. 219-226.

Strudler, Alan. "On the Ethics of Deception in Negotiation." *Business Ethics Quarterly* 5.4 (1995): 805-822.

Public Employees' Right to Strike

Mary Gibson

[This is an excerpt (pp. 108–116) from Chapter Four of Gibson's book. The first part of the chapter deals with the rights of workers in the private sector to organize and join unions, bargain collectively, and strike.]

1   Let us now consider the main arguments advanced against the right of public employees to strike.[1] (In view of the clarification above, I should say that I shall understand arguments against the right to strike as supporting specific legislative prohibition, and arguments for the right as supporting specific legislative recognition.)

2   Perhaps the oldest argument – if it can be called an argument – is based on the doctrine of sovereignty. (This is the same doctrine urged in support of claims to governmental immunity to lawsuits by individuals, e.g., for negligence; hence, "the doctrine of sovereign immunity.")[2] As originally conceived, this doctrine was appealed to as justification for denying public employees not only the right to strike, but the right to bargain as well:

> What this position comes down to is that governmental power includes the power, through law, to fix the terms and conditions of government employment, that this power cannot be given or taken away or shared and that any organized effort to interfere with this power through a proc-

ess such as collective bargaining is irreconcilable with the idea of sovereignty and is hence unlawful. [Hanslowe, 1967, 14–15]

Another formulation of the view is provided by Neil W. Chamberlain:

> In Hobbesian terms, government is identified as the sole possessor of final power, since it is responsive to the interests of all its constituents. To concede to any *special* interest group a right to bargain for terms which sovereignty believes contravenes the *public* interest is to deny the government's single responsibility. The government must remain in possession of the sole power to determine, on behalf of all, what shall be public policy. [Chamberlain, 1972, 13]

3   Applying the doctrine specifically to the right to strike, Herbert Hoover said in 1928 that "no government employee can strike against the government and thus against the whole people" (Aboud and Aboud, 1974, 3). And in 1947, Thomas Dewey stated that "a strike against government would be successful only if it could produce paralysis of government. This no people can permit and survive" (Aboud and Aboud, 1974, 3).

4   On the other side, Sterling Spero wrote in 1948:

> When the state denies its own employees the right to strike merely because they are its employees, it defines ordinary labor disputes as attacks upon public authority and makes the use of drastic remedies, and even armed forces the only method for handling what otherwise might be simple employment relations. [Spero, 1948, 16]

From Mary Gibson, *Workers' Rights*. NJ: Rowman & Allanheld, 1983. © 1983 by Mary Gibson. Reprinted with permission of Rowman and Littlefield Publishers, of which Rowman & Allanheld is a division, and the author.

5   Even if one accepts the doctrine of sovereign authority, it has been argued, it does not follow that collective bargaining or striking by public employees must be prohibited. Legislatures have often waived sovereign immunity in other areas of law. In most jurisdictions, individuals are now able to sue public bodies for negligence, for example. And since sovereignty refers to the people's will as expressed in legislative action, the concept does not preclude – indeed, it seems to require – that the people may, through their representatives, enact legislation authorizing government to engage in collective bargaining and permitting public employees to strike.

6   A related objection to the claim that sovereignty precludes strikes by public employees distinguishes between what might be called legal and political sovereignty. Legal sovereignty, according to this view, exists in order to meet the need for a peaceful, final, and enforceable means of settling disputes within society. Political sovereignty, on the other hand, refers to the process by which decisions are made in a political system. The American political process, it is pointed out, provides for no ultimate sovereign authority.

7   It might be added that the role attributed to government by the idea of legal sovereignty – that of a neutral or impartial third party for settling disputes – is clearly inappropriate where government itself is one of the parties to the dispute, e.g., as the employer in a labor-management dispute. This is so whatever one may think, in general, of the depiction of government as a neutral in disputes between private parties.

8   It has also been pointed out that the sovereignty argument as advanced by governmental units sounds suspiciously like the management prerogatives arguments private employers advanced against the rights of workers in the private sector to organize, bargain, and strike. If those arguments are properly rejected for the private sector, it is not clear why they should be accepted for the public sector. It is worth asking, moreover, what our reaction would be to the sovereignty argument if it were advanced by the government of another country as justification for prohibiting strikes by its citizen-employees. As the Executive Board of the Association of Federal, State, County, and Municipal Employees (AFSCME) has said, "Where one party at the bargaining table possesses all the power and authority, the bargaining process becomes no more than formalized petitioning" (Eisner and Sipser, 1970, 267).

9   A somewhat different version of the sovereignty argument relies on the claim that the public has rights, and these rights outweigh the right of public employees to strike. Hugh C. Hansen, for example, says:

> In a democracy, the people should decide what services the government will supply. The right to strike is a powerful weapon, subject to abuse, which would indirectly give workers the power to make those decisions. A public employee strike is only successful if it hurts the public.... The public has rights; it should not be reluctant to assert them. [Hansen, 1980]

This sort of appeal to the rights of the public, however, is subject to what seems to me a decisive objection. As Ronald Dworkin has argued, it eliminates the protection which recognition of individual rights is supposed to provide:

> It is true that we speak of the 'right' of society to do what it wants, but this cannot be a 'competing right' of the sort that may justify the invasion of a right against the Government. The existence of rights against the Government would be jeopardized if the Government were able to defeat

such a right by appealing to the right of a democratic majority to work its will. A right against the
Government must be a right to do something
even when the majority thinks it would be wrong
to do it, and even when the majority would be
worse off for having it done. If we now say that
society has a right to do whatever is in the general benefit, or the right to preserve whatever sort
of environment the majority wishes to live in,
and we mean that these are the sort of rights that
provide justification for overruling any rights
against the Government that may conflict, then
we have annihilated the latter rights. [R.
Dworkin, 1978, 194]

10   Thus, if we take seriously the claim that
workers in general have a right to strike, we cannot justify abrogating that right by appeal to a
conflicting right of the public to decide what
services government will supply. (Note that
Dworkin is not here objecting to the idea of
group rights in contrast to that of individual
rights; it is only the idea of the rights of society
as a whole, or of a democratic majority, as potentially competing with the rights of individuals, corporations, or other corporate-like entities
within the society, that threatens to annihilate
the latter rights.)

11   If we reject the argument from sovereignty,
then, there are two further arguments against the
right of public employees to strike that pick up
different threads from the arguments discussed
so far. One appeals to preservation of the normal American political process, and the other to
the essentiality of government services. The
former may be dealt with more quickly, so let
us consider it first.

What sovereignty should mean in this field is not
the location of ultimate authority – on that the
critics are dead right – but the right of government, through its laws, to ensure the survival of

the "'normal' American political process." As
hard as it may be for some to accept, strikes by
public employees may, as a long run proposition,
threaten that process. [Wellington and Winter,
1969, 1125-26]

12   But what is this normal political process? "Is
something abnormal because it does not operate in conjunction with the standard political
process and procedures of a particular era? Does
the normal political process automatically exclude any methods or goals which will disrupt
existing power relations?" (Aboud and Aboud,
1974, 4). And if a group "distorts" the political
process by having more power than the average
interest group, are public sector unions the only,
or even the most salient examples? (Note that,
by Dworkin's argument above, the "right of government ... to ensure the survival" of the normal
political process cannot be understood simply as
a right to prevent individuals or groups from affecting and influencing the political process
through the exercise of their rights.)

13   Is it true that recognizing the right of public
employees to strike would give them such irresist-
ible power that the political process would be seriously enough distorted to justify denying them
that right? To argue that it would, it seems to me,
one would have to base one's case on one or
more independent reasons for thinking such disproportionate power would ensue. One of these
– essentiality of government services – we shall
examine next. Two others – absence of a competitive market in the public sector, and the idea
that public employees have influence over their
wages and working conditions through lobbying
and voting – we shall consider briefly below.

14   The claim that government services are essential may be thought to provide support for
prohibition of strikes by public employees in one
or more of at least three ways. First, it may be ar-

gued that, since these services are essential, it is intolerable that they be interrupted, even temporarily, as they would be by a strike. A second argument is that if essential services *are* interrupted, the public will put enormous pressure on government to restore them, and government will have little choice but to cave in to union demands, no matter what they are. Thus, if such strikes were permitted, public employee unions would be in an extraordinarily powerful position. Indeed, one opponent of the right to strike in the public sector likens public employee strikes to sieges or mass abductions because, in such a strike, an "indispensable element of the public welfare, be it general safety, health, economic survival, or a vital segment of cultural life such as public education, is made hostage by a numerically superior force and held, in effect, for ransom" (Saso, 1970, 37). A third argument is that, since government services are essential, the individual recipients of those services have a right to receive them. A strike that interrupted such services would, therefore, violate the rights of the would-be recipients, and, since the services are essential, the right to receive them must be an important right. These rights of individual recipients, then, may be said to compete with and outweigh any right of public employees to strike. (This appeal to the rights of individual members of the public does not run afoul of Dworkin's objection, above, which rejects only appeals to the rights of society, or the majority, as a whole.)

15   Clearly, however, not all government services are essential in the ways required for these arguments to be sound. In addition, somewhat different kinds and degrees of essentiality may be required by each of the three different arguments.

16   First, from the fact that a given service, such as public education, for example, is essential to society and its members over the long term, it by no means follows that any temporary interruption of such a service is intolerable. Public education is routinely interrupted for summer vacation, spring and fall breaks, holidays, and snow days. Time lost due to (legal or illegal) strikes by school employees can be, and is, made up by scheduling extra days and/or hours of classes. Are transportation services provided by municipal bus lines essential in ways that those provided by privately owned bus companies are not? If hospital workers in voluntary hospitals have the right to strike, why are public hospital employees different? Are their services any more essential? Upon reflection, it appears that few, if any, public services are essential in the way required to make the first argument sound, i.e., that even temporary interruption of them would be intolerable. Many who reject the first argument as applied to most government services do, nonetheless, accept it for two specific categories of service, those provided by police and firefighters. We shall return to these possibly special cases below.

17   In response to the second argument, that enormous public pressure to end a strike and restore services would force government to yield even to unreasonable union demands, there are at least three things to be said. First, in the absence of the economic pressure that a strike in the private sector exerts on the employer, public pressure to restore services is the only real leverage public employees can bring to bear on management to come to terms. Striking workers, of course, forfeit wages and place their jobs on the line in the public sector just as in the private sector. So the pressure on workers to arrive at an agreement and end a strike is very strong indeed. In contrast, the public sector employer is likely to have tax revenues continue to accrue

during a strike, while saving on the wage bill. Without public pressure for the restoration of services, management could comfortably wait out almost any strike, thus rendering the strike weapon totally ineffectual.

18   Second, the impact on tax rates of wage and benefit packages provides a strong incentive for public sector employers to bargain hard. "For the public employer, increases in the tax rate might mean political life or death; hence, unions are not likely to find him easy prey" (Aboud and Aboud, 1974, 6). And, as AFSCME's Victor Gotbaum points out:

> An automobile can increase in price 300 percent. Your food can go up 200 percent. If your taxes go up even less of a percentage, somehow the public is being raped by public employees. That is not so. In fact, our own studies show that the wage bill has not been going up that high since the arrival of unionism, taxes have not increased at a greater pace than costs in other areas, and yet we get this funny comparison that somehow when workers in the public sector strike, they get a helpless hopeless citizen. [Gotbaum, 1978, 161]

19   A third response to the second argument is that it is essential to identify the source of the public pressure. As Ronald Dworkin's argument above establishes, public disapproval or displeasure at being inconvenienced or made somewhat worse off does not justify the abrogation of a right. Certainly, then, the anticipation of public pressure arising from such displeasure cannot justify the abrogation of the right to strike. Thus it seems that prohibition of public sector strikes could be justified only by showing that they constitute a very direct and serious threat to the public safety or wellbeing, or that exercise by public employees of the right to strike would somehow violate more important rights of other members of society, as the third

argument from essentiality of government services maintains. The claim that *any* strike would seriously and directly threaten the public safety or wellbeing does not seem at all plausible applied across the board to public employees. Again, it appears most plausible in the case of police and firefighters, although even here a blanket prohibition may be far more restrictive than is justifiable. We shall return to this question below.

20   Now let us consider the third argument, that the individual recipients of government services have rights to those services which would be violated if they were interrupted by a strike. First, from the fact that an individual has a right to a government service it does not follow that the right is violated if the service is temporarily interrupted. Even a very important right to a given service need not be violated by a temporary interruption, as it would be, let us suppose, by permanent cessation of the service. Moreover, from the fact that individuals have very important rights to certain services it does not follow that the onus is entirely upon government workers to provide those services without interruption under whatever conditions management chooses to impose. The right is against government or society as a whole, whose obligation it is to create and maintain conditions in which qualified workers are willing to work and provide those services.

21   It is worth noting, too, that in many instances the issues over which government employees are likely to strike are issues on which the interests of the recipients of government services coincide with those of the providers. Welfare workers demanding lighter case loads, teachers insisting on smaller classes, air traffic controllers complaining about obsolete equipment, understaffing, and compulsory overtime

are all instances of government workers attempting to secure adequate conditions in which to do their jobs. The rights of the recipients of these services are not protected by prohibiting the providers from using what may be the only effective means of securing such conditions – quite the contrary. Even where this is not the case, there appear to be no grounds for a general claim that strikes by public employees would violate the rights of the recipients of governmental services. If such a case is to be made, it must be made in much more particular terms with respect to specific categories of service. Once again, the chief candidates presumably will be policing and firefighting, to be discussed below.

22   Let us now briefly consider two additional reasons which have been offered in support of the claim that recognizing the right of public employees to strike would give them such power as to seriously distort the political process: absence of a competitive market in the public sector, and the claim that public employees have the opportunity to influence their wages and working conditions through lobbying and voting.

23   The absence of competitive market forces in the public sector has been said to lend disproportionate power to striking public employees in two ways. First, it is argued that in the private sector market forces such as elasticity of demand for the employer's product and the extent of nonunion competition limit the ability of an employer to absorb increased labor costs. Since employees recognize these limits, and have no interest in putting the employer out of business, they have reason to limit their demands accordingly. In the absence of such forces, it is held, public employee unions have little reason to restrict their demands to reasonable levels. This argument seems to ignore the fact that all striking workers have a very direct incentive to reach a settlement – they lose

wages each day that they are out. Even with a strike fund, strikers' incomes are drastically reduced, and in a prolonged strike, any existing strike fund is in danger of being exhausted. Moreover, unions in the public sector are not entirely insulated from competitive labor. The threat of permanent job loss through layoffs or even complete elimination of public agencies is very real. Santa Monica, California, for example, ended a strike of city employees by threatening to contract out its sanitation work. In Warren, Michigan, a similar threat was carried out (Burton and Krider, 1972, 277).

24   The second way in which the absence of market forces is said to result in greatly increased power for potential or actual strikers in the public sector is that public employers, not needing to minimize costs to remain competitive and profitable, will not bargain hard. As we saw above, however, the pressure to keep tax rates down can also provide an effective incentive for hard bargaining. Indeed, in many cases, the absence of a competitive market can work to strengthen the hand of the employer rather than that of the union, since the economic pressure a private sector strike brings to bear on the employer is absent, or greatly reduced, in the public sector.

25   Our final candidate for an argument showing that granting public employees the right to strike would seriously distort the political process is the claim that, unlike private sector workers, public employees and their unions have the opportunity to affect their wages and working conditions through the political process, so that if they had the right to strike as well, they would wield undue power. Thus it has been argued that, through collective bargaining, public employee unions can acquire the maximum concessions management will offer at the bargaining table, and then they can apply political pressure,

through lobbying efforts and voting strength, to obtain additional concessions. If the right to strike were added, according to this argument, public sector bargaining would be heavily weighted in favor of employees.

26   But the capacity of public employee unions to influence legislative decisionmaking is a necessary (and often inadequate) counterweight to the tendency of legislators, responding to public pressure to keep taxes down, to solve difficult and ubiquitous fiscal problems at the expense of public employees. Representatives of each of the different categories of government workers must attempt to bring their concerns to the attention of legislators in an effort to avoid being lost in the budgetary shuffle. Further, although they constitute a growing percentage of the workforce, public employees as a group are unlikely to constitute anything approaching a voting majority in any given jurisdiction. And, although public employees as a group may constitute a potentially significant voting block, those workers directly affected by negotiations over any particular contract will almost certainly be a tiny minority. Thus, whatever truth there may be to this argument, it seems grossly inadequate to the task of showing that if on top of their right as citizens to participate in the political process they had, as workers, the right to strike, the political process would be so seriously distorted as to justify prohibiting the exercise of one of these important rights.

27   We have been unable to find any justification for a general prohibition of strikes by public employees. I conclude that public employees generally, like workers in the private sector, have the moral right to strike, and that right ought to be recognized and protected by law, as it is for all other workers.

[Gibson deals next with whether police and firefighters constitute a special case; included in this last section is a discussion of whether arbitration is a satisfactory substitute for the right to strike.]

NOTES

1. For many of these arguments and responses, I rely on Aboud and Aboud, 1974.
2. The federal government has successfully appealed to sovereign immunity as a defense against suits charging the government with negligence in exposing shipyard workers and their families to asbestos during World War II (*New York Times*, September 18, 1982, 36).

REFERENCES

Aboud, A., and G. Aboud. 1974. *The Right to Strike in Public Employment*. New York State School of Industrial and Labor Relations, Ithaca: Cornell University Press.

Burton, J. F., and C. Krider. 1972. "The Role and Consequences of Strikes by Public Employees." In J. J. Lowenberg and M. H. Moskow, eds., *Collective Bargaining in Government*. Englewood Cliffs: Prentice Hall. (Cited in Aboud and Aboud, 1974.)

Chamberlain, N. W. 1972. "Public vs. Private Sector Bargaining." In Lowenberg and Moskow, 1972 (quoted in Aboud and Aboud).

Dworkin, R. 1978. *Taking Rights Seriously*. Cambridge, MA: Harvard University Press.

Eisner, E. G., and I. P. Sipser, 1970. "The Charleston Hospital Dispute: Organizing Public Employees and the Right to Strike." *St. John's Law Review* 45, no. 2 (Dec.): 254-72.

Gotbaum, V. 1978. "Public Service Strikes: Where Prevention Is Worse than the Cure." In DeGeorge and Pichler, eds., *Ethics, Free Enterprise and Public Policy*. New York: Oxford University Press, 1978.

Hansen, H. C. 1980. "Pro and Con: Should Public Servants Have the Right to Strike?" *Family Weekly*, July 13.

Hanslowe, K. L. 1967. *The Emerging Law of Labor Relations in Public Employment*. New York State School of Industrial and Labor Relations. Ithaca: Cornell University Press. (quoted in Eisner and Sipser, 1970.)

Saso, C. D. 1970. *Coping With Public Employee Strikes*. Chicago: Public Personnel Association. (Quoted in Aboud and Aboud.)

Spero, 5. 1948. *The Government as Employer*. (Quoted in Eisner and Sipser, 1970.)

Wellington, H. H., and R. K. Winter. 1969. "The Limits of Collective Bargaining in Public Employment." *Yale Law Journal* 77: 1107-27. (Quoted in Aboud and Aboud, 1974.)

Questions

1. Prior to the selection included in this text, Gibson states the following: "If you have a right to withhold your labor, you have the right to quit your job and the right to put your job on the line in negotiations with your employer. Since you also have the right (both morally and constitutionally) to freedom of association, which provides the basis for the right to concerted action, it is hard to see how you can fail to have a right to strike (and hence also to threaten to strike). If this argument is sound with respect to workers in the private sector, a powerful reason is needed to block its application to the public sector..." (107). *Is* it sound with respect to workers in the private sector?

2. (a) Explain the argument based on the doctrine of sovereignty.

   (b) What three objections does Gibson raise (P5, 6, 8)?

3. How does Dworkin respond to the argument that the public's rights outweigh the public workers' right to strike?

4. What three arguments are given to support the claim that the public sector unions, by having the right to strike, threaten the normal political process?

5. Outline Gibson's treatment of the "essential services" argument. Be sure to explain all three lines of the argument, and her objections to each line (P16; P17, 18, 19; P20), as well as to the overall argument (P15).

6. Outline Gibson's treatment of the "competitive market" argument. Be sure to explain the two lines of argument, as well as her objection to each line.

7. What does Gibson think of the argument that, unlike private sector workers, public sector workers can influence their working conditions though lobbying and voting (the normal political process) and therefore don't need the right to strike (P26)?

8. Choose one of the arguments against the public worker's right to strike and assess Gibson's objections to it. Are her objections sound? Can you think of any replies to any of her objections?

9. Suppose public sector workers' right to strike *does* threaten the normal political process — is this a (morally) bad thing? What assumption supports that claim?

10. Can you think of any other reasons why public sector workers should or should not be able to go on strike? (Consider ethical approaches not covered by Gibson.)

Ethics in Negotiation:
Oil and Water or Good Lubrication?

H. Joseph Reitz, James A. Wall, Jr., and Mary Sue Love

1   In his 1996 year-end column for *Forbes*, merchant banker and economist John Rutledge describes two weeks of negotiations over an acquisition for a private equity fund. The hours of bargaining were tense, long, hard, and far more complicated than he had envisioned. Nevertheless, he reports:

> Despite all the haggling, we ended on a friendly note. All of us – buyer, seller, lender – shook hands and clinked champagne glasses. As we were leaving, the seller said he would like to discuss teaming up with us in a joint venture. I beamed. Some buyers wouldn't have liked this. They think if the seller doesn't hate them at the end of a deal, they haven't squeezed out every last drop of money. I disagree. We believe that when someone wants to do repeat business with us, it is the highest form of praise. Allowing your opponent in a transaction to walk away with his dignity, his humor, and his bearing intact, and with a pretty good deal in his pocket, is the right way to do business.

2   Rutledge then lists a set of principles learned from his first business partner and admonishes his readers to

... walk away from a deal, any deal, rather than violate your principles to win it.... The twist, of course, is that business organizations organized around principles are often more successful and make more money than those organized around the idea that greed is good. Nice guys often finish first.

3   Rutledge's thesis that ethical negotiating is not only the right thing to do but frequently is also more profitable represents an argument more common today than in the so-called "decade of greed" in the 1980s – and one that finds more receptive audiences.

4   Should business people take this as an article of faith? Or can reason bring us to similar conclusions? In probing that question, we shall list a number of questionable negotiation tactics or behaviors and evaluate them according to four commonly used ethical criteria. This will help us assess the costs and benefits of ethical versus unethical negotiation tactics.

Questionable Negotiation Tactics and Ethical Criteria

5   We all have a general idea of what negotiation is: two parties attempting to work out a trade of items or services that is acceptable to both sides. Each side has an array of tactics to employ in achieving this trade. Below are ten popular tactics, the ethics of which have been challenged over the years:

H. Joseph Reitz, James A. Wall, Jr., and Mary Sue Love, "Ethics in Negotiation: Oil and Water or Good Lubrication?" *Business Horizons* 41.3 (May/June 1998): 5-15. © 1998 by Indiana University Kelley School of Business. Reprinted with permission of the publisher and the authors.

1. *Lies* – Statements made in contradiction to the negotiator's knowledge or belief about something material to the negotiation.

2. *Puffery* – Exaggerating the value of something in the negotiation.

3. *Deception* – An act or statement intended to mislead the opponent about the negotiator's own intent or future actions relevant to the negotiations.

4. *Weakening the opponent* – Actions or statements designed to improve the negotiator's own relative strength by directly undermining that of the opponent.

5. *Strengthening one's own position* – Actions

Figure 1. Questionable Tactics

Tactic	Description/Clarification/Range
Lies	Subject matter for lies can include limits, alternatives, the negotiator's intent, authority to bargain, other commitments, acceptability of the opponent's offers, time pressures, and available resources.
Puffery	Among the items that can be puffed up are the value of one's payoffs to the opponent, the negotiator's own alternatives, the costs of what one is giving up or is prepared to yield, importance of issues, and attributes of the products or services.
Deception	Acts and statements may include promises or threats, excessive initial demands, careless misstatements of facts, or asking for concessions not wanted.
Weakening	The negotiator here may cut off or eliminate the opponent some of the opponent's alternatives, blame the opponent for his own actions, use personally abrasive statements to or about the opponent, or undermine the opponent's alliances.
Strengthening one's own position	This tactic includes building one's own one's own resources, including expertise, finances, position and alliances. It also includes presentations of persuasive rationales to the opponent or third parties (e.g., the public, the media) or getting mandates for one's position.
Nondisclosure	Includes partial disclosure of facts, failure to disclose a hidden fact, failure to correct the opponents' misperceptions or ignorance, and concealment of the negotiator's own position or circumstances.
Information exploitation	Information provided by the opponent can be used exploitation to exploit his weaknesses, close off his alternatives, generate demands against him, or weaken his alliances.
Change of mind	Includes accepting offers one had claimed one would not accept, changing demands, withdrawing promised offers, and making threats one promised would not be made. Also includes the failure to behave as predicted.
Distraction	These acts or statements can be as simple as providing excessive information to the opponent, asking many questions, evading questions, or burying the issue. Or they can be more complex, such as feigning weakness in one area so that the opponent concentrates on it and ignores another.
Maximization	Includes demanding the opponent make concessions that result in the negotiator's gain and the opponent's equal or greater loss. Also entails converting a win-win situation into win-lose.

or statements designed to improve the negotiator's own position without directly weakening that of the opponent.

6. *Nondisclosure* – Keeping to oneself knowledge that would benefit the opponent.

7. *Information exploitation* – Using information provided by the opponent to weaken him, either in the direct exchange or by sharing it with others.

8. *Change of mind* – Engaging in behaviors contrary to previous statements or positions.

9. *Distraction* – Acts or statements that lure the opponent into ignoring information or alternatives that might benefit him.

10. *Maximization* – The negotiator's single-minded pursuit of payoffs at the cost of the opponent's payoffs.

6   How do negotiators decide if such tactics – laid out in greater detail in Figure 1 – are ethical? Our interviews with business people have yielded such comments as:

• "A lie is not a lie when a lie is expected."

• "When someone tells the truth, that's good; when someone lies, that's wrong. It's that simple."

• "What's right or wrong really depends on the situation."

7   The variety in comments vis-à-vis the first tactic indicates that opinions can vary as to what is ethical. Fortunately, moral reasoning can help negotiators assess the ethical nature of lies and other tactics. Summarized in Figure 2, the four criteria most widely used in business ethics today are the *Golden Rule*, *utilitarianism*, *universalism*, and *distributive justice*.

The Golden Rule

8   Most managers tend to explain ethical behavior as a function of personal values. One of the most frequently cited values is the Golden Rule: "Do unto others as you would have them do unto you." A relatively popular principle, perhaps its most famous and vocal advocate in industry was J.C. Penney, who used it in building and running his business from his youth until his nineties. In practice, it requires decision-makers to apply the same standards of fairness and equity to their own actions that they would demand of others.

Universalism

9   A more complex ethical base is universalism, which argues that the rightness or wrongness of actions can be determined *a priori*, or before the actual outcomes of those actions can be realized. Based on a system of individual rights and obligations founded by philosopher Immanuel Kant, it argues that human beings are incapable of foreseeing all the outcomes of their decisions

Figure 2. Ethical Criteria

Criteria	Explanation/Interpretation
Golden Rule	Do unto others as you would have them do unto you.
Universalism	People are not to be used as a means to an end.
Utilitarianism	Do the greatest good for the greatest number of people.
Distributive Justice	Everyone is better off because of this act.

and actions, and thus should be held morally accountable for the *way* they made them.

10   For an act or decision to be moral, it must meet several criteria:

1. It must respect the inherent worth and dignity of those involved or affected; people must never be used primarily as a means to an end.

2. It must be universally applicable to all human beings facing similar situations – there are no special treatments.

3. It must be consistent with all other universal moral principles.

11   Consider the dilemma of downsizing. Universalism would permit downsizing for sound economic reasons, but it would require informing all those being laid off of that decision when it is made. Withholding such information from employees to keep them working with the same level of dedication and effort would be unethical because it would be using them primarily as a means to an end. Unaware of their impending doom, they might make family, career, or financial decisions they would not have made with valid information about their employer's plans.

Utilitarianism

12 In contrast to universalism, utilitarianism judges the rightness or wrongness of actions and decisions by their consequences. It argues that human beings ought to seek those alternatives that produce the greatest amount of good for the greatest number of people, or to maximize the total good produced. When seeking the greatest net good, one must consider all people likely to be affected by a set of alternatives and the array of outcomes (both good and bad) each alternative might generate for each person.

Distributive Justice

13 John Rawls's ethical concept of justice implies that individuals have an obligation to exercise their own rights in a way that permits others to enjoy theirs. Justice occurs when all individuals get what they deserve; injustice, when people are deprived of that to which they have a right. In brief, this ethical norm asks, "Is everyone (the group) better off because of this act?" And for each person, it asks, "Would you be willing to trade places with any of the other parties after this act takes place?"

14   Rawls's concept of justice, like universalism, focuses on the *process* by which outcomes are distributed rather than on the outcomes themselves. Like Kant's universalist perspective, Rawls attempts to derive a set of principles that would be acceptable to all rational people.

15   In considering the justice of any process, we are asked to assume a *veil of ignorance*. That is, we act as if we are ignorant of our *own* roles in the situation, and assume we could be assigned *any* role. Would we be willing to abide by our decision if we might be any of the players affected by it? According to Rawls, the veil of ignorance leads us to construct processes in which:

1. all members of the process could agree to be a part of it, regardless of the position they might happen to occupy in the process;

2. each person would have an equal right to the most extensive liberty that can accommodate similar liberties for others;

3. inequalities work to the benefit of all;

4. these inequalities are attached to positions that are accessible to all.

Using Multiple Criteria

16 Evaluating bargaining tactics raises the question of which of these four criteria takes precedence.

If a tactic is condoned by one criterion and condemned by another, what is a negotiator to do?

17   In the first place, if applied correctly, these criteria ought to yield similar results. They are not designed to bring about different answers; rather, they are different ways of looking for the same answer. Which criterion one uses can be a matter of personal preference or may be dictated by the nature of the dilemma. Utilitarianism is useful when the number of affected parties is relatively small and known and the outcomes are relatively predictable. However, when the number of affected parties is large, knowledge of their preferences is unreliable, or outcomes are unpredictable, then other criteria are more useful. When dealing with unfamiliar situations (new technology), unfamiliar parties (new markets), or complex issues (mergers and acquisitions), principle-based criteria such as universalism are going to be more reliable than those, such as utilitarianism, that require predictions about very uncertain future events.

Ethical Negotiations

18 Having delineated these four standards, we shall now apply them to the ten questionable negotiation tactics, from lying to maximizing.

Lies

19 A lie is a statement made by a negotiator that contradicts his knowledge or beliefs about something material to the negotiations. In negotiating, lies are intended to deceive the opponent about values, intents, objectives, alternatives, constraints, and beliefs. Examples include:

• "Why should I buy it from you for $10,000 when I've got another seller willing to let me have one just as good for $8,500?" — when the buyer has no such alternative.

• "I can't possibly pay $10,000. I have only $8,500 to spend"; or "My client has directed me to pay no more than $9,000" — when the negotiator has no such constraints.

20 **Lying and the Golden Rule**. Most religions, including Christianity, Judaism, and Islam, contain strict injunctions against lying. Some religions, however, permit lying when it is the only possible way to prevent a greater harm. For example, you may lie to someone in a murderous rage in order to prevent a homicide, or to a drunken, abusive person in search of his usual victims. These exceptions are really not inconsistent with the Golden Rule. The question would be, "Would you prefer to be lied to if that were the only way to keep you from committing a terrible deed?" The rational answer is yes.

21 The examples of lying in negotiations, however, do not prevent a greater harm. They are simply examples of immediate self-interest, of doing harm by deceit to further your own interest. The question would be, "Would you prefer that others deceive you to enrich themselves at your expense?" The rational answer is no.

22 **Lying and Universalism**. In his late years, Kant argued that honesty was so important to the concept of intrinsic human worth and dignity that *no* lie could be justified. The argument is that human beings rely on information to make decisions for themselves. And to make the best decisions, they must have the truth. When others deprive them of the truth through lies, the victims of those lies may be led to make faulty decisions.

23 Some will propose that lying is permissible when you believe your opponent is lying. They argue, in fact, that lying is the only defense against an opponent who lies. But this argument

is flawed. First, there are other options, one of which is to terminate the negotiation. Second, you can try to discover the truth that will expose the lie, thus turning a disadvantage into an advantage. If you cannot possibly ascertain the truth, then you must admit that you only believe your opponent to be lying; you don't know it as fact. Such a belief is not sufficient to justify a lie.

24 **Lying and Utilitarianism**. At first blush, it might seem that utilitarianism could make a case for lying under certain circumstances. A negotiator might think, "This lie helps my company a lot and doesn't harm my opponent very much." However, utilitarianism requires us to consider all the possible consequences to all the people potentially affected by the action – and to consider all the people so affected as equals. We cannot weight the interests of some, such as ourselves, as greater than the interests of others.

25 A further problem with attempting to justify lying through utilitarianism is that one must consider the effects of the lying itself. Beyond the direct effects of a lie are the indirect effects of harm done to society in general by increasing cynicism and decreasing trust. The liar also suffers some loss of self-esteem by admitting that his success, however noteworthy, was achieved by dishonorable means. Cynicism and lack of trust entail significant costs for any society, which requires more laws, surveillance, and sanctions – none of which add value to a transaction – to be in place before enacting agreements.

26 **Lying and Distributive Justice**. Distributive justice requires us to be willing to take the role of either party in the situation. Would we willingly trade places with the party being lied to? No, because being lied to increases our chances of making a decision that is not in our best interests.

27 Second, does a lie decrease the freedom to act of any of the parties? Yes; consistent with the maxim that the truth frees us to make the best decisions, a lie reduces that freedom. One can also argue that a lie decreases the freedom of the liar, whose subsequent statements and actions are now constrained to be (or appear to be) consistent with the lie. Suppose a buyer lies about her reservation price, claiming she could never pay more than $8,000 for an object for which she is willing to pay $9,000, and for which the seller is asking $11,000. If the seller reduces his price to $10,000, the buyer cannot reinforce that concession by raising her offer above $8,000, lest her lie be exposed. Lies constrain the freedom of both the victim and the liar.

28 None of the four ethical models can justify lying in negotiations. Lying is seen to be what it is – an act of self-interest usually taken as a convenient alternative to (a) the hard work of preparing for negotiations, including improving one's knowledge about an opponent, or (b) walking away from a negotiation when one comes to believe the opponent is lying. Only when a lie is the only possible means of preventing a greater harm to another could it possibly be justified. Such an exceptional circumstance is extremely rare in most negotiations, and those circumstances, such as a hostage negotiation, would be dramatic enough to be relatively obvious.

Puffery

29 Puffery is exaggerating the value of something, such as its cost, condition, or worth. Negotiators will often exaggerate the value of alternatives, what they are giving up or are prepared to give up, the importance of issues, product or service attributes, or the value of their case. Examples:

• "I have a six-figure offer from another company" – when no such offer has actually been made, or the offer is less than six figures.

• "This union will never give up the right to strike" – when job security is actually more important.

• "I consistently get up to 33 miles per gallon" – when in fact that happened only once in the car's lifetime.

• "We have enough evidence right now to put your client away for 20 years" – when the real evidence at hand is less than convincing.

30   Clearly, puffery is simply a euphemism for lying. Every one of these statements contradicts the negotiator's knowledge or beliefs. Exaggeration may be considered by some as a milder form of lying in that there is a shred of truth in it; nevertheless, a statement that contradicts the truth is a lie. Like lies, exaggerations are intended to deceive and gain advantage at another's expense.

Deception

31   A deception is an act or statement intended to mislead another about one's own intent or future actions relevant to the negotiations. These include false promises or empty threats, excessive initial demands, careless statements of fact, and asking for things not wanted. Examples include:

• "If you give us the contract, we'll begin shipments in 30 days" – when such a delivery date is known to be impossible (false promise).

• "If we don't settle this right now, the whole deal is off and we'll just find somebody else" – when the negotiator has no intention of losing this deal (empty threat).

• "In order to accept a position on your board, I would expect to receive 20,000 shares

of stock, luxury class travel and lodging, and to be named chair of the personnel committee" – when what the negotiator really wants is 10,000 shares and a seat on the personnel committee (excessive demands, asking for things not wanted).

• "We need at least a $50,000 contribution from loyal supporters like you because our people tell us that the opposition plans to eliminate Medicare for people like you if they are elected" – when the negotiator knows that the opponents will only seek to halt increases in Medicare spending (careless statement of facts).

32   Some of these deceptive tactics clearly fall into the first category of lies. False promises and empty threats are statements made in contradiction to the negotiator's knowledge or beliefs. We have already determined that lies are unethical. But what about excessive demands, careless statements of fact, asking for things not wanted, or distracting statements?

33   Deception as a category of acts is clearly designed to profit at others' expense – to lead others into acts that are not in their self-interest, or away from an act that is. In this light, deceptive acts can be seen to be unethical.

34   None of us wants to be deceived, so deception fails the Golden Rule. It does not treat the deceived parties with respect, but takes advantage of their trust or vulnerability, so it fails the test of universalism. It does not create the greatest good for the greatest number of people, but only allows the deceiver to profit at the expense of the deceived, violating the standards of utilitarianism. And it limits the deceived person's choices, failing the test of distributive justice. In the end, then, deception fails all four tests of ethical behavior.

Weakening the Opponent

35 A tactic for improving your relative position is to weaken that of your opponent, either psychologically or economically. Direct attacks are generally aimed at lowering another's self-esteem, often through guilt or embarrassment. Indirect attacks include closing off another's alternatives or undermining his support or alliances.

36 Frequently, the means for weakening one's opponent involve lying, deception, or exaggeration. You could blame your opponent for damage caused by others or of unknown origin, or create the impression that he was the author of harm done to you or others when no real harm had been done. We have already demonstrated that such tactics are unethical.

37 But what about those cases in which the negotiator can weaken an opponent by telling the truth? The morality of the tactic depends on a number of factors. Information about your own position ("Our company will be bankrupt if we increase wages by that much") would meet ethical criteria. Such admissions are usually painful, and you should be permitted to make personal sacrifices under any of the frameworks we have studied. They typically involve uncertainty and risk for the discloser; the opponent may ignore or even exploit such knowledge.

38 However, when the information concerns the opponent, the situation becomes murkier. Can you ethically publicize personal information about an opponent that would undermine his support or embarrass him in some way? If you obtained that information in confidence during the negotiations, you may not use it to do your opponent harm for your benefit. It would be permissible only if revealing the information would prevent a greater harm to others, such as disclosing evidence of criminal activity. If you did not obtain the information in confidence, the moral question would shift to one of intent: Would you be morally required to reveal the information if you and your opponent were not negotiating? In other words, your benefit in the revelation should not influence your decision.

39 The difference between taking risks for oneself and doing direct harm to another is best understood in the context of distributive justice. A key maxim is whether an action would increase or decrease the other's freedom. Risk-taking and self-disclosure increase an opponent's options, so they are permissible. Harming him reduces his options, and thus requires other justification.

Strengthening One's Own Position

40 A host of tactics are designed to improve one's own position without doing direct harm to the opponent. Instead of involving lying, deception, or exaggeration, they entail ability, effort, and intelligence. Moreover, conceptually at least, they are available to all parties in a negotiation.

41 Again, distributive justice tells us inequalities are permitted as long as all parties have the opportunity to pursue them. If you work harder, train better, prepare more effectively, or create and follow a more successful strategy than your opponents, you have done them no direct harm. You are willing to permit them to do their best in preparation and execution. We are all permitted to improve ourselves; none of the four ethical frameworks deny self-improvement.

42 Under the Golden Rule, we are willing to permit others to strengthen themselves. According to utilitarianism, the net benefits of strengthening go to those who have done the best job — a "survival of the fittest" outcome. Under universalism, one can argue that preparation and discipline in execution actually enhance the dig-

nity of one's opponent. To be well-prepared is to show respect for the other; shoddy preparation is actually demeaning to an opponent.

Nondisclosure

43 We have determined that negotiators are ethically required to tell the truth – lying, deception, and exaggeration are wrong. But are they required to tell the *whole* truth? May a negotiator withhold factual information that could be of use to an opponent? The answer depends on the nature of the hidden truth.

44   If failure to disclose the truth would harm one's opponent, it would be unethical. Hiding a product or service defect or flaw that would mislead the other about the value of the item being bargained for would be wrong. If, to induce a potential buyer into paying a higher price, you fail to disclose a lien on property or a mechanical problem with an automobile you are attempting to sell, you are wrong. Just so, potential buyers who fail to disclose information revealing that they are, in fact, unlikely to be able to make payments on a purchase are acting unethically.

45   However, you are not required to disclose personal information that could be harmful to your case. You need not reveal that you are able and/or willing to pay far more for an item than the asking price. And you are not required to disclose your reservation price, although you are not permitted to lie about it.

46   Likewise, if you – as a buyer – suspect that the value of an offered item is greater than the asking price, you are not required to disclose that fact to the seller, presuming the seller has the competence to assess the value of the object. It would be wrong to take advantage of someone incapable of evaluating the worth of an object.

47   From a different perspective, are you permitted to disclose the true value of an object to a misinformed seller? Yes; there is nothing wrong with being more generous in a negotiation than you are morally required to be, as long as you are negotiating for yourself. However, if you are acting as an agent for another, you are required to obtain the best deal that is legally and ethically permissible, so you cannot disclose the true value.

Exploiting Information

48 Effective negotiators uncover information about themselves, their opponents, and the object of a negotiation during both the preparation phase and the negotiation itself. If that information is gained by legal and ethical means, no ethical proscription forbids a negotiator from using it. If you learn that your opponent *really* wants what you have to offer – in fact, values it more than he is disclosing – you are permitted to raise your asking price. If you learn that your opponent has fewer options than he suggests, thereby raising his valuation of what you have to offer, you may do likewise. As long as that information is legally and ethically accessible to both parties, you are permitted to use it to strengthen your position.

49   Are you permitted to use information obtained by illegal or unethical means? Certainly not if you had a hand in the unethical or illegal act – committed it yourself or induced someone else to commit it. But what if information so gained became public knowledge, and you had nothing to do with either the discovery or the publication of that information? Then you would be permitted to exploit it. Earlier, we concluded that one is not permitted to do direct harm to an opponent; however, if the harm has already been done by another, one may take advantage

of it. If a police report of a burglary reveals that your opponent has a greater need or ability to pay for an item over which you are negotiating, you are *permitted* to use the information to your advantage. May you use it to defame your opponent, thereby decreasing his options or weakening his alliances? No, because that would be doing direct harm to him that would not be done without your action.

Change of Mind

50 Sometimes in the course of negotiations, something happens to alter the attraction of the object for one of the parties. The need is diminished or increased; an attractive alternative appears or vanishes; one's ability to pay is changed. May you abruptly change your negotiating position in light of these new circumstances? As long as you are not breaking a commitment or agreement, you are permitted to change your mind. You may decide to accept an offer you said you would never accept, or to pay a higher price than your original reservation price. If you intentionally lied about your reservation price, the act of lying was wrong. However, paying more than you said you would pay or accepting less than you said you would accept is not wrong – your act is doing no harm to your opponent; in fact, it benefits him.

51   May you withdraw an offer you have made? Yes, providing your withdrawal meets the legal requirements and the opponent has not accepted the offer. However, once the opponent has *accepted* an offer or commitment in any way, you may not ethically withdraw it even if it is legal to do so. Reneging on agreements is wrong from all standpoints. You would not wish others to do so to you. It does more harm than good, not only to your opponent but to the general level

of trust among negotiators. And you certainly would not be willing to trade places with the person who accepted your offer.

52   Of course, you are permitted to ask an opponent to withdraw his acceptance of your offer or release you from your commitment because of changed circumstances. However, if he refuses to do so, then you are morally bound to your agreement.

Distraction

53 Negotiators are sometimes tempted to protect a weakness or conceal their interest in a particular issue by distracting their opponents. As long as the distractive tactic did not involve lying, puffery, or outright deception, is one ethically permitted to distract an opponent?

54   We concluded earlier that you need not disclose harmful information about yourself if the nondisclosure would do no harm to another. We can assume that the other is entitled to a fair outcome in the negotiation; however, he is not *entitled* to maximize his outcomes at your expense. He may attain them through his skill, your ineptitude, or other factors; you are not depriving him of his rights by limiting his outcomes to something between fair and maximization.

55   Distraction as a tactic does not reduce an opponent's options, according to distributive justice. It also provides him with information – if he is skilled enough to uncover it – about your perceptions of what *you* believe to be important and what you believe *he* considers to be important. If you evade answering certain questions, your opponent may learn that you do so to protect a weakness. Burying issues that you see as important or surrounding critical questions with questions you consider trivial reflect your own

judgments. They may not be correct; they do not limit the opponent's options; they provide an opponent with opportunities to learn from them; they certainly involve risk on your part. Neither the Golden Rule nor universalism would prohibit distraction.

Maximization

56 Is it ethical to pursue your own payoffs at another's expense? Yes, but it depends on the manner in which the gain is pursued. Keep in mind that a negotiation has two facets. First, one side usually does not have the same goals as the other, yet both share a goal in that they want to have an exchange with the other side. A machine shop operator buying bolts from a manufacturer has a goal that differs from the manufacturer's. The operator wants a low price and the manufacturer seeks a high one. Yet they both want an exchange, because the machine shop operator needs bolts to produce machines and the manufacturer prefers money to an inventory of bolts.

57 In the negotiated exchange, the two sides usually bargain over a number of items. And the value of each item differs for each side. In the bolt negotiation, there might be four issues: anti-rust coating, bolt strength, delivery schedule, and method of payment. For the machine shop operator, the first two items would be very important. He needs anti-rust coating so that the bolts don't rust in inventory, and he must have strong bolts in order to produce high-quality machines. Because these two characteristics are important, he is willing to pay handsomely for them.

58 By contrast, the bolt manufacturer knows he can put an anti-rust coating on the bolts rather inexpensively, and, with some minor modifications of his production process, produce very strong bolts. Consequently, the bolts are of low cost to him. However, the delivery schedule is important to the manufacturer, as is the method of payment. Specifically, he would prefer to make deliveries when he is sending bolts to other customers in the city, and he wants the shop owner to use a standard invoicing system that cuts the amount of paperwork.

59 In this setting, it would be unethical for the manufacturer to maximize his own goals – at the machine-shop owner's expense – on every item. To do so would violate the Golden Rule; he probably would not want the operator to behave in this manner. It violates the universalism criterion because it exploits the opponent; that is, it uses the opponent for the benefit of the negotiator rather than permitting the opponent, as well as the negotiator, to share adequately in the negotiation benefits. It also violates the utilitarianism criterion because this approach does not provide the greatest good to the greatest number. Rather, it forces the negotiation into a win-lose result and does not allow the two sides to improve their total joint benefit. Likewise, it violates the distributive justice criterion because everyone is not better off from this act.

60 How, then, should the negotiator bargain if all items are fixed sum ("My loss is your gain") and of equal value to the negotiator and opponent? The utilitarian criterion proffers no guidance here because there is no variation in the total value; rather, all points have equal total value. Moreover, distributive justice provides modest instruction because everyone will not be better off in the various agreement points.

61 However, the universalism and Golden Rule criteria do assist us. The former dictates that the negotiator must consider the well-being of the opponent. Therefore, it posits that the negotiator can press his own interests up to the

point at which the well-being of the opponent is endangered. The Golden Rule's dictate is consistent with this idea; the negotiator should pursue his own interests only as far as he would want the opponent to do so.

Applying Ethics to Negotiations: Oil on Water?

62 A cynic's retort to these evaluations might be, "Ethics are fine in theory. I can negotiate ethically and sleep well at night, but I'll be hungry tomorrow, and next week." In other words, some might expect that ethical bargaining would lead to low payoffs, or no agreement, or one that costs them their job. How do we respond to that?

63 True, ethical bargaining does entail risks and sometimes seems to place a negotiator in a vulnerable position. Yet the ethical route, for operational as well as moral reasons, is the preferable one, because unethical negotiation has four major costs that are often overlooked:

- rigidity in future negotiations;
- a damaged relationship with the opponent;
- a sullied reputation; and
- lost opportunities.

Rigid Negotiating

64 Even when it is successful, unethical behavior has a personal cost for negotiators. If their lies, deceptions, and puffery yield high-outcome agreements, they will repeat those behaviors in subsequent negotiations, because such actions have paid off. In addition, they will tend to attribute their success to such acts. Consequently, unethical negotiators will sacrifice some of their flexibility, creativity, and openness to others' ideas, thereby trapping themselves into a rigid

bargaining approach that will eventually be matched by their opponents.

65 Keep in mind that unethical negotiating is not as advantageous as it may seem. One may lie about an alternative; but doesn't silence about an alternative prove as valuable as the lie? Wouldn't the comment "I'd better find another buyer" be just as potent as the statement "I've got another buyer"? Moreover, it is a wiser strategy to interrupt the negotiation, find another buyer, and let the original opponent know about it than to lie about already having another buyer.

Damaged Relationships

66 Unethical negotiation also mars the relationship between the two sides, causing emotional fallout (such as anger) as well as higher operational costs. When the negotiation is a single event — such as the sale of building materials — a negotiator who has been the victim of unethical behavior is less likely to implement the deal fully, perhaps not delivering all the materials. Or he will be less than cooperative when post-agreement problems arise, such as if some of the building materials are defective or do not meet construction specifications.

67 When negotiations are of a repeated nature, the costs of unethical behavior mount. Today's bargainer becomes an embittered enemy rather than tomorrow's customer. Such an enemy might refuse to bargain with an unethical opponent, could return to the table with some open Machiavellian tactics of his own, or, more devastatingly, could voice no complaints but secretly seek revenge in the next round.

Sullied Reputation

68 Seldom do victims of unethical behavior hold their tongue, in public or across the bargaining

table. At times, they are even apt to embellish. Thus, an unethical reputation often permeates the business environment and precedes or accompanies its owner to the bargaining arena. Consequently, the opposing negotiator expects unethical behavior. A building contractor once commented about a subcontractor, "He'll lie to you, cheat you, steal from you, and then brag about it, if you give him a chance."

69   Once an opponent has experienced unethical behavior, he will prepare to counteract your unethical tactics in the future. Moreover, he will suspect that they are present, even if they are not. And often he will use them as excuses for his own obstinate behavior.

Lost Opportunities

70 The most detrimental effect of unethical behavior comes in the negotiation itself. The explanation for this is somewhat complex, but with assistance from a simple example it can be quickly understood: The essence of a productive negotiation is trading a *package* of issues in which each side concedes heavily on issues that are of low cost (or value) to it in return for major concessions on issues that are of high cost (or value) to it.

71   A company supplying tractor seats to John Deere probably finds that the cost of painting them green and packing them ten to a carton for shipment is not very difficult. If Deere places high value on green seats packed ten to a carton, it would be wise for the supplier to agree (or concede) on these issues. In turn, the firm could have John Deere — with its large storage facilities — accept the supplier's entire production run and store it until used. This concession would cost Deere quite little and would be a major benefit to a small company with limited storage facilities.

72   Most negotiations have manifold issues like these — namely, they are of low cost to one side and high value to the other. For the negotiators, the key is to find as many of these issues as possible and arrange trades among packages of them. In such trades, the first step is to determine which issues — of those currently under negotiation — have differential value to the two sides. To locate these, the parties must exchange valid information. If either side lies, deceives, or engages in puffery or distracts the other, it is very difficult, if not impossible, to determine the win-win trades, because the opponent does not receive accurate information. Moreover, the unethical behavior, if detected, motivates the opponent to withhold information (that he feels will be used against him) about the cost and values of the issues.

73   Not only does unethical behavior undermine the first step toward package trading, it also precludes the second: discovery of new issues. Productive negotiations are those that grow beyond the issues on the table. A simple expansion is one in which both sides agree on a two-year contract, even though the negotiation began with a one-year frame. A more complex expansion, taken from our earlier example, might be that Deere and its seat supplier jointly discover that Deere has vibration-reduction expertise that the supplier could use in its production machines. And the supplier has discovered a method for mixing and applying paint that makes it highly chip-resistant — which Deere would no doubt find useful. With an open, trusting negotiation, the two sides probably would be able to ferret out the two new issues and, through some creative discussions, arrange a trade on these or explore the prices for each technology transfer.

74   Here the impact of unethical bargaining is clear. Not only does it undermine the negotiators' capabilities to reach win-win agreements on the current issues, it also interferes with discussions that would bring new, mutually profitable issues to the table.

75 Coming full circle, then, we agree with John Rutledge that ethical negotiation is not only morally right, it is frequently more profitable. Business men and women often feel they move into a different environment when they negotiate – one in which anything goes and the rules are understood by all players.

76   Yet negotiations today are not a separate function; they are an integral part of all business environments. Joint ventures, purchasing options, labor contracts, leasing agreements, salaries and benefits, day-to-day disputes, mergers, and spinoffs are all negotiated. And in such bargaining, ethical rules must apply. The four we have touched on – the Golden Rule, universalism, utilitarianism, and distributive justice – rule out several negotiation tactics, guide the use of some, and permit the use of others.

77   This guidance does not make negotiating easy. With their high stakes, complexity, deadlines, uncertainty, emotions, and stress, negotiations will always remain tough going. But those who take care to negotiate ethically should find the process better for them – personally, interpersonally, and economically.

REFERENCES

Richard T. DeGeorge, *Business Ethics*, 4th ed. (New York: Prentice-Hall, 1994).

Larue Tone Hosmer, *Moral Leadership in Business* (Burr Ridge, IL: Richard D. Irwin, 1994): Ch. 4.

J.C. Penney, *View from the Ninth Decade* (New York: Thomas Nelson & Sons, 1985).

John Rawls, *A Theory of Justice* (Cambridge, MA: Harvard University Press, 1971).

John Rutledge, "The Portrait on My Office Wall," *Forbes*, December 30, 1996, p. 78.

Questions

1. Choose one of the ethical approaches covered in Section II that Reitz, Wall, and Love do *not* consider and, as you read, apply it to each of the ten negotiation tactics they consider, comparing the outcome with those described.

2. In Section II, lying was concluded to be wrong by Kant according to his "universalize" imperative. Reitz, Wall, and Love conclude it to be wrong by his "respect" imperative – explain (P22).

3. Do you agree with the authors' definition of deception as given in P33? If not, does this change whether or not deception is morally acceptable (see P34)?

4. Some philosophers argue that there is no moral difference between actively doing X and passively not-doing Y if the result is the same (for example, "pulling the plug" on a terminally ill person is neither more nor less wrong [or right] than not putting him/her on the ventilator in the first place – in both cases, what you do or not-do results in his/her death). Do you think, contrary to Reitz, Wall, and Love, that the same can be said for lying and nondisclosure?

5. How can the morality of what you do change according to whether you are acting for yourself or acting for another? That is, do you agree with the authors in P47?

6. In P49, the authors seem to say that doing harm is wrong but taking advantage of it, exploiting it, is okay.

   (a) Is that a correct reading?

   (b) According to the four criteria used throughout, is that conclusion sound? Read especially, and compare with, P59.

   (c) Would those who argue that we should not use the knowledge gained by the morally unacceptable experiments done by Nazi doctors on Jewish people agree or disagree with the authors?

7. The authors' assessment of distraction is that it is morally acceptable.

   (a) Do you agree with the distributive justice analysis they provide?

   (b) Do you agree with their conclusion that (i) the Golden Rule and (ii) universalism would also allow it?

8. "If applied correctly, these criteria ought to yield similar results" (P17). Do you agree? For the four criteria used by the authors or for all ethical criteria?

9. Which of the four costs of "unethical" negotiation that the authors describe would be most significant for labour/management negotiation?

Case Study – The McDonald's Union

During the summer of 1998, McDonald's restaurants had its first unionized outlet in North America. This occurred at the McDonald's in Squamish, British Columbia, and was spearheaded by two teenage girls who were tired of the poor treatment by managers there.

McDonald's has been a very profitable company over the years; with more than 14,000 restaurants across North America, it is perhaps the world's pre-eminent fast-food eatery. It has a long history of employing youth, partly because its main market is young people and young families, but also because of the flexibility and low cost of young workers. While McDonald's proudly boast that thousands of new employees happily join the restaurant chain every year,

some critics use the company's name to vilify any low-paying, dead-end employment as a "McJob."

Two previous attempts to unionize McDonald's in Canada – one at Orangeville, Ontario, and the other at Longeuil, Quebec – failed to win certification in the early 1990s. Another attempt at an outlet in Saint-Hubert, Quebec, succeeded, but the ruling came shortly after the restaurant was closed.

The issue that sparked the union drive at the Squamish outlet was clearly not money. It was a classic case of employees rebelling against poor working conditions – in particular, according to the organizers, against mistreatment by abusive and heavy-handed managers. Jennifer

Wiebe and Tessa Lowinger, 16 and 17 respectively, were employees at the Squamish McDonald's restaurant, Lowinger having worked there for two years. The two girls found that some managers at the restaurant berated young employees for making mistakes. One employee was yelled at in front of customers and made to cry. Wiebe says that she once became sick at work and wasn't allowed to leave until the next shift arrived. The girls talked to other workers and heard similar stories. They noted that employees had to find their own replacements if they called in sick, and there were various safety concerns as well.

The girls spoke with Tessa's father, a Canadian Auto Worker (CAW) member who put them in touch with a CAW youth organizer. Working together, they began talking with the other employees, urging them to sign union cards. They recognized the risks: they might lose their jobs; they might be unsuccessful; even if successful, the restaurant might close. They moved fairly quickly and managed to get the majority they needed on time; on August 19, the union was certified by the B.C. Labour Board.

The organizers were of the view that the union might never have happened had the McDonald's managers behaved in a decent and professional manner. Jennifer Wiebe stated, "We wanted to be treated the way we treated management – with respect. We didn't yell at them and call them stupid for doing something. I mean, they made mistakes too, right?"

It was surprising to the girls how quickly McDonald's moved once they heard of the union drive: they held meetings to hear complaints; they introduced new incentives, such as free meals; they fixed faulty electrical outlets; they bought a new stereo for the staff room. As one employee later put it, "If they were always like that, I wouldn't be for the union."

REFERENCES

Gray, John. "Is Labour's Mac Attack a Losing Battle?" *The Globe and Mail* 9 Sep. 1998: A1+.

Lu, Vanessa. "McMemories Resurface." *The Toronto Star* 28 Aug. 1998: A4.

Lu, Vanessa. "Stand Up, Speak Out, Unionists Say." *The Toronto Star* 28 Aug. 1998: A4.

Questions

1. Some business consultants advise that decent, ethical treatment of employees is good for business, aside from being the "right thing to do." Which is the better motive?

2. Is unionization the only (or even the best) way to deal with the alleged "bad" behaviour of some McDonald's managers?

3. As the owner of the Squamish McDonald's, what would be your plan from this point on in order to keep union demands and grievances to a minimum? (Should that *be* your intent?)

CHAPTER 7
PROFIT

What to Do? - No Limits, Ltd.

You are an upper-level manager of a very successful company, No Limits, Ltd. Call it a midlife crisis, call it an awakening, but the thought occurred to you that *maximizing* profit may not be the be-all and end-all of life, let alone of business — more importantly, it may even be immoral to get everything you can all the time. You're considering suggesting a profit ceiling to the Board of Directors.

Maybe relaxing the bottom line will enable you to pay a fairer price to your suppliers or afford the costlier but more environmentally responsible materials; maybe it will enable you to lower prices; maybe it will enable you to increase wages and benefits; maybe it will enable you to afford peripheral programs that have been on the proverbial back burner forever.

However, you begin to consider the possible downside of a profit ceiling. Current and potential future investors are likely to sell or not buy your company's shares — why would someone settle for a 6% rate of return when they can get 7% or 8% elsewhere? What broker would recommend the stocks of a company that has put a voluntary limit on its profits?

Then you get to thinking about your own interests. As a senior executive of the company, you receive bonuses if profits are higher. Those bonuses help to fund some extras which improve your family's quality of life; for example, part of the bonus money goes toward your children's university education. And, you recognize that those bonuses have, in fact, been earned with a lot of after-hours work, creative thinking, and commitment to your employer. Finally, you know that profits are never guaranteed: high (even obscenely high) profits are simply a reflection of successful risk-taking *this year* — you know it can all turn around next year.

But, you think to yourself, instead of limiting profits, maybe the company should use the profits that they make to enhance its stability and reputation and hence increase the level of job security for all its employees. Perhaps the company could give part of its after-tax profit to certain charities. Perhaps some of the profits could go to worthy environmental projects or community recreation programs. Perhaps the company could institute a profit-sharing program with its workers; this would improve productivity as well as the quality of future job applicants. But are these profits justifiably the company's to spend – or are they dirty money? Maybe you should suggest the profit ceiling after all.

What do you decide to do?

Introduction

Many students participating in discussions about ethical issues in business apparently take the pursuit of profit as a given. But it's not, not from an ethical point of view. And, remember, that's the point of view we're taking in this book, that's what this book is all about. From a *business* perspective (whatever that is – I'd argue that there *isn't* just one unified "business" point of view), perhaps the pursuit of profit is a given. But from an *ethical* perspective, it must be justified – and it must be so on *ethical* grounds. (See, for example, Arnold's position in Jacobsen's essay in this chapter.)

Most business students seem to assume that profit is *good*. Certainly many assume that the pursuit of profit (perhaps even the maximization of profit) is the *reason* for being in business. (Let me remind them that a not-for-profit business is a business, too.) Some even assert that the pursuit of profit is a *right*. And, of course, I'm going to try to get you to question those assumptions and, in the process, to justify profit – on ethical grounds.

You may, of course, decide that you don't care about ethical justifications, you don't care about whether what you're doing is right or wrong. (Can I be the same way? Especially with regard to what I do to you?) Okay, then you *can* consider profit, or power, or whatever, to be your given, your unquestioned need-not-be-jus-

tified priority. But then you should have closed this book and withdrawn from this course long ago – because this is about business *ethics*, about the *moral reasons for our decisions, our actions*. (Take another look at Section I if you need to.)

Or you may want to do the right thing, but argue that the pursuit of profit can sometimes override morality (assuming that the pursuit of profit can't be ethically justified, can't be morally good). This is the question Goldman examines, and he concludes in the negative:

> [T]he manager is not to violate moral rights in the interest of his corporation ... [h]e must make decisions within a moral framework defined by principles and rights *applicable with the same force* in *non*professional contexts. Adherence to such principles does not require any special expertise at judging cumulative economic effects; often it requires only the removal of institutional blinders. (284–5, my emphasis)

Let's first define our terms. Accounting profit is different from economic profit, and the layperson's definition/understanding is different still. But simply put, profit is the difference between income (revenues) and expenses (costs). Actually, that's the definition for loss, too – if the difference is positive, it's called profit; if the difference is negative, it's called loss.

The complicated part is what's included in "expenses." If everything is included – everything required to maintain the business, such as fair payment for everyone's labour, including that of the owner, fair return to investors, reserve funds for upgrading, etc. – then there's no need, no reason, for profit: the very existence of a profit (or loss) indicates a miscalculation – either you charged more than you should have for your product and/or you paid less than you should have (or vice versa). And if your profit is thus the result of some unfairness (the "should" being a *moral* "should") then the ethical remedy seems clear: just charge/pay what you should have – decrease your price and/or increase your wages, returns, etc. (or vice versa). Otherwise, your profit is getting back more than you put out, and as such, it would be considered undeserved, unfair. (What's wrong with breaking even? Isn't that a win-win situation? Whereas profit – if your profit exists because of someone else's loss – is a win/lose situation.)

Note, however, that this analysis assumes that there is, can be, a fixed fair price for things. But this is not so in a free market system – in such a system, there is no "fair," there is only "whatever the market will bear."

Note, also, that the implication is that the miscalculation entails an injustice – and this isn't necessarily so. Maybe the surplus (or deficit) wasn't the result of exploitative pricing or waging, but of unexpected sales or supplies (there could be a number of reasons for "legitimate" profit, but we don't need to go into them). One can't know the future, one can only predict it; so if sales were unforeseeably higher or lower than anticipated, well, where's the injustice in that miscalculation? So the very *existence* of profit need not be morally unacceptable; however, the *distribution* of that profit may be.

And the distribution problem is compounded by the fact that everything is usually *not* included in expenses. So should the profit be used for upgrading and expansion? Should it go to the shareholders? Should the owner pocket it? Let's consider the moral acceptability of each of these in turn.

Upgrading and expansion may well be good. Be careful, though, of the circular argument: profit is good because it enables expansion, and expansion is good because it increases profit. And be careful not to *assume* that growth is good. Sometimes growth, certainly *unlimited* growth, is not necessarily good. Consider cancer. Consider that life may be better when we limit our growth. After all, isn't there a point at which you have enough? Don't we all learn, when we're about two years old, to "say when"? ("No," one of my students once quipped, "we didn't learn that lesson. That's why we're in Business.")

If, however, with upgrading, better products and services can be provided (better, not just more – unless we truly don't have enough), why not provide them? And if, with expansion, more jobs (good jobs, needed jobs) can be created, why not create them? But then, why not build this into your price as an operating or development cost? (This particular justification for profit is closely related to the notion of social responsibility; while interesting, that discussion is a little beside this discussion of profit, so it's in a separate section at the end of this introduction.)

Okay, what about your shareholders? Is it true that if someone invests in your company, giving you money to use, you have an obligation to give them the best return on their money? The best? Why not set a fair rate of return and make that your obligation? Have you asked your shareholders if they were willing to accept a lesser return in order to lower prices or increase wages or whatever? Perhaps there are more people than you think who would rather be (morally) right than be rich. And why not include that return as an expense, rather like the interest on a loan?

And what about stakeholders – all those who are affected by your company (consumers, suppliers, the local community, perhaps even the global community)? Why do you have a responsibility only to, or even first to, your shareholders? Recall that distributive justice according to contribution is not the only option. (See Freeman; Weiss; and Donaldson and Preston for discussions of this.)

Next, let's consider the entrepreneur – doesn't s/he deserve to profit from, to benefit from, his/her endeavours? Perhaps it is this argument that causes the most moral outrage – on both sides. Certainly most people would agree that one deserves payment for one's work. But as long as the entrepreneur takes his/her payment from the profit rather than, or in addition to, taking it from the expenses (as a fixed wage), there are two ethical problems: the payment is potentially extra (if indeed s/he is also getting/taking a wage) – and that needs to be justified; the payment is potentially excessive (in the case of high profits) – and that needs to be justified.

One justification appeals to the hard work, the late hours often extending over years, that the owner has put in. Well, most people work hard for many years – are they not as entitled to an eventual payback that exceeds their normal wage? Certainly profit-sharing plans seem to endorse such entitlement. As for the late hours, which is often used as justification for profit-dependent bonuses for a select few at the top as well for as the owner, yes, perhaps they put in twice as many hours, but they'd have to work 100 times as hard during each of those hours to justify some of those bonuses – I don't think that's even possible. (Maybe they've never experienced how hard it is to be on the assembly line or to be a secretary – there are different kinds of "hard" when it comes to work.) Some companies, perhaps thinking along these lines, put a proportional limit on incomes – those at the top can't make more than, for example, four times as much as those at the bottom.

Another justification appeals to the risk taken by the entrepreneur. Again, I think many would agree that one deserves payment for risk-taking (if one is paid at all – consider the risks of pregnancy and childbirth). But why isn't it a fixed amount? Miners, police officers, firefighters, and many other workers risk their health, often even their lives, and supposedly their wages reflect that. But it's a fixed amount, and it's often a much lower amount than most entrepreneurs' profit. Why should a person get more for risking money (and often not even their own money, certainly seldom money they need – i.e., for food, clothing, and shelter) than for risking health or life? No dangerous occupation pays several million dollars per year (except in sports – and some of those occupations are not even that dangerous). At the very least, there's a consistency issue here.

Yet another justification appeals to the motivating role of "extra" and "excessive": without profits (or, more accurately, without the expectation of profit), there would be little incentive to do what entrepreneurs do. First, it is arguable that people *are* motivated by economic self-interest (and even if they are, it's arguable that they are happiest and healthiest when so motivated). Second, most of us who are motivated by economic self-interest are motivated by payment (our basic wage/salary), not profit (the extra, the excessive payment) – why should the entrepreneur be any different? And, in any case, that the entrepreneur is different – does require extra and excessive – does not make it right. But nor does it make it wrong. Merely saying that profit motivates doesn't seem to be ethically relevant. (Fear and curiosity motivate, too, but whether either is morally good is independent of those observations. In order to prove that X is good because X motivates, one would need to establish that "motivating" in itself is good – and I suspect that would strongly depend on what one is motivated to do!)

Still others point to the equally excessive incomes of some actors and athletes. This, however, is a red herring – their incomes may be equally undeserved, so pointing them out adds nothing to the case for deserved profit (though it may add something to the case for societal consistency).

Furthermore, if profit is actually income, the entrepreneur's income, why isn't it taxed at the same rate as other forms of income such as wages, salaries, and interest? Corporate tax rates are lower, in general, than rates of tax on income. And why do some large profitable corporations get away without paying any tax at all? Well, but they don't – really. Every year, the media publicize the fact that several hundred profitable corporations pay no tax, but this is usually because of tax credits or deductions which simply allow the firm to defer taxes to some future period of time. In any case, again, this is a red herring: that profit is not taxed doesn't prove that it's not income – it may just prove that our tax system is inconsistent.

So the heart of the ethical issue seems to be not only the existence of profit (does it imply a legitimate miscalculation or an injustice), but also the distribution of profit (if its existence is just, who should get it – the shareholders, the owner/s, the other people who work to make the company what it is, the customers). Consider, for example, the billions of dollars in profit made by the very banks who have laid off thousands of workers. Were some of those billions made *because* the jobs were eliminated? (Is that why such a profit existed?) Shouldn't some of the those billions be used to reinstate those jobs? (Were the profits fairly distributed?)

Social Responsibility

Some argue that not only does business have a right to pursue profit, it has a responsibility to do so – it's in the best interests of the community that it does so. (See, for example, Friedman – and all of his critics.) However, perhaps one should question the initial assumption: does a business have any social responsibility (let alone the responsibility to pursue profit)? Why should it have any more or any less such responsibility than individuals? We might say that we all have a responsibility to make the world a better place, or at least to refrain from making it a worse place – why should a business be any different? Is a business a person? (See French; Ladd; and Goodpaster and Matthews for answers to that question.)

One might suggest that a business has more social responsibility simply because it has more power. (The top 200 corporations in the world have almost twice as much economic clout as 4/5 of humanity [Fraser].) So do individuals with greater power – political, economic, etc. – have more responsibility? That's certainly a notion worth considering.

For example, many seem to think that businesses should provide health care and a pension to its employees. But if those are basic needs, why shouldn't they be the government's responsibility? (We do assume that the state should cover everyone's basic needs.) And indeed, in Canada, the government does provide basic health care and a pension. (But not food – why not?) So why does business also provide those benefits? Are they extras? To entice employees? To compensate employees? Isn't the pay you're offering sufficient? Wouldn't it be better, more respectful of people's autonomy, to just pay your employees the "extra," so they can decide for themselves whether to set up a personal pension/healthcare supplement? Isn't it a bit patronizing for the business to just decide to do that for them? (Is it patronizing for the state to do so?)

Or is it that the government programs are inadequate? Well, why should business have to pick up the slack?

Some justify social responsibility, and indeed any ethically correct behaviour, on the grounds that it's good for business – i.e., doing the right thing is profitable. But understand that that's not an ethical argument – the end is not goodness, but profit; goodness is seen as a means to that end. (Perhaps these businesses call investments "ethical" and label their products "green" when they are not – it's "just" a way of maximizing profit.)

Some argue that business isn't any more equipped to solve social problems than the ordinary citizen – and such endeavours should be left to those who know something about them, presumably social experts and policy makers. Boatright (350) points out that not only do they lack the expertise, they also lack the legitimacy: no one elected business people to run society.

But they do. Legitimately or not, business, especially big business, does run society in many respects. Michalos describes a very good example: Canada's Business Council on National Issues was founded on the idea that "corporations and their leaders have a responsibility not merely to their traditional constituents but to society as a whole" (225)– to "help build a strong economy, progressive social policies, and healthy political institutions" (226). However, Michalos points out that "some Canadian companies and families have more than one voice at the Council's table. For example, the Bronfman family interests may be expressed through the C.E.O. of Brascan Ltd., John Labatt Ltd., Noranda Inc., Noranda Forest Inc., MacMillan Bloedel Ltd., Norcen Energy Resources Group, or Joseph E. Seagram and Sons" (226). He adds that "the most glaring absentee is a representative from the Canadian Federation of Independent Business" (226) and he concludes that "it would be more accurate for the Council to describe itself as the 'voice of big business'" (226).

Furthermore, as for doing what it says it's to do, for society as a whole, Michalos points out that the Council has never suggested that there is anything wrong with a tax system that allows big companies to frequently pay no income tax or with a system that makes lobbying expenses in the private interests of businesses tax-deductible while those expenses in the public interests of antipoverty groups are not tax-deductible.

Even our standard of living is measured by economic performance indicators (including employment statistics), by trade in goods and services. By business. And so perhaps, having this power, they do have the responsibility.

The Ethics of Economics: A Postscript

By considering the morality of profit, we are actually just looking at the tip of an iceberg: what should be prerequisite, perhaps, is considering the morality of capitalism (the economic system built on private ownership of production and the free market that gives rise to this pursuit of profit), as well as the morality of other systems, such as socialism (social ownership of production and centralized planning). (See De George and Shaw for starting points.) Included in such examinations would be the notions of competition and cooperation, as well as the role of government – what should be its rights and responsibilities? (The Sethi et al. anthology has a few good essays in this area.)

Maybe pursuit of profit isn't so much the problem as the distribution of wealth (recall the distribution of profit discussion) – i.e., most of it seems to end up in the hands of a very, very few. According to the *Human Development Report 1998*, the world's 225 richest people (that's about .000004% of the world's population) have, combined, just about as much wealth as the bottom half of the world's people have, combined.)

Consider Michalos' observation:

[A]fter people around the world have made Steven Spielberg rich by their individually modest but collectively huge purchases of his products, they might well have second thoughts about putting all that power into the possession of one person. After all, ignoring luck, the virtue that allowed Spielberg to accumulate his vast fortune may be far out of proportion to his virtue in spending it. For all I know, Spielberg is a saint and every dime he spends is well-spent, and there certainly are many others with more money and perhaps less virtue of any kind than he has. But my point is that an economic and political system that would allow such people to spend all their money, say, buying and levelling large chunks of the re-

maining forest of cash-starved Third World countries or promoting North American football around the world is a dangerous system. It seems to me that the world would be a better place for more people if no one were allowed to have such power. Since twenty of the twenty-two countries in the OECD [Organization for Economic Cooperation and Development] have some sort of wealth taxation, modest as it is in every country, other people apparently have shared some of my intuitions about these things. (222–223)

(Canada is one of the two that does not. Guess who the other is.)

Perhaps the most effective critiques of our current system come from E.F. Schumacher and Marilyn Waring. Schumacher says this:

The judgment of economics ... is an extremely fragmentary judgment; out of the large number of aspects which in real life have to be seen and judged together before a decision can be taken, economics supplies only one – whether a thing yields a money profit to those who undertake it or not. (35)

(See Jacobsen's essay in this chapter for a similar point.) Schumacher goes on to say:

[The modern economist] is used to measuring the "standard of living" by the amount of annual consumption, assuming all the time that a man who consumes more is "better off" than a man who consumes less. A Buddhist economist would consider this approach excessively irrational: since consumption is merely a means to human well-being, the aim should be to obtain the maximum of well-being with the minimum of consumption. (47–48)

Waring also questions what we value and how we measure what we value, and she comes up with some very disturbing answers. For example, as long as income passes through the system, it's considered a contribution to growth, which is considered a good thing. So the Exxon Valdez oil spill, because it generated clean-up jobs, was a good thing! (So would be the car accident that maims three people, because it makes work for insurance companies and auto shops and physiotherapy clinics....) And "Ben," who spends his days in a bunker practicing to push the button that will annihilate the planet is more valuable, is contributing more to society than "Cathy," who spends her days in the home, nurturing children into maturity. As Waring says, "this is not a sane state of affairs" (20).

REFERENCES AND FURTHER READING

Arrow, Kenneth J. "Social Responsibility and Economic Efficiency." *Public Policy* 21 (Summer 1973).

Boatright, John R. *Ethics and the Conduct of Business.* 2nd ed. Englewood Cliffs, NJ: Prentice Hall, 1997.

De George, Richard T. *Business Ethics.* 5th ed. Englewood Cliffs, NJ: Prentice Hall, 1999. (See chapters 6 and 7.)

Donaldson, Thomas and Lee E. Preston. "The Stakeholder Theory of the Corporation." *Scaling the Corporate Wall: Readings in Business and Society.* Ed. S. Prakash Sethi, Paul Steidlmeier, and Cecilia M. Falbe. 2nd ed. Englewood Cliffs, NJ: Prentice Hall, 1997. 233-252.

Estes, Ralph. *Tyranny of the Bottom Line: Why Corporations Make Good People Do Bad Things.* SF: Berrett-Koehler Publishers, 1996.

Fraser, Chris. "Taking Stock." *Conscience Canada* 76 (November 1994): 4.

Freeman, R. Edward. "The Politics of Stakeholder Theory." *Business Ethics Quarterly* 4.4 (1994): 409-412.

French, Peter A. "Corporate Moral Agency." *Business Ethics: Readings and Cases in Corporate Morality.* Ed. W. Michael Hoffman and Jennifer Mills Moore. NY: McGraw Hill, 1984. 163-171.

Friedman, Milton. "The Social Responsibility of Business is to Increase its Profits." *New York Times Magazine* 13 Sep. 1970. Rpt. in *Business Ethics in Canada.* Ed. Deborah C. Poff and Wilfrid J. Waluchow. 3rd ed. Scarborough: Prentice Hall Allyn and Bacon Canada, 1999. 43-47.

Goldman, Alan H. "Business Ethics: Profits, Utilities, and Moral Rights." *Philosophy & Public Affairs* 9.3 (1980): 260-286.

Goodpaster, Kenneth E., and John B. Matthews, Sr. "Can a Corporation Have a Conscience?" *Business Ethics: Readings and Cases in Corporate Morality.* Ed. W. Michael Hoffman and Jennifer Mills Moore. NY: McGraw Hill, 1984. 150-162.

Grant, Colin. "Friedman Fallacies." *Journal of Business Ethics* 10.12 (December 1991): 907-914.

Ladd, John. "Morality and the Ideal of Rationality in Formal Organizations." *Ethical Issues in Business: A Philosophical Approach.* Ed. Thomas Donaldson and Patricia H. Werhane. 2nd ed. Englewood Cliffs, NJ: Prentice Hall, 1983. 125-136.

Michalos, Alex. "Issues for Business Ethics in the Nineties and Beyond." *Journal of Business Ethics* 16.3 (February 1997): 219-230.

Mulligan, Thomas. "A Critique of Milton Friedman's Essay 'The Social Responsibility of Business Is to Increase Its Profits'." *Journal of Business Ethics* 5.4 (August 1986): 265-269.

Phillips, Jr., Charles F. "What is Wrong with Profit Maximization?" *Issues in Business and Society*. 3rd ed. Ed. W.T. Greenwood. Boston: Houghton Mifflin, 1977. 77-88.

Schumacher, E.F. *Small Is Beautiful: Economics as if People Mattered.* London: Sphere Books, 1974.

Sethi, S. Prakash, Paul Steidlmeier, and Cecilia M. Falbe. *Scaling the Corporate Wall: Readings in Business and Society*. 2nd ed. Englewood Cliffs, NJ: Prentice Hall, 1997.

Shaw, William H. *Business Ethics*. 2nd ed. Belmont, CA: Wadsworth, 1996. (See chapters 3, 4, and 5.)

United Nations Development Programme. *Human Development Report 1998*. NY: Oxford University Press, 1998.

Weiss, Joseph W. *Business Ethics: A Managerial, Stakeholder Approach*. Belmont, CA: Wadsworth, 1994.

Waring, Marilyn. *If Women Counted: A New Feminist Economics*. SF: Harper and Row, 1988.

Economic Efficiency and the Quality of Life

Rockney Jacobsen

ABSTRACT. A classical moral defense of profit seeking as the social responsibility of business in a competitive market is examined. That defense rests on claims about the directness of relationships between (a) profit seeking activity and standards of living and (b) standards of living and the quality of life. Responses to the classical argument tend to raise doubts about the directness of the first relationship. This essay challenges the directness of the second relationship, argues that the classical argument is invalid, and claims that an alternative description of the social responsibility of business is entailed by the classical premises.

Rockney Jacobsen, "Economic Efficiency and the Quality of Life." *Journal of Business Ethics* 10.3 (March 1991): 201-209. © 1991 by Kluwer Academic Publishers. Reprinted with permission of the publisher and the author.

I.

1   Profits, we are told by the classical and neoclassical strains in economic thought, are the best measure of a firm's contribution to the welfare of others. If our contributions to the social good are relevant to what we merit or deserve, then profits clearly seem to be deserved. The classical story is sometimes told in a more dramatic form: the mechanisms of the free market work to yield a high quality of life for a community when, and only when, the participants in the market are driven by a motive of profit maximization. If the participants suffer a motivational lapse and direct their market activities to ends other than profits, the machine falters, and the community lapses into hard times; thus, if the participants in the free market bear a responsibility for the well-being of bystanders, then that responsibility can only be met by engaging in the pursuit of profits.

2   These kinds of stories about the relationships between economic activity and ethics, ending with claims about the moral status of profit seeking, have been widely challenged outside the classical[1] traditions in economic thought. The dispute tends to focus on the truth or falsity of claims about the capability of a free market, fueled by the energies of profit seekers, to deliver the promised goods efficiently to the community. It thus becomes a series of skirmishes over how direct the relationship is, at various points, between increasing profits and increasing contributions to the social well-being. If the relationship turns out to be direct, the classical liberal or contemporary libertarian is thought to win the day; if the relationship is discovered to be indirect or, better yet, inverse, then the case is thought to be lost.

3   I will not enter into the fray along this front, for two reasons. First, the claims about the delivery capabilities of a free market of competing profit seekers is often acknowledged to be an empirical claim which, according to its proponents, has not yet been subjected to an adequate or fair test in the market place.[2] Thus, if the consequences of profit seeking in any particular case can be shown to be morally odious, the defender of profit seeking is more likely to call for revisions in the economic system than concede that the odious consequences derive from a motive to acquire profits. Secondly, I suspect that the moral upshot of disputes about the status of profit seeking depend less on the soundness of classical economics than is generally assumed. My strategy in what follows will be to grant as much as possible to the claims of classical economics, but question the moral consequences which are thought to follow. Since his writings are the most articulate contemporary expression of the classical cause, I will use the libertarian views of Milton Friedman[3] as my chief stalking horse. Although most of my attention will be directed towards an argument which operates only as "deep background" to Friedman's own presentation of his case, we will see in the final section how the ruin of this classical argument takes the wind out of the contemporary libertarian addenda.

II.

4   I noted in opening that the classical argument can take more or less dramatic forms, resulting in a stronger or weaker conclusion; in its weaker form, the argument concludes that profit seeking is always morally justifiable (morally permissible); in its stronger form, the argument concludes that profit seeking is morally obligatory. Both conclusions agree in suggesting that there is certainly nothing wrong with pursuing profits — that it is not morally forbidden. I will state and examine an argument for both the weaker and stronger conclusions; the argument will be found lacking, but in noting how it fails, we shall see an alternative statement of the social responsibilities of business emerge.

5   The central classical argument for these conclusions, which I will refer to as the economic efficiency argument, is of distinguished pedigree, making an early appearance in the writings of Adam Smith. In a deservedly famous passage, Smith, writing of merchants who intend only their own interest and gain, says that in a free competitive market such a merchant is

> led by an invisible hand to promote an end which was no part of his intention. Nor is it always the worse for society that it was no part of it. By pursuing his own interest, he frequently promotes that of the society more effectually than when he really intends to promote it. I have

never known much good done by those who affected to trade for the public good.[4]

This passage, which Friedman quotes[5] with obvious approval, does not actually state an argument, but the spirit of one shines clearly through. The justification of the pursuit of private interest and gain in the market place is derived from the fact that such a pursuit promotes the public interest or good; furthermore, designs on the part of merchants to promote the public good directly will be less efficient in doing so than is the pursuit of gain and may even damage the public interest. If pursuing individual profits effectively promotes the public welfare, then it is morally justified; if pursuing individual profits is the *only* effective means of promoting social ends, then it is morally obligatory, and if pursuing desirable social ends directly is destructive of those ends, it is morally forbidden.

6   The first premiss employed in such reasoning may be stated as follows:

(1)   A free competitive market, in which the participants act always so as to maximize their individual profits, is the most (or, the *only*) efficient mechanism for the production and distribution of safe, high quality, affordable goods and services for consumers.

This claim about the delivery capabilities of a free market is offered both in defense of a certain design for the market place — it must be free and competitive — and in defense of a profit motivation on the part of its participants. My strategy will be to suppose that both parts of the claim are true, and see what follows. I will, therefore, suppose that a free competitive market is the most (or, the only) efficient mechanism for the delivery of the goods, and, the efficiency of the mechanism depends upon the self-interested pursuit of profits on the part of persons doing business in the market place. The additional

premisses needed to support the desired conclusion are less contentious and less frequently criticized. I suggest the following premisses as a plausible route to the weaker and stronger conclusions of the classical argument:

(2)   The production and distribution of safe, high quality, affordable goods and services for consumption increases the standard of living throughout the community by alleviating scarcity and its attendant moral evils — hunger, disease, crime, etc.

(3)   Alleviation of, and security against, scarcity and its attendant evils is an essential part of promoting and maintaining a high quality of life for persons, human well-being, human flourishing, the good life, etc., and these are morally good things.

7   Before completing the argument, we should pause here to deflect a misunderstanding which might otherwise affect the outcome of the argument. The joint claim of the first three premisses might easily be obscured by talk about "the quality of life", "human well-being", etc. The claim being made is not that the maximal contribution which *persons in business* can make to our quality of life is made by the self-interested pursuit of their own profits. Rather, the somewhat weaker claim is being made that the maximal contribution such persons can make to our quality of life *in their capacity as persons in business* is made by their self-interested pursuit of profits. Milton Friedman does not deny[6] that I can make, and even *should* make other contributions to the quality of your life in other capacities — e.g., as your friend, as your spouse, as your priest, etc. But, in doing business with you, I can make the fullest contribution to your welfare which it is possible for me to make *in that capacity or role*, by pursuing my own profits in a free and competi-

tive market. Contributions which I might make by serving you well in other capacities may be far greater than any I can make by doing business with you. But in making such contributions to your well-being I can only be viewed as meeting the responsibilities which accrue to me in the roles of friend, spouse, or priest; I am not thereby meeting the responsibilities of business. The question we should have before us is not "what can I do to contribute to the quality of your life?" but, rather, "what can I do, *qua* businessman, to meet the responsibilities which I have in that capacity?"

8   With this qualification in mind, the argument can be completed as follows:

(4)   Participants in a free competitive market can (or, can only) promote and secure a high quality of life throughout a community by acting always so as to increase their profits.

(5)   Those who can contribute to the promotion of moral goods, or the alleviation of moral evils, are morally justified in doing so (or, have a moral responsibility to do so).

(6)   Participants in a free competitive market are morally justified in (or, have a moral responsibility for) acting always so as to increase their profits.

We are in a position to see that, even granting the truth of the premises of this argument, there are difficulties in supposing that it supports any moral advice or moral prescriptions which can be used to guide participants in the market place as they do business. In the following sections, I will point to three weaknesses in argument, in order of increasing degree of seriousness, and *enroute* arrive at an alternative statement of the responsibilities of business. Only in the concluding section will I address directly Friedman's libertarian addenda to the argument. We shall see that when the economic efficiency argument is

answered, and its import better understood, then those addenda lose their force.

III.

9   It should first be noticed that to concede the argument in its entirety is not yet to concede that persons in business are justified in, or obligated to, pursue profits. The moral justification which the economic efficiency argument provides for either permitting or requiring the pursuit of profits does not depend upon the implausible assumption that there is something intrinsically good about making profits; rather, the pursuit of profits is argued to have intrinsically desirable consequences for the quality of life in our communities. The entire weight of the argument is borne by those consequences. Thus, if there should arise any need for a trade-off between promoting the ends of profit seekers and promoting social ends, then only those trade-offs which favor the promotion of socially desirable ends will receive the moral backing of the efficiency argument. But our present economy is agreed by all sides to be one in which such trade − offs *are* required.[7] Trade restrictions, corporate taxes, and a whole net of government constraints on business make ours a market in which there is not a direct relationship between increasing profits and increasing the quality of our lives. Consequently, even if the argument is sound, the conclusion which it yields is not that participants in any actual market are morally justified in pursuing, let alone morally obliged to pursue their individual profits at every point in their market activities. It may well be true that this only points to flaws in our economic systems as they stand, and the defender of the argument will, perhaps, justly respond that the point only requires us to urge deregulation of the present market. None-

theless, the conclusion we are forced to by the economic realities is that the efficiency argument cannot be used to support saying that persons in business ought always to act in such a way as to increase their profits. Furthermore, the nature of the support which the argument does try to throw behind profit seeking reveals that at all points where our less than free and competitive market requires a trade-off between the public good and profits, morality will demand that we sacrifice profits for the public good. If an increase in the quality of our lives can work to ground the morality of profit seeking in a free economy, then surely it will work to ground the charge that profit seeking is immoral at any point that it decreases the quality of life.

IV.

10 It might be thought that the case made in the previous section only establishes that, in our fallible world, the moral advice to people in business to pursue their profits is defeasible on special occasions and, so, allows occasional exceptions. We should therefore see what happens in a less imperfect world. Let us suppose that not only are the premisses of the argument true, but that we also have an ideal libertarian market, of perfect freedom and perfect competition. In this happy world, a firm's profits are thought to be a perfect measure of the contributions which the firm makes to our standard of living. Consumers will be assured that those contributions, in the form of goods and services, which business is capable of making to our well-being are being made to the fullest, and business can be assured of the greatest profits commensurate with that contribution. In such a world, the entrepreneur who lived according to the maxim "act always so as to increase your profits" would at the same time always act so as to increase the standard of living throughout the community. Nonetheless, I shall argue that even in such a world, there are limits on the extent to which the pursuit of profits receives moral justification *via* the economic efficiency argument.

11 Recall that the moral justification which the pursuit of profits receives from the economic efficiency argument derives solely from the contribution which that pursuit makes to the *quality of our lives*; it does not derive from the intrinsic value of the activity of seeking profits, but, nor does it derive from the contribution which pursuing profits makes to the *standard of living* in the community. It is only in so far as seeking profits promotes the quality of life that we defend profit seeking; but, even in an ideal economy, how far is that? The third premiss of the argument states, quite plausibly, that the "delivery of the goods" is an essential part of promoting human well-being. The larger, more complex, and more interdependent human communities become, the more likely it is to be true that that part of a life of desirable quality will be provided by market mechanisms. Our standard of living, as it is measured by production and consumption, may be granted to be an essential component in our quality of life without thereby granting very much of moral interest. Perhaps there are rare individuals (though this is doubtful) who measure the quality of their lives by their standard of living alone, where that standard is viewed in terms of the goods and services made available for them to use as they will. But in general, however much we differ in what we take a high quality of life to contain, our view of it is much more capacious than our view of our standard of living. Most of us view it as containing certain ingredients which it is no part of the capabilities of a market, however perfect, to

deliver — such "intangibles" as love, friendship, virtues, enjoyable activities, and so on.

12 So long as there is a difference between what makes up a high standard of living and what makes up a high quality of life, there will be limits to the extent to which the economic efficiency argument can justify the pursuit of profits. The reason is this: the moral value which we place on any increase in our standard of living derives from the contribution which that increase makes to our quality of life; but so long as our standard of living is only one of the components of our quality of life, then the moral value of an increasing standard of living will obey a principle of "diminishing moral utility". Equivalent consecutive increases in the standard of living will not yield equivalent consecutive increases in the quality of life; as our standard of living increases up to a certain point, the contribution which such increases make to the quality of our lives will diminish towards zero. Let us see why.

13 Suppose, contrary to what has been suggested, that increases of equivalent size in a person's standard of living always resulted in increases of equivalent size in that person's quality of life. Now consider the case of a person who lacks love, friendships, the promise of salvation, or whatever in your view goes into a high quality of life beyond a high standard of living. Suppose that this person has the same high standard of living as others in the community, but that they, unlike him, also have the intangibles to which he has been denied access. We would surely think that those who have an abundance of these "intangible goods" are better off than the one who lacks them. But, now, suppose that the man who lacks the intangibles acquires the means to increase his wealth, and so, his standard of living, without limit. By hypothesis, as he

does so, he will at some point acquire a higher, more desirable quality of life than the others, despite the fact that, unlike them, he will never be blessed with the intangibles. Thus, it would appear, love, friendship, and the like, are no essential part of the quality of life we enjoy. Any quality of life which can be achieved by having those things can also be reached, and even surpassed, merely by acquiring a high enough standard of living. But this consequence runs entirely against the grain of our view of a desirable quality of life as containing such intangibles, however much we may differ as to what they are. The consequence is avoided by denying that increases in our standard of living are always accompanied by commensurate increases in our quality of life, and conceding that there are limits on the extent to which greater access to goods and services can make for a better life. No doubt an increase in our standard of living which lifts us from hunger and disease to satiation and health will be assigned a high moral value; but the move from economic sufficiency to affluence need not be thought to have as great a value to us, and the further move from affluence to opulence will have even less value. At some point, further affluence will always become superfluous in the pursuit of a better life.

14 We can see now why the fact of diminishing moral utility limits the range of the efficiency argument in justifying the pursuit of profits. In a community in which a level of affluence is reached which is sufficient for doing its part in contributing to a desirable quality of life, further increases in our standard of living cease to make any additional contribution, and, so, further profit seeking cannot be given moral justification by citing consequences for the quality of our lives. The very best that the economic efficiency argument can do to defend the pursuit of profit,

even in an ideal economy, is justify the pursuit of profit up to the point where the community has reached some level of economic sufficiency or affluence; beyond that point, profit seeking lacks the backing of the argument. Furthermore, before that point is reached, but as it is more and more closely approached, the strength of the support which the efficiency argument gives to profit seeking diminishes.

15   I have not made the claim that our society has already reached the point of zero moral returns from profit seeking; but it seems arguable that we are approaching it, and the claim is always worth seriously entertaining. The market place, fueled as it is by the profit motive, stands to benefit from obscuring our sense of how close we might be, and when we may have had enough of what it can provide.

V.

16 I have argued thus far that even if the economic efficiency argument is sound, it does not yield moral advice or prescriptions for persons who do business in our present economies; also, it has been argued that the considerations raised in the efficiency argument do not support unlimited pursuit even in an ideally free and competitive market. Both arguments against the classical cause have assumed that the argument for the cause contains only true premisses; the first counterargument assumes the soundness of the efficiency argument and the second counterargument challenges only the range of application of the conclusion. In this section, the soundness of the argument will be challenged.

17   It may be replied to the considerations raised in the preceding sections that they show only that profit seeking is not *always* morally justified or obligatory. Nonetheless, in so far as our present markets approximate a free and competitive ideal, and in so far as our standard of living has not (or, has not *clearly*) reached a point of zero moral returns on profit seeking, some (or even much) profit seeking is still justified by the efficiency argument. Furthermore, nothing I have said addressed directly the stronger form of the argument which leads to the conclusion that profit seeking is morally obligatory. If maintaining and securing our standard of living depends upon profit seeking, and if directing the attention of persons in business to desirable social ends and, thereby, away from profit seeking would undermine the efficiency of the market to such an extent that we would run the serious risk of lapsing into scarcity and its attendant evils, then participants in the world of business are morally obliged to pursue their individual profits.

18   But it is, we shall now see, a mistake to suppose that these considerations, even if all true, would support thinking that business has a social responsibility to pursue profits. Seeing why they fail will lead us to an alternative statement of the responsibilities of business.

19   Let us assume, once again, that the first premiss of the efficiency argument is true, and that when and only when market participants (in an ideally free and competitive market) pursue their individual profits, can we be assured of security against the evils of scarcity. We noted earlier that the economic efficiency argument gives whatever justification it does to market activities only by reference to the contributions which such activity makes to the quality of our lives. That fact would not be changed simply because the economy was so arranged that we had a perfectly direct relationship between increasing profits and increasing (or maintaining) the quality of our lives. But it is only supposing that a

perfectly direct relationship between these two factors does make a difference to the *source* of our rights and obligations which could lead us to suppose that there is a moral responsibility on the part of business to increase its profits. An analogy should make clear why this is so.

20   Consider a boiler tender who is responsible for keeping the pressure in a boiler within a specified range; he proceeds by opening and closing valves and adjusting the temperature while watching a pressure gauge. As long as the gauge is functioning properly and is properly calibrated, all he need attend to is the position of the needle on the gauge. If he should come to describe his own responsibility as being that of keeping the needle within a certain range, his description of his responsibilities is perfectly harmless, but it is a harmless *mis*-description of his responsibilities. That it is a misdescription, and not merely an alternative reformulation of his duty, is shown by the fact that if the gauge were faulty, he would be clearly duty bound to try as best he could to keep the pressure within its proper range, despite the fact that, then, the needle would no longer stay within the range which ought to, but does not, indicate that pressure. In such a situation, to let the pressure go where it will, in order to ensure that the needle stays where it ought, would be the height of negligence. To take his "harmless" misstatement of his responsibilities seriously would be an invitation to catastrophe.

21   In a world of perfect pressure gauges, our boiler tender would not be forced to choose between describing his duty as a duty to keep the needle in a certain position or describing it as a duty to keep the pressure in a certain range; in practice, they will come down to the same thing. Likewise, if we grant that the first premiss of the economic efficiency argument is true, and if we supposed that we lived and worked in a perfectly free and competitive market where profits were a perfect gauge of a firm's contributions to our quality of life, then it would be a harmless *mis*-statement of the responsibilities of business to say that their sole social responsibility was to increase their profits. Nonetheless, what the efficiency argument supports as a proper description of the social responsibilities of business is not increasing profit, but, rather, producing and distributing safe, high quality, affordable goods and services for consumers. In the case of the boiler tender, it was only because maintaining the pressure and positioning the needle on the gauge came down to the same thing (given an ideal gauge) and because *maintaining the pressure was his real responsibility*, that we were at all tempted to accept the misstatement of his responsibility as keeping the needle in position. Likewise, it is only because delivering the goods and making profits are thought to come down to the same thing (in an ideal market), and because the delivery of the goods is the social responsibility of business, that we are at all tempted to accept the misstatement of the responsibility of business as increasing profits.

22   If we think that delivery of the goods, to whatever extent is sufficient for maintaining a desirable quality of life, is a desirable social end, then what this argument shows is that business does, after all, have a moral responsibility to promote desirable social ends. According to my conclusion, it is *no part* of the social responsibility of business to increase its profits though, assuming the truth of the first premiss of the economic efficiency argument, and taking into account the considerations raised in previous sections, pursuing profits may sometimes be morally permissible. In the following and concluding section I will raise and address two objections to my conclusion.

VI.

23 The doctrine that firms have a social responsibility, combined with the claim that they have no responsibility to make profits, is argued (by the contemporary libertarian descendants of Adam Smith) to have dangerous consequences.[8] The libertarian addenda to the classical efficiency argument proceed by indicating the dangerous social and political consequences of the doctrine of social responsibility. Since I have argued for a version of that doctrine and rejected in total the strong libertarian conclusion that business has a social responsibility to increase its profits, it will be necessary to speak directly to the so-called "dangerous" consequences.

24   It might first be objected that by following a moral prescription to meet their social obligations, and not attending to profits, corporate executives will be distracted from that course of action on which the efficient operation of the market depends. Businesses attending to their social responsibilities, and not to their profits, are like the boiler tender who attends to the pressure in the tank, and not to the needle on the pressure gauge. Even if their responsibility is to promote certain social ends, they cannot accurately gauge how well they are doing that except by attending to their profits. Even if profits are not a perfect measure, in our less than perfectly free and competitive market, of a firm's contributions to our quality of life, they are nonetheless the best measure we have. The problem here is epistemic, not moral. Just as the boiler tender has no way to gauge the pressure other than by watching the pressure gauge, so the person in business has no way to gauge contributions to our quality of life, except by attending to profits. To allow boiler tenders and firms to exercise their own best judgement without re-

course to such aids as gauges and profits is to invite catastrophe. But this objection is misguided.

25   The heart of the defense of the free competitive market, and the pursuit of profits, was the assumption that business best promotes the public good by seeking profits precisely because it will discover that the best way to make profits is to provide safer, cheaper, lower cost goods and services for consumers. Thus, the self-regulatory nature of the market which is meant to lead (albeit unintentionally) to desirable social ends requires that persons in business will be able to judge what counts as a safer, higher quality, or lower priced commodity. But that is all that I have argued they have a social responsibility to do. If they can do those things well enough for the purposes of the defenders of the first premiss of the economic efficiency argument, then they can do it well enough for the purposes of meeting their social responsibilities *qua* business.

26   A second objection which might be leveled against my conclusions derives from the contractual agreements which are made by individuals in doing business. Thus, a corporate executive, for example, is described by Milton Friedman as

> an employee of the owners of the business. He has a direct responsibility to his employers. That responsibility is to conduct the business in accordance with their desires, which generally will be to make as much money as possible...[9]

Now this point, by itself, does nothing at all to support the claim, which Friedman is defending, that corporate executives have a social responsibility to increase profits. As is well-known, no one has a responsibility to keep any contracts or agreements if it should turn out that what has been promised, agreed, or contracted to, is itself immoral. But, even if we add the additional premiss that making profits is not immoral, such responsibilities as Friedman mentions would not count as moral or social responsibilities. Even though society has a strong interest in seeing that just agreements and contracts are kept, and so we have a general obligation to keep our agreements, it does not follow that the contents of our agreements have a similar status. Thus, although I may owe a general duty to society to keep my promises, and though I have promised to lend you my car for the weekend, it does not follow that I owe a duty to society to lend you my car for the weekend. Though it turns out, that, on this occasion, the only way I can meet my obligation to society to keep my promise is by lending you my car, my doing *that* (lending the car to you) is not a duty owed to society. My doing that is no part of what society has an interest in, though my keeping my promises is.

27   Friedman's worry, thus far, simply mistakes the notion of a social responsibility. But he goes further:

> What does it mean to say that the corporate executive has a "social responsibility" in his capacity as a businessman? If this statement is not pure rhetoric, it must mean that he is to act in some way that is not in the interest of his employers.[10]

and:

> The executive is exercising a distinct "social responsibility", rather than serving as an agent of the stockholders or the customers or the employees, only if he spends the money in a different way than they would have spent it.[11]

Friedman is here creating a false dilemma. He represents as incompatible alternatives the options of meeting social responsibilities and abiding by agreements with employers and stockholders. But if the social responsibility which a person has *in his capacity as a businessman* is simply the production and distribution of

safe, quality, affordable goods and services, then, according to the doctrines of the free market, by meeting *those* responsibilities, he will be keeping his agreements to make profits for his employers. They are not incompatible alternatives; rather, the one is supposed to be the most efficient means to the other. If that turns out not to be true, then the moral defense of the free market collapses.

28   Finally, an objection to the view that business has a social responsibility to promote desirable social ends, and no responsibility to increase profits, comes from those who, like Friedman, are concerned to protect the liberties of persons in a free society. The promotion of social ends is the business of those we elect to represent our interests. By inviting corporate executives to promote social ends, we are in effect inviting private citizens to exercise their sometimes considerable influence to shape policy according to their personal visions of what makes for a better quality of life. When there is no consensus as to what makes for a better quality of life, we do not want powerful corporate executives, whom we cannot remove by the ballot, forming public policy according to their private visions.

29   This argument against the doctrine that businesses have a social responsibility mistakenly supposes that the social responsibilities of businessmen go beyond doing what they can to ensure the production and distribution of safe, high quality, affordable goods and services. But nothing in the efficiency argument supports that supposition. What it supports saying is only that business has a moral responsibility for the delivery of the goods. Of course, not all the responsibilities which persons in business have accrue to them in their capacity as businessmen. Meeting the responsibilities *of that role* does not in-

volve activities which could threaten the liberties of free persons or which could undermine the roles of elected representatives. On the other hand, by doing what they can to meet those responsibilities which they take themselves to have *outside* of their roles in business, businessmen may well undertake to do things which have dangerous consequences. But so may we all. Any individual with sufficient power or wealth is capable of doing things which either promote or destroy the quality of life of others, and we should no doubt maintain close controls on the extent to which any person is capable of so influencing others. Friedman's fear that businesses, when aiming to promote some vision of a better life for the community, will undermine our liberty to pursue our own and varied visions, is not a fear of the consequences which might ensue if businesses meet *their* social responsibilities. The responsibilities which come with doing business – i.e., effectively delivering the goods – are too narrow to pose that threat. The responsibilities which individuals may take themselves to have as citizens, as members of a political party, as members of a church group, and so on, *do* pose the threat which Friedman sees, but even there the threat is contained by limiting the powers of individuals to impose their views on others, not by *denying* that there are such responsibilities.

30   The error which I have just been attributing to Friedman dates back to Plato. In his argument with Thrasymachus in the first book of the *Republic*, Socrates argues that the doctor who charges a fee is acting in two different capacities. In charging a fee, he is acting *qua* businessman. So, on the account which emerges, it becomes the function of the person (who happens also to be a doctor) to make money *in so far as he is doing business*. But my suggestion has been that this

dichotomy – the doctor/businessman dichotomy – is a false dichotomy. Even though it is not the doctor's function to make money but, as Plato rightly says, to promote the health of his patients, it may still be true that the function of the businessman is to promote health, if the businessman *is* a doctor, and his line of business is practicing medicine. In a world in which medical services are acquired in the market place, to practice medicine is to do one's business, and so one's function *in that line of business*, is to promote health. Likewise, if one is engaged in the business of manufacturing automobiles, one's social "function" is to produce a safe, quality product at a reasonable price.

31   We thus find that granting the assumption that a free competitive market is the most (or, the only) effective mechanism for promoting a better quality of life does not have the consequence that persons in business have a responsibility to increase their profits; it does not have the consequence that it is always (or, even in general) morally permissible to seek profits; nor does that initial assumption conflict with the doctrine that business has a social responsibility to promote certain desirable social ends. Whether or not that initial assumption should be granted is yet another problem.

NOTES

1. I will be using the expression "classical" more broadly than usual, referring to systems of thought which share certain assumptions about the self-regulatory nature of the market. It thus encompasses the theories of Smith and Ricardo, the neoclassical or "marginalist" theories of Marshall and his followers, as well as contemporary libertarian figures like Hayek and Friedman.

2. See, for example, Narveson, Jan: 'Justice and The Business Society', in *Ethical Theory and Business*,

2nd ed., Tom L. Beauchamp and Norman E. Bowie (eds.), Prentice-Hall, Inc., Englewood Cliffs, New Jersey. Especially pp. 620-1.

3. 'The Social Responsibility of Business Is to Increase Its Profits', *New York Times Magazine* (Sept. 13, 1970); reprinted in 1983, *Ethical Issues in Business*, 2nd. ed., Donaldson and Werhane, (eds.), Prentice-Hall, Inc., New Jersey. Page numbers cited below are from this reprint. Also see Friedman, M.: 1962, *Capitalism and Freedom*, The University of Chicago Press, especially Chapter VIII.

4. *The Wealth of Nations*, Bk. IV, Chapter ii.

5. Friedman, *op. cit.*, p. 133.

6. On the contrary, he insists on it. Discussion of his conclusion often proceeds by ignoring this important qualification. His *New York Times Magazine* essay emphasizes the need for the qualification in several explicit passages, though his earlier defense of what I am calling "the stronger conclusion" does not make the qualification explicit (see *Capitalism and Freedom, op. cit.* pp. 133-6).

7. All sides agree that the pursuit of profits in the present market has morally undesirable consequences in particular cases; what they disagree about is the diagnosis and the cure. Libertarians trace the cause to inadequate freedom or competition, and so call for revisions in the present system to increase these; their opponents trace the cause to excessive zeal in the pursuit of profit, and so call for closer regulation of market activity. But all agree that things are not as they should be in the market place.

8. See Levitt, Theodore: 1958, 'The Dangers of Social Responsibility', *Harvard Business Review* (Sept. – Oct.).

9. *op. cit.*, 'The Social Responsibility of Business Is To Increase Its Profits', p. 239.

10. *Ibid.*, p. 240.

11. *Ibid.*, p. 240.

Questions

1. What are the six premises of the economic efficiency argument, according to Jacobsen?

2. What is Jacobsen's point in Section III?

3. (a) What relationship between standard of living and quality of life does Jacobsen establish in Section IV?

   (b) Rewrite the third premise, by adding no more than four words, to embody his point.

4. Explain Jacobsen's point about what the social responsibility of business is, with reference to the boiler tender analogy.

5. Consider the notion that profit can be maximized by producing and distributing unsafe, low-quality goods and services.

   (a) Which premise would this, if true, undermine?

   (b) What then would be the implication for the conclusion that "profits ... are the best measure of a firm's contribution to the welfare of others" (P1) and are therefore deserved?

6. The starting point for Jacobsen's paper is based on a consequentialist approach – profit is morally acceptable because of the consequences of its contribution to the social good. What defence of profit-seeking might the following suggest?

   (a) an intuitionist

   (b) a Kantian

   (c) a natural law proponent

   (d) a religionist

7. Chris Sarlo comments (private correspondence) that Jacobsen incorrectly identifies the argument he examines as the libertarian one. According to Sarlo, the libertarian defense of profit-seeking is as follows:

    "Each person is entitled to their own life and the free use of their own (rightly acquired) property (this would include the things that you own, the things that you create, and the things that you bring into being as the result of contracts you have made with others). As long as they do not interfere with the rights of others to use and enjoy their property, people are free to make choices and profit from the property they own. The important point for those who respect the primacy of individual property rights is that each of us is entitled to benefit from (profit from) any non-coercive use of our property, including our human capital. The beneficial economic effects of a profit and loss system are a happy byproduct."

    (a) Is this an argument for the moral *acceptability* of profit-seeking or the moral *goodness* of profit-seeking?

    (b) Do you agree that each person has a right to their own life and property?

    (c) What are the tricky spots of this view? (Which parts will be difficult to determine?)

Are Profits Deserved?

Grant A. Brown

ABSTRACT. N. Scott Arnold has argued forcefully that, for the most part, those who win profits (and suffer losses) in a market economy deserve them. According to Arnold, profit opportunities arise when there are malallocations of resources, which entrepreneurs initiate changes in production to correct. If they succeed, they simultaneously further the essential point of the market system — to meet the needs and wants of consumers — and they make profits; if they do not, then they stand to suffer losses. I argue that the structure of modern corporate enterprises tends to channel income into the hands of those whose entrepreneurial contribution is diminishingly small — namely stockholders — and away from those within the firm who genuinely participate in the entrepreneurial role.

Grant A. Brown, "Are Profits Deserved?" *Journal of Business Ethics* 11.2 (February 1992): 105-114. © 1992 by Kluwer Academic Publishers. Reprinted with permission of the publisher; the author could not be located.

1   Do those who win profits (and suffer losses) in a market economy deserve them? N. Scott Arnold has argued that, in general, they do.[1] In this paper I wish to raise some doubts about this claim, at least so far as it applies to familiar mar-

ket systems in the western world. Arnold believes that if we consider the correct positive account of how and why profits (and losses) come about in a market economy, we will be well on our way to seeing that they are deserved by those who bring them about, i.e., by "entrepreneurs." I begin, then, by summarizing the account he provides.

Arnold's account

2   We must first identify the role played by entrepreneurs in production, as distinct from that of capitalists, on the one hand, and of workers, on the other. These three basic roles can be defined in terms of what each provides or does in the productive process. Capitalists, of course, are defined as the providers of capital; and workers as the providers of labour. The role of the entrepreneur is more complicated to state. As the etymology of the word indicates, entrepreneurs may be characterized as those who acquire control over capital and labour (through loans and labour contracts, say), and thereby "bring together the needed factors of production. Entrepreneurship consists essentially of organizing production – deciding what to produce, when to produce it, and how much to produce at what price" (p. 388) – "or to set the broad parameters within which these decisions are to be made and to hire people to work out the details" (p. 396). "Entrepreneurship is not management; indeed, often entrepreneurs hire others to manage the firm" (p. 388).

3   Now, if entrepreneurs are to earn an income (referred to in this discussion as "profit") after paying their capitalists, workers, and suppliers the going rate for their factor inputs, then they must exercise particular talents. They must be "alert to inefficiencies in existing ways of doing business" (p. 397). "In the most dramatic cases,

the entrepreneur is a great innovator and gambler. He conceives of a whole new product or service ... [or] figures out a way to drive down production costs (e.g., by adopting a certain technological or organizational innovation)" (p. 388). This brings about profit as Arnold explains:

The marginal value product of some of his factors of production will go up, since he is using less of them, let us suppose, to produce the product. However, he is paying the factor owners the going rate. The spread between cost and price is profit. A similar situation arises when a new product is produced and marketed for which there is great demand. Obviously, these situations cannot last, since competitors will imitate successful entrepreneurs; as a result, factor prices will tend to be bid up and product prices will tend to be driven down. Thus there will be a tendency for profits to be wiped out as a new equilibrium is approached.... [T]he main source of profits in the final analysis is the malallocation of factors of production. This malallocation results from the fact that technology, consumer tastes, and other ultimate determinants of value are in a constant state of flux. Since no one is omniscient, some factors of production are always being used in nonoptimal ways. The successful entrepreneur is the one who is alert to differences in the marginal value products of factors of production and is in a position to do something about it.... Other potential entrepreneurs are unaware of these discrepancies; otherwise they would have been competed away. The successful entrepreneur, then, can be characterized as someone who exploits social ignorance about the malallocation of resources. (pp. 388-389)

4   The various roles identified above are elucidated *functionally*, in terms of what contribution each makes to the productive process. Thus capitalists, entrepreneurs, and workers are not

necessarily distinct individuals within a firm: one individual may play all three roles, or a collection of individuals may jointly play any single role. Indeed, typically these roles are highly fragmented within modern corporate structures – a point I shall return to later in my critique. The significance of this point for present purposes is to avoid a possible confusion, namely to conflate profit, the income of the entrepreneur, with producer surplus or return on investment. Producer surplus is the difference between the market price for a particular good and the lowest price for which the producer would be willing to go into business of providing that good. When someone fulfills not only the role of entrepreneur, but is also a provider of investment capital or a supplier of natural resources or a skilled labourer, producer surplus may include some amounts which are attributable to interest or factor rents (as well as to great efficiency). Return on investment always includes an (imputable) interest component. The entrepreneur's income does not – *by definition* – include interest, factor rents, salary, or wages.[2] Arnold is not concerned in the article in question to claim that market wage and salary scales, factor rents, and interest rates are deserved.[3]

5 Arnold next provides an account of the concept of desert, particularly within an institutional setting. Since I do not wish to take exception to this account, I will summarize it briefly. Arnold's account explains what determines two things: (a) the basis of desert claims; and (b) the nature of the objects of desert (rewards or punishments). As for the former, the "basal reason" for a desert claim is determined by the essential goals or purposes of the institution within which the desert claim is being made. For example, the essential point of athletic competitions is to determine who, among a given group, is the most

skilled in some specified way; hence *being* the best among the group is the basal reason for deserving that recognition, as well as whatever prize may go along with it. The best athlete *deserves* this, even though others may try harder or have more virtuous characters.[4]

6 It is important to note that recognition and prizes do nor always go to the most deserving athlete – that is, the most *talented* one. Sometimes they go to the one who was more lucky – who happened to *perform* better. Here we must distinguish between desert claims and claims of entitlement. Entitlements are (property) rights generated by the rules of an institution: he who crosses the finish line first is entitled to the gold medal. This is true even if the most talented athlete (the one who *deserved* the gold medal) lost the race only because he was accidentally tripped up by a third party. Desert claims do not usually establish entitlements; nevertheless, well-designed institutions will minimize the gap between entitlement and desert by minimizing the gap between ability (or basal reason) and performance (or rules of entitlement).

7 The general character of the objects of desert is also determined by the institution's essential goals. If one of the essential goals of an institution is to give positive recognition to a complex of characteristics, the rules that specify what rewards are due to the most deserving can be criticized on the grounds that they are inappropriate for that goal. The rewards offered might be judged ugly or offensive or, what is perhaps more common, insufficiently attractive to motivate the best potential participants to participate in the institution (p. 392). Further, where the things deserved and the basal reasons for desert are both variable quantities, it is intuitively appealing that these should be related by a principle of proportionality. Grades on academic tests generally fit this

bill: students' mastery of the material and relevant skills can range from nil to complete, and on a well-designed test this is reflected in a grading scale from 0 to 100 per cent, or (if the subject matter does not admit of such precise grading) from F to A. This proportionality principle is a consequence of the root idea of desert, namely that there should be a "fit" between the basal reason and the things deserved.

8   Finally, in order to bring together his positive account of how profits come about in a market economy with his conception of desert, Arnold must identify the essential purpose of a market system. A market, he says, is a production-distribution system which allocates, via voluntary exchange, (rights over) scarce goods and resources. The social point of this allocational system is (to permit people) to meet those wants and needs of consumers which can be satisfied by scarce and exchangeable goods and services (p. 396) – though not necessarily to do so in a consequentialist, maximizing manner. Now, as we saw, entrepreneurs are the ones who decide upon the basic structure or configuration that productive resources will take; and if they do this successfully, then they will improve the overall efficiency of the system. Their income, profit, is dependent upon correcting malallocations of resources: either by bringing to bear some kind of new discovery or technological advance, or by catering to changes in the preferences of consumers. "This suggests that the basal reason for a desert claim on behalf of entrepreneurs is their alertness to an inoptimal allocation of resources.... But why do they deserve the profits they uncover rather than, say, a pat on the back and a letter of commendation?" (p. 397).

9   Arnold gives three reasons for the fittingness of profits as a reward for successful entrepreneurial activity (p. 397). First, to the extent that entrepreneurs are not allowed to keep the profits they uncover, this reduces the incentive to introduce socially useful innovation in production, which defeats the essential goal of the institution. Second, allowing entrepreneurs to keep profits tends to give control over productive resources to those who have demonstrated a capacity to use such resources wisely. The successful entrepreneur usually reinvests some of his profits in an attempt to capture more. Finally. winning large profits by some serves as an effective signal to competitors to follow suit by making the appropriate changes. Conversely and similarly, if entrepreneurs were not made to suffer the losses they bring about when unsuccessful, they would have little incentive to exercise due caution in their entrepreneurial activities, thereby squandering social wealth. Allowing entrepreneurs to suffer their losses also takes resources out of the hands of those who have demonstrated an inability to use them wisely. And the losses incurred by some entrepreneurs will send an effective signal to others not to repeat their mistakes. In short, allowing entrepreneurs to keep profits and suffer losses appropriately brings control over productive resources together with personal responsibility for results; and it does this in a way that satisfies the proportionality principle: the bigger the entrepreneur's profits (or losses), the more serious had been (is) the malallocation of resources.

10   It remains to identify more concretely who the entrepreneurs are in a modern market system. Says Arnold:

Not all – or even most – entrepreneurs are inventors with a little marketing skill. In a capitalist economy, they are the independent business men, the promoters, the managers of large corporations with significant stock holdings, the arbitrage experts in the stock market, the instigators of hostile takeovers, and so on – and to a lesser extent, anyone who owns any stock in a firm; in short, entrepreneurs are the ones who decide where and how capital should be invested. (p. 397)

The entrepreneurial function

11 Much of the production in our market system takes place within very complex organizations, i.e., large, publicly held corporations. In order to evaluate Arnold's conservative claims about who deserves the profit arising therefrom, we must determine whether or not he is right in identifying the actors who play the role of entrepreneur within these corporations, as well as what their relative contributions to that function are. I contend that once the entrepreneurial function is more carefully located within the productive process, it will become apparent that many – perhaps most – of those who participate in this role do not directly share in the deserts (profits and losses). Others, whose entrepreneurial contribution is tenuous at best, reap profits and losses where they do not deserve them.

12 I begin by examining the structure of a modern corporate enterprise, in particular the relationship between stockholders (whom Arnold counts as entrepreneurs) and the managers (most of whom he does not). Legally speaking, this relationship is characterized as follows:

(1) corporate officers like the president and the treasurer are agents of the corporation itself; (2) the board of directors is the ultimate decision-making body in the corporation (and in a sense the group most appropriately identified with "the corporation"); (3) directors are not agents of the corporation but are *sui generis*; (4) neither officers nor directors are agents of the stockholders; (5) both officers and directors are "fiduciaries" with respect to the corporation and its stockholders.[5] Clark continues:

By statute in every state, the board of directors of a corporation has the power and duty to manage or supervise its business. The stockholders do not. To appreciate this point fully, consider the following activities: setting the ultimate goal of the corporation – for example, whether its legal purpose will be to maximize profits; choosing the corporation's line of business – for example, whether it will engage in retailing general merchandise or refining oil; hiring and firing the full-time executives who will actually run the company, and exercising supervisory power with respect to the day-to-day operations of the business. Stockholders of a large publicly held corporation *do not* do these things; as a matter of efficient operation of a large firm with numerous residual claimants they *should not* do them; and under the typical corporate statute and case law they *cannot* do them."[6]

13 The upshot is that stockholders exercise extremely limited control over production within large, publicly held corporations. They can vote for or against "organic corporate changes" (mergers, charter amendments, and dissolution) – but only if the board has formally voted to approve the change and has put it before the stockholders. The stockholders themselves cannot initiate or force through such a change even with 100 percent support. "To influence corporate managers, then, stockholders can vote for directors and approve or veto director-initiated organic changes, but cannot do much else. The important part of this description is the negative clause."[7] Given this, can one reasonably count "anyone who owns any stock in a firm" an entrepreneur? Legally, stockholders do not and cannot do any of the activities which Arnold

identifies with the entrepreneurial function. What might lead Arnold to think that they do?

14   One possibility is the thought that stockholders have considerable indirect control over production through trading activities on the stock market. It does not matter how or even if stockholders vote at their meetings; what matters is their "voting with their feet" by selling their shares if they see things going badly, or by retaining them or buying more if they anticipate things going well.[8] This view is incoherent, since for every trade on the stock market there is a willing buyer and a willing seller. The former anticipates that the stock will increase in value (relative to other investment opportunities), while the latter anticipates that the stock will decrease in value. So what message does this exchange send to the managers of the corporation? The point is that the stock market is a *secondary* market which does not directly involve the corporation itself, any more than selling used Pintos involves the Ford Motor Company. All the stock market does is change the principals of the corporation; so far as the day-to-day operations of the corporation go, these changes are quite irrelevant. Indeed, empirical evidence suggests that the link between financial markets and real economic activity is becoming rather tenuous. Lester Thurow observes that "1988 was the fastest year of economic growth during the decade, [yet this growth came] in the aftermath of the most severe stock market collapse since 1929."[9]

15   Perhaps the argument could be rescued if we restrict it to stockholders who obtained their stock in the *primary* market, i.e., to purchasers of new stock issues. For clearly, in this case, the enterprise offering stock will be affected by people's decisions to buy or not: purchasing the stock tells managers to go ahead with the expansion (or whatever), and not doing so indicates that there is a lack of confidence in the enterprise. Now, it should be noticed how severely this restricts the scope of Arnold's claim: "Over a forty-year interval, on average, 98.5% of common stock purchased by investors in a given year involved the purchase of already existing shares rather than newly issued shares [*The Wheat Report* (1969)]."[10] Yet even this restriction will not rescue the case for including stockholders as entrepreneurs. For it remains the case that purchasers of new stock still give over control of production to others. There appears to be no relevant difference, for present purposes, between the purchaser of new stock and the bank manager who offers a loan: both base their decisions on the expected viability of the proposal; both could scuttle the proposal by refusing to offer the funds; and both largely concede control of the funds once they offer them.

16   Of course, the stockholder does share more directly in the *risk* of the venture than does the normal lender or the bondholder, since the stockholder buys into the enterprise and is the last to receive proceeds, after the firm's other commitments have been met. Stockholders are residual claimants, whose claims are not underwritable. In compensation for taking this greater risk, stockholders expect higher returns. But all this is irrelevant to the case at hand, since the distinction between equity and debt is in no way related to the role of the entrepreneur according to Arnold's account (which I accept). Moreover, Arnold explicitly rejects the common view that risk-bearing is a basal reason for the desert of profits. His reason for rejecting this is that risk and profitability are not in general directly related: big risks do not necessarily lead to big profits or losses, nor small risks to small profits and losses.[11] Thus the proportionality

principle would as a rule be violated if risk were the basal reason for the desert of profit. Stockholders cannot be counted as entrepreneurs given the legal separation of ownership and control within large, publicly held corporations, since control of productive forces is necessary to the entrepreneurial function (pp. 397, 399).

17   Since the common view, that profit is a reward for bearing risk, is very attractive to many theorists, I add another reason for rejecting it. Suppose we decide to flip a coin: if it comes up heads you win $1, and if it comes up tails I win $1. Now suppose it comes up tails: does that mean I *deserve* the $1 for accepting the risk of the game, quite apart from being *entitled* to it by the rules of the game? One might be lead to think so if one were to commit the error of thinking that since I do not deserve *not* to have the $1, therefore I must deserve to have it. But this is a false dichotomy I neither deserve it nor deserve not to have it.[12] I would rather say that I simply got lucky; desert does not enter into games of pure chance at all. When we move to games of partial chance and partial skill, such as betting on the ponies, desert does enter into it: the more skillful better deserves to win more than the less skillful.[13] But here the desert is proportional to skill, not to the bearing of risk as such. The "as such" here is important, since skill is shown by the manner in which one *handles* risk. For example, the skillful bettor knows enough to reduce risk by betting less on races that are harder to predict. By reducing risk, he wins more – and deserves to win more; his betting is more rational. Similarly, one who is willing to take risks in proportion to the expected return deserves to win more than one who is highly risk-averse. This is because the former is more rational and thus more skillful than the latter, it is not because he simply is willing to undertake risks which the latter will not.

18   This line of reasoning may provide a basis for saying that (some) profits and losses earned in the stock market are deserved after all. More skilled traders can perhaps make "abnormal profits"[14] at the expense of the less skilled – and when they do they deserve them. But if my general rejection of the idea that stockholders deserve profit is sound, then even skillful traders do not deserve *all* the profit accruing to their investments; only the abnormal profit *margins* which their superior skill reaps. It bears noting, however, that many analysts believe that it is not possible to consistently earn abnormal profits, barring trading on insider information. Abnormal profit is very largely a matter of luck, and to that extent is not really deserved after all. Thus this wrinkle is not much comfort to Arnold, since (1) inasmuch as luck accounts for much of the abnormal profits people get, it is undeserved on any account; (2) in any case, abnormal profit margins are typically only a small part of all the profit accruing to stockholders; and (3) skill in trading is not Arnold's basal reason for desert – stock traders still do not organize production.

19   According to the above analysis, the stock market is essentially a mechanism for matching more risk-seeking providers of capital with genuine entrepreneurs. Stockholders are basically capitalists who have chosen to be paid for their investment according to a loose profit-sharing scheme, rather than as a fixed rate of interest. Being basically capitalists and not genuine entrepreneurs, stockholders therefore do not deserve the profits their investments generate. I hasten to add that they might still be justified in receiving the return they do, for two reasons. First, at least part of their return is attributable to their role as capitalists; I have not argued that capitalists should not receive interest on their capital. Second, desert is only one kind of justi-

fication which is available. Stockholders have chosen to be paid for their investment on the basis of a profit-sharing scheme, and stock-issuing entrepreneurs find this an acceptable arrangement. An agreement exists between the stockholder and the corporation, which entitles the stockholder to a share in the company profits. Thus their claim to a share of the profits is contractually based rather than desert based. By definition, only entrepreneurs bring about profits; so only they *can* deserve them, not capitalists or workers. This does not mean that only entrepreneurs have a legitimate claim to profits, all things considered, since desert claims can be "trumped" by entitlements.

20   To summarize this section: the fundamental flaw in the idea that stockholders are entrepreneurs is that the decisions they make are not related *in the appropriate way* to decisions about how to organize production. All kinds of decisions affect how productive forces are deployed, including those of bank managers, (prospective) bondholders, union leaders, politicians, and ordinary workers. (Workers can "vote with their feet", too, by leaving the company if they see bad times ahead; but this does not make them entrepreneurs.) In order to be an entrepreneur, an agent's decisions must deploy or initiate changes in the deployment of productive forces. Stockholders, as such, as not initiators; they merely *respond to* the profits and losses generated by the genuine entrepreneurial activity of those within the firm who have (mis)perceived profit opportunities and have acted upon them.

Entrepreneurs within the corporation

21 Since stockholders cannot be considered entrepreneurs, we must look inside the corporation for those who fulfill this role. We have already noted that the board of directors is "the ultimate decision-making body in the corporation." That is, it sets the "broad parameters" within which decisions are to be made about what to produce, how to produce it, and at what price, and they hire others (the corporate officers) to "work out the details." According to Arnold's own words, then, the board of directors is a prime candidate for the role of entrepreneur. Unfortunately, this does not sit well with his conservative views about who deserves profit, since members of the board are not remunerated (or penalized) according to how profitable the firm is under its direction. When board members are paid at all (and there was a time when most were not), they are paid a fixed sum, regardless of the astuteness of their decisions. If they are to be counted as entrepreneurs, as it appears they should be, then on Arnold's own account they do not get what they deserve.

22   Is the board of directors the only body of decision-makers within the corporation which can be counted as entrepreneurs? No. If it is puzzling why Arnold includes stockholders in his list of entrepreneurs, it is equally puzzling why he excludes the officers of the corporation from occupying that role. For the officers also undertake many of the activities he attributes to entrepreneurs; successful ones are alert to inoptimal ways of doing business, and are in a position to do something about it. One should think that here is another prime candidate for the role of entrepreneur in a modern corporate enterprise. Yet Arnold explicitly states that entrepreneurship is not management. (He admits that managers of large corporations who have significant stock holdings count as entrepreneurs – presumably because he thinks that any stockholder counts as such. But we have just rejected this contention.)

23   A clue to Arnold's thinking might be found when he says that entrepreneurs "set the broad parameters within which these decisions are to be made and ... hire people to work out the details. (Deciding whom to hire is often the most critical task an entrepreneur executes)" (p. 396). The suggestion is that entrepreneurs make the important, innovative, high-level decisions regarding how to structure production, and the officers exercise the merely technical skills necessary to bring the product or service onto the market: they "work out the details." But this is obviously a grotesque distortion of the role of the officers of modern corporations. There is no plausibility to the idea that managerial skill is merely technical, though certainly there are technical aspects to it. Yet this is the only basis I can imagine on which Arnold might refuse counting managers as entrepreneurs. The reason that deciding whom to hire is often the most critical task an entrepreneur executes is that, in fact, the hireling is doing most of the entrepreneurial work for him! Again, if we heed Arnold's own words, we must conclude that the officers of corporations also participate in the entrepreneurial role. And we should observe again, as in the case of board members, that typically the officers' remuneration is not strictly proportional to the profitability of the firm, hence not proportional to their deserts.

24   Indeed, I want to go further and suggest that the entrepreneurial role is often even more highly fragmented within modern corporations, in some cases extending throughout the ranks, down to the shop floor. The fundamental point is that one need not have "ultimate" control over productive forces to be an entrepreneur, nor are all of those who do have "ultimate" control over productive forces entrepreneurs. To be an entrepreneur, all that is required is that one has *some*

discretion over how productive forces are deployed, and that one should use this discretion to initiate changes in production. If the changes brought about by an agent's discretionary control of productive forces adapt appropriately to changes in technology, consumer tastes, or the other ultimate determinants of value which are continually in flux, then profits will arise; if they do not, then losses will be incurred. The only questions which remain are: Who else, besides the board of directors and the officers, have discretion over how productive forces are deployed? And who else initiates changes in production?

25   Of course, the answers to these questions will vary from one enterprise to another, but something can be said in a general way to indicate that the entrepreneurial role is not usually restricted to top management. Large corporations usually employ a whole department of people whose job it is to come up with the innovations which make the firm profitable on a continuing basis. Top management may instruct researchers to look for a "cure" for wrinkles, but the researchers themselves have a great deal of discretion as to how they pursue this objective. They may even discover some entirely different cosmetic in the process, which is highly profitable to market. Researchers within corporations are the major innovators of advanced capitalism. Thus I would maintain that they also participate in the role of entrepreneur in modern corporations – though they are not recognized as such by Arnold. This may be because Arnold's imagination, like many others', is captured by the paradigm of an entrepreneur as a lone wolf who is a "great innovator and gambler." The fact that researchers are salaried employees does not show that their work is not entrepreneurial; it shows only that they do not

get paid what Arnold's account indicates they deserve – i.e., according to the "gaps" their discoveries create between the marginal value product of the factors of production and their price.

26 Once we have gone this far, though, why not further? Sometimes, indeed, ordinary labourers will act to realize profit opportunities for their employers. Consider the construction labourer who finds ways of saving many man-hours on a particular job. If the boss had tendered a bid on that job based on calculations including significantly higher labour costs, then the worker increases the gap between cost and price, which the owner of the company keeps as profit. According to my analysis, which is a more refined version of Arnold's position, this profit was created and is deserved by the worker.[15] Arnold, in fact, may not dispute this, for he says:

> ... [I]t should not be assumed that existing market systems perfectly apportion the objects of desert to those who deserve them, even aside from the usual vagaries due to luck.... A worker who makes a suggestion which allows a firm to produce more efficiently, thereby allowing it to capture for a time some (pure) profits, would deserve some of those profits. In a capitalist system, such a worker sometimes gets these profits in the form of a bonus, but sometimes he does not, in which case he is not getting his deserts. However, he may not deserve all the profits his suggestion generates. Those in control may have exercised entrepreneurial alertness in hiring him over someone else or in setting up a work environment more conducive to creative suggestions from employees. Finally, not all apparently good suggestions will produce benefits for the firm. It takes a special talent to separate the good ideas from the apparently plausible but ultimately unsuccessful ones. (pp. 400–401)

27 What I think Arnold does not appreciate is the *extent* to which entrepreneurial activity is possible for many employees throughout the modern corporate structure. Virtually everyone has some discretion in how he does his job; almost no job is merely technical and rigidly defined. Arnold's conservative outlook makes him always want to move the credit for successful innovation up the ladder of command, to some identifiable, high-level decision-maker; but the extent to which this is legitimate is highly debatable. It would help if we had a theory which tells us how to calculate the relative importance of each party's entrepreneurial contribution to a complex innovative process, and thus determine what each contributor deserves. Arnold does not even gesture at such a theory, so his claim that those who win profits in general deserve them must remain a mere article of faith. (In my view, the issue of who *deserves* what share of the profits is usually moot, or of only academic interest, since particular labour contracts or legal statutes generally "trump" claims of desert anyway. This is where my position is in sharpest disagreement with Arnold's.)

28 A further problem looms for Arnold's claim that those who win profits in a market system in general deserve them. Profits, according to Arnold, arise when "gaps" exist between the marginal value product of a factor in its use in the firm as compared to its market cost. Suppose an entrepreneur decides to produce new-fangled widgets because he anticipates a surge in consumer demand for them. After production has begun, it turns out that demand is not as strong as anticipated, and the price is only equal to the cost of production. The entrepreneur earns no profit, and deserves none. Yet there may still be "gaps" between the marginal value product of *some* factors in their use in the firm as compared

to their market cost. (I will call these gaps "epi-profits.") For example, employees in the firm may have worked with much greater than average enthusiasm; or managers may have introduced an innovative way of structuring production very early on, thereby cutting costs. The price the entrepreneur can demand for the widgets is much lower than he anticipated; but, luckily for the entrepreneur, the costs are also slightly less than anticipated – which is why they end up being equal. In other words, the entrepreneur's decision to go into production of new-fangled widgets was a mistake which resulted in a malallocation of resources. He was saved from suffering the losses he deserved only by the creation of epi-profits by his employees. Now, once we have seen (as I argued above) that employees deserve the profits they create when the firm has overall profitability, there is no reason why we should not say that those who create epi-profits also deserve them, regardless of the overall profitability of the firm. Of course, it may be self-defeating for some members of the corporation to insist on getting their deserts. Doing so, and forcing investors and top level entrepreneurs to suffer losses (rather than breaking even), may simply result in the closure of the firm, hence the loss of their jobs. What this shows is that investors and top-level entrepreneurs frequently get more than they deserve because of their greater *power* over the process of production relative to that of the other members.

Patents and bankruptcy laws

29 So far I have argued that, for various reasons, profits and losses (and epi-profits and epi-losses) frequently go to those who do not deserve them, primarily because of prior contractual or legal arrangements. I will now argue that familiar

market systems typically include institutional rules deliberately designed to allow entrepreneurs to reap profits beyond what Arnold's account suggests they may deserve, and also to avoid the full extent of losses they may deserve. In particular, I have in mind patents and bankruptcy laws.

30 Arnold assumes the perfectly competitive model, according to which profits are "ephemeral": they get competed away as new firms imitate successful ones. But patents prevent other firms from entering into competition in the production of new goods, thereby assuring that the patentholder will be able to maintain virtually monopolistic powers over prices for a period of time. Bankruptcy laws, on the other hand, allow entrepreneurs to absolve themselves of certain losses they have incurred, pushing them onto creditors and former employees. These institutional rules do not enhance the tendency to bring control over productive resources together with personal responsibility for results, or to do so in a proportionate way. The gains they bring to entrepreneurs cannot, therefore be considered deserved on Arnold's account – even on that account as refined above.

31 I hasten to add, once again, that patent and bankruptcy laws may still be justifiable, all things considered. Modern market societies tend to value entrepreneurial activity very highly, and there is a clear danger that it would be undersupplied in a perfectly competitive market without these protections. No doubt a cost-benefit analysis would show that these institutional rules are useful to society. But utilitarian considerations cannot function as basal reasons for desert claims, as Arnold, quoting Feinberg, acknowledges: "... to say 'S deserves x because giving it to him would be in the public interest' is simply to misuse the word 'desert'" (p. 393). Desert

is a "backward-looking" principle, whereas social utility is a "forward-looking" one.[16] Thus the social utility of an institutional rule cannot be used as a basis of desert claims for specific results brought about by that rule. Since it is impossible to determine even roughly what distorting effects these areas of law have on the creation and distribution of profits and losses in specific cases, conservative conclusions such as Arnold endorses can hardly be defended.

32   Finally, it must be noted that local improvements in the efficiency of particular firms do not necessarily lead to global improvements for society as a whole. In a depressed economy, an entrepreneur may rationalize production by cutting back on employees, who then remain unemployed for several years. This might maintain profits for investors while pushing a malallocation of resources onto society as whole. Even in favourable circumstances, the entrepreneurs who profit by rationalizing production contribute to only one side of the equation that results in improved overall efficiency; those who hire on the displaced workers at a later time make an arguably more valuable contribution to this equation. Arnold recognizes this when he says, "... in particular cases, these benefits might not materialize. However, the tendencies are in that direction, and in justifying institutional rules, that is the relevant consideration" (p. 413). But this is not good enough, for Arnold's claim is not the weak one that these institutional rules are justified. His claim is stronger, namely that those specific people who win profits and suffer losses in a market system *deserve* them. This claim is not well supported by pointing to mere tendencies. It seems to me that Arnold underestimates the counter-tendencies to his thesis which exist in the market.

Conclusion

33 I have not argued that the way markets distribute profit and loss is fundamentally wrong. On the contrary, I have argued that often conservative distributions can be defended on grounds of contract, efficiency, social utility, and even the self-interest of those who do not get their full desert. Of course, contracts are in part responsive to what the people making them think they deserve; but they are also responsive to the relative powers of the parties involved. Thus entitlement and desert to a significant extent go separate ways in the market. My main contention is that *desert* cannot be used as a systematic justification for such distributions of profits and losses as we typically find. This is important to realize, I think, because desert is a particularly strong category of moral appraisal, and it is well to undermine the unjustified moral superiority often felt by the relatively prosperous vis-à-vis the relatively poor.

NOTES

1. Arnold, N. Scott: 1987, 'Why Profits Are Deserved', *Ethics* 97 (January, pp. 387–402). References enclosed in brackets in the text refer to this source.

2. Arnold does not heed the distinctions among the sources of producer surplus when he concludes, "One surprising consequence of this analysis is that capital gains taxes are, *prima facie*, immoral" (p. 399). This claim is under-supported by the arguments in his paper for the fundamental reason that capital gains sometimes include interest and factor rents, which he has not addressed at all.

3. I should also state explicitly that profit is a form of income arising within a system of rules (in particular rules upholding voluntary exchange) which define the market. It would be a conceptual mis-

take to call the income from activities such as extortion and fraud "profit," just as it would be a conceptual mistake to call the proceeds of a mugging "wages." Neither I nor Arnold wish to defend such non-market means of generating income, let alone argue that their proceeds are deserved.

4. The view (e.g.) that virtuous persons deserve happiness involves a non-institutional desert claim. I do not discuss non-institutional desert claims in this paper, though it should be recognized that they can co-exist with institutional desert claims based on other considerations and warranting other kinds of reward. Another issue I ignore is whether or nor the institution of rise market can itself be justified. This is obviously important, since institutional desert claims are morally weak if the institution is itself immoral. These two issues are beyond the scope of this paper.

5. Clark, R. C.: 1985, 'Agency Costs versus Fiduciary Duties', in J. W. Pratt and R.J. Zeckhanser, eds., *Principals and Agents: The Structure of Business* (Boston, Mass.: Harvard Business School Press), p. 56. The important distinction here is between agents and fiduciaries. In the principal-agent relationship, the principal retains the power to control and direct the activities of the agent, continuously and throughout the entire period of agency. In the principal-fiduciary relationship, on the other hand, the fiduciary is responsible for acting on behalf of the principal according to his best judgment, and without direction from the principal. Common examples of fiduciaries are executors and trustees.

6. Ibid., pp. 56-7.

7. Ibid., p. 58.

8. This way of putting the case was suggested to me in personal correspondence by Jan Narveson.

9. Quoted in the *Financial Post*, 'Links between Growth Rates, Financial Markets Growing Tenuous', 28 March 1990, p. 27.

10. Beaver, W. H.: 1981, *Financial Reporting: An Accounting Revolution* (Prentice-Hall, Englewood Cliffs, N.J.), p. 39.

11. Arbitragers, who are entrepreneurs, can sometimes make huge profits while beating no risk whatever. Contrariwise, workers can and sometimes do share in the risk of an enterprise by taking part or all of their income as a proportion of profits instead of being paid a fixed wage or salary; but doing so does not thereby make them entrepreneurs.

12. Perhaps it might be said that I "deserve" the $1 in the same way that I "deserve" to have the conditions of all my agreements met; but insofar as this makes sense, it involves quite another idea of "desert."

13. A more skillful bettor is one who makes a higher return per dollar wagered. What he deserves, actually, is this *higher yield*. Obviously if a less skillful bettor wagers ten times the amount that a more skilled bettor wagers, then he may earn a greater nominal amount, and deserve to earn a greater nominal amount. What he generally gets, and deserves to get, is a lower yield.

14. "Abnormal profit" is the profit margin above the weighted average return of all stocks in the market.

15. One might defend labour unions as a mechanism which helps workers to recover some of the profitability that they have brought to a firm. But it is a very inaccurate means of achieving the goal of matching desert and reward. Besides, labour unions do not accept the transfer of losses to the workers when they are responsible for them. Most employees' wages or salaries are fixed in advance by choice, by mutual agreement between the contracting parties. I must reiterate that this does not

show that the work they do is not entrepreneurial; it shows only that contracts over-ride desert claims as a moral (or at least legal) justification for giving people what they get in a market system.

16. *That* someone deserves some treatment (reward or punishment) is a function of what the person *has done* in the past; though *what* the person deserves may be *influenced by* utilitarian considerations. For example, that Jones has killed an innocent person is a basal reason for her deserving punishment, but the *level* or *kind* of punishment may be a function of both (1) the nature of the crime committed (a backward-looking consideration); and (2) the deterrent effect of the punishment (a forward-looking consideration). To say, however, that Jones *deserves* to be hung by the neck until death because this would be in the public interest (independently of whether or not she committed any crime) is conceptual nonsense. In the specific case of profits, Arnold argues (and I agree) that profits are deserved as a reward for correcting malallocations of resources because: (1) keeping profits (a material reward) "fits" the action of efficiently using society's resources (a material benefit); and (2) allowing entrepreneurs to keep profits set up socially useful incentives. It is conceptually possible that the latter considerations not be operative (i.e., that punishments do not lead people to avoid crime; that not getting to keep profits has no effect on incentives); but it is empirically very unlikely.

Questions

1. According to Arnold,

   (a) What is an entrepreneur?

   (b) How does profit come about?

2. Is it entrepreneurial ability or performance that results in profit? If the latter, then wouldn't Arnold say entrepreneurs are entitled to, rather than deserve, profit?

3. Who does Arnold identify as deserving of profit, and who does Brown identify as deserving of profit? Does Brown disagree with Arnold's conception of desert or with his identification of who fits the terms?

4. Explain Brown's last sentence.

5. Why does Brown reject the view that profit is a reward for bearing risk (P16–17)?

6. (a) Why does Brown discuss patents and bankruptcy laws?

   (b) Do you think they're fair?

   (c) Do you think they're otherwise justifiable?

7. If a company has an employee participation program, then might all employees deserve profit?

8. Brown says "[b]y definition, only entrepreneurs can bring about profits; so only they *can* deserve them, not capitalists or workers" (P19). But since the entrepreneur cannot bring about profits without the capital or the labour – i.e., s/he needs and uses the resources of both the capitalist and the worker – why shouldn't they also be deserving of the profit (with or without an employee participation program)?

Case Study – Tembec: Losses to Profits

In 1998, Tembec, a pulp and paper and wood products mill based in Temiscaming, Quebec, celebrated its 25th anniversary. What is remarkable about Tembec is that it was resurrected by its employees after having been shut down by its former owners in 1972. It was left for dead because of persistent financial losses. Today, Tembec is very much alive and profitable.

In the spring of 1972, the closure of a mill owned and operated by Canadian International Paper (CIP) caught the 550 employees by surprise. The company had instituted a plan for modernization of the mill and had hired several people, including engineer Frank Dottori, to assist with the plan. However, CIP pulled the plug before any modernization was implemented.

Within a few months, a group led by Dottori began to reopen the mill. They convinced a number of employees to invest their severance pay in the project. They brought on board some very experienced people to add credibility. Finally, they managed to obtain some funding from the provincial and federal governments for the new company. Tembec was born and began operations in August, 1973.

Tembec earned a profit of $9.3 million in its first year and has been consistently profitable ever since. It has used some of its profits to modernize, building some state-of-the-art facilities. It has expanded into new lines (particle board, flooring, furniture-quality wood) and established or purchased production facilities in Timmins, Mattawa, Ville Marie, Huntsville, and other locations. It has even become an international company, with a facility in France and sales offices in Switzerland and China.

Integral to its success has been its employee profit-sharing plan by which Tembec employees are given shares and automatically participate in profits. This means that every employee has a strong vested interest in the health of the company. Employee participation through dialogue and problem solving is actively promoted at Tembec.

Tembec has established a set of corporate principles and guidelines intended to steer the company as it moves forward into the future. For example, the "social responsibility" guideline directs the company to spend at least 1% of its pre-tax profits to "promote health, education, culture and recreation that contribute to improving the individual and collective quality of life ... in the community." The "environmental responsibility" guideline recommends that it "establish policies and guidelines in all phases of [its] operations which provide for responsible stewardship and sustained yield and development of [its] resources, while protecting the health and safety of employees, customers and the public." Finally, under the heading of "ethics," the company strives to "conduct business and relationships with respect, openness and integrity."

Despite the employee profit-sharing arrangement and the commitment to social and environmental responsibility, Tembec clearly operates with the same fundamental principles as any other private corporation. Its stated aim is to be profitable. In its 1998 annual report, it pledges to restrict capital investments to projects which meet minimum return (profit) guidelines, to cut costs by a minimum of $25 million, and to improve management accountability and effectiveness. These are the strategies of a corporation actively engaged in a competitive market.

In an economy dominated by private, for-profit companies, Tembec is clearly a success story. Due largely to the faith and vision of its employees, it took a losing situation and turned it into a winner. Its willingness to share its profits with its workers can be regarded as a model to other Canadian companies.

REFERENCES

Tembec. *Annual Report 1997.*
Tembec. *Annual Report 1998.*

Questions

1. Profit-sharing may be a good business decision because it results in workers who have a vested interest. For what reasons might be it a good ethical decision?

2. Tembec's stated commitment to social and environmental responsibility as well as ethical standards (though the former may be the latter) may be viewed by some as a public relations exercise that will not be effective unless specific measures and systems are put in place to ensure the desired outcome. As well, a profit-sharing plan may be viewed as an effective way of co-opting workers into acceptance of the typical "corporate mentality" of profits before all else. How would you respond to these sorts of critiques?

3. Why don't all private, for-profit companies have a profit-sharing plan for their employees? Can you think of some reasons why employees might not be interested in such a plan?

4. Does profit-sharing make "obscenely high" profits more morally acceptable?

CHAPTER 8
CANADIAN ISSUES

What to Do? – Canadian Natural Resources, Inc.

It is 2025. And as the International Water Management Institute projected back in 1999, a billion people are living in countries facing absolute water scarcity. Water tables have fallen on every continent; major rivers run dry for part of every year, a longer part each year.

You are the CEO of Canadian Natural Resources, Inc. (True to form, Canada has neither completely privatized nor completely socialized its businesses.) The country finds itself in a unique, but not surprising, position: it is the largest nation on the planet (the former U.S.S.R. and the former U.S.A. have since subdivided into smaller nations because of, respectively, ethnic/economic and racial/religious/right-to-bear-arms conflicts; and China split in two, one half capitalist, the other socialist). More importantly, the natural resources and the population density of Canada are enviable, to say the least.

Several countries want to buy fresh water from Canada. Due to a combination of overpopulation (whether because of sociocultural/religious, educational, or healthcare reasons,

you don't know), environmental changes, and less-than-democratic governance, these countries are desperate for water, not only for agricultural purposes (industrial purposes have long ceased to be a consideration), but also for drinking. Simply put, people will die if they don't get water. (Then again, you realize, they may die anyway.)

You have two major concerns. One, whether achieved by truck convoys, pipelines, or iceberg tows, getting the water from here to there will surely involve the re-routing of rivers and the lowering of lake levels – which is sure to worsen things, environmentally speaking.

Two, if you don't sell the water to them, they will probably come and take it; ironically, while fresh water is scarce, fuel for transport and tow is not. Or, as has been suggested by at least one nation, they will simply explode their entire nuclear arms arsenals (which they have, thanks to Canadian sales a few decades ago) as well as their nuclear power reactors (can you spell "Candu"?), creating worldwide radiation hazards.

Though it's not like we're swimming in the stuff (that was made illegal several years ago), unless there's a dramatic change in immigration policies or a further change in climate patterns (the former is unlikely, but the latter is not), Canada has enough fresh water for its current, and probably its future, population. You *could* sell the excess.

But why just the excess: why should you look after Canadians first? Is a Canadian life worth more than, say, an African life?

And at what price? Is it right to let the free market call the shots? People are dying – what about compassion and generosity? But what about justice – whose fault is the overpopulation? Okay, but we're an industrialized nation; surely the climate changes leading to the desertification are partly our fault. But what about the despotic government? Yeah, but it's not like we did anything to stop it. Well, it wasn't any of our business … In any case, you suspect it'll be a while before they can pay, whatever the price.

What do you decide to do?

Introduction

Culture and politics affect business in any country, and Canada is no exception. Three issues that can have a bearing on business ethics may be considered of special importance in Canada.

The first involves the French-English relationship – maintaining the "distinct" society of French Canadians continues to be a challenge. (See the Pasquero essay in this chapter.) Language rights, understood by many to be part of cultural rights, is often at the core of this challenge. You may recall the example in Section II, dealing with whether Quebec businesses should (be allowed to/be forced to) advertise and conduct business only in French. First, one must determine whether language *is* part of culture. Second, one must determine *whether* anyone has a *right* to a particular culture. Third, does that right extend to their doing business? These questions are not just important for the French – what about the Asian population in British Columbia? Canada's multiculturalism gives rise to many distinct groups who may (or may not) want to preserve their culture – and business certainly could have a part in that.

Further, does it matter whether the business is public or private? Essential or not? In answering these last two questions, one will recognize that whatever rights were established at the outset must compete with other rights – and others' rights.

The second special issue involves the First Nations. While language and cultural rights are no doubt relevant, perhaps property rights are at the moment (still) more important. This may seem odd to say, given that the First Nations view property differently than the Europeans, who created the current "Canadian" system, which tends to recognize individual property rights and only certain kinds of property transfers. One big question is whether a business should operate on property whose ownership has not yet been settled. (Don't forget that legal decisions are not necessarily morally correct – and we're concerned here with moral decisions.)

A prime example of this is the oil and logging development in Lubicon Cree territory in Alberta. According to the Lubicon Legal Defence Fund, in the mid-1970s the Lubicon filed a notice under law warning developers that title to the land in question was contested, but the Province of Alberta ignored the notice and dismissed the case. The subsequent development destroyed the hunting that the Cree depended on for food and income; by 1982, there were 400 oil wells within a 15-mile radius of the Lubicon community, and 90% of the community's population was on welfare (compared to 10% prior to the development). Negotiations between the Lubicon and the federal government continued, more or less, but ten years later, Daishowa owned cutting rights to 10,000 square miles of the Lubicon territory. A boycott seemed to succeed in stalling a clear-cut; as a result, the company filed a lawsuit to make the boycott illegal – it lost and has now agreed not to log until a land settlement has been reached between the Lubicon and the governments. (Such a settlement has not yet been reached; nevertheless, the provincial government is accepting tenders for timber rights on that same land.) The oil and logging companies may have had a legal right to develop the land, but did they have a moral right?

The Oka Crisis in 1990 involved similar issues of unresolved land claims: land being turned into a golf course by developers was claimed by Mohawk leaders to be theirs, land which included a burial site; a month-long confrontation (the Quebec government had asked the Canadian army for assistance) near Kanesatake (also known as Oka) resulted in loss of life.

According to Nozick, property is justly owned if the history of transfers has been just. In the case of Canada, *has* the history of transfers been just? Was a fair price paid? Was deceit or other manipulation, such as force (or smallpox), involved? (See the Cragg and Schwartz paper in this chapter for a look at the role historical injustice can have in business today.)

Another contentious issue is whether First Nations people should have the right to hunt and fish when and where non-First Nations people do not have that right. Isn't that discrimination? Some justify it on the basis of need: First Nations are allowed because it's their livelihood, but for non-First Nations people, it's just sport. But what about commercial hunting and fishing? Then is it not livelihood for both? (See *Windspeaker* for some good pieces on these issues.) The Maritime provinces certainly have an interest in these matters.

Forbes raises another interesting issue when he proposes a First Nations Intellectual Property Act that would "provide that royalties must be paid for the use of native American inventions and products including kayaks, toboggans, tipis, rubber, design motifs, plants, medicinals, tribal names and personal names." Citing the attempt by chemical and biomedical corporations to establish ownership of herbs, herbal extracts, food plants, and plant fibres, as well as the past appropriation (theft?) by Europeans of North American foods and medicines (such as corn, potatoes, cacao, peanuts, quinine, and golden seal), he speculates that "the payment of royalties on Native American inventions might well be enough to completely replace the federal contributions to tribes in the U.S. and Canada."

A third issue of significance to Canada is our proximity to the U.S.A. Sharing a large unprotected border with the country that sings "We are the World" – and is in many ways right about that – must give rise to a few special ethical issues in business. Certainly many Canadians objected to the Free Trade Agreement (FTA) – and not just on economic grounds. Indeed, non-economic considerations (about cultural identity and about sovereignty and about Canada's ability to continue its social safety net) dominated the controversy over the North American Free Trade Agreement (NAFTA).

"Canadian content" rules are intended to preserve our culture against American influence. Do such rules restrict or enhance consumers' freedom of choice? Do they ensure or hinder entrepreneurs' access to a level playing field? Are government subsidies and tax incentives given to the arts unfair to non-cultural businesses? What about the tariffs imposed on imports that are competitors to Canadian-made products – governmental intervention or interference?

An example of Canada-U.S. friction as a result of the ambiguity of the FTA on cultural matters is the "split run" magazine debate. Many American magazines are marketed to Canada; understandably, American businesses may be reluctant to advertise in Canada-bound magazines – they would be throwing away their money. Such magazines, therefore, would like to attract Canadian advertising dollars for their Canada-bound magazines. However, in order to qualify to have Canadian advertising in a magazine sold in Canada, the magazine must *be* Canadian. As a result, in the mid-1990s, some U.S. magazines (notably *Sports Illustrated*, but also a number of others) put out a "Canadian edition" of their magazine by adding several pages of Canadian content at the beginning, but otherwise leaving the bulk of the magazine's content intact.

Many Canadian magazine publishers then complained to the federal government that the existing protection afforded Canadian magazines was insufficient: Canadian advertising dollars would go to these American magazines rather than to "real" Canadian magazines, and Canadian culture would suffer (presumably many Canadian magazines would decline without those advertising dollars). Canadian publishers argued that this split run tactic was simply a device to get around the regulation and should not be allowed.

The federal government responded, in 1999, with Bill C-55 which attempted to tighten up the definition of a Canadian magazine and to continue to provide some protection for Canadian culture. The U.S. government has argued, in its opposition to C-55, that the FTA guarantees non-discrimination of each country's firms in the other's market; they even threatened to retaliate by limiting Canadian exports in selected areas of trade if a resolution wasn't reached. Is this just business or is Canadian culture at stake? How/Are the two connected? What is the *ethical* problem here? And what is the solution?

And "content" may not be the only element subject to American influence. Any Canadian business may have trouble attracting and keeping qualified personnel as long as the financial climate is more attractive south of the border. Not only its personnel, but the business itself may just as well move south; after all, it's a global economy now, right? Gwyn questions this view that corporations should not owe any allegiance to Canada and wonders whether *some* contract, "whether social or legal or commercial or cultural," shouldn't obligate corporations to the nation-states in which they happen to be located.

REFERENCES AND FURTHER READING

Boyd, Colin. "Business Ethics in Canada: A Personal View." *Journal of Business Ethics* 16.6 (April 1997): 605-609.

Brooks, Len. "Business Ethics in Canada: Distinctiveness and Directions." *Journal of Business Ethics* 16.6 (April 1997): 591-604.

Di Norcia, Vincent. *Hard Like Water*. Toronto: Oxford University Press, 1998. 167-171.

Forbes, Jack D. *Columbus and Other Cannibals: The Wetiko Disease of Exploitation, Imperialism and Terrorism*. NY: Semiotexte-Autonomedia, 1992.

Forbes, Jack D. "Intellectual Property Rights of Indigenous Peoples." *Windspeaker* Classroom Edition 3. <http://www.ammsa.com>

Goar, Carol. "Carving out a Place for our Culture." *The Toronto Star*. 6 Mar. 1999: B2.

Gwyn, Richard. "The True Allegiance of Canadian Corporations." *The Toronto Star* 28 Apr. 1999: A17.

Hill, Roger and Pamela Sloan. "A New Era in Corporate Aboriginal Relations." *Canadian Business Review* 23.1 (Spring 1996): 22-25.

Hill, Roger and Pamela Sloan. *Corporate Aboriginal Relations*. Toronto: Books for Business, 1995.

"Hunters and Harvesters." *Windspeaker* Classroom Edition 1. <http://www.ammsa.com>

"Let's Talk about Fish" *Windspeaker* Classroom Edition 2. <http://www.ammsa.com>

Levitt, K. *Silent Surrender: The Multinational Corporation in Canada*. Toronto: Macmillan, 1970.

Marchak, P. *In Whose Interests: An Essay on Multinational Corporations in a Canadian Context*. Toronto: McClelland and Stewart, 1979.

McDonald, Michael. "Business Ethics in Canada: Integration and Interdisciplinarity," *Journal of Business Ethics* 16.6 (April 1997): 635-643.

McQuaig, Linda. *The Quick and the Dead: Brian Mulroney, Big Business and the Seduction of Canada*. Toronto: Viking, 1991.

Michalos, Alex. "Non-academic Critics of Business Ethics in Canada." *Journal of Business Ethics* 16.6 (April 1997): 611-619.

Sustainability and Historical Injustice: Lessons from the Moose River Basin[1]

Wesley Cragg and Mark Schwartz

ABSTRACT. Our paper examines the role of distributive justice in the pursuit of sustainable development. One goal of the paper is to challenge the assumption that sustainability is an exclusively forward looking idea. The tool of analysis is a case study of a proposed hydro electric development on the Mattagami River in Northern Ontario. We look at the conflicts the project has generated as arising in large measure from historical injustices inflicted on aboriginal project stakeholders. Two principles of distributive justice are identified and then used to evaluate three proposals for resolving those conflicts advanced by the principal stakeholders, Ontario Hydro, the First Nations affected, and the provincial government. We conclude that sustainability has moral structure, and go on to evaluate the distributive justice dimension of that structure and its implications for sustainable resource development.

Introduction

1 Sustainable development is about environmentally friendly economic growth and the elimination of poverty through equitable distribution of

Wesley Cragg and Mark Schwartz, "Sustainability and Historical Injustice: Lessons from the Moose River Basin" *Journal of Canadian Studies* 31.1 (Spring 1996): 60-81. © 1996 by *Journal of Canadian Studies.* Reprinted with permission of the publisher and the authors.

economic wealth. Thought of this way, sustainable development is about the future. It is also about the past – or perhaps more accurately about escaping a past in which economic growth was more often than not environmentally destructive and distributively unjust. Finally, the idea of sustainability, as articulated by the Brundtland Commission and the increasingly converted business community, is inherently optimistic.

2 It is this optimism that sustainable economic growth remains a genuine possibility at this stage of human economic history that is most frequently questioned by critics. Can we find in nature the resources and the capacity to support the growth that will be required if the grinding poverty in which much of the world now lives is to be overcome? And can we find in ourselves the political and moral resources required to ensure that wealth is fairly distributed?

3 These questions offer profound challenges in their own right. Yet they appear to leave unaddressed some central environmental and social problems whose focus is not so much the future as the past. Indeed much of the current sustainable development rhetoric implicitly suggests a posture popularized by Prime Minister Trudeau in his first term of office when he argued, faced with aboriginal discontent, that a political system could only be held responsible for its own actions, and that it should not be asked to correct historical injustices for two rea-

sons. First, history could not be changed and those harmed could not be compensated. Second, to require those now living to bear costs for which they are not responsible would be unfair. Trudeau's position on this question was subsequently rejected by his government. It is now widely recognized that creating the conditions in which poverty and social inequity can be addressed requires that we face not just the future, but also the grievance-generating historical events which have shaped the present.[2]

4 Is there a lesson here for discussions of sustainable development? If so, what attention should be paid to historical injustices in the pursuit of sustainable development? Looked at globally, the legacy of injustice seems so complex that it defies analysis, let alone resolution. Discrete examples, on the other hand, may not have that character. A good example is Ontario Hydro's proposal for restructuring and developing the hydroelectric potential of the Mattagami River in northeastern Ontario. The Mattagami River north of Kapuskasing was first harnessed in 1928 to provide power for a pulp mill which in turn gave life to the northern community of Kapuskasing. The same part of the river was redeveloped in the 1960s by Ontario Hydro to assist in meeting the peak power demands of a rapidly growing industrial economy. Those developments had a significantly positive impact on the developing economy of the north, and a significantly negative impact on both the river itself and the subsistence economies of the river basin's original inhabitants.

5 In the last decade, faced with what were then thought to be accelerating demands for energy, Ontario Hydro proposed a redevelopment of what has come to be known as the Mattagami Complex. Although most other aspects of Hydro's planning have been shelved in response to greatly reduced growth in Ontario's economy, this particular proposal is still under active study. Blocking the development have been Native grievances linked directly to the environmentally damaging impacts of the original development.

6 What is at issue, then, is the meaning of sustainability in a setting in which there is strong support for resource development juxtaposed with deeply felt historically grounded grievances connected with previous exploitation of natural resources. Added to this are serious concerns about the environmental impacts for the river and the river basin of both the current complex and its redevelopment.

7 This article approaches the Mattagami project from an economic and ethical perspective. In particular, we examine three approaches to resolving both past and present issues raised by the project. The first was developed by Ontario Hydro in the context of its now shelved 25 year plan, aimed at what might be called compensatory justice based on economic analysis. Second, the First Nations in the area are calling for a recognition of their right to self-government followed by co-planning and co-management of resource development. Finally, the Ontario government now is advocating a process-oriented solution based on equitable participation in the decision making process.

8 We begin with the case itself, examined from the perspective of distributive justice and sustainable development. We then turn to a description and evaluation of the three alternatives outlined above and draw some lessons on the moral structure of the concept of sustainability. We conclude with some observations about the nature of the exercise and a postscript describing how the case has evolved over the period of our study.

The Case[3]

9   The Moose River Basin is an area larger in size than Ireland. The Mattagami is one of three rivers that empty into James Bay via the Moose River. The ecosystems of the region, in common with other boreal and sub-arctic areas, are fragile and easily damaged. The Ontario Hydro complex which is the focus of our study consists of four dams on the Mattagami River 60 to 100 kilometres north of Kapuskasing. Vegetation in the vicinity of the four dams consists mainly of boreal forests. The basin's wildlife population includes moose, bear, beaver, fox, otter and numerous species of birds, amphibians and fish.

10   Aboriginal settlement would appear to date back as much as 5,000 years. European settlement dates to 1776 when the Hudson's Bay Company opened a post on Moose Factory Island. In the early 1900s railway lines opened up the area to agriculture, mining and lumbering. In the following years, private hydroelectric developments were established in the basin to provide power to new resource industries.

11   In 1922, the "model" town of Kapuskasing was built around a pulp and paper mill which was operated by the Spruce Falls Pulp and Paper Company and owned by Kimberly Clark and the owners of *The New York Times*. The first of four dams in the complex, the Smoky Falls station, was built by Spruce Falls in 1928 to supply inexpensive hydroelectric power to the mill. This dam destroyed a beautiful natural water fall and caused long term environmental damage, but not on the scale of later hydroelectric developments. In the 1960s Ontario Hydro added three more dams: Little Long (1963), Harmon (1965), and Kipling (1966). Unlike the Smoky Falls station, however, these were "peaking" stations, operating only five hours per day and requiring "headponds" whose water levels were to fluctuate up to three metres each day. Also required was a spillway which would operate during the spring runoff. The spillway was created by diverting water into Adam Creek, a small natural water course adjacent to the river itself. The resulting erosion has created river banks 20 to 30 metres in height and washed millions of cubic metres of soil down the river.

12   The hydroelectric developments of the 1960s have had a significant impact on the basin's ecology and its Aboriginal inhabitants. Construction of the dams provided employment for some Aboriginal peoples. Connecting the communities of Moose Factory and Moosonee to the Ontario power grid has resulted in important improvements for the communities affected. These developments have also been accompanied by a deterioration in water quality; fluctuating water levels leading to trapped fish, sandbars and silted-over spawning beds; erosion; significant flooding; a loss of food and habitat for beavers and other animals; and the destruction of historic Cree settlement sites, historic portages, fur trade sites and cemeteries. Aboriginal inhabitants have also linked noise from generators to declining populations of birds, otter, mink and fox in the area of the dams and complained of deterioration in the quality of the fur from beaver, muskrat and otter. The dams' construction roads have improved access for non-Native hunters, generated competition for resources and provided greater access for logging companies whose cutting activities have also had a negative impact on fur-bearing mammals and fish. Finally, the use of the rivers for transportation has been seriously affected by the fluctuating water levels. All of these impacts not only have taken a toll on the traditional way of life of the

basin's Aboriginal inhabitants but also appear to have been accompanied throughout by an absence of consultation, mitigation or compensation by Ontario Hydro.

13 In 1990, Ontario Hydro submitted to the Ontario government an environmental assessment calling for a redevelopment of the four dams to increase the hydroelectric generation capacity of the Mattagami River. Additional generating units were proposed for the Little Long, Harmon and Kipling stations. The base load Smoky Falls station was to be retired, and a new peaking power station constructed adjacent to it. The goal was to optimize energy production from the river by building a new "in-step" operation which Ontario Hydro projected would provide enough new energy to supply the electricity demands of 150,000 homes. In its environmental assessment, Ontario Hydro predicted that the redevelopment would cause little new damage and would reduce environmental impacts from existing operations.

14 In 1991, the owners of the Spruce Falls Pulp and Paper Company, having failed to find a buyer for an increasingly uneconomic operation, announced their decision to shut down most of the Kapuskasing mill operation with the possible loss of 1,200 direct and 6,200 indirect jobs in a town of 11,000. The resulting political crisis caused the Ontario government to intervene. As a result, the company was sold by Kimberly Clark and *The New York Times* to its employees. As part of the package, the Smoky Falls station was sold to Ontario Hydro on the condition that the environmental assessment process found the redevelopment proposal acceptable. Alternatively, the Ontario government would be required to pay Ontario Hydro $247 million.[4]

15 This article focusses on the debates and proposals generated by the ensuing environmental assessment process. The project's stakeholders include the following:

Ontario Hydro, the proponent of the Mattagami extension proposal. Although the urgency for finding new sources of power has now vanished, until recently the project was regarded as an efficient way of providing inexpensive hydroelectric power to the Ontario grid.

The Aboriginal peoples now living in the Moose River Basin. Most affected by the dams in question are the Aboriginal residents of Moosonee, about 900 in number, and Moose Factory, a community of about 2,200 Aboriginal inhabitants. In total there are about 10,000 Aboriginal inhabitants in the basin area. For these people, ongoing land claims and their traditional way of life are of deep significance.

The Ontario government, with a political, economic and financial stake in discussions and negotiations accompanying the environmental assessment process.

The non-Aboriginal residents of surrounding communities where unemployment is high and opportunities for economic development have been warmly welcomed.

Other stakeholders include the more distant municipalities, labour unions, independent power producers, tourist operators and environmental groups.

The Structure of Injustice

1) Distributive Justice and the Concept of Sustainable Development

16 Ontario Hydro's proposed Mattagami Complex extension poses a complex challenge to the application of the notion of sustainable development. That complexity derives in large measure from the nature of the environmental impacts of

earlier developments as set against the likely benefits of further development. Economic analysis suggests, as we already have pointed out, that redevelopment of the complex would bring substantial economic benefits to the town of Kapuskasing, to the economy of the northeastern region of the province and to Ontario Hydro consumers; analysis also suggests that the proposed development would have beneficial environmental impacts. This of course is a significant component of Ontario Hydro's case for development. If we focus exclusively on the future, the proposal might therefore seem to be sustainable. Nevertheless, it has generated considerable controversy and deep opposition, particularly from the Native population. It is in our opinion virtually impossible to understand the breadth and substance of that opposition without exploring the links between sustainability and distributive justice.

17   The idea of sustainable development has been reformulated in numerous ways by critics of the Brundtland Commission's definition. Criticism, however, has not managed to undermine the importance of the role the idea continues to have in the thinking of those concerned with the impact of modern industrial development on the world's environment. It has continued to play this role in part, we suggest, because of the particular way in which the idea of sustainable development has helped to bring environmental concerns into dialogue with economic ones. Under-riding that dialogue is a set of moral imperatives. This is evidenced by two things. First, sustainable development is at its most fundamental level about sharing the planet's resources with the future in equitable ways. Second, underlying the concept is a conviction that non-sustainable development carries with it morally significant costs that are cumu-

lative and will be passed on to future generations. The harnessing of the great rivers draining the Canadian Shield illustrates these points; discussions of future developments unavoidably confront them.

18   What then is the moral structure of sustainable development?[5] We propose that it must include the following principle: *The costs of resource development should be borne by those who will reap its benefits.*[6] This principle is clearly a principle of distributive justice. Failure to respect it, we propose, must unavoidably lead to injustice, that is, to the imposition of morally significant costs not balanced by benefits to those on whom they are imposed. We shall argue that sustainable resource development which is insensitive to this principle may occur, but if so it is by accident and not by design.

2) Cost Benefit Analysis and the Problem of Externalities

19 For much of the century Ontario Hydro, a publicly owned provincial public utility, has studied and exploited the hydraulic potential of the great rivers draining the Canadian Shield. The province of Ontario has been the direct beneficiary of hydroelectric development undertaken by Ontario Hydro in pursuit of this mandate.

20   Even a cursory survey of the evidence shows that hydroelectric development in the north has not been constrained or guided by principles of sustainable development in the past. The dams and turbines constructed on northern rivers have diverted and altered the flow of rivers in environmentally significant ways, resulting in the creation of the huge reservoirs needed to ensure reliable energy delivery over long time periods in response to fluctuating demand. The resulting energy has

been delivered at relatively low monetary cost to the residents of Ontario with considerable economic benefit. On the other hand, substantial costs have been imposed on Native communities in the absence of meaningful consultation and countervailing benefits recognizable as such by those affected. The legacy of these developments is reflected in an acute sense of grievance which now dominates discussion of Northern Ontario resource use. It is reflected as well in substantial environmental problems that now confront Native and non-Native communities in the north.[7]

21   What is the source or origin of the injustice that has been imposed on Native communities in the north? A first clear candidate is moral insensitivity on the part of planners, developers and the Crown corporation itself. The histories that are now being collected and the accounts of Aboriginal peoples that are now being assembled in defence of self-government claims suggest that much of the development has taken place in an environment in which the fact that the land was occupied and under use by an indigenous population was simply ignored.[8] A second candidate is the Friedmanite character of modern economic activity. The task of business, Friedman has argued, is to operate as profitably as possible within the constraints set by law. So long as they work within the law, managers are not responsible for monitoring or compensating costs that have no direct impact on profits. Responding to inequities resulting from economic activities is deemed more properly the responsibility of governments.[9] Finally, it might be argued that the injustice resulting from northern hydro development is a direct consequence of the structure of the planning process that guided the development of the hydraulic potential of the north of Ontario.

22   It is this third explanation that holds the key to the problems of injustice on the one hand and unsustainability on the other. Ontario Hydro's mandate is an economic one. Ontario Hydro is directed by law to maximize economic benefits and minimize costs which must be passed on to consumers. In the past, where hydroelectric installations were concerned, the costs Ontario Hydro could not avoid passing on to consumers were those costs resulting from construction, transmission and maintenance of its northern generating facilities as well as whatever compensation the law required be paid to those (private property owners for example) with a legal right to compensation. Legally speaking, Ontario Hydro was entitled to regard all other costs as externalities and therefore not its responsibility. For the most part, this was the path Ontario Hydro chose to follow. Given its mandate, the approach taken is hardly surprising.

23   Ontario Hydro's past approach to the development of Ontario's northern rivers is best characterized as "least cost" planning. It is an approach to planning that Litchfield argues has dominated energy planning by utilities throughout North America until very recently.[10] It reflects a Friedmanite approach to the issue of corporate social responsibility. Finally, it is an approach which, taken by itself in the absence of alternative non-corporate responses to environmental and human impacts, is obviously open to the charge of moral insensitivity. In the case under consideration, no adequate strategies for dealing with external (to Ontario Hydro) costs were put in place by the government. As a consequence, the full burden of carrying those costs was shifted to the Cree population and their communities.

24   It is this legacy which underlies the conflicts which Ontario Hydro's proposals for the rede-

velopment of the Mattagami Complex have generated. It remains a legacy in spite of the fact that all of the parties to the conflict acknowledge the inadequacies of past planning and development and have committed themselves to the idea of sustainable development in planning and assessing new projects. The central dilemma concerns what role that legacy should play in creating a sustainable development strategy for the Mattagami River.

The Structure of Environmental Conflict

1) Economic Analysis and Compensatory Justice

25 Ontario Hydro's proposal for redeveloping the Mattagami Complex derives from its mandate "to provide a reliable supply of electrical power and energy to the people of Ontario, at the lowest long-term feasible cost."[11] Its proposal is designed to assist it to meet its obligations by expanding the four existing sites so as to extract the greatest possible energy potential of the river with the least possible adverse environmental effects.

26 It is clear from both the *Environmental Assessment Summary* and *The Demand Supply Plan Report* that the proposed extensions are designed to increase the peak energy capacity of Ontario Hydro. Its case for the project rests on "least-cost" planning that incorporates all (but only) those costs to be "borne directly by Hydro."[12] Ontario Hydro acknowledges that "(c)osts and benefits for the Ontario community beyond these direct costs are not factored into cost comparisons."[13] In this respect the approach used in developing the current proposal is no different from that which Hydro has used in developing

all its hydraulic sites in Northern Ontario in this century.

27 In spite of the similarities with past planning methods, however, the approach used to plan the Mattagami Extension represents important differences. Among other things, it incorporates a commitment to take into account social and environmental as well as the economic impacts in the planning process. This change is clearly significant. Given a commitment to "least cost" planning, how is it to be accounted for?

28 The answer lies in two places. First, it lies with Ontario's Environmental Assessment Act which aims at "the betterment of the people of Ontario by providing for the protection, conservation and wise management in Ontario of the environment."[14] That act defines the environment broadly, to include the natural environment as well as "the social, economic and cultural conditions that influence the life of man or a community,"[15] and has led to significant changes in the regulatory environment in which energy planning must now take place in Ontario. As a result, in planning the Mattagami Extension, Ontario Hydro has been required by law to take into account costs which previously it had externalized. Second, it is clear from the *DSP Environmental Analysis* offered in justification of the Mattagami extension that not only the law but also Ontario Hydro's own thinking has undergone significant changes since the 1960s. Respect for the principles of sustainable development is now Ontario Hydro policy.[16] This has been interpreted to mean that project planning must consider environmental protection and conservation, regional economic stability, recreation, health, heritage protection and Aboriginal concerns. More striking for our purposes, however, is recognition that sustainable development carries the moral implication that "Gen-

erally, it is preferable that those who bear the risks also share equitably in the benefits."[17] To be committed to sustainable development is thus understood to require qualified respect for the principle of distributive justice.

29   The planning and internal environmental assessment process which appears to have emerged as a result of these changes can be summarized as follows:

1) Meet the electrical power needs of the province in the most sustainable manner possible;

2) Integrate environmental as well as economic costs in all cost calculations;

3) Inform and consult with the public in identifying benefits and costs;

4) Mitigate all adverse impacts where economically feasible;

5) For all residual impacts and where economically feasible, provide substitute off-setting benefits for losses;

6) Compensate fairly for all adverse residual impacts where mitigation or substitution is not possible.

Ontario Hydro's own assessment has led it to conclude that tested against these criteria the Mattagami Extension represents the lowest cost option available to it and that the criteria constitute a fair basis for responding to the concerns of all those likely to benefit or suffer as a result of the development. The redevelopment will allow a more efficient and productive use of the hydraulic potential of the river than the present installations allow. The construction phase will provide jobs. Permitting the redevelopment will justify the purchase of the Smoky Falls station from the Spruce Falls Pulp and Paper Company, saving tax dollars and indirectly strengthening the economic viability of the mill and consequently of Kapuskasing by contributing to the continued provision of low cost power through the Ontario grid. These economic benefits are to be accompanied by minimal environmental damage and the potential for certain environmental improvements.[18] For example, there will be little impact on soil, vegetation, wildlife and aquatic habitat. There will be a reduction in shoreline erosion in headponds, downstream erosion in Adam Creek, and in the passage of fish through the Adam Creek control structure.

30   Ontario Hydro does acknowledge that negative environmental impacts may occur as a result of the redevelopment that it is proposing. However, they claim that those that do occur will be mitigated. For example, although there may be additional angling and hunting pressure on fish and wildlife populations from the construction workforce, measures will be taken to both restrict and discourage excessive hunting and angling activities during the construction period.[19] Although the peaking operations will increase the water level fluctuation downstream of the Kipling station, Hydro proposes to maintain minimal water levels to prevent the dewatering of aquatic habitat. A new spawning habitat will be created in the Smoky Falls' tailrace[20] to compensate for the loss of spawning grounds as a result of the redevelopment.[21] Ontario Hydro's environmental assessment also acknowledges that there will be some residual impacts. For example, Hydro proposes to "cooperate with trappers to identify yields before the project and compensate financial losses resulting from project activities."[22] It has also offered to compensate for impacts on aboriginal harvesting activities.

Ontario Hydro will seek to provide fair compensation for all subsistence users and licensed trappers in the project area, for any losses that may result from the undertaking. With their co-operation, funding will be provided to area First Nations to define both pre- and post-development levels of aboriginal harvesting.[23]

Furthermore,

> Should impacts be identified, options such as financial compensation, replacement of losses in kind (e.g., provision of fish, fowl, etc. from other sources) or other equivalent impact management measures (e.g., to establish new trap lines, relocate cabins, etc.) will be offered.[24]

The commitment to inform and consult is reflected in "public information and feedback" as "the cornerstones of the public involvement program for the Mattagami River Extensions Environmental Assessment Study."[25] And if it is acknowledged that Hydro's relationship with the Nishnawbe-Aski First Nations is strained,[26] some attempts have been made to rectify the situation, including the appointment of a Corporate Aboriginal Affairs Coordinator.[27]

31   Finally, Ontario Hydro has undertaken to deal with the grievances to which the earlier developments on the river have given rise. However, at the time of the original environmental assessment, it rejected the view that settling those grievances is or should be an element in any environmental assessment carried out under the Environmental Assessment Act.

32   Ontario Hydro's position on the Mattagami Extension represents an attempt to achieve important economic goals within a sustainable development framework. However, the resulting development model has failed to win agreement, particularly on the part of Aboriginal stakeholders. From their perspective, Ontario Hydro's approach, which Ontario Hydro acknowledges, was implemented without substantial Cree consultation, has two defects. The first is its fundamentally utilitarian structure: the overriding objective is the provision of adequate supplies of reliable, low cost electricity to the people of Ontario. The key to the exercise is identifying "low cost" or "lowest cost options." Achieving their goal, however, becomes extremely difficult unless the monetary value of costs and benefits can be accurately determined, and herein lies the difficulty for many of the participants.[28] Hydro's environmental assessment, for example, identifies the following as priorities: low cost reliable electric power, efficient use of water resources, environmental protection, conservation, regional economic stability, recreation, health, heritage protection and Aboriginal concerns. By contrast if we probe the documents assembled in response to the *Demand/Supply Plan*, we discover the following as Aboriginal concerns: a deep sense of obligation to the land or "mother earth," treaty rights, control over those land areas on which they have relied for subsistence, and finally a profound sense of obligation to the Creator, their traditional way of life, and aboriginal rights. It is not at all clear how one would seek to assess the cost of environmental impacts from the perspective of this set of concerns.[29]

33   The importance of the ability to cost impacts is further emphasized by the way this approach to planning relies on the substitution of off-setting benefits for costs incurred and, failing that, on compensation. Values readily quantified easily can be assimilated to this approach. The risk, however, is that values that cannot be quantified will be ignored just because the methodology has no way of dealing with them.[30] In short, the problem in using a mitigation and compensation approach is that it appears to call for what has been described as the commodification of values. It is perhaps not surprising that the methodology and its application have given rise to offence and criticism. Aboriginal reactions to

Ontario Hydro's plans reflect that kind of judgment. To propose financial compensation for polluted water, or poisoned fish, or the loss of traditional hunting grounds, or flooded grave sites is from a Native perspective to misunderstand in a profound way the nature of the losses for which compensation is being offered.

34   The second defect in Ontario Hydro's approach lying at the heart of the First Nations' refusal to cooperate is a deep sense of historical grievance, one grounded not simply in the costs that have been imposed as a result of hydroelectric development, but rather reacting to the contempt for Native values, and the way of life in which they have traditionally been enshrined, implied by the way development in the north has typically taken place. It is unlikely that a planning and assessment process, which assumes that adequate mitigation, substitution and compensation are in principle available for all unavoidable negative impacts, could respond to that sense of injustice. These sentiments are captured by the alternative solution to the conflict proposed by First Nation leaders.

2) Respecting Rights: The Self-Government Option

35 The First Nations' response to the Mattagami Extension proposal has three components. First is a commitment to sustainable development, which the Native People's Circle on Environment and Development suggests has always been a guiding concept for them. This commitment, they go on to say, is reflected in the view that "the land and its resources [must] be preserved for the benefit of past, present, and future generations."[31]

36   For Aboriginal peoples, sustainability also is closely linked to economic wellbeing. What

separates this view from that of Ontario Hydro, however, is how best to achieve that goal. As Randy Kapashesit, Chief of the MoCreebec First Nation, points out: "Ontario Hydro's notion of economic development is not supportive of the kind of economy that is reflective of our own culture, values, traditions and environment."[32] For Hydro, the land is a resource to be used. From a Native perspective, the land is something deserving great respect, a source of cultural, aesthetic and spiritual as well as economic well-being. The land is seen as of great value in its own right. Its health is viewed as directly linked to the well-being of Native peoples.[33]

37   The implications of these two perspectives for dealing with the concept of sustainability are striking. What for Ontario Hydro are impacts properly discussed with a view to substitution and providing financial compensation raise questions for the Aboriginal peoples about their capacity to sustain a way of life. In short, from an Aboriginal perspective, sustainability is impossible in the absence of respect for the land. Unavoidably, therefore, sustainability raises the issue of historical grievances, the second component in the Aboriginal perspective on the Mattagami extensions.

38   Why is this so? The Aboriginal position on grievances is succinctly set out by Chief Kapashesit in a statement to the Environmental Assessment Board created to evaluate Ontario Hydro's 25 year *Demand/Supply Plan*; he argues that "Justice requires that ... past grievances be settled before future projects are even considered. It is immoral for Ontario Hydro to be talking about future projects when they have not entered settlements to compensate for the damage they inflicted by past projects."[34] At first glance this stance may appear paradoxical. If, as we have been suggesting, the objectionable character of

Ontario Hydro's proposal for resolving conflicts over the Mattagami Extension rests in part in the suggestion that the way to deal with residual impacts of the development it is proposing is through compensation, how is it possible that Aboriginal leaders should propose that serious grievances be resolved through compensation?

39   The question is important. It is also relatively easily answered. Those historical grievances now hold enormous symbolic value for the Native peoples of the north. They represent the failure on the part of an alien and insensitive culture to give to the land slated for development as well as the life dependent on it the profound respect which are their due. The Native inhabitants' response to this failure is analogous to the outrage which would greet a proposal to burn the contents of Canada's libraries to heat the city of Toronto, or the art hanging on the walls of the Louvre to light the city of Paris.

40   To understand the analogy requires seeing books and paintings as renewable resources, which in a sense they are. There is no shortage of either authors or painters to renew our libraries or art galleries. But to see books and paintings in this light would be clearly unacceptable, indeed offensive for many people raised in a European culture. Native peoples regard our response to water as a renewable natural resource in a similar way. At issue in both cases is an implied disrespect for things of great value and, by implication, for the people who value them. What then could count as compensation? Or more properly, what is the role of compensation in cases such as this? Compensation cannot replace valued items with things of equal value. What compensation can do is restore a sense of respect or acknowledge in a significant way the nature of the offence which has been given.[35] It is unlikely that a people so offended could accept as sincere a commitment to change that offered nothing by way of restitution for activities said now to be regretted and not to be repeated.

41   The third component of the Aboriginal position on the proposed Mattagami Extension is the demand that there be no further development until the rights of the First Nation communities to self-government have been recognized. Recognition is to include control over the development of natural resources in areas of Native jurisdiction. The logic of this demand flows directly from the importance of sustainability to the traditional Native way of life and the failure on the part of those developing the north to respect values of central importance to the Native communities affected. Control over the land and uses imposed would ensure that future development was appropriately responsive to those values.

42   As with the Ontario Hydro proposal for the Mattagami Complex, this solution to the current impasse has clear strengths. If we accept that sustainability is as Native leaders have claimed a fundamental value in Aboriginal culture, it would move environmental values to a much more significant place in the evaluation of development proposals than has been the case previously. It would ensure respect for the interests of a minority who have been required historically to carry substantially more than their fair share of the costs of development.

43   The idea of a veto for Aboriginal or local communities over development proposals in areas like Northern Ontario has been advanced in a number of formats and contexts and is not unique to the Aboriginal peoples of northeastern Ontario. For example, the environmental assessment *Guidelines for the Great Whale River Hydroelectric Project* require that "the proposed (Great Whale) project must ... respect the rights of local communities to determine their future

and their own societal objectives."[36] But is this proposal consistent with the moral principle that those who benefit from an activity should carry the costs it generates? To satisfy this principle requires a careful accounting of the interests of all those who have a stake in any decisions about the future of, for example, the Mattagami Complex. What is being proposed would appear simply to shift control over development from one stakeholder, Ontario Hydro, to another. It is not obvious that the effect of such a shift would be a fair sharing of the costs and benefits of decisions affecting the use of nature's resources.

44   There are two immediate objections to this interpretation of this second option seen from a northeastern Ontario Aboriginal perspective. What First Nation stake-holders are calling for in this case is co-planning and co-management of resources;[37] surely a demand of this nature is not inconsistent with principles of distributive justice. Further, the demand for self-government is a rights claim. It is not based on an appeal to principles of distributive justice or sustainable development. As such it might well be argued that it is immune to moral arguments seeking to balance costs and benefits of actions and policy decisions for those affected.

45   These are important considerations. What they seem to point to is a weakness in the analysis of the moral underpinnings of the idea of sustainable development. The principle that those who reap the benefits of a development project should bear the costs can be operationalized acceptably only where there is substantial agreement on what is to count as a cost or a benefit. However, the concepts of cost and benefit are culturally sensitive, and one form of moral insensitivity is insensitivity to this fact. Historical injustice is frequently the result, undermining, on the part of those affected, trust in the willingness

of its perpetrators to change their ways. The demand for self-government can be seen as a response to that breakdown in trust.

46   Whether the idea of self-government, accompanied as it almost always is with a desire to exercise control over natural resources, is an acceptable response to the fact of historical injustice is too large a question for this paper.[38] Seen from the perspective of sustainable development and its moral underpinnings, however, it raises an instructive point. If we accept that individuals themselves are usually the best judges of their own interests, then in practice it is unlikely that a principle like the one we have highlighted will find morally acceptable implementation in the absence of equitable participation in decision making by those likely to be affected.[39] And while acknowledging that this point does raise significant difficulties for shaping decision making so that it reflects adequately the interests of future generations, it does point to the need to add a principle of equitable participation as a practical requirement for sustainable development.

47   It is considerations of this sort which lead to the third option presented by stakeholders for resolving the conflict generated by the Mattagami Extension proposal.

3) Operationalizing the Principle of Equitable Participation

48   As the stakeholder analysis in part one indicates, the Ontario Government had a substantial financial, economic and political interest in resolving the conflict that emerged in response to the Mattagami Extension proposal. In response to a report it commissioned in July 1991 and extensive informal negotiations with First Nation representatives, the provincial government un-

dertook to create two consultative processes. Both were designed to resolve conflict over the Mattagami Extension proposal while laying the framework for constructive resolution of the longer term resource use planning issues. Both processes reflected an acknowledgement that the short term and longer term issues could not be resolved unless both non-Native concerns about the economic future of the region and Aboriginal concerns about the right to equitable participation in resource development and resource management were addressed.

49   First, the Ontario government undertook to create a "technical group" whose mandate was to review "how the design and/or operation of the (Mattagami Complex) Project could be modified to achieve the primary objective of environmental enhancement as well as the production of energy." The government proposed that the group have four members, two appointed by the government and two by the Moose River James Bay (Aboriginal) Coalition and/or its members, on behalf of Moose Factory, New Post and MoCreebec First Nations. In proposing this group, the government committed itself to providing the financial and technical resources the group would need to assess the Mattagami extension project, to consult broadly and to report back to the government and the elected chiefs and councils of the New Post, Moose Factory and MoCreebec First Nations.[40] The intention was to bring the environmental assessment process to a successful conclusion while recognizing the importance of First Nation self-government concerns by appointing an advisory group with an equal number of Native and non-Native members. Further, the technical group was to be given a mandate to report with recommendations to the appropriate bodies on any issues of concern identified in the consulta-

tive process. In proposing the committee, the minister implied a willingness to be guided in his decisions on the project by a consensus report that met with Aboriginal approval.

50   The second element in the government proposal was the creation of a baseline data collection project, given the task of describing the existing biophysical, social, cultural and economic environmental conditions in the Moose River Basin. These data could then be used to identify a base line against which the cumulative impacts of resource development in the basin could be measured.[41] The government also proposed that "traditional knowledge" as well as data gathered using the techniques of modern science should be included in the data base.

51   Here, the government was responding to a fundamental Native environmental concern, namely, that the environment should be looked at holistically. In responding to resource development proposals, Native spokespeople argued that what matters is not the aggregate environmental impact of any particular development looked at in isolation but the cumulative impact of resource development in the Moose River Basin looked at together. Native groups also argued that cumulative impacts could only be calculated against pre-established environmental benchmarks. Identifying such benchmarks for the Moose River Basin before further development was approved was therefore a fundamental First Nation demand.

52   The proposals advanced by the Ontario government and accepted by the Moose Cree First Nation as a single package focus on matters of process. They assume that, if a fair dispute resolution process can be established, sound environmental and economic decisions will be forthcoming. As such, the Ontario government proposals are not derived directly from

a commitment to sustainable development or to the equitable sharing of the costs and the benefits of resource development. The option proposed does seem to rest on a moral principle, however, namely that of equitable participation.[42] Are there important connections between these two principles? As a matter of practice, the answer is surely yes.

53 We have already suggested that the deep sense of grievance that Native leaders have carried into the Mattagami Extension debate can be understood as a legitimate moral response to the lack of respect exhibited in the past for their peoples' values by resource developments. It is at least arguable that the Native peoples of Northern Ontario would not have been treated as they were had they been granted the right to equitable participation. It is equally difficult to see how in practice distributive justice or sustainable development could be guiding principles of resource development where equitable participation on the part of those likely to be adversely affected was denied.

The Moral Structure of Sustainability

54 What lessons can be learned from the debate that has been generated by Ontario Hydro's Mattagami Extension proposals? There would seem to be several.

1. Commitment to sustainable development by itself is not likely to lead to consensus on environmentally acceptable development unless we are able to unpack carefully the moral structure of that idea. This need may not be obvious in morally homogeneous cultural settings, but where the moral underpinnings of the idea are not carefully considered, consensus may reflect little more than a pervasive cultural bias. It was not the presence of Native peoples in Northern Ontario that made hydraulic development of northern rivers unsustainable. What their presence has done, though all too slowly and at great cost, is to make the unsustainable character of that development visible.

2. Distributive justice is an important component of sustainable development. The relevant principle of distributive justice is that those who benefit from resource development should bear the costs it generates. Injustice results when significant costs are externalized. Hence, externalizing costs is simply incompatible with a commitment to distributive justice and hence to sustainable development.[43]

3. The identification, measurement and sharing of costs and benefits of development is a key element in assessing sustainability. This process, however, is culturally sensitive. That is to say, what counts as a cost and a benefit will be a function of the values and patterns of life of those affected. Because of this, moral insensitivity is both a significant obstacle to assessments of sustainability and a source of injustice.

4. One form of moral insensitivity to which least cost planning seems particularly prone is the monetization of costs. Monetizing all costs assumes the homogeneity of values. But more importantly, it assumes that everything valued, particularly anything which is a part of the natural environment, can be instrumentalized in monetary terms. Our study suggests that this view clashes with the need for cultural sensitivity in identifying, assessing and sharing costs and benefits. The issue is not whether in some cultures at least there are things which are so valuable they cannot be given up whatever the circumstances, but rather how the cost or perhaps the loss of things of that sort is to be assessed.

5. In practice, ensuring equitable participation in processes which are directed toward the identification, measurement or sharing of costs is a requirement of sustainable development. This is not because it is in principle impossible for people to identify and measure impacts from the perspective of those with a different cultural background. Rather, it is a requirement first because it is reasonable to assume that adults are the best judges of the value of things seen from their own perspective, and second because overcoming moral insensitivity in practice is a difficult challenge and one which is likely to be met only imperfectly much of the time in the absence of the active cooperation and participation of those whose perspective is in question.

6. Finally, while historical injustice is not an infallible indicator of unsustainability, it does stand as a powerful symbol of moral insensitivity. Moral sensitivity is not a necessary condition of sustainable development. However, where it is absent, sustainability can only be realized by accident, not by design.

Final Observations and a Concluding Postscript

55 This paper is an exercise in applied ethics. Our purpose in writing it has been to identify the moral values that underpin the pursuit of sustainability, values that must be respected if it is to be achieved. The argument of this paper is designed to support two conclusions in this regard. First, sustainable development does indeed have a moral structure. Second, the moral structure of sustainability has three components. The first two are principles of distributive justice: *those who benefit from resource development should bear all its costs; costs and benefits of resource development should be distributed fairly.* The third is a practical corollary of the first two: *equitable participation in planning and management of resource developments on the part of those on whom a particular development is likely to have an impact is in practice necessary if moral insensitivity in identifying and "costing" costs and benefits likely to accrue from development and injustice in the distribution of costs and benefits is to be avoided.*

56 Our analysis has not outlined a strategy for eradicating historical injustice in this or any of its many manifestations, although the article does purport to identify some of the political, legal, economic and social roots of historical injustice. Neither does it make substantive recommendations about policies, procedures or initiatives required if sustainable development is to be achieved in social environments in which historical injustice is a seriously complicating factor. Ethical analysis alone cannot provide answers to these questions. It can help to expose the moral structure of historical grievances. It can also help to identify morally necessary conditions for their resolution. However, the task of rectifying those injustices requires a depth and breadth of practical wisdom only one part of which is moral insight. Also needed will be a considerable degree of cultural knowledge, practical political skills, political and economic analysis and so on.

57 For some, this conclusion will appear a counsel of despair. In our view, however, it is a simple acknowledgement that moral values are only one of the keys to unlocking sustainable futures.

A Concluding Postscript

58 In 1994, the Ontario government gave approval for the Mattagami Complex project, thus avoiding the $247 million payment. A condition of

that approval, however, is a proviso that any future Mattagami complex redevelopment will be overseen by a "Mattagami Extensions Coordinating Council" consisting of equal representation from the First Nations and the Ontario government. This uniting of Aboriginal and provincial interests appears to be unprecedented for Ontario's environmental assessment process.

59   Whether the complex will be redeveloped in the future is now a moot point. However, in 1995, Ontario Hydro signed an agreement for the settlement of past grievances with one First Nation, and is currently in negotiations with several others. Such actions appear to reflect a new direction for Ontario Hydro, based on recommendations made by its Task Force on Sustainable Energy Development, recommendations such as securing greater stakeholder involvement and strengthening partnerships with Aboriginal communities.[44] Also in 1995, the Ministry of Natural Resources launched the "Environmental Information Partnership" for the Moose River Basin consisting of First Nations, the federal government and the Ontario government, a continuation of the original baseline data collection project. The goal of the partnership is to develop an information management system for the Moose River Basin that will assist in the identification and evaluation of potential cumulative effects of any planned developments within the Basin. Integral to that information management agreement is recognition that Aboriginal environmental knowledge has a legitimate place along with modern science in that identification process.

60   Meanwhile discussions on Aboriginal self-government are still pending amongst the First Nation, federal and Ontario governments.[45] Based on these recent developments, it appears to be the case that several of the "lessons" to be

learned from the conflict are beginning to be put into practice. Whether or not there will emerge a complete resolution to the conflict which is morally satisfactory to the major stakeholders remains to be seen.

NOTES

1. The authors acknowledge funding support for this research on the part of the SSHRCC (Strategic Grants Program), York University's Haub Program in Business and the Environment and York University's Faculty of Administrative Studies Small Research Grants Program.

   This paper is a product of an interdisciplinary environmental ethics research project studying four resource use proposals for northeastern Ontario and northern British Columbia. We wish to acknowledge the contribution of Maria Radford who did much of the original document research. Co-investigator David Pearson, project partner Ralph Wheeler from the Ministry of Natural Resources, project partner Mario Durepos from Ontario Hydro, and Paul Wilkinson and Associates all have provided assistance at various stages. The Ontario Aboriginal Research Coalition, created to direct research into the effects on Ontario's First Nations of Ontario Hydro's 25 Year Plan, financed the collection of oral histories. Chief Ernest Beck and David Fletcher of the Moosecree Factory First Nation, Chief Randy Kapashesit of the MoCreebec First Nation, and John Turner of the Mushkegowuk Tribal Council provided guidance and on-site assistance. Our thanks also go to David Fletcher, for continuing assistance throughout, and to Ontario Hydro, who arranged a site visit to the Mattagami Complex.

2. For a statement of Trudeau's position and a discussion of the issues raised by it, see A.W. Cragg, *Contemporary Moral Issues* Third Edition (Toronto: McGraw-Hill, 1992), Chapter 5, "Native Rights."

3. The information in the following case is based on Ontario Hydro's *Environmental Assessment*, Aboriginal Witness Statements (Adams, Conway, Roderique, J. Sutherland, P. Sutherland), and an exhibit from J. Morrison used during the DSP Environmental Assessment Hearing.

4. K. Noble, "Kapuskasing Deal Best for Everybody," *The Globe and Mail*, B4.

5. For an attempt to identify cross-cultural moral principles appropriate for resource development decisions which goes beyond a discussion of the moral principles imbedded in the concept of sustainable development, see Michael McDonald, Jack T. Stevenson and Wesley Cragg, "Finding a Balance of Values: An Ethical Assessment of Ontario Hydro's Demand/Supply Plan" *Report to the Aboriginal Research Coalition of Ontario* (1992), and Wesley Cragg, Michael McDonald and Jack T. Stevenson, "The Demand/Supply Plan and the Moose River Basin" (unpublished). These reports are complementary ethical analyses of the Ontario Hydro 25 year *Demand/Supply Plan*. The analysis is a direct moral evaluation which alludes to the concept of sustainable development but is not based on it; for a discussion of the need for value based analysis see Litchfield et al., "Integrated Resource Planning and the Great Whale Public Review," Background Paper, No. 7, Great Whale Environmental Assessment (Great Whale Environmental Public Review Office, 1994).

6. It could be argued that a fuller and wider application of this principle than proposed here might require that it be qualified by phrases like: "In the absence of genuinely voluntary agreement to the contrary, the costs, etc." This caveat is ignored here, since introducing it would not modify the argument which we propose to advance in what follows. The principle itself is defended by Andy Brookin "Obligations to Future Generations: A Case Study," *Contemporary Moral Issues*, ed. A.W.

Cragg (Toronto: McGraw/Hill Ryerson, 1993)359. Brook ties this principle to two others: Liberty – Our actions must not result in preventable and foreseeable restriction of others' opportunities (which disease, pain, mutation or costs of avoiding these would do); Freedom from pain – Our actions must not result in preventable and foreseeable pain (or discomfort or diminution of ability) in others.

In turn Brook ties these three principles to a fourth which he claims under-rides all three: Prior to considerations of individual distinguishing qualities of moral relevance, each person has the same value as any other. For the purposes of this paper, the distributive justice principle is the key one: Brook's account offers a defence of that principle and proposals for others that a full examination of the ethics of resource extraction should use as well.

7. For the purpose of this discussion we propose to use as our definition of the term "environment" the meaning set out in by Ontario statute in the Environmental Assessment Act:

i) air, land or water,

ii) plant and animal life, including man,

iii) the social, economic and cultural conditions that influence the life of man or a community,

iv) any building, structure, machine or other device or thing made by man,

v) any solid, liquid, gas, odour, heat, sound, vibration or radiation resulting directly or indirectly from the activities of man, or

vi) any part or combination of the foregoing and the interrelationships between any two or more or them. (Revised Statutes of Ontario, 1980, s. 1(c)).

8. See Aboriginal Witness Statements, DSP Environmental Assessment Hearing, Exhibits: 829-886, 947-951, 1018-1019.

9. See for example M. Friedman, "The Social Responsibility of Business is to Increase its Profits," *The New York Times Magazine*, September, 1970.

10. Litchfield et al., "Integrating Resource Planning ...," 1994.

11. Ontario Hydro, *Environmental Assessment: Hydroelectric Generation Station Extensions Mattagami River*, October 1990, 2-1.

12. Litchfield et al., "Integrated Resource Planning ...," 4, describe this as the traditional planning model for utilities in North America in this century.

13. Ontario Hydro, *Demand/Supply Plan Report*, DSP Environmental Assessment Hearing, Exhibit #3, December 1989, 6-13.

14. Presently the Environmental Assessment Act R.S.O. 1990, c.E.18. *Ibid.*, s. 2.

15. *Ibid.*, s. 1(c).

16. Ontario Hydro, *Demand Supply Plan Environmental Analysis*. DSP Environmental Assessment Hearing, Exhibit #4, December 1989, 3-3.

17. *Ibid.*, 3-5.

18. Ontario Hydro, *Environmental Assessment Summary: Hydroelectric Generation Station Extensions Mattagami River*, October 1990, 18.

19. *Ibid.*, 23.

20. A channel which carries away water which has passed through the generating station.

21. Ontario Hydro, *Environmental Assessment Summary*, 24-5.

22. *Ibid.*, 6-13.

23. *Ibid.*, 6-48.

24. *Ibid.*

25. *Ibid.*, 8-11.

26. The First Nations in the Moose River Basin refused to cooperate with Ontario Hydro's environmental assessment.

27. Ontario Hydro, *Environmental Assessment Summary*, 8-11.

28. These difficulties are the subject of ongoing debate among economists and others. An accessible (to the lay person) discussion is offered in Litchfield et al., "Integrated Resource Planning..." For a more detailed examination of the limitations of cost/benefit analysis from the perspective of distributive justice see McDonald, Stevenson and Cragg, "Finding a Balance of Values."

29. This conclusion is not unique to the authors of this paper. Two recent attempts at costing impacts relevant to these concerns by major utilities, Ontario Hydro in its 25 Year Plan and Quebec Hydro with regard to the Great Whale project, seem to have led to the same conclusion. Ontario Hydro put off assessing these costs to the formal environmental assessment process which of course was never completed. What they appear to have concluded was that costing would have to be arrived at through some process of negotiation after the developments they were seeking had been approved in principle. Quebec Hydro's environmental assessment from "Grande-Baleine Complex: Feasibility Study," Hydro Quebec, August 1993, is worth quoting in this regard:

   The financial evaluation of sociocultural impacts is ... difficult. Many believe economists do not have the right to put a price tag on goods or values for which it is difficult, if not impossible, to imagine a market. Such people may find it reprehensible that economists perform economic assessments of certain aspects of Native culture.

   Further:

   In the case of other externalities, which are generally social or cultural, an approach aimed at establishing an economic value appears neither appropriate nor possible. (Part 2, Book 8, 37).

30. For a discussion of this point see, Litchfield et al., "Integrated Resource Planning..."

31. Native People's Circle on Environment and Development, Report prepared for the Ontario Round Table on Environment and Economy, 1992, 4.

32. R. Kapashesit, "Evidence in Chief," DSP Environmental Assessment Hearing, Exhibit #1019, n.d. 7.

33. Native People's Circle, Report, 4.

34. Kapashesit, "Evidence in Chief," 7.

35. There are no relevant studies that we know of in environmental ethics that probe this perspective. However, there are relevant studies in other areas. Philosophy of law and punishment is a good example. Punishment of offenders is often seen as a form of compensation for offensive actions. This theme is explored at length by Jean Hampton and Jeffrey Murphy in their book *Forgiveness and Mercy* (Cambridge: Cambridge University Press, 1988). H.L.A. Hart explores a similar theme in *Punishment and Responsibility* (Oxford: Clarendon Press, 1963), particularly "Punishment and the Elimination of Responsibility," 183. See also A.W. Cragg, *The Practice of Punishment: Toward a Theory of Restorative Justice* (London: Routledge, 1993). It should also be noted that Paul Wilkinson has pointed out (private correspondence) that compensation of the sort to which Chief Kapashesit refers need not be thought of in purely financial terms; he argues that "compensation might take a symbolic form such as the erection of a monument, a public apology, environmental remediation, economic development to replace lost opportunities, or many other forms." Wilkinson also points out that acceptance of financial compensation should not be construed as a recognition by concerned First Nations of its appropriateness, given the nature of the harms experienced.

36. *Guidelines for the Great Whale River Hydroelectric Project,* #113.

37. D. DeLauney, "Report of the Provincial Representative: Moose River Basin Consultations," prepared for the Ministry of Natural Resources, April 1992, 7.

38. Will Kymlicka goes some distance in an unpublished paper entitled "Concepts of Community and Social Justice" prepared for a conference on "Global Environmental Change and Social Justice," at Cornell University, September 1993; in it he explores the interplay of the right to self-determination of minorities with principles of distributive justice concerned with a fair distribution and use of natural resources.

39. The idea of equitable participation has been most carefully examined in the context of medical ethics, where it is now widely accepted that it is the competent patient's judgement of his or her own interests which should guide treatment and not that of the health care provider. See T. Beauchamp and J. Childress, *Principles of Biomedical Ethics* (New York: Oxford University Press, 1979) 62, 153; and Edmund Pellegrino, "Trust and Distrust in Professional Ethics," *Trust and the Professions: Philosophical and Cultural Aspects* (Washington, DC: Georgetown University Press, n.d.) 81.

40. Ministry of Natural Resources, "Draft Terms of Reference/Work Plan for the Technical Group," 28 July 1993, 1.

41. Ministry of Natural Resources, "Moose River Basin Baseline Data Collection Project, Background Report," August 1993, 2.

42. Cragg, McDonald and Stevenson, "Finding a Balance ...," 20.

43. It does not follow, of course, that any project with externalized costs is unsustainable. It does follow on the other hand that it is unjust to externalize costs for which there are inadequate compensating benefits recognizable as such by those on whom the costs are imposed.

44. Ontario Hydro, *Report of the Task Force on Sustainable Energy Development: A Strategy for Sustainable Energy Development and Use for Ontario Hydro*, 18 October 1993,32-5.

45. The members of the research team of which this project is a part consist of Wesley Cragg, Principal Investigator and co-investigators John Lewko, David Pearson and Craig Summers (Laurentian University). For further information about the project, please write Wesley Cragg, Faculty of Administrative Studies, York University, 4700 Keele St., North York, Ontario, M3J 1P3; e-mail: wcragg@mail.fas.yorku.ca.

BIBLIOGRAPHY

Adams, T. "Witness Statement," DSP Environmental Assessment Hearing, Exhibit #855, December, 1992.

Allen, G. "Ontario Backs Mill Buyout Plan," *The Globe and Mail*, 20 June 1991, A4.

Bay and Basin Bulletin: The Moose River Basin Project Newsletter, Vol. 1, No.2, January, 1995.

Beauchamp, T. and Childress, J. *Principles of Biomedical Ethics*. New York: Oxford University Press, 1979.

Bennett, Kearon. "Small Hydro Research Summary Report," Appendix G, DSP Environmental Assessment Hearing, Exhibit #926, November, 1992.

Brook, A. "Obligations to Future Generations: A Case Study," *Contemporary Moral Issues*. Toronto: McGraw/Hill Ryerson, 1993, 359.

Brundtland Commission. *Our Common Future*. Oxford: Oxford University Press, 1987.

Cheena, G. "Witness Statement," DSP Environmental Assessment Hearing, Exhibit #883, December, 1992.

Conway, T. "Impacts of Prior Development," DSP Environmental Assessment Hearing, Exhibit #890, December, 1992.

Cragg, A.W. *Contemporary Moral Issues*. Toronto: McGraw-Hill Ryerson, 1992.

Cragg, A.W. *The Practice of Punishment: Toward a Theory of Restorative Justice*. London: Routledge, 1993.

Cragg, A.W., McDonald and Stevenson. "Finding a Balance of Values: An Ethical Assessment of Ontario Hydro's Demand/Supply Plan," November, 1992.

DeLauney, D. "Report of the Provincial Representative: Moose River Basin Consultations," prepared for the Ministry of Natural Resources, April, 1992.

Environmental Assessment Act, R.S.O. 1980, c. 140.

Environmental Assessment Act, R.S.O. 1990, c. E.18.

ESSA (Environmental and Social Systems Analysts Ltd.). "Hypotheses of Effects of Development in the Moose River Basin Workshop Summary - Final Report," DSP Environmental Assessment Hearing, Exhibit #719, March, 1992.

Faries, B. "Witness Statement," DSP Environmental Assessment Hearing, Exhibit #876, December, 1992.

Fowlie, L. "Town That Refused To Die," *Financial Post*, 28-30 December 1991, 16.

Friedman, M. "The Social Responsibility of Business is to Increase Its Profits," *The New York Times Magazine*, 13 September 1970.

"Guidelines: Environmental Impact Statement for the Proposed Great Whale River Hydroelectric Project," Evaluating Committee, Kativik Environmental Quality Commission, Federal Review Committee North of the 55th Parallel, Federal Environmental Assessment Review Panel, published by Great Whale Public Review Support Office, 1155 Sherbrooke St. West, Suite 1603, Montreal, Quebec (H3A 2N3).

Hampton, J. and Murphy, J. *Forgiveness and Mercy*. Cambridge: Cambridge University Press) 1988.

Hart, H.L.A. *Punishment and Responsibility*. Oxford: Clarendon Press, 1963.

Jones, I. "Witness Statement," DSP Environmental Assessment Hearing, Exhibit #950, December, 1992.

Kapashesit, R. "Evidence in Chief," DSP Environmental Assessment Hearing, Exhibit #1019.

Keir, A. "Socio-Economic Impact Assessment: Reference Document of Hydroelectric Generating Station Extensions Mattagami River," prepared for Ontario Hydro Corporate Relations Branch, Volumes 1-2, January 1991.

Kymlicka, W. "Concepts of Community and Social Justice." Unpublished. Presented at "Global Environmental Change and Social Justice" conference at Cornell University, September, 1993.

Linklater, M. "Witness Statement," DSP Environmental Assessment Hearing, Exhibit #877, December, 1992.

Litchfield, James, Hemmingway, Leroy and Raphals, Philip. "Integrated Resource Planning and the Great Whale Public Review," Background Paper No.7, Great Whale Environmental Assessment, Great Whale Public Review Office, 1994.

MacDonald, R. "Witness Statement," DSP Environmental Assessment Hearing, Exhibit #852, December, 1992.

Mackie, R. "Can't Afford Mill Bailout, Premier Says," *The Globe and Mail,* 15 July 1991, A8.

Ministry of Natural Resources. "Draft Terms of Reference/Work Plan for the Technical Group," 28 July 1993.

Ministry of Natural Resources. "Moose River Basin Baseline Data Collection Project, Background Report," August, 1993.

Mittelstaedt, M. "Hydro Looking To End Environmental Hearing," *The Globe and Mail,* 13 November 1992, A5.

Mittelstaedt, M. "Ontario Gives Hydro Project Go-Ahead," *The Globe and Mail,* 6 October 1994, B1O.

Morrison, J. "Colonization, Resource Extraction and Hydroelectric Development in the Moose River Basin: A Preliminary History of the Implications For Aboriginal People," DSP Environmental Assessment Hearing, Exhibit #869 November, 1992.

Mugiskan, Chief W. "Witness Statement," DSP Environmental Assessment Hearing, Exhibit #866, December, 1992.

Nation, K., and Noble, K. "U.S. Firm Rejects Newsprint Mill Deal," *The Globe and Mail,* 29 June 1991, B1, B4.

Native People's Circle on Environment and Development, Report prepared for the Ontario Round Table on Environment and Economy, 1992.

Noble, K. "Kapuskasing Deal Best For Everybody," *The Globe and Mail,* 15 August 1991, Section B1, B4.

Ontario Hydro. *Demand/Supply Plan Report,* DSP Environmental Assessment Hearing, Exhibit #3, December, 1989.

Ontario Hydro. *Demand Supply Plan Environmental Analysis,* DSP Environmental Assessment Hearing, Exhibit #4, December, 1989.

Ontario Hydro. *Environmental Assessment: Hydroelectric Generating Station Extensions Mattagami River,* October, 1990.

Ontario Hydro. *Environmental Assessment Summary: Hydroelectric Generating Station Extensions Mattagami River,* February, 1991.

Ontario Hydro. *Report of the Task Force on Sustainable Energy Development: A Strategy For Sustainable Energy Development and Use For Ontario Hydro,* 18 October 1993.

Pellegrino, Edmund. "Trust and Distrust in Professional Ethics." *Ethics, Trust and the Professions: Philosophical and Cultural Aspects.* Washington D.C.: Georgetown University Press.

Philp, M. "Spruce Falls Mill May Close," *The Globe and Mail,* 20 March 1991, B3.

Roderique, J. "Witness Statement," DSP Environmental Assessment Hearing, Exhibit #875, December, 1992.

Sears, S.K. and Peterson, M. "Integrated Ecosystem-Based Planning for Hydroelectric Generation Development in a Remote Northern Ontario River Basin," DSP Environmental Assessment Hearing, Exhibit #382, May, 1991.

Submission Letters re: Review of Environmental Assessment for the Proposed Hydroelectric Generating Station Extensions on the Mattagami River. 1992, Ministry of the Environment, Environmental Assessment Branch. 1992.

Sutherland, J. "Witness Statement," DSP Environmental Assessment Hearing, Exhibit #873, December, 1992.

Sutherland, P. "Witness Statement," DSP Environmental Assessment Hearing, Exhibit #874, December, 1992.

Questions

1. Do you agree with Trudeau's statement?

2. Explain how Cragg and Schwartz's conception of sustainable development is based on distributive justice theory (P18, P28). How is the First Nations' definition of sustainable development different (P35)? And how is Ontario Hydro's definition different from that of the First Nations (P36–37)? What principle does the Ontario government proposal add to that of sustainable development (P52–53)?

3. (a) Explain how the (past) injustice resulting from Ontario Hydro development in the North was due to a relativistic moral perspective that equates right with law (P22–23); explain how the same perspective may lead to (future) justice (P28).

   (b) Define "externalities" and explain how the injustice was due to an egoistic moral perspective.

4. Identify the parts of the paper that show application of each of the following:

   (a) a consequentialist approach

   (b) a Kantian approach

   (c) a rights-based approach

   (d) a justice-based approach

5. Which of the three proposals (Ontario Hydro, First Nations, Ontario government) do you think is the best, ethically speaking? Be prepared to support and defend your opinion.

6. (a) Suppose you are the ethics consultant representing the Ontario government appointed to the Mattagami Extensions Coordinating Council. What are the top five items on your "things to do" list?

   (b) Suppose you are the ethics consultant representing the First Nations appointed to the Mattagami Extensions Coordinating Council. What are the top five items on your "things to do" list?

   (c) Suppose you are the next generation CEO of Ontario Hydro intending to call each of the representatives. What will you say?

Business Ethics and National Identity in Quebec: Distinctiveness and Directions

Jean Pasquero

1 In North America, business ethics is defined largely in American terms. As part of the continent, Quebec is certainly influenced by the ethical movement that has swept the business scene in the last ten to fifteen years. Yet, business ethics in Quebec presents particular characteristics, which set it apart from the mainstream Anglo-Saxon framework with which we are familiar.

2   This essay will not present a survey of business ethics literature in Quebec; it will rather try to analyze the nature and meaning of this distinctiveness for both practice and theory. The critical difference is that, unlike the US where it is defined largely in individual terms, in Quebec business ethics is tightly linked to one central issue, the preservation of a "national identity". Therefore, understanding the obligations of business people and firms requires to put them within a societal context.

3   The paper includes five parts. In the first part, we broadly contrast the American and the Quebec discourses on ethics, providing a framework for the analysis of business ethics in Quebec. The next three parts discuss the details of the framework. In the last part, we apply this framework to a sample of recent business eth-

Jean Pasquero, "Business Ethics and National Identity in Quebec: Distinctiveness and Directions" *Journal of Business Ethics* 16.6 (April 1997): 621-633. © 1997 by Kluwer Academic Publishers. Reprinted with permission of the publisher and the author.

ics issues and discuss their meaning for both theory and practice.

Contrasting two discourses on business ethics

4 Business ethics as discussed in Quebec is quite different from the discourse in the US. The difference originates mostly in the level at which the discourse is held.

A difference of level

5 The first difference is one of quantity. The discourse on business ethics in the US is characterized by its vitality. From a marginal addition to curricula in a few select business schools at its beginning, it has now taken the form of a wide-ranging social and intellectual movement. Business ethics in the US embraces at least three dimensions: a philosophical reflection about individual needs and values; a critical analysis of prevailing business practices; and a conventional market, with its producers, consumers, and promoters. The movement is more than a media success, however; it is also generating an unprecedented theoretical creativity, and it holds the potential for a lasting transformation of some traditional practices of American capitalism.

6   By contrast, the discourse on business ethics in Quebec is not prevalent in neither the

media, business schools or business circles. At best, it is still embryonic.[1,2,3] It is marked by few surveys of practices, few vocal business critics, and still fewer scholars. The American brand of business ethics does make inroads in Quebec, but mostly by appropriation: large firms discreetly import practices from the US when dealing with classic ethics issues, while a few isolated scholars try to strengthen their reflection by capitalizing on the US trend.

7   Nevertheless, the real difference between the discourse on business ethics in the US and in Quebec is not a quantitative, but a qualitative, one. Quebec is certainly not spared the business ethics issues that American firms face, but these issues are overshadowed by a discourse set at a different level. The theme is indeed actively discussed, but it is not labelled as such. Business ethics in Quebec is primarily cast in terms of social responsibilities. Its primary focus is not the transformation of the values and practices of individual business managers. It is the cooperation of business firms and key decision-makers to the sustainment of one overwhelming goal collectively valued at the societal level, the preservation of Quebec's identity within the North American mosaic.

8   This paper holds that the discourse on business ethics is largely culture-bound. For present purposes, let us define culture as including both the values shared by a community and the institutions that help sustain these values. The specificity of business ethics in Quebec will be made more apparent from a comparison with the roots of the US discourse on ethics.

The roots of the US discourse on ethics

9 The American discourse on business ethics is supported by three traditions. First is the old tradition of liberal democracy, inherited from the 18th century. This tradition values individualistic ideals of self-accomplishment and equality, which find their consecration in the ownership of a small business. Its hero is still the law-abiding entrepreneur who earns an honest and independent living by offering some valuable service to his or her community, and whose values reflect those of this community. This tradition is deeply distrustful of power in general, notably the power of big business, and that of government. It holds that ethics is better ensured when power is divided among responsible equals – today called stakeholders – whereas the concentration of power among unelected holders is associated with a lack of ethics. In this egalitarian tradition, the ultimate value is fairness.[4] Business ethics is interpreted as a return to the traditional democratic ideals of the American Republic, through a renewed social contract between business and society. It is based on interpersonal relationships: Decision makers will act ethically when they respect their stakeholders, that is when they treat them fairly.

10   The second tradition is that of puritanism. The work ethic celebrated by Max Weber is inseparable from a certain rigorism in moral judgment, which leaves little room for flexibility. Behaviours, people, institutions are judged as either good or bad. The courts, which are often called upon as the ultimate arbiters of business ethics, reinforce this tendency by casting ethical issues into an either-or, binary framework. In addition, religious and cultural diversity does not completely override a certain pressure for moral and social conformity. Any departure from the most exacting standards of behaviour deserves attention, and can become the object of public opprobrium. In this tradition, business ethics is considered as a movement of moralization to purge business of its intrinsic vices.

11   The third tradition is that of utilitarianism. The business ethics movement in the US is also fuelled by the consideration of material interests: avoiding scandals, curbing governmental intervention, warding off pressure group activism, motivating the work force or increasing market share. Firms must act as good corporate citizens, because the alternative is more costly. Business ethics becomes a commodity. It can be implemented organizationally through internal programs and employee training. Its effects can be measured and incorporated into economic decision-making. In this tradition, the motivation for business ethics rests not in individual moral conviction, but in the threats arising from non-compliance with society's expectations as defined by the prevailing social powers.

The roots of the Quebec discourse on ethics

12   The business ethics discourse in the US, and that of Quebec follow two opposite trajectories. In the US, it starts with the individual, raises to the level of the corporation, and eventually to society; in Quebec it starts with societal concerns, filters down to the level of the firm, and eventually reaches individuals. To some extent, these traits are typical of those of small states confronted to world markets.[5]

13   Indeed, the particular experience of Quebec in North America makes its treatment of business ethics two steps removed from that prevailing in the United States. Quebec is first part of Canada. As such, it shares many of the traits that make Canada distinct from the US, notably a greater emphasis on the provision of public goods. For example, Canadians on the whole show a special interest in forging a national culture, are deeply attached to their extended social security system, and collectively hold a more

sympathetic attitude toward government intervention. Canada has often been described as the European alternative to the United States in North America. Secondly, within Canada, Quebec is somewhat unique among the ten Canadian provinces, thus further removing its experience from that of the US experience: it enjoys a cultural heritage and institutions of its own that cannot be found elsewhere with such concentration. Some of the typical Canadian traits are reinforced in Quebec, others have taken a distinct twist over time, and some traits are specific to the province. As a rough approximation, if one were to place Canada and Quebec on a continuum with the market-oriented US at one end and the mix economy countries of Western Europe at the other, both entities would fall somewhat in the middle. Yet, English Canada would be closer to the US and Quebec closer to Europe, with each probably closer together than to either pole.

14   The centrality of societal concerns in Quebec finds its roots in a deeply entrenched commitment to the preservation of the identity of the province. Three structural factors interplay to give the province a distinct identity in North America: identity preservation, institutional modernization, and consociative democracy. Each factor contributes a dimension to the framework within which business ethics in Quebec must be understood: collective rights, economic nationalism, and social solidarity:

identity preservation	→	collective rights
institutional modernization	→	economic assertion
consociative democracy	→	social solidarity

Accounts of the influence of a society's distinctive traits on business practices are traditionally divided into two categories: cultural explanations, and institutional explanations. A comprehensive framework should consider both.[6] In the case of Quebec, it is best to consider them jointly, as they cannot be analytically dissociated. A distinct cultural heritage has provided the province with specific needs and institutions; these institutions are in turn consciously cultivated and expanded by the social and political forces of the province to sustain the distinctiveness of its character.

15   Each of the three elements of the above framework will now be considered in turn.

Identity preservation and collective rights

16 The notion of collective rights lies at the heart of the specificity of the business ethics discourse in Quebec, just as it permeates all aspects of the social political life of the province. Quebec does have a strong Charter of individual rights, which even predates that of Canada. It does also however recognize the existence of some collective rights over and beyond individual rights in matters dealing with the survival of the province's identity.

17   Collective rights are rights that are granted to communities or groups rather than to individuals. The notion is common in European countries. In Quebec, the preservation of the French culture and especially of the French language – fundamental components of the francophone identity – is considered as a collective right benefitting the whole French-speaking community. This conception is akin to that of a public good, that is, a good that must be provided by political authorities to compensate for the failures of private individual exchange. Only government can provide public goods and enforce collective rights. The notion clashes with the traditional Anglo-saxon notion of individual rights, which ignores the rights of communities, or severely limits them, and considers social political choices as matters of personal preferences. One problem is that protecting the collective rights of one group usually creates individual obligations for the members of other groups without a direct offsetting counterpart. In Quebec, the debate over the legitimacy of collective rights, especially linguistic rights, is a source of daily frictions. Two groups, the francophone and the anglophone, coexist on the same territory, each claiming majority status, and each holding radically different views on the subject.

18   The recognition of collective rights finds its source in the traditional sentiment of cultural vulnerability held by the French-speaking population of the province. The notion deeply divides the heterogeneous population of Quebec along emotional lines. As with all matters of identity, perceptions rule realities, and objective facts are of little use in sorting out conflicting interpretations. One objective reality on which all observers will agree, however, is that cultural vulnerability is at the core of the Quebec psyche. Another is that the issue is extremely complex, and that no treatment can really render full justice to its intricacies. The following account will try to make sense of the contentions shaping business ethics debates in Quebec.

19   Since identity in Quebec is tightly linked to history and geography, a short overview will help. The population of Quebec exceeds 7 million, including 82% (about 6 million) whose mother tongue is French, and 18% (about 1 mil-

lion) who speak English either as mother tongue or as adopted tongue. Irrespective of language (that is, ignoring the linguistic crossovers), the 1991 federal census establishes that of 100 Quebecers today, 75 are descendants of the original 10,000 colonists from France who settled in the St. Lawrence valley in the late 17th century, 5 are from British descent who have settled in Quebec since the British conquest of French Canada in 1759, and most of the remaining 20 are more recent immigrants who trace their origins outside these two countries. Since the discovery of Canada by Jacques Cartier in 1534, Quebec has undergone three different regimes: French rule until the British conquest of 1759, British colonial rule until the formation of Canada in 1867, and since then membership within the Confederation of Canada. The ten provinces that presently make that confederation enjoy a considerable degree of autonomy when compared to American states. Within Canada, Quebec's demographic weight has steadily declined to the present proportion of slightly under 25% (which means that the 82% French-speaking component of Quebec only makes 20% of the total Canadian population).

20   Against this background, the sentiment of cultural vulnerability of French Quebec is kept acute by three underlying threats: cultural vulnerability, split identity, and institutional strain. Each leads to an affirmation of collective rights as a protection against an otherwise unstoppable loss of identity.

Cultural vulnerability

21 French Quebecers define their identity as the legacy of three centuries of resistance to assimilation, and the fierce preservation of a unique culture which predates most other European cultures on the continent. However, with a population barely reaching 2% of the Canadian-American whole, French Quebec is obsessed with the survival ("survivance") of that culture within this "sea of anglophones". The problem is complicated by the fact that most new immigrants to Quebec whose mother tongue is neither French nor English elect English – the language of the continent – as their working language, thus accelerating the erosion of the weight of French and Francophone culture within Canada. Resisting the cultural and political consequences of this erosion is therefore held as a moral obligation.

Split identity

22 Depending on the perspective, French-speaking Quebecers constitute both a majority (82% of the total population of the province), and a minority (the largest cultural minority within Canada as the result of a conquest by a foreign empire). The population is split between its affiliation with Quebec, where its ancestral roots are, and with Canada, which it has helped form as one of the original two "founding nations" in 1867 but within which a sizable part of the French-speaking group has never felt comfortable. Now, if the 82% French Quebecers see themselves as the majority group of the province, the 18% English-speaking group refuse to see themselves as a minority within Quebec, and prefer to define themselves as members of the Canadian majority. The result is that two "majorities" try to coexist on the same territory. In private as well as public life, the issue of where an individual's primary loyalty lies always ends up surfacing, constituting a permanent ethical problem.

Institutional strain

23 The previous threats to cultural survival – that is, to the values and institutions that the French community has developed over time and with which it feels most comfortable – are amplified by the official Canadian policy of multiculturalism. Situated midway between the American "melting pot" tradition of adherence to a basic set of patriotic values and the French "integration" tradition of total socialization into the host country's culture, the Canadian policy of multiculturalism seeks to preserve the authenticity of the various groups that make up the "Canadian mosaic". Cultural diversity is not only tolerated, it is encouraged, both symbolically and materially, by federal programs and legislative protections. Recent immigrants as well as existing "cultural communities" are not expected to espouse any particular Canadian identity, and the choice always remains an individual one. It is guaranteed by a federal Charter of Rights firmly rooted in individual rights.

24 This policy directly clashes with Quebec's concerns for "cultural survival". English Canada, and especially the several dozen protected cultural communities, view multiculturalism with pride. They see it as a continuous source of national enrichment, with the English language as the natural unifying factor. Conversely, French Quebec perceives it as deeply divisive, since it creates a permanent source of inter-cultural conflicts within Quebec, making the language of the majority an endless object of contention, and casting any effort by the French majority to promote its own language on its own territory as an aggression against Canadian multicultural values. The clash between these two equally legitimate conceptions of cultural identity permeates everyday life in Quebec. Not a single day passes without headlines on some language or identity issue, with conflicting, and generally incompatible analyses, predictable from the language of the reporting media.

25 Since language is the prime vehicle of a community's values, language issues become ethical issues, and for business, the language firms choose to communicate with their various stakeholders becomes an issue of business ethics.

Institutional modernization and economic assertion

26 The second element in the contextual framework of business ethics issues in Quebec is economic assertion. Although tightly related to the theme of identity preservation, it nevertheless deserves a separate treatment. Economic assertion is a form of nationalism. It consists mainly in a voluntary effort led conjointly by the public and private sectors to modernize the economic institutions of Quebec and secure an acceleration of economic development by gaining a greater control of the main economic instruments of the province. It raises thorny questions on the legitimacy of the role of business, the role of government and the nature of the relationships between the two. Modernization has rested on two complementary strategies: promoting francophone control, and government leadership.

Promoting francophone control

27 Popular accounts date the birth of modern Quebec on a specific day, June 22, 1960. On that day a new government was elected, with the avowed objective to finally bring the dormant province and its sluggish economy into modernity. It launched a comprehensive program of institu-

tional reforms putting an end to the traditional conservatism which the elites of the province had long believed was the most effective strategy to secure its cultural survival. This program, mostly empirical, came to be known later as the Quiet Revolution, and is still part of the mobilizing myths of French Quebec. Long overdue, it was "revolutionary" only in the speed of its implementation and in the depth of the institutional transformations it was able to bring about. Among various objectives like thorough reforms in public administration and social security or overhauling an obsolete education system, the program was geared to boost the autonomy of the province through a greater control of its economic decision centres by its francophone element.[7,8] At that time, the economy of Quebec was largely dominated by external interests, as the French-speaking business class, long unable to develop fully for social or religious reasons, was strangely absent from the main decision-making centres.

Government leadership

28 The modernization strategy gave the state the central role as coordinator of a vast effort of private industrial redevelopment. It was multifaceted. Instruments included the formation of a core of large firms under francophone control, through fusion, acquisition or expansion; the creation of a few key state industrial groups (power, mines, forestry, usually invested with a dual mission of production and regional development); government and local procurement contracts, preferential rates to heavy industry (especially energy), and various legislative (mostly fiscal) dispositions favourable to business. The traditional lack of access of Quebec firms to large capital financing was solved first through the creation of specially designed capital pools, usually state corporations established in concertation with industry, and later through specific legislation making it easier to channel local savings into local investment.

29 The model of mixed economy developed in the mid 1960s is still in place today. At one time it has even be designated by the controversial term of "Quebec, Inc."[9,10] The net result has been a displacement of economic power from the anglophone minority to the francophone majority, and a full deployment of francophone talent in business. Many of today's business success stories owe their success to this model. For example, the food chain that now controls 40% of the highly competitive Quebec market was originally a loose association of small retailers with no economic clout. It was assembled into a single large company under the leadership of the Quebec civil servant pension fund (Caisse de dépôts et placements du Québec), one of the capital pools formed in the 1960s with a mission to promote industrial development in Quebec. At present, the Caisse owns shareholder participation in more than 100 Canadian firms, and holds minority board membership on a select number of large holdings. As another example, if Montreal boasts the presence of two or three of the ten largest engineering firms in the world, it is largely due to the contracts regularly handed out for twenty years by the state-owned power company for the construction of the huge dams in the Great North of the province.

30 The consequence of this economic nationalism[11] for the treatment of business ethics are profound. First, the impact of government influence on economic matters cannot in Quebec be considered as only negative. The image of the state as oppressor or intruder yields before the image of the state as guarantor or catalyst. This

legitimizes the role of government as one source of collective values, including business values.

31   Second, many present-day prosperous business firms, and much of the business elite, owe their success to the joint endeavours of their social political milieu. This raises the question of what society can now expect from them in return for the help provided when they needed it most. Consequently, good corporate citizenship from the largest francophone firms is not only the discrete exercise of social responsibilities. It is also the payment of a debt which the public perceives it holds against business. For example, firms are always expected to defend what the public defines as "the interests of the province", which can mean anything from taking a pro-Quebec stance in a federal-provincial dispute, to refusing to sell out to outside interests, through the encouragement of domestic suppliers.

32   Third, the tight links between government and business raise the question of the legitimacy of their relationships. When private firms are used by government to enhance public interests, the question of whose interests are really served cannot be easily eschewed.

Consociative democracy and social solidarity

33   The third element of our framework for business ethics in Quebec is the social solidarity that permeates the relationships among the various decision-makers. Again, this element includes both cultural and institutional components. Cultural components refer to traditions which value the search for consensus. Institutional components refer to the tight network of leaders and organizations which animate the social political process, and which represent a wide cross-section of society. This ethics of solidarity values personal

relationships and participative decision-making in multi-stakeholder arenas.[12] These arenas host much of the social construction of the reality of Quebec. They emerge as a fundamental source of economic and social values, for society in general and for business in particular. As the role of government gradually evolves from that of entrepreneur to that of catalyst,[13] this form of consociative democracy is likely to become even more salient in the future. It rests on three pillars: conviviality, cooperativism, and concertation.

Conviviality

34   The culture of French Quebec is marked by an ethics of conviviality variously described by scholars as inherited from its ancestral rural roots, its Catholic tradition, a long experience of family business, and the relative homogeneity of a community without a sharp social structure.[14] This ethics values social justice, quality of life and open social relations. The population expects its business leaders to demonstrate the same qualities. Firms which espouse these values are typically revered and held as role models.[15] At the societal level, this ethics translates into social democratic values, which are fundamentally shared by all political parties, and which find their expression in various programs of the welfare state. One consequence, which also holds for Canada, is that at this level government assumes many of the social responsibilities abandoned to private corporations in the US. For example, compensation for occupational safety hazards is exclusively managed by a state agency to ensure social justice among all the workers of the province; for the same reasons, health care is provided freely and for all by the state system; and ethical issues like corporate political contributions are severely lim-

ited by law to modest amounts, virtually barring corporations from exerting influence in that way. At the business level, the Quebec Chamber of Commerce, a provincial federation of local chambers, has produced a detailed chart to the social responsibilities of business, where it officially defines 18 categories of social obligations to eight classes of stakeholders.[16] The document was officially adopted by its general assembly in 1982.

Cooperativism

35 Quebec enjoys a strong cooperative sector in various areas. The most salient institution is the Desjardins credit union group, with a capital of more than 40 billion US dollars, 1300 autonomous district units, and 4 million savings and banking accounts in Quebec alone. This network of cooperatives has grown so central in Quebec's economic and social political life that it is customarily referred to as the Desjardins "movement". Its strength and influence are unique. Founded at the beginning of the century in rural Catholic parishes as a marginal alternative to the established Anglo-saxon banking system, it eventually developed into its most powerful competitor. Behind the values explicitly cultivated by the movement are those of self-help and self-reliance. Each customer must first buy one ownership share at a symbolic price, thus becoming an owner-customer member. Each district unit is overseen by an autonomous board of democratically elected owner-customer members from this unit (their total numbers 18,000, all non-paid volunteers). This board is expected to adapt the unit's loan strategies to the social and economic needs of its immediate environment. From its original local credit unions, the movement has grown to the dimensions of a financial empire, including banking, insurance, brokerage and capital investment activities. In direct competition with the major private Canadian banks, it is particularly efficient and technologically innovative. Its organization, consolidated into 11 regional federations, is both highly complex and highly democratic. At the provincial level, leaders from the movement are active members of the social political process, and are expected to use the clout of their organization to foster policies and initiatives of public interest. For example, the Desjardins movement is deeply involved in the provincial forum against unemployment. It has supported or contributed in developing various government policies of public interest, and is regularly used by government as an outlet for services to the general public. The movement is regulated by a Quebec law specifically adapted to its needs as an instrument of social and economic development.

36 Overall, the Desjardins movement constitutes a central element of Quebec's socio-economic distinctiveness. Its corporate status escapes all conventional categories: Neither private, nor public, nor strictly cooperativist, nor even typically not-for-profit, it is profoundly original. Its policies and practices also defy conventional thinking. For Desjardins, social responsibility is not an add-on to otherwise conventional financial strategies. Social responsibility, as it defines it at both the customer and the societal levels, lies at the core of its mission. Desjardins is a permanent counterpoint to pure market ideologies. Words like solidarity, democracy, self-development, popular education or social justice are common in its vocabulary. The population, which regards the movement as a symbol of its collective worth, holds especially exacting demands towards its performance. Desjardins is not only expected to act in a socially responsible manner, it also has to. The

general public is particularly sensitive to any issue in which the authenticity of the movement could be jeopardized, and the evolution of its role, conduct and philosophy is subject to permanent scrutiny. The powerful presence of Desjardins on the daily Quebec scene cannot but deeply influence the terms of the discourse on business ethics.

Concertation

37 Business ethics in Quebec is also marked by the particular process in which social political issues develop. In addition to the Desjardins movement, the province also houses a dense network of peak organizations. Business, farming, labour and educational interests are each represented by one or several associations which regularly meet at the provincial level. A host of interests are represented by other peak organizations of lesser scope. Business interests are organized around the familiar North American pattern of chambers of commerce or sectorial associations. However, much like Europe but in contrast to most of North America, business has also given itself a powerful employers' council (Conseil du Patronat du Quebec, or CPQ), which includes the largest private employers, francophone and anglophone, as well as the largest state corporations. Interestingly, this council was founded in 1969 as a response to a challenge by the largest union leader who was deploring the lack of a clear business voice in disputed public arenas. Today the CPQ plays an active role in public debates and is regularly consulted by government. Its president routinely meets with other interest groups in various arenas, most notably the boards of government agencies where business stakes are particularly high, and in public hearings on societal issues as varied as constitu-

tional matters, educational reform or employee training.

38 This general process of policy formation is known as concertation.[17] Some authors have traced its origins in some corporatist traditions of the clerical Quebec of the early 20th century, others in the development of cooperativism, still others in the social democratic bent of its political parties or in the social activism of its labour unions.[18,19,20] Concertation takes various institutional forms: government-sponsored, as in the "socio-economic summits", of which more than 30 have been held in the past 20 years at the national, sectorial or regional levels (most of them are organized by the Secretariat for concertation); privately organized, as in the Quebec Forum on employment, a semi-permanent arena seeking to forge consensus on diagnosis and action against unemployment among a vast cross-section of business, social and popular groups, and from which government is absent; government supported, as in the various provincial and municipal roundtables on environmental protection, where government is only one of the partners.

39 The results of this constant interaction between political, social and economic forces can sometimes be surprising. For example, in accordance with government and business, the two largest unions have formed their own risk capital funds, which collect tax deductible retirement savings for investment into capital-short promising small businesses.[21,22] In another vein, the employers' council is known to have decided not to use a particularly controversial court decision made in its favour (the unconstitutionality of a union-supported law against strikebreakers). At the same time, the otherwise quite militant labour unions have been actively cooperating with a number of companies to develop original sys-

tems of participative decision making, exchanging flexibility for worker involvement in major technological and employment changes.

40   Concertation does not equate with consensus. In no way does it eliminate conflict between government, business, labour and social interests. Nor is it so prevalent as in some European states. It does however provide arenas where many of these interests can be revealed, discussed and prioritized, and where old values are adjusted and new values formed. Ethical standards and social expectations towards not only business, but also its major stakeholders, emerge from the social political process as a natural outcome of public life. Rather than being left at the discretion of business firms, they are jointly assumed by a multiplicity of participants. To the extent all sectors of society can find a voice in this process the legitimacy of the standards of business behaviour that it produces is democratically sanctioned. Concertation does suffer from shortcomings, which this paper does not need to discuss; but despite its weaknesses, it sets a stage for the debate around business ethics and social responsibilities that is profoundly different from the existing models prevalent in the mainstream North American literature.

A sample of business ethics issues in Quebec

41   In this section we will briefly analyze a sample of salient business ethics issues in Quebec to illustrate the import of the above framework. The sample is not representative but typical. Each issue holds at least one dimension characteristic of the Quebec scene. Similarities or contrasts with the Canadian and American scenes will be highlighted when warranted.

Identity preservation

42   Issues tied to identity preservation involve collective rights. The issue of the "francization" of business is particularly telling. It will be given special attention.

43   *The "francization" of business.* The francization of business is a peculiar form of affirmative action. It has drawn considerable attention in the last 20 years in Canada and abroad, for it is based on linguistic regulation and therefore is an area where collective rights permanently clash with individual rights. The purpose is to redress a historical imbalance between anglophones and francophones in managerial positions, and especially between the use of English and the use of French in business communications. These objectives are accomplished through legislation requiring business firms to "francisize" their communications with their various stakeholders, that is to use French rather than English as the common language of commerce within Quebec. The onus falls on business firms to change their linguistic practices to accommodate the rights of the linguistic majority of the province.

44   Legislation has been necessary for the same reasons it is for conventional affirmative action. What sets this form of intervention apart however is its particular twist. Affirmative action is normally conceived in the US and Canada as a strategy to emancipate minorities. In Quebec, it was conceived to emancipate a majority, the French-speaking segment of the population, trapped for complex historical and geographical reasons in a disproportionately unfavourable situation. The collective rights of the French majority thus clash with the individual rights of the members of the linguistic minority, who are denied the right to remain unilingual in a bilingual society. Business firms are then required to

walk a fine line between respecting the letter and especially the spirit of the linguistic laws, while accommodating the requests of their anglophone employees and workers. This issue will not wither away. After more than 20 years of francization, many firms still do not hold their certificate of compliance, and although undeniable, the gains of the French language have not yet been spectacular.[23,24,25]

45 Interestingly, linguistic regulation is not confined to Quebec, and it is likely that it will spread around the world in parallel with globalization. In the United States, for example, a number of states and the federal government itself have started toying with this approach, to protect the English language against the rapid gains of Spanish. The US situation is not entirely comparable to that prevailing in Quebec, however, since in both cases the same language, English, is by far the dominant force. Nevertheless, the case of francization in Quebec is a good illustration of the complex interplay between culture, identity, social forces and business ethics.

46 *Quotas in radio programming.* Another ethics issue around collective rights is the imposition of a minimum "French content" in radio programming, including popular songs in French, in order to better reflect and sustain local culture against international commercial music. This issue is also raised in the rest of Canada ("Canadian content") and in several European countries, for the same reason of identity preservation.[26] It is unknown in the US.

47 *Compulsory movie dubbing.* Most audiences around the world watch US made films in their native language, after a delay of several months for dubbing purposes. In Quebec, a recent law stipulates that the English original cannot be shown if the French version is not made available within the next 60 days, so that

francophones have a reasonable chance to see the movie in their own language. This issue has aroused the ire of Hollywood, under the claim of "unfair trade barriers". It is obviously not raised in English Canada, but it is in Western Europe under various guises. In fact, these trade barriers are never considered as such in the province: They are just regarded as minimal protection of a basic collective right.

48 *Business political stances.* In a society highly conscious of its vulnerability within the great North American space, politics is a way of life. Business leaders do not escape the necessity to take public stances on controversial matters. When the issues are particularly emotional, notably when they involve collective identity, public outcry can be such as to pass for censorship of business positions. Instances occurred during the 1995 referendum on the sovereignty of Quebec. The ethical conflict here is one of freedom of expression against deference to the general public's sensibilities.

Institutional modernization

49 Ethical issues tied to institutional modernization involve questions about the role of government, the role of business and the nature of the relationship between the two.

50 *Free trade agreement.* Against the will of the unions, and of most of the voters, successive governments of Quebec have forcefully endorsed the free trade agreement between Canada, the US and Mexico. Business was also massively in favour of the project. Political and business leaders view the extension of international competition as a powerful incentive to complete the transformation of Quebec into a modern, efficient economy. Labour unions oppose the treaty for fear of losing jobs, farmer

unions for fear of losing the stability their industry has patiently assembled, and the general public for fear that the social security system be dismantled under the pressure of American business competition to lower costs. The issue here is a case of a joint government-business coalition against popular desires.

51   *Pay equity.* Part of present-day institutional modernization is pay equity, that is same pay for comparable work. Government, supported by unions and various interest groups, wants to impose pay equity programs to private business through legislation. Business is not opposed to the principle, but to the costs (an estimated 1% of aggregate remuneration), and prefers incentive rather than coercive measures. Previous experience in other economies has shown that large-scale pay equity programs have contradictory effects. They raise the revenues of the better protected segments of the target population at the expense of the less well protected, especially non unionized sectors, the unemployed and new entrants. A transfer of funds to the first group will weaken the chances of the second. In a period of growing long-term unemployment, the ethics issue the various stakeholders face is one of priority: which group has more legitimate claims.

52   *Privatizations.* As the role of the Quebec government changes from doer to helper, the privatization of public assets becomes a modernization strategy. More than 50 operations of privatization have been conducted in Quebec since 1986. Indeed, privatization is today a very ambiguous notion. It ranges from a simple opening of state assets to private capital, to the total alienation of state-controlled assets, through a vast combination of flexible partnerships with private industry and the not-for-profit sector. The ethics issue raised for government is the choice between private interest and public interest utilitarianism. In the former case, government simply sells to the highest bidder, and uses the one-short proceeds against its deficit. In the latter, it structures the deal around strategic concerns, with the risk of making it less financially attractive for itself. In both cases, the private buyer faces the issue of the legitimacy of its purchase.

Consociative democracy

53 Ethics issues tied to consociative democracy involve questions of solidarity among the various groups which constitute civil society.

54   *Tuition fees.* In Quebec, university tuition fees have been kept at the same nominal level for 20 years, then doubled, then doubled again. They are still the lowest in Canada. The reason is the widely shared objective of higher education democratization, an area where Quebec has had to catch up with its neighbours. Student fees are exactly the same across all universities, for world class luminaries like McGill and small regional centres alike. Fees cover less than 20% of expenses and most of the remainder comes out of an annual government subsidy. The issue is one of equity. In an era of youth unemployment and severe constraints on public finances, who should pay for university education: students, presumably the primary beneficiaries, cannot find the jobs necessary to reimburse the present costs; taxpayers, although direct or indirect beneficiaries, are now burdened with new responsibilities, like the financing of an increasingly costly health care system; companies, which claim they already contribute through all kinds of channels; professors, whose job security comes to be regarded as an exorbitant privilege? Public opinion now expects business to increase its share of the collective burden. These ques-

tions regarding stake-holders obligations are all linked to a social democratic ethic.

55 *Wage cuts for jobs.* In various forums, fighting unemployment has been determined to be a collective priority. A number of solutions have been examined or tested, like work time reduction or shared time jobs. None seems to have any significant impact on the unemployment rate. A more efficient and growing practice is for workers to accept wage cuts to save the jobs of their younger colleagues. These schemes require the collaboration of labour unions and employers, in the name of an inter-generational ethics.

56 *Job training.* The Quebec economy needs job training badly. An issue similar to that for higher education arises. Who should pay for job training: the taxpayer, through the state vocational system; the students themselves, by accepting lower rates; or business, through voluntary or compulsory programs? Free riding makes it irrational for an average company to invest in job training when its competitors don't. Following a European practice, the government has decided to get around the problem by requiring all companies above 50 employees to devote 1% of their aggregate remuneration annually to job training. As usual, business favours the objective, but opposes the coercive and bureaucratic nature of the program. It must however publicly confront its expectations to those of other groups. The mutual obligations of each group of stakeholders are debated in several places, most notably the Quebec Forum on employment, a concertation arena led by the Desjardins movement. Here again, the definition of business obligations emerges from the social political process rather than from the individual initiative of private of managers. The ethics issue is therefore the conflict between managerial discretion and social obligation.

Conclusion

57 This paper has shown that business ethics is cast in a distinctive manner in Quebec because the social political tissue of the province is itself distinct. The nature of business ethics is deeply rooted in the national identity of the community. Three underlying forces combine to create a unique context: identity preservation, institutional modernization, and consociative democracy. Each in turn sets the conditions leading to a specific brand of business ethics: the pursuit of collective rights, the will to economic assertion, and social solidarity.

58 As such, the Quebec reality departs considerably from the American discourse on business ethics. Scholars have generally underestimated the importance of tying business frameworks to societal context. This paper is a call to develop alternative theorizing, starting from a holistic level of conceptualization in order to access the meaning of corporate and individual level beliefs and practices in business ethics.

NOTES

1. Dion, Michel: 1992, *L'éthique et le profit* (Fides, Montréal).

2. Macdonald, Roderick (ed.): 1995, *Valeurs de l'entreprise québecoise* (Fides, Montréal).

3. Pradès, José: 1995, *L'éthique de l'environnement et du développement* (Presses Universitaires de France, Paris coll. Que sais-je, no. 2967).

4. D'Iribarne, Philippe: 1989, *La logique de l'honneur. Gestion des entreprises et traditions nationales* (Seuil, Paris).

5. Katzenstein, Peter J.: 1985, *Small States in World Market & Industrial Policy In Europe* (Cornell University Press, Ithaca, NY).

6. Sainsaulieu, Renaud: 1987. *Sociologie de l'organisation et de l'entreprise* (Presses de la Fondation nationale des sciences politiques, Paris).

7. Vaillancourt, François et Carpentier, J.: 1989, *Le contrôle de l'économie du Québec* (Centre de recherche en développement économique, Montréal).

8. Gagnon, Alain G. (Ed.): 1994, *Québec: Etat et société* (Québec-Amérique, Montréal) [1994. Quebec: State and society (2nd ed.) (Methuen, Toronto)].

9. Fraser, Matthew: 1987, *Quebec Inc. French-Canadian Entrepreneurs and the New Business Elite* (Key Porter Books, Toronto).

10. Paquet, Gilles: 1995, *Québec Inc.: mythes et réalités*, in Jean-Pierre Dupuis (ed.), *Le modèle québecois de développement économique* (Presses Interuniversitaires, Cap-Rouge, QC).

11. Keating, Michael: 1996, *Nations Against the State: The New Politics of Nationalism in Quebec, Catalonia and Scotland* (St. Martin's Press, New York).

12. Clarke, Adele E.: 1991, 'Social Worlds/Arenas Theory as Organizational Theory', in David R. Maines (ed.), *Social Organization and Social Process. Essays In Honor of Anselm Strauss* (Aldine-deGruyter, New York).

13. Séguin, Francine et Bélanger-Martin, Luc: 1993, 'De l'Etat-entrepreneur à l'Etat-mailleur', *Gestion* 18(3), 82-90.

14. Aktouf, Omar, Bédard, Renée et Chanlat, Alain: 1992, 'Management, éthique catholique et esprit du capitalisme: l'exemple québecois'. *Sociologie du travail* 1(92), 83-89.

15. Aktouf, Omar et Chrétien, M.: 1987, 'Le cas Cascades. Comment se crée une culture d'entreprise', *Revue française de gestion* 65-66, 156-166.

16. Chambre de commerce du Québec: 1982, *Rapport du comité sur la responsabilité sociale de l'entreprise*, Montréal.

17. Tremblay, Diane-Gabrielle, and Noël, Alain: 1993, 'Beyond Quebec Inc.? Concertation in a High Unemployment Society', *Inroads* 2, 74-85.

18. Archibald, Clinton: 1983, *Un Québec corporatiste?* (Editions Asticou, Hull, QC).

19. Tremblay, Diane-Gabrielle (ed.): 1995, *Concertation et performance économique: vers de nouveaux modèles?* (Presses de l'Université du Quebec, Montréal).

20. Bélanger, Paul et Lévesque, Benoît: 1995, 'La modernité par les particularismes. Le modèle québecois de développement économique', in Jean-Pierre Dupuis (ed.), *Le modèle québecois de développement économique* (Presses Interuniversitaires, Cap-Rouge, QC).

21. Fournier, Louis: 1991, *Solidarité Inc.: Un nouveau syndicalisme créateur d'emplois* (Québec-Amérique, Montréal).

22. Fournier, Louis: 1993, 'The Quebec Solidarity Fund: A Profound Revolution in the Labour Movement', *Inroads* 2, 87-91.

23. Champagne, René: 1995, *Evolution de la présence francophone parmi les hauts dirigeants des grandes entreprises québecoises entre 1976 et 1993* (Office de la langue française, Québec).

24. Ministère de la culture et des communications: 1996, *Bilan de la situation de la langue française*, (Publications du Québec, Montréal).

25. Béland, Paul: 1991, *L'usage du français au travail: Situation et tendances* (Conseil de la langue française, Québec).

26. Globerman, Steven: 1983, *Cultural Regulation In Canada* (Institute for Research on Public Policy, Montreal).

Questions

1. Should entrepreneurs in Quebec be obligated to preserve a "national identity" (P2)?

2. Pasquero compares business ethics in Quebec with those in the U.S. rather than with those in the rest of Canada. Speculate as to why he did that.

3. Pasquero describes three major elements, focusing on eight specific characteristics, to establish his claim that business ethics in Quebec are different than business ethics in the rest of North America. Consider and assess the strength of each of the eight points; that is, do you think that Quebec, and hence business, and hence business ethics in Quebec, are as distinct as Pasquero claims they are? Before you answer, be sure to consider his sample of business ethical issues in Quebec, P41–56.

4. For any one of the issues he describes (in his sample section), outline the moral conflict(s) involved and figure out a way to reconcile the conflict(s). (More than one way would be even better.) If you used any of the ethical decision-making approaches covered in Section II, identify which one(s).

Case Study – Hockey:
A Disappearing Canadian Cultural Icon

Is the globalization of hockey removing one of the last remaining uniquely Canadian symbols of our national identity?

From its inception in 1917 to about 1970, hockey was 'the' Canadian game. It was the game that most Canadian boys (and many girls) played in winter on frozen ponds and outdoor rinks. It was the sport Canadians preferred to watch in arenas across the country and, later, on television. During the "glory years" of professional hockey, from the 1940s to the late 1960s, four of the six teams in the National Hockey League (NHL) were based in the U.S.; however, the vast majority of the players were born in Canada and learned their hockey in Canada. During this time, hockey was widely acknowledged as Canada's national sport.

Change happened on two fronts. One, the proportion of non-Canadian NHL players increased steadily. Two, the NHL, pushed into action by both the growing interest in hockey in the U.S. and the establishment of a rival league (the World Hockey Association [WHA]), greatly expanded the number of teams in the late 1960s and early 1970s. By 1977, only one of the fourteen new NHL teams was Canadian. The rationale was that new franchises (remember that professional teams are businesses, franchises to be bought and sold, owned and managed) were selected on the basis of their likely commercial viability, and most of the big money markets were in the U.S.

Further expansion did include three new Canadian teams; however, two of those three survived only a short time and the franchises were bought by American interests in Colorado and Phoenix. Currently, the existence of at least two other (smaller market) Canadian teams is threatened due to persistent financial losses. The possibility exists that, in a short while, there will be only two or three Canadian teams (out of about thirty) in the NHL. In addition, Canadian-born players are no longer in the majority in the NHL.

Many Canadians have expressed disappointment with these profound changes in our national game. Among hockey fans, there is a real sense of loss and a feeling that we have somehow let the "Canadian game" slip away from us. Blame for the predicament is largely put on "big money" interests that have made hockey more a business than a sport and a "greedy players' union" that has driven the average salary close to $1,000,000 per year.

In recent years, various levels of government have been asked to intervene and assist some of the weaker franchises. In many cases, local governments have assisted teams with tax deferrals, subsidized land, special transit routes, and even part ownership of the arena. They have argued that the favourable economic impact of the NHL franchise on the local community (due to additional tourism, in particular) justifies the spending of public monies in this way.

During the 1998–99 hockey season, the issue of differential treatment of NHL franchises by local governments in Canada and in the U.S. received considerable publicity. Owner of the Ottawa Senators, Rod Bryden, pointed out that property taxes on arenas in Canada were considerably higher than in the U.S., and that new arenas for NHL teams built in the U.S. often had public funding whereas new buildings in Canada were constructed with private funding only. These considerations, as well as the adverse change in the Canada-U.S. exchange rate, have made it much more difficult to run an NHL franchise in Canada. Bryden has argued that unless governments in Canada address these matters, we will continue to lose NHL franchises to the U.S.

REFERENCES

Hudson, Kellie. "Premier Rules Out 'handouts' for NHL." *The Toronto Star* 8 Apr. 1998: A3.

"Information from Round Table Discussion with Rod Bryden." 2 Mar. 1999. Ottawa Senators Media Relations Department. <http://www.ottawasenators.com/news/press/1999/nr020-e.html>

Questions

1. Should Canadian municipalities adjust the level of their business property taxes to that in comparable U.S. cities in order to be "competitive"?

2. (a) What reasons can be given to support, on ethical grounds, the use of public money to help professional hockey teams?

   (b) What reasons can be given to oppose, on ethical grounds, the use of public money to help professional hockey teams?

   (c) Should hockey and other sports be considered "Canadian culture" with respect to government subsidies (whether one supports or opposes such subsidies)?

3. (a) Some might argue that in *recreational* hockey (and recreational arts), culture can, and should, be maintained, but as soon as it becomes *professional*, as soon as it becomes *a business*, culture can't, and shouldn't, be an issue. Do you agree? Why/not?

   (b) Do you think that being the manager of a sports team or an arts centre would change your opinion?

CHAPTER 9
INTERNATIONAL BUSINESS

What to Do? – The Processing Fee

Part of the process of setting up shop in a certain foreign country involves obtaining a certain permit. You discover that your application for the permit has not been forwarded to the appropriate person; nor will it, apparently, until you pay the clerk a "processing fee" equal to 40% of the permit fee. There is no mention of this processing fee in the guidelines for permit acquisition – it seems to be blatant bribery, and you are reluctant to start doing that kind of thing.

And yet, it also seems expected – there is no shame or secrecy about the request. You know the clerk's wages are minimal, and you suspect that such clerks may actually depend on such additional payments, much like waiters in Canada depend on tips. However, tips are paid after the fact, and even non-tipping customers get served.

You reconsider the financial wisdom of your plans: if these sorts of expenses are common, your financial projections will be significantly off. You even reconsider the ethical wisdom of your plans: do you really want to do business this way?

But then you wonder, call it bribery or not, why is it so wrong?

What do you decide to do?

Introduction

Many ethical questions arise when one does business with/in nations other than one's own, and they present themselves at every stage of the business cycle.

To begin, consider your financing, your stockholders. Should you let your company be partially, or mostly, foreign-owned? To be fair, responsibilities entail rights: do you want non-Canadians to have any rights of influence or control? To those who, like Einstein, think "nationalism is an infantile disease," this may be a non-issue: humanity transcends political boundaries, what's the problem?

Well, the problem, some may respond, is that value systems often have an unnerving respect for political boundaries: do you want someone who believes that some people are "untouchable," for example, to have any influence over your company?

(Of course, values vary *within* political boundaries as well, and this is an equally important ethical question for domestic ownership: do you want a Canadian racist, for example, to have any influence over your company?)

Next, let's consider your acquisition of materials. The ethics of "cross-border shopping" are the same, whether you're an individual buying clothes or a business buying supplies. And again, for some, the "Buy Canadian!" campaign was merely a show of patriotism (or a convenient display of self-interest).

But, given our existing economic system, it could be more than that: when you buy here, you keep the jobs here, so there's less unemployment (so more are happy), so there's less stress on the social systems, so taxes go down – or at

least don't go up (so more are happy). Now, of course, every one of those "so" statements is arguable, but the general gist is that there are economic consequences for many people, besides yourself (presumably you shop non-Canadian because it's cheaper – at least in the short term) and these are consequences that you may want to consider when deciding what to do.

However, the flip side of "Buy Canadian" is "Buy Nicaraguan" (or whatever) – reverse boycotting. Consider the Bridgehead line of products; consider the Body Shop's purchasing policies. You may want to support a certain nation for certain reasons – and so certain cross-border shopping may be the right thing to do.

Next, let's consider production. Should you outsource – out of Canada? Should you set up a branch of your company in another country? The nationalist and economic/quality of life issues raised in the preceding paragraphs are writ larger here. It's not a matter of indirectly keeping the jobs here, but a matter of *directly* doing so. And yet what if the Mexican needs the job more than the Canadian? Is nationalism a sort of collective egoism that puts self-interest first, defining "self" just a little more broadly?

Now, if you *do* establish in other countries, there are further ethical questions to answer. One is "do you conduct yourself and your business according to *their* ethical standards or according to your own (assuming they're different)?" The moral relativist would say to do the former; the moral absolutist would say to do the latter. The utilitarian would consider the consequences – and the big thing here is that the consequences may be quite different in one's own country than in the other country *for the same action* (so you really have to know the customs, the local cultures, to, at the very least, avoid giving unintentional offence, and to, at best, adequately judge the consequences of your action). See the Kohls and Buller article for some specific strategies for resolving cross-cultural conflict; they identify seven different strategies and suggest that one's choice depends on the context, which is classified according to the centrality of and social consensus about the issue, as well as the power you have and the urgency for action. Wines and Napier also address this issue.

But note that I said "assuming they're different" – there may be many values and principles that both (all) countries have in common that can be maintained. Consider, for example, the rights listed in the *United Nations Declaration of Human Rights.* Consider also the *Caux Round Table Principles for Business* (perhaps the first international ethics code created in collaboration by business leaders in Europe, Japan, and the U.S.). And these common values may – or may not – be sufficient. See De George, Donaldson, and Weiss for discussions of international codes of ethics. And lest you assume that when the standards *are* different, your own are *higher*, read Singer's article. For a very practical approach to ethics in international business, see chapter 11 of the Treviño text.

However, deciding on absolute/universal values and principles is only a first step. Translating them into action may present problems, which can be magnified in international business. For example, maybe both countries value respect for people, but in the one, this is shown by paying for X and in the other, it is shown by *not* paying for X.

Hugh Lehman has written an excellent analysis of the importance of context with re-spect to wages, examining the possible interpretations of setting wages in Third World nations according to the "equal pay" principle: does that mean we should (1) pay workers the same number of dollars per hour as they're paid in our own country for that job (which might make a factory worker a member of the rich elite and draw all the skilled workers from local companies which can't compete with those wages, harming those local companies); does it mean we should (2) pay enough so that their standard of living in their country is the same as that of workers at comparable jobs in our country (which would certainly make them very well off – factory workers here can generally afford a house, car, phone, and TV); or does it mean we should (3) pay enough so that their standard of living relative to other people in their country is the same as the standard of living of their comparable workers relative to other people in our country (which might mean they starve – lower class here is okay, but lower class there...).

The same sort of analysis would be needed for other employment rights issues; discrimination can be particularly thorny – what if the other country believes that it's immoral for women to work? Or that it's okay for children to do so, even chained to the machines (see Di Norcia [185], referring to the Asian carpet industry)?

The decision to become a transnational is not a simple one. On the positive side, transnational companies can benefit their host countries by providing jobs, capital, technology, and training, and by boosting the local economy directly and indirectly (e.g., through local purchases). However, they can also be detrimental by widening class divisions, encouraging urbanization, providing unnecessary and harmful consumer goods, changing the way – and quality – of life, supporting morally corrupt governments because they are pro-business, preempting the development of local business, causing local unemployment through the use of capital-intensive technology, and causing environmental destruction. (Both Cavanagh and De George provide good discussions of these benefits and detriments.) Along with the power to do all of the above comes the responsibility not to do whichever are morally wrong. (Which are?)

Next, let's look at marketing. One issue to consider is *how* you advertise in other countries. Recall the case of Nestle's infant formula discussed in Chapter Two – it provides a number of lessons about marketing in developing countries, and highlights a number of questions one should ask: Will your potential consumer understand the ad? Will it be unduly manipulative, given the context in which it will appear? (*We* may not be suckered in by a character in a lab coat, but people in countries where medical personnel are rare and revered may be.) Or would you be patronizing and stereotyping to market your product in a special way just for them?

Another issue is *whether* you market your product in another country. Should you/we sell nuclear reactor parts to a country that could and might use them in nuclear weapons? Isn't there something wrong with pushing high-priced status symbol non-necessities (jeans and running shoes – and *Dallas* reruns – come to mind) to a country that can barely feed itself? (Coca Cola now reaches areas where there is no clean drinking water.) On the other hand, don't all people, even those living at subsistence level, deserve some modest diversions, some little shred of luxury to make their humdrum lives a bit more bearable?

Consider also "dumping" – selling a product in a foreign market at a lower price than in the home market, a price that doesn't cover export costs. Many consider dumping to be mor-

ally wrong because it damages competition and hurts workers in the other country. In fact, it can be illegal if it reduces competition. But since when is competition more important than people? What if the product is much needed and would be unaffordable to many at "competitive prices"? Wouldn't the *right* thing be to sell it at that low price, to dump it?

Of course, that's a consequentialist analysis. An intent analysis may render a different judgement: if your reason for dumping were to enter and capture a market – get in with low prices, get people wanting your product, then increase the price – perhaps dumping is *not* the right thing to do.

Let's expand the intent analysis: why are you interacting with other countries in the first place? To escape home tax laws? Labour laws? Environmental laws? Safety laws? Well, without the tax advantages, the cheaper labour, and the lenient standards, you say, I'd have no reason to go to other countries. Hm. You can't think of any reasons other than those of self-advantage? Well, what's wrong with self-advantage as long as you do no harm to others? But aren't you doing harm by avoiding those taxes, by doing more environmental damage than you would in your own country?

Not only might you ask whether you're morally obligated *not* to market your product in another country, you may want to ask whether you're morally obligated *to* market your product to another country? If you're sitting on cheap water purification tablets, are you morally compelled to market them to countries without clean water?

This brings us to sales – and pricing. The issue shares some features with that of wages. Should you charge the same price in the Third World market as you do in the First World market? Should you charge a price at all? Perhaps the right thing to do would be to give your product away. Consider the case of the pharmaceutical company Merck and the cure for river blindness: those who needed it simply could not afford it – so they did indeed give it away. And why not? If income from Third World sales is not necessary to the survival of your company and your product *is* necessary to the survival of Third World people ... But what about your obligations to your shareholders? Well, which is more important, curing blindness or higher returns?

One might consider that merely doing trade with, selling anything to, another country is a gesture of support. This is the notion underlying Klein's suggestion that the Export Development Corporation, a crown corporation that finances export and investment deals, "take measures to ensure the projects it supports in no way contribute to the denial of human rights, labour rights or to environmental damage" (A21). Be careful, however, of the false dichotomy: in addition to "do" or "not do," there may be a third option, "do with strings attached." The Sullivan Principles, adopted by multinationals operating in South Africa, are such strings (see the Werhane article).

Let's next consider product safety and product quality. Is it morally permissible to sell products that wouldn't pass *our* safety standards in a country with*out* such standards? Perhaps it depends on the harm – severity, likelihood, duration, etc. And the alternatives – is it a drug that would nevertheless in most cases improve their life? (Or is it a croquet set whose mallet heads come off too easily?)

Lastly, focusing on business with so-called "developing" countries (though recognizing that international business is often with other developed countries), perhaps we have to ask, "Why *is* the Third World still developing and still so poor?" (Though perhaps we need to reconsider our terms – in many ways, such countries may be far more developed than so-called developed countries: can we really say that at 2 kg/person/day, the world's most prolific garbage producer – yup, that's us – is developed?)

The First World has had the resources to remedy illness, malnutrition, etc. worldwide for quite a while. According to The United Nations *Human Development Report 1998*, it would take a mere US$40 billion to provide basic education, health, nutrition, safe water, and sanitation for everyone in the world. There is more spent on ice cream in Europe ($11 billion) than on water and sanitation for all ($6 billion). What's our problem? What is it about our system that makes it so impossible to distribute these benefits to all who need and want them? Do we lack the ability? Or the will? Why can't we figure this out?

Many developing countries are so crippled by foreign debt, they can't keep up with the interest, let alone chip away at the principal. According to Michalos,

> The Ecumenical Coalition for Economic Justice pointed out that "Total less developed country debt has doubled from approximately US$819 billion in 1982 to US$1,712 billion in 1993 despite their having repaid over US$14 trillion in debt service. The reasons for such massive payments include the compounding effect of high real interest rates and the need to take on new debt just to service old loans." (220)

Can we honestly say this state of affairs is just? Canada's debt forgiveness suggests it's not; since 1978, more than $1.3 billion of Official Development Assistance (ODA) debts have been cancelled (Marleau).

But how did they get into such debt – by living beyond their means? Have they squandered their money on candy and cracker jacks? (and croquet sets?) Or are they just not trying, not working hard enough? Or have their corrupt governments taken it all for themselves – and their wargames? Do their elected governments sell their resources to buy mercenaries to fight the mercenaries hired by those trying to get those resources? (See the Grant article.) Or did we, do we, steal their stuff – and call it colonialism and free trade?

REFERENCES AND FURTHER READING

Amba-Rao, Sita C. "Multinational Corporate Social Responsibility, Ethics, Interactions and Third World Governments: An Agenda for the 1990s." *Journal of Business Ethics* 12.7 (July 1993): 553-572.

Cavanagh, Gerald F. *American Business Values with International Perspectives*. 4th ed. NJ: Prentice Hall, 1998.

Chossudovsky, Michel. *The Globalisation of Poverty: Impacts of IMF and World Bank Reforms*. London: Zed Books, 1997.

De George, Richard T. *Business Ethics*. 5th ed. NJ: Prentice Hall, 1999. (Chapters 19, 20, and 21 deal with "Moral Issues in International Business")

De George, Richard T. *Competing with Integrity in International Business*. NY: Oxford, 1993. 19-21.

De George, Richard T. "International Business Ethics: Russia and Eastern Europe." *Social Responsibility: Business, Journalism, Law, and Medicine* 19 (1993): 5-23.

Di Norcia, Vincent. *Hard Like Water: Ethics in Business*. Toronto: Oxford University Press, 1998.

Donaldson, Thomas. *The Ethics in International Business*. NY: Oxford University Press, 1989.

Frederick, William C. "The Moral Authority of Transnational Corporate Codes." *Journal of Business Ethics* 10.3 (March 1991): 165-177.

Grant, Dale. "Canadians Cry 'Havoc,' and Let Slip the Dogs of War." *The Toronto Star* 9 Mar. 1999: A19.

Klein, Naomi. "Dusting the Cobwebs off Canada's Conscience." *The Toronto Star* 4 Feb. 1999: A21.

Kohls, John, and Paul Buller. "Resolving Cross-Cultural Ethical Conflict: Exploring Alternative Strategies." *Journal of Business Ethics* 13.1 (January 1994): 31-38.

Lehman, Hugh. "Equal Pay for Equal Work in the Third World." *Journal of Business Ethics* 4 (1985): 487–491. Reprinted in *Business Ethics in Canada*, 2nd edition. Ed. Deborah C. Poff and Wilfrid J. Waluchow. Scarborough, ON: Prentice Hall Allyn and Bacon, 1991. 444–449.

Marleau, Diane. "Canada's Role in Alleviating Poverty in the Third World." *The Toronto Star* 19 Mar. 1999: A17.

Mayer, Don, and Anita Cava. "Ethics and the Gender Equality Dilemma for U.S. Multinationals." *Journal of Business Ethics* 12.9 (September 1993): 701-708.

Michalos, Alex. "Issues for Business Ethics in the Nineties and Beyond." *Journal of Business Ethics* 16.3 (February 1997): 219-230.

Pogge, Thomas W. "The Bounds of Nationalism." *Rethinking Nationalism* (*Canadian Journal of Philosophy* Supplementary Volume 22). Ed. Jocelyne Couture, Kai Nielsen, and Michel Seymour. Calgary: University of Calgary Press, 1998. 463-504.

Singer, Andrew W. "Ethics: Are Standards Lower Overseas?" *Across the Board* (September 1991): 31-34.

Skelly, Joe. "The Caux Round Table Principles for Business: The Rise of International Ethics." *Business Ethics* (March/April 1995): 2-5.

Taka, Iwao. "Business Ethics: A Japanese View." *Business Ethics Quarterly* 4.1 (January 1994): 53-78.

Treviño, Linda K., and Katherine A. Nelson. *Managing Business Ethics: Straight Talk about How to do it Right.* 2nd ed. NY: John Wiley and Sons, 1999.

United Nations Development Programme. *Human Development Report 1998.* NY: Oxford University Press, 1998.

Weiss, Joseph W. *Business Ethics: A Managerial, Stakeholder Approach.* Belmont, CA: Wadsworth, 1994. 242-244.

Werhane, Patricia H. "The Moral Responsibility of Multinational Corporations to be Socially Responsible." *Emerging Global Business Ethics.* Ed. W. Michael Hoffman et al. Westport, CT: Quorum Books, 1994. 136-142.

Wines, William A. and Nancy K. Napier. "Toward an Understanding of Cross-Cultural Ethics: A Tentative Model." *Journal of Business Ethics* 11.11 (November 1992): 831-841.

Ethics and Multinational Corporations vis-à-vis Developing Nations

James R. Simpson

ABSTRACT. The ethical dilemma of large-scale multinational corporations is presented. The list of complaints and issues is summarized. A case is made for the concept of multinationals being inherently beneficial in today's world of high technology and dependence on international trade. The difficulty is extreme power wielded by some groups. It is concluded that a philosophical ideal is for control on size and power as well as international rules to prevent abuses of power. The concern is that today the worthiness of being relatively small is slowly but surely being eroded.

James R. Simpson, "Ethics and Multinational Corporations vis-à-vis Developing Nations" *Journal of Business Ethics* 1 (1982): 227-237. © 1982 by D. Reidel Publishing Co., Dordrecht, Holland and Boston, U.S.A. Reprinted with permission of Kluwer Academic Publishers; the author could not be located.

"For the World Managers the underdeveloped world is the supreme management problem.... A Global Shopping Center in which 40 to 50 percent of the potential customers are living at the edge of starvation without electricity, plumbing, drinkable water, medical care, schools, or jobs is not a marketable vision." (Richard J. Barnett and Ronald E. Muller, *Global Reach.*)

Advances in world economic and political structure should be positively related to globalization of the private productive system but, for the most part, the required institutional changes in national government have not taken place, with consequent and predictable political and societal tensions. The lag between technological advance and institutional change was envisioned by Marx in his analysis of the historical progression of capitalism to communism and is, ironically, probably doing more to foster interest in socialism among the educated than any discontent which might be fomented among the so-called proletariat. The situation is of such magnitude that economic liberalists will have to depend on a major redefinition of legislation and philosophy of production and distribution, especially those relating to large corporations with a multinational dimension, to prevent Marx's prophecy of the inevitable movement to communism from being fulfilled.

2   Parallel to the new internationalism of business has been the coining of new jargon. The rise of the 'global corporation', as Barnett and Muller euphemistically call it (they dislike the term 'multinational' corporation for that implies international ownership while globals are almost always owned by one company from one country), has led to the creation of what they term a 'global shopping center' to serve the 'world customer'. The global corporations are operated by 'globalists' and, as might be expected, they 'think globally'. Apart from the challenge of making profits through integrating global marketing with superior management techniques, is the creation of what Daniel Boorstin calls the 'consumption community', which is a bond transcending race, geography, and tradition based on drinking, eating, smoking, wearing and driving identical things.[1] The World Managers who are orchestrating the 'Great Crusade' are convinced that they have a 'historic mandate' to participate in the creation of a 'postpolitical world order'.

3   Many Globalists in the top decision-making ranks believe that politicians have created chaos in the world with their patriotic wars, antiquated borders, and national pride, and that it falls to the international businessmen to save the world. They further argue that social progress stems from the little decisions on production and mar-

keting rather than those of politicians. To them, the great steps forward in a country's progress come about through internationalizing production so that widely dispersed productive facilities can be integrated by such innovations as containerized shipping and automated record keeping into what is, conceptually, a global factory without geographical ties. Although most global corporations, in terms of management and ownership, are either American, British, Dutch, German, French, Swiss, Italian, Canadian, Swedish, or Japanese, they are gradually becoming companies without a country. Carl Gerstacher, chairman of Dow Chemical Company, reportedly even dreams of buying land owned by no nation for his headquarters. A unique feature is that unlike corporate philosophies of just a decade ago, overseas factories and markets are no longer viewed simply as adjuncts to home operations. Rather, the world is visualized as one economic unit with the nation state as an obstacle to planetary development. The irony is that even though many 'futurists' are discussing and planning for a world without borders, the twentieth century is characterized by a wave of nationalism.[2]

4   It is generally agreed that the driving force behind the global concept is a revolution in managerial organization which has made it possible to centralize industrial planning on a global scale.[3] A key to success is delegation of authority with supreme efforts being made to build the global factory into one big happy participating family. As top managers increasingly receive stocks, options, bonuses, overrides, and special opportunities as a part of their income, the distinction between them and owners begins to disappear, and they acquire the same personal interest in maximizing corporate growth and profits as the largest shareholders. Loyalty is a watchword and,

while the globals base their appeal for allegiance on building a faith in their being a principal means of bringing world peace and progress, "its most powerful appeal for loyalty is to the general public, and its message is simple and insistent: Consumption is the key to happiness and the global corporation has the products that make life worth living".[4] The Globalists as well as the Club of Rome[5] are in agreement that there will be a shortage of many products sought by an international community at the global shopping center due to rising populations and depletion of natural resources, and are naturally concerned about a lack of inputs.

5   Recognizing the dangers from potential resource scarcity as well as other conflicts about globals, at least three groups have arisen in direct opposition to the multinational's efforts to fill the shelves and construct new stores. The first of the global managers' mortal enemies are advocates of a 'zero growth economy'. Second are members of the 'anticonsumption movement' who are especially concerned with finding solutions to the problems of global poverty. The third is a group which resists global centralization on a variety of economic, political, moral, scientific, or aesthetic grounds. This third group can be further subdivided into several subgroups, one of which consists of those whose economic interests are affected, such as organized labor in developed countries which views the cheap manpower of LDC's as a real threat. An example of this opposition is the United States' textile industry.

6   The second sub-group of 'enemies' are those motivated as much by political feelings as economic interest. Of special significance are officials and bureaucrats of LDC's who are bent on promoting even greater feelings of nationalism. Paramount in a third subgroup are concerned

reformers, idealistic young people, and followers of other economic systems (such as communism) who view the large corporation as another tool of capitalism designed to further exploit the world's masses. There is also a countercorporate movement emerging within universities, and the global managers are reported to be sufficiently upset that they are bringing pressure on universities by reducing grants and through reminders that the funds of most universities are usually tied up in stocks. As an offensive tactic, there is a proposal by the globals to create a University of the World, whose

> curriculum would be geared to the needs of the 'real world' – i.e. the emerging Global Shopping Center. Criticism of the underlying values and assumptions of the establishment would be muted. Doubt, searching for alternative visions, and other inefficient intellectual activities would be discouraged.[6]

7   The discussion about globals is confined to a new corporate structure comprising a few hundred businesses which deal internationally. They represent the culmination of a process which has led to a concentration that is dangerous in the sense that the globals do not compete according to the traditional liberal economic philosophy.[7] It is this lack of competition and the undesirable effects from their size which form the crux of the global corporation problem vis-à-vis society. Although we must recognize that growth is the driving force behind oligopolistic competition, the late Joseph Schumpeter, a giant among economists, feared that large corporations would rob capitalism of its vitality by dichotomizing the structure into owners who do not manage and managers who do not own. John Kenneth Galbraith, well known for his book, *The Affluent Society*, feels that large corporations become laws into themselves thus pre-

venting Adam Smith's 'invisible hand' from acting as an effective market regulator. The global manager takes a different view though, for to him bigness is next to godliness. It is a law of nature, or to be more exact, of life, since a lack of growth would mean losing confidence from the stock market and other money lenders. Bigness is also important in social hierarchy. The manager (or any employee for that matter) of IBM is more esteemed than one from a little company of 100 employees making parts for the big computer manufacturers. In the same vein, the ambassador from a large industrialized country is held in higher esteem and is more 'important', than one from a small, recently formed African nation. This leads us to one of our tasks which is to determine how a small person's or nation's dignity can be raised in the face of the global corporation problem and how development can be given needed stimulus. First we must examine the globals in more detail.

A closer look at globals

8 Global corporations have been around for a long time. Witness the East India Company of the 1800's and the banana companies which came into their own after the turn of this century. The real proliferation in globals came about after the Korean War, though, as better methods of communication became available, transportation was improved, the cost of labor rose rapidly in the developed countries, and there was a general growth in the size and scale of business. Along with improved managerial techniques came a discovery of tax loopholes in the developed countries and encouragement by leaders in various developing nations to build plants in their countries. As the globals ventured forth, they were well received; the news spread

that the LDC's offered many advantages for setting up business not found in developed countries.[8] Furthermore, as international economic development has taken place, the sheer size of markets in many LDC's has made them attractive. Finally, if a global locates within a common market, it realizes many economic and political advantages which are not available if it is situated in a developed country which does not belong to a common market.

9 The principal longer term problem facing the world managers is how to legitimize their actions. They base their claim to a world role on superior management skills, their corporation's efficiency, and a belief that they can bring about world peace through international trade. The globalists support proposals for breaking down world borders and believe that governments are behaving irrationally because they are tied to territories with such uneconomic goals as pride, prestige, and power. The 'transnational corporations' claim great achievements in their contributions toward an unprecedented standard of living in their own countries and argue that they can assist in replicating this economic progress in other countries if given a chance. The global managers argue that a person's self esteem is, in large part, determined by what is purchased. It can be interjected that the sales of transnational corporations come about largely through advertising, which can have both positive and negative effects. On the positive side, most advertised products, such as transistor radios or bicycles, are processed products which have a higher economic multiplier than many of the so-called basic necessities such as milk, bread, rice and fish. In effect, for every dollar's worth of sales there is more economic activity generated in the economy due to more processing. More people are given jobs and incomes improve. On the

other side of the coin, advertising leads to the consumption of goods which have a questionable tradeoff with the basic necessities, such as a father purchasing a brand name shampoo while his children are malnourished. Advertising also leads to a dependence on satisfying the desire for goods.

10   Irrational consumption habits in LDC's should not necessarily be blamed on the advent of T.V., radio, and billboards, no matter how important the globals have been in promoting their use. Since the dawn of civilization, men have squandered their money on wine, women, and song. Thus, if it is deemed desirable that consumption habits be 'improved' in some manner, the problem should be recognized as one of mounting an educational program to accomplish this. Objective reasoning indicates that it is illogical to expect large corporations to take over the function of improving consumption habits *except* to the extent that they are in the business of processing and marketing the type food deemed 'acceptably nutritious'. This brings us to the topic of globals being change agents or adopting a social role.

11   While no attempt is being made here to determine the extent to which multinational corporations are engines of development or retard the growth of LDC's, a few comments are in order. First, exhaustive studies are required to determine their input, and certainly it will be difficult to generalize as each country is different. The key point is that global corporations, like any other business, operate to make a profit. They assist in developing a social conscience only to the extent they deem it advisable or the top management happens to have more of an altruistic outlook. It should hastily be pointed out that *if the company were owned by the state, it would have no more altruism than a private corpora-*

tion. In fact, there would probably be less spirit of benevolence since state corporation managers in a socialist system receive their rewards from fulfilling production quotas, not in improving the common weal. Anyone who has attempted to solicit donations or assistance will testify that it is harder to get them from government than from private business. The point is that private corporations can be instruments of development, but only within the context of their production and sales capabilities and it is irrational to expect any other attitude.

12   The arguments and counterarguments about global corporations being major suppliers of capital, their providing technology when it would be otherwise unavailable, and their helping solve balance-of-payments problems are quite complex. Statistics can be manipulated to prove almost any point and, certainly, abuses by globals have been many and varied. Furthermore, the past serves only as a reference point. What is becoming clear is that globals are enjoying a greater control over technology, finance capital, and marketing. The difficulty, as with any oligopoly or monopoly, is that they frequently have an inordinate amount of power which can be, and frequently is, used to the detriment of other businesses.[9] One factor is that global corporations are not major suppliers of foreign capital to poor countries and often compete with local corporations for scarce financing. A bank would rather loan to Sears, Roebuck and Company than to a new national department store chain because it is less risky.

13   Knowledge is the critical component of power.

The same power that enables corporations in Latin America to conceal their ownership, plans, and intracorporate dealings and hence frustrate government control over them operates also in the United States. It is one key structural reason why, in our view, the world's richest society is looking more and more like an underdeveloped country.[10]

The power shifts which have occurred as a result of global transformations in the private productive system have not been reflected in governmental modifications either in the LDC's or in the first world countries. The relative loss of power by governments is translated as a detriment to small businesses because there is little countervailing power to resist corporate take-over mainly because of structural weakness in major public institutions which theoretically are expected to balance off the power of global corporations. This situation is exactly what global corporations desire, for they want to stimulate government-big business relationships in which the future is planned to meet tomorrow's challenge. The world managers see government's future role as development of a good business climate which will create the needed infrastructure for a global economy. This is why global corporations require a different kind of nation state, one that provides them with stability, since anticipation and projection of the future are vital for efficient planning. It is also why they will do business with fascists, communists, or dictators if there is a profit. They don't like dealing with a state, but state planning does provide an element of stability.

14   If the government of a global corporation's home country were to be in league with its multinational corporations to a greater extent than at present, the result would be frightening. Think, for example, of the pressure now brought to bear on weaker countries which dare to stand in the path of U.S. based global corporations. The major role which the globals have played in setting foreign policy both of their own 'home' country as well as the 'host' country in which they operate is well known. The names of ITT in Chile, Litton Industries in Greece, United Fruit in Costa Rica, and Gulf in Bolivia are cases in point. What appears on the horizon, though, is a clash between governments and global corporations, as neither one is desirous of giving up the planning function that each have accepted as their own domain. To protect their interests, governments have gained a secure foothold on the futurism bandwagon in predicting, planning, and prevention. Numerous government committees in all countries dedicated to these functions have sprung up in the past few years.[11] A bill introduced in the United States Congress by Senators Humphrey and Javets entitled the Balanced Growth and Economic Planning Act of 1975 is the first attempt at centralized national planning in the United States since the 1930's. The clear trend in the United States is a growing demand for tighter coordination between national policy and corporate policy, and while this seems admirable on the surface, there are drawbacks.

15   Some further considerations of the United States experience are instructive in considering policy about globals as there is evidence that increased planning directed at *coordinating* policies with big business is not the ethical solution for regulating globals. In the United States, big government is not able to control an ever bigger business because

politicians who achieve high office and the public administrators they appoint have little desire to control the expansion and exercise of corporate power. The dominant ideology in midcentury America is the celebration of growth and bigness. No government dedicated to steady, spectacular economic growth as the prime tool for maintaining social peace can afford to take a tough line with corporations.[12]

The same holds true in most other developed countries. Oddly enough, big business has achieved its power through a conception that the best people to manage, advise, and assist the government are those from big business. The result has been a big business-big government interlock. (An interlock, in business terms, is a corporation electing an executive or director of another corporation to be on its board of directors.) In the United States, there has not appeared to be an overt fundamental conflict in corporate and public interests so that the federal government has regulated the economy by people 'on loan' from corporations and banks. The result is that government is able to exercise little countervailing power against big corporations. In Japan, there is outright collaboration between government and business, management, and labor.

16   Considering that the power to dominate seems to be a principal element of concern about multinationals, a major question is: How big is too big? A few statistics provide some illuminating facts. The largest ten 'world corps' are, by sales, bigger than some 80 nations as measured by GNP, and the largest 40 firms are bigger than some 64 nations. Whereas the world's GNP increases at about five percent annually, the world's multinational community grows at some ten percent annually. With assets of more than $200 billion along with human and financial resources that come with that financial power, the multi's have access to data that is unavailable to the majority of nations.[13] The problem of size is not new and has faced U.S. government and academics since the late 1800's when the Sherman Antitrust Act was passed. In the 1960's, conglomerates received a lot of bad press, and orders from justice departments to break up their power were commonplace. Although attention in the 1980's continues to be focused on the size and power of corporations, there are no hard and fast guidelines in what is one of the most cloudy areas of jurisprudence. The sad and disagreeable thing is that many governments are losing their regulatory power because they do not have a clear policy on what they should be regulating.

> What once were laws in such areas as tax, banking, securities, and controls are now looked upon in the sophisticated corporate world as little more than shoals to be avoided by careful steering. The U.S. government is a little like the orchestra conductor who discovers midway through the symphony that the principal players have left.[14]

17   The list of complaints, some with reason, others without justification, is long. In an effort to summarize the issues, the following list has been prepared:

– Just being big is 'bad'.

– Bigness reduces bargaining power of governments and competitors.

– Global corporations (G.C.'s) enter into cartels which hurt smaller businesses.

– G.C.'s only deal in high profit items and leave low profit items for nationals.

– G.C.'s promote luxury items rather than necessities.

– G.C.'s earn excess profits.

– G.C.'s do not reinvest in the country.

– G.C.'s exploit LDC's natural resources.

– They unfairly compete with local companies for scarce development capital.

– G.C.'s transfer prices deviate considerably from market prices to avoid taxes.

– G.C.'s reap double benefits by selling to themselves.

– They have little "social consciousness."

– They are not development agents.

– G.C.'s exploit indigenous labor.

– They introduce machinery rather than using labor intensive techniques.

– Global corporations reduce jobs in the developed countries.

– Globals fail to introduce new technology, and when they do it is a type which LDC's least need, or it is antiquated.

– They over-use advertising.

– They desire to make the world homogenous, i.e. reduce cultural differences and this is 'bad'.

– The developed countries benefit rather than the LDC's.

– Large corporations plan centrally and act globally, but nation states do not.

– Globals are able to escape national regulation.

– They have an inordinate amount of power in their own and host countries, and interfere in policy making.

– Global interdependence has transformed the world political economy in such a way that former stabilizing effects are now destabilizing effects.

18   Prior to discussing the allegations, some more evidence – from the viewpoint of ethics – will assist in evaluating the case. We must recall that moral judgments, and this is the crux of this article for we are making a determination if globals are 'good' or 'bad', should be made with full knowledge of the relevant facts to be objective. The situation must be viewed impartially, but with sympathy. Furthermore, another formal requirement for a moral judgment is universality, i.e. that the judgement would hold in a relevantly similar situation. But let's get into the problem.

Ethics and the global corporation

19 Problems of moral philosophy are divided into three parts: value, the good, and duty. The pros and cons of the multi's from a moral point of view can be discussed within this organizational framework. The problem of value, it will be recalled, revolves around goodness and badness, opinions, attitudes, customs, law, interest, obligation, virtue, control over people; i.e. values or properties which people hold dear. With respect to globals, the heart of the problem revolves around their size. Recognizing that economic organization on a 'sufficiently' large scale is necessary to reach even minimum productive efficiency, the difficulty, from both a practical and ethical viewpoint, is that conflicts of interest arise which threaten order and progress toward many of the values held in highest esteem such as human dignity and the belief by economic liberalists that the 'little guy' should be able to develop a business by working hard enough and possessing the necessary business acumen.

20   In all fairness to globals, they do use their size and scale to enhance economic freedom by promoting upward mobility and greater choice making. In this sense, they contribute to modernity of the LDC's. On the opposite tack, and probably the most damaging of all arguments, is that power situations arise which cause conflicts of interest and subsequent social problems. By having unequal power, globals can also restrict the range of choice to consumers by driving out competition and consequently reducing freedom of the less powerful. On the personal level, they can act in a negative manner through advertising to coerce us into accepting partial freedoms.

21   Let's move on to the problem of 'the good' and its special case, happiness. Can globals be

shown to be intrinsically good, i.e. worthwhile on their own account? If one listens to the global managers, one will come away believing that globals are the salvation of humankind on a par with happiness. More sober analysis in the academic field known as industrial organization leaves one less optimistic. In fact, it is generally concluded that as concentration of power and sales grows, the social function of the market as a price regulator and resource allocator is diminished. Concentration also leads to violations of good market conduct such as tax evasion, overuse of advertising, escaping certain regulations, and inordinate amounts of interference in policy making, thus fulfilling many of the allegations set forth in the last section. Following up further on the problem of 'the good', we recall that intrinsic (ultimate goods) are ones which are valuable in and of themselves, while non-intrinsic or instrumental goods are those which are valuable by virtue of their being related to intrinsic goods. As such, globals, just like any other corporation or type of business, are non-intrinsic in nature and, furthermore, are instrumental in nature, i.e. those valuable as a means to achieve an intrinsic good. The upshot of the matter is that being a global corporation, or any type of business organization for that matter, is simply a means to an end. It is a tool to assist us achieve happiness or some other higher good rather than being a higher good. Thus, in judging whether globals are 'good' or 'bad', the problem is determining how well they contribute to intrinsic goods or the highest good (whatever that may be). In effect they are judged on their conduct and performance – the same thing that economists hold in their theory of industrial organization.

22   To what extent are globals' actions appropriate to their position and to what degree do their actions reflect conduct resulting from a sense of morality and justice, i.e. duty? Adopting a normative position to define what 'ought' to be the ideal action, it is clear that globals cannot be lumped together. Just as any business organization, some do carry out their 'social duty' in a commendable fashion while others abuse power vested in them. Witness the flurry in 1976 from discoveries of bribes paid by globals and other large corporations to government officials all over the world. On the more positive side we observe that they *generally* do fulfill their duty of improving the condition of humankind by providing some articles for life sustenance, enhancement, and luxury. However, they also place emphasis on esteem through materialism, thus probably reducing some inner-self rewards.

23   In all likelihood, globals do help attain the 'good life' by providing an ever greater amount of goods and services but, to the extent that advertising 'forces' people to accept their products after which there is a feeling of repentance, they detract from quality of life. They provide new jobs and services to us through higher standards of living. They 'pull' development by stimulating wants and desires which in turn generates greater economic activity, but negates principles of austerity. They help attain happiness through economic means, but foster homogenation of cultural values. They do help humankind become masters of their own destiny by helping raise standards of living, but are a potential hazard to economic freedom to the extent that they are interlocked with government. They increase freedom of choice by providing more goods and services, but reduce freedom for the individual entrepreneur or small businessman to self-actualize. In brief, they have desirable traits but difficulties with respect to conduct. How then, should they be finally judged from a moral point of view?

An assessment

24 The fundamental objectives of economic policy – full employment, relatively stable prices, equitable income distribution, and quality of life – are compatible with the profit motive providing it is controlled. 'Think, maybe we can avoid work' is a sign frequently observed in both public and private offices. Governments in LDC's could well heed this advice with respect to multinational corporations. By writing the rules clearly, delineating their goals, and using psychology, LDC's can use globals to gain desired development. One place to start is with the world managers themselves.

25 The Global Manager receives satisfaction from the use of imagination, which translates into the generation of corporate profits. Probably, there are few managers who are concerned with reaching some *absolute* profit level, as a profit figure is just a number. There is nothing magic about 40 percent versus 15 percent, for it is *relative* profits which are important to them. The manager is concerned about what others are doing, so the game is played by pitting one corporation's balance sheet against another's. We can hypothesize that global corporations work at the international level because there is a higher percentage of profits abroad than within their home country, as well as a chance to increase sales and consequently total profits. Probably there are also other economic and non-economic goals. The challenge to the manager is seeing how much profit he can make *within the rules of the game.*[15] Naturally, they will complain and attempt to change the rules, as this is an integral part of good management – it is a rationale for lobbying. If rules are made which set restrictions on all global corporations, none are disadvantaged in terms of the others. If the rules are set even at fairly disadvantageous levels, it is likely that the global managers will not complain too loudly *providing* they are maintained for everyone, i.e. that stability accompanies them. A spinoff would be greater innovation. Overall, the key to using globals is fomenting regulations that take advantage of the firm's propensity for profits; the sin is leaving loopholes in the law or 'rules of the game'.

26 As Professor Gordon has pointed out, it is difficult to measure the extent of the multinational's influence on the culture, economics, and political structure of the third world and, consequently, it is difficult to set goals or controls. The magnitude of the global's power is impressive, though. Consider, for example, that United Brands has higher net sales than the GNP of Panama or Costa Rica, Del Monte is higher in sales than Honduras is in GNP, and Quaker Oats is higher than Paraguay. This can lead to a playing, by multi's, of one nation against another. Gordon says

> One must wonder why Third world governments have been so directly subject to the control of multinational enterprises. Using Latin America as an example, the governments tend to be feudalistic, highly structured, and centralized, and thus easier to penetrate than a broadly based government.[16]

27 Recognizing that globals need to be controlled, the United Nations General Assembly recently published a history-making document called the 'Charter of the Economic Rights and Duties of States'. In the second chapter 'transnational corporations', (TNC's) are considered in some detail with the major point being that sovereign states have the right to deal with and regulate TNC's. Recognizing that many states don't have the sophistication to deal with TNC's, the Economic and Social Council

(ECOSOC), a United Nations agency, established a Commission on Transnational Corporations as well as an Information and Research Center, both of which are aimed at a comprehensive and continuous monitoring of the TNC's.[17] A similar project is being carried out in the U.S. Congress.[18] Among the first action programs have been special workshops to assist in training government officials in negotiating techniques, taxation laws, and bargaining.[19] This positive action follows up on the 1973 Algiers conference out of which it was decided to establish a center for studying the 500 leading global corporations.

28   By 1975, the United Nations launched a 48 member intergovernmental body called The Commission on Transnational Corporations which is charged with drafting a code of conduct for transnational corporations. Their subgroups deal with accounting practices, corruption, data retrievals, original research, impact of multi's and conduct workshops.[20]

29   In summary, when we realistically and rationally study the problem, we cannot help but believe there is nothing 'wrong' or 'bad' about corporations doing business on an international level.[21] The difficulty lies in their wielding an exorbitant amount of power. The approach to take, then, from both moral and practical stands seems to be obtaining general world agreement on regulating globals, as our concern about them falls back to their size.[22] There seems to be nothing wrong with a multinational corporation that is relatively small and controlled.[23] However, the worthiness of being little is slowly but surely being eroded as a part of the liberal economic ethic as the corporation and the state merge into one being.[24]

30   What should be done? Specific legislation should be enacted in both host and client countries, as well as at the international level, to effectively control the size and activities of globals while concomitantly encouraging them to be innovative.[25] It implies recognition that the problem is much like pollution control; all nations must participate to optimize benefits and prevent any one organization or nation from being unduly disadvantaged. We are living in an international era and, realistically, it is not feasible to propose doing away with international corporations.

31   The challenge, in which philosophers can play an important role, is drafting the guidelines for dealing with globals from an ethical point of view, recognizing that the end purpose of production and consumption is furthering the happiness of the entire world's population.[26] The problem is defining economic organization in such a way that our physical and mental well-being are promoted to the greatest possible extent. It is recognizing that there is a difference between growth and equity and between growth and development.

NOTES

1. As cited by Richard J. Barnett and Ronald E. Muller, *Global Reach* (Simon and Schuster, New York, 1974), p. 33.
2. See Lester R. Brown, *World Without Borders* (Random House, New York, 1972), especially Chapter II on the multinational corporation.
3. Abdul A. Said and Luiz R. Simmons (eds.), *The New Sovereigns: Multinational Corporations as World Powers* (Englewood Cliffs, New Jersey, Prentice-Hall, Inc., 1972).
4. Barnett and Muller, *Global Reach*, p. 89.
5. Donella H. Meadows *et al.*, *The Limits to Growth* (The New American Library, Inc., Signet Books, New York, 1972).
6. Barnett and Muller, *Global Reach*, p. 118.

7. For more detail, see Robert Staiffer, *Nation-Building in a Global Economy: The Role of the Multinational Corporation* (Sage Publications, Inc., Beverly Hills, California, 1974).

8. A summary of the difficulties faced by multinationals is given by Joseph P. Cummings in 'Is the Fear Justified?' and Dion de Beer in 'What Multinationals Should Know'. Both are in the summer, 1977 *World* published by PMM & Co., pp. 8-10 and 11-17 respectively. A major conclusion is that comprehensive planning and reporting in a context of mutual trust and respect are needed for multinationals to fulfill their true role.

9. For example, when the global corporations invade a country, "available statistics indicate that the usual outcome is that the family business is sold off". Barnett and Muller, *Global Reach*, p. 139.

10. *Ibid.*, pp. 252-253.

11. Constance Holden, 'Futurism: Gaining a Toehold in Public Policy', *Science* 189 (1975), 120-124.

12. Barnett and Muller, *Global Reach*, p. 248. For more information on this theme, see Richard Barnett, *The Lean Years* (Simon and Schuster, New York, 1980).

13. See *Action UNDP*, United Nations, New York, May/June, 1977, p. 2.

14. Barnett and Muller, *Global Reach*, p. 261.

15. A number of books and articles have been written on business practice ethics. See for example, Frank Knight's *The Ethics of Competition* (George Allen and Urwin, London, 1951) or Marquis W. Childs and Douglas Cater, *Ethics in a Business Society* (Mentor Books, New York, 1963).

16. Gordon, Michael W., 'The Impact of the Multinational Corporations and the Third World', ed. by K. R. Simmonds, *Legal Problems of Multinationals* (British Institute of International and Comparative Law, London, 1977), pp. 21-42.

17. For complimentary report see *The Impact of Multinational Corporations on Development and on International Relations*, U.N. Publication Sales No. E.74.11.A.5 (United Nations, New York, 1974). Another good reference is Raymond Vernon, *Storm Over the Multinationals* (Harvard Univ. Press, Cambridge, Mass., 1977).

18. See for example 'A Congressional-Parliamentary Draft Code of Principles on Multinational Enterprises and Governments', office of Congressman Sam M. Gibbons, U.S. House of Representatives, 1976. Activities and publications on multinationals are put out by the International Management and Development Institute, 2600 Virginia Ave. N.W., No. 905, Washington, D.C. 20037 in their bimonthly release *International Corporate Citizenship*.

19. For a summary of the U.N. document and the workshop see *Action UNDP*, United Nations, New York, May/June, 1977. Other periodicals on multi's are *Multinational Monitor*, Corporate Accountability Research Group, P.O. Box 19312, Washington, D.C. 20036, and *The New Internationalist*, 113 Atlantic Ave., Brooklyn, N.Y. 11201.

20. For a summary of the Commission's activities see 'Getting the Measure of the Transnationals', *Development Forum*, Volume V, No. 4, May, 1977, p. 2.

21. Ray Goldberg concludes "the evidence shows" there are many examples of the new breed of socially useful, as well as functionally practical, multinational corporations. *Am. J. Agr. Econ.* 63 (1981), 374.

22. The problem can be conceptualized in the framework similar to pollution control, i.e., no single LDC will be hurt if all nations adopt the same regulations on globals, just as no one individual company will be disadvantaged with respect to the rest if all are subjected to the same controls. The difficulty arises when one company has an advantage, such as a large multi obtains favorable interest rates while a small company has to pay higher rates.

23. One way to bring about reduction in size is trust-busting'. This same principle could hold on an international level. For a good discussion on the United States situation in food, see Russell C. Parker, 'Antitrust Issues in the Food Industries', *Am. J. Agr. Econ.* 58 (1976), 854 – 860. For methodology, see Bruce W. Marion and Thomas L. Spoerleder, 'An Evaluation of the Economic Basis for Antitrust Policy in the Food Industry', *Am. J. Agr. Econ.* 58 (1976), 867 – 873.

24. The Honorable Ted Weiss of New York, for example, has argued that "the corporate state is not individualistic, it is collectivist to the extreme. It is not humanitarian, it is animalistic." See his speech 'Development of the Corporate State' given to the House of Representatives Wednesday, April 30, 1980, *Congressional Record* (126), p. 68.

25. The following suggestions are given to stimulate thought on worldwide control of globals. Certainly I do not possess the credentials for setting up complete guidelines on this complex issue, but at least the following list brings some ideas together and demonstrates that economics cannot be separated from ethics. Many of these proposals are being incorporated in draft legislation in the United States and the EEC.

(1) Demand competitive bids when appropriate, rather than depending on a brand name.

(2) Set worldwide minimum wages through international corporations.

(3) Fight for stronger bargaining on investment, such as time limits and pricing control.

(4) Look toward worldwide bargaining in which the LDC's form committees to study proposals of global corporations so that one G.C. cannot play one country against another.

(5) Use the United Nations and congress of various countries to develop a good set of standards, ethics and procedures for relations between multinationals and nation-states.

(6) Consider strikes as a last resort as this diminishes confidence from potential investors, especially smaller ones.

(7) Place greater emphasis on auditing global corporations.

(8) Organize and coordinate international trade plans with other LDC's.

(9) Place greater emphasis on common market policies.

(10) Set up rules and improve coordination between the internal revenue service of foreign countries and tax offices in local countries.

(11) A novel approach – If you can't lick 'em, join 'em. The LDC's could create their own global corporations just as the Union of Banana Exporters is doing in Central America. See *Action UNDP* (United Nations, New York), May-June, 1977, p. 1, for information on COMUNBANA.

(12) Promote 'Nadarism'.

(13) Encourage relatively small businesses in the developed countries to invest in LDC's, especially by showing how invested capital can be repatriated.

(14) Find ways to keep more finance capital in the country. Do not allow large foreign companies to borrow finance capital on local money markets, but help small foreign companies in obtaining loans.

(15) Increase coordination between LDC's and developed countries on the problem of globals rather than fomenting diametric opposition.

26. For more detail, see Martin A. Alugbuo, 'American Multinational Corporations: What Role Could They Play in Fostering Good Business Ethics in the Lesser Developed Countries?' Staff Paper Series No. 160-77, Unemployment and Underemployment Institute, Southern University and A&M College, Baton Rouge, Louisiana, 1977. Caterpillar Tractor Co. has published *A Code of Worldwide Business Conduct*, Peoria, Ill., 1977. The

Interreligious Task Force on U.S. Food Policy presented their view in 'Multinational Corporations and Global Development', *Hunger* (24), July, 1980.

Questions

1. Do you think the best, most-likely-to-be-successful, road to world peace is economic (the global shopping centre, international trade) or political (nation states of tradition and geography)? Or some third option?

2. "The global managers argue that a person's self esteem is, in large part, determined by what is purchased" (P9). Do you agree?

3. (a) Despite Simpson's note that "globals cannot be lumped together" (P22) and that "it will be difficult to generalize as each country is different" (P11), perform a utilitarian analysis of multinational corporations, listing and weighting their benefits and drawbacks. (Don't restrict yourself to P17 – Simpson speaks of good and bad consequences of MNCs throughout.)

   (b) Is your end evaluation compatible with your (i) intuition? Is it compatible with your view of (ii) rights? (iii) justice? (iv) virtuous behaviour?

4. What is Simpson's answer to the question "how big is too big?"

5. What would you include in the legislative guidelines for globals that Simpson suggests as a solution?

Business Ethics and the International Trade in Hazardous Wastes

Jang B. Singh and V.C. Lakhan

ABSTRACT. The annual production of hazardous wastes which was less than 10 million metric tonnes in the 1940s is now in excess of 320 million metric tonnes. These wastes are, in the main, by-products of industrial processes that have contributed significantly to the economic development of many countries which, in turn, has led to lifestyles that also generate hazardous wastes. The phenomenal increase in the generation of hazardous wastes coupled with various barriers to local disposal has led to the thriving international trade in these environmentally hazardous substances. This paper examines the nature of the international trade in hazardous wastes and the ethical issues associated with such business activity.

1 The export of hazardous wastes by the more developed countries to the lesser developed nations is escalating beyond control. The ethical implications and environmental consequences of this trade in hazardous wastes highlight the need for international controls and regulations in the conduct of business by corporations in the more developed countries. In the late 1970's, the Love Canal environmental tragedy awakened the world to the effects of ill conceived and irresponsible disposal of hazardous by-products of industries. Today, the media focuses its attention on the alleged illegal dumping of hazardous wastes in the lesser developed countries (see Barthos, 1988, and Harden, 1988). The most recent dramatic case so far is that of Koko, Nigeria where more than eight thousand drums of hazardous wastes were dumped, some of which contained polychlorinated biphenyl (PCB), a highly carcinogenic compound and one of the world's most toxic wastes (Tifft, 1988). The government of Nigeria has detained a number of Nigerians in connection with the incident and President Babangida has indicated that they may face a firing squad if found guilty of illegal dumping. Previous to this was the media documentation in the spring of 1987 of an American barge laden with 3,000 tonnes of garbage being turned back to the United States by the Mexican navy. The barge had already tried, unsuccessfully, to dump its noxious cargo in North Carolina, Alabama, Mississippi and Louisiana. The Mexican navy action was aimed at preventing the barge from dumping its cargo in Mexico.

2   The three cases cited above serve as disturbing examples of the international trade in hazardous wastes. Not all of the activities involved in this trade are illegal. In fact, governments are often directly involved in the business of hazardous wastes. This paper examines various char-

Jang B. Singh and V.C. Lakhan, "Business Ethics and the International Trade in Hazardous Wastes" *Journal of Business Ethics* 8.11 (November 1989): 889–899. © 1989 by Kluwer Academic Publishers. Reprinted with permission of the publisher and the authors.

acteristics of the international trade in hazardous waste and discusses the ethical implications of such business activity.

The international trade in hazardous wastes and attendant problems

3 Miller (1988) defined hazardous waste as any material that may pose a substantial threat or potential hazard to human health or the environment when managed improperly. These wastes may be in solid, liquid, or gaseous form and include a variety of toxic, ignitable, corrosive, or dangerously reactive substances. Examples include acids, cyanides, pesticides, solvents, compounds of lead, mercury, arsenic, cadmium, and zinc, PCB's and dioxins, fly ash from power plants, infectious waste from hospitals, and research laboratories, obsolete explosives, herbicides, nerve gas, radioactive materials, sewage sludge, and other materials which contain toxic and carcinogenic organic compounds.

4 Since World War II, the amount of toxic by-products created by the manufacturers of pharmaceuticals, petroleum, nuclear devices, pesticides, chemicals, and other allied products has increased almost exponentially. From an annual production of less than 10 million metric tonnes in the 1940's, the world now produces more than 320 million metric tonnes of extremely hazardous wastes per year. The United States is by far the biggest producer, with "over 275 million metric tonnes of hazardous waste produced each year" (Goldfarb, 1987). The total is well over one tonne per person. But the United States is not alone. European countries also produce millions of tonnes of hazardous wastes each year (Chiras, 1988). Recent figures reported by Tifft (1988) indicate that the twelve countries of the European Community produce about 35 million tonnes of hazardous wastes annually.

5 The problems associated with hazardous wastes started to gain world-wide attention after 1977 when it was discovered that hazardous chemicals leaking from an abandoned waste dump had contaminated homes in a suburban development known as Love Canal, located in Niagara Falls, New York. This event triggered a frantic search for new ways and places to store hazardous wastes, and an introduction of new environmental regulations to store, handle, and dispose of hazardous wastes. With the "not in my backyard" (NIMBY) syndrome in the developed societies, the manufacturers and creators of hazardous wastes began to escalate the practice of dumping their wastes in the lesser developed countries.

6 Table 1 mainly provides an extensive list of companies which are exporting various toxic wastes to the lesser developed countries. Figure 1 maps the various routes. It is seen that the United States and certain European countries are now turning to areas in Africa, Latin America, and the Caribbean to dump their wastes. Historically, the trade in wastes has been conducted among the industrialized nations. A major route involving industrialized nations is that between Canada and the United States. The movement of wastes from the United States into Canada is governed by the Canada-U.S.A. Agreement on the Transboundary Movement of Hazardous Waste which came into effect on November 8, 1986 (Environment Canada). In 1988, the United States exported 145,000 tonnes. Of this amount, only one third was recyclable, leaving approximately 96,667 tonnes of hazardous organic and inorganic wastes such as petroleum by-products, pesticides, heavy metals, and organic solvents and residues for

disposal in the Canadian environment. Of interest is the fact that Canada restricts the import of nuclear waste, but not toxic, flammable, corrosive, reactive, and medical wastes from the United States.

7   Most of the United States hazardous wastes are shipped from the New England states, New York and Michigan and enter Ontario and Quebec which in 1988 received approximately 81,899 and 62,200 tonnes respectively. The neutralization and disposal of the imported hazardous wastes are done by several Canadian companies, with the two largest being Tricil and Stablex Canada Inc. Tricil, with several locations in Ontario, imports wastes from more than 85 known American companies, which it incinerates and treats in lagoons and landfill sites. Stablex Canada imports a wide variety of hazardous wastes from more than 300 U.S. companies. It uses various disposal methods, including landfills and cement kilns which burn not only the components needed for cement but also hazardous waste products. With the established Canada-U.S. Agreement on the Transboundary Movement of Hazardous Waste, companies like Tricil and Stablex may increase their importation of hazardous wastes generated in the United States. As it stands, the United States Environmental Protection Agency estimates that over 75% of the wastes exported from the U.S. is disposed of in Canada (Vallette, 1989). This estimate will likely have to be raised in the near future. Canada-United States trade in hazardous wastes is not a one-way route. It is believed that all of the hazardous wastes imported by the United States (estimated at 65,000 tonnes in 1988) is generated in Canada (*Ibid.*).

8   An especially controversial trend in the international trade in hazardous wastes is the development of routes between industrialized and "lesser developed countries". For example, according to the United States Environmental Protection Agency, there have been more proposals to ship hazardous wastes from the United States to Africa during 1988, than in the previous four years (Klatte *et al.*, 1988).

9   African nations have recently joined together to try to completely ban the dumping of toxic wastes on their continent. They have referred to the practice as "toxic terrorism" performed by Western "merchants of death". Some African government officials are so disturbed by the newly exposed practices that they have threatened to execute guilty individuals by firing squad. Recently, Lagos officials, seized an Italian and a Danish ship along with fifteen people who were associated with transporting toxic wastes in the swampy Niger River delta, into Nigeria. This occurred shortly after the discovery of 3,800 tonnes of hazardous toxic wastes, which had originated in Italy. Local residents immediately became ill from inhaling the fumes from the leaking drums and containers which were filled with the highly carcinogenic compound PCB, and also radioactive material.

10   Companies in the United States have been responsible for sending large quantities of hazardous wastes to Mexico. Although Mexico only accepts hazardous wastes for recycling, which is referred to as "sham re-cycling", there are numerous reports of illegal dumping incidents. Two Californian companies have proposed the shipping of 62,000 tonnes of hazardous wastes each year to Guyana for incineration. They are also close to concluding a deal with the Guyana Government "to build a giant toxic waste incinerator in that country". The companies have suggested that "the incinerator ash be sold as fertilizer and building materials" (Morrison, 1988, p. 8). Guyana is one of a large number of

Table 1. Identification of Actual Waste Shipments and Active Proposals

	Importing Country	Name of Firm	Point of Export	Type of Waste
1	Argentina	American Security International	Florida, USA	Solvents/ Chemical Sludge
2	Benin	Sesco Ltd.	Gibraltar	Non-Nuclear Toxic Waste
3	Benin	Government of France	France	Radioactive Wastes
4	Brazil	Applied Technologies	USA	Unspecified Toxic Wastes
5	Brazil	Ashland Metal Co.	Pennsylvania, USA	N/A
6	Brazil	Delarre Metals Inc.	California, USA	N/A
7	Brazil	Astur Metals Inc.	Puerto Rico, USA	N/A
8	Canada	Over 400 Firms	Mainly points in New England, New York and Michigan	Petroleum By-products, Pesticides, Heavy Metals and Organic Solvents and Residues
9	Dominican Republic	Arbuckle Machinery	Texas, USA	PCB Wastes
10	Dominican Republic	Franklin Energy Resource	New York, USA	Refuse
11	Dominican Republic	World Technology Co.	Italy	Toxic Liquid Wastes
12	Equatorial Guinea	Unspecified British	UK	Chemical Wastes
13	Gabon	Denison Mining	Colorado, USA	Uranium Tailing Wastes
14	Guinea	Bulkhandling Inc.	Philadelphia, USA	Toxic Incinerator Ash
15	Guinea-Bissau	Hamilton Resources	UK	N/A
16	Guinea-Bissau	B/S Import-Export Ltd.	UK	Pharmaceutical Industrial Wastes
17	Guinea-Bissau	Hobday Ltd.	UK	Pharmaceutical Industrial Wastes
18	Guinea-Bissau	Intercontrat SA	Switzerland	Pharmaceutical Industrial Wastes
19	Guinea-Bissau	Lindaco Ltd.	Michigan, USA	Pharmaceutical Industrial Wastes
20	Guyana	Pott Industries	California, USA	Industrial Oil Wastes
21	Guyana	Teixeria Farms International	California, USA	Paint Sludge
22	Haiti	Palino and Sons	Philadelphia, USA	Toxic Incinerator Ash

Table 1 (continued)

	Importing Country	Name of Firm	Point of Export	Type of Waste
23	India	Jack & Charles Colbert	USA	Lead Tainted Hazardous Wastes
24	Mexico	Arm Co. Steel	Missouri, USA	N/A
25	Mexico	Border Steel Mills	Texas, USA	N/A
26	Mexico	Chapparral Steel	Texas, USA	N/A
27	Mexico	Nucor Steel, Nebraska	Nebraska, USA	N/A
28	Mexico	Nucor Steel, Texas	Texas, USA	Furnace Dust
29	Mexico	Nucor Steel, Utah	Utah, USA	Furnace Dust
30	Mexico	Razorback Steel	Arkansas, USA	N/A
31	Mexico	Sheffield Steel Corp.	Oklahoma, USA	N/A
32	Mexico	Federated Metal	New Jersey, USA	Lead Wastes
33	Mexico	B.F. Goodrich	Texas, USA	PCB's, Mercury Cinders
34	Mexico	Diamond Shamrock	Texas, USA	PCB Wastes
35	Mexico	Bayou Steel Corp.	Louisiana, USA	Furnace Dust
36	Nigeria	Jack & Charles Colbert	USA	Lead Tainted Hazardous Wastes
37	Paraguay	American Securities Int	Florida, USA	Solvents/Chemical Sludge
38	Peru	American Securities Int.	Florida, USA	Solvents/Chemical Sludge
39	Senegal	Intercontrat, S.A.	Switzerland	N/A
40	South Africa	American Cyanimid	New Jersey, USA	Mercury-Laced Sludge
41	South Africa	Quanex	Texas, USA	PCB Wastes
42	South Korea	Jack & Charles Colbert	USA	Lead Tainted Hazardous Wastes
43	Surinam	Mine Tech International	Netherlands	PCB Wastes
44	Tonga	Omega Recovery	California, USA	Hazardous Wastes
45	Uruguay	American Security Int.	Florida, USA	Solvents/Chemical Sludge
46	Zimbabwe	Jack & Charles Colbert	USA	Lead Tainted Hazardous Wastes

This table includes information mainly on actual waste shipments and active proposals for shipments from Europe and the United States to less developed countries.

Source: Klatte *et al.*, 1988.

developing countries whose economic plight makes it willing to accept proposals such as this, despite the long term human and environmental costs (*Ibid.*, p. 9).

11   Given the fact that hazardous wastes are:

(1) toxic;

(2) highly reactive when exposed to air, water, or other substances that they can cause explosions and generate toxic fumes;

(3) ignitable that they can undergo spontaneous combustion at relatively low temperatures;

(4) highly corrosive that they can eat away materials and living tissues;

(5) infectious, and

(6) radioactive;

Miller (1988) has, therefore, emphasized correctly that the proper transportation, disposal, deactivation, or storage of hazardous wastes is a grave environmental problem which is second only to nuclear war.

12   The practice of transporting and dumping hazardous wastes in lesser developed nations, where knowledge of environmental issues is limited is causing, and will pose, major problems to both human health and the environment. Several comprehensive studies have outlined the detrimental impacts which hazardous waste can have on humans and natural ecosystems. Epstein *et al.* (1982) have provided a thorough and dramatic coverage of the impacts

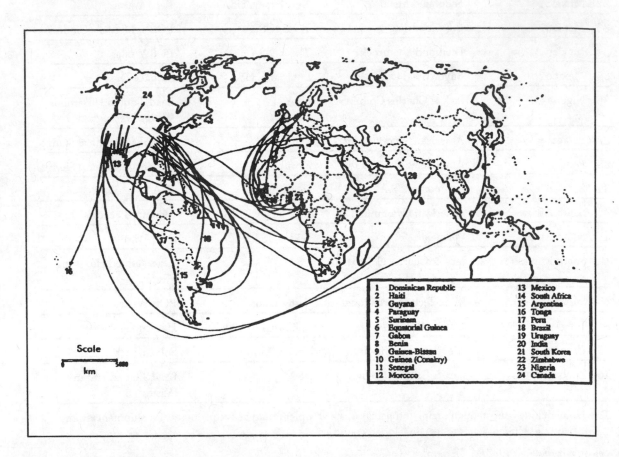

1	Dominican Republic	13	Mexico
2	Haiti	14	South Africa
3	Guyana	15	Argentina
4	Paraguay	16	Tonga
5	Surinam	17	Peru
6	Equatorial Guinea	18	Brazil
7	Gabon	19	Uruguay
8	Benin	20	India
9	Guinea-Bissau	21	South Korea
10	Guinea (Conakry)	22	Zimbabwe
11	Senegal	23	Nigeria
12	Morocco	24	Canada

Figure 1. Location of active waste shipments.

of hazardous wastes, while Regenstein (1982), in his book *America the Poisoned*, gives a good overview of the implications of hazardous wastes. Essentially, hazardous wastes not only contaminate ground water, destroy habitats, cause human disease, contaminate the soil, but also enter the food chain at all levels, and eventually damage genetic material of all living things. For instance, when hazardous wastes enter water bodies, they are taken up by Zoo plankton, which single cell fish ingest while feeding. Other higher-level organisms also accumulate these substances, so that tissue concentrations become higher at higher levels of the food chain. The accumulation and biological magnification which occurs exposes organisms high on the food chain to highly dangerous levels of many chemicals. Understanding toxic chemical repercussions is still barely out of the dark ages, but it is known that metals present in water are toxic for fish. The metals irritate their gills and cause a mucus to build up on them, which eventually causes the fish to suffocate (Chiras, 1988). When hazardous wastes are deposited in the soil it is taken up by food crops, which eventually affect livestock as well as humans. When the ash enters the air, it also has the ability to cause pollution. Even though air is a finite resource capable of cleansing itself, it cannot entirely get rid of all pollutants. Besides causing respiratory problems in the local inhabitants, air pollution will damage the crops and reduce the yields. The rate of photosynthesis will be decreased with harmful effects on animal respiratory and central nervous systems (Miller, 1988).

13   The hazardous wastes can also directly threaten human health through seeping into the ground and causing the direct pollution of aquifers, which supply "pure" drinking water. To-day, in the United States, a long list of health related problems are caused by hazardous chemicals from "leaking underground storage tanks" (LUST). Investigations now show that human exposure to hazardous wastes from dumpsites, water bodies, and processing and storage areas can cause the disposed synthetic compounds to interact with particular enzymes or other chemicals in the body, and result in altered functions. Altered functions have been shown to include mutagenic (mutation-causing), carcinogenic (cancer-causing), and teratogenic (birth-defect causing) effects. In addition, they may cause serious liver and kidney dysfunction, sterility and numerous lesser physiological and neurological problems (see Nebel, 1987).

The ethical implications

14   The very notion of dumping one's wastes in someone else's territory is repulsive. When the Mexican navy turned back an American barge laden with garbage, one Mexican newspaper columnist commented that "the incident serves to illustrate once again the scorn that certain sectors of U.S. society feel toward Mexico in particular and Latin America in general" ("Mexico Sends Back", April 27, 1987, p. F9). Others have pointed to the export of wastes as an example of neo-colonialist behaviour. An official of an environmental organization expressed this view in the following manner: "I am concerned that if U.S. people think of us as their backyard, they can also think of us as their outhouse" (Porterfield and Weir, 1987, p. 343). In addition to arousing emotions such as those described above, the international trade in hazardous wastes raises a number of ethical issues. The rest of this paper examines some of these.

The right to a livable environment

15 The desire for a clean, safe and ecologically balanced environment is an often expressed sentiment. This is especially so in industrialized countries where an awareness of environmental issues is relatively high – a fact that is gaining recognition in political campaigns. However, expression of the desire for a clean, safe environment is not the same as stating that a clean, safe environment is the right of every human being. But the right of an individual to a livable environment is easily established at the theoretical level. Blackstone (1983) examines the right to a livable environment from two angles – as a human right and as a legal right. The right to a clean, safe environment is seen as a human right since the absence of such a condition would prevent one from fulfilling one's human capacities.

> Each person has this right qua being human and because a livable environment is essential for one to fulfill his human capacities. And given the danger to our environment today and hence the danger to the very possibility of human existence, access to a livable environment must be conceived as a right which imposes upon everyone a correlative moral obligation to respect. (Blackstone, 1983, p. 413) .

Guerrette (1986) illustrates this argument by reference to the Constitution of the United States. He proposes that people cannot live in a chemically toxic area, they cannot experience freedom in an industrially polluted environment, and they cannot be happy worrying about the quality of air they breathe or the carcinogenic effects of the water they drink (Guerrette, 1986, p. 409). Some even argue (e.g., Feinberg, 1983) that the right to a livable environment extends to future generations and that it is the duty of the present generation to pass on a clean, safe environment to them.

16 Establishing the right to a livable environment as a human right is not the same as establishing it as a legal right. This requires the passing of appropriate legislation and the provision of a legal framework that may be used to seek a remedy if necessary. Such provisions are more prevalent in the industrialized countries and this is one of the push factors in the export of hazardous wastes to the lesser developed countries. This points to the need for a provision in international law of the right to a decent environment which with accompanying policies to save and preserve our environmental resources would be an even more effective tool than such a framework at the national level (Blackstone, 1983, p. 414). As ecologists suggest, serious harm done to one element in an ecosystem will invariably lead to the damage or even destruction of other elements in that and other ecosystems (Law Reform Commission of Canada, 1987, p, 262) and ecosystems transcend national boundaries. The need for international law in this area has not led to the formulation of the same. However, there have been campaigns to stop the flow of hazardous wastes across national boundaries. In a current campaign, the international environmental group, Greenpeace, is calling for a global ban on the transboundary movement of wastes. Greenpeace is basing its appeal on Principle 21 of the 1972 Declaration of the United Nations Conference on the Human Environment which declares that each state is responsible for ensuring that activities within their jurisdiction or control do not cause damage to the environment of other states or of areas beyond the limits of their own national jurisdiction (Klatte *et al.*, 1988, p. 3).

17 A more direct harmful effect of the international trade in hazardous wastes is the damage to the health of workers involved in the trans-

portation and disposal of these toxic substances. For example, prolonged exposure to wastes originating in Italy and transported by a ship called Zanoobia is suspected of causing the death of a crew person and the hospitalization of nine others (Klatte *et al.* 1983, p. 12). Whereas worker rights in work-place health and safety are gaining wider recognition in many industrialized nations this is not so in the "less developed" countries which are increasingly becoming the recipients of hazardous wastes. Widespread violation of workers right to a clean, safe work environment should therefore be expected to be a feature of the international trade in hazardous wastes.

Racist implications

18 The recent trend of sending more shipments of hazardous wastes to Third World countries has led to charges of racism. *West Africa*, a weekly magazine, referred to the dumping of toxic wastes as the latest in a series of historical traumas for Africa. The other traumas cited by the magazine were slavery, colonialism and unpayable foreign debts. An article in another African magazine viewed the dumping of wastes in Koko, Nigeria as follows:

> That Italy did not contemplate Australia or South Africa or some other place for industrial waste re-echoes what Europe has always thought of Africa A wasteland. And the people who are there, waste beings. (Brooke, 1988, p. A10)

Charges of racism in the disposal of wastes have been made before at the national level in the United States. A study of waste disposal sites found that race was the most significant among variables tested in association with the location of commercial hazardous wastes facilities. The findings of this national study which were found to be statistically significant at the 0.0001 level showed that communities with the greatest number of commercial hazardous wastes facilities had the highest concentration of racial minorities (Lee, 1987, pp. 45-46). The study found that although socio-economic status appeared to play a role in the location of commercial hazardous wastes facilities, race was a more significant factor.

19 In the United States, one of the arguments often advanced for locating commercial waste facilities in lower income areas is that these facilities create jobs. This is also one of the arguments being advanced for sending wastes to poor lesser developed countries. An examination of Table 1 would reveal that nearly all the countries receiving hazardous wastes have predominantly coloured populations. This is the reason why charges of racism are being made against exporters of wastes. However, it must be noted that even though the trend of sending wastes to countries such as those listed in Table 1 has recently gained strength, the bulk of the international trade in hazardous wastes is still within industrialized Europe and North America which have predominantly non-coloured populations.

20 For example, the United States Environmental Protection Agency estimates that as much as 75% of the wastes exported from the US. is disposed of in Canada (Klatte *et al.*, 1988, p. 9). Another striking example is that a dump outside Schonberg, East Germany, is the home of well over 500,000 tonnes of waste a year from Western Europe ("Rubbish Between Germans", March 1, 1986, p. 46). Thus, while charges of racism in the export of hazardous wastes are being made by some Third World leaders, figures on the international trade in such substances do not substantiate these claims.

Corporate responsibility

21 The international trade in hazardous wastes basically involves three types of corporations — the generators of wastes, the exporters of wastes, and the importers of wastes. These entities, if they are to act in a responsible manner, should be accountable to the public for their behaviour.

> Having a corporate conscience means that a company takes responsibility for its actions, just as any conscientious individual would be expected to do. In corporate terms, this means that a company is accountable to the public for its behaviour not only in the complex organizational environment but in the natural physical environment as well. A company is thus responsible for its product and for its effects on the public. (Guerrette, 1986, p. 410)

Using Guerrette's definition of corporate responsibility, it seems clear that a corporation involved in the international trade in hazardous wastes is not likely to be a responsible firm. The importer of hazardous wastes is clearly engaged in activities that will damage the environment while the exporter being aware that this is a possibility, nevertheless, sends these wastes to the importer. However, it is the generator of hazardous wastes that is the most culpable in this matter. If the wastes are not produced then obviously their disposal would not be necessary. Therefore, in view of the fact that virtually no safe method of disposing hazardous wastes exists, a case of corporate irresponsibility could easily be formulated against any corporation involved in the international trade in these substances.

Government responsibility

22 Why do countries export wastes? A major reason is that many of them are finding it difficult to build disposal facilities in their own countries because of the NIMBY syndrome mentioned earlier. Other reasons are that better technologies may be available in another country, facilities of a neighboring country may be closer to a generator of waste than a site on national territory and economies of scale may also be a factor. However, to these reasons must be added the fact that corporations may be motivated to dispose of waste in another country where less stringent regulations apply ("Transfrontier Movements", March 1984, p. 40). It is the responsibility of governments to establish regulations governing the disposal of wastes. In some countries, these regulations are stringent while in others they are lax or non-existent. Moreover, some countries have regulations governing disposal of wastes within national boundaries as well as regulations relating to the export of hazardous wastes. For example, companies in the United States that intend to export hazardous wastes are requested to submit notices to the Environmental Protection Agency (EPA) and to demonstrate that they have the permission of the receiving country (Porterfield and Weir, 1987, p. 341). However, the effectiveness of these controls is in question. The General Accounting Office has found that "the E.P.A. does not know whether it is controlling 90 percent of the existing waste or 10 percent. Likewise it does not know if it is controlling the wastes that are most hazardous" (*Ibid.*). Moreover, there is evidence indicating that other U.S. government agencies are encouraging the export of hazardous wastes. The Navy, the Army, the Defence Department, the Agriculture Department and the Treasury Department are some government agencies that have provided hazardous wastes to known exporters. Also, major U.S. cities, sometimes with the approval of the State Department, have been

suppliers to the international trade in hazardous wastes (Porterfield and Weir, 1987, p. 342).

23 While more stringent regulations, higher disposal costs, and heightened environmental awareness are pushing many companies in industrial countries to export hazardous wastes, it must be, nevertheless, realized that the governments of lesser developed countries are allowing such imports into their countries because of the need for foreign exchange. These governments are willing to damage the environment in return for hard currency or the creation of jobs. One must assume that on the basis of cost-benefit analysis these governments foresee more benefits than harm resulting from the importation of hazardous wastes. However, these benefits go mainly to a few waste brokers while the health of large numbers of people is put at risk. In some cases, decisions to import wastes are made by governments which hold power by force and fraud. For example, Haiti which has imported wastes (see Table 1) is ruled by a military dictatorship and Guyana which is actively considering the importation of industrial oil wastes and paint sludge is ruled by a minority party which has rigged all elections held in that country since 1964. The ethical dilemma posed by this situation is that of whether or not an unrepresentative government of a country could be trusted to make decisions affecting the life and health of its citizens. In fact, a larger question is whether or not any government has the right to permit business activity that poses a high risk to human life and health.

24 Generally, governments of waste generating countries, in reaction to political pressure, have imposed stringent regulations on domestic disposal and some restrictions on the export of hazardous wastes; however, as the examples above illustrate, the latter restrictions are not strictly enforced, hence, indicating a duplicitous stance on the part of the generating countries. The governments of importing countries, in allowing into their countries, wastes that will disrupt ecosystems and damage human health, deny their citizens the right to a livable environment.

Conclusion

25 Hazardous wastes are, in the main, by-products of industrial processes that have contributed significantly to the economic development of many countries. Economic development, in turn, has led to lifestyles which also generate hazardous wastes. To export these wastes to countries which do not benefit from waste generating industrial processes or whose citizens do not have lifestyles that generate such wastes is unethical. It is especially unjust to send hazardous wastes to lesser developed countries which lack the technology to minimize the deleterious effects of these substances. Nevertheless, these countries are increasingly becoming recipients of such cargoes. The need for stringent international regulation to govern the trade in hazardous wastes is now stronger than ever before. However, this alone will not significantly curb the international trade in hazardous wastes. International regulation must be coupled with a revolutionary reorganization of waste-generating processes and change in consumption patterns. Until this is achieved the international trade in hazardous wastes will continue and with it a plethora of unethical activities.

BIBLIOGRAPHY

Barthos, G.: 1988, 'Third World Outraged at Receiving Toxic Trash', *The Toronto Star* June 26, pp. 1,4.

Blackstone, W. T.: 1983, 'Ethics and Ecology' in Beauchamp, T.L. and Bowie, N. E. (Eds), *Ethical*

Theory and Business 2nd. edition (Prentice-Hall, Inc., Englewood Cliffs, New Jersey) pp.411-424.

Barthos, G.: 1988, 'Third World Outraged at Receiving Toxic Trash', *The Toronto Star* June 26, pp. 1,4.

Brooke, J.: 1988, 'Africa Fights Tide of Western Wastes', *The Globe and Mail* July 18, p. A10.

Chiras, D. D.: 1988, *Environmental Science* (Benjamin Commings Publishing Co. Inc., Denver).

Environment Canada: 1986, *Canada-U.S.A. Agreement on the Transboundary Movement of Hazardous Waste* (Environment Canada, Ottawa).

Epstein. S. S., Brown. L. O., and Pope, C.: 1982, *Hazardous Waste in America* (Sierra Club Books, San Francisco).

Feinberg, J.: 1983, 'The Rights of Animals and Unborn Generations', in Beauchamp, F. L and Bowie, N. E., (Eds), *Ethical Theory and Business* 2nd. edition (Prentice-Hall Inc., Englewood Cliffs, New Jersey) pp. 428-436.

Goldfarb, T. D.: 1987, *Taking Sides: Clashing Views on Controversial Environmental Issues* (Dushkin Publishing Co. Inc., Connecticut).

Guerrette, R. H.: 1986, 'Environmental Integrity and Corporate Responsibility' *Journal of Business Ethics* Vol. 5, pp. 409-415.

Harden. B.: 1988, 'Africa Refuses to Become Waste Dump for the West', *The Windsor Star,* July 9, p. A6.

Klatte, E., Palacio, F., Rapaport, D., and Vallette, J.: 1988, *International Trade in Toxic Wastes: Policy and Data Analysis* (Greenpeace International, Washington, D.C.)

Law Reform Commission of Canada: 1987, 'Crimes Against the Environment' in Poff, D. and Waluchow, W., *Business Ethics in Canada* (Prentice-Hall Canada Inc., Scarborough), pp. 261-264.

Lee, C.: Summer 1987, 'The Racist Disposal of Toxic Wastes', *Business and Society Review* Vol. 62, pp. 43-46.

Miller, T.: 1988, *Living in The Environment,* (Wadsworth Publishing Co., California).

Montreal Gazette: April 27 1987, 'Mexico Sends Back U.S. Barge Filled With Tonnes of Garbage', p. F9.

Morrison, A.: 1988 'Dead Flowers to U.S. Firms that Plan to Send Waste to Guyana', *Catholic Standard,* Sunday, May 8.

Nebel, B. J.: 1987, *Environmental Science* (Prentice-Hall, Inc., New Jersey).

OEGD Observer: March 1984, 'Transfrontier Movements of Hazardous Wastes: Getting to Grips with the Problem', pp. 39-41.

Porterfield, A. and Weir, D.: 1987, 'The Export of U.S. Toxic Wastes', *The Nation,* Vol. 245, Iss. 10 (Oct. 3), pp. 341-344.

Regenstein, L.: 1982, *America the Poisoned* (Acropolis Books, Washington D.C.).

The Economist: March 1, 1986, 'Rubbish Between Germans', p. 46.

Tifft, S.: 1988, 'Who Gets the Garbage', *Time* July 4, pp. 42-43.

Vallette, J.: 1989, *The International Trade in Wastes: A Greenpeace Inventory* 4th edition (Greenpeace International, Luxembourg).

Questions

1. What happens when hazardous waste is not properly transported, deactivated, and disposed of or stored?

2. How could you argue that the right to a livable environment extends to future generations?

3. What fact weakens the claim of racism (with respect to the international trade in hazardous wastes)?

4. Which of the three types of corporations found responsible by Singh and Lakhan do you think bears most responsibility – why?

5. What conditions do you think must be met if trade in hazardous waste is to be morally acceptable? (Consider the rights- and con- sequence-based arguments presented by Singh and Lakhan, but consider other ethical approaches to decision-making as well.)

Case Study – Microcredit: The Case of Calmeadow

Two decades ago, Muhammed Yunus began making $1 loans, mainly to Bangledeshi villagers. He started what has come to be known as the microcredit phenomenon. Now his Grameen Bank is praised as having helped reduce poverty in one of the world's most impoverished nations.

Calmeadow, an organization based in Toronto, was established in 1983 by two business executives looking to utilize the microcredit model. It was initially a grant-giving foundation and started its overseas program partnering with ACCION International and supported by the Canadian International Development Agency (CIDA).

Calmeadow International has established programs of microcredit, research, and advocacy in a variety of developing countries including South Africa, Guinea, Kenya, Bangladesh, the Philippines, Cambodia, Bolivia, and Colombia. Their Toronto office has one of the largest col lections of microfinance resources in the world. In the long term, Calmeadow intends that its loan programs be sustainable in the sense that revenues from past loans cover the funds needed for new loans. Achieving this goal would free them from dependence on external funding.

It is important to note that while Calmeadow makes microcredit available to people with good business ideas but little collateral, the loans are by no means without cost. Most loans now have a 12% interest rate, which is high by current conventional (bank) loan standards. Most borrowers must form a "loan group" which acts partly as a support group, but also serves to protect the lenders' interest. The group members vouch for each other in getting the loans initially, and members are partly liable if another member defaults. As well, members of the group cannot qualify for new loans until all group members have reimbursed their loans in full.

Calmeadow is not the only institution in Canada involved with microloans. The Bank of Nova Scotia (now referred to as "Scotiabank") is currently extending microcredit to 3,000 clients in Guyana, helping them build small businesses. In Thailand, Bata (a Canadian shoe manufacturer) has helped set up worker co-ops. CIDA is also involved, providing about $50 million to micro-enterprise development. A major CIDA microcredit project in Russia is currently assisting Russian banks to lend to micro- and small-scale businesses.

The microcredit movement has been connected to women's business enterprises from the earliest beginnings in Bangladesh. The majority of the borrowers so far have been women; in many developing countries, women are the traders and small business operators. With modest infusions of seed money, small groups of women have been able to engage in successful enter-prises greatly helping to both alleviate poverty and improve women's independence. As Marleau points out, "Microcredit is not a pana-cea, but it is demonstrably part of the solution to women's poverty." Clearly, the hope is that if women can escape poverty, so will their chil-dren; economic development most often pro-ceeds in small steps.

REFERENCES

Barthos, Gordon. "Canadian Firms Mix Con-science, Commerce." *The Toronto Star.* 5 Jun. 1998: A19.

Calmeadow website. <www.calmeadow.com>

"Canada's Foreign Aid Funds Hope For Many." Editorial. *The Toronto Star* 1 Feb. 1998: D2.

Le Gras, Gilbert. "Microcredit Spawning Small Businesses." *The Toronto Star.* 19 Aug. 1998: E5.

Marleau, Diane. "Plight of Millions of Women Desperate." *The Toronto Star.* 6 Mar. 1998: A24.

Questions

1. Don't organizations such as Calmeadow let the commercial banks "off the hook"? Shouldn't the banks be extending loans to people who need them? Why can't banks devote some of their enormous profits to such projects?

2. Should we have any ethical concern about the need for borrowers of microcredit to have a group support system? Doesn't this discriminate unfairly against people who are alone or who do not have an extensive so-cial network?

3. Why would a large commercial bank (like Scotiabank) be involved in microcredit in Guyana? Is this likely to be a profitable ac-tivity for the bank? If you were a Scotiabank shareholder, what questions would you ask the CEO about such a project?

CHAPTER 10
BUSINESS AND THE ENVIRONMENT

What to Do? – Surprise Toxins

You've just discovered that your company is standing on a toxic dump of sorts. If you do nothing, chemicals will continue to leach out, polluting lakes and streams in the community (such water is used not only for recreational purposes, but also for drinking). However, as far as you can see, doing something means either selling your business property (and you'd have to withhold the truth to get a sale) or excavating and arranging proper disposal (which means you'd go bankrupt).

You feel it's a little unfair – after all, you're not the one who dumped the toxins. But, it is your land now. Along with property rights come responsibilities.

Could you say you bought the land under false pretenses? Suddenly *caveat emptor* comes back to haunt you. Truth be told, you didn't actually ask about the toxicity of the land; no one actually lied about it – they simply didn't tell you (apparently property assessments don't routinely check for this kind of thing). And, well, you don't tell prospective customers about the down-side of what you're selling, either.

No one seems to have dropped dead from the contaminated water (which still sparkles prettily in the sun) – but you know that such harm could be long-term, even next-generational. It may be that drinking the water isn't nearly as bad as, say, eating the fish that live in it (less concentrated), but you don't know.

Your business is not essential – the community can survive without it, as can you and your employees.

What do you decide to do?

Introduction

It may seem strange to have a special chapter about the environment; after all, the chapter on product safety should cover it, as long as the full cycle is considered (raw material acquisition, manufacture, use, *and* disposal). And as long as one recognizes that business should, for some reason, be concerned about the impact of that full cycle on the environment. But what might that reason be? Well, there are several possibilities.

From an egoistic point of view, you should be concerned about sustainability: if your source material runs out, you're out of business. Ditto if you run out of dumping grounds, or they become scarce and disposal costs increase – there goes your profit. (Can you develop a fully recyclable product, eliminating the disposal problem? Consider the ice cream cone.) Quite simply, the environment has economic value to business.

That is, if *you* have to pay for disposal. And here's an important ethical issue: traditionally, the impact of business operations on the environment has been considered an "externality" – the expenses have not been borne by either the producers or consumers, but rather they have been passed on to others not really involved with the business. But is this morally right? Why should others bear the consequences of your profit-making? Justice theories come in handy here.

Business may say, "well, it's not my fault, or not only my fault, after all you *bought* X, *you* wanted it!" (See Bowie, who argues that if consumers are not willing to pay more for environmentally friendly products, it is not the responsibility of business to "correct" that "market failure.") But as long as environmental costs are externalities, the consumer may not really know what s/he's buying: if the cost to the en-

vironment were included, s/he may well decide *not* to buy it, may not want it *that* badly, not badly enough to have something destroyed or even a little damaged.

If the responsibility for the environment falls solely to the government, then we all share it, through our taxes. Which sounds fair enough, since we all "use" the environment. But why should I pay to clean up the mess you made, or paid to have made, because you had to have stone-washed jeans and steak?

From a utilitarian point of view, if you're running your business according to the stakeholder model, you should be concerned about the effects of your business on your customers, your employees, the community, perhaps even society-at-large if you have that much influence/power. And, in the case of environmental effects, you do: environmentally speaking, *everything connects*.

Given this interconnectedness, by the way, these issues overlap with international issues; as mentioned in the international issues chapter, one important ethical question is whether you're doing business in other countries *because* they have lower environmental standards – should you do that? Just because you can? (And why does a dog – never mind.)

Consider the following:

Since its massive use in the 1940s, the footsteps of DDT can be followed from wheat, to insects, to rodents, to larger animals and birds, and to man. In its wake it left whole species of animals more or less extinct or with serious reproductive problems. To illustrate the degree of interaction involved and the insignificance of time and distance, traces of DDT can now be found in the flesh of polar bears. (Law Reform Commission of Canada, 22)

Consider global warming, acid rain, the ozone layer – rarely do the consequences remain where the action happened.

Or when. Your stakeholders include future generations. Consider Chernobyl.

And insofar as your stakeholders depend on the environment for life itself – well, they'll be affected. Now, two things must be said here. First, this is a very instrumental view of the environment: that is, the environment is valued only insofar as it does good *for us* (see Baxter for this view). And as long as "us" is human beings, it's a very speciesist view as well. After all, we're as much a part of the beaver's or tree's environment as the beaver or tree is part of ours.

One could take, instead, the intrinsic view: the environment has value in and of itself (see Rolston for this view; see Stone too, who argues not only for value, but also for rights). So even if we didn't need to breathe and drink, even if we didn't find starry night skies stunningly beautiful, still we should do no harm to the environment. The environment itself may be considered a stakeholder (see Starik, as well as Hoch and Giacalone): it can be affected by business decisions.

The second consideration, and surely the developers among you are sputtering about this, is that the environment doesn't sustain us *just as is*. Ever hear of mining? Agriculture? Paper doesn't grow on trees, you know! If we didn't develop the environment, we'd still be hunters and gatherers – well, maybe not even that (hunting and gathering involve intervention). And every development, even agriculture, causes some environmental destruction. It's a trade-off.

And therein lies an important ethical question: Is X worth Y? For example, are cars worth smog? Is a cheap burger worth the loss of rainforests? Baxter has something to say about this, too.

Before you answer, consider your alternatives: crop rotation "costs" less than other agricultural methods that wreak havoc on the topsoil; solar and wind power costs less than nuclear or hydroelectric power, etc. So maybe you *can* have your cake and clean air too. But it's not easy to figure this out: producing plastic bags requires 20-40% less energy than producing paper bags (Fredericksen and Jones), but paper bags decompose in the dump while plastic bags don't – so which should you go with? Hopefully, environmental scientists, *independent* environmental scientists, can tell us.

Who decides whether the trade-off is worth acting on? Utilitarian theories and justice theories may well say it should be whoever would be affected – which is, given the interconnectedness, pretty much everyone, yes? So, what are you saying, you might ask: I have to get everyone's permission before I open my business? Well, if your business creates by-product A which does B which affects C which makes a hundred lakes toxic for half a century, yes. Even if it makes one lake toxic for ten years, yes. No?

See the paper by Cragg, Pearson, and Cooney about ethics, surface mining, and the environment, the opening of which can apply far beyond the mining business:

Adopting an ethical stance requires that a company bargain fairly in building contractual relationships with voluntary stakeholders. Genuine voluntary involvement requires informed choice. And informed choice requires, in turn, that a company disclose information available to it which could reasonably be expected to affect in a material way a stakeholder's decision to become involved. ...[It also] requires that a mining company carefully distinguish voluntary and involuntary stakeholder relationships...[and] that a company seek and support a fair distribution of costs and benefits for all stakeholders.... Finally, an ethical company has an obligation to avoid harmful impacts on stakeholders from which recovery is likely to be difficult or onerous or perhaps impossible. This will require a willingness not to initiate projects that are likely to impose unacceptable human or environmental risks or costs. (229–230)

This may be where government plays a part: by setting regulations (e.g., don't change the climate), isn't it granting or withholding permission on behalf of "everyone"? So, as long as you conform to the regulations, you're okay? (How is the government doing on this regulation thing? Those of you with Minamata disease from mercury, or skin cancer from the ultraviolet, is it doing all right?)

But what if your by-product A wasn't the only cause? One smokestack may be okay, it may be within the coping threshold of the natural environment. But two may not be. So are you in the wrong only if your smokestack is the second one? Or, if another factory wants to set up, and you're the first one, should you cut your exhaust in half, should you share responsibility? Does it matter what the alternatives are? (Can the second factory set up somewhere else? Is there a way to manufacture your product with less exhaust?) Does it matter what you're making? (Do we need it? badly?)

How do we decide if X is worth Y? Unless we can use some common measure (like money?), we're measuring apples against oranges. We can put a monetary price on paper, cars, and burgers. But should we, could we, put a dollar value on the starry sky, the quiet, the loon's call, drinkable water, breathable air – life itself? If we say we can't, because we say they're "priceless," then they're certainly worth more than what's on the other side of the equation. Mark Sagoff is one (among many – see also Kelman) who questions whether we should put a price on the environment, whether we should figure in how much people would be willing to pay for environmental qualities: "What is wrong with that? ...Not all of us think of ourselves simply as *consumers*." See Shrader-Frechette for a response to his critique.

But of course it's not so black and white. Surely a few cars – police cars and ambulances, at least – are worth a little air pollution and noise. And, well, the freight trucks that get food to my local stores (even bananas that come all the way from the tropics? But if we don't buy them, what else can those tropical countries sell?) are worth a little pollution. And where do we draw the line? Two-car households? Single-occupant trips? Bananas from the tropics?

The utilitarian approach, weighing the consequences on both sides, is not the only way to approach this decision. We could look at it as a conflict of rights: my right to a certain quality of life against your right to profit (i.e., a certain quality of life?) – my clean air or your Porsche? See Blackstone for an analysis of this right to a livable environment.

Right to private property is also invoked in this context. But are rights ever absolute? Does the right to private property include the right to do anything you want to your property, on your property, regardless of harm to others? See Harbrecht for an interesting angle on this issue.

Perhaps a principle-based approach can be enlightening. Do no harm. Period. So find yourself a nontoxic way to make money. Is that really too much to ask? (Is it really that simple?)

Much environmental destruction has resulted from the "bigger/more is better" view of development, a view that might just have been excusable back when natural resources seemed infinite and causal connections were not understood. But that view is becoming less and less accepted; many are endorsing sustainable growth rather than unlimited growth. Such a model, according to DesJardins, proposes three things:

1. Businesses should not use renewable resources at rates that exceed their ability to replenish themselves. ...

2. Businesses should use nonrenewable resources only at the rate at which alternatives are developed or loss of opportunities compensated. ...

3. Businesses cannot produce wastes and emissions that exceed the capacity of the ecosystem to assimilate them. (455)

See Cragg, who argues that sustainable development is possible even in the mining business, and Beckerman for a counter to DesJardins.

As a solution to this ongoing environmental destruction, some have proposed, economic strategies such as pollution taxes and the sale of licenses to pollute. Some advocate that such licenses could be traded internationally. So the undeveloped world could get rich, or at least debt-free, by selling its hardly necessary pollution licences to the industrialized world. Is that morally right? To *sell* pollution rights? Well, why not – why should this right be *in*alienable? But is it morally right to even *have* pollution rights? Or even pollution taxes – they imply the right, just for a price. Well, we could set limits – recall the trade-off idea.

Is government regulation the better way? The more just way? For a discussion of the market-based approach compared to the "command-and-control" (government regulation) approach, see Stavins and Whitehead. See also Freeman, who explains that of the two remedies for market failure, the government regulation approach suits environmental concerns better than the property rights approach because the environment is not easily divisible.

Indeed, the free market need not be environmentally *un*friendly: see Anderson and Leal, as well as Taylor, for a defence of "free market environmentalism"; then see Tokar for a criticism of such a view, one that turns environmental protection into a profit-making commodity, and Smith for succinct replies to four arguments supporting free-market environmentalism. (See also Simon and Partridge for another version of the Palmer and Peacock debate in this chapter.)

Speaking of the marketplace, Poff makes the argument that the global economy with its increasing weakening of national boundaries (through privatization, deregulation, and liberalization of national economies) makes environmental sustainability impossible. Any country strengthening its environmental protection laws unilaterally will be at a competitive disadvantage, hence the need for nations to negotiate internationally.

A rather (but not completely) different question about business and the environment is "Who owns it?" Consider this, reported by De George: "One drug company extracted the multimillion-dollar cancer drug, vincristine, from Madagascar rosy periwinkle, paying just a few dollars for the plant. The company made millions, and Madagascar received nothing" (573). Was that morally right? Why/not? Did they pay too little? Or did they pay too much? That is, should the periwinkle even have been for sale? Should vincristine be for sale? Can the company claim ownership of – can it patent – vincristine? Can it patent the periwinkle?

What about the fish that swim in the ocean – who owns them? Everyone? No one? Whoever catches them? (Who owns you?)

Despite the fact that very, very few Canadian corporate codes even discuss environmental affairs (6.7% of 75 respondents, from 461 queried, of the top 500 corporations in Canada [Lefebvre and Singh]), being in business is not incompatible with being environmentally responsible. Consider, for example, 3M (makers of Scotch Tape and Post-It notes): they eliminated CFCs and PCBs, and "[reduced] contaminant emission by 134,00 tons, waste water by 17,000 tons, sludge and solid wastes by 426,00 tons...[saving] over US$500 million" (Di Norcia 1998, 148). Not bad, eh?

References and Further Reading

Anderson, Terry L., and Donald R. Leal. "Free Market versus Political Environmentalism." *Harvard Journal of Law and Public Policy* 15.2 (Spring 1992): 297-310.

Baxter, William F. *People or Penguins: The Case for Optimal Pollution.* NY: Columbia University Press, 1974.

Beckerman, Wilfred. *Two Cheers for the Affluent Society: A Spirited Defense of Economic Growth.* NY: St. Martin's Press, 1974.

Blackstone, William T. "Ethics and Ecology." *Philosophy and Environmental Crisis.* Ed. William T. Blackstone. Athens, GA: University of Georgia Press, 1974.

Bowie, Norman. "Morality, Money, and Motor Cars." *Business, Ethics, and the Environment: The Public Policy Debate.* Ed. W. Michael Hoffman, Robert Frederick, and Edward Petry, Jr. NY: Quorum Books, 1990. 89-97.

Cragg, Wesley. "Sustainable Development and Mining: Opportunity or Threat to the Industry?" Canadian Institute of Mining, Metallurgy, and Petroleum Conference, Montreal, May, 1998.

Cragg, Wesley, David Pearson, and James Cooney. "Ethics, Surface Mining and the Environment." *Resource Policy* 21.4 (December 1995) 229-235.

De George, Richard T. *Business Ethics.* 5th ed. NJ: Prentice Hall, 1999.

DesJardins, Joseph R. "Sustainable Development and Corporate Social Responsibility." *Contemporary Issues in Business Ethics.* Ed. Joseph R. DesJardins and John J. McCall. 3rd ed. Belmont, CA: Wadsworth, 1996. 452-456.

Di Norcia, Vincent. "Environmental and Social Performance." *Journal of Business Ethics* 15.7 (July 1996): 773-784.

Di Norcia, Vincent. *Hard Like Water: Ethics in Business.* Toronto: Oxford University Press, 1998.

Frankel, Carl. *In Earth's Company: Business, Environment, and the Challenge of Sustainability.* Branford, CT: New Society Publishers, 1998.

Fredricksen, Liv, and Laura Jones. "The Green Team." <http://www.fraserinstitute.ca/forum/1998/june/environment.html>

Freeman III, A. Myrick. "The Ethical Basis of the Economic View of the Environment." *The Environmental Ethics and Policy Book: Philosophy, Ecology, Economics.* Ed. Donald VanDeVeer and Christine Pierce. CA: Wadsworth, 1994. 307-315.

Frosch, Robert, and Nicholas Gallapoulos. "Strategies for Manufacturing." *Scientific American* 261.3 (September 1989): 144–152.

Harbrecht, Doug. "A Question of Property Rights and Wrongs." *National Wildlife* 32.6 (October/November 1994): 4-11.

Hoch, David, and Robert A. Giacalone. "On the Lumber Industry: Ethical Concerns as the Other Side of Profits." *Journal of Business Ethics* 13.5 (May 1994): 357-367.

Hoffman, W. Michael. "Business and Environmental Ethics." *Business Ethics Quarterly* 1.2 (1991): 169-184.

Kelman, Steven. "Cost-Benefit Analysis: An Ethical Critique." *Regulation* (January-February 1981): 74-82.

Kelman, Steven. "Economists and the Environmental Muddle." *The Public Interest* 641 (Summer 1981): 106-123.

Law Reform Commission of Canada, *Crimes Against the Environment* (Working Paper 44, Protection of Life Series). Ottawa: Ministry of Supply and Services Canada, 1985.

Lefebvre, Maurice, and Jang B. Singh. "The Content and Focus of Canadian Corporate Codes of Ethics." *Journal of Business Ethics* 11.10 (October 1992): 799-808.

Partridge, Ernest. "Holes in the Cornucopia." *Ethical Issues in Business: A Philosophical Approach.* Ed. Thomas Donaldson and Patricia H. Werhane. 6th ed. NY: Prentice Hall, 1999. 574-591.

Poff, Deborah. "Reconciling the Irreconcilable: The global economy and the environment." *Journal of Business Ethics* 13.6 (June 1998): 439-445.

Rolston III, Holmes. "Are Values in Nature Subjective or Objective?" *Environmental Ethics* 4 (Summer 1982): 125-151.

Sagoff, Mark. "At the Shrine of Our Lady of Fatima *or* Why Political Questions Are Not All Economic." *Arizona Law Review* 23 (1981): 1283-98.

Sagoff, Mark. *Economy of the Earth* NY: Cambridge University Press, 1990.

Shrader-Frechette, Kristin. "A Defense of Risk-Cost-Benefit Analysis." *Environmental Ethics: Readings in Theory and Application.* Ed. Louis P. Pojman. 2nd ed. CA: Wadsworth, 1998. 507-514.

Simon, Julian. "Scarcity or Abundance?" *Ethical Issues in Business: A Philosophical Approach.* Ed. Thomas Donaldson and Patricia H. Werhane. 6th ed. NY: Prentice Hall, 1999. 565-573.

Smith, Tony. "Free Market Environmentalism: Against." *The Ag Bioethics Forum* 6.2 (November 1994): 2, 5-7.

Starik, Mark. "Should Trees have Managerial Standing? Toward Stakeholder Status for Non-Human Nature." *Journal of Business Ethics* 14.3 (March 1995): 207-217.

Stavins, Robert N., and Bradley W. Whitehead. "Market-Based Incentives for Environmental Protection." *Environment* 34.7 (September 1992): 7-11, 29-42.

Stone, Christopher. *Should Trees have Standing? Toward Legal Rights for Natural Objects.* Los Altos, CA: W. Kaufmann, 1974.

Taylor, Robert. "Economics, Ecology and Exchange: Free market Environmentalism." *Humane Studies Review* 8.1 (Fall 1992): 2-8.

Tokar, Brian. "Trading Away the Earth: Pollution Credits and the Perils of 'Free Market Environmentalism'." *Dollars and Sense* (March/April 1996). Rpt. in *Taking Sides: Clashing Views on Controversial Environmental Issues.* Ed. Theodore D. Goldfarb. 7th ed. Guilford, CT: Dushkin, 1997. 15–21.

Corporate Responsibility

Wayne Stewart and Peter Dickey

1 It used to be so easy. The widely accepted business "truth," that the "business of business is business," created a distinct limit on corporate and managerial responsibility, and is often still used for that purpose. This truth is useful, too, as a means of reducing the complexity of the enterprise to a manageable level in the best traditions of scientific management. This tenet narrows the scope of responsibility accepted by corporations to pursuit of profit in the service of a single master – the shareholder.

2 Increasingly, as complexity reaches chaotic proportions, corporations are compelled to accept societal realities, to expand their sphere of activity and their scope of responsibility. The distinct boundaries of the past are being destroyed by growing awareness of interdependencies. All segments of society, including corporations, are being forced to face the world in its complexity and to deal with it as a whole.

3 The complexity faced by modern corporations is enormous. Corporate managers are faced with a multitude of demands and objectives. In addition to creating wealth and jobs and thereby improving the human standard of living, their generally accepted traditional role, corporations are increasingly expected to serve their communities and to protect the environment.

Wayne Stewart and Peter Dickey, "Corporate Responsibility" has been previously published in *Ethics and Climate Change: The Greenhouse Effect*, Ed. Harold Coward and Thomas Hurka. Waterloo: Wilfrid Laurier University Press, 1993. 99–113. © 1993 by Wilfrid Laurier Press. Reprinted with permission of the publisher and the authors.

4 Adding to the difficulty are the differences among corporations, which come in all sizes and forms. They are small and large, private and public, operating locally and internationally, serving a small market and the world. It is no longer easy being a corporation. Although

> there are some, some economists in particular, who still hold that the business corporation is amoral and exists for the sole purpose of maximizing the return to its shareholders, I believe that this is not only nonsense, but inconceivable. Business enterprises are made up of people and they bring to the work place their own sense of morality (van Wachem 1992).

Separation, the creation of limits and boundaries, as a strategy is no longer either adequate or viable. Concepts of the corporate role and corporate responsibility must be rethought and expanded. The potential negative consequences for the environment (see Hare, "The Challenge" in [*Ethics and Climate Change: The Greenhouse Effect*]) must be accepted and dealt with. The business of business must be more than just business in the narrow sense that this term has acquired.

5 In this chapter we address the responsibility of corporations to protect air quality from greenhouse gas emissions, leaving aside other corporate objectives even as we recognize that conflicts may result (particularly between wealth generation and environmental protection). We will draw on our own experience for examples, which will thus focus on large, private oil companies. We will then extend the argument to small and public corporations in a summary

fashion. Our experience indicates that many corporations are sincerely struggling to understand their new responsibilities and to integrate economic, social, environmental, and ethical concerns. This is not an easy task; we hope that the suggestions offered in this chapter will help.

1. Attitudes and Approaches: Causes and Changes

6 The sincere efforts of many corporations to find a new way of conducting their business is a result of a growing recognition that the "old model" no longer works. In that old model, corporate managers developed their plans solely on the basis of economic considerations, made whatever arrangements were necessary with government, and proceeded to implement. Those who objected were treated in an adversarial fashion. Plans were kept secret from objectors until public hearings were called, and these were often held only if the opposition was adequately strong and the opponents were adequately powerful. The result, naturally, was that economic considerations prevailed and new manufacturing facilities were built at lowest cost/highest output with little consideration of future impact. The majority of older natural gas processing plants in Alberta were planned and constructed using this model. Fossil fuel specifications and characteristics have to date mostly been established solely through business-government dialogue.

7 Increasingly, particularly as environmental awareness grows, and with that, the power of environmental activist groups, corporations utilizing this old model are beset with ongoing complaints and difficulties. Activists refuse to remain silent on issues that they consider important; they often hound the corporation until the problem is rectified or the offending practice changed. Employees at operating facilities developed under the old model must live in the community, facing the activist pressure regularly, often lining up against their neighbours. This is understandably an unpleasant mode of existence, particularly in small communities.

8 In itself a corporation is a legal, impersonal entity. To grasp corporate attitudes, one must understand the attitudes of its managers and employees, for the corporation is empty without its people. Corporations therefore reflect the culture of the society in which they exist, and notions of corporate duty are merely an extension of the attitudes of individuals within the culture. North American culture contains strong strains of secular humanism and materialism. Many people live solely for immediate self-gratification; their interest is focused entirely inwardly, on themselves. Our entire system often seems set up to provide for individual gratification.

9 A further cultural norm is the focus on the individual and his or her rights, which in the extreme leads to complete isolation. We have compartmentalized our society, constructing little boxes and drawing sharp, decisive boundaries between each, allowing little overlap and encouraging even less. We adopt different roles, attitudes, and even moral values depending on which box we happen to be occupying.

10 Corporations are, naturally, influenced by these cultural norms. It is small wonder that the corporate focus is on the short-term bottom line. With the passage of time, even in light of sophisticated planning models (we could argue, because of these models), this myopia seems to worsen. Corporate boards, historically content with sound annual results, increasingly seem to demand good performance in the present quarter. Executives are turned over and out for fail-

ure to achieve projections for the present three-month period. The negative results of this short-term focus are exacerbated by the general level of chaos existent today.

11   Corporate responsibility is often seen in a limited, narrow way, with the sole responsibility of corporate executives being to maximize current profit. One result of this attitude is that costs are understated in an attempt to increase profit. If there is any consideration of duty at all, that duty falls only on the shareholder of record in the present quarter and, increasingly, to the corporate executives and senior managers themselves.[1] Reward systems in current corporate practice generally focus solely on the bottom line and discourage all but a very narrow notion of responsibility. The question of ethics rarely enters the picture at all.

12   Corporate managers often get caught up in the craziness that results, and chaos builds upon itself. When the blue suit goes on, personal values are left behind. Employees limit their personal involvement with an "I just work here" attitude. As the chaos grows, people try simply to cope, to survive the next corporate down-sizing. Stress increases along with hours of work; at the same time, reflection on duty decreases, as does action to fulfil duty. As one quarter ends the next starts, and the cycle is repeated. Given this relentless pressure, it is small wonder that corporate responsibility has attracted neither attention nor enthusiasm from within the corporation.

13   There are signs of change, some suggesting that a small measure of intervention and assistance may be sufficient to catalyze an extension of corporate responsibility and action in support of it. The Canadian Chemical Producers' Association produced one of the first Canadian moves towards environmental responsibility with their Responsible Care program (which has subsequently become a global model for chemical producers). In their detailed document on the program, they identify as a driving force "the implicit social contract that member companies have with society in general and involved communities in particular, to behave ethically and responsibly" (1991, 12). But nowhere in the document is there any elaboration of the term *ethically.* At best, the authors suggest that ethics requires meeting needs and concerns; the hope seems to be that if enough people are consulted, someone will surely include ethical concerns that can be addressed. It is not obvious that the authors understood what the term *ethical responsibility* implied, and they have provided few hints on the implications for action.

14   On a more personal level, and not surprisingly, some corporate executives today let their actions be guided by the potential impact on their progeny, most often their grandchildren. Doug Baldwin (1992) of Imperial Oil recently stated, "I'm not willing to force my grandson Riley to sit down to a banquet of the negative consequences of my actions today." This kind of remark points to an understanding that personal values must be aligned with actions while one is functioning in the corporate executive "box," and provides much to be optimistic about for the future.

2. The New Model

2.1 Sustainable Development

15 There are at present several positive stimuli that point towards alignment of corporate interests and an expanded sense of responsibility. Perhaps the most promising is the concept of sustainable development arising from the report of the World Commission on Environment and Development (1987). This concept requires humanity "to ensure that it meets the needs of the present

without compromising the ability of future generations to meet their own needs." It further "requires meeting the basic needs of all and extending to all the opportunity to fulfil their aspirations for a better life" (p. 8).

16   The Canadian federal government responded quickly to the Commission report, establishing a round table process beginning with the National Round Table on the Environment and the Economy and fostering overlapping provincial equivalents. Corporate leaders were included in the various round tables, have participated in forging new partnerships, and have become active supporters of the concept. Jack MacLeod (1992c), CEO of Shell Canada Limited since 1985 and a charter member of the National Round Table since 1988, recently stated, "I have become committed to the concept personally."

17   The concept of sustainable development has the potential to bring corporations and environmental groups together in the search for solutions, as it contains something for both. Development is accepted as a prima facie good, but not when untrammelled; it must be sustainable. The potential for alignment and harmony between two seemingly incompatible interests suggests huge possibilities.

18   Sustainable development has stimulated international co-operation on many levels. One example is the international Business Council for Sustainable Development, on which Ken McCready, CEO of TransAlta Utilities, and Paul Stern, CEO of Northern Telecom, are the Canadian representatives. This group of international business leaders has "committed to sustainable development" as defined by the World Commission. The Canadian Business Council on National Issues has also accepted the concept and urged its members to adopt sustainable development principles (see MacLeod 1992a).

2.2 Lesson from Japan

19   The success of Japanese corporations on the world market provides a second stimulus. North American companies have been very slow to identify the factors that have contributed to Japanese success, focusing ever more inward in obvious frustration at their inability to compete. It is readily apparent now that among those factors are a long-term view, a genuinely strategic approach, and employee contracts and reward systems that value long-term success. The long-term focus may well be the single most important factor, for it instills added responsibility to ensure the survival of the enterprise, and the availability of resources, into the future.

2.3 Consumer Attitudes

20   Another important factor in aligning corporate interests and ethics is increasing consumer awareness of environmental issues and the desire of consumers to do something to help. The most recent Decima quarterly report (1992) indicates that lifestyles continue to change out of concern for the environment, with 83 per cent of respondents reporting some change in lifestyle, up from 58 per cent in June 1987. Canadians are beginning to accept the premise that lifestyle standards will have to conform to standards of environmental protection. Fully 91 per cent report that they have made positive changes (Decima 1992). According to the same report, over half feel that environmentally inferior products should cost more where alternatives are available, in effect carrying a "sin tax" (pp. 93–94).

21   This general consumer thrust is emphasized by Carson and Moulden (1991, 5), who state, with supporting evidence, that "recent ... surveys show that millions of people in North America now have a stated interest in the future of the planet and

are willing to change their habits to prove it." Customers are sending corporations powerful messages and the corporations are hearing them, as they must in order to flourish in the marketplace.

2.4 Stakeholders

22 Another important influence is the expansive concept of the stakeholder; corporations are expanding their understanding of those who hold a legitimate interest in corporate activities beyond their shareholders. Stake-holders can include government, employees, customers, those living in proximity to plants and facilities (community), activist groups, and the public. (In our experience with public consultation, groups are incorporated into the process more or less in the order given here.) As the concept of the stakeholder comes to include more groups, important new ideas and perspectives are brought into corporate decision making. The franchise is extended, and the corporation often benefits through better ideas, lower costs, and firmer relationships with important stakeholders. Inclusion of environmental groups, with their attendant biases and ideas, has proven to be a great help in improving environmental practice. In the new sour gas plant at Caroline, Alberta, Shell Canada used the expanded notion of stakeholders, incorporating community groups in the planning process. The result was that many contentious issues were resolved prior to the public hearing process. Given impetus by the positive results at Caroline, the concept was expanded still further at a subsequent gas development in the Ram area (in the foothills of Alberta west of Rocky Mountain House). Environmental groups, such as the Canadian Parks and Wilderness Society and Ducks Unlimited, were brought into discussions at the interest stage, and development plans were made with extensive input.

23 There are many who endorse expansion of the stakeholder concept. Jack MacLeod (1992b), for instance, states that "a key mandate of Round Tables is to help forge new partnerships ... [to] resolve issues and overcome barriers towards a more sustainable future" and goes on to praise these new partnerships. The International Business Council makes it very clear that "we must expand our concept of those who have a stake in our operations to include not only employees and shareholders but also suppliers, customers, neighbours, citizens' groups, and others" (Schmidheiny 1992, 8). This changed attitude is welcomed by environmental groups such as the Canadian Parks and Wilderness Society, whose members have consistently worked to strengthen relationships with corporations and help corporate executives understand environmental issues (see the discussion of the Ram gas plants above). Carson and Moulden (1991, 42) quote Bryn James, formerly of Greenpeace (generally held to be among the most radical of environmental activist groups), as saying "environmentalists have got to roll up their sleeves and get to work with industry. There's no point standing on the sidelines shrieking abuse." The co-operation and changed approach of environmental groups is critical if solutions are to be found. Morbid environmentalism, the kind that presupposes the end of the world, will only lead to inaction ("There is no point") and fulfilled prophecy.[2] Indeed, even on a narrow view of stakeholders – encompassing only the shareholder – responsibility is expanding. Shareholders are increasingly holding equity in corporations that display sound environmental practice and accept increased responsibility for protection of the natural environment. The growth and popularity of "green funds" is evidence of this change.

2.5 Life-cycle Costing

24 Finally, as a result of consumer pressure and government regulation, environmental problems are being assigned to their source – the "polluter pays" principle. Corporations can no longer escape responsibility by shedding the problem – by selling contaminated land or shipping toxic waste to landfill sites. As one example of the impact of the polluter pays principle, consider Shell Canada, which implemented an extensive reclamation program to return the Oakville, Ontario, refinery site to a state suitable for residential and commercial development – a project that took fully eight years to complete.

25 This principle, and its implications, is leading corporations to adopt life-cycle (or full) costing practices, which include the full and final impact of production and use in the cost of a product. (For further discussion of the concept of full costing, see van Kooten, "Effective Economic Mechanisms" in [Ethics and Climate Change: The Greenhouse Effect].) Full cost accounting also encourages practices that reduce future costs and harms through adjustment of product attributes, location and design of production facilities, and various other means. The Canadian Petroleum Association was an early proponent of this approach, including in their Environmental Code of Practice (1988, 5) a requirement that companies "assess the potential effects of their projects and ... integrate protective measures ... to prevent or reduce impacts upon the environment." The Canadian Chemical Producers' Association (1991, 5) "codes span the complete life cycle of chemicals from original development through to use and ultimate disposal or destruction."

26 These factors provide positive stimuli to responsible action and afford the opportunity for alignment of personal and corporate values.

There are many signs in the corporate world that this alignment is beginning to take place. To support this movement, we now turn to the question of ethics: What is the corporate duty and to whom is it owed?

27 In this analysis, we reject the notion of corporations as amoral institutions: "Corporations are not passive receptors of external direction; they use their economic power aggressively often to forestall the impact of environmental regulation" (Lydia Dotto, personal communication, September 3, 1992). They must be seen to hold responsibility from an ethical as well as an economic viewpoint.

3. Corporate Ethical Responsibility

28 We have identified a number of stimuli that point towards an expanded sense of responsibility for the corporation and have offered a number of examples of positive corporate responses.

29 To address the question of ethics, however, we return to and rely on the typology provided by Hurka (see "Ethical Principles" in [Ethics and Climate Change: The Greenhouse Effect]). We start from the basic assumption that "if an act or policy has good consequences ... this counts ethically in its favour" (p. 24). We hold that corporate ethics revolves around consequences – that a corporate act is good if it produces consequences for some individual or group of people. The issue, then, is to determine to whom the corporate duty is owed – whom the corporation should seek to benefit – and to define what counts as a good for that person or group.

3.1 A Narrow View

30 Even under the old model (where "the business of business is business"), corporations can be seen to have ethical responsibilities. To produce

profits can be held to be ethical, for that produces a good for the shareholder. On the maximizing principle, the corporation should produce the greatest profit possible. To do so today, of course, requires consideration of issues beyond economics. Success in the marketplace requires responsible environmental practice and products that are environmentally acceptable. To fulfil its ethical responsibility to the shareholder – to maximize its profits – the corporation must market products that consumers will buy. And it must also become known as an environmentally responsible company. If it is to profit from the development of new resources, a company must be seen to act responsibly – or the development will not be allowed to proceed.

31   If employees are added to the list of those to whom a corporation owes a duty (which still maintains the narrow view), the list of goods grows. Now the corporation has a duty to create and sustain jobs, to ensure security, and to offer a pleasant living environment. Once again, the corporation must make a profit. It must also ensure that relationships in the community are good so that employees live in peace with their neighbours. This inexorably draws the corporation into discussions with community groups.

32   Shareholders, too, are redefining their good. Long-term success has always been important, as is evidenced by the holding term of equity in large companies. And increasingly, shareholders are paying attention to and rewarding companies that act responsibly on environment issues.

33   These duties can be concisely expressed as a duty to be frugal and efficient and to use resources wisely and sparingly. This suggests that corporate ethical responsibility extends beyond humans to include natural resources as well. If a corporation holds long-term survival as an objective, it must ensure that resources are available as raw material in the future. Following this approach, corporate profits will increase and environmental damage will be reduced by the same action.

3.2 An Expanded View

34   As the list of relevant stakeholders expands, so does the list of goods that must be provided. If the corporation, for example, includes an environmental group as a stakeholder, it might find amongst its list of goods air quality, water quality, and protection of wild land and animal rights. An expanded list of goods, of course, complicates the issue, for conflicts inevitably arise and the corporation is faced with the problem of balancing competing interests. In addition, as van Kooten points out (see "Effective Economic Mechanisms" in *[Ethics and Climate Change: The Greenhouse Effect]*), many of these goods are difficult or impossible to value. Shell has resorted to the use of a values matrix that includes both quantitative and qualitative indices, but inevitably the quantitative measures are given greater credence. In the end, one ends up with a satisficing approach, where an attempt is made to produce a reasonably good outcome on each of the many dimensions important to a specific case.

3.3 Temporal Considerations

35   The foregoing discussion considers the interests of humans living here and now. One could argue that attention to shareholder goods suggests responsibility for the future, but the discussion so far has considered only shareholders of current record.

36   Corporations appear increasingly to accept ethical responsibility for future generations of humans. The very definition of sustainable development (see sec. 2.1) considers the interests of future generations, although it stops short of

intergenerational equity. (It says we need only leave unimpaired "the ability of future generations to meet their own needs," and leaves open to current generations the difficulty, or the opportunity, to define what "their needs" will be.) That many corporations and business groups have accepted the principle of sustainable development suggests acceptance of an expanded responsibility, for future human beings.

37 Corporate executives, too, are increasingly concerned about the future that they are creating by their actions and the legacy that will remain for their progeny (see the earlier mention of Doug Baldwin's concern, sec. 1). This also suggests acceptance of a duty to future humans.

38 Corporations can best fulfil this duty by projecting future impacts and implementing action now to mitigate or avoid those impacts. This approach has been taken by Shell, for example, in the new lubricants plant in Brockville, Ontario. Corporations must also ensure that research required for future mitigation is begun early enough for the results to be available when needed.

3.4 Geographic Considerations

39 If a corporation has an ethical duty to humans living here and now, that duty is owed to the same people regardless of where the corporation operates. If that duty imposes a set of standards and operating principles here, those standards also apply in a remote location in cases where the environmental impact respects no boundaries. In order to fulfil responsibilities to Canadians, the corporation must apply Canadian standards while operating in Africa, for example, for the impact of greenhouse gases cannot be confined to Africa. Once the ethical duty is accepted, on whatever basis, it must be applied universally. (Note that this may not be so when the impact

can be confined, for the list of goods specific to the operating locale may well be very different from ours.) On issues that have global impact, the ethical duty is the same no matter where the operation takes place. This principle is accepted and applied by the Canadian Chemical Producers' Association (1992, 1) in its statement that "the codes apply to Canadian member company operations inside and outside Canada."

3.5 Additional Thoughts on Corporate Responsibility

40 Corporate activity has made a significant contribution to the increase in anthropogenic greenhouse gases in the atmosphere. As Table 1 indicates, 44 per cent of the carbon dioxide produced annually by humans in Canada results from direct industrial activity, and an additional 30 per cent is due to residential use of corporate products. Corporations cannot escape responsibility by assigning blame to other parties. Corporate managers have argued that they only produce products that consumers want, and therefore the consumer is responsible. The role of advertising in influencing demand (in the case of greenhouse gases, the emphasis on speed and distance driving on the open road in oil company advertising, for example) effectively counters this argument.

41 Corporations have also been known to argue that consumers are ultimately in control; if we want harmful products off the market, we must get consumers to stop using them. Or we might get governments to regulate use, to level the playing field. Oil companies' reluctance to remove lead from gasoline illustrates how effective regulation can be. The companies pleaded that consumers wanted high-performance gasolines that required lead, when the underly-

ing corporate reasons included higher manufacturing costs. When regulation was introduced, lead was removed quickly, and even ahead of schedule, with little or no adverse consumer reaction. It is just not possible to achieve responsible consumer consumption in the face of the advertising onslaught that occurs today. The budgets of groups attempting to encourage reduced consumption are simply overwhelmed by those of the corporations, who are intent on increasing the size of the pie. This suggests to us an additional ethical responsibility, once a product is known to be harmful.

42   The additional responsibility that accrues to those who "should have known at the time of

Table 1. Carbon Dioxide Emissions, 1990

By fuel	Megatons	%
Coal (direct use)	15.7	4
Oil (direct use)	201.5	46
Gas (direct use)	122.2	28
Electricity (production)	95.3	22
Total	434.7	100
By sector		
Industry		
Energy industry	76.5	18
Other industry	114.5	26
Total Industry	191.0	44
Transport		
Commercial and industrial	64.4	15
Personal	64.4	15
Total Transport	128.8	30
Residential	67.2	15
Commercial	47.7	11
Total	434.7	100

Source: Adapted from Friends of the Earth and Canadian Climate Action Network (1990, 54).

Note: The original data had combined all transport data into one category. Researchers have calculated that 50 per cent or more of transportation carbon dioxide emissions results from personal transportation.

acting that the harm would result" (Hurka, "Ethical Principles" in *[Ethics and Climate Change: The Greenhouse Effect]*, p. 36) also applies to the corporation. It is no longer at issue that corporations produce greenhouse gases. It is not yet clear, however, exactly what harm will accrue to humans as a result, and corporate executives have no superior wisdom to help them understand the dilemma. Hare's conclusions (see "The Challenge" in *[Ethics and Climate Change: The Greenhouse Effect]*) will help corporate executives such as Jack MacLeod (1992c), who speaks for many when he says, "It is not clear to me ... whether the climate change will in fact become life-threatening. The hypotheses and evidence lend themselves to conflicting conclusions."

43   Finally, one is left with the problem of defining the good that corporations must work to produce. A review of the issues defined by stake-holders will show that greenhouse gases do not rank high on the list. Air quality issues such as those concerning sulphur and lead emissions, water quality, protection of wild lands and animals, and even noise pollution are given higher priority. Herein, of course, lies the crux of a global issue for which a cost/benefit analysis cannot meaningfully be conducted. (See Danielson, "Personal Responsibility" in *[Ethics and Climate Change: The Greenhouse Effect]* for a description of the atmospheric commons.) Jack MacLeod (1992c) echoes Dr. Hare's conclusions with the words, "I do not believe that one must be in terror of global climate change to become committed to sustainable development." This is one case where the corporation must do what is right even though it is not in its short-term business interest, simply because it is the right thing to do.

44   The potential consequences to humankind from global climate change caused by greenhouse gases are enormous. Corporations have

an ethical responsibility whether one takes a narrow approach or expands upon that. Corporations must accept that responsibility and act on it, and many of them are doing just that, by embarking on a prudent series of actions highlighted by energy conservation and efficiency improvement measures.

3.6 Small Companies and Public Corporations

45 The same line of reasoning applies to small companies. For them, however, the conflict between the objectives of wealth generation and environmental protection is often more severe, as many small companies struggle simply to survive. Arguments from ethics do not change, but a different definition of the good might lead to rather different actions. The profit motive and customer pressure will, however, require responsible environmental practice to conserve resources. Small companies are often in a good position to provide leadership, as Mohawk Oil is doing on alternative fuels, because they are more flexible and able to adjust to changed realities more quickly.

46 Public companies have an additional ethical responsibility that derives from their public trust. They must also, we hold, support the direction of government regulation (in turn a response to public pressure) by providing leadership and modelling desired behaviour. Once the public articulate their definition of a good, public corporations must respond by providing that good for they have an ethical responsibility to do so.

4. Corporate Responsibility in Practice

47 We have argued that corporations have an ethical responsibility to limit the potential negative consequences of greenhouse gas emissions. We suggest the following principles as a guide in meeting that responsibility.

1. The separation of the corporation from the rest of life must be eliminated. Corporations are merely an economic instrument composed of and attending to a series of stakeholders and groups and to the individuals that compose them. Corporations have no independent identity, no reason for being except to serve their stakeholders. Corporate leaders must stop seeing the corporation as a separate entity and begin to recognize interdependencies that exist at a number of levels. These leaders must align personal and corporate values. The desire of corporate executives that their grandchildren enjoy full and good lives must be reflected in the policies and practices undertaken by the corporation.

2. Effective long-term planning must replace the current focus on short-term profit, and the long-term approach must be implemented and supported by corporate systems. Reward systems must be reworked to direct attention to long-term success and away from only short-term gain.

3. Life-cycle (full) cost accounting practices must be adopted. The full impact of a product must be accounted for in design and costing, for the entire life of the product. This involves accurately valuing all resources, including raw materials, labour, energy, air, water, land, and the impact of emissions. The impact of ultimate disposal will also have to be valued and included.

4. Corporate associations must be further developed and must be challenged to promote collective, voluntary, responsible action. Corporations must take the lead in educating their consumers about potential environ-

mental impact and designing their products to limit negative effects.

5. An expanded concept of stakeholders and their legitimate involvement in decision making should be accepted. Ideas from all sources should be considered and integrated into corporate decision making.

6. Corporations must voluntarily apply equivalent standards regardless of where they are operating. Duty cannot be confined within national borders when the impacts of actions refuse to be so restricted.

7. Corporations must operate in an efficient manner, using minimum resources to ensure both short-term profit and long-term supply of raw material.

5. Conclusion

48 Corporations have an ethical duty to act responsibly on environmental matters. Even from the narrow viewpoint of business as a generator of wealth for the shareholder, a duty to ensure profits now and into the future requires responsible environmental action. For a corporation that intends to survive into the future, corporate duty is owed to people who will inherit that future. Enlarging the concept of the stakeholder, the corporation must be a good place for employees, who will require the respect of their community; it must ensure adequate long-term returns for its shareholders; it must satisfy its customers; and it must attend to the issues and ideas of interest groups. All of these objectives require acceptance of responsibility. In order for there simply to be a future for these stakeholders, corporate action today must be ethical and responsible.

49 Corporations operating in the marketplace can be a potent force for change. Evolving consumer preference, nurtured by information on product attributes and responsible use and expressed in changed purchasing habits, in combination with full cost pricing, has the potential to move society towards a combination of increased demand for sustainable products (lower resource use and reduced impact) and the practice of sustainable consumption (less single use, less energy intensive products). Corporate power, used in the right manner, can have significant influence on this movement.

50 Change involves a number of factors, including awareness of the need for change, commitment to action, and leadership. Sustainable development and its outcomes are providing the stimuli for these factors. Corporate leaders, such as Jack MacLeod and Doug Baldwin, involved with mature multistakeholder networks, are providing leadership for the change in course. And involvement in external activities is resulting in internal change.

51 The current scientific data suggest a warming trend of global proportions caused by greenhouse gases (see Hare, "The Challenge" in *[Ethics and Climate Change: The Greenhouse Effect]*). Corporations have a duty, shared with other institutions and with individuals, to take precautionary measures to limit the possible negative impacts of this trend. Jack MacLeod (1992c), speaking about his company's sustainable development policy, states that its creation "was driven by the personal motivations of members of our senior management and our collective determination to protect the legitimacy of our corporation." In this and the actions of other responsible corporations there is much cause for optimism.

NOTES

1. See, for example, MacLeod (1992a). Jack MacLeod is widely regarded as progressive on the issue of corporate responsibility to the environ-

ment through sustainable development. In this paper, he speaks of obligations to "employees, customers, other stakeholders and the public," presumably lumping shareholders in the "other stakeholder" category but clearly giving primacy to employees, of which, of course, he is one.

2. I make this claim on the basis of a discussion with Steve Allen, principal of Sunnyside Public School (K-6) in Calgary, in August 1992; he suggested that many young children believe they will be dead before they reach the age of twenty – a belief that is the result of "morbid environmentalism" as preached by many environmental groups.

REFERENCES

Baldwin, D.D. 1992. Sustainable development: An opportunity or a threat? Paper presented at Conference on Energy Efficiency, Calgary, June 19.

Canadian Chemical Producers' Association. 1991. *Responsible care: A total commitment.* Ottawa.

Canadian Petroleum Association. 1988. *Environmental code of practice.* Calgary.

Carson, P., and J. Moulden. 1991. *Green is gold: Business talking to business about the environmental revolution.* Toronto: Harper Business.

Decima Research. 1992. *Decima Quarterly* (Spring).

Friends of the Earth and Canadian Climate Action Network. 1990. *The carbon dioxide report for Canada.* Ottawa.

MacLeod, J.M. 1992a. Sustainable development: Progress in Canada. Paper presented at the Ninth Clean Air Congress, Montreal, August 30–September 4, 1992.

MacLeod, J.M. 1992b. Sustainable development: Progress on the Canadian agenda. Panel contribution at the International Productivity Symposium, Oslo, June 15–18, 1992.

MacLeod, J.M. 1992c. Toward a more sustainable future. Keynote address to the Inuit Circumpolar Conference, Tuktoyaktuk, July 20, 1992.

Schmidheiny, S. 1992. *Changing course: A global business perspective on development and the environment.* Cambridge: MIT Press.

van Wachem, L.C. 1992. Industry, democracy andn the values of business. Paper presented at the annual meeting of the London Chamber of Commerce, July 3, 1992. London, England.

World Commission on Environment and Development. 1987. *Our common future.* Oxford: Oxford University Press.

Questions

1. Stewart and Dickey take the utilitarian definition of right/good as their starting point and proceed to determine (a) "to whom" a corporation is responsible, and (b) "what counts as a good" for each. What are their conclusions?

2. What is their strongest basis for claiming corporate responsibility to limit greenhouse gas emissions?

3. What is their response to the objection that consumers are in control and therefore *they* are the ones responsible (for environmental damage)?

4. Stewart and Dickey argue for additional responsibility on two counts (P42 and P46); can you think of other grounds for additional responsibility?

5. (a) Which of the seven suggestions made in Section 4, "Corporate Responsibility in Practice," do you think will be most difficult to implement?

   (b) What specific things can you imagine yourself doing in your imagined position at your imagined place of business to facilitate its implementation?

If a tree falls...

John Palmer, Eugene Tan, and Kent A. Peacock

Letter to the Editor, John Palmer

"We can continue to log our brains out, and we probably won't run out of wood for another 50 years. But we will run out, because current management is not sustainable."

1   The above quotation from a touchy-feely tree-hugger is pure and simple hogwash. Why? Because the writer has an incomplete understanding of economics.

2   Will we run out of timber for logging? Not likely. As current supplies are harvested, the decline in supply will cause prices to rise. Furthermore, as population and wealth increase, so will the demand for timber, also putting upward pressure on prices.

3   But these higher prices provide important signals. They encourage people who would like to earn some profits to plant more trees. And they encourage potential buyers to look for substitutes for timber and to cut down on their use of lumber.

4   We will not run out of timber, because, despite the warnings of naive tree-huggers, prices will rise, eliciting responses that promote conservation and more production.

5   If the tree-huggers really believe we will run out of timber, they should buy up lots of land and plant lots of trees. And they and their progeny will be rich beyond their wildest dreams, if their predictions of doom and gloom are correct.

6   But if they *do* plant more trees now, there will be more trees in the future, and their predictions will be wrong. And even if the doomsayers don't plant the trees, some people will; the anticipation of future profits will keep us from running out of timber.

7   There is a heavy shadow of doubt clouding this rosy picture, though. It comes from the spectre of government intervention in the timber market in two ways.

8   First, as the government gets involved in tree-planting and the leasing of timber lands, the incentive for lumber companies to practice conservation is diminished. "Why conserve," they reasonably ask themselves, "if the government is going to undercut our actions with their own programs?"

9   Second, government intervention designed to keep prices low will further deter private conservation efforts. "Why plant more trees," people will reasonably ask, "if we can't sell them for a price high enough to cover all our costs?"

10   And so the more the government tries to keep future prices down, the more it deters private conservation efforts.

11   Will we run out of timber? Only if we implement really stupid government policies that discourage private conservation.

Letter to the Editor, Eugene Tan

1   On March 13, an article by John Palmer, a professor of economics, appeared in *The Gazette*. He accused environmentalists (tree-huggers) of hav-

ing an incomplete understanding of economics and of naivety. He pleaded for unencumbered markets to control forestry practices. Palmer's article affirmed that corporate North America is leading us down the path towards environmental degradation. The road to hell is paved with sickening rationalizations.

2 The Greek roots of economy and ecology are inextricably linked. Economy, from *oikonomic*, means the management of the household, whereas ecology, from the root *oikos* plus *logos*, means household.

3 But Palmer suggests that the free market will provide all that we need when it becomes profitable.

4 Palmer maintains that an incomplete understanding of economics has led to the naive view that trees are becoming endangered. The market will provide all that we need. Scientific reality maintains:

- The widespread destruction of trees for timber or farmland has contributed to global warming;
- Logging practices practically ensure soil destruction, harming future growth;
- Planting trees for short-term economic gain is an asinine proposition because trees take substantial time to grow;
- So much is wasted that demand-side economics just makes sense;
- One of the leading causes of animal species extinction is loss of habitat.

5 Has simple economics accounted for these factors or are they the 'externalities' evoked by many economists when a model goes wrong? The presence of externalities means that economists don't understand all factors involved. I fail to see how Dr. Palmer's 'complete' understanding of economics would preserve vital resources.

6 Palmer's article is guilty of the heinous crime of which he accuses environmentalists. Economists simply have an incomplete understanding of ecology and cannot begin to account for the infinite number of variables and nuances in an ecosystem. Physician, heal thyself.

The Economics of Extinction, Kent A. Peacock

1 Professor John Palmer condemns "tree-huggers" for failing to understand economics. Don't worry about running out of trees, he tell us, market forces will guarantee that timber producers will do the right thing and make sure that there are lots of trees for the future. The only thing, he says, that could cause us to run out of timber would be government intervention in environmental management, since that would remove the incentive for private conservation.

2 I wish I could agree with this rosy picture of the magic of market economics; life would be so much simpler. But the relationships between market forces and ecological necessities are far more complex and problematic than Palmer is apparently aware. Of course there is an incentive to conserve a resource, or renew it if one knows how; that is elementary. However, the free-market boosters forget that all too often there are also enormous short-term *disincentives* to conservation and renewal. Sometimes it is highly economically advantageous to *wipe out* a

University of Western Ontario *Gazette*, March 19, 1992. © 1992 by Eugene Tan. Reprinted with permission of the author.

Kent A. Peacock, "The Economics of Extinction" in Kent A. Peacock, Ed., *Living with the Earth: An Introduction to Environmental Philosophy*, pp. 338–341. © 1996 by Harcourt Brace & Company, Canada, Ltd. All rights reserved. Reprinted with permission of the publisher and the author.

resource rather than conserve it. This dismal process is known as the *economics of extinction*, and it is worthwhile, although unpleasant, to remind ourselves how it works.

3   As a resource (say timber, whales, cod, rhino horns) becomes more and more scarce, its market value approaches infinity. Market value often has little to do with the actual value of the resource for human welfare; we do need timber, but no one has any real need for pulverized rhino horns. Nevertheless, they command such a fabulous price on certain markets that poachers will risk death to hunt down the few remaining rhinos. No incentive to conserve can override the immediate gain to be made from cashing in the resource. Furthermore, any measure which could increase the supply (say, establishing a rhino ranch) would tend to lower its market value; the more effective the renewal method, the more it would tend to cancel out the scarcity value of the resource. Add to all this the fact that measures to renew and conserve a resource can be economically risky and have costs, often large, which may not be recoverable in the short term at all. Hence, when a resource is scarce there are positive *disincentives* to renew it. The scarcer the resource, the more it is in demand, and the harder it is to renew, the more these disincentives tend to operate. If nothing but pure market forces govern, the result (and this has happened time and again in history) is very often the extinction or commercial exhaustion of the resource, not its preservation.

4   Another practice that contributes to extinction is *discounting the future* when carrying out an economic cost-benefit analysis. This means that we often apply a discount to the value of a resource that we will not be able to profit from right away; the longer we will have to wait to use it, the more we discount it. This is just an academic way of saying that we often grab all of something for

ourselves now, and let the future take care of itself. Sometimes people have even deliberately destroyed remaining stocks of a resource so that no one else can profit from it; butterfly collectors used to burn out the hillsides that were home to rare species so that they would have the only remaining specimens to sell (see Rolston 1989.) The grab-it-all-now factor is especially likely to operate if the resource is very expensive or impossible to renew, if there is a very high immediate demand for it, or if its renewal is so slow that the money invested in the harvesting technology cannot be recovered if one waits for the resource to renew itself. (The latter is the case for whales; see Dobra 1978.) We need something like the *seventh-generation rule* of many Native North American peoples — before you act, consider the effect on the seventh generation to follow!

5   Nothing I have said here should be news to anyone familiar with economics or the long and tragic history of resource depletion. Let's talk about forestry, for instance, since Palmer brought the subject up; the eroded, desiccated area of the world now known as Lebanon is a very good example of what can happen if the needs of commerce are allowed to determine the fate of a resource. (To be sure, commercial exploitation is not the only reason for the deforestation of the Levant — but it was one of the major reasons.) Three thousand years ago, Lebanon had at least two million acres in timber, the famous cedars of Lebanon. (See the selection in *Living with the Earth* by Carter and Dale, Chapter 4.) In fact, the topography, climate, and tree types were remarkably similar to those of British Columbia today. For several centuries, while the trees held out, forestry was the basis for the thriving Phoenician commercial empire. Eventually, though, the ecology collapsed, and with it the prosperity of the society it supported. Bil-

lions of tons of topsoil washed into the sea and the forests disappeared completely except for a few guarded sacred groves. The country today has only the remotest resemblance to its lush and fertile condition in biblical times.

6   And this is just a typical example; there is very little historical evidence to support the faith that market forces by themselves can guarantee adequate renewal and conservation of resources, and much evidence against it. What almost always seems to happen is that the immediate demand for a resource outweighs the perceived advantage to be gained by long-term measures. Many societies in the past have desperately attempted to reforest, to replenish topsoil or conserve stocks of fish or game; only a few have succeeded, because the short-term pressure to exploit the resource was always too great.

7   Still speaking of forestry, Palmer also shows no sensitivity to the really tough biological and technical problems posed by reforestation. In fact, it is very unclear that we really know how to replace the forests that we are harvesting so rapaciously. Foresters would have us believe that they are competent to replace them with "managed" forests as good as or better than those that they clear-cut away. This, like the belief in the power of the "invisible hand" itself, is mostly an article of faith; there is insufficient evidence that present methods work, and some evidence that they do not (in the sense that they may lead to a long-term but inevitable decline in the vitality of the ecology). I am certainly not saying that sustainable harvesting of forest products is impossible, but I am saying that we have not yet found a completely reliable method, especially if we insist on continuing to be able to harvest at the rate and scale that we now find necessary.

8   The biggest problem we face right now is just the problem that Aldo Leopold identified many years ago: there is very little correspondence between the market value of a "resource" such as a plant or animal species and its real value to the health and functioning of the ecology. We must figure out how to devise an economic system that reflects ecological reality, or our hi-tech culture will go the way of all the other failed cultures whose ruins lie weathering in the deserts they created.

REFERENCES

Clark, C. 1973. "The Economics of Overexploitation," *Science* 181, 630–634.

Dobra, Peter M. 1978. "Cetaceans: A Litany of Cain," *Boston College Environmental Affairs Law Review* 7(1), 165–183.

Invited Response, John Palmer

1   On a recent trip to Alberta, I was subjected to a lengthy lecture from a retired gentleman about all the trains passing his house, carrying lumber from British Columbia to the east. He was quite concerned about all the trees being cut down in British Columbia. I suggested that if his concerns have merit, he could do his grandchildren a great service by buying up a bunch of land and planting trees on it – he'd be able to leave them an extremely valuable resource.

2   The point of this story, and of my original brief editorial, is simply this: people respond to incentives. When people expect prices to rise in the future, some will respond by trying to make sure they have more to sell then, when prices are higher. The second point of the editorial was that government programs which keep timber prices low will inhibit both the incentives (prices) and

the response (private reforestation), thus creating more future deforestation than we would have with an unfettered market.

3   The key to having the market work effectively is that there be well-defined and well-enforced property rights. Only if people can rely on being able to capture future gains will they make decisions to conserve now and plant more for the future. We don't have persistent shortages of wheat, eggs, or cattle for this very reason: people know they can reap what they have sown. We do have persistent shortages, however, of things for which property rights cannot be well-defined or well-enforced, such as whales, even though whales, like cattle, are replenishable resources.

4   The difference in sustainability between whales and cows is not the fault of the market economy. Non-market economies have the same problems of over-exploitation of resources. Rather, the difference between whales and cows is that property rights to cows are relatively easily defined and enforced. Property rights to whales aren't, and so whales have been seriously over-hunted to the brink of extinction.

5   The same thing can happen to our forests. We have a myriad of government programs that continue to erode property rights and the expectations that people will be able to reap what they have sown. For example, stumpage fees on government lands are set so low that in many instances private reforestation doesn't pay.

6   Note that nowhere have I discussed other values of having forests. The only point I wished to make initially was that we won't run out of wood (see the initial quotation on which I based the original editorial) if market forces are allowed to work. I was very disappointed that those commenting on my original piece chose to ignore this simple point and raise other issues I did not have the space to address in that editorial. I do, however, discuss the concepts of externalities and other market failures at length in my book, *The Economic Way of Thinking* (Paul Heyne and John Palmer, 1st Canadian edition, Prentice Hall, 1999).

Questions

1. (a) What assumption about human behaviour does Palmer's free market environmentalism, and indeed all free market theory, rest on?

   (b) What evidence do we have that that assumption is indeed fact?

2. (a) Is there an element of the paper tiger fallacy in Tan's response to Palmer?

   (b) Which of the scientific facts that Tan lists does most damage to Palmer's argument?

3. (a) Explain "the economics of extinction."

   (b) What ethical approach(es) would support the poacher's actions as morally right?

   (c) Both Palmer's tree-planters and Peacock's poachers seem to be acting out of self-interest, so why does the one renew resources and the other wipe them out?

   (d) Even if Palmer is right, there are problems, Peacock says and Tan implies, with the solution of just planting more trees. What are they?

4. (a) (i) Explain Palmer's point about the danger of government regulation, to which neither Tan nor Peacock responded.

(ii) Assess Smith's response: "Citizens have a right to a livable environment, and enforcing rights is part of the legitimate function of government. The thesis that responsibility for the environment should be left entirely in the hands of private economic agents is as ludicrous as the idea that rights to freedom of speech or freedom of religion should be left entirely to the market" (see this chapter's "References and Further Reading" list for citation).

(b) (i) Find out what "the tragedy of the commons" refers to and explain how it supports Palmer's view.

(ii) What relevance does Peacock's telling of "the tragedy of the Lebanon forests" have here?

(c) How can (and why should) we make sure whales don't become extinct, given Palmer's comment that both market and non-market economies fail in this regard?

Case Study – Ballard Power Systems: Zero Emission Vehicles

Ballard Power Systems, a Vancouver-based technology company, has developed a fuel cell that will power vehicles without producing exhaust emissions. This new fuel cell technology has been many years in the works and is now at the testing stage.

The fuel cell is an engine that combines hydrogen (from methanol, natural gas, or petroleum) with oxygen (from air) to generate electricity without combustion, leaving only heat and water vapour as byproducts.

This new technology is revolutionary and has the potential to eliminate much of the airborne pollution in our major cities within a generation. The commercial viability of the fuel cell received a major boost with the new regulations in California, America's most populous state, which require that 10% of cars sold have no exhaust emissions by 2003.

The fuel cell development is sufficiently significant for some of the major oil companies (such as Royal Dutch/Shell, Texaco, and Atlantic Richfield) to become involved in the testing process. Ballard has also formed alliances with Daimler-Benz and Ford for the commercialization of fuel cells in vehicles, and with GPU International and ALSTOM for the commercialization of fuel cells in stationary electric power plants.

These new developments have boosted the market value of Ballard shares: between April 1998 and April 1999, the share value of Ballard Power rose by almost 100%. The company has become a major player in the high tech industry, having a current net worth of $4.3 billion.

Currently, the vehicles that use Ballard's fuel cells are very expensive and would not be affordable by many people, despite the added fuel efficiency and zero exhaust emission. As well, test vehicles do not have quite the same performance as many of the better automobiles now on the market. However, supporters of the fuel cell technology argue that with further refinements and mass production, cost and performance issues will disappear.

Of more concern, however, is the claim by some detractors that the fuel cell may not be entirely "zero emission." After all, there must be some disposal of whatever is left of the base fuel once the hydrogen has been separated. As well, there will be heavy metals used in the cell which must be disposed of when the cell eventually dies. There is also concern that the water vapour produced will contribute to the greenhouse effect.

Supporters of the fuel cell are confident that, with further testing in powering real vehicles, these concerns will be allayed. Furthermore, not only will auto emission problems be solved: if the base fuel of choice is methanol (which is not a fossil fuel and can be manufactured from corn), use of the earth's non-renewable resources with current automobiles will decrease.

The Ballard company clearly believes they have a winner. In a news release on April 20, 1999 they stated:

> Ballard fuel cells offer the automobile industry the potential to offer commercial vehicles that will be comparable to conventional powered cars in passenger space, acceleration, speed, range, lifetime, and refuelling time. In addition, they will provide higher fuel efficiency and lower noise, vibration, and air emissions than vehicles powered by internal combustion engines. This combination makes fuel cells the most likely alternative technology to power the vehicles of the next century.

REFERENCES

Acharya, Madhavi. "Fuel-cell Maker Launches Tests in California." *The Toronto Star* 20 Apr. 1999: D4.

Ballard website. <http://www.ballard.com>

Fuhs, David. "Fuel Cell Technology Operates like a Battery." Posting to "The Debating Room." 10 Nov. 1998. <http://www.mcspotlight.org/debate/capitalism/messages/3567.html>

Questions

1. This new fuel cell technology holds the promise of greatly reducing air pollution and improving fuel efficiency, both of which are good. Do you think this was the primary motivation of the Ballard company in developing this technology? (Does motivation matter?)

2. Why would oil companies, who have such a vested interest in the internal combustion engine, be interested in the fuel cell technology?

3. Would you purchase a car equipped with the fuel cell engine if it were 10% more expensive than comparable conventional cars? 20% more expensive? 30%? Why/not?

CHAPTER 11
THE MEDICAL BUSINESS

What to Do? – The Fetal Tissue Transplant Business

As government continues to privatize services such as health care, opening it up to marketing and profitability, the medical technology business may provide attractive opportunities. Indeed, one of these opportunities has caught your attention: fetal tissue transplants.

In addition to the now-common organ and bone marrow transplants, fetal tissue transplants may prove to be life-saving. Fetal tissue (from aborted fetuses or from lab cultures) can be used to treat brain and spinal cord injuries, and some forms of epilepsy, as well as Parkinson's and Alzheimer's disease.

It is true that the Human Genome Project may render these conditions obsolete, but that is unlikely to happen for a while. And certainly as the baby boomers age, which is happening now, the demand for a cure at least for Alzheimer's will surely increase.

However you have some concerns about the supply. You can't imagine a company actually coercing anybody, but you're not sure it's right for someone to even voluntarily sell their fetus. And yet surely that's better than just throwing it away. (It?)

But in any case, it's not really your decision. (Or at least, that's not the decision you're trying to make at the moment.) Nevertheless, if you become part of the fetal tissue transplant business, wouldn't you be endorsing whatever it takes to keep you in business? You'd certainly be benefiting from it.

What do you decide to do?

Introduction

Business reaches into all areas of life, and each kind of business is a little different; these differences may give rise to unique ethical issues – not all products and services (or employees, or clients/customers) should be considered in the same light.

Consider the education business. Many people think there's something morally wrong with students having to go into debt to pay tuition; the implication is that there should be a change in pricing, perhaps through a change in salaries or subsidies. But we go into debt for houses and cars – why not for education? If you really want it now and can't afford it, you borrow the money and thus go into debt; otherwise, you save for many years, and then you buy it all on your own. Some would respond that education is different: it's not a possession – it's a need; access to education is a fundamental right that should be available to all. Well, food is a need, too; surely access to food should be a fundamental right – but we have to pay for it.

Consider the sports business. Perhaps there the biggest ethical challenge is to justify the incredible amounts of money spent – not only on athletes' salaries, but on the activity itself. My guess is that building and operating a sports stadium costs more than building and operating a school. (Certainly your high school football team may well have cost more than all the other teams put together.)

Consider the military business. There's another one plagued with justifying exorbitant expenses. The ethics of rigid hierarchy and obedience is another issue to be considered (and one that has recently been highlighted by media coverage of military hazing rituals). And of course there's the primary service the military provides – killing. How right is that? (Not killing, but *protecting, defending. That's* okay, isn't it?)

Consider government business. No, that's redundant – when the president of General Motors becomes the Secretary of Defense, one has to wonder whether the government isn't just a front for big business. Does expertise in the auto industry qualify one to be in defense? (Well, if you consider all products and services to be interchangeable, if everything's just a "commodity"…) But running a Ministry *has* to be a bit different than running a company. One is public sector, the other is private sector: as a government body, you work by the people for the people. (And pigs fly.)

Choosing the medical business as the special focus for this chapter wasn't completely arbitrary: both the current trend toward privatization and the development of medical technologies seem to present new challenges to the business – and you, today's students, will be the ones facing them.

For example, there will probably be serious resource allocation problems; whether the resource is hospital beds, AZT, or organs, you may have to "choose" your customers – you may have to choose who lives and who dies. Is a utilitarian approach appropriate here? Or a justice-based approach?

Client confidentiality may be increasingly important – and perhaps problematic: do you or do you not give certain information to your patients' sexual partners? To blood donor clinics? To insurance companies? Whose rights take precedence? (Do you even give the information, say about a terminal illness or a genetic predisposition, to the client him/herself? Do you respect the person by telling or by not telling?)

Should you, and how should you, advertise your services and products? Will you hold yourself to "higher" ethical standards in this regard? Why/not?

And what about those services and products? Will you consider fetal tissue research an ethically acceptable business endeavour? Live organ transplant? Post argues against the commercialization of body parts: only the poor will need to sell their organs and fetuses and only the rich will be able to buy them — this will exacerbate class inequities and it may also result in low-quality parts. Matthews argues in favour of it, refuting both of Post's concerns: a poor person could use the money from the sale of a kidney to start a business and perhaps escape poverty; free market mechanisms increase rather than decrease product quality. Furthermore, an organ market would save lives. See also Chadwick who provides a Kantian argument against such a market. Then see Tadd's response to Chadwick; he argues that there's no difference between selling one's body parts and selling one's labour.

What about abortion? Physician-assisted suicide? Euthanasia? Religionists would argue against these, appealing to the sanctity of life. Blood transfusions are also considered morally unacceptable by some.

What about in vitro fertilization? Sex selection? Natural law theorists might draw their line here.

What about genetic screening? Genetic research?

Should you patent your "products"? What is your motive for patenting — merely to recover expenses for discovery? (And is that just an ego-

istic approach or could it be utilitarian?) Di Norcia notes that "manipulating patents is the most popular means of suppressing a technology" (120) and says the oil companies have suppressed solar energy technology. Would you do that: suppress an alternative remedy or cure so that yours is the one everyone buys?

Is it right to test your products on animals who are unable to refuse consent? Does it matter whether your product is life-saving or just life-enhancing? Does it matter whether it benefits only humans or the animals used for testing as well? Does it matter what effect, what degree of harm, your testing has on the animal — discomfort, pain, death?

Must you test all of your products to certain safety? By then, some prospective customers could be dead. Should people have the right to buy drugs or procedures that are not completely tested — especially if that's their last chance and they're going to die otherwise? What risk is acceptable? Whose decision is that?

Management/union issues may be especially problematic in the medical business — should physicians and nurses be able to go on strike? Does management have an extra responsibility to make sure that doesn't happen? Why/not?

Of course, there are many of the usual ethical issues as well: product safety issues (remember the Red Cross "tainted blood" affair?), workplace safety issues (consider the potential for contagion), discrimination issues (would it be unjust discrimination to refuse to hire an HIV-positive surgeon?). But perhaps these issues are more acute in the medical business because they often involve life and death, or at least serious quality-of-life consequences.

Reconsider the profit issue. According to Zimmerer and Preston (see Donaldson and

Werhane, 186), Plasma International Company bought blood in underdeveloped countries, then sold it with a price mark-up in the U.S. When it was in great demand because of a disaster, they marked it up even more, and made quite a profit. Is that morally right? Not just exploiting underdeveloped countries, not just capitalizing on others' misfortune, but capitalizing on life and death? Do you want to consult a doctor whose bottom line is his/her profit margin? (See Relman and Wicks for opposing views about whether medicine is better or worse off as a free market enterprise.)

Here's another question: should doctors be able to refuse demands for futile treatment? Well, are *other* businesses obligated to provide whatever the customer wants? Should the patient be considered a customer? To what extent is the medical business like other businesses? (See Agich and Wicks.)

REFERENCES AND FURTHER READING

Agich, George J. "Medicine as Business and Profession." *Theoretical Medicine* 11 (1990): 311-324.

Chadwick, Ruth F. "The Market for Bodily Parts: Kant and Duties to Oneself." *Journal of Applied Philosophy* 6.2 (1989): 129-139.

Di Norcia, Vincent. *Hard Like Water: Ethics in Business.* Toronto: Oxford University Press, 1998.

Donaldson, Thomas and Patricia H. Werhane. *Ethical Issues in Business: A Philosophical Approach.* 5th ed. NJ: Prentice Hall, 1996.

Matthews, Jr., Merrill. "Have a Heart, But Pay For It." *Insight* (January 9, 1995). Reprinted in *Taking Sides: Clashing Views on Controversial Moral Issues.* Ed. Stephen Satris. 5th ed. Guilford, CT: Dushkin Publishing Group, 1996. 114–117.

Post, Stephen G. "Organ Volunteers Serve Body Politic." *Insight* (January 9, 1995). Reprinted in *Taking Sides: Clashing Views on Controversial Moral Issues.* Ed. Stephen Satris. 5th ed. Guilford, CT: Dushkin Publishing Group, 1996. 118–121.

Relman, Arnold S. "What Market Values are Doing to Medicine." *The Atlantic Monthly* 269.3 (March 1992): 90-104.

Tadd, G. V. "The Market for Bodily Parts: A Response to Ruth Chadwick." *Journal of Applied Philosophy* 8.1 (1991): 95-102.

Wicks, Andrew C. "Albert Schweitzer or Ivan Boesky? Why We Should Reject the Dichotomy between Medicine and Business." *Journal of Business Ethics* 14.5 (May 1995): 339-351.

Ethics, Pricing and the Pharmaceutical Industry

Richard A. Spinello

ABSTRACT. This paper explores the ethical obligations of pharmaceutical companies to charge fair prices for essential medicines. The moral issue at stake here is distributive justice. Rawls' framework is especially germane since it underlines the material benefits everyone deserves as Kantian persons and the need for an egalitarian approach for the distribution of society's essential commodities such as health care. This concern for distributive justice should be a critical factor in the equation of variables used to set prices for pharmaceuticals.

Introduction

1 A perennial ethical question for the pharmaceutical industry has been the aggressive pricing policies pursued by most large drug companies. Criticism has intensified in recent years over the high cost of new conventional ethical drugs and the steep rise in prices for many drugs already on the market. One result of this public clamor is that the pricing structure of this industry has once again come under intense scrutiny by government agencies, Congress, and the media.

2 The claim is often advanced that these high prices and the resultant profits are unethical and unreasonable. It is alleged that pharmaceutical companies could easily deliver less expensive

Richard A. Spinello, "Ethics, Pricing and the Pharmaceutical Industry" *Journal of Business Ethics* 11.8 (August 1992): 617–626. © 1992 by Kluwer Academic Publishers. Reprinted with permission of the publisher and the author.

products without sacrificing research and development. It is quite difficult to assess, however, what constitutes an unethical price or an unreasonable profit. Where does one draw the line in these nebulous areas? We will consider these questions as they relate to the pharmaceutical industry with the understanding that the normative conclusions reached in this analysis might be applicable to other industries which market *essential* consumer products. Our primary axis of discussion, however, will be the pharmaceutical industry where the issue of pricing is especially complex and controversial.

The problem

3 Beyond any doubt, instances of questionable and excessive drug prices abound. Azidothymide or AZT is one of the most prominent and widely cited examples. This effective medicine is used for treating complications from AIDS. The Burroughs-Wellcome Company has been at the center of a spirited controversy over this drug for establishing such a high price — AZT treatment often costs as much as $6,500 a year, which is prohibitively expensive for many AIDS patients, particularly those with inadequate insurance coverage. The company has steadfastly refused to explicate how it arrived at this premium pricing level, but industry observers suggest that this important drug was priced to be about the same as expensive cancer therapy.[1] In dealing with its various constituencies, Burroughs has relied on two key arguments

to justify this price: high research and development cost and the threat of obsolescence. Burroughs maintains that in order to recoup its oppressively high research and development costs for this medication, it has no choice but to charge a price in the range of $6,500 per year. The company also defends its pricing policy by noting that proceeds from the sale of AZT will be used to finance other drugs for AIDS which are more effective than present treatments. Of course, if there is a superior second generation of the AZT medication, the drug will soon become obsolete. Moreover, once the patent expires, generic competition could erode the drug's current market share. Hence the need to generate substantial profits very quickly.

4   The lack of more reasonable prices for drugs such as AZT can be attributed to the functioning of the American free market and the oligopolistic nature of the drug industry. Prices in other countries are often much lower since they are the result of a negotiation process between drug companies and their host governments. For example, the average price of Roche Products' valium is $9.70 in the United States but $3.60 elsewhere. Most European governments determine pricing levels by bargaining with pharmaceutical companies. The end result is that these prices cover companies' manufacturing and distribution costs and, to a much lesser extent, research and development costs. But since these companies pass on such costs to their customers in the United States, they can still make a reasonable profit at these lower price levels.[2]

5   Thus, there are many inequities in the distribution of pharmaceutical products. Within the United States, certain medicines are simply inaccessible for many people due to the industry's pricing scheme. High drug prices have the most negative impact on the elderly and the chronically ill. The elderly, for example, are usually forced to pay for their prescription drugs, since Medicare does not cover their drug costs unless they are in a hospital. In addition, the American consumer ends up subsidizing lower drug prices for other countries in which medicine is often available at much lower prices. As a result, many of the industry's most vocal critics contend that the only solution to this injustice is government regulation, perhaps in the form of the European model.

6   But the major pharmaceutical companies strongly resist any form of regulation as a serious threat to the stability of their powerful industry. This industry has consistently put forward the same arguments for high prices as those advanced by Burroughs. These focus on the premise that premium prices are justified due to the excessive costs of developing new drugs. This rationale is based on the most fundamental principle of free market economics: high risk deserves high rewards. Beyond question, there *are* great risks involved in researching and developing new drugs, especially since such a small percentage make it through the long and costly process. Moreover, even if a drug is a commercial success, there is always the impending threat of product liability problems and expensive law suits. Finally, the industry maintains that earnings received from breakthrough drugs such as AZT are necessary to stimulate future research and compensate for many commercially unsuccessful drugs.

7   Regardless of the merit of these arguments, the superior financial performance of the pharmaceutical industry in recent years is beyond dispute. In studies which compare the performance of various U.S. industries, the pharmaceutical industry has consistently been the leader in several important categories such as return on

sales, return on assets, and return on common equity. For example, the drug industry currently boasts a return on sales of 20%. Also, its return on common equity of 31.9% compares quite favorably with the average return of 11.7% and is the highest of all the industry groups tracked by *Business Week*.[3] These figures reveal that at least according to some criteria drug companies and their stockholders are receiving substantial returns for the risks they take.

Ethical questions

8   The behavior of Burroughs and the tendency of most drug companies to charge premium prices for breakthrough medicines raises serious moral issues which defy easy answers and simple solutions. As Clarence Walton observed, "no other area of managerial activity is more difficult to depict accurately, assess fairly, and prescribe realistically in terms of morality than the domain of price" (1969, p. 209). This difficulty is compounded in the pharmaceutical industry due to the complications involved in ascertaining the true cost of production.

9   To be sure, every business is certainly entitled to a *reasonable profit* as a reward to its investors and a guarantee of long-term stability. But the difficulty is judging a reasonable profit level. When, if ever, do profits become "unreasonable?" It is even more problematic to determine if that profit is "unethical," especially if it is the result of premium prices.

10 Obviously, the issue of ethical or fair pricing assumes much greater significance when the product or service in question is not a luxury item but an essential one such as medicine. Few are concerned about the ethics of pricing a BMW or a waterfront condo in Florida. But the matter is quite different when dealing with vital commodities like food, medicine, clothing, housing, and education. Each of these goods has a major impact on our basic well-being and our ability to achieve any genuine self-fulfillment. Given the importance of these products in the lives of all human beings, one must consider how equitably they are priced since pricing will determine their general availability. Along these lines several key questions must be raised. Should free market, competitive forces determine the price of "essential" goods such as pharmaceuticals? Is it morally wrong to charge exceptionally high prices even if the market is willing to pay that price? Is it ethical to profit excessively at the expense of human suffering? Finally, how can we even begin to define what constitutes reasonable profits?

11 Also, the issue of pricing must be considered in the context of the pharmaceutical industry's lofty performance guidelines for return on assets, return on common equity, and so forth. On what authority are such targets chosen over other goals such as the widest possible distribution of some breakthrough pharmaceutical that can save lives or improve the quality of life? Pharmaceutical companies would undoubtedly contend that this authority emanates from the expectations of shareholders and other key stakeholders such as members of the financial community. In addition, these targets are a result of careful strategic planning that focuses on long-term goals.

12 But a key question persistently intrudes here. Should *other* viewpoints be considered? Should the concerns and needs of the sick be taken into account, especially in light of the fact that they have such an enormous stake in these issues? In other words, as with many business decisions, there appear to be stark tradeoffs between superior financial performance versus

humane empathy and fairness. Should corporations consider the "human cost" of their objectives for excellent performance? And what role, if any, should fairness or justice play in pricing decisions? It is only by probing these difficult and complex questions that we can make progress in establishing reasonable norms for the pricing of pharmaceuticals.

Free market vs. regulation

13 Of course, many would question the validity of basing drug prices on anything other than pure economic factors. Milton Friedman and his followers have argued persuasively that the only social responsibility of business is to increase profits. According to this "free market" philosophy, the responsible course of action is to charge whatever price the market will accept. Thus, if the market will support an annual price of $8,000 a year for a drug such as AZT, that should be the end of the matter. Managers who fail to price in a fashion that will maximize profits are shirking their primary fiduciary duty to stockholders. Therefore if executives in the pharmaceutical industry refrained from raising prices for a social objective, they would be unfairly imposing a tax on shareholders. When managers go beyond economic and financial data in their decisions, they become political agents with a social agenda. This is regarded by Friedman as a pernicious state of affairs which "will undermine the very foundations of our free society," since managers lack the wisdom and ability to resolve complex social problems such as the equitable distribution of pharmaceutical products (1979, p. 90).

14 One problem with this narrow view of corporate responsibility is that it fails to appreciate that corporate decisions often have a powerful social impact. The strategic decisions of large organizations "inevitably involve social as well as economic consequences, inextricably intertwined" (Mintzberg, 1989, p. 173). Thus such firms are social agents whether they like it or not. It is virtually impossible to maintain neutrality on these issues and aspire to some sort of apolitical status. The point for the pharmaceutical industry and the matter of pricing seems clear enough. The refusal to take "non-economic" criteria into account when setting prices is itself a moral and social decision which inevitably affects society. Companies have a choice – either they can explicitly consider the social consequences of their decisions or they can be blind to those consequences, deliberately ignoring them until the damage is perceived and an angry public raises its voice in protest.

15 If companies do choose, however, to be attentive and *responsible* social agents they must begin to cultivate a broader view of their environment and their obligations. To begin with, they must treat those affected by their decisions as people with an important stake in those decisions. This stakeholder model, which has become quite popular with many executives, allows corporations to link strategic decisions such as pricing with social and ethical concerns. By recognizing the legitimacy of its stake-holders such as consumers and employees, managers will better appreciate all the negative as well as positive consequences of their decisions. Moreover, an honest stakeholder analysis will compel them to explore the financial and human implications of those decisions. This will enable corporations to become more responsible social agents, since explicit attention will be given to the social dimension of their various strategic decisions.

16 Quite simply, then, the assumption that corporations are pure economic agents represents

a facile approach to this issue. Hence the free market philosophy of Friedman offers little guidance for reaching a solution to the dilemma of fair pricing in the pharmaceutical industry. At the other extreme, we find the solution offered by a framework of government regulations, but this too seems to be fraught with difficulties. Obviously, there would be severe practical and procedural problems if an attempt were made to directly regulate drug prices through a government agency such as the FDA. To begin with, there is the problem of exclusive trademark and patent rights. If the investment supporting these patented drugs is treated as a cost, firms would be able to raise prices by increasing these costs, and this would open the door for all sorts of abuses. Similar problems would arise with the regulated pricing of generic drugs. If, for example, generic drug prices were based on an industry wide basis, the price would most likely be determined by calculating the industry's average cost. Inefficient firms with above average costs, however, would fail to make a profit at this price and would be forced to withdraw from the market. As these firms exit, competition is diminished, and in the long run fewer players will probably mean higher costs and higher prices. Indeed, the problem with any regulatory solution is that it provides no real incentives for efficiency and cost controls. Hence relying exclusively on cumbersome government regulations to solve the problem of high drug prices seems completely unfeasible.

17 Given the inadequacy of regulating prices or letting them be determined by the marketplace, the only viable means of realizing fair pricing appears to be some form of self-regulation. According to Goodpaster and Matthews, the most effective solution to this and most other moral dilemmas is one "that permits or encourages corporations to exercise independent, noneconomic judgment over matters that face them in their short- and long-term plans and operations" (1989, p. 161). In other words, the burden of morality and social responsibility does not lie in the marketplace or in the hand of government regulation but falls directly on the corporation and its managers.

18 Companies that do aspire to such moral and social responsibility will adopt *the moral point of view*, which commits one to view positively the interest of others, including various stakeholder groups. Moreover, the moral point of view assigns primacy to virtues such as justice, integrity, and respect. Thus, the virtuous corporation is analogous to the virtuous person. each exhibits these moral qualities and acts according to the principle that the single-minded pursuit of one's own selfish interests is a violation of moral standards and an offense to the community. The moral point of view also assumes that both the corporation and the individual thrive in an environment of cooperative interaction which can only be realized when one turns from a narrow self – interest to a wider interest in others.

Pricing policies and justice

19 This brings us back to the specific moral question of fair pricing policies for the pharmaceutical industry. The moral issue at stake here concerns justice and more precisely distributive justice. As we have remarked, justice has always been considered a primary virtue and thus it is an indispensable component of the moral point of view. According to Aristotle, justice "is not a part of virtue but the whole of excellence or virtue" (1962, p. 114). Thus, there can be no virtue without justice. This implies that if corporations are serious about assimilating the moral point of

view and exercising their capacity for responsible behavior, they must strive to be just in their dealings with both their internal and external constituencies. Moreover, traditional discussions on justice in the works of philosophers such as Aristotle, Hume, Mill, and Rawls have emphasized distributive justice, which is concerned with the fair distribution of society's benefits and burdens. This seems especially relevant to the matter of ethical pricing policies.

20   Corporations which control the distribution of essential products such as ethical drugs like AZT can be just or unjust in the way they distribute these products. When premium prices are charged for such goods an artificial scarcity is created, and this gives rise to the question of how equitably this scarce resource is being allocated. The consequence of a premium pricing strategy whose objective is to garner high profits would appear to be an inequitable distribution pattern. As we have seen, due to the expensiveness of AZT and similar drugs they are often not available to the poor and lower middle class unless their insurance plans cover this expense or they can somehow secure government assistance which has not been readily forthcoming. However, if this distribution pattern can be considered unjust, what determines a just distribution policy?

21   There are, of course, many conceptions of distributive justice which would enable us to answer this question. Some stress individual merit (each according to his ability) while others are more egalitarian and stress an equal distribution of society's goods and services. Given a wide array of different theories on justice, where does the manager turn for some guidance and straightforward insights?

22   One of the most popular and plausible conceptions of justice is advanced by John Rawls in his well known work, *A Theory of Justice.* A thorough treatment of this complex and prolix work is beyond the scope of this essay. However, a concise summary of Rawls' work should reveal its applicability to the problem of fair pricing. Rawls' conception of justice, which is predicated on the Kantian idea of personhood, properly emphasizes the equal worth and universal dignity of all persons. All rational persons have a dual capacity: they possess the ability to develop a rational plan to pursue their own conception of the good life along with the ability to respect this same capacity of self-determination in others. This Kantian ideal underlies the choice of the two principles of justice in the original position. Furthermore, this choice is based on the assumption that the "protection of Kantian self-determination for all persons depends on certain formal guarantees – the equal rights and liberties of democratic citizenship – plus guaranteed access to certain material resources" (Doppelt, p. 278). In short, the essence of justice as fairness means that persons are entitled to an extensive system of liberties *and* basic material goods.

23   Unlike pure egalitarian theories, however, Rawls stipulates that inequities are consistent with his conception of justice so long as they are compatible with universal respect for Kantian personhood. This implies that such inequities should not be tolerated if they interfere with the basic rights, liberties, and material benefits all deserve as Kantian persons capable of rational self-determination. In other words, Rawls espouses the detachment of the distribution of primary social goods from one's merit and ability because these goods are absolutely essential for our self-determination and self-fulfillment as rational persons. These primary goods include "rights and liberties, opportunities and power, income and wealth" (Rawls, 1971, p. 92). What-

ever one's   nception of the good life,
these goo   means to realize
that pla   ould prefer
more r   unequal

be   it
di   the

24   or our
                                             material
                                             persons.
                                         ree self-de-
                                        l of material
                                     tee of abstract
                                    m of expression
                                 he primary social
                              , goods, like income
                          xtent health care (in-
                        , be considered as one
                      ods since it is obviously
n.   suit of one's rational life
plan. The   distribution of health care
should not be con ngent upon ability and merit.
Also it would be untenable to justify an inequitable distribution of this good by means of
Rawls' difference principle. It is difficult to imagine a scenario in which the unequal distribution of health care in our society would be more
beneficial to the least advantaged than a more
equal distribution which would assure all consumers access to hospital care, medical treatment, medicines, and so forth. If we assume that
the least advantaged (a group which Rawls never
clearly defines) are the indigent who are also
suffering from certain ailments, there is no advantage to any inequity in the distribution of
health care. Unlike other primary goods such as
income and wealth, it cannot be distributed in
such a way that a greater share for certain groups
will benefit the least advantaged. In short, this

is a zero sum game – if a person is deprived of
medical treatment or pharmaceutical products
due to premium pricing policies, that person has
lost a critical opportunity to save his life, cure a
disease, reduce suffering, and so on.

25   Thus, at least according to this Rawlsian
view of justice with its Kantian underpinnings,
there seems to be little room for the unequal distribution of a vital commodity such as health
care in a just society. It follows, then, that the just
pharmaceutical corporation must be far more
diligent and consider very carefully the implications of pricing policies for an equitable distribution of its products. The alternative is
government intervention in this process, and as
we have seen, this has the potential to yield gross
inefficiencies and ultimately be self-defeating. If
these corporations charge premium prices and
garner excessive profits from their pharmaceutical products, the end result will be the deprivation of these goods for certain classes of
people. Such a pricing pattern systematically
worsens the situation of the least advantaged in
society, violates the respect due them as Kantian
persons, and seriously impairs their capacity for
free self-determination.

26   It should be emphasized, however, that this
concern for justice does not imply that pharmaceutical companies should become charities by
distributing these drugs free of charge or at
prices so low they must sustain meager profits
or even losses. To be sure, their survival, long-
term stability, and ongoing research are also vital to society and can only be guaranteed
through substantial profits. Thus, the demand for
justice which we have articulated must be balanced with the need to realize key economic
objectives which guarantee the long-term stability of this industry. As Kenneth Goodpaster
notes, "the responsible organization aims at con-

gruence between its moral and nonmoral aspirations" (1984, p. 309). In other words, it does not see goals of justice and economic viability as mutually exclusive, but will attempt to manage the joint achievement of both objectives.

27   We are arguing, then, that pharmaceutical companies should seek to balance their legitimate concern for profit and return on investment with an equal consideration of the crucial importance of distributive justice. There must be an explicit recognition that for the afflicted certain pharmaceutical products are critical for one's well-being; hence they are as important as any primary social good and are deserved by every member of society. As a result these products should be distributed on the widest possible basis, but in a way that permits companies to realize a realistic and reasonable level of profitability.

28   It is, of course, quite difficult to define a "reasonable level of profitability." In many respects the definition of "reasonable" is the crux of the matter here. Unfortunately, as outsiders to the operations of drug companies we are ill prepared to judge whether development costs for certain drugs are inflated or truly necessary. As a result, these corporations must be trusted to arrive at their own definition of a reasonable profit, given the level of legitimate costs involved in researching and developing the drug in question. But we can look to some case histories for meaningful examples that would serve as a guide to a more general definition. One of the most famous controversies over drug prices concerned the Hoffman-LaRoche corporation and the United Kingdom in which the government's Monopoly Commission alleged that Hoffman-LaRoche was charging excessive prices for valium and librium in order to subsidize its research and preserve its monopoly position. In the course of the prolonged deliberations between the British government and the company reasonable profits were defined as "profits no higher than is necessary to obtain the 'desired' performance of industry from the point of view of the economy as a whole."[4] In general, then, under normal circumstances reasonable profits for a particular product should be consistent with the average return for the industry. Exceptions might be made to this rule of average returns if the risks and costs of development are inordinately and unavoidably high.

29   Thus, based on this Rawlsian ideal of justice I propose the following thesis regarding ethical pricing for pharmaceutical companies: for those drugs which are truly essential, the just corporation will aim to charge prices that will assure the widest possible distribution of these products consistent with a reasonable level of profitability. In other words, these companies will seek to minimize the deprivation of material benefits which are needed by all persons for their self-realization by imposing restraints on their egocentric interests in premium prices and excessive profits. Since only some pharmaceutical products can be considered as truly "essential," it remains to be seen which of those products should be subject to the imperative of justice. Moreover, we must present some sort of methodology for reaching this determination.

A tentative model for evaluating the role of justice in pricing decisions

30 As we have observed, for companies producing essential goods such as pharmaceuticals, the moral imperative of justice is one element in a complex equation that includes the need for profit, a respectable return on investment, and many other factors. Obviously some drugs are

far more important than others and hence the issue of their just distribution must be weighted much more heavily than it would be for other medicines. The weight given to the concern for distributive justice in this equation will be directly proportionate to some measurement of how critical this drug is to patients. For pharmaceutical products, this can be determined by considering the nature of the illness, the efficacy of the particular product, the availability of low-price substitutes, and so forth. The framework in Table 1 includes the key questions for determining the importance of a pharmaceutical product for society. The way in which these questions are answered will determine the role which should be played by the demands of distributive justice in the pricing equation.

Table 1. Questions for Considering the Relative Importance of a Pharmaceutical Product

- What is the nature of the malady? Is it life threatening or physically and/or mentally disruptive? Does it deprive the afflicted of their physical or mental well-being (e.g., schizophrenia) or is it more of an inconvenience (e.g., baldness)?
- Do patients have other options? Is there any other therapeutic recourse? Is this medication a last resort for the illness in question?
- Are there other drugs available for similar effectiveness and if so how affordable are these drugs?
- At the planned pricing level will people likely be deprived of treatment?
- How "experimental" is this drug considered to be? What is the likelihood that government agencies and insurance companies will offer assistance so that it can be afforded by everyone who needs it?
- Who is the likely end-user of the drug? The chronically ill? The elderly? Special consideration should be given to these groups who bear the biggest burden of high drug prices.

31   This brief framework serves as a general guide for pharmaceutical managers, which will enable them to discern how essential the product is, the likelihood of its affordability, and the probability of government assistance for the indigent. The more critical the product and the less likely it will be affordable to certain segments of society, the more prominent should be the consideration given to distributive justice in pricing policy deliberations. Justice cannot be the exclusive concern in these deliberations, but must be given its proportionate weight depending upon the way in which the questions in this framework are addressed. Thus, as pricing decisions duly consider factors such as production and promotion costs, etc., they should also take into account the element of distributive justice. Clearly, however, drugs that are less important for society because they deal with less serious ailments should not be subject to the same demands of justice as those for diseases which are truly life threatening or debilitating. Hence drug companies should have much more flexibility in pricing medicines for these less critical ailments.

A collaborative approach

32 There is no doubt that pharmaceutical executives would raise many objections to the proposal on fair pricing which we are advocating. Thus, despite their concern about these issues, the likelihood of any significant change is probably quite slim. Unfortunately, the premium pricing policy of these companies is perpetuated by industry-wide peer pressure for above average returns and the quasi-monopoly status of certain brand name drugs. Also, if a company unilaterally sought to distribute some of its products more equitably, it would probably find itself in an anomalous position in the drug

industry with no followers. In the face of this threat, it is difficult to envision one of the pharmaceutical companies taking the initiative and complying with Rawls' distribution criterion, even if there is some concession that in principle this is the right thing to do. Hence the current impasse which many argue can only be overcome by decisive intervention and regulation, perhaps in the form of "European style" controls of drug prices.

33   Although these arguments have some merit, they should not interfere with a proper ethical resolution to the intractable dilemma of high returns versus accessibility and a reasonable pricing scheme. Of course the apprehension that following the right course of action will jeopardize one's competitive position is quite common and is frequently brought forth to justify all sorts of corporate inaction and indifference on ethical matters. It is a variation of the traditional but jaded claim that ethics cannot be reconciled with economics.

34   As we have been at pains to insist here, however, ethical values can be integrated with economic success. But in order to accomplish this, it is necessary to transcend traditional thinking which posits a sharp dichotomy between morality and the economic criteria of success. As Laura Nash and others have argued, this "bottom line" mentality erects many barriers between managers and the marketplace. An exclusive and relentless focus on profit, continued growth, and increased market share tends to shut off much of the legitimate feedback from customers. For example, the demise of the automobile industry in the 1970s and '80s can partially be attributed to Detroit's narrow focus on these criteria and its unwillingness to listen to its customers.

35   On the other hand, when the focus shifts from pure economic measures of success to the relationship between corporations and their customers, the prevailing concerns become value creation and mutual benefit (Nash, 1990, pp. 91–94). In other words, mutual benefit is the essence of a sound business relationship, and this is achieved by delivering created value. When we consider the problem of pricing from this perspective, it becomes clear that an essential part of value creation in the pharmaceutical industry is the provision of medicines to those who need them at a fair and reasonable price. Moreover, listening to the concerns of its customers and various other constituencies on this matter is also an important aspect of value creation and a key to long-term success. Thus, by adopting a framework that centers on mutually beneficial *relationships* and value creation, pharmaceutical executives will come to realize that pricing is not a remote ethical problem that can be dismissed by invoking the principle of free market economics. Rather, it is a grave business problem which impedes these corporations from delivering value and impairs the critical relationship with their customers.

36   But even if the companies in question accept this line of reasoning, how should they proceed? A unilateral action might be well intentioned but it will probably not settle this acute industrywide problem. Instead, the optimal solution must follow a more complicated path that entails a collaborative effort in which the major firms work with government agencies such as the FDA to develop a tenable pricing framework that addresses the social costs of high prices. Both the industry and government share responsibility for dealing with this problem given the community's need for reasonably priced medicine. Also, as we have argued previously, if government regulators act independently they will not have access to the information, and special-

ized competence necessary to make the most effective decisions. A collaborative approach, on the other hand, will ensure that the community will be well-served and it will also preserve the level playing field for all the firms involved. It will also allow these companies to retain control of the pricing process and avoid the intricate problems associated with explicit price controls of any sort.

Final observations

37 Let us now summarize and conclude. Our aim has been to attempt an ethical analysis of pricing in the pharmaceutical industry in order to make some normative recommendations. This analysis might also be applied to other industries which are in the business of supplying essential commodities. We have argued that if these pharmaceutical companies seek to be responsible and adopt the moral point of view, they must practice the primary virtue of justice. No person can be considered virtuous and moral if he or she is unjust, and the same can be said for the corporation. Although there are several conflicting notions of distributive justice, the conception delineated by John Rawls seems both compelling and practically feasible. It is grounded in a Kantian view of the person which stresses the need for both abstract rights and concrete material resources for one's rational self-determination.

38   We have argued with some insistence that an essential commodity such as health care is analogous to the primary social goods considered by Rawls since it is so crucial for one's self-determination. Hence its distribution should not be contingent on one's abilities and standing in the community. Thus pharmaceutical firms must be prepared to impose some restraints on profits for the sake of distributive justice. The alter-

native is a more comprehensive involvement of government in this process which will lead to cumbersome pricing regulations that are likely to be ineffectual in the long run.

39   Given the importance of profitability and the long-term stability of these companies, however, justice cannot be their exclusive concern. Rather, the imperative of justice must be balanced with the need to realize key financial objectives. We are simply arguing that these objectives should not be pursued to the exclusion of justice, which must be responsibly and fairly factored into the pricing equation. Moreover, the weight given to justice in that equation will depend on how critical the product is, and this depends on the nature of the illness, the availability of substitutes, and so forth.

40   We have also pointed out that since this is such an entrenched and complex industry-wide problem, it cannot be resolved by any unilateral policy changes by a particular firm. Rather, the major producers must act in concert in collaboration with the government in order to ensure a fair pricing scheme.

41   This analysis does not by any means eliminate the frustrations regarding ethical pricing which were cited earlier by Walton. We can offer no definitive, quantitative formulae or comprehensive criteria to assure that pricing in this industry will always be fair and just. As with most moral decisions, much will depend on the individual judgment and moral sensitivity of the managers making those decisions. But if managers are sincere in their quest for the primary virtue of justice, the general guidelines proposed here will offer some modest assistance for this foray into the uncharted territory of fair pricing. It seems beyond doubt that responsible and fair pricing in the pharmaceutical industry is a serious moral imperative, since for so many con-

sumers it is a matter of well-being or infirmity and perhaps even life or death.

42   We might consider once again the wisdom of Aristotle on this topic of justice. In the *Nicomachean Ethics* he writes that "we call those things 'just' which produce and preserve happiness for the social and political community" (1962, p. 113). If corporations respond to the demands of justice for the sake of the common good, it will help promote the elusive goal of a just community and a greater harmony between the corporation and its many concerned stakeholders.

NOTES

1. Holzman, D.: 1988, 'New Wonder Drugs at What Price?', *Insight* (March 21), pp. 54–55. For more recent data on drug prices, see 'Maker of Schizophrenia Drug Bows to Pressure to Cut Costs', *The New York Times* (Dec. 6, 1990), pp. A1 and D3.

2. Kolata, G.: 1991, 'Why Drugs Cost More in U.S.', *The New York Times* (May 24), p. D3.

3. 'Corporate Scorecard', *Business Week* (March 18, 1991), pp. 52ff.

4. 'F. Hoffman-LaRoche and Company A.G.', Harvard Business School Case Study in Matthews, Goodpaster, Nash (eds.), *Policies and Persons* (McGraw Hill Book Company N.Y., 1985).

REFERENCES

Aristotle: 1962, *Nicomachean Ethics,* trans. by M. Oswald (Library of Liberal Arts, Bobbs Merrill Company, Inc., Indianapolis).

Doppelt, G.: 1989, 'Beyond Liberalism and Communitarianism: Towards a Critical Theory of Social Justice', *Philosophy and Social Criticism* 14 (No. 3/4).

Friedman, M.: 1979, 'The Social Responsibility of Business is to Increase Profit', in T. Beauchamp and N. Bowie (eds.), *Ethical Theory and Business* (Prentice Hall, Englewood Cliffs, N.J.).

Goodpaster, K.: 1984, 'The Concept of Corporate Responsibility', in T. Regan (ed.), *Just Business: New introductory Essays in Business Ethics* (Random House, New York).

Goodpaster, K. and Matthews, J.: 1989, 'Can a Corporation Have a Conscience', in K. Andrews (ed.), *Ethics in Practice* (Harvard Business School Press, Boston).

Mintzberg, H.: 1989, 'The Case for Corporate Social Responsibility', in A. Iannone (ed.), *Contemporary Moral Controversies in Business* (Oxford University Press, New York).

Nash, L.: 1990, *Good Intentions Aside: A Manager's Guide to Resolving Ethical Problems* (Harvard Business School Press, Cambridge).

Rawls, J.: 1971, *A Theory of Justice* (Harvard University Press, Cambridge).

Walton, C.: 1969, *Ethos and the Executive* (Prentice Hall, Inc., Englewood Cliffs. N.J.).

Questions

1. "The refusal to take 'non-economic' criteria into account when setting prices is itself a moral ... decision" (P14) – explain.

2. How does Spinello reconcile justice theory with virtue ethics?

3. How do health care and medicine fit into the Kantian/Rawlsian theory, according to Spinello?

4. What do you think of the definition of "reasonable profit" given (P28)?

5. How does distinguishing between essential and nonessential medicines when pricing increase the potential for justice?

The Morality of Human Gene Patents[1]

David B. Resnik

ABSTRACT. This paper discusses the morality of patenting human genes and genetic technologies. After examining arguments on different sides of the issue, the paper concludes that there are, at present, no compelling reasons to prohibit the extension of current patent laws to the realm of human genetics. However, since advances in genetics are likely to have profound social implications, the most prudent course of action demands a continual reexamination of genetics laws and policies in light of ongoing developments in science and technology.

1   Should individuals or corporations be allowed to hold patents on human genes? In the last few years, this question has generated a great deal of moral, political, and legal controversy. A dispute over the ownership of human gene therapy technology erupted a few years ago, when the National Institutes of Health (NIH) and Genetic Therapy Incorporated were awarded patents on techniques for modifying cells outside a patient's body (Beardsley 1995). Opponents of this patent argued that it was too broad and that it would prevent fair competition and slow research. Several years ago, the United States Patent and Trade Office (PTO) rejected NIH's bid to patent thousands of human gene fragments (Zurer 1994). Critics of this patent bid argued

that human genes are not inventions and cannot, therefore, be patented. In 1996, the United States Congress considered a measure, the Ganske-Wyden Bill (HR1 127), that would have prevented the PTO from awarding patents that do not involve a new machine or compound. In 1995, a group of 186 religious leaders called for a moratorium on patents on human and animal genes on the grounds that genes are creations of God rather than human inventions (Andrews 1995). As knowledge of human genetics and biotechnology continues to advance, the demand for patents will increase and more controversies about human gene patents will surface.

2   Although human genetics raises many important legal questions concerning the interpretation and application of patent laws, this paper will discuss the morality of patenting human genes. After examining arguments on different sides of this issue, the paper will conclude that there are, at present, no compelling reasons to prohibit the extension of current patent laws to the realm of human genetics. However, since advances in genetics are likely to have profound social, political, and medical implications, the most prudent course of action demands a continual reexamination of genetics laws and policies in light of ongoing developments in science and technology.

Terminological Preliminaries

3   Before discussing some of the different moral perspectives on this issue, it will be useful to say a bit more about the terms describing items that

David B. Resnik, "The Morality of Human Gene Patents" *Kennedy Institute of Ethics Journal* 7.1: 43–61. © 1997 by the Johns Hopkins University Press. Reprinted with permission of the publisher and the author.

might be patentable. The term "gene" (or "geno-type") should not problematic, but more needs to be said about the difference between human genes and nonhuman genes. Although some genes, such as those that regulate the production of human growth hormone, occur only in human populations, many genes that occur in human populations also occur in primate, mammalian, and other animal populations (King and Wilson 1975, Suzuki and Knutdson 1989). It would be a mistake to think of *human* genes as genes that occur only in human populations, since many genes that play an important role in nonhuman populations also play an important role in cellular regulation, growth, development, and physiology in human populations. The most reasonable view on this distinction is to say that biological context determines the humanness of genes: a gene is a human gene if and only if it contributes to the structures or functions of human beings. Thus, genes that code for hair proteins are human genes even though many of these genes also occur in chimpanzee populations, but genes that regulate pollen production in plants are not human genes because they do not contribute to the structures or functions of human beings.[2] It is important to understand the complexity of the distinction between human and nonhuman genes, since a ban on the patenting of all genes that occur in human populations would also imply a ban on the patenting of genes that occur both in human and nonhuman populations.

4   A second point worth mentioning at this juncture is that the units of heredity include entities both smaller and larger than genes. Genes are the basic units of heredity and protein synthesis in human populations; they are made out of DNA base pairs and are housed in chromosomes. Genes range in size from a few hundred to several million base pairs. Each human somatic cell has 46 chromosomes, and each chromosome contains thousands of genes. The entire collection of genes in a cell is called the genome, and the genome for any given human being consists of more than 100,000 different genes and 3 billion base pairs (Suzuki and Knutdson 1989). Units smaller than chromosomes but larger than genes include gene clusters, gene families, and chromosome regions. It is important to place genes in this molecular perspective, since people may attempt to patent not only genes, but smaller units, such as DNA sequences (gene fragments) or perhaps even larger units, such as gene clusters or portions of a genome.

5   Finally, it should be noted that there are many different technologies relating to human genetics that might be the subject of patent disputes. These technologies include methods for isolating, weighing, sequencing, analyzing, and synthesizing DNA, RNA, or proteins; techniques for injecting DNA, RNA, or proteins into cells; cloning techniques; recombinant DNA technologies; and the list goes on and on.

6   Thus, patents might be sought for: parts of the human genome (human gene fragments or sequences, genes, gene clusters, gene families, chromosome regions) or genetic technologies (methods or processes for sequencing, analyzing, synthesizing, cloning, studying, or modifying the human genome).

Intellectual Property Laws in the United States

7   Although the main focus of this paper is on moral, not legal, issues in human gene patents, it is useful to review patent laws in the United States in order to understand the kind of legal protections that could be available to those seek-

ing human gene patents. Items that are patented become a type of "intellectual property." All property rights can be thought of as a penumbra of legal entitlements to control something, and ownership of a thing consists of a collection of these rights over that thing. Intellectual property can be distinguished from tangible property in that it can be shared without diminishing the owner's ability to use it. In economic terms, intellectual properties are nonrivalrous goods (Dreyfuss 1989). Even though it is possible to share intellectual property, societies may decide to enact laws that give the owners of intellectual goods some control over how their properties are used by others. In the United States, property law allows for several different types of intellectual property, including copyrights, patents, trademarks, and trade secrets. A legal basis for U.S. intellectual property laws can be found in the United States Constitution. Article 1, Section 8, Clause 8 states "The Congress shall have power ... to promote the progress of science and the useful arts by securing to the authors and inventors the exclusive right to their respective writings and discoveries." For the purposes of this paper, I will discuss two types of intellectual property, patents and copyrights.

8   According to the United States patent laws, a patent is a legal permission granted by the PTO that gives the patent holder the right to exclude others from making, using, or selling an invention within the United States, its territories, or possessions for a 20-year period. Patents cannot be renewed. To obtain a patent, one must "reduce the invention to practice," which involves making the invention or a model of it, and submit an application to the PTO. The invention must "work" — i.e. it must do what it is supposed to do. The patent application becomes public — people can study the invention — although rights to control the invention remain private. In most cases, the PTO will grant a patent if the inventor provides a specification of the invention that will allow someone skilled in the relevant technical field to make and use it (Foster and Shook 1989). In the last 200 years, the courts and legislatures have refined and developed patent laws. A useful summary of a these laws is that a patent is new, useful, and nonobvious invention (Barber 1990). United States courts have ruled that some types of things cannot be patented, such as, ideas, scientific principles or theories, or mere results. Things that are not useful or original also cannot be patented, nor can inventions designed for the sole purpose of violating the legal rights of others.

9   A copyright is a renewable, legal protection granted by the United States government to allow an author to control the reproduction of an original work. A copyright does not give the author legal rights over the ideas expressed by the original work; it only gives him or her rights over his or her particular expression of the ideas. Copyrightable materials include: literary, dramatic, audiovisual, and choreographic works; pictorial, graphic, and sculptural artwork; music; motion pictures; and sound recordings (Barber 1990). A copyright gives an author the right to reproduce his or her own work or authorize others to reproduce it, to prepare derivative works from the original or authorize others to do so, to perform or display a work publicly or authorize others to do so. Although a copyright owner has exclusive rights to control his or her works, the doctrine of "fair use" allows others to use the author's works without the author's permission. While there have been many disputes about "fair use," the courts have allowed unauthorized copying of small portions of copyrighted works for educational purposes so long as the copying does not substantially diminish

the commercial value of the copyrighted work (Dreyfuss 1989).

10   Given this thumbnail sketch of patent and copyright laws in the United States, one can see that there is a legal basis for some forms of ownership pertaining to human genes, including (1) ownership of artificial human genes or artificial combinations of genes; (2) ownership of works describing human genes or scientific ideas or principles pertaining to human genetics; and (3) ownership of processes for analyzing, sequencing, copying, fabricating, or manipulating human genes.

11   As far as patent rights are concerned, there is a legal basis for patenting original – i.e., invented, non-naturally occurring – human genes, DNA sequences, parts of chromosomes, or combinations thereof; processes for manufacturing, analyzing, sequencing, or recombining human genes would also to be patentable. However, patent laws would not allow anyone to own naturally occurring human genes or combinations thereof; nor would patent laws allow anyone to own scientific principles pertaining to human genetics, such as the central dogma of molecular biology. Copyright laws would also permit some forms of ownership relating to human genes. For instance, a book, monograph, or paper describing human genes (or virtually any aspect of human genetics) could be copyrighted, although the ideas contained in this original work would be available to the public under the doctrine of "fair use."

12   Thus, it would appear that there is a legal basis for extending intellectual property laws to the realm of human genetics and for allowing human gene patents on original (or artificial) human genes. Thus far, individuals and corporations have found patents to be the most profitable and advantageous form of protection for

genetic discoveries and innovations, and most of the controversies relate to gene patents (Oman 1995). But should current patent laws be applied to human genetics? Are human gene patents immoral even if they have a legal basis?

The Moral Basis of Intellectual Property

13   In order to address these important questions, it is helpful to examine some traditional moral arguments relating to intellectual property, since they can provide a moral basis for human gene patents. Arguments for intellectual property can be treated as either "forward-looking" or "backward-looking" (Goldman 1989). For the sake of brevity, this paper focuses on only two of the most influential arguments for intellectual property, the desert approach and the utilitarian approach.

14   According to the desert approach to intellectual property, intellectual property rights should be granted in order to give people just rewards for their contributions and efforts (Davis 1989). If you invent a machine, you deserve to be able to have some control over that machine; if you write a book, you deserve to have control over its dissemination. The desert approach to intellectual property traces its history to the Lockean view that one acquires property (in general) by "mixing one's labor" with something (Kuflik 1989). The desert approach is "backward-looking" in that it focuses on just rewards for past actions.

15   The main problem with this approach is that current intellectual property laws do not appear to serve as effective vehicles for giving authors and inventors just rewards for their contributions and efforts (Dworkin 1989, Kuflik 1989). A person may work her entire life on an invention but

fail to profit from it if she is not the first person to obtain a patent for it. A graduate student may do most of the work for a scientific paper yet not even be listed as an author. The law seems to reward results, not contributions and efforts. If we want to understand the moral foundation for our current patent and copyright laws, we would do best to look at the arguments that support those laws. (One might reply that this argument only shows that our current laws are immoral, but I am not concerned with overthrowing our current system in this essay.)

16   The utilitarian approach seems to provide the moral foundation for most of our intellectual property laws, and it is by far the most influential rationale for them (Dworkin 1989, Nelkin 1984). According to the utilitarian approach, intellectual property laws can be justified in so far as they maximize socially valued outcomes. This approach is "forward-looking" in that it focuses on ways to produce future results. Stated in this fashion, the argument leaves open the question of what constitutes a socially valued outcome. As Dworkin (1989) points out, there is considerable disagreement about the ends that intellectual property should promote even among people who agree with the utilitarian rationale for intellectual property. Should intellectual property promote justice, social infrastructure, public health, the free flow of information, quality control of products, human happiness, economic prosperity, or some other kind of goal? Although there is a wide variety of goals that one might want to promote, many of them can be advanced by nurturing the growth of science and technology. Whether the growth of science and technology is treated as valuable in itself or merely as a means to these other goals is an important question that will not be answered here. In any case, one can view the growth of science and technol-

ogy as valuable either as an end in itself or as a means to other ends. The utilitarian rationale for intellectual property thus can be stated as follows: intellectual property is justified insofar as it contributes to the progress of science and technology (Nelkin 1984, Dworkin 1989).

17   Patent laws can promote the progress of science and technology in several ways. Without patents, many people and corporations would use secrecy to protect their inventions (Bok 1983). Although trade secrets often produce socially valued outcomes, patents offer the added advantage of allowing inventors to make knowledge available to the public while protecting their property rights and financial interests. Since openness promotes progress in science and technology and secrecy generally has the opposite effect, patents can promote progress by facilitating openness in science and technology and by discouraging secrecy (Bok 1983). A period of secrecy usually prevails when a company or inventor is in the process of obtaining a patent or perfecting an invention, but patents encourage companies and inventors to disclose their secrets. Although the aggressive, competitive pursuit of patents can sometimes hinder scientific and technological progress by stifling cooperation and openness, it is likely that secrecy and competition would prevail over openness and cooperation in science if our society had no laws to protect intellectual property.

18   Although openness is important in science and technology because it can help nurture cooperation and trust among scientists, there are also some economic arguments for openness in science and technology. From an economic perspective, openness helps to free-up markets for products by helping to prevent companies from monopolizing information crucial to product development. Free markets contribute to

progress in science and technology by encouraging fair competition among companies and researchers, since fair competition encourages companies to invest in research and development in order to get a competitive edge. Patents can therefore promote progress in science and technology by offering incentives to conduct and sponsor research and by allowing researchers and corporations to profit from their investments in research (Bowie 1994). Although the pursuit of truth usually provides enough motivation for individual scientists to conduct research, corporations will not sponsor research without economic incentives. Since patents generally offer a greater return on investments than copyrights, this economic perspective helps us to understand why corporations (and individuals) often pursue patents instead of copyrights. As far as human genes are concerned, a patent on an invention for copying a human gene is likely to be more profitable than a copyright on a paper describing that gene.

A Utilitarian Perspective on Human Gene Patents

19 The foregoing utilitarian perspective on intellectual property can provide a moral basis for extending patent laws to human genetics if we assume that extending those laws is likely to promote the progress of science and technology relating to human genetics. Patent laws would be a primary catalyst in the genetic revolution in much the same way as various laws have helped to stimulate progress in computer science, agriculture, manufacturing, and other endeavors (Volti 1995). Pharmaceutical companies, for example, depend on patents for their products in order to reap profits from high development costs. Indeed, it is likely that the pharmaceuti-

cal industry will lead the way in applications for patents (and copyrights) pertaining to human genetics, since genetic innovations and discoveries will have implications for new treatments and drugs. Although patents will encourage some secrecy in genetic research while companies are developing inventions, the practice of patenting human genes will encourage disclosure instead of secrecy. The practice of patenting human genes may hamper research in the short-run, but in the long-run it will foster research and product development by promoting openness and cooperation.

20   New discoveries and innovations in human genetics will not only have important scientific and economic benefits, but they will also yield important medical payoffs by leading to improvements in human health and well being. For example, advances in genetics aid in the treatment of diseases that have a genetic basis, such as Huntington's chorea, diabetes, cystic fibrosis, and cancer. Such advances also have important social and economic consequences, since people who are healthy generally lead happier lives than those who are not as healthy, and improvements in health should help to reduce health care costs.

21   Since a complete utilitarian analysis of a moral issue considers the possible bad, as well as the good, consequences, we also need to address the possible bad consequences of human gene patents. Although the practice of patenting human genes may yield medical, scientific, technological, and economic dividends, it may also generate negative consequences. The practice of patenting human genes could contribute to a variety of negative consequences, such as:

(1) The widespread use of genetic tests by employers, insurance companies, the government, and other organizations;

(2) Harms to future generations as a result of tampering with the human genome – i.e. mutations, and the like;

(3) The loss of genetic diversity in the human population as a result of the attempt to eliminate genetic diseases or improve the human genome;

(4) Genetic discrimination and bias;

(5) A radical alteration of our conception of ourselves from persons with dignity to commodities with a market-value;

(6) The exacerbation of existing social inequalities resulting from genetic engineering;

(7) The further erosion of privacy as various people and agencies gain access to genetic information;

(8) The employment of genetics to develop biological weapons; and

(9) The exploitation of third world nations who provide the resources for gene harvesting (Mead 1996).[3]

22   Many readers will note that these bad consequences could occur regardless of whether society allows the patenting of human genes. These are possible consequences of the genetic revolution itself; they are not consequences of the practice of patenting human genes, per se. The NIH, the National Science Foundation (NSF), and other agencies that fund scientific research will still provide ample funding for the development of genetics and related technologies even if society provides no legal protections to promote industrial investments in research. Moreover, if society does not allow companies to profit from human gene patents, they will still sponsor secret genetic research and product development, since genetic research and development will still be profitable (Gardner 1995). As the potential profits of genetic discoveries and innovations become more apparent, biotechno-logical, pharmaceutical, agricultural, and other firms will invest more money in research and development even if human gene patents are not available.

23   Since these possible bad consequences would result from the genetic revolution itself, one might argue that they do not constitute an argument against the practice of patenting human genes. In order to mount a utilitarian attack on the practice patenting human genes, we need to discover or postulate causal connections between this practice and specific, negative consequences. At this point in time, we might postulate that human gene patents could cause social, political, and medical harms by encouraging the industrialization of genetic research. Human gene patents could help to promote the development of undesirable and dangerous products and technologies by industry, such as devices for enhancing human offspring or techniques for making dangerous organisms or medicines. However, as I argued earlier, the industrial involvement in genetic research facilitated by human genes patents could also have a wide variety of good consequences. Moreover, there could also be some negative consequences of forbidding human gene patents, since industrial research could still take place under a veil of secrecy, and secret scientific research creates its own social problems, including a lack of accountability, regulation, and control. From a utilitarian perspective, gene patents are a double-edged sword.

24   The upshot of this discussion is that our predictions and forecasts about the social, political, economic, and medical effects of human gene patents are pure speculation. Although we can dream up various scenarios, we cannot foresee the future of the genetic revolution or specific applications of genetic technology. Given these

uncertainties, one might argue that we should abandon the utilitarian approach to assessing human gene patents, since any decisions we make at this point would be pure guesswork. We should not formulate social policies until we have "all the facts" or at least enough facts to make justifiable decisions. However, we cannot afford to wait until we have all the facts. Like it or not, the genetic revolution will continue its march, and we need to formulate some policies despite ignorance and uncertainty. The decision to abstain from any policy decisions is an act of omission that could force us to make hasty, careless decisions in the future.

25 If we need to make some policy decisions about human gene patents despite ignorance and uncertainty and we accept the idea that a utilitarian perspective can play a role in informing those decisions, then how should we develop an utilitarian analysis of human gene patents? I would suggest that the best we can do at this point is conduct a general assessment of the role of human gene patents in the development of genetic science and technology and attempt to weigh these possible benefits and harms. In conducting this general assessment, we should be mindful that it is difficult to forecast the progress of science and technology and that it is therefore also difficult to make reasonable assessments of the good or bad consequences of genetic science and technology (Volti 1995). Throughout history we have seen both science and technology put to good and bad uses: nuclear science and technology led to the atom bomb but they also led to nuclear medicine; the automobile gave people more freedom to travel but it also generated pollution and congestion; rockets launch weather satellites but they also deliver bombs.

26 Since the future is not an open book, our science and technology assessments can be viewed as decisions under uncertainty: we can at best make educated guesses about the future, based on our current knowledge of science, technology, and society. The best way to approach the issue of human genes patents, therefore, is to assign probability estimates (educated guesses) to various outcomes and revise those probabilities in light of new evidence about the effects of gene patenting as this practice develops and the genetic revolution unfolds. We can then use these probabilities to formulate social policies and change those policies in light of new evidence. Thus, the extension of patent laws to human genetics at this point in time is on sound moral ground, provided that we are willing to revise our laws in light of scientific, technological, and social changes and consequences. This decision strategy follows what could be called the Bayesian approach to decision making in that it instructs us to maximize our social utilities based on Bayes's rule for conditionalizing probabilities on the evidence (Resnik 1987).

27 However, the Bayesian approach has some serious difficulties that we need to avoid in making science and technology policies. The main problem is that Bayesian methods for revising probabilities in light of new evidence may never advance us beyond our initial educated guesses to reliable knowledge (Howson and Urbach 1989). If this occurs, and our initial, educated guesses are biased, then our social policies based on those guesses will also be biased. While many writers have argued that Bayesian methods will go beyond biased opinions and converge on objective knowledge in the long run (Howson and Urbach 1989), we have to make decisions for the short run – i.e., at a point in time when our "knowledge" may be mere biased opinion. Given these problems with applying Bayesianism to social policy, this approach will

always need to be tempered by a certain degree of a caution and humility.

28   To summarize this section, a utilitarian perspective provides a moral foundation for the practice of human gene patents but it also requires a willingness to change those laws in light of new evidence and developments.

Nonutilitarian Arguments against Gene Patenting

Human Gene Patents and Human Dignity

29 The remainder of the paper will examine three nonutilitarian arguments against human gene patents. All of these arguments hold that the practice of patenting human genes is morally wrong, regardless of its benefits or harms for society. The first argument takes a Kantian perspective on human gene patents and proceeds something like this: (1) the practice of patenting human genes treats persons as property; (2) it is morally wrong to treat persons as property; thus, (3) the practice of patenting human genes is morally wrong. Gene patenting is wrong because it treats persons as things that can be bought, sold, traded, or modified. For the purpose of discussing this argument, this paper will assume a Kantian perspective on personhood: a person is a rational, autonomous, moral agent (Kant 1964). This perspective assumes that a human person is not the same thing as a human body, since there might be human beings that are not autonomous, moral agents – e.g., zygotes – and there might be autonomous, moral agents that are not human beings – e.g., dolphins.[4] Human beings are members of the species *Homo sapiens*, but not all members of this species are persons (Warren 1973).

30   Although this Kantian perspective merits consideration as an objection to the practice of patenting human genes, it does not offer a sound argument against this practice because the practice of patenting human genes does not treat persons as property. Gene patenting does not treat persons as property because it only allows individuals or corporations to own inventions for analyzing, sequencing, manipulating, or manufacturing human genes. Ownership of a process for making or manipulating a part of a human body does not (automatically) constitute ownership of a person. A human gene patent would be analogous to a patent for making or manipulating other kinds of human body parts, such as hair, bones, or hearts. If the patenting of technologies for transplanting, growing, analyzing, or modifying bone marrow is morally acceptable, then the patenting of human genetic technologies should also be morally acceptable.

31   So, this Kantian perspective would appear to regard the practice of patenting human gene processes as morally acceptable, since it would not violate the rights and dignities of persons. However, we can imagine extreme cases in which gene patenting might treat persons as property. Biotechnology companies now own patents on various kinds of genetically engineered mice, and these patents entail ownership of the whole animal (Looney 1994). What if a biotechnology company attempted to patent a genetically engineered human?[5] Would this kind of patent constitute ownership of a person?

32   One might argue that patents on genetically engineered humans would treat persons as property, since patenting a genetically engineered human being would be ownership of a process for making something that could become a person. If the biotechnology patents on genetically engineered mice extend to the whole animal, then patents on genetically engineered humans being should also extend to the whole (human)

animal. Since patents give patent holders the right to control the buying, selling, and production of their inventions, a patent on a genetically engineered human being would be tantamount to slavery, since the patent holder could control the production and marketing of the body associated with the person.

33   Thus, I think the Kantian perspective on human genes patents provides us with good reasons for not allowing individuals or corporations to patent processes for making entire human beings, even though it would still allow more modest types of gene patents.

The Practice of Patenting Human Genes and Our Humanness

34 On the other hand, one might argue that the prospect of patenting human beings the way we patent mice raises issues that go beyond Kantian concerns about the ownership of persons, which brings up a second nonutilitarian argument against the practice of patenting human genes. One might challenge the metaphysical separation of human body and human person that has been assumed thus far and argue that humanity is closely connected to biological characteristics (Parens 1995). One might argue that the practice of patenting human genes, though it does not violate the rights of persons in most cases, threatens our understanding of humanity itself and our notions of what makes a being human. The human body occupies a key role in how we conceive of ourselves. It is dehumanizing to think of bodies as property because who we are depends on our relationship to our bodies: if my body is property, then I am property. The practice of patenting human genes is dehumanizing in that it changes our view of humans from beings with dignity and respect into objects to be

bought, sold, or modified (Kass 1985, 1992). Our humanness is morally "sacred," and we should not allow anything to undermine it.

35   Though this argument has some popular appeal, it rests on some dubious scientific assumptions or questionable moral intuitions, depending upon how it is read. If read as an argument concerning the social/cultural consequences of certain practices, such as the practice of patenting human genes, then it is a kind of forward-looking, "slippery slope" argument that claims that these practices will lead us toward total disrespect for human beings and human dignity (Heyd 1992, Resnik 1994). But this argument rests on the dubious sociological/psychological assumption that we will go down this slippery slope. We have for many years treated bodies as objects or commodities in some fashion, yet we do not treat living humans, nor even dead human bodies, purely as objects or commodities. In the Western World, we champion human rights although we treat bodies as objects by modifying them, replacing body parts, studying bodies, selling body parts, and so on. Why should we think that the practice of patenting human genes will be any more "dehumanizing" than our present and past uses of the human body? Taken to its extreme, this reading of the argument would suggest that we should not even perform dissections of the human body on the grounds that this practice will take us down a slippery slope toward vivisection (Anderson 1994).

36   The argument can also be understood as a critique of specific ways of treating the human body. It is simply wrong, the argument asserts, to treat the body as an object that can be bought, sold, modified, and so on. It is wrong because the body is part of our humanity; it is part of what makes us human beings, and we should not tamper with our humanity. But this argument

would seem to rest on some questionable moral intuitions about what constitutes "our humanness" and its moral sacredness. One might argue that "our humanness" depends more on psychological, intellectual, social, and other traits than on bodily features. "Our humanness" cannot be equated with the number of arms or legs we have, the shape of our eyes, the curvature of our spine, or even the number of chromosomes we have; "our humanness" is more closely related to our aspirations and dreams, our ideas and values, our personality and emotions, and our actions and attitudes (Anderson 1994).

37   Of course, there may indeed be no way to resolve this issue; who we are may depend on who we think we are. If I view my humanness as closely connected to my body, then my humanness is, for me, closely connected to having a specific kind of body, but another individual might view her humanness as closely connected to her mind, and another might view her humanness as closely connected to her clothing or her automobile. The question "what makes me a human being?" may have a different answer for every individual who asks it. We can now see how this argument begins to unravel. If the argument that views gene patenting as dehumanizing boils down to a purely subject-dependent answer about what constitutes humanness, then it cannot serve as a basis for a public policy banning gene patenting.

38   Having said that much against this argument, I should note that there may be some general consensus about properties of the human body that are intimately linked to humanness. For instance, most people might say that a being who is immortal is not human; or perhaps most people would agree that a being who has no feelings or emotions is not a human. But even if gene patenting allowed the creation of beings who we would not call human beings, this does not imply that it is dehumanizing. It would only be dehumanizing if it allows us to treat *ipso facto* human beings as nonhuman.

39   Finally, there is the question of why our humanness should be treated as morally sacred. Why should we refrain from changing human beings or directing human evolution? There are of course religious answers that can be given: tampering with the human genome is "playing God," usurps God's authority, and so on (Kass 1985, Andrews 1995). However, for the purposes of this essay, I will only consider secular critiques of patent laws, since a discussion of the legitimacy of religious arguments in public policy debates would take us too far afield. The main reasons for not tampering with human evolution through genetic engineering have more to do with the possible bad consequences of the genetic revolution (discussed earlier) than with the erosion of our humanity (Resnik and Langer, forthcoming).

Human Genes as Common Property

40 The final nonutilitarian critique of the practice of patenting human genes is the assertion that these resources should be viewed as common property, belonging to no single individual or corporation (Looney 1994). Since human beings have so many genes in common, we can no more claim ownership of human genes than we can claim ownership of the air. However, this "common property" approach to human genes rests on a mistaken view of human gene patents. The practice of human gene patenting does not allow anyone to own naturally occurring human genes, since patents only apply to inventions. Individuals or corporations could attempt to patent a processes for copying, sequencing, modifying, and analyzing human genes, but

ownership of these processes would not constitute ownership of our naturally occurring, common, human genes. Gene patents would apply to inventions that are not shared among all the people of the world and are not natural phenomena. As analogy, water cannot be patented but companies can patent inventions that make, analyze, or purify water.

Conclusion: Proceed with Caution

41 Intellectual property rights for various forms of scientific and technical information relating to human genetics will undoubtedly occupy center stage in future legal, ethical, and political debates. It is important to give serious thought to any decisions to treat human genes as property, since these decisions will in all likelihood have a dramatic effect on the development of science, technology, and society. This paper has considered several moral arguments for and against the practice of human gene patenting and has found no compelling moral reasons to forbid human gene patents at this time. Patents on genetically engineered humans should not be allowed, since these patents would amount to slavery, but this technology does not yet exist. If we want to obtain the potential benefits of the genetic revolution, then we need to be willing to take some risks, including those associated with the extension of patent rights to the realm of human genetics. However, this paper should not be treated as an unabashed endorsement of the patenting of human genes, since this practice could have some very disturbing social, political, and medical consequences. The most reasonable position at this time is to proceed with caution, examine various applications for human gene patents as they arise, and be willing to change our laws and social policies in light of new evidence. We cannot close the Pandora's box of human genetics, nor should we attempt to run away from its curses and plagues. The best policy is to try to manage these potential evils as they enter our society.

NOTES

1. I would like to thank Susanna Goodin, Michael Harkin, and two anonymous reviewers for the *Kennedy Institute of Ethics Journal* for their helpful comments and criticism.

2. In this paragraph (and in the rest of this essay), "human being" refers to a member of the species *Home sapiens.*

3. For more on the possible consequences of advances in genetics (both good and bad), see Wilkie (1993), Kass (1985), Suzuki and Knutdson (1989), and Resnik and Langer (forthcoming).

4. I adopt this perspective on personhood in order to articulate a Kantian approach to human gene patents. I recognize that this perspective raises many controversial questions about what constitutes a person, but it is not my aim to settle those questions in this essay.

5. Although we cannot yet genetically engineer human beings like we design mice, "designer sperm" come very close to "designer humans" (see Coghlan 1994).

REFERENCES

Anderson, French. 1994. Genetic Engineering and Our Humanness. *Human Gene Therapy* 5: 755-59.

Andrews, Edmund. 1995. Religious Leaders Prepare to Fight Patents on Genes. *New York Times* (13 May): N1, L1.

Barber, Hoyt. 1990. *Copyrights, Patents, and Trademarks.* Blue Ridge Summit, PA: Tab Books.

Beardsley, Tim. 1995. Patently Obvious: Want to Do Gene Therapy? Ask Sandoz. *Scientific American* 273 (3): 45.

Bok, Sissela. 1983. *Secrets.* New York: Pantheon Books.

Bowie, Norman. 1994. *University-Business Partnerships.* Lanham, MD: Rowman and Littlefield.

Coghlan, Andy. 1994. Outrage Greets Patent on Designer Sperm. *New Scientist* 142 (1920): 4-6.

Davis, Michael. 1989. Patents, Natural Rights, and Natural Property. In *Owning Scientific and Technical Information,* ed. Vivian Weil and John Snapper, pp. 241-49. New Brunswick, NJ: Rutgers University Press.

Dreyfuss, Rochelle. 1989. General Overview of the Intellectual Property System. In *Owning Scientific and Technical Information,* ed. Vivian Weil and John Snapper, pp. 17-40. New Brunswick, NJ: Rutgers University Press.

Dworkin, Gerald. 1989. Commentary: Legal and Ethical Issues. In *Owning Scientific and Technical Information,* ed. Vivian Weil and John Snapper, pp. 250-52. New Brunswick, NJ: Rutgers University Press.

Foster, Frank, and Shook, Robert. 1989. *Patents, Copyrights, and Trademarks.* New York: John Wiley and Sons.

Gardner, William. 1995. Can Genetic Enhancement be Prohibited? *Journal of Medicine and Philosophy* 20 (1): 65-75.

Goldman, Alan. 1989. Ethical Issues in Proprietary Restrictions on Research Results. In *Owning Scientific and Technical Information,* ed. Vivian Weil and John Snapper, pp. 69-82. New Brunswick, NJ: Rutgers University Press.

Heyd, David. 1992. *Genethics: Moral Issues in the Creation of People.* Berkeley, CA: University of California Press.

Howson, Christopher, and Urbach, Peter. 1989. *Scientific Reasoning: The Bayesian Approach.* La Salle: Open Court.

Kant, Immanuel. 1964. *Groundwork for the Metaphysic of Morals,* trans. H. J. Patton. New York: Harper Torchbooks.

Kass, Leon. 1985. *Toward a More Natural Science.* New York: Free Press.

———. 1992. Organs for Sale? Propriety, Property, and the Price of Progress. *The Public Interest* 107: 76-82.

King, Mary-Claire, and Wilson, Ann. 1975. Evolution at Two Levels in Humans and Chimpanzees. *Science* 188 (11 April): 107-16.

Kuflik, Arthur. 1989. Moral Foundations of Intellectual Property Rights. In *Owning Scientific and Technical Information,* ed. Vivian Weil and John Snapper, pp. 219-40. New Brunswick, NJ: Rutgers University Press.

Looney, Barbara. 1994. Should Genes Be Patented? *Law and Policy in International Business* 26 (1): 231-72.

Mead, Aroha. 1996. Genealogy, Sacredness, and the Commodities Market. *Cultural Survival Quarterly* 20 (2): 46-53.

Nelkin, Dorothy. 1984. *Science as Intellectual Property.* New York: Macmillan.

———, and Lindee, Susan. 1995. *The DNA Mystique: The Gene As a Cultural Icon.* New York: W. H. Freeman.

Oman, Ralph. 1995. Biotech Patenting Issues Raise Ethical Concerns. *The National Law Journal* 17 (36): C42.

Parens, Eric. 1995. Keeping the "Body" and "Soul" Together. *Human Gene Therapy* 6: 3-7.

Resnik, David. 1994. Debunking the Slippery Slope Argument against Human Germ Line Gene Therapy. *Journal of Medicine and Philosophy* 19: 23-40.

———, and Langer, Pamela. Forthcoming. *Moral and Political Issues in Human Germ-Line Gene Therapy.* Austin, TX: RG Landes.

Resnik, Michael. 1987. *Choices: An Introduction to Decision Theory.* Minneapolis: University of Minnesota Press.

Suzuki, David, and Knutdson, Peter. 1989. *Genethics.* Cambridge, MA: Harvard University Press.

Volti, Robert. 1995. *Society and Technological Change*, 3d edition. New York: St. Martin's.

Warren, Mary Anne. 1973. On the Moral and Legal Status of Abortion. *The Monist* 57: 43-61.

Wilkie, Thomas. 1993. *Perilous Knowledge: The Human Genome Project and Its Implications.* London: Faber and Faber.

Zurer, Pamela. 1994. NIH Drops Bid to Patent Human Gene Fragments. *Chemical and Engineering News* 72 (8): 5-6.

Questions

1. After careful definition of terms, Resnik examines and rejects as inadequate four arguments against human gene patents (on moral bases). Do you agree with his assessment in each case? (If not, why not?)

2. He therefore concludes that it is, at least for now, morally acceptable to patent human genes. Do you accept his conclusion, or do you think there are other arguments he did not consider that are strong enough to support prohibiting such patents? (If so, what are they? Consider all the ethical approaches covered in Section II!)

3. "The pharmaceutical giant Merck ... is convinced that more money and more benefit will derive from letting all comers exploit the genetic map in order to make tests or drugs that they can then patent. ... The company is sponsoring a group at Washington University in St. Louis to find genes and put the information up on the internet for free. This has created a truly remarkable situation in which two corporate giants are engaged in a race where one is giving away what the other wishes to patent." [The 'other' is SmithKline Beecham, which "has formed an alliance with an American company, Human Genome Sciences, to map, sequence, and patent as much of the human genome as possible."] (Arthur Caplan, *Due Consideration: Controversy in the Age of Medical Miracles,* New York: John Wiley & Sons, 1998, 41–42.) Comment.

Case Study –
The St. Michael's-Wellesley Hospital Merger

Should a Catholic hospital be compelled to offer services (such as abortion) that conflict with Catholic beliefs?

This issue came to the fore in the spring of 1998 when the Ontario government merged Wellesley Hospital in Toronto with St. Michael's, a few blocks away. The two buildings would be operated and administered by St. Mike's, but much of the former Wellesley would be closed. This was one of a number of hospital mergers in 1997–8 recommended by the Ontario Hospital Restructuring Commission, which was established to examine and find ways to make the hospital system in Ontario more effective and efficient.

As soon as the merger was proposed, opponents expressed concern. "Why close Wellesley?" asked many, including its doctors and nurses. It was apparently busy and served people who were poor or had so-called '"alternate lifestyles." What was particularly worrisome for many of the Wellesley patients was the absence of services such as abortion, contraception, and AIDS treatment at the Catholic hospital: prior to closing, doctors at Wellesley did up to 1,500 abortions a year; they also had an extensive HIV/AIDS program including treatment and prevention. Many patients expressed a real fear that they would have to seek treatment further afield if the "new" St. Mike's followed its traditional policy of refusing to offer services the hospital administration found morally unacceptable.

Michele Landsberg, a *Toronto Star* columnist, wrote about these concerns in May 1998. She objected to a statement by Jim O'Neill, Director of Services at St. Mike's, who was quoted as stating, "Our core values have served us well for over 100 years and those values are not going to change." Landsberg pointed out that although St. Mike's was a Catholic hospital, it was also a public hospital built with public money. They have an obligation, according to Landsberg, to serve all of the public and not deny services that people need because of their religious beliefs; the services in question were especially needed in that neighbourhood of Toronto. Landsberg argued that it would be immoral for any public hospital to limit women's choices and infringe on their reproductive rights. She concluded by stating, "How can this hospital justify taking over the assets of another public hospital and promptly cancelling services the public needs, wants, and is entitled to?"

By mid-1998, the Province of Ontario had 220 publicly funded hospitals, including 28 under Catholic governance. According to an *Ottawa Citizen* article by April Lindgren, "Hospitals under Catholic governance adhere to the *Catholic Health Care Ethics Guide*, which says contraception is 'morally unacceptable', bans sterilization as a means of birth control, and says that abortion of an embryo or fetus is 'immoral'." Physicians at Catholic hospitals are asked to "sign on" to the Catholic ethics guide. Many, of course, do so quite willingly; as Peter Lauwers pointed out, why should people have to perform procedures (such as abortion) which violate their beliefs and values?

REFERENCES

Landsberg, Michele. "St. Mike's Religious Rules Undemocratic." *The Toronto Star* 30 May 1999: L1.

Lauwers, Peter D. "Wellesley's Sore Losers Need to Move On Now." *The Toronto Star* 6 Jun. 1998: C3.

Lindgren, April. "Hospital Closings Spark New Debates: Catholic Integration Cuts Abortion, Birth Control." *The Ottawa Citizen* 14 Jun. 1998: A5.

Questions

1. Should patients who need and want services such as abortion and contraception be forced to go beyond their neighbourhood to find these services? Beyond their town/city? Beyond their province?

2. Is the hospital administration justified in asking its physicians to sign onto a particular ethics guide? Is there a way that both the rights of the hospital workers (not to violate their beliefs/values) and the rights of the hospital users (to have access to needed services) can be respected?

3. Why are publicly funded hospitals run by religious organizations, in any case? Should that be permitted?

4. (a) Should privately funded hospitals be allowed to restrict their services in this way? Maria Cosillo (quoted in the Lindgren article) says that "the purpose of hospitals is to serve patients, not to promote certain values" – to what extent, if any, do you agree?

   (b) Should any other privately funded businesses be allowed to restrict their services according to their beliefs and values? Do you think Cosillo's comment can be said of *every* business or just some, like the medical business?

CHAPTER 12
ETHICAL INVESTING

What to Do? –
Put Your Money Where Your Morals Are!

You have just been hired by a fund management company to create several new mutual funds aimed at a dual target market: people who don't think they have enough money for that kind of thing, and people who want to get into "ethical investing" (once they realize they *do* have enough money). You need to design a decision-making process for selecting companies to be included in these funds.

What do you do?

Introduction

Ethical investing is not typically a topic in business ethics texts, but I have decided to include it for several reasons. First, as the opening decision-making scenario suggests, if you end up working in the financial services sector, you may have to decide which investments can and should be included in your ethical investment portfolio. How do you do that? What counts as an ethical, a morally good, investment? (Will *your* business qualify to be part of someone's ethical investment portfolio?) And should you do that – or should the client be able to pick and choose?

Second, your business, whatever its nature, may well be making some investments of its own, and I hope that, having read this book, you'll want to consider the ethics of your investment decisions.

Third, ethical investing is experiencing a bit of popularity at the moment, and what with the traditional savings account having gone out of favour, many individuals are investing instead. Hopefully, you will want to do the right thing with your own personal investments.

But last, this topic makes an excellent last chapter, bringing us back to the big question, the only question: what is moral goodness – *what is the right thing to do?* As I suggested in the first paragraph of this chapter, to define "ethical investing," you'll have to define "ethical" (i.e., "ethically correct" a.k.a. "morally good" a.k.a. "right").

However, even before we consider *ethical* investing, we should consider *investing* – is investing itself ethically correct? By definition, investments (well, *good* investments) enable you to get back more than you put in. Isn't that unfair?

Where did that extra come from? Assuming a sort of conservation of mass principle, it had to come from somewhere, from someone. So if you got more out of the deal, doesn't someone else get less? Your profit is someone else's loss. (Or maybe not – recall the discussion in the chapter on profit.) Consider Forsey's comments:

> The claim than an 'ethical' mutual fund can bring principles and corporate profits cozily together is at bottom a moral fraud. Even if the screening process could be made to work more or less as intended, any significant corporate profit still has to come from someone else's labour or from the finite and precious resources of the Earth itself. Nothing comes from nothing, so if you're getting a windfall, someone else is getting shafted. (2)

Or are your dividends just your payment for letting someone else use your money? People pay you for the use of your time and effort, and your property, why not also for the use of your money? But then why aren't dividends a fixed amount – like wages or rental fees?

Another point to consider with respect to investing in general, as De George explains (475–6), is that when you invest in a company, you are buying a part of it. Ownership has its privileges, but it also has its responsibilities. As part owner, you are partly responsible for what it does (or does not do). And yet, investors often don't even know what companies they're part owner of (consider retirement and mutual funds), what companies they're supporting – let alone what those companies are doing. (How can you find out what a company does or does not do? Check the supplementary list at the end of this chapter.) Perhaps one is morally obligated to get into "shareholder activism." See Alinsky, perhaps the first to organize "ordinary" citizens to influence corporations through shareholding; see also the book by Rosenberg about Robert Monks who, among other things, started Institutional Investor Services, a research organization, and Institutional Shareholder Services, an organization whose mandate is to extend shareholder rights in corporations.

Now, with respect to *ethical* investing, some people use a *negative screen*. That is, they *exclude* all companies that do X, Y, and Z – ethically bad actions such as (arguably) discriminate, pollute, or contribute to the arms trade. However, for this method to be completely successful, your list of no-nos will have to be complete. And that might be difficult. (Did you screen out "obscenely high salaries for its CEOs"?)

Some use a *positive screen*: they *include* all companies that do A, B, and C – ethically good actions such as (arguably) develop environmentally-friend technologies, provide a safe workplace, or operate a daycare for employees' kids.

Of course, you could use a combination of negative and positive screens. And, of course, it can be tricky. Referring to ethical screening processes and drawing attention to the potential difficulties, Leonard J. Brooks asks, "Why is it unethical for a company to provide food or telephones or pencils to the military? On the other hand, why are banks considered ethical investments, even though they lend to the companies that supply the food, phones and pencils?" (1).

Whichever way you go, you'll soon find out that, like people, companies are not usually all good or all bad. What do you do with a solar heating company that never hires First Nations people? Do you put it in your ethical investment fund or not? And that gets us to the *real* big question: *How do you solve moral conflicts?*

Consequentialist theories, you may recall, provide one way. You can rank your options according to the severity or extent (or whatever) of the consequences. So, for example, supporting solar technology may actually contribute to saving the planet – which, you may decide, is more important than offering jobs to a few specific people. So you support the company.

What about principle- or value-based theories? How do you decide which principle or value takes priority? One way is according to logical primacy. For example, if we don't save the planet, *no one's* going to get jobs – because no one's going to exist. Saving the planet must logically precede equal employment opportunities. So you support the company.

However, logical primacy may not always work: life is logically prior to pleasure, but many would say that a life without (at least a certain amount of) pleasure isn't worth living, so they'd put pleasure before life.

One could rank according to some other criteria. Perhaps rational values are worth more than emotional ones – so justice outranks compassion, for example.

But don't forget, in any case, to be creative and consider alternatives: you could, along with your investment cheque, send a letter to that solar company endorsing their environmentally responsible attitude but encouraging them to reconsider their employment equity policy.

And remember not to be discouraged by the inability to make *pure and perfect* moral decisions – making *better than* decisions is an achievement in itself.

REFERENCES AND FURTHER READING

Alinsky, Saul. *Rules for Radicals.* NY: Random House, 1971.

Brooks, Leonard J. "Ethical Investing: Helpful or Heresy." *The Corporate Ethics Monitor* 9.5 (September-October 1997): 1.

De George, Richard T. *Business Ethics.* 5th ed. NJ: Prentice Hall, 1999.

Forsey, Helen. Letter. *This Magazine* 32.3 (November/December 1998): 2.

Hollingworth, Sarah. "Green Investing – A Growing Concern?" *Australian CPA* 68.4 (May 1998): 28-30.

Mackenzie, Craig. "The Choice of Criteria in Ethical Investment." *Business Ethics (A European Review)* 7.2 (April 1998): 81-86.

Nitkin, David. "Ethical Investing In Canada: The First Decade." *The Corporate Ethics Monitor* 9.5 (September-October 1997): 76-78.

Olive, David. "Ethical Investing and Ranking." *The Corporate Ethics Monitor* 9.4 (July-August 1997): 63-64.

Rosenberg, Hilary. *A Traitor to His Class: Robert A. G. Monk and the Battle to Change Corporate America.* NY: John Wiley & Sons, 1999.

FINDING OUT ABOUT WHAT COMPANIES DO...

Alperson, M. et al. *The Better World Investment Guide.* NY: Prentice Hall, 1991.

Ellmen, Eugene. *Canadian Ethical Money Guide.* Toronto: James Lorimer, 1997.

Ethicscan (Box 50434, Toronto, Ontario M6A 3B7) provides company profiles based on a great number of things (code of ethics, direct job creation, employment of women, hiring and promotion programs, charitable donations, community relations, progressive staff policies, employee gain-sharing opportunities, labour relations/heath and safety, environmental management, environmental performance, international relations, business practice issues, Canadian sourcing, and candour); they have a website (www.ethicscan.on.ca); they also publish *The Ethical Shopper's Guide, The Corporate Ethics Monitor,* and *Shopping with a Conscience.*

Lydenberg, Steven D. et al. *Rating America's Corporate Conscience.* Cambridge, MA: Addison Wesley, 1986.

The National Boycott Newsletter. The Institute for Consumer Responsibility (6506 28th Avenue, N.E., Seattle, WA 98115).

The Ethics of Investing

William B. Irvine

ABSTRACT. In this paper, I examine various popular notions concerning the ethics of investing. I first consider and reject the absolutist view that it is always wrong to invest in "evil" companies and the view that what makes investments in evil companies morally objectionable is the fact that by making such investments, investors are taking steps to benefit from the wrongdoing of others. I then defend the view that what makes certain investments morally objectionable is the fact that by making such investments, investors enable others to do wrong. According to this view, when weighing the purchase of a certain company's stock, investors should ask themselves the following question: "Would this sort of investment, if made by many people, enable others to do wrong?" If the answer to this question is yes, and if an investor nevertheless makes the investment in question, he can justifiably be accused of moral wrongdoing.

1 Since the late Sixties, investors have become growingly concerned with the ethical implications of their investments. The idea, basically, is that there is an ethical dimension to investing and, in particular, that there are times when it is morally wrong to buy the stock of a company.

2 In this paper, I will consider and reject certain popular notions concerning the ethics of investing. I will then present and defend my own views on this topic. As we shall see, it is my contention that there are indeed times when investments are morally objectionable and that in at least some of these cases, the investments in question are objectionable because they enable people and/or companies to do wrong.

3 Before beginning my examination of the ethics of investing, it will be useful to discuss some of the things we should keep in mind when thinking about this topic.

4 We should, in the first place, be careful to distinguish between the ethical dimensions of investing and the aesthetic dimensions of investing. Many an investor avoids certain stocks because they do not appeal to his imagination. I know, for example, people who wouldn't consider buying stock in a certain coffin manufacturing company. When these people avoid the stock in question, they don't do so on moral grounds: They don't think there is anything morally objectionable about coffins or about the way the company in question manufactures them. Rather, they avoid the stock because they would be depressed by its presence in their portfolio. Similarly, consider the investor who refuses to buy the stock of a certain company because he doesn't like the taste of the soft drink it manufactures. This investor's refusal to buy the stock is presumably made on aesthetic rather than on moral grounds.

5 Mutual funds that bill themselves as "socially responsible" have an unfortunate tendency to confuse the ethical and aesthetic dimensions of investing. This, at any rate, is the conclusion

William B. Irvine, "The Ethics of Investing" *Journal of Business Ethics* 6.3 (April 1987): 233–242. © 1987 by D. Reidel Publishing Company. Reprinted with permission of Kluwer Academic Publishers and the author.

I draw from their stated investment policies. One fund, for example, tells us that it is interested in making investments in companies which, in the conduct of their business, "contribute to the enhancement of the quality of life in America."[1] Another tells us that it is interested in investing in companies that "make a significant contribution to society through their products and services and through the way they do business."[2] It is not clear whether these policy statements are intended to be aesthetic declarations or ethical declarations.

6   In this paper, I will be concerned exclusively with the *ethical* dimensions of investing.

7   A second distinction I would like to draw concerns two ways in which an investment decision can have ethical implications. Some investments have ethical implications because of contractual obligations the investor has created for himself; other investments – as I shall argue below – have ethical implications because of certain non-contractual obligations the investor has.

8   Perhaps the difference between contractual and non-contractual obligations can be better understood if we consider a case from outside the realm of investing. If you have promised to feed me, you have an obligation to do so. The obligation in question is contractual since it exists because of an agreement you voluntarily entered into. If, on the other hand, you have never promised to feed me, but you have plenty of food and I am starving to death, most people would agree that you have an obligation – a non-contractual obligation since it doesn't stem from any agreement you voluntarily entered into – to feed me. Most people would, after all, agree that we have a moral obligation to help our fellow human beings when they are in dire need and when helping won't require great sacrifice on our part.

9   In parallel fashion, an investor might create contractual obligations for himself, say by promising to invest other people's money in a certain way. If he invests their money against their expressed wishes or if he invests in a way that creates a conflict of interest – if, for example, he buys stock for their account that he is simultaneously selling from his own – he will unquestionably be doing something wrong. On the other hand, even though an investor is under no contractual obligations, it might be (and in what follows will be) argued that he is nevertheless under certain non-contractual obligations that prohibit him from making certain investments. These are obligations "to society as a whole" that he has regardless of any particular promises he has made or contracts he has entered into.

10   In this paper, I will be concerned exclusively with the ethical implications of investing that stem from the *non-contractual* obligations of investors.

11   Finally, it is important that in what follows we not mistake egoistical investing for ethical investing. Suppose, for example, that the widget-makers' union adopts the following investment strategy: Buy (in equal dollar amounts) all and only the stocks of companies that employ members of the widget-makers' union. Such an investment policy is concerned not with the well-being of people in general, but with the well-being of members of the widget-makers' union. Furthermore, such an investment policy might lead the union to make investments in companies whose activities, while beneficial to members of the widget-makers' union, are harmful to others. Consequently, the investment strategy described above is one that reflects egoistical concerns rather than ethical concerns.

12 Let me begin my examination of the ethics of investing by rejecting one popular view concern-

ing the issue. According to the view in question, we can judge the moral rightness or wrongness of an investment by applying what I shall call the Evil-Company Principle: If a company is at present "evil," it is morally wrong for us to buy its stock. The advocates of the Evil-Company Principle will tell us, for example, that they refuse to buy the stock of any company that owns and operates a nuclear power plant or of any company that manufactures cigarettes. According to these people, the mere fact that such companies are now engaged in wrongdoing – or, at any rate, what they perceive to be wrong-doing – makes it wrong for us to buy their stock.

13   Actually, the advocates of the Evil-Company Principle are not in agreement about just what sort of evil the principle is concerned with. To understand the nature of this difference, let us take a moment to distinguish between two sorts of evil companies, those that are directly evil and those that are indirectly evil.

14   A *directly evil* company is a company which, in the very act of conducting its business, engages in wrongdoing.[3] An *indirectly evil* company, on the other hand, is one which manufactures products that enable others to engage in wrongdoing. Thus, a company that uses slave labor to manufacture, say, pencils would count as directly evil, since in the very act of conducting its business it commits the moral wrong of treating people as slaves. On the other hand, a company whose main product is a poison whose only known use is to cause people horrible lingering deaths would count as indirectly evil, since it manufactures a product that enables other people – namely, the company's customers – to do wrong. It is, of course, possible for a company to be directly evil but not indirectly evil and vice versa. It is likewise possible for a company to be both directly and indirectly evil: An example of this would be a company that used slave labor to manufacture the poison described above.

15   There are, to be sure, legitimate questions about whether particular companies count as evil in either of the above senses. Consider, for example, cigarette manufacturers. Suppose that cigarettes were harmful only to those who chose to use them and that there were no problems concerning the health risks smoking creates for nearby non-smokers. Would cigarette manufacturers then count as indirectly evil? It depends on whether you think it is morally wrong for a person to engage in an activity that harms only himself. If you think it is, you will classify cigarette manufacturers as indirectly evil; otherwise you will not.

16   Once we have distinguished between directly and indirectly evil companies, we can divide the investors who advocate the Evil-Company Principle into various categories. There are, in the first place, investors who think it wrong to purchase the stock of companies that are *either* directly *or* indirectly evil. There are, in the second place, investors who think it wrong to purchase the stock of directly evil companies, but who have no qualms about purchasing the stock of an indirectly evil company. And, amazing as it may seem, there are investors who (seem to) think that it is wrong to purchase the stock of indirectly evil companies, but who have no qualms about purchasing the stock of directly evil companies. I know, for example, investors who shy away from buying the stocks of cigarette manufacturers (assuming, of course, that these companies are indeed indirectly evil), but who would not hesitate to buy the stocks of various directly evil companies.

17   The Evil-Company Principle, although popular, is clearly flawed. After all, we can eas-

ily imagine circumstances under which it would be morally permissible to buy the stock of even a company that is, at present, extremely evil. To keep our discussion concrete, let us imagine a company – call it XYZ Company – that uses slave labor to manufacture the deadly poison described above. XYZ Company, then, is an example of a company that is both directly and indirectly evil, so no matter which version of the Evil-Company Principle an investor may favor, he will be opposed to purchasing the stock of XYZ Company. Suppose that one day, the president of XYZ Company comes to you and announces that he has seen the error of his ways. He offers to sell you a certain amount of his company's stock and promises you that if you buy the stock, he will use the money you invest to rebuild his plants. In particular, he tells you that he plans to introduce machinery so that his manufacturing process will no longer require slave labor, and he tells you that with the new machinery, he will be able to stop manufacturing the deadly poison described above and will instead turn his energies to manufacturing chemicals that are beneficial to mankind. Additionally, he promises that instead of selling his slaves, he will free them and use his company's profits to compensate them for past injustices. Under such circumstances, I think you would be morally blameless if you bought the stock.

18   Given, however, it isn't necessarily wrong to buy the stock of an evil company, we must abandon the Evil-Company Principle: From the mere fact that a company is evil (in some sense of the word), it does not follow – and we are not entitled to conclude – that it is morally wrong to buy the stock of the company. Instead, we should take a conditional approach to investment ethics: It is morally wrong for us to buy the stock of an evil company *only under certain*

circumstances. What we must now determine is the nature of these circumstances.

19   In what follows, let us suppose that XYZ Company is the slave-owning, poison-manufacturing entity described above, but that it has no intention of releasing its slaves and no intention of ceasing its production of the deadly poison in question. Indeed, suppose that the president of the company has publicly stated that he will use any additional capital he can raise to buy more slaves so that he can produce even more of the poison in question. Many would agree that it would, under these circumstances, be wrong to buy XYZ stock. The question we will now address is, *Why* would it be wrong?

20   Some investors will respond to this question by invoking what I call the Tainted-Profits Principle, which says that it is morally wrong for a person to take steps to benefit from the wrongdoing of others. According to these investors, what makes it wrong for me to buy the stock of XYZ Company is the fact that its profits are tainted, so that by becoming a part owner of the company in question and sharing in its tainted profits, I myself become morally tainted.

21   There are at least two ways I might profit from the wrongdoing of XYZ Company. In the first place, the company might distribute some of its profits to me in the form of dividends. These dividends, however, would be blood money, and by accepting them, I would in effect become an accomplice to the crimes of XYZ Company. In the second place, even if XYZ Company does not pay dividends, the value of its stock might appreciate; and if it did, I would once again profit from the wrongdoing of others. Since the Tainted-Profits Principle tells us that any investment that enables me to profit from the wrongdoing of others is morally wrong,

the principle would classify as morally wrong a purchase of XYZ stock.

22   The Tainted-Profits Principle, although commonly appealed to, is clearly false, at least in the form stated above. To see why, consider the following case. Suppose there is a great deal of burglary in my neighborhood. There are many ways in which I might take steps to benefit from this wrongdoing. I might, to begin with, go into the guard business and offer my services to my neighbors as a night watchman; or I might go into the insurance business and sell burglary insurance to my neighbors; or I might go into the tool business and open a store that specializes in the sale of crowbars, tools to pick locks with, glass cutters, etc. In going into any of these three businesses, I will be taking steps to benefit from the wrongdoing of others. Consequently, according to the Tainted-Profits Principle, my going into any of these three businesses will be wrong. This consequence, however, is counterintuitive. Most people would hold that while I may be doing something wrong if I open the tool shop described above, I won't be doing anything wrong if I go into the guard business or the insurance business. What makes my going into the tool business morally objectionable is the fact that my doing so has the effect of *enabling* the wrongdoing I am seeking to benefit from: By selling the tools described, I make it easier for burglars to break into houses. On the other hand, my going into the insurance business will presumably have no effect (or, at any rate, will have a negligible effect) on the wrongdoing I am seeking to benefit from, and my going into the guard business will have the effect of *disenabling* the wrongdoing I am seeking to benefit from.

23   In conclusion, then, it isn't necessarily morally objectionable for a person to take steps to benefit from the wrongdoing of others. What *is* morally objectionable is taking steps in a way that enables others to do wrong.

24   This problem with the Tainted-Profits Principle suggests a somewhat different principle that might be invoked to show that it is morally wrong for me to purchase XYZ stock. This principle, which I call the Enablement Principle, is concerned not with the fact that by buying the stock of a directly evil company I am taking steps to benefit from the wrong that it does, but instead with the fact that by buying the stock of an evil company I sometimes make it easier for others to do wrong.

25   The Enablement Principle can be stated as follows: It is morally wrong for a person to do something that enables others to do wrong. Thus, even if I don't profit from my investment in an evil company, my investment – as long as it enables others to do wrong – will be morally objectionable.

26   Notice that the Enablement Principle differs in at least one important respect from the Evil-Company Principle and the Tainted-Profits Principle. These last two principles were applicable only to a company that is *currently* engaged in wrongdoing. (In the case of the Tainted-Profits Principle, notice that I can't take steps to benefit from the wrongdoing of a company that isn't doing wrong.) The Enablement Principle, on the other hand, is concerned not so much with whether a company is now engaged in wrongdoing as it is with how our investing in the company will affect its ability to do wrong in the future. The Enablement Principle, then, is a "forward-looking" ethical principle, and I take this to be a plus.

27   Even though the Enablement Principle is an improvement over the Tainted-Profits Principle, it will still have its critics.

28   Act-utilitarians, for example, might reject the principle on the grounds that there are cases in which it is morally permissible to do things that enable others to do wrong. Suppose, for example, that one evening a gang of hooligans comes to my door and tells me that unless I provide them with a baseball bat so that they can go around my neighborhood smashing windows, they will spend the evening beating up old people. Suppose that I am powerless to stop them from engaging in either of these activities and that I have good grounds for thinking that if I provide them with a baseball bat, they *will* go around smashing windows instead of beating up old people. (In particular, I am confident that they won't use the baseball bat to beat up old people.) A utilitarian might argue that in these circumstances I have a moral obligation to give them the baseball bat, even though in doing so I am enabling them to do wrong. A utilitarian would remind us that what I am *really* doing is enabling them to do the lesser of two evils, a course of action that the utilitarian will heartily recommend.

29   We can think of similar cases that might arise when we are making investment decisions. Suppose, for example, that the situation is such that if XYZ Company cannot sell stock, it will go out of business, and its former slaves will starve to death as a consequence. If this were indeed the case, a utilitarian might argue that it would not be wrong for us to buy the stock of XYZ Company, even though in buying the stock, we are enabling others to do wrong. They would argue that the harm done if the slaves starve to death outweighs the harm done in treating them as slaves and that we have an obligation to do the thing which has the least harmful consequences.

30   While this criticism does indeed carry weight, I do not think it is fatal to the Enablement Principle. If we agree with the intuitions of the utilitarian, we can simply revise the principle as follows: It is wrong for me to do something that enables others to do wrong, *unless my failure to do the thing in question will have even worse consequences.* Of course, not everyone will share the utilitarian's intuitions, so not everyone will want to make this change.

31   Another objection that might be raised against the Enablement Principle is the following. Suppose that I bought a pair of shoes from a store and that the owner of the store used the money I paid him to buy a gun, which he subsequently used to murder his wife. Suppose, too, that the owner didn't reveal his murderous intentions to me before I bought the shoes and, indeed, that there was no way I could have discovered them. (Perhaps when I was buying the shoes, the owner hadn't yet decided to murder his wife; perhaps the thought came to him only as I was leaving the store.) By buying the shoes, I have done something that enables someone else to do wrong. According to the Enablement Principle, then, my buying shoes was wrong. Many people, however, would say that my buying shoes was a case of "innocent enabling" and consequently that I did nothing wrong in buying them.

32   In investing, similar cases of innocent enabling might occur. Suppose, for example, that because I have purchased the stock of a company, the company is able to pay one of its employees, who in turn uses his pay to do evil things. In an indirect way, my stock purchase has enabled him to do wrong; nevertheless, few people would want to say that it was wrong, under these circumstances, for me to have purchased the stock.

33   In light of the above objection, we might revise the Enablement Principle to take into ac-

count the beliefs of the enabler. This revised version of the principle would read as follows: It is morally wrong for a person to do something that *he realizes* enables others to do wrong. This version of the Enablement Principle distinguishes between cases of innocent enabling and cases of knowing enabling; it classifies only the latter cases as morally objectionable. Thus, in the case of my shoe purchase, since I did not realize that the purchase would enable the store's owner to do wrong, the above revision of the Enablement Principle does not classify my purchase as morally objectionable. On the other hand, if I *had* realized that the owner would use my money in the way he did, the above revision of the Enablement Principle tells us that my buying the shoes was morally objectionable.

34   If we make this change in the Enablement Principle, we will want to use the revised Enablement Principle in conjunction with a second ethical principle, namely, the principle that we have a moral obligation to make *some* effort to determine the likely consequences of our actions. Using these two principles, we can show that there are cases in which the enabler, even though he didn't realize he was enabling others to do wrong, *should* have realized it and was therefore wrong in acting the way he did.

35   The above revision of the Enablement Principle, like the original version, has consequences for investors. According to the revised version of the Enablement Principle, whenever an investor realizes that his purchase of stock enables others to do wrong, his purchase is morally objectionable; and whenever an investor doesn't realize that his purchase of stock enables others to do wrong but *should* realize it, his purchase is likewise morally objectionable

36   Should we, then, abandon our original version of the Enablement Principle in favor of this revised version? Not necessarily. Notice, after all, that some people will think that the original version of the principle is correct in classifying my shoe purchase as morally objectionable. Consider, in particular, act-utilitarians. They will point out that since my refraining from purchasing shoes would have had better consequences than my purchasing shoes, it was wrong for me to purchase shoes. They will not worry about the fact that I couldn't have known that my purchase would have the terrible consequences it did. This is because they judge acts by their consequences, not by the intentions of the agents.

37   We now have before us three different versions of the Enablement Principle, the original version, the utilitarian version, and the version that takes into account the beliefs of the enabler. I will not attempt to show that one of these versions is superior to the others. I do not need to, since the remarks that follow – with some minor changes – are compatible with any of the three versions. Although my remarks are stated in terms of the original version, the reader may, if he wishes, substitute either of the other two versions.

38   In summary, while people might differ over the exact statement of the Enablement Principle, most people will admit that the intuition behind the principle – that some activities are morally objectionable in as much as they enable others to do wrong – is basically correct. It is this intuition that I am appealing to in the remarks that follow.

39 Even those who accept the Enablement Principle might challenge its *applicability to* investment ethics. According to the principle, it is wrong for us to buy the stock of a company whenever doing so enables others to do wrong. It might be suggested, though, that as a practical matter, the stock purchases of "average" investors (i.e., typical American private investors) rarely, if ever,

enable anyone to do wrong; thus, the Enablement Principle will rarely, if ever, classify the stock purchases of average investors as morally wrong.

40   There are two forms that this criticism can take. Let us refer to these as the Old-Stock Objection and the Small-Purchase Objection.

41   According to the Old-Stock Objection, average investors, when they purchase stock, virtually always purchase *old* stock. That is, when they buy stock, they almost always buy it not from the company that originally issued it, but instead from some other investor. Indeed, even when they buy "new issue" stock, they are really buying it not from the issuing company, but from a middleman – namely the underwriter of the issue – who has already (in effect) paid the company for the stock. For the average investor, then, no stock is new stock.

42   Given that this is the case, though, it looks as if the average investor's stock purchases will rarely, if ever, affect a company's ability to conduct its business. For notice that when an investor purchases "old" stock, the money he invests flows not to the company that originally issued the stock, but to the investor who sold him the stock. Since, however, the money he invests does not flow to the company in question, it is hard to see how his investment can affect the company's ability to conduct its business and thereby enable anyone – either inside the company or outside of it – to do wrong.

43   If the above objection is correct, then it does indeed look as if the Enablement Principle will rarely, if ever, prohibit the stock purchases of average investors.

44   In reply to the Old-Stock Objection, let me say this. Even though an investor purchases old stock, and even though his money consequently does not flow to the company that issued the stock, I think that his investment can nevertheless make it easier for the company to conduct its business, in as much as it indirectly enhances the company's ability to raise new capital. Notice, to begin with, that a company's ability to issue new stock depends upon the willingness of investors to buy the stock when it is no longer new. In particular, no underwriter will buy a company's new stock unless there are investors who will buy it – no longer new – from the underwriter. If investors systematically shunned a company's old stock, the company would find it quite difficult to issue any new stock. Notice, too, that a company that found it difficult to issue new stock would be regarded as less creditworthy by lenders than a company that could readily issue new stock. After all, this latter company has a source of cash – viz., the sale of new stock – that the former company does not. Thus, investors' reluctance to buy a company's old stock would not only make it more difficult for the company to issue new stock, but would also make it harder for the company to borrow money. In short, investors' reluctance to buy a company's old stock makes it harder for the company to raise capital. Conversely, the willingness of investors to buy a company's old stock makes it easier for the company to raise capital and thus makes it easier for the company to conduct its business.

45   What this shows is that when I buy old stock, my purchase can make it easier for the company to conduct its business, even though the money I invest doesn't flow to the company in question. The causal connection between my purchase of a company's old stock and the company's ability to conduct its business is indirect, but it is nevertheless real.

46   Like the Old-Stock Objection, the Small-Purchase Objection tells us that the Enablement

Principle, while perhaps true, is of limited applicability to the stock purchases of average investors. Where the two objections differ is over the reason why this is so. According to the Old-Stock Objection, the Enablement Principle will almost never classify the stock purchases of average investors as wrong because average investors almost always buy old stock; according to the Small-Purchase Objection, the Enablement Principle will almost never classify the stock purchases of average investors as wrong because the stock purchases of average investors are almost always small.

47   To better understand the Small-Purchase Objection, consider the following reasoning. If a company has a million shares of stock outstanding and I purchase 100,000 of them, my purchase might drive up the price of the stock and thus, in an indirect way, make it easier for the company to conduct its business. (If the stock price increases, the ability of the company to raise new capital generally also increases.) If, however, a company has a million shares of stock outstanding and I purchase two of these shares, my purchase will in no way affect the stock's price and consequently will in no way affect the company's ability to conduct its business. Indeed, it is likely that the only person in the company who even realizes that I made my purchase is the person whose job it is to keep track of shareholders.

48   Granted, however, that a small purchase of a company's stock has virtually no effect on the company in question, it is hard to see how the purchase can enable the company or anyone outside the company to do wrong. Consequently, it looks as if the Enablement Principle will almost never classify small purchases of stock — i.e., the sorts of purchases average investors almost always make — as morally wrong.

49   In reply to the Small-Purchase Objection, let me say this: I agree that small purchases of stock do not, in and of themselves, affect the ability of a company to do its business; nevertheless, I don't think this gets the average investor off the hook, morally speaking. The real question, from a moral point of view, is not whether his one purchase affects the ability of the company to conduct its business, but rather whether his purchase, if imitated by many other investors, would affect the ability of the company to conduct its business.

50   What I am doing at this point is invoking what ethicists call the Universalizability Principle. There are any number of cases in which the behavior of one person won't make any real difference to the world. Consider the standard ethical example: walking across newly-seeded grass. If one person walks across newly-seeded grass, it won't harm the grass. Nevertheless, it is presumably wrong for even one person to walk across the grass. After all, if everyone followed his reasoning — that this one case of walking won't hurt the grass — the results would be undesirable. Thus, walking on the grass is wrong, not because one act of walking in and of itself will cause any harm, but because the act is not universalizable: If everyone who was in a position to do the act went ahead and did it, harm would be done.

51   There are, to be sure, any number of problems we encounter when we try to give a precise statement of the Universalizability Principle. It looks, for example, as if the principle can be used to show that celibacy is wrong, or that living in America is wrong. (How would you like it if *everyone* were celibate? Our species would soon be extinct. How would you like it if *everyone* lived in America? Think of the miserable living conditions that would result.) The principle

does, however, have strong intuitive appeal, and there is reason for thinking the problems described can be overcome.[4]

52   We can use the Universalizability Principle in conjunction with the Enablement Principle to show that even though a small purchase of stock won't affect a company's ability to conduct its business, the consequence of many investors making (or attempting to make) such an investment would indeed affect a company's ability to conduct its business. Therefore, even the decisions of a small investor have ethical implications.

53 Suppose, then, that we accept the Enablement Principle. What, exactly, does this principle tell us about the ethics of investing?

54   Basically, the principle gives us the following piece of advice: When we are weighing the purchase of a certain company's stock, we should ask ourselves the following question: "Would this sort of investment, if made by many people, enable others to do wrong?" If the answer to this question is yes, and if we nevertheless purchase the stock, we can justifiably be accused of moral wrongdoing.

55   Thus, the Enablement Principle tells us that it is wrong for me to buy the stock of a *directly* evil company if the company has no plans to change its mode of operation. My purchase of the stock of such a company will, after all, enable the company to go on being directly evil, in as much as it will enhance the company's ability to raise new capital. If, on the other hand, the company does have plans to change its mode of operation, then my purchase of its stock might or might not be morally objectionable.

56   Similarly, the Enablement Principle tells us that it is wrong for me to buy the stock of an *indirectly* evil company that has no plans to change

the products it manufactures. After all, if my purchase enables the company to manufacture products which in turn enable those who purchase the products to harm others, then my purchase will indirectly enable others to do wrong. The "others" in question, it is worth noting, will not be the employees of the company, but will instead be the purchasers of the company's products. (Remember that the Enablement Principle does not limit the "others" I enable to do wrong to the employees of the company whose stock I am purchasing.)

57   Besides classifying our purchases of the stocks of certain evil companies as objectionable, the Enablement Principle will also classify our purchases of the stocks of certain morally upright companies as objectionable. Suppose, for example, that a morally upright company has plans to "go bad," and that our purchase of its stock will somehow help it carry out these plans. Because our purchase of the company's stock would enable it to do wrong, the Enablement Principle would classify our purchase as objectionable, even though the company we are investing in is not, at the time of the investment, evil.

58   Above I have applied the Enablement Principle only to stock purchases. It should be apparent, though, that the principle is likewise applicable to other sorts of investments. It might be argued, for example, that a variant of the Enablement Principle will tell us that it is wrong, under certain circumstances, to buy a company's *bonds* or *warrants*.[5] Such purchases can, after all, enable a company to conduct its business by enhancing the company's ability to raise capital, and can thus, under some circumstances, enable others to do wrong.

59   Although the Enablement Principle condemns the above sorts of investment activities,

it is silent concerning the morality of other investment activities. Consider, for example, cases in which investors sell a stock short.[6] Although purchases of a company's stocks, bonds, and warrants, might enhance the company's ability to raise new capital, the short sale of a company's stock, if it has any effect on a company, has just the opposite effect. When an investor sells a stock short, it has the effect of increasing the supply of the stock and this in turn places downward pressure on the price of the stock. (This is not to say that short selling will necessarily cause the price of the stock to fall. If demand for the stock increases more than the supply of the stock, the price of the stock will rise despite short-selling.) This downward pressure will harm rather than help the company: It will, after all, hinder the company's ability to raise new capital and thus hinder the company's ability to conduct its business. Given, however, that a short sale of a company's stock does not enhance a company's ability to conduct its business, the Enablement Principle will nor classify the sale as morally objectionable.

60   Suppose, then, that an investor, after hearing of the disaster that occurred in Bhopal, India, in December of 1984, in which a gas leak at a Union Carbide plant killed and injured thousands of people, reacted by calling his broker and asking him to sell Union Carbide stock short. (In doing so, the investor would be hoping to profit from the decline in Union Carbide stock that he thought would take place as a result of the Bhopal disaster.) Since this transaction does not enable anyone to do wrong — notice, in particular, that it does not somehow enable Union Carbide to harm more Indians than it otherwise would — the Enablement Principle will not classify the transaction as morally objectionable.

61   I, for one, do not have any problems with this conclusion. This is because I don't think that the above investor, in selling Union Carbide stock short, did anything morally objectionable. Perhaps we can accuse him of cold-heartedness — what else can you say about a person who reacts to the Bhopal tragedy by calling his broker to profit from it? — but I don't think we can accuse him of moral wrongdoing.

62   Before ending my discussion of the ethics of investing, let me make a few closing remarks.

63   In the first place, it is worth noting that in investing, as in other aspects of life, there are incentives to be immoral. If enough investors shun a stock because they realize that it would be morally wrong for them to buy it, the price of the stock will likely fall. If it falls enough, though, the stock in question could become quite attractive. Suppose, for example, that a stock that pays a dividend of $1 per share falls, because of investor avoidance, to a price of $5 per share. As the price falls, the yield of the stock will climb to 20 percent, which in turn will make the stock quite attractive to investors. Investors will, as a consequence, have a real incentive to do the immoral thing and buy the stock in question. If they wish to be moral persons, however, investors have to learn how to fight this temptation, the same way as they have learned to fight the temptation to buy stolen tires at bargain prices.

64   In the second place, I would like to point out that ethical investors will have to work a bit harder than unethical investors to find acceptable investments. All an unethical investor has to do is find stocks that look promising from a financial point of view; an ethical investor, after finding stocks that look promising from a financial point of view, must go on to ask whether the stocks in question are acceptable from a moral point of view.

65   Some investors, on hearing this, will complain that they don't have the time or energy to inquire into the moral acceptability of investments. In reply to this complaint, let me say this. I don't think the process of investigating the moral acceptability of an investment is as time-consuming as the above investors make it out to be. It would indeed be time-consuming – not to say impossible – for an investor to make *absolutely certain* that a company was morally upright before investing in it. He would have not only to read the company's financial documents, but also to visit its plants, talk to its employees, etc. As it so happens, though, morality does not require us to be absolutely certain of the moral implications of our actions before acting; instead, it requires only that we make a "reasonable effort" to inquire into these moral implications before acting.

66   Consider a parallel case from outside the realm of investing. Suppose a stranger comes to your door and offers to sell you a slightly used set of tires for a remarkably low price. If you buy the tires without asking any questions, we will hold you morally blameworthy if the tires turn out to be stolen. If, on the other hand, you make a "reasonable effort" to determine their true ownership before buying them (e.g., if you ask to see purchase receipts), we won't hold you morally blameworthy if they in fact turn out to be stolen (and the receipts turn out to be counterfeits). As a buyer of tires – and as a buyer of stocks – you have a moral obligation to ask a few questions before you enter into a transaction.

67   It is, to be sure, difficult to say exactly what constitutes a "reasonable effort" to inquire into the moral implications of our investments. I think it is clear, though, that any investor who buys stocks in companies without the least idea of what the companies do or how they do it is not fulfilling his moral obligations as an investor. On the other hand, I think that an investor who has read a company's annual report and assimilated the information contained in it has gone a long way toward making a "reasonable effort." If I am correct in this belief, then the work involved in being an ethical investor isn't all that burdensome. Indeed, many investors, in the process of determining that a company is attractive from a financial point of view, will already have read the company's annual report and will be in a good position to form an opinion concerning the moral acceptability of the investment.

68   I would also like to point out that even if it did require a substantial amount of work to determine the moral acceptability of an investment, the ethical investor will nevertheless be willing to do the work in question; and if he feels unable to do it, he will give up investing altogether. In the same way as it is sometimes inconvenient to buy food instead of stealing it or to keep promises instead of breaking them, it will sometimes be inconvenient to inquire into the moral status of a company before investing in it. The inconveniences of being moral, however, in no way lessen our obligation to be moral, and this is a point investors must not forget.

69   Finally, I would like to mention that while I think that the Enablement Principle is correct and is an important tool for investors to use when making investment decisions, I do not pretend that it tells us all there is to know about the ethics of investing. It tells us that one sort of investment is wrong; as our discussion of contractual obligations shows, however, it is not the only sort of investment that is morally objectionable.

70   Furthermore, there are other ethical principles that may sometimes override the

Enablement Principle. Consequently, although the Enablement Principle is indeed an important ethical principle, it is just one of many ethical principles that an ethical investor must appeal to when determining the moral acceptability of an investment.

NOTES

1. From the October 1, 1984 Prospectus of the Dreyfus Third Century Fund.

2. From the January 1, 1984 Prospectus of the Calvert Social Investment Fund.

3. Some companies, of course, sell not goods but services to the public. If the services such a company offers are morally objectionable, then the company in question will count as directly evil, since the objectionable activity is done by the company "in the very act of conducting its business."

4. For a nice discussion of the problems of the principle of universalizability as well as possible solutions of these problems, see Kurt Baier's *The Moral Point of View* (Ithaca: Cornell University Press, 1958), pp. 208-213.

5. A warrant is a right to buy the stock of the company for a certain price during a certain time period.

6. For non-investors, short selling is a paradoxical activity, for it is a way to make money from a *decline* in stock prices. To sell a stock short is simply to sell borrowed stock. Suppose, for example, that a certain stock is trading at $10 a share. You might sell it short by borrowing 100 shares of it and selling them, gaining $1000 from the sale. Now suppose the stock declines to $8 a share. You can buy 100 shares back for $800; once you return these 100 shares to whoever lent their to you, you will have no further obligations. Notice, however, that you will have a profit of $200, since the $800 you repurchased the stock for is less than the $1000 you sold it for.

Questions

1. Is Irvine's objection to the Evil-Company Principle (applicable to both strands of it) strong enough for you to reject the principle?

2. The utilitarian approach presents a strong objection to Irvine's Enablement Principle. What is it and what does he do about it?

3. In tandem with his third version of the Enablement Principle, Irvine suggests that "we have a moral obligation to make some effort to determine the likely consequences of our action" (P34). Do you agree? How much "some" would be enough?

4. Explain and assess the Old-Stock Objection and the Small-Purchase Objection.

5. A version of the Tainted-Profits Principle has been invoked to suggest that universities refuse certain donations. Consider Irvine's objection to the principle and decide whether this application of it has any merit.

Capitalist Crunch

Anders Hayden

1   During last winter's RRSP blitz, Vancouver-based Ethical Funds Inc. (EFI) launched an aggressive ad campaign with the slogan "Not in my portfolio," offering investors the "winning combination" of "profits and principles" and the opportunity to "feel good about your finances." EFI's slick brochure began with pictures of Asian kids smoking cigarettes, tanks in Tiananmen Square, and despoiled landscapes – practices their investors supposedly aren't sullied by. Next came images of mountain-top panoramas, flourishing rainforests, and happy nuclear families peering at sunsets over breaking waves, all ending with a full-page call to "Do the right thing."

2   This campaign, with its attacks on the "ugly corporate practices" behind the profits of other mutual funds, helped push EFI's assets above the $2-billion mark. It also attracted greater scrutiny of EFI's own ethically questionable behaviour.

3   In March, *The Vancouver Sun* broke the story that EFI was investing in three companies violating its ethical screens: tobacco-owner Imasco, military-supplier Bombardier, and gold miner Placer Dome, which EFI had dropped as an individual holding two years earlier following a large mine spill in the Philippines. EFI had invested in these companies through Toronto 35 Index Participation Units (TIPS), an abstract fund reflecting performance of the Toronto Stock Exchange's top 35 companies. In fact, this unscreened investment was the single largest holding of Ethical Growth Fund – the flagship of EFI's eight funds.

4   After the bad press, EFI decided TIPS would no longer be held. But because alternative money market investments cannot match the returns of TIPS, investors will almost certainly take a financial hit. It's the kind of real-world trade-off between profits and principles that EFI claims to have transcended.

5   Back in 1986 when Ethical Growth Fund was introduced by VanCity Credit Union, many financial analysts argued that ethical considerations could not be brought into investment without seriously reducing rates of return. Twelve years later, Ethical Growth is earning more than conventional investments, and was even named 1998 "Fund of the Year" by mutual fund guru Gordon Pape. The other Canadian "ethical" fund families – Clean Environment, Investor's Summa, and Desjardins Environment – also produce above-average returns. Competitive returns and rapid growth of assets give advocates of socially conscious investment hope of finally gaining respect on Bay Street.

6   But a closer look at EFI, Canada's largest ethical fund family, reveals that its trumpeted high returns have been made possible by ethically dubious investments, such as the unscreened investment in TIPS and large holdings of Canada's ethically suspect banks, not to mention screening criteria so weak that a

Anders Hayden, "Capitalist Crunch" *This Magazine* 32.1 (July/August 1998): 23–26. © 1998 by Anders Hayden. Reprinted with permission of the author.

number of the planet's worst corporations make the grade. Furthermore, EFI has not only failed to use its potential clout as an active shareholder, it has helped thwart progressive shareholder actions.

7   The case of EFI also raises questions for the broader ethical investment community, a young movement which has been preoccupied with financial performance anxiety and has yet to develop widely accepted ethical standards for the industry. And it triggers the big question of whether it is possible to succeed ethically in today's financial casino economy, a system based on making paper mega-profits off the labour of others, a structure that is itself on questionable ethical ground.

8   Screening is the foundation upon which "ethical" mutual funds are built. Negative screens rule out firms that do not live up to particular values, and positive screens favour good practices. EFI's screens cover tobacco, military weapons, nuclear energy, racial equality, industrial relations, and the environment. Sounds promising, but the wording of its commitments is often vague, such as "progressive industrial and employee relations" and "environmentally conscious practices," or utterly minimal, like "compliance with labour and environmental laws". In fact, despite EFI's promise of "the peace of mind that comes with knowing you are not contributing to the exploitation of people or the environment," these criteria do not rule out investing in environmentally unsustainable activities or paying workers less than a living wage.

9   EFI uses a "best of sector" approach to put screening into practice. But even Michael Jantzi, president of Michael Jantzi Research Associates, which provides best-of-sector analysis for clients including EFI, openly admits the approach "does mean compromise." It was designed to allow investment in large sectors of the Canadian economy, like resource extraction, which might be off-limits with stronger criteria. Jantzi, nonetheless, maintains that the approach is sound: "We don't believe social investors are looking for perfection, but for change."

10   David Nitkin, president of EthicScan, a Toronto ethics consultancy firm, cautions that "best of sector may still be grossly inappropriate in environmental and social terms." For instance, a logging firm with unsustainable practices may be the best of a bad lot. Nitkin favours a more rigorous standard of "ethical practice," for example, sustainably managing forests, even if few companies meet it at present.

11   But at EFI, even the weak best-of-sector standard isn't applied to Canada's big banks, all five of which appear in its funds. The target of public wrath over exorbitant profits and CEO salaries, high service charges, and miserly small business lending and community reinvestment, banks are among EFI's largest holdings, accounting for about 16 per cent of Ethical Growth Fund. This is particularly ironic since EFI is owned by the Canadian credit union system.

12   Critics such as economist Jim Stanford of the Canadian Automobile Workers (CAW) argue that the banks have lobbied for economic policies such as zero inflation, government cutbacks, and deliberate efforts to depress labour markets: "The interests of the financial sector run counter to those of most Canadians. Don't invest in one of the most reactionary vested interests in Canada and call it ethical."

13   But Jantzi, who says he's "sick of bank bashing," highlights the banks' progressive work-family policies, workplace diversity, and charitable contributions. "Banks do some positive things," he says, before adding what may be the more relevant point: "You cannot eliminate them from

contention. They represent about 15 per cent of the market."

14 The most fundamental ethical problem with banks is, in the words of David Olive, a senior writer at the *Financial Post*, that they "lend to just about everybody – from tobacco firms to arms dealers. Banks are complicit in everything their clients do." And so, by extension, are investors in ethical funds with bank stock – an uncomfortable fact that the ethical investment movement has yet to come to terms with.

15 The combination of banks and TIPS means that over 20 per cent of Ethical Growth Fund has, in effect, been unscreened until recently. Surprising enough, but that's before looking at what gets through EFI's weak screens. Ethical North American Equity Fund, for instance (EFI's "best performer" with staggering one-year returns of 66.1 per cent), has embraced a number of the corporate world's ethical bottom feeders. Disney, one of 1996's 10 worst corporations according to *Multinational Monitor*, a muckraking American magazine founded by Ralph Nader, appears in the fund. While CEO Michael Eisner's 1996 compensation was estimated at $190 million (U.S.), Disney contractors pay Third World workers as little as $1 a day to make Mickey Mouse T-shirts in sweatshop conditions.

16 Nike, number seven on *Multinational Monitor*'s 1997 10 worst corporations list (for making "both the swoosh and sweatshops famous") was also held by Ethical North American in 1997. It was dropped in the second half of the year, but EFI would not say whether it was the result of long-running ethical concerns raised by social activists or simply a response to Nike's limp financial performance.

17 EFI also invests in U.S. healthcare firms, which *Left Business Observer* editor Doug Henwood calls "corporate substitutes for a civi-lized single payer system that profit from denying people care." Sun Healthcare, an Ethical Balanced Fund investment, has not only faced charges of fraudulent billing at home, it is aggressively expanding into Canada, hoping to profit from the erosion of our healthcare system through its subsidiary, Columbia. Meanwhile, U.S. based Columbia/HCA Healthcare is held by Ethical North American, despite climbing to number eight on 1997's 10 worst corporations chart. According to the *Monitor*, it "cut costs, slashed staff and put profits before patients" and is currently facing charges from the U.S. government of forging a "systematic corporate scheme" to defraud federal health programs. Richard Rainwater, the company's co-founder, proclaims, "The day has come when somebody has to do in the hospital business what McDonald's has done in the fast-food business and what Wal-Mart has done in the retailing business."

18 For good measure, Wal-Mart, the folks who demand total loyalty from their low-wage part-timers, were caught red-handed intimidating unionizers in Windsor, Ontario, and turn downtowns into ghost towns through predatory pricing, also fed Ethical North American's profit machine in 1997.

19 EFI's funds embrace many Canadian firms of questionable repute, as well. Examples include: Bell Canada (massive downsizings at a time of high profits); Canadian Occidental Petroleum (offshore drilling in Nigeria – a country notorious for human rights abuse – and a subsidiary of Occidental Petroleum, *Multinational Monitor*'s sixth worst corporation of 1997); Magna International ("a pattern of threats and intimidation of workers to prevent unionization," say CAW reps); Northern Telecom and Nova (both with projects linked to Burma's oppressive regime); Power Financial Corporation

(a 1,418 per cent increase in the CEO's already seven figure compensation – 1997's worst case of Canadian CEO excess); and Seagram's (one of *Multinational Monitor*'s 10 worst firms in 1996 for breaking a decades-old voluntary ban in the U.S. on broadcast advertising for hard liquor.)

20 A further illustration of EFI's inadequate screening process occurred when Ethical Growth Fund, despite claiming nuclear-free status, purchased Ontario Hydro bonds in June 1997. Margaret Yee, senior vice-president of EFI, ascribes this ethical meltdown to a case of "human error," adding that, "within three days of finding the mistake, we divested." But, according to Eugene Ellmen, author of the annual *Canadian Ethical Money Guide* and unofficial watchdog for the industry, this lapse "shows that the ethical advisory committee is not on active watch of the portfolio."

21 Yee says EFI learned from this nuclear incident, and has since hired a full-time ethics officer. This theme of learning and trying to improve runs throughout our interview. She emphasizes the thoroughness of EFI's screening, but when confronted with a lengthy list of questionable EFI holdings, she refuses to comment on particular firms. Repeating "it always goes back to our ethical principles" like a mantra, Yee leaves me with the impression that most of the tough questions EFI has faced until now have been about financial performance rather than their ethical *raison d'être*.

22 Yee does admit that in ethical investment "there are lots of grey areas." And, she adds, "All we offer is one investment option. It's up to individuals to decide if they agree before investing." That contradicts the inspirational rhetoric of EFI's ad campaign, but Yee's point about the responsibility of investors to read the fine print is a good one.

23 Are other "ethical" funds in Canada any better than EFI? Desjardins Environment investors will have to be prepared to stomach four of five big banks and arms supplier Bombardier, while asking themselves what aluminum smelters, multinational oil companies, auto parts-makers, and shopping mall builders are doing in an "environment" fund. Investor's Summa takes a stronger stand than EFI on alcohol, gambling and pornography, but has no labour relations screen and counts all five big banks among its 1997 top 10 holdings.

24 Some ethical investors have turned to bank-free Clean Environment funds. But, ironically, fund manager Ian Ihnatowycz does not consider Clean Environment to be an "ethical" investment since he does not screen out any particular offences. In principle, the fund targets firms developing environmental technologies that contribute to "sustainable growth." Its portfolio includes Ballard Power Systems, producer of potentially revolutionary fuel cells. However, "environmental technologies" is a loose term, and can also include companies whose technologies may actually cause net environmental damage. One of the main holdings is Philip Services, which has lobbied for privatization of municipal water services. The fund also includes many non-environmental firms, from frozen yogurt makers to that ethical favourite, Disney.

25 In 1991, the Ethical Investment Research Information Service in the U.K. estimated that 19 of 23 ethical, socially screened, or green mutual funds in that country were "scams." But Ellmen doesn't think any of the Canadian funds merit that tag, maintaining that "fund managers are trying to do a sincere job to get companies that fit their guidelines."

26 Still, rumours of at least one scam circulate within the industry. One insider tells of a fund

manager ridiculing his wife for buying household "green" products, adding "the only thing green about our environment fund is the commission cheque I receive every month." When the fund dropped environmental objectives from its prospectus, the manager was asked why the investment criteria were changed. "We did not change the investment criteria," he replied. "But we did decide not to emphasize the green aspect of the fund for marketing purposes." He added, in a classic double entendre, "We are as socially concerned today just as in the past."

27 Nitkin has a similar story to share. Although he won't name names, he cringed when an "ethical" fund client told him, "Ethical funds are BS. I'm advertising myself as ethical to take advantage of the movement."

28 A major irony in ethical investment is the lack of accepted standards for ethical practice within the industry. "It's an open secret at least some of the funds are seriously questionable in terms of their standards," says Nitkin. He perceives a glaring lack of rules governing screening criteria, portfolio choices, marketing, and what can be labelled an ethical or environmental fund. In fact, the closest thing to a standard for being part of the club is inclusion of social, environmental, or ethical criteria in a fund's prospectus. But no independent body regulates fund practices.

29 Robert Walker, Executive Director of the Social Investment Organization (SIO), formed in 1989 to promote socially responsible investment, says his organization is considering a statement of principles for investment advisors in its directory. As for regulating the funds themselves, no specific plans exist, although, Walker says, the idea is "at the back of our minds."

30 Nitkin, however, urges the SIO to act: "If we can set standards for used car dealers and the securities industry, why not for the ethical funds? This should be the core of what they're doing. If nothing else, it better not stink from inside." Nitkin went public with his concerns last October in a letter to *The Globe and Mail*'s Report on Business. For his efforts, he felt "savaged" by the "ethical investment establishment." His intent was to offer constructive criticism but, he concluded, "We are now in a stage of uncritical belief."

31 Of course, it is not always easy to find ethical standards everyone can agree on. In the U.S., some funds screen in favour of firms with same-sex benefits, while others, such as the Timothy Plan, screen out "sinful" pro-homosexual and pro-choice firms. Or take the example of Noranda, an EFI holding that has been hailed as a leader in environmental management and reporting, but, as David Olive points out, is "the U.S. Interior Department's poster boy for bad environmental practices after its handling of tailings at a Colorado gold mine."

32 Doug Henwood's pet peeve is zero tolerance for tobacco. Why screen out cigarettes and invest in finance, a "parasitical" sector feeding off the real economy, he asks? He sees this as "cheap moral bombast involving no significant challenge to the social order."

33 So if funds such as EFI are not ethical enough, what can be done? Some critics believe dialogue can push the funds in a more ethical direction. "I don't want to trash ethical funds. They're still new and their clout is increasing," says Daniel Gennarelli, co-ordinator of the Task Force on the Churches and Corporate Responsibility. "But I would like to see their decision-making over ethical issues mature."

34 Gennarelli challenges the funds to engage in dialogue with firms over their questionable practices, support shareholder activism to change

company ways, and even go to the courts if necessary to overcome company resistance to shareholder actions. "If they're not committed in these areas of action, then I'd have to shrug and say it's just slick marketing," he says.

35   There's little sign yet of such commitment, at least from EFI. In fact, EFI actually voted against a shareholder resolution to cap CEO salaries at the Royal Bank, on the grounds that executive pay is a "governance" issue not an "ethical" one. In contrast, the B.C. Federation of Labour, supported by the SIO and others, recently used its voice as a shareholder in major retailers to pressure them into joining a coalition calling for a national task force to eliminate child and sweatshop labour.

36   Socially conscience investors who are not satisfied with the ethical funds, and who are prepared for lower returns, can look into "alternative" investments like community loan funds, co-operatives and micro-enterprises. Walker also sees room for a "groovier" mutual fund that goes beyond screening to target investment in cutting-edge companies with a strong social vision.

37   One example that sets the ethical bar a lot higher is the Ecumenical Development Co-operative Society (EDCS). It provides loans for environmentally sound, co-operative development projects in Third World communities. No 66 per cent returns here – a maximum two per cent is paid to investors. But then again, you aren't giving your money to Disney or the banks.

38   Stanford calls for visionary alternatives to the "hogwash" of ethical funds, such as social investment pools of democratically owned capital financing the provision of useful goods and services for moderate returns of two or three per cent. Until then, "the number one thing a truly ethical investor should do is be active in the struggle for public pensions and a society where we take care of everyone, whether or not they have a big mutual fund."

39   Bringing ethics into investment is clearly far more difficult than the hype suggests. If the promise of ethical investment is to actually be fulfilled, putting ethical rigour before financial performance, accepting the responsibilities of active shareholding, and adopting ethical standards for the industry would all be places to start. More honesty about the trade-offs involved, less self-righteous promotion, and a healthy uneasiness about making paper profits off the labour of others might help too. With hundreds of billions of dollars in pension savings crying out to be used more ethically, it is time to find ways to truly do the right thing.

Questions

1. Explain Nitkin's objection to the best-of-sector approach.

2. Should "the banks" be in an ethical investment fund?

3. Is there anything "wrong" with an investment return of 2–3% (as per the EDCS and Stanford's suggestion)?

4. Prepare a proposal for the SIO regarding screening criteria for ethical funds. Consider submitting it to the SIO.

Case Study – Investing in China

Just as indirect foreign investment by way of including foreign stock in one's investment portfolio is subject to ethical examination, so too is the direct foreign investment of setting up and operating a business in a foreign country – both provide capital to the country. Indeed, not only foreign investment, but also foreign trade – which also provides capital – may be subject to ethical examination.

This is especially, and currently, true with respect to China. Because of its record of human rights abuses (religious and political persecution – China is the country of the famed Tiananmen Square massacre of students protesting for democracy, forced abortions and sterilizations, sale of organs from condemned prisoners, etc.), doing business in and with China may be considered ethically unacceptable.

Some think that doing business in and with such a country supports the repressive regime by providing products, revenue, infrastructure, and legitimacy. Arguments once made about South Africa are also applicable to China, with slight modifications:

> The argument generally made for ethical investing, divestment, disinvestment, and sanctions is that these measures will isolate South Africa, cut its access to international markets, increase the cost of obtaining needed supplies, reduce or eliminate the import of capital, and in time create enough economic hardship so that the government will be forced to make concessions and eliminate apartheid. (Paul and Aquila 695)

Some, however, think that doing business in and with a repressive regime is the way to change it because companies can introduce and uphold democratic values, as well as provide employment and thus empowerment for its peoples: "trading with China is the best way to promote freedom and prosperity in that country" ("Deal Not Up to Our Standards"). And some think that all of this is none of a company's business.

As just suggested, the decisions involving China today are not unlike those involving South Africa 15 or 20 years ago. Some companies stayed and some left (and some decided not to get involved in the first place). Many of those who stayed decided not to conform to the racist policies and procedures of the apartheid system; in fact, in April 1978, the Canadian government issued "The Code of Conduct Concerning the Employment Practices of Canadian Companies Operating in South Africa," a code that covered general working conditions, collective bargaining, wages, training and promotion, race relations, and fringe benefits. But even now, with some degree of hindsight and the chance to observe cumulative and long-term effects, opinion is divided: government and business leaders in South Africa acknowledge that international efforts proved successful in dismantling the apartheid system, but some question the effect of sanctions on the very people they were intended to help – during the trade sanction years, poor South Africans were hard hit and poverty increased.

Certainly the contemporary business community reflects these mixed opinions with respect to China. Levi Strauss Canada has pulled out of China because of its human rights record. Toronto-based Bata (a shoe company) refuses to manufacture in China because of the safety and child labour issues, but it is setting up stores there. Several Canadian companies are involved in the Three Gorges dam project – controversial not only for involvement in China but also for the dam's environmental impact – but Ontario Hydro is no longer one of them. And several of Canada's top life insurance companies have set up shop in China, a spokesperson for Manufacturer's Life explaining that they were comfortable with the way they will operate with respect to their employees and their customers, and they will be providing a needed product.

In fact, at the 1998 annual general meeting of the Canada China Business Council, a private sector, nonprofit membership organization incorporated in 1978 to facilitate and promote trade and investment between Canada and China, Canadian Prime Minister Jean Chretien claimed that 350 Canadian firms now have offices or investments in China. He also announced the following agreement with China's Premier Zhu Rongji:

> to pursue the following three goals over the next five years: first, to double direct investment in our two countries; second, to give a major boost to the number of small and medium sized firms that are doing business in our respective countries; and third, to lead Team China and Team Canada missions in the next few years. (Chretien 6-7)

Indeed, Chretien's Team Canada trade mission in 1994 generated $8.6 billion in business/trade deals. Canada has even sold a couple Candu nuclear reactors to China.

Of course, our government's role in business with China has not gone uncriticized. Davison notes:

> our government leaders are far more interested in playing the role of business agent and national advertiser on behalf of Canadian corporate interests, than in highlighting the situations of human rights in other countries.... [O]ur government leaders stay silent, and shy away from any critical comment regarding violations committed by governments which are the worse offenders in the world because the same governments represent and control lucrative markets and other forms of financial opportunity for Canadian businessmen. (44–45)

Davison concludes that "we have, in a certain way, sold our morals, ethics and values, in order to ensure that rich Canadians can continue to profit from the terrible and unfortunate plights of repressed people in other lands" (45). And yet, the South Africa situation seems to suggest that it may be possible to do "good" business in a "bad" country.

REFERENCES

Bond, Kenneth M. "To Stay or to Leave: The Moral Dilemma of Divestment of South African Assets." *Journal of Business Ethics* 7.1-2 (January/February 1988): 9-18.

Chretien, Jean. "Canada-China Business Council." *Presidents & Prime Ministers* 7.6 (November/December 1998): 6-7.

Culpeper, Roy. "Making Global Trade Work for All People: Canadian Governments and Businesses could be Leaders in promoting Rights and Values along with Trade." *The Hamilton Spectator* 10 Feb. 1989: A9+.

Davison, Charles B. "Trading in Rights." *Law Now* 20.6 (June/July 1996): 44-45.

"Deal Not Up to Our Standards." *The Financial Post* 12 Dec. 1996: 12.

"Development & Peace Catches Attention of Levi's Head Office." *Catholic New Times* 20.4 (February 18, 1996): 1, 11.

Freeman, Linda. *How Canada Failed South Africa.* Toronto: University of Toronto Press, 1998.

Paul, Karen, and Dominc A. Aquila. "Political Consequences of Ethical Investing: The Case of South Africa." *Journal of Business Ethics* 7.9 (September 1988): 691-697.

Rainbow Revolution Exploration. <http://www.rainbow-revolution.com>

Spoke, Frederick. "Business in China: Change creates Opportunity." *Ivey Business Journal* 63.3 (March/April 1999): 12-13.

Swift, Alan. "Bata Sells Business in 'Corrupt' Nigeria." *The Toronto Star* 8 Oct. 1997: D10.

Yellin, Susan. "Life Insurers Alammed for 'Repressive' Nations Offices." *The Financial Post* 13 Nov. 1996: 10.

Questions

1. Which ethical theories do you think provide most help with the decisions about investing in China?

2. Canada's First Nations reserves have been referred to by some as another form of apartheid. Should other nations take economic actions (divestment, disinvestment, sanctions) against Canada on this basis?

3. "A recent study by the International Centre for Human Rights and Democratic Development recommended that the Department of Foreign Affairs and International Trade maintain a registry, flagging countries that are serious human-rights abusers, and providing guidelines for Canadian businesses so they can avoid activities that bolster the repressive capacity of the regime" (Culpeper).

   (a) Do you think this is a good recommendation?

   (b) What sorts of guidelines would you need?

Section IV

Institutionalizing Ethics

INSTITUTIONALIZING ETHICS

Introductory Note

An ethically good workplace depends, to a large extent, on having people who understand and engage in ethically good decision-making. However, some companies institutionalize or formalize their ethics as well (and hopefully it is "as well" rather than "instead"), adding a sort of organizational behaviour to individual behaviour.

Ethics Offices/Officers/Committees

First, companies can create an ethics office and appoint or hire an ethics officer; often an ethics committee is formed. Ethics officers, note Ferrell and Fraedrich, are responsible for the following:

> coordinating the ethical compliance program with top management, the board of directors, and senior management; developing, revising, and disseminating a code of ethics; developing effective communication of ethical standards; establishing audit and control systems to determine the effectiveness of the program; developing consistent means of enforcing codes and standards; reviewing and modifying the ethics program to improve its effectiveness. (178)

In addition (or as part of the ethics program), the ethics officer or committee may act as a support system for people trying to do the right thing. At the very least, ethics officers are usually available for consultations to help resolve ethical dilemmas.

Unfortunately, it seems to me, ethics officers are usually high-ranking people in the company: Kelley notes that "in many cases, the job is reserved for longtime company loyalists" (20). I say this is unfortunate because I'm not at all convinced that "the cream rises to the top" with regard to promotions, to how one becomes high-ranking; nor am I at all convinced that company loyalty is a good thing for ethics officers to have.

Perhaps even more unfortunately, these people hardly ever have any ethics training or expertise; sometimes they're from the legal department (and we now understand the iffy relationship between legality and morality); often they're from the human resources department (okay, so they've got good "people skills" — which may just mean they're good at sweeping things, and people, under the carpet). This is especially unfortunate because we have people across the country who are specially trained in applied ethics; to our collective shame, business people often don't have much use for philosophers, nor do philosophers often have much use for business people.[1]

But perhaps that doesn't matter if, as Kelley notes, quoting Michael Josephson, president of the Joseph and Edna Josephson Institute of Ethics, "most ethics officers don't even have the clout to come close to over-riding the bottom-line-ism that governs most business goals" (20).

Ethics Programs

An ethics program can include a number of things. Certainly a code of ethics is a typical component (see below). The development of ethical policies and procedures is also part of the ethics program, insofar as this is not covered by the code.

An educational component is also a typical part of the program, and, if good, will attend not only to *what* the ethical policies are, but also to *how* they are to be applied; as you have (I hope) discovered, putting ethical theory into practice is not always straightforward.

Various educational strategies are used: guest speakers and presentations (especially by ethics consultants – see below), study groups, videos, workshops involving role-playing or ethics games, brochures, newsletters, orientation packages and sessions, and seminars. But I have to wonder whether many of these do more than scratch the surface. Rigorous ethical thinking is critical thinking, and this is not likely to be achieved with a brochure or a morning workshop; I suspect even the "study groups" fail to be more than discussion groups.

Some ethics programs include a whistle-blowing system that encourages (or at least enables) and protects those who disclose wrongdoing. Some companies have 24-hour ethics "hot lines." Among the mechanisms listed by Lindsay, Lindsay, and Irvine, in addition to those already mentioned, are a reward system and a judiciary board. (See their study for more about how companies manage their ethics.) In-house surveys may be conducted to determine just what is needed in the company (such a survey could determine current levels of ethical awareness as well as current practices). And ongoing assessment tools are often put in place to monitor the program.

According to Paine, many ethics programs focus on compliance ("to prevent, detect, and punish" [527]), but she criticizes such programs, suggesting instead an "integrity strategy" approach ("to define and give life to an organization's guiding values, to create an environment that supports ethically sound behaviour, and to instill a sense of shared accountability among employees" [531]). Murphy (1989) notes two other problems with ethics programs: they can be too issue-centred and too narrow in scope.

Nevertheless, ethics programs are especially valuable, Murphy (1989) notes, when the company conducts business in many different locations; an ethics program can increase consistency in decision-making. Perhaps simply increasing awareness levels is sufficient justification for ethics programs: identifying an issue as ethical is a necessary prerequisite to handling it well.

Codes of Ethics

Along with education, often prior to it, but sometimes in tandem with it, the development of a code of ethics is a primary responsibility of the ethics office/r. After its initial development, updating and enforcing the code are also important. Shaw states that the ethics committee should have

full authority and responsibility to communicate the code and decisions based on it to all corporate members, clarify and interpret the code when the need arises, facilitate the code's use, investigate grievances and violations of the code, discipline violators and reward compliance, and review, update, and upgrade the code. (180)

Some codes are implicit and are therefore more appropriately called corporate culture than corporate code, and some are explicit. Of the explicit codes, some are mere mission statements or corporate credos; others are extensive statements of policy and procedure.

One of the common criticisms of company codes of ethics is that they are just for show; no one really takes them seriously, let alone actually abides by them.

Another criticism, and this one may explain the previous one, is that codes are bound to be too simplistic to be effective. As you now know, a list of values or principles can only go so far — as far as moral conflicts: at that point, unless those values or principles are ordered by importance, they're not very helpful. — And as far as specifics: at that point, unless all the relevant extenuating circumstances are covered, they're not very helpful. (See Hosmer for more on this point.)

So why bother? Well, they may be a reminder to be ethically involved. Then again, they may be just PR (and BS). Or they may actually succeed in some way. For that to happen, Newton notes, there must be input from all levels of the company during its development, the code must be defensible by reasoned argument, and people at all levels must be bound by it. Murphy (1988) recommends that it be specific, public, blunt and realistic about violations, and periodically revised.

Interestingly enough, and dismayingly enough, Lefebvre and Singh found (through a 1992 study of 75 codes of ethics, all for Canadian companies) that the focus of codes of ethics is the protection of the firm: "They are principally concerned with conduct against the firm ... very few of the codes refer to issues concerning product safety, product quality, relations with consumers, or environmental affairs" (abstract). (See their article for a detailed analysis of 61 criteria.) Also of dismaying interest is that those 75 codes were all they got out of queries to 461 of the top 500 companies in Canada. Things have gotten a little better: according to the 1999 KMPG Business Ethics Survey Report, 85% of 200 Canadian companies surveyed had codes — but the executives who were surveyed said that the most important reason for investing in ethical initiatives was to protect or enhance their reputations.

This focus on conduct against the firm is particularly interesting when considered along with the observation of one ethics officer (Prachar, formerly at Teledyne) that 80% of the ethics issues brought to him were human resource related, involving "people who thought they should have been allowed to try for a particular job opening, or someone who thought they were unfairly disciplined, where the boss yelled at them unfairly in front of others, showing a lack of mutual respect" (as reported by Kelley, 21).

In addition to company codes of ethics, one should consider industry-wide codes: they may be quite valuable (see Arrow) if adhered to (see Maitland), because the risk of losing competitiveness by being morally right is reduced if everyone does the same morally right thing. For example, if every business in your field is bound to be environmentally responsible, then your environmentally responsible choices won't "cost" you. However, such self-regulation may be insufficient; some argue that government regulation is necessary.

Ethics Consultants

A company can also, or instead, hire an ethics consultant. This is a relatively new profession; according to Brooks, as of 1995, there were "upwards of 15 ethics consultants and academic consultants practising in Canada" (75). Although external consultants often perform the same tasks as in-house officers, especially those of providing training programs and developing codes of ethics, there can be differences. For one thing, companies will often hire out-of-house for their audits, whether financial or social or ethical – for obvious reasons (increased impartiality, increased disclosure by employees, etc.).

Ethics consultants may also provide a number of other services. For example, Grainger and Associates, based in Ottawa, provides ethics counselling and program assessments. Ethicscan, based in Toronto, publishes a newsletter (*The Corporate Ethics Monitor*) and provides information for ethical investors and shoppers. They have a database of corporate social performance for 1500 companies, and they publish *The Ethical Shoppers' Guide to Canadian Supermarket Prices* and *Shopping with a Conscience: The Informed Shoppers' Guide to Retailers, Suppliers, and Service Providers in Canada.*

Many consultants belong to the Ethics Practitioners' Association of Canada (Toronto), a professional organization which provides a directory of members and their services. Other resources for ethics consultants, as well as ethics officers, include the Canadian Centre for Ethics and Corporate Policy (Toronto), the Clarkson Centre for Business Ethics (Toronto), and the Centre for Professional and Applied Ethics (Van-

couver). Most of these organizations have websites – you may want to check them out.

Ethics Audits

Financial audits can have an ethical audit role, to the extent that they could expose and/or prevent fraud. Legal reviews can also have an ethical audit role to the extent that they prevent illegal behaviour; such illegal behaviour is also considered immoral. Environmental audits also involve ethical performance, to the extent that use of the environment is an ethical issue. The Global Reporting Initiative (GRI), established in 1997 and convened by the Coalition for Environmentally Responsible Economies (CERES), has proposed Sustainability Reporting Guidelines which encompass

> three aspects or dimensions of enterprise performance – the environmental, the social, and the economic aspects, as well as the relationships between them.... [Their] aim is eventually to elevate sustainability reporting to a level equivalent to and as routine as financial reporting in terms of comparability, auditability, and gneerally acceptaced practices. (Willis 3)

Social audits, which measure the social impact of a business, can also have an ethical role, insofar as social impact is part of morally good behaviour. Reports of social audits are available through Ethicscan, as mentioned above, and published in books such as *Rating America's Corporate Conscience* put out by the Council on Economic Priorities.

An ethical audit, however, is a little different, in that it measures how well the company is doing with respect to ethical policies and practices. "An ethical audit," according to Murphy, "would pose questions about manufacturing practices, personnel policies, dealings with suppliers, financial reporting and sales techniques to find out if ethical abuses may be occurring" ("Implementing Business Ethics," 109). Ferrell and Fraedrich say that an ethics audit "would provide a systematic and objective survey of the ethical condition of the organization" (185) and list over twenty questions that might be asked. Treviño and Nelson also provide questions to ask, based on Wilkins, divided into those for auditing the formal system and those for auditing the informal system.

Closing Note

If ethics officers and ethics committees consist of upper management only (as seems to be the norm), who are focused in a broadly egoistic way with behaviour against the firm (as would be expected, and as found by Lefebvre and Singh), you'll probably *not* have a morally good business because many of the issues covered in this text (advertising, product safety/quality, employee rights, environmental responsibility) will simply not be addressed.

"A glossy code of conduct, a high-ranking ethics officer, a training program, an annual ethics audit – these trappings of an ethics program do not necessarily add up to a responsible, law-abiding organization whose espoused values match its actions," says Paine (537). Nor, say I, do they necessarily add up to a responsible *morals-abiding* organization, in which values (not necessarily those of the company – not all companies are ethically sound) are matched with action.

Now that you've made it to the end of this text, you should have a better (clearer, richer) understanding of values, virtues, principles – of ethics. So on to the action part – go ye and do the right thing! (Or at least ask the right questions!)

Note

1   The profession of philosophy is especially known for its critical inquiry skills: "[philosophers] ask sequenced questions to reveal presuppositions or inconsistencies, [they] give focused examples to clarify ideas or evoke intuitions, [they] pose counter-examples to refine or, if necessary, refute a view, [they] lay out connected reasons to show how a view can be grounded or why it should be accepted" (Audi 144).

REFERENCES AND FURTHER READING

Arrow, Kenneth J. "Business Codes and Economic Efficiency." *Public Policy* 21 (Summer 1973). Rpt. in *Ethical Theory and Business*. Ed. Tom L. Beauchamp and Norman E. Bowie. 5th ed. NJ: Prentice Hall, 1997. 124-126.

Audi, Robert. "Philosophy in American Life: The Profession, The Public, and The American Philosophical Association." *Proceedings and Addresses of The American Philosophical Association* 72.5 (May 1999): 139-148.

Brooks, Leonard J. "Business Ethics in Canada: Distinctiveness and Directions." *Journal of Business Ethics* 16: 591-604. Rpt. in *Business Ethics in Canada*. Ed. Deborah C. Poff and Wilfrid J. Waluchow. 3rd ed. Scarborough: Prentice Hall Allyn and Bacon, 1999. 70-84.

Cava, Anita, Jonathan West, and Evan Berman. "Ethical Decision-making in Business and Government: An Analysis of Formal and Informal Strategies." *Spectrum: The Journal of State Government* (Spring 1995): 28-36.

Ferrell, O.C., and John Fraedrich. *Business Ethics: Ethical Decision Making and Cases*. 3rd ed. Boston: Houghton Mifflin, 1997.

Flynn, Gillian. "Make Employee Ethics Your Business." *Personnel Journal* (June 1995): 30-32, 34, 36, 38-39, 41.

Hosmer, LaRue Tone. *The Ethics of Management.* Burr Ridge, IL: Irwin Press, 1987.

Kelley, Tina. "Charting A Course To Ethical Profits." *New York Times* 8 Feb. 1998: 1,12. Rpt. in *Annual Editions: Business Ethics 99/00.* Ed. John E. Richardson. Guilford, CT: Dushkin, 1999. 20-24.

Lefebvre, Maurica, and Jang B. Singh. "The Content and Focus of Canadian Corporate Codes of Ethics." *Journal of Business Ethics* 11.10 (October 1992): 799-808.

Lindsay, R. Murray, Linda M. Lindsay, and V. Bruce Irvine. "Instilling Ethical Behaviour in Organizations: A Survey of Canadian Companies." *Journal of Business Ethics* 15 (1996): 393-407. Rpt. in *Business Ethics in Canada.* Ed. Deborah C. Poff and Wilfrid J. Waluchow. 3rd ed. Scarborough: Prentice Hall Allyn and Bacon, 1999. 91-106.

Maitland, Ian. "The Limits of Business Self-Regulation." *California Management Review* 27.3 (1985). Rpt. in *Ethical Theory and Business.* Ed. Tom L. Beauchamp and Norman E. Bowie. 5th ed. NJ: Prentice Hall, 1997. 126-135.

McNamara, Carter. *Complete Guide to Ethics Management: An Ethics Toolkit for Managers.* <http://www.mapnp.org/library/ethics/ethxgde.htm>

Murphy, Patrick E. "Implementing Business Ethics." *Journal of Business Ethics* 7 (1988): 907-915. Rpt. in *Annual Editions: Business Ethics 97/98.* Ed. John E. Richardson. Guilford, CT: Dushkin, 1999. 107-115.

Murphy, Patrick E. "Creating Ethical Corporate Structures." *Sloan Management Review* (Winter 1989): 81-87. Rpt. in *Annual Editions: Business Ethics 97/98.* Ed. John E. Richardson. Guilford, CT: Dushkin, 1999. 212-218.

Newton, Lisa H. "The Many Faces of the Corporate Code." *Institutionalizing Corporate Ethics Programs.* Proceedings of the Conference "Corporate Visions and Values", Fairfield University, November 1991. Rpt. in *Ethical Issues in Business: A Philosophical Approach.* Ed. Thomas Donaldson and Patricia H. Werhane. 6th ed. NJ: Prentice Hall, 1999. 519-526.

Paine, Lynn Sharp. "Managing for Organization Integrity." *Harvard Business Review* (March/April 1994): 106-117. Rpt. in *Ethical Issues in Business: A Philosophical Approach.* Ed. Thomas Donaldson and Patricia H. Werhane. 6th ed. NJ: Prentice Hall, 1999. 526-538.

Treviño, Linda K., and Katherine A. Nelson. *Managing Business Ethics: Straight Talk About How To Do It Right.* New York: John Wiley & Sons, 1995.

Shaw, William. H. *Business Ethics.* 2nd ed. Belmont, CA: Wadsworth, 1996.

Wilkins, A.L. "The Culture Audit: A Tool for Understanding Organizations." *Organizational Dynamics* (Autumn, 1983): 24-38.

Willis, Alan. "International Sustainability Reporting Guidelines Released for Comment." *Management Ethics* (April 1999): 3-4.

Appendix I
Excerpts from 'The Originals'
(Ethical Theories)

Utilitarianism

Jeremy Bentham, *An Introduction to the Principles of Morals and Legislation*

from Chapter 1, Of the Principle of Utility

I. Nature has placed mankind under the governance of two sovereign masters, *pain* and *pleasure*. It is for them alone to point out what we ought to do, as well as to determine what we shall do. On the one hand the standard of right and wrong, on the other the chain of causes and effects, are fastened to their throne. They govern us in all we do, in all we say, in all we think; every effort we can make to throw off our subjection, will serve but to demonstrate and confirm it.

...

VI. An action then may be said to be conformable to the principle of utility, or, for shortness' sake, to utility, (meaning with respect to the community at large) when the tendency it has to augment the happiness of the community is greater than any it has to diminish it.

...

X. Of an action that is conformable to the principle of utility, one may always say either that it is one that ought to be done, or at least that it is not one that ought not to be done. One may say also, that it is right it should be done; at least that it is not wrong it should be done: that it is a right action; at least that it is not a wrong action. When thus interpreted, the words *ought*, and *right* and *wrong*, and others of that stamp, have a meaning: when otherwise, they have none.

from Chapter 4, Value of a Lot of Pleasure or Pain, How to be Measured

IV. To a *number* of persons, with reference to each of whom the value of a pleasure or a pain is considered, it will be greater or less, according to seven circumstances: to wit, the six preceding ones; *viz.*

1. Its *intensity*.
2. Its *duration*.
3. Its *certainty* or *uncertainty*.
4. Its *propinquity* or *remoteness*.
5. Its *fecundity*.
6. Its *purity*.

And one other; to wit:

7.   Its *extent*; that is, the number of persons to whom it *extends*, or (in other words) who are affected by it.

V. To take an exact account then of the general tendency of any act, by which the interests of a community are affected, proceed as follows. Begin with any one person of those whose interests seem most immediately to be affected by it: and take an account,

1.   Of the value of each distinguishable *pleasure* which appears to be produced by it in the *first* instance.

2.   Of the value of each *pain* which appears to be produced by it in the *first* instance.

3.   Of the value of each pleasure which appears to be produced by it *after* the first. This constitutes the *fecundity* of the first *pleasure* and the *impurity* of the first *pain*.

4.   Of the value of each *pain* which appears to be produced by it after the first. This constitutes the *fecundity* of the first *pain*, and the *impurity* of the first pleasure.

5.   Sum up all the values of all the *pleasures* on the one side, and those of all the pains on the other. The balance, if it be on the side of pleasure, will give the *good* tendency of the act upon the whole, with respect to the interests of that *individual* person; if on the side of pain, the *bad* tendency of it upon the whole.

6.   Take an account of the *number* of persons whose interests appear to be concerned; and repeat the above process with respect to each. *Sum up* the numbers expressive of the degrees of *good* tendency, which the act has, with respect to each individual, in regard to whom the tendency of it is *good* upon the whole: do this again with respect to each individual, in regard to whom the tendency

of it is *bad* upon the whole. Take the *balance*; which, if on the side of *pleasure*, will give the general *good tendency* of the act, with respect to the total number of community of individuals concerned; if on the side of pain the general *evil tendency*, with respect to the same community.

VI. It is not to be expected that this process should be strictly pursued previously to every moral judgment, or to every legislative or judicial operation. It may, however, be always kept in view: and as near as the process actually pursued on these occasions approaches to it, so near will such process approach to the character of an exact one.

VII. The same process is alike applicable to pleasure and pain in whatever shape they appear: and by whatever denomination they are distinguished: to pleasure, whether it be called *good* (which is properly the cause or instrument of pleasure), or *profit* (which is distant pleasure, or the cause or instrument of distant pleasure), or *convenience*, or *advantage*, *benefit*, *emolument*, *happiness*, and so forth: to pain, whether it be called *evil* (which corresponds to *good*), or *mischief*, or *inconvenience*, or *disadvantage*, or *loss*, or *unhappiness*, and so forth.

John Stuart Mill, *Utilitarianism*

from Chapter II, What Utilitarianism Is

The creed which accepts as the foundation of morals, Utility, or the Greatest Happiness Principle, holds that actions are right in proportion as they tend to promote happiness, wrong as they tend to produce the reverse of happiness. By happiness is intended pleasure, and the absence of pain; by unhappiness, pain, and the privation of pleasure. To give a clear view of the moral standard set up by the theory, much more requires to be said; in particular, what things it includes in the ideas of pain and pleasure; and to what extent this is left an open question....

Now, such a theory of life excites in may minds, and among them in some of the most estimable in feeling and purpose, inveterate dislike. To suppose that life has (as they express it) no higher end than pleasure – no better and nobler object of desire and pursuit – they designate as utterly mean and grovelling; as a doctrine worthy only of swine....

... Human beings have faculties more elevated than the animal appetites, and when once made conscious of them, do not regard anything as happiness which does not include their gratification.... But there is no known Epicurean theory of life which does not assign to the pleasures of the intellect, of the feelings and imagination, and of the moral sentiments, a much higher value as pleasures than to those of mere sensation....

...

... It is better to be a human being dissatisfied than a pig satisfied; better to be Socrates dissatisfied than a fool satisfied. And if the fool, or the pig, is of a different opinion, it is because they only know their own side of the question. The other party to the comparison knows both sides.

...

I have dwelt on this point, as being a necessary part of a perfectly just conception of Utility or Happiness, considered as the directive rule of human conduct. But it is by no means an indispensable condition to the acceptance of the utilitarian standard, for that standard is not the agent's own greatest happiness, but the greatest amount of happiness altogether...

...

I must again repeat, what the assailants of utilitarianism seldom have the justice to acknowledge, that the happiness which forms the utilitarian standard of what is right in conduct, is not the agent's own happiness, but that of all concerned. As between his own happiness and that of others, utilitarianism requires him to be as strictly impartial as a disinterested and benevolent spectator. In the golden rule of Jesus of Nazareth, we read the complete spirit of the ethics of utility. To do as one would be done by, and to love one's neighbour as oneself constitute the ideal perfection of utilitarian morality. As the means of making the nearest approach to this ideal, utility would enjoin, first, that laws and social arrangements should place the happiness, or (as speaking practically it may be called) the interest, of every individual, as nearly as possible in harmony with the interest of the whole; and secondly, that education and opinion, which have so vast a power over human character, should so use that power as to establish in the mind of every individual an indissoluble association between his own happiness and the good of the whole; especially between his own happiness and the practice of such modes of conduct, negative and positive, as regard for the universal happiness prescribes: so that not only he may be unable to conceive the possibility of happiness to himself, consistently with conduct opposed to the general good, but also that a direct impulse to promote the general good may be in every individual one of the habitual motives of action, and the sentiments connected therewith may fill a large and prominent place in every human being's sentient existence ...

...

Again, Utility is often summarily stigmatized as an immoral doctrine by giving it the name of Expediency, and taking advantage of the popular use of that term to contrast it with Principle. But the Expedient, in the sense in which it is opposed to the Right, generally means that which is expedient for the particular interest of the agent himself....

Again, defenders of utility often find themselves called upon to reply to such objections as this – that there is not time, previous to action, for calculating and weighing the effects of any line of conduct on the general happiness.... The answer to the objection is, that there has been ample time, namely, the whole past duration of the human species. During all that time mankind have been learning by experience the tendencies of actions; on which experience all the prudence, as well as all the morality of life, is dependent. ...

Kantian Ethics

Immanuel Kant, *The Foundations of the Metaphysics of Morals*

(translated by T. K. Abbott)

from First Section: Transition from the Common Rational Knowledge of Morality to the Philosophical

THE GOOD WILL

Nothing can possibly be conceived in the world, or even out of it, which can be called good, without qualification, except a Good Will. Intelligence, wit, judgment, and the other *talents* of the mind, however thy may be named, or courage, resolution, perseverance, as qualities of temperament, are undoubtedly good and desirable in many respects; but these gifts of nature may also become extremely bad and mischievous if the will which is to make use of them, and which, therefore, constitutes what is called *character*, is not good. It is the same with the *gifts of fortune*. Power, riches, honour, even health, and the general well-being and contentment with one's condition which is called *happiness*, inspire pride, and often presumption, if there is not a good will to correct the influence of these on the mind, and with this also to rectify the whole principle of acting, and adapt it to its end. The sight of a being who is not adorned with a single feature of a pure and good will, enjoying unbroken prosperity, can never give pleasure to an impartial rational spectator. Thus a good will appears to constitute the indispensable condition even of being worthy of happiness.

...

A good will is good not because of what it performs or effects, not by its aptness for the attainment of some proposed end, but simply by virtue of the volition, that is, it is good in itself....

WHY REASON WAS MADE TO GUIDE THE WILL

...[A]nd since, nevertheless, reason is imparted to us as a practical faculty, *i.e.* as one which is to have influence on the *will*, therefore, admitting that nature generally in the distribution of her capacities has adapted the means to the end, its true destination must be to produce a *will*, not merely good as a *means* to something else, but *good in itself*, for which reason was absolutely necessary. ...

THE FIRST PROPOSITION OF MORALITY

We have then to develop the notion of a will which deserves to be highly esteemed for itself, and is good without a view to anything further, a notion which exists already in the sound natural understanding, requiring rather to be cleared up than to be taught, and which in estimating the value of our actions always takes the first place, and constitutes the condition of all the rest. In order to do this, we will take the notion of duty, which includes that of a good will, although implying certain subjective restrictions and hindrances. These, however, far from concealing it, or rendering it unrecognizable, rather bring it out by contrast, and make it shine forth so much the brighter. ...

THE SECOND PROPOSITION OF MORALITY

The second proposition is: That an action done from duty derives its moral worth, *not from the purpose* which is to be attained by it, but from the maxim by which it is determined, and therefore does not depend on the realization of the object of the action, but merely on the *principle of volition* by which the action has taken place, without regard to any object of desire. ...

THE SUPREME PRINCIPLE OF MORALITY: THE CATEGORICAL IMPERATIVE

But what sort of law can that be, the conception of which must determine the will, even without paying any regard to the effect expected from it, in order that this will may be called good absolutely and without qualification? As I have deprived the will of every impulse which could arise to it from obedience to any law, there remains nothing but the universal conformity of its actions to law in general, which alone is to serve the will as a principle, *i.e.* I am never to act otherwise than so *that I could also will that my maxim should become a universal law.*

...

... I only ask myself: Canst though also will that thy maxim should be a universal law? If not, then it must be rejected, and that not because of a disadvantage accruing from myself or even to others, but because it cannot enter as a principle into a possible universal legislation, and reason extorts from me immediate respect for such legislation....

from Second Section: Transition from Popular Moral Philosophy to the Metaphysic of Morals

FIRST FORMULATION OF THE CATEGORICAL IMPERATIVE: UNIVERSAL LAW

...

There is therefore but one categorical imperative, namely, this: *Act only on that maxim whereby thou canst at the same time will that it should become a universal law.* ...

FOUR ILLUSTRATIONS

...

2. Another finds himself forced by necessity to borrow money. He knows that he will not be able to repay it, but sees also that nothing will be lent to him, unless he promises stoutly to repay it in a definite time. He desires to make this promise, but he has still so much conscience as to ask himself: Is it not unlawful and inconsistent with duty to get out of a difficulty in this way? Suppose, however, that he resolves to do so, then the maxim of his action would be expressed thus: When I think myself in want of money, I will borrow money and promise to repay it, although I know that I never can do so. Now this principle of self-love or of one's own advantage may perhaps be consistent with my

whole future welfare; but the question now is, Is it right? I change then the suggestion of self-love into a universal law, and state the question thus: How would it be if my maxim were a universal law? Then I see at once that it could never hold as a universal law of nature, but would necessarily contradict itself. For supposing it to be a universal law that everyone when he thinks himself in a difficulty should be able to promise whatever he pleases, with the purpose of not keeping his promise, the promise itself would become impossible, as well as the end that one might have in view in it, since no one would consider that anything was promised to him, but would ridicule all such statements as vain pretences. ...

... Some actions are of such a character that their maxim cannot without contradiction be even *conceived* as a universal law of nature, far from it being possible that we should *will* that it *should* be so. In others this intrinsic impossibility is not found, but still it is impossible to *will* that their maxim should be raised to the universality of a law of nature, since such a will would contradict itself. ...

SECOND FORMULATION OF THE CATEGORICAL IMPERATIVE: HUMANITY AS AN END IN ITSELF

...

If then there is a supreme practical principle or, in respect of the human will, a categorical imperative, it must be one which, being drawn from the conception of that which is necessarily an end for everyone because it is *an end in itself*, constitutes an *objective* principle of will, and can therefore serve as a universal practical law. ... Accordingly the practical imperative will be as follows: *So act as to treat humanity, whether in thine own person or in that of any other, in every case as an end withal, never as means only.* We will now inquire whether this can be practically carried out.

...

FOUR ILLUSTRATIONS

...

Secondly, as regards necessary duties, or those of strict obligation, towards others; he who is thinking of making a lying promise to others will see at once that he would be using another man *merely as a mean*, without the latter containing at the same time the end in himself. For he whom I propose by such a promise to use for my own purposes cannot possibly assent to my mode of acting towards him, and therefore cannot himself contain the end of this action. This violation of the principle of humanity in other men is more obvious if we take in examples of attacks on the freedom and property of others. For then it is clear that he who transgresses the rights of men intends to use the person of others merely as means, without considering that as rational beings they ought always to be esteemed also as ends, that is, as beings who must be capable of containing in themselves the end of the very same action.

Virtue Ethics

Aristotle, *Nicomachean Ethics*

(translated by James E. C. Weldon)

from Book I

... This being so, if we define the function of man as a kind of life, and this life as an activity of the soul or a course of action in accordance with reason, and if the function of a good man is such activity of a good and noble kind, and if everything is well done when it is done in accordance with its proper excellence, it follows that the good of man is activity of soul in accordance with virtue, or, if there are more virtues than one, in accordance with the best and most complete virtue. But we must add the words "in a complete life." For as one swallow or one day does not make a spring, so one day or a short time does not make a man blessed or happy. ...

from Book II

Virtue then is twofold, partly intellectual and partly moral, and intellectual virtue is originated and fostered mainly by teaching; it therefore demands experience and time. Moral virtue on the other hand is the outcome of habit. From this fact it is clear that moral virtue is not implanted in us by nature, for a law of nature cannot be altered by habituation. Thus a stone, that naturally tends to fall downwards, cannot be habituated or trained to rise upwards. It is neither by nature then nor in defiance of nature that virtues are implanted in us. Nature gives us the capacity of receiving them, and that capacity is perfected by habit.

...

... But virtue is concerned with emotions and actions, and here excess is an error and deficiency a fault, whereas the mean is successful and laudable, and success and merit are both characteristics of virtue.

It appears then that virtue is a mean state, so far at least as it aims at the mean. ...

W. D. Ross, *The Right and the Good*

W. D. Ross, *The Right and the Good.* Oxford: Oxford University Press, 1967. Reprinted by permission of Oxford University Press.

... Of *prima facie* duties I suggest, without claiming completeness or finality for it, the following division.[1]

(1) Some duties rest on previous acts of my own. These duties seem to include two kinds, (a) those resting on a promise or what may fairly be called an implicit promise, such as the implicit undertaking not to tell lies which seems to be implied in the act of entering into conversation (at any rate by civilized men), or of writing books that purport to be history and not fiction. These may be called the duties of fidelity. (b) Those resting on a previous wrongful act. These may be called the duties of reparation. (2) Some rest on previous acts of other men, i.e. services done by them to me. These may be loosely described as the duties of gratitude. (3) Some rest on the fact or possibility of a distribution of pleasure or happiness (or of the means thereto) which is not in accordance with the merit of the persons concerned; in such cases there arises a duty to upset or prevent such a distribution. These are the duties of justice. (4) Some rest on the mere fact that there are other beings in the world whose condition we can make better in respect of virtue, or of intelligence, or of pleasure. These are the duties of beneficence. (5) Some rest on the fact that we can improve our own condition in respect of virtue or of intelligence. These are the duties of self-improvement. (6) I think that we should distinguish from (4) the duties that may be summed up under the title of 'not injuring others.' No doubt to injure others is incidentally to

fail to do them good; but it seems to me clear that non-maleficence is apprehended as a duty distinct from that of beneficence, and as a duty of a more stringent character. It will be noticed that this alone among the types of duty has been stated in a negative way. An attempt might no doubt be made to state this duty, like the others, in a positive way. It might be said that it is really the duty to prevent ourselves from acting either from an inclination to harm others or from an inclination to seek our own pleasure, in doing which we should incidentally harm them. But on reflection it seems clear that the primary duty here is the duty not to harm others, this being a duty whether or not we have an inclination that if followed would lead to our harming them; and that when we have such an inclination the primary duty not to harm others gives rise to a consequential duty to resist the inclination. The recognition of this duty of non-maleficence is the first step on the way to the recognition of the duty of beneficence; and that accounts for the prominence of the commands 'thou shalt not kill,' 'thou shalt not commit adultery,' 'thou shalt not steal,' 'thou shalt not bear false witness,' in so early a code as the Decalogue. But even when we have come to recognize the duty of beneficence, it appears to me that the duty of non-maleficence is recognized as a distinct one, and as *prima facie* more binding. We should not in general consider it justifiable to kill one person in order to keep another alive, or to steal from one in order to give alms to another.

...

(2) If the objection be made, that this catalogue of the main types of duty is an unsystematic one resting on no logical principle, it may be replied, first, that it makes no claim to being ultimate. It is a *prima facie* classification of the duties which reflection on our moral convictions seems actually to reveal. And if these convictions are, as I would claim that they are, of the nature of knowledge, and if I have not misstated them, the list will be a list of authentic conditional duties, correct as far as it goes though not necessarily complete. The list of *goods* put forward by the rival theory is reached by exactly the same method — the only sound one in the circumstances — viz, that of direct reflection on what we really think. Loyalty to the facts is worth more than a symmetrical architectonic or a hastily reached simplicity. If further reflection discovers a perfect logical basis for this or for a better classification, so much the better. ... (20-23)

1   I should make it plain at this stage that I am *assuming* the correctness of some of our main convictions as to *prima facie* duties, or, more strictly, am claiming that we *know* them to be true. To me it seems as self-evident as anything could be, that to make a promise, for instance, is to create a moral claim on us in someone else. Many readers will perhaps say that they do *not* know this to be true. If so, I certainly cannot prove it to them; I can only ask them to reflect again, in the hope that they will ultimately agree that they also know it to be true. The main moral convictions of the plain man seem to me to be, not opinions which it is for philosophy to prove or disprove, but knowledge from the start; and in my own case I seem to find little difficulty in distinguishing these essential convictions from other moral convictions which I also have, which are merely fallible opinions based on an imperfect study of the working for good or evil of certain institutions or types of action.

Alasdair MacIntyre, *After Virtue*

Alasdair MacIntyre, *After Virtue*. Notre Dame: Notre Dame Press, 1981. © 1981 by University of Notre Dame Press. Reprinted by permission of the publisher and the author.

A practice involves standards of excellence and obedience to rules as well as the achievement of goods. To enter into a practice is to accept the authority of those standards and the inadequacy of my own performance as judged by them. It is to subject my own attitudes, choices, preferences and tastes to the standards which currently and partially define the practice.

...

But what does all or any of this have to do with the concept of the virtues? It turns out that we are now in a position to formulate a first, even if partial and tentative definition of a virtue: *A virtue is an acquired human quality the possession and exercise of which tends to enable us to achieve those goods which are internal to practices and the lack of which effectively prevents us from achieving any such goods.* Later this definition will need amplification and amendment. But as a first approximation to an adequate definition it already illuminates the place of the virtues in human life. For it is not difficult to show for a whole range of key virtues that without them the goods internal to practices are barred to us, but not just barred to us generally, barred in a very particular way. ...

... In other words we have to accept as necessary components of any practice with internal goods and standards of excellence the virtues of justice, courage and honesty. For not to accept these, to be willing to cheat as our imagined child was willing to cheat in his or her early days at chess, so far bars us from achieving the standards of excellence or the goods internal to the practice that it renders the practice pointless except as a device for achieving external goods.

...

I have defined the virtues partly in terms of their place in practices. But surely, it may be suggested, some practices – that is, some coherent human activities which answer to the description of what I have called a practice – are evil. So in discussions by some moral philosophers of this type of account of the virtues it has been suggested that torture and sado-masochistic sexual activities might be examples of practices. But how can a disposition be a virtue if it is the kind of disposition which sustains practices and some practices issue in evil? My answer to this objection falls into two parts.

First I want to allow that there *may* be practices – in the sense in which I understand the concept – which simply *are* evil. I am far from convinced that there are, and I do not in fact believe that either torture or sado-masochistic sexuality answer to the description of a practice which my account of the virtues employs. But I do not want to rest my case on this lack of conviction, especially since it is plain that as a matter of contingent fact many types of practice may on particular occasions be productive of evil. For the range of practices includes the arts, the sciences and certain types of intellectual and athletic game. And it is at once obvious that any of these may under certain conditions be a source of evil: the desire to excel and to win can corrupt, a man may be so engrossed by his painting that he neglects his family, what was initially an honourable resort to war can issue in savage cruelty. But what follows from this?

It certainly is not the case that my account entails *either* that we ought to excuse or condone such evils *or* that whatever flows from a virtue is right. I do have to allow that courage sometimes sustains injustice, that loyalty has been known to strengthen a murderous aggressor and that generosity has sometimes weakened the capacity to do good. But to deny this would be to fly in the face of just those empirical facts which I invoked in criticising Aquinas's account of the unity of the virtues. That the virtues need initially to be defined and explained with reference to the notion of a practice thus in no way entails approval of all practices in all circumstances. That the virtues – as the objection itself presupposed – *are* defined not in terms of good and right practices, but of practices, does not entail or imply that practices as actually carried through at particular times and places do not stand in need of moral criticism. And the resources for such criticism are not lacking. There is in the first place no inconsistency in appealing to the requirements of a virtue to criticise a practice. Justice may be initially defined as a disposition which in its particular way is necessary to sustain practices; it does not follow that in pursuing the requirements of a practice violations of justice are not to be condemned. Moreover I already pointed out ... that a morality of virtues requires as its counterpart a conception of moral law. Its requirements too have to be met by practices. ...

...

Secondly without an overriding conception of the *telos* of a whole human life, conceived as a unity, our conception of certain individual virtues has to remain partial and incomplete. Consider two examples. Justice, on an Aristotelian view, is defined in terms of giving each person his or her due or desert. To deserve well is to have contributed in some substantial way to the achievement of those goods, the sharing of which and the common pursuit of which provide foundations for human community. But the goods internal to practices, including the goods internal to the practice of making and sustaining forms of community, need to be ordered and evaluated in some way if we are to assess relative desert. Thus only substantive application of an Aristotelian concept of justice requires an understanding of goods and of the good that goes beyond the multiplicity of goods which inform practices. As with justice, so also with patience. Patience is the virtue of waiting attentively without complaint, but not of waiting thus for anything at all. To treat patience as a virtue presupposes some adequate answer to the question: waiting for what? Within the context of practices a partial, although for many purposes adequate, answer can be given: the patience of a craftsman with refractory material, of a teacher with a slow pupil, of a politician in negotiations, are all species of patience. But what if the material is just too refractory, the pupil too slow, the negotiations too frustrating? Ought we always at a certain point just to give up in the interests of the practice itself? The medieval exponents of the virtue of patience claimed that there are certain types of situation in which the virtue of patience requires that I do not ever give up on some person or task, situations in which, as they would have put it, I am required to embody in my attitude to that person or task something of the patient attitude of God towards his creation. But this could only be so if patience served some overriding good, some *telos* which warranted putting other goods in a subordinate place. Thus it turns out that the content of the virtue of patience depends upon how we order various goods in a hierarchy and *a fortiori* on whether we are able rationally so to order these particular goods.

I have suggested so far that unless there is a *telos* which transcends the limited goods of practices by constituting the good of a whole human life, the good of a human life conceived as a unity, it will *both* be the case that a certain subversive arbitrariness will invade the moral life *and* that we shall be unable to specify the context of certain virtues adequately. These two considerations are reinforced by a third: that there is at least one virtue recognised by the tradition which cannot be specified at all except with reference to the wholeness of a human life – the virtue of integrity or constancy. 'Purity of heart,' said Kierkegaard, 'is to will one thing.' This notion of singleness of purpose in a whole life can have no application unless that of a whole life does.

Feminist Ethics

Nel Noddings, *Caring: A Feminine Approach to Ethics & Moral Education*

from Nel Noddings, *Caring: A Feminine Approach to Ethics & Moral Education.* Berkeley: University of California Press, 1984. © 1984 by The Regents of the University of California. Reprinted with permission of the publisher and the author. Notes and references are omitted.

Many persons who live moral lives do not approach moral problems formally. Women, in particular, seem to approach moral problems by placing themselves as nearly as possible in concrete situations and assuming personal responsibility for the choices to be made. They define themselves in terms of *caring* and work their way through moral problems from the position of one-caring. This position or attitude of caring activates a complex structure of memories, feelings, and capacities. Further, the process of moral decision making that is founded on caring requires a process of concretization rather than one of abstraction. An ethic built upon caring is, I think, characteristically and essentially feminine – which is not to say, of course, that it cannot be shared by men, any more than we should care to say that traditional moral systems cannot be embraced by women. But an ethic of caring arises, I believe, out of our experience as women, just as the traditional logical approach to ethical problems arises more obviously from masculine experience. (8)

...

... The source of my obligation is the value I place on the relatedness of caring. This value itself arises as a product of actual caring and being cared-for and my reflection on the goodness of these concrete caring situations. (84)

Alison M. Jaggar, "Feminist Ethics: Some Issues for the Nineties"

from Alison M. Jaggar, "Feminist Ethics: Some Issues for the Nineties." *Journal of Social Philosophy* 20.1-2 (Spring/Fall 1989): 83-84. Reprinted by permission of the *Journal of Social Philosophy* and the author. Some notes and references may be omitted.

Feminist approaches to ethics are distinguished by their explicit commitment to rethinking ethics with a view to correcting whatever forms of male bias it may contain. Feminist ethics, as these approaches are often called collectively, seeks to identify and challenge all those ways, overt but more often and more perniciously covert, in which western ethics has excluded women or rationalized their subordination. Its goal is to offer both practical guides to action and theoretical understandings of the nature of morality that do not, overtly or covertly, subordinate the interests of any woman or group of women to the interests of any other individual or group.

While those who practice feminist ethics are united by a shared project, they diverge widely in their views as to how this project may be accomplished. These divergences result from a variety of philosophical differences, including differing conceptions of feminism itself, a perennially contested concept. The inevitability of such disagreement means that feminist ethics cannot be identified in terms of a specific range of topics, methods or orthodoxies. For example, it is a mistake, though one to which even some feminists occasionally have succumbed, to identify feminist ethics with any of the following: putting women's interests first; focusing exclusively on so-called women's issues; accepting women (or feminists) as moral experts or authorities; substituting "female" (or "feminine") for "male" (or "masculine") values; or extrapolating directly from women's experience.

Even though my initial characterization of feminist ethics is quite loose, it does suggest certain minimum conditions of adequacy for any approach to ethics that purports to be feminist.

1. Within the present social context, in which women remain systematically subordinated, a feminist approach to ethics must offer a guide to action that will tend to subvert rather than reinforce this subordination. Thus, such an approach must be practical, transitional and nonutopian, an extension of politics rather than a retreat from it. It must be sensitive, for instance, to the symbolic meanings as well as the practical consequences of any actions that we take as gendered subjects in a male dominated society, and it must also provide the conceptual resources for identifying and evaluating the varieties of resistance and struggle in which women, particularly, have tended to engage. It must recognize the often unnoticed ways in which women and other members of the underclass have refused co-operation and opposed domination, while acknowledging the inevitability of collusion and the impossibility of totally clean hands.

2. Since so much of women's struggle has been in the kitchen and the bedroom, as well as in the parliamentary chamber and on the factory floor, a second requirement for feminist ethics is that it should be equipped to handle moral issues in both the so-called public and private domains. It must be able to provide guidance on issues of intimate relations, such as affection and sexuality, which, until quite recently, were largely ignored by modern moral theory. In so doing, it cannot assume that moral concepts developed originally for application to the public realm, concepts such as impartiality or exploitation, are automatically applicable to the private realm. Similarly, an approach to ethics that is adequate for feminism must also provide appropriate guidance for activity in the public realm, for dealing with large numbers of people, including strangers.

3. Finally, feminist ethics must take the moral experience of all women seriously, though not, of course, uncritically. Though what is feminist will often turn out to be very different from what is feminine, a basic respect for women's moral experience is necessary to acknowledging women's capacities as moralists and to countering traditional stereotypes of women as less than full moral agents, as childlike or "natural." Furthermore, as Okin (1987), among others, has argued, empirical claims about differences in the

moral experience of women and men make it impossible to assume that any approach to ethics will be unanimously accepted if it fails to consult the moral experience of women. Additionally, it seems plausible to suppose that women's distinctive social experience may make them especially perceptive regarding the implications of domination, especially gender domination, and especially well equipped to detect the male bias that has been shown to pervade so much of male-authored western moral theory.

On the surface, at least, these conditions of adequacy for feminist ethics are quite minimal – although I believe that fulfilling them would have radical consequences for ethics. I think most feminist, and perhaps even many nonfeminist,[1] philosophers would be likely to find the general statement of these conditions relatively uncontroversial, but that inevitably there will be sharp disagreement over when the conditions have been met. Even feminists are likely to differ over, for instance, just what are women's interests and when they have been neglected, what is resistance to domination and which aspects of which women's moral experience are worth developing and in which directions. ...

NOTE

1   'Nonfeminist' here refers to philosophers who do not make their feminist concerns explicit in their philosophical work; it is not intended to imply that such philosophers do not demonstrate feminist concern in other ways.

Naturalistic Theories

Aristotle, *Nicomachean Ethics*

(translated by James E. C. Weldon)

from Book 1

Perhaps, however, it seems a commonplace to say that happiness is the supreme good; what is wanted is to define its nature a little more clearly. The best way of arriving at such a definition will probably be to ascertain the function of man. For, as with a flute player, a sculptor, or any artist, or in fact anybody who has a special function or activity, his goodness and excellence seem to lie in his function, so it would seem to be with man, if indeed he has a special function. Can it be said that, while a carpenter and a cobbler have special functions and activities, man, unlike them, is naturally functionless? Or, as the eye, the hand, the foot, and similarly each part of the body has a special function, so may man be regarded as having a special function apart from all these? What, then, can this function be? It is not life; for life is apparently something that man shares with plants; and we are looking for something peculiar to him. We must exclude therefore the life of nutrition and growth. There is next what may be called the life of sensation. But this too, apparently, is shared by man with horses, cattle, and all other animals. There remains what I may call the active life of the rational part of man's being. Now this rational part is twofold; one part is rational in the sense of being obedient to reason, and the other in the sense of possessing and exercising reason and intelligence. The active life too may be conceived of in two ways, [In other words, life may be taken to mean either the mere possession of certain faculties or their active exercise.] either as a state of character, or as an activity; but we mean by it the life of activity, as this seems to be the truer form of the conception.

The function of man then is activity of soul in accordance with reason, or not apart from reason. ...

Thomas Aquinas, *Summa Theologica*

from Question 90

First Article: Whether law is something pertaining to reason?

... It belongs to the law to command and to forbid. But it belongs to reason to command, as was stated above. Therefore law is something pertaining to reason.... Law is a rule and measure of acts, whereby man is induced to act or is restrained from acting; for *lex (law)* is derived from *ligare (to bind)*, because it binds one to act. Now the rule and measure of human acts is the reason, which is the first principle of human acts, as is evident from what has been stated above. For it belongs to the reason to direct to the end, which is the first principle in all matters of action....

Intuitionism

W. D. Ross, *Foundations of Ethics*

W. D. Ross, *Foundations of Ethics.* Oxford: Oxford University Press, 1939. Reprinted by permission of Oxford University Press.

In such action, in its earliest form, there was no thought of duty. We must suppose that when a certain degree of mental maturity had been reached, and a certain amount of attention had been, for whatever reason, focused on acts which had hitherto been done without any thought of their rightness, they came to be recognized, first rather vaguely as *suitable* to the situation, and then, with more urgency, as *called for* by the situation. *Thus* first, as belonging to particular acts in virtue of a particular character they possessed, was rightness recognized. Their rightness was not deduced from any general principle; rather the general principle was later recognized by intuitive induction as being implied in the judgements already passed on particular acts.

...

Our insight into the basic principles of morality is not of this order. When we consider a particular act as a lie, or as the breaking of a promise, or as a gratuitous infliction of pain, we do not need to, and do not, fall back on a remembered general principle; we see the individual act to be by its very nature wrong.

Rights Theories

Ronald Dworkin, *Taking Rights Seriously*

Ronald Dworkin, *Taking Rights Seriously.* Cambridge: Harvard University Press, 1977. Excerpt is from an essay previously published in an issue of *The New York Review of Books*, 1977 or prior. © 1963-77 by New York Review, Inc. Reprinted with permission from *The New York Review of Books.*

from 3. Controversial Rights

It makes sense to say that a man has a fundamental right against the Government, in the strong sense, like free speech, if that right is necessary to protect his dignity, or his standing as equally entitled to concern and respect, or some other personal value of like consequence. It does not make sense otherwise.

So if rights make sense at all, then the invasion of a relatively important right must be a very serious matter. It means treating a man as less than a man, or as less worthy of concern than other men. The institution of rights rests on the conviction that this is a grave injustice, and that it is worth paying the incremental cost in social policy or efficiency that is necessary to prevent it. But then it must be wrong to say that inflating rights is as serious as invading them. If the Government errs on the side of the individual, then it simply pays a little more in social efficiency than it has to pay; it pays a little more, that is, of the same coin that it has already decided must be spent. But if it errs against the individual it inflicts an insult upon him that, on its own reckoning, it is worth a great deal of that coin to avoid.

Justice Theories

Aristotle, *Nicomachean Ethics*

(translated by D. P. Chase)

from Chapter VI, That Distributive Justice implies four proportional terms.

Well the unjust man we have said is unequal and the abstract 'Unjust' unequal: further it is plain that there is some mean of the unequal, that is to say the equal or exact half (because in whatever action there is the greater and the less there is also the equal, i.e. the exact half). If then the Unjust is unequal the Just is equal, which all must allow without further proof: and as the equal is a mean the Just must be also a mean.

Now the equal implies two terms at least: it follows then that the Just is both a mean and equal, and these to certain persons; and, in so far as it is a mean, between certain things (that is the greater and the less), and, so far as it is equal, between two, and in so far as it is just it is so to certain persons. The Just then must imply four terms at least, for those to which it is just are two and the terms representing the things are two.

And there will be the same equality between the terms representing the persons as between those representing the things: because as the latter are to one another so are the former: for if the persons are not equal they must not have equal shares; in fact this is the very source of all the quarrelling and wrangling in the world when either they who are equal have and get awarded to them things not equal, or, being not equal, those things which are equal. Again the necessity of this equality of ratios is shown by the common phrase 'according to rate,' for all agree that the Just in distributions ought to be according to some rate, but what that rate is to be all do not agree; the Democrats are for freedom Oligarchs for wealth others for nobleness of birth and the Aristocratic party for virtue.

The Just, then, is a certain proportionable thing. For proportion does not apply merely to number in the abstract but to number generally, since it is equality of ratios and implies four terms at least, (that this is the case in what may be called discrete proportion is plain and obvious, but it is true also in continual proportion for this uses the one term as two and mentions it twice; thus A : B : C may be expressed A : B : : B : C. In the first B is named twice; and so, if, as in the second, B is actually written twice, the proportionals will be four:) and the Just likewise implies four terms at the least, and the ratio between the two pairs of terms is the same because the persons and the things are divided similarly. It will stand then thus, A : B : : C : D, and then permutando A : C : : B : D, and then (supposing C and D to represent things) A + C : B + D : : A : B. The distribution in fact consisting in putting together these terms thus: and if they are put together so as to preserve this same ratio the distribution puts them together justly. So then the joining together of the first and third and second and fourth proportionals is the Just in distribution, and this Just is the mean relatively to that which violates the proportionate, for the proportionate is a mean and the Just is proportionate. Now mathematicians call this kind of proportion geometrical: for in geometrical proportion the whole as each part to each part. Furthermore this proportion is not make up one term.

The Just then is this proportionate and the Unjust that which violates the proportionate; and so there comes to be the greater and the less: which in fact is the case in actual transactions, because he who acts unjustly has the greater share, and he who is treated unjustly has the less, of what is good: but in the case of what is bad this is reversed: for the less evil compared with the greater comes to be reckoned for good because the less evil is more choiceworthy than the greater and what is choiceworthy is good and the more so the great good.

This then is the one species of the Just.

Mill, *Utilitarianism*

from Chapter V, On the Connexion Between Justice and Utility

Most of the maxims of justice current in the world, and commonly appealed to in its transactions, are simply instrumental to carrying into effect the principles of justice which we have now spoken of. That a person is only responsible for what he has done voluntarily, or could voluntarily have avoided; that it is unjust to condemn any person unheard; that the punishment ought to be proportioned to the offence, and the like, are maxims intended to prevent the just principle of evil for evil from being perverted to the infliction of evil without justification. The greater part of these common maxims have come into use from the practice of courts of justice, which have been naturally led to a more complete recognition and elaboration than was likely to suggest itself to others, of the rules necessary to enable them to fulfil their double function, of inflicting punishment when due, and of awarding to each person his right.

That first of judicial virtues, impartiality, is an obligation of justice, partly for the reason last mentioned; as being a necessary condition of the fulfilment of the other obligations of justice. But this is not the only source of the exalted rank, among human obligations, of those maxims of equality and impartiality, which, both in popular estimation and in that of the most enlightened, are included among the precepts of justice. In one point of view, they may be considered as corollaries from the principles already laid down. If it is a duty to do to each according to his deserts, returning good for good as well as repressing evil by evil, it necessarily follows that we should treat all equally well (when no higher duty forbids) who have deserved equally well of us, and that society should treat all equally well who have deserved equally well of it, that is, who have deserved equally well absolutely. This is the highest abstract standard of social and distributive justice; towards which all institutions, and the efforts of all virtuous citizens, should be made in the utmost possible degree to converge. But this great moral duty rests upon a still deeper foundation, being a direct emanation from the first principle of morals, and not a mere logical corollary from secondary or derivative doctrines. It is involved in the very meaning of Utility, or the Greatest-Happiness Principle. That principle is a mere form of words without rational signification, unless one person's happiness, supposed equal in degree (with the proper allowance made for kind), is counted for exactly as much as another's. Those conditions being supplied, Bentham's dictum, 'everybody to count for one, nobody for more than one,' might be written under the principle of utility as an explanatory commentary. The equal claim of everybody to happiness in the estimation of the moralist and the legislator, involves an equal claim to all the means of happiness, except in so far as the inevitable conditions of human life, and the general interest, in which that of every individual is included, set limits to the maxim; and those limits ought to be strictly construed. As every other maxim of justice, so this, is by no means applied or held applicable universally; on the contrary, as I have already remarked, it bends to every person's ideas of social expediency. But in whatever case it is deemed applicable at all, it is held to be the dictate of justice. All persons are deemed to have a *right* to equality of treatment, except when some recognised social expediency requires the reverse. ...

John Rawls, *A Theory of Justice*

By way of general comment, these principles primarily apply, as I have said, to the basic structure of society. They are to govern the assignment of rights and duties and to regulate the distribution of social and economic advantages. As their formulation suggests, these principles presuppose that the social structure can be divided into two more or less distinct parts, the first principle applying to the one, the second to the other. They distinguish between those aspects of the social system that define and secure the equal liberties of citizenship and those that specify and establish social and economic inequalities. The basic liberties of citizens are, roughly speaking, political liberty (the right to vote and to be eligible for public office) together with freedom of speech and assembly; liberty of conscience and freedom of thought; freedom of the person along with the right to hold (personal) property; and freedom from arbitrary arrest and seizure as defined by the concept of the rule of law. These liberties are all required to be equal by the first principle, since citizens of a just society are to have the same basic rights.

The second principle applies, in the first approximation, to the distribution of income and wealth and to the design of organizations that make use of differences in authority and responsibility, or chains of command. While the distribution of wealth and income need not be equal, it must be to everyone's advantage, and at the same time, positions of authority and offices of command must be accessible to all. One applies the second principle by holding positions open, and then, subject to this constraint, arranges social and economic inequalities so that everyone benefits.

These principles are to be arranged in a serial order with the first principle prior to the second. This ordering means that a departure from the institutions of equal liberty required by the first principle cannot be justified by, or compensated for, by greater social and economic advantages. The distribution of wealth and income, and the hierarchies of authority, must be consistent with both the liberties of equal citizenship and equality of opportunity.

It is clear that these principles are rather specific in their content, and their acceptance rests on certain assumptions that I must eventually try to explain and justify. A theory of justice depends upon a theory of society in ways that will become evident as we proceed. For the present, it should be observed that the two principles (and this holds for all formulations) are a special case of a more general conception of justice that can be expressed as follows.

All social values — liberty and opportunity, income and wealth, and the bases of self-respect — are to be distributed equally unless an unequal distribution of any, or all, of these values is to everyone's advantage.

Injustice, then, is simply inequalities that are not to the benefit of all. Of course, this conception is extremely vague and requires interpretation.

As a first step, suppose that the basic structure of society distributes certain primary goods, that is, things that every rational man is presumed to want. These goods normally have a use whatever a person's rational plan of life. For simplicity, assume that the chief primary goods at the disposition of society are rights and liberties, powers and opportunities, income and wealth. (Later on in Part Three the primary good of self-respect has a central place.) These are the social primary goods. Other primary goods such as health and vigor, intelligence and imagination, are natural goods; although their possession is influenced by the basic structure, they are not so directly under its control. Imagine, then, a hypothetical initial arrangement in which all the social primary goods are equally distributed: everyone has similar rights and duties, and income and wealth are evenly shared. This state of affairs provides a benchmark for judging improvements. If certain inequalities of wealth and organizational powers would make everyone better off than in this hypothetical starting situation, then they accord with the general conception. (61-62)

Robert Nozick, *Anarchy, State, and Utopia*

Robert Nozick, *Anarchy, State, and Utopia.* NY: Basic Books, 1974. © 1974 by Basic Books, Inc. Reprinted by permission of Basic Books, a member of Perseus Books, L.L.C. and the author. Notes have been omitted.

from Chapter 7, Distributive Justice

SECTION I, THE ENTITLEMENT THEORY

The subject of justice in holdings consists of three major topics. The first is the *original acquisition of holdings*, the appropriation of unheld things. This includes the issues of how unheld things may come to be held, the process, or processes, by which unheld things may come to be held, the things that may come to be held by these processes, the extent of what comes to be held by a particular process, and so on. We shall refer to the complicated truth about this topic, which we shall not formulate here, as the principle of justice in acquisition. The second topic concerns the *transfer of holdings* from one person to another. By what processes may a person transfer holdings to another? How may a person acquire a holding from another who holds it? Under this topic come general descriptions of voluntary exchange, and gift and (on the other hand) fraud, as well as reference to particular conventional details fixed upon in a given society. The complicated truth about this subject (with place-holders for conventional details) we shall call the principle of justice in transfer. (And we shall suppose it also includes principles governing how a person may divest himself of a holding, passing it into an unheld state.)

If the world were wholly just, the following inductive definition would exhaustively cover the subject of justice in holdings.

1. A person who acquires a holding in accordance with the principle of justice in acquisition is entitled to that holding.

2. A person who acquires a holding in accordance with the principle of justice in transfer, from someone else entitled to the holding, is entitled to the holding.

3. No one is entitled to a holding except by (repeated) applications of 1 and 2.

The complete principle of distributive justice would say simply that a distribution is just if everyone is entitled to the holdings they possess under the distribution.

A distribution is just if it arises from another just distribution by legitimate means. The legitimate means of moving from one distribution to another are specified by the principle of justice in transfer. The legitimate first "moves" are specified by the principle of justice in acquisition. Whatever arises from a just situation by just steps is itself just. The means of change specified by the principle of justice in transfer preserve justice. ...

Almost every suggested principle of distributive justice is patterned: to each according to his moral merit, or needs, or marginal product, or how hard he tries, or the weighted sum of the foregoing, and so on. The principle of entitlement we have sketched is *not* patterned. There is no one natural dimension or weighted sum or combination of a small number of natural dimensions that yields the distributions generated in accordance with the principle of entitlement. The set of holdings that results when some persons receive their marginal products, others win at gambling, others receive a share of their mate's income, others receive gifts from foundations, others receive interest on loans, others receive gifts from admirers, others receive returns on investment, others make for themselves much of what they have, others find things, and so on, will not be patterned. ...

HOW LIBERTY UPSETS PATTERNS

It is not clear how those holding alternative conceptions of distributive justice can reject the entitlement conception of justice in holdings. For suppose a distribution favored by one of these nonentitlement conceptions is realized. Let us suppose it is your favorite one and let us call this distribution D_1; perhaps everyone has an equal share, perhaps shares vary in accordance with some dimension you treasure. Now suppose that Wilt Chamberlain is greatly in demand by basketball teams, being a great gate attraction. (Also suppose contracts run only for a year, with players being free agents.) He signs the following sort of contract with a team: In each home game, twenty-five cents from the price of each ticket of admission goes to him. (We ignore the question of whether he is "gouging" the owners, letting them look out for themselves.) The season starts, and people cheerfully attend his team's games; they buy their tickets, each time dropping a separate twenty-five cents of their admission price into a special box with Chamberlain's name on it. They are excited about seeing him play; it is worth the total admission price to them. Let us suppose that in one season one million persons attend his home games, and Wilt Chamberlain winds up with $250,000, a much larger sum than the average income and larger even than anyone else has. Is he entitled to this income? Is this new distribution D_2, unjust? If so, why? There is *no* question about whether each of the people was entitled to the control over the resources they held in D_1; because that was the distribution (your favorite) that (for the purposes of argument) we assumed was acceptable. Each of these persons chose to give twenty-five cents of their money to Chamberlain. They could have spent it on going to the movies. or on candy bars, or on copies of *Dissent* magazine, or of *Monthly Review*. But they all, at least one million of them, converged on giving it to Wilt Chamberlain in exchange for watching him play basketball. If D_1 was a just distribution, and people voluntarily moved from it to D_2, transferring parts of their shares they were given under D_1 (what was it for if not to do something with?), isn't D_2 also just? If the people were entitled to dispose of the resources to which they were entitled (under D_1), didn't this include their being entitled to give it to, or exchange it with, Wilt Chamberlain? Can anyone else complain on grounds of justice? Each other person already has his legitimate share under D_1. Under D_1, there is nothing that anyone has that anyone else has a claim of justice against. After someone transfers something to Wilt Chamberlain, third parties *still* have their legitimate shares; *their* shares are not changed. By what process could such a transfer among two persons give rise to a legitimate claim of distributive justice on a portion of what was transferred, by a third party who had no claim of justice on any holding of the others *before* the transfer? ...

...

The general point illustrated by the Wilt Chamberlain example ... is that no end-state principle or distributional-patterned principle of justice can be continuously realized without continuous interference with people's lives. ... To maintain a pattern one must either continually interfere to stop people from transferring resources as they wish to, or continually (or periodically) interfere to take from some persons resources that others for some reason chose to transfer to them. ...

APPENDIX II
RELEVANT CANADIAN LAW AND LANDMARK CASES

prepared by Chrisopher B. Gray

Chapter 1 – Whistleblowing

The common law has always enforced the employee's duty of loyalty and confidentiality, but has always made an exception in the public interest.[1] The main threat to this exception is the doctrine of employment at will, which allows an employer to dismiss for any reason or even for no reason an employee who does not have an employment contract for a definite period of time, in order to maintain harmony and productivity in the workplace. In Canada, this primarily U.S. doctrine has been countered by the availability of proceedings against dismissal without just cause. The first statutory protections were to give immunity from prosecution to co-offenders who revealed their wrongdoing.

The leading Canadian case at common law is the BCGEU arbitral decision, where arbitrator Joseph Weiler decided that, while "the duty of fidelity does not mean that the Daniel Ellsbergs [reporting the Pentagon strategists' papers] and Karen Silkwoods [revealing negli-

gence in the nuclear industry] must remain silent," there is an obligation to work through internal mechanisms first, before going public, unless there is a significant reason not to.[2]

Several Canadian statutes contain whistleblowing provisions, mostly in the areas of environmental law and occupational health and safety.[3] In one case under these, the employee was awarded compensatory damages for warning of the disposal of toxic chemicals, and was considered for reinstatement if the employer ever recommenced operations.

New protections for whistleblowing are in the *Competition Act*:[4]

"Any person who has reasonable ground to believe that a person has committed or intends to commit an offence under this Act, may notify the Commission of the particulars of the matter and may request that his or her identity be kept confidential with respect to the notification." (65(1))

"No employer shall dismiss, suspend, demote, discipline, harass, coerce or otherwise disadvantage an employee, or deny an employee a benefit of employment by reason that (a) the employee, acting in good faith and on the basis of reasonable belief"

has given that information (66.1(1)).

These provisions apply only to offences under the *Competition Act*, not elsewhere; and only to its criminal offences (conspiracy, bid-rigging, discriminatory and predatory pricing, price maintenance, and misleading advertising or deceptive marketing practices), but not to its non-criminal matters which the Competition Tribunal can review (mergers, abuse of dominant position, refusal to deal, consignment selling, exclusive dealing, tied selling, market restriction, and delivered pricing).

For these reasons, and since the legislative approach had not worked well in the States, mostly because workers know that employers can always penetrate anonymity, Mr. Justice Charles L. Dubin in his commissioned report on the bill preceding these amendments to the *Competition Act* recommended a non-legislative regime.[5] Legislation is explicit and clear, can provide punitive and not merely compensatory damages, creates a criminal offence against retaliating employers, and encourages reporting to authorities instead of to media, and within firms before going to authorities. Legislation, however, is redundant beyond common law protections, is unlikely to result in reinstatement, deals with matters in competition law less criminalisable than the offences in environmental law, and takes longer to implement. The Parliament did not agree.

Chapter 2 - Advertising

In 1999 the federal *Competition Act* updated its offences in advertising. Setting the literal against the general meaning, or the reverse, will not exculpate from false and misleading advertising or from deceptive telemarketing. These "deceptive marketing practices" also include misleading statements about guarantees, performance, replacement, ordinary price, testing, testimonials, and contests. Disclosure of information was already required about the likely compensation to be earned by participants in multi-level and pyramid marketing plans.[6]

The *Combines Investigation Act* made an offence of "double ticketing" with a high and a low advertised price and of "bait and switch" selling whereby one advertises at a bargain price a product that he does not supply in reasonable quantities.[7]

The Supreme Court's 1989 decision in *Irwin Toy* assimilated advertising to political debate, in judging the limits of restriction upon free speech in advertising.[8] A broad test was used, to protect commercial advertising: if it "conveys or attempts to convey a meaning, it has expressive content and prima facie falls within the scope of the guarantee." Nonetheless, the court permitted Québec's restriction upon advertising directed at children as a legitimate limit upon that right.

Advertising for illegal products is illegal; and advertising for disfavoured products is disfavoured. The *Tobacco Act* fortified the prohibition on sales to youth and the health messages on products required by two earlier acts. The new act prohibits advertising of tobacco products; the exception is information and brand-preference inducement only in publications seen mostly by adults. Advertising of tobacco is also prohibited on non-tobacco products associated with youth or a lifestyle. A reduced visibility is required on sponsorship materials. The restriction upon advertising of tobacco sponsorship of sporting events was subsequently allowed a five-year phase-in period.[9]

No advertising or selling of prepackaged products is allowed unless they are labelled to describe the net quantity in terms of an official unit of measurement, under the *Consumer Packaging and Labelling Act*.[10] False or misleading representations on this quantity are whatever qualifies that information or is likely to deceive in regard to it, as to the type, quality, performance, function, origin or method of manufacture. Furthermore, the shape of the container must not make this deception likely. The nature, quality, age, size, material content, and composition must be on the label. When a number of servings are advertised, so must be the amount of each serving.

In cases under the *Competition Act*, it is not false or misleading to advertise beds at a "special lower price," if the business ordinarily sells at an outrageous price, even if the special price is also outrageous.

Where competitors ordinarily sold mink coats at the advertised price, advertising a price below the "ordinarily sold" price is not misleading, even if the seller itself had not sold at that price. But a sale which goes on 114 days of the year does not make prices charged on other days the "ordinary prices" below which sale prices may be advertised.[11]

A "Three Dollar offer, coupon refund and recipes, offer inside," which did not state that three proofs of purchase were required is not misleading, since the average food purchaser has become more sophisticated in his role as "the average credulous person" whom the ad must be shown likely to deceive. Irving Oil's "6 cents off per gallon" beside a gas pump was misleading, however, when gas was sold at the same price as neighbouring stations.[12]

Saying "You may already have qualified to win" is not deceptive when winners have already been fairly selected. Nonetheless, saying "the best possible dollar value and saving on every item, every day" when there are lower (drugstore) prices to be found is no longer "puffery" as it might have been considered before the act, but is misleading and an offence.[13]

Chapter 3 – Product Safety

The requirement for mandatory disclosure of information is the most pervasive form of product safety regulation in Canada. The *Hazardous Products Act* requires warnings of safety risks in advertising of products from charcoal sacks to science sets. The *Weights and Measures Act* requires specific information to be stated in selling goods. The *Food and Drugs Act* prohibits labelling foods as, e.g., "low calorie," unless they meet standards set out in the act. Provincial legislation, such as Ontario's *Pesticides Act*, also achieves product safety by mandatory disclosure.[14]

Alternative ways of ensuring product safety are to have governments deliver goods directly, to nationalize private industry, to use tax policy, subsidies, licensing and certification, to set performance standards and design standards, to ban products, or to require insurance for their sale. Requiring disclosure is far less intrusive a legal intervention than these alternatives. Product safety regulation is carried on more directly by the Product Safety Branch of the Department of Consumer and Corporate Affairs under the *Hazardous Products Act*, as well as by the Department of Health and Welfare pursuant to the *Food and Drugs Act*.

The business contract to supply products yields a relationship between no one but its parties; this is called privity of contract. Only they are obliged by it. In the most common business contract, the sales contract, only the seller has the duties to pass a good title and to deliver the goods, at the right time, in the right quantity, and in the right quality. The contract is with the retailers, not with the customers. Customers, then, have no legal complaint under their contract.[15]

At the peak of their success in the 1970s, consumer protection acts adjusted the provisions between merchants in order to include fairness toward parties without commercial experience and know-how.[16] Recent initiatives have revived waning interest in the consumer protection approach to product safety, particularly through fortifying product warranties.[17] For example, a contractual clause is null which states that a test report obtained by one party will make proof of its claims. The reason is that not only the other party but the court as well is kept in ignorance of its validity.[18]

The courts have searched how to escape privity of contract, by looking to third parties' reasonable reliance upon others' contracts. Reliance has led to merging the contractual regime with torts and fostered the remedy of restitution by reason of "unconscionable" conduct or "unjust enrichment." The inclination particularly by juries to hold producers strictly liable for harms done by their products, that is, liable without proof of negligence or intent, has also been a response to manufacturer's shield of privity. This has tended to make the producers into insurers against the harms, since they stand in a better financial, controlling, and knowledgeable position to do this than ultimate consumers do.

Most members of the European Community since 1985 and several provinces in Canada have adopted legislation that enforces the principles of strict products liability on the part of manufacturers.[19] The crisis in the affordability, availability, and adequacy of liability insurance in the wake of such huge mass tort claims as the asbestos, DES, and Agent Orange litigations in North America has given pause as to the effectiveness of strict product liability, however. It is difficult to determine whose manufacturing activities should be asked to "internalize" the liability costs into their market prices. This even prejudices the low income consumers who are primarily to be protected, by requiring them to pay the same premium for safety in their product prices as do the higher income consumers. The tendency to allow anyone who has more profits to be sued collapses strict liability into absolute liability without any defence.

Husky, an oil driller, leased its rig from the builder, St. John, which needed a heating system with a ground breaker to keep its pipes from freezing. Its manufacturer, Raychem, failed to provide the breaker. The pipes froze, and the rig went for repairs. Husky had left the system on even after it showed failure. The Supreme Court agreed with a 60% liability on the builder for failure in its duty to warn about a defective product. But because the builder had by its contract excluded any liability on its part except for installation, its liability was eliminated.

In a far-reaching dissent, two judges refused to accept that exclusion, because St. John's duty to warn arose independently of the contract and had not been explicitly excluded by the contractual words; these normally would be taken to exclude only warranties for workmanship and materials. The dissent also, nonetheless, refused any claim for economic loss here.

"However, this *prima facie* duty of care is negatived by policy considerations. The most serious problem is that of indeterminate liability. If the defendants owed a duty to warn the plaintiffs, it is difficult to see why they would not owe a similar duty to a host of other persons who would foreseeably lose money if the rig was shut down as a result of being damaged."[20]

Chapter 4 – Employee Rights

Employees rights are established both under caselaw and in prominent statutes. Both in Québec[21] and in the commonlaw provinces,[22] legislation typically amplifies labour codes with specific protections. Ontario's *Health and Safety Act*, for example, requires employers to provide protective equipment, maintain it, and ensure its use. The employer must ensures that instruction on safety is given, that supervisors are competent in safety, and that every precaution for safety is taken. The availability, storage, and use of harmful products is monitored, and workers are scrutinized for their fitness and their exposure in working with these (s.15, and Part IV generally). In turn, the obligation on workers is to make use of this information and equipment, and not to create further risks, as by any "prank, contest, feat of strength, unnecessary running or rough and boisterous conduct." Workers may refuse to work where they have reason to believe that their health or safety is in danger from the equipment or the physical condition of the workplace. Employers may not take reprisals for workers' exercise of this entitlement. That right does not apply in occupations which are dangerous by their nature, such as policing.

Recourse for wrongful dismissal is available at both civilian and common law. Under statute as well a right to be rehired after a firing without just and sufficient cause can lie, even when the employee is not unionized. Seasonal work-

ers during three years for City of Brossard had this right violated when no connection could be shown between their firing and their conduct and capacity to do the work.

The employer's bad faith conduct is also considered in compensation.

"The point at which the employment relationship ruptures is the time when the employee is most vulnerable and hence most in need of protection. In recognition of this need, the law ought to encourage conduct that minimizes the damage and dislocation (both economic and personal) that result from dismissal. To ensure that employees receive adequate protection, employers ought to be held to an obligation of good faith and fair dealing in the manner of dismissal ....[A]t a minimum in the course of dismissal employers ought to be candid, reasonable, honest and forthright with their employees and should refrain from engaging in conduct that is unfair or is in bad faith by being, for example, untruthful, misleading or unduly insensitive."[23]

Elsewhere, however, where there is no claim in tort or contract, the court's majority has not inferred a general requirement of "good faith" reasons for dismissal. "The law has long recognized the mutual right of both employers and employees to terminate an employment contract at any time provided there are no express provisions to the contrary." A minority of three on this point, however, added to the breach "an implied contractual term to act in good faith in dismissing an employee."[24]

Employees' privacy is increasingly protected as the technology to undermine it is increasingly perfected. While employers have long had the right to discipline even for off-duty ac

tivities which undermine their business or reputation,[25] polygraph tests cannot be demanded
from workers and polygraph evidence sometimes has been held inadmissible. Similarly for
fingerprinting employees and medical examinations to verify the employee's own medical certificate for justifying an absence.[26]

The duty to accommodate disabled work-
ers is one instance of the general difficulty of fitting occupational health and safety rules with
human rights. In *Alberta Human Rights Commission v. Central Alberta Dairy Pool*, the Supreme
Court reversed its earlier decision, and held that
a defence of "bona fide occupational qualification" was not applicable in cases of adverse impact discrimination, such as the hard hat rule
which adversely affected the Sikh, Bhinder.[27]
The employer's only defence in these is to show
that it would suffer undue hardship in accommodating employees who are disparately affected by apparently neutral employment rules
of general application. Both in the instance
where employers try to exclude workers on
health and safety ground or the workers seek a
safer work environment, the interface is not neat.

Disabled persons, AIDs patients, child-bear-
ing women, chemically or electrically sensitive
persons, older workers, injured returning workers, women, and other "non-traditional" workers fall under the effect of this ruling. Pregnant
waitresses employed at strip bars, flight attendants who wear contact lenses, millworkers and
carpenters' assistants with limited English,
armed forces personnel with asthma, heart conditions and epilepsy have won accommodation.
Such was Laurene Wiens, a woman of child-
bearing capacity who won an INCO job involving exposure to nickel carbonyl which harms
foetuses; such was Mira Heincke who won accommodation by a job change to the Emrick

Plastics packing plant and away from her spray
painting job when pregnant.[28] On the other
hand, longshoremen barred from employment
due to lack of physical co-ordination, insulin-
dependent diabetics refused work as railway
trackmen, eyeglass wearers denied bus-driving
jobs, persons deprived of careers in the armed
forces because of short stature, poor eyesight,
and kidney stones all had their rejections upheld
due to the health and safety rationale put forward by their employers.[29]

Chapter 5 - Discrimination

The imbalance in employment power is reflected in the legal treatment of vulnerable
groups of employees. While discrimination in
employing a protected group has been extended
to a business' non-intentional but "systemically"
disproportionate presence of its members in the
workforce since 1985,[30] remedies for first-hand
mistreatment still abound.

Disability is a prime target. When Betty-Lu
Clara Gibbs became disabled as a result of mental disorder, she took sick leave and replacement
income under an insurance policy that was an
employment benefit. The policy did not replace
income past two years for mental illness unless
the employee was in a mental institution. All levels held this provision discriminatory under s.
16(1) of *Saskatchewan Human Rights Code*.

"In defining the purpose of schemes, reference should thus not be made to specific
disabilities and specific target groups. To
permit this is to permit the kind of reasoning which led tribunals and courts in the
past to deny benefits to pregnant women, on
the ground that the schemes in question
were intended to compensate for illness

only. The focus of the inquiry should be placed on the need being provided for rather than on the class of person being compensated."[31]

Age discrimination is akin to disability. Pilots retired at age 60 alleged discrimination since most employees in Canada are required to retire at 65. The Supreme Court denied their appeal because the hearing board had no authority to declare laws invalid. But a minority of two commented that "usual practice may be unjustifiable, having regard to the egregiousness of the infringement or the insubstantiality of the objective alleged to support it. Each case must be looked at on its own circumstances."[32]

Gender discrimination in business remains present. A restauranteur demanded that his waitresses wear tight clothes and, when Isabelle Guimont refused to "undress to work," told her she didn't have the figure for it and fired her. The commissioner awarded lost wages, tips, and moral damages for violation of the Québec Charter, explaining:

"It is still quite common that women have to sell their sexual appearance at the same time they are selling something else. In this case, the owner made an arbitrary decision based on a stereotype of what an ideal woman is. I think this ruling sends a message that women must be treated with respect both in and outside the workplace."[33]

While the principle of equal pay for equal work has been codified by the International Labour Convention 100 since 1951, it was not until 1977 that the federal government brought in legislation which implemented the principle. Since then, most provinces have followed with their own statutes, but only a few affect the private sector besides the public sector.[34] The principle of pay equity incorporates the concept of "equal pay for *work of equal value*," and not only that of "equal pay for *equal work*." The principle's primary focus is upon disparities between the rewards for one type of work perceived as work for women and the rewards for another type of work perceived as work for men, while the types are comparable in terms of their economic value. The Public Service Alliance of Canada lodged one of the first complaints on behalf of librarians whom it represented, claiming back pay to equalize their rewards to those of historical researchers. The first profession is predominantly female; the latter, male. After taking from 1979 to 1998 to reach final decision, the Canadian Human Rights Tribunal made awards to rectify the wage gaps.[35]

Harassment at business carries business law beyond merely discrimination. A McDonald's manager was fired for genital touching of an employee who was subject to him. Although he had been twice rebuffed, the labour investigator dismissed the complaint because the manager had positive job evaluations, and the event occurred outside the workplace. The Superior Court reversed this holding, and said that it was not reasonable to conclude that there was only an error in judgment, because of his past bad conduct.[36]

Zero tolerance by employers for sexual harassment, however, is not sufficient grounds for discipline by termination. Instead, factors must be considered which mitigate or aggravate the offence: the employer's tolerance of harassment or "horseplay," whether others had been disciplined, the nature and gravity of the acts, their repetition or isolated occurrence, the harasser's seniority, record and demeanour, and generally the principles of progressive discipline need to be taken into account.[37]

While what in Québec are called moral damages may be available for business discrimination and harassment, more often there is no injury sufficiently evident to win these compensatory damages. This is the occasion for exemplary damages. New to Québec in 1975 under its Charter, despite their availability in Roman law, their availability for outrageous and scandalous behaviour and to express disapproval of actions contrary to fundamental values of the society is of longer standing at common law.[38]

Chapter 6 – Management/ Union Matters

Corporate relations with employees remain a bellwether of commercial trust and reciprocity, even though public favour for unions is at one of its nadirs right now. While North American unions remain most successful in the public administration sector, the construction and manufacturing industries are only 20% unionized.

Labour statutes are prominent in every jurisdiction.[39] They envisage the privately organized labour organisations of the atomistic market in 1944 when the Wartime Labour Relations Regulations of Order in Council P 1003 set up the initial labour statutes. These may be insufficient for public service labour and for the precarious employment and lessened protectionism today. Since most do follow a similar pattern in trying to achieve fair and peaceful commercial relations, however, a survey of the Québec *Labour Code* can suffice, although it is more labour-friendly than some others, while Ontario's swung in the 1990s first to labour-fawning and then to labour-hostile provisions.

Both employers and employees have the right to join in their respective associations, but solicitation cannot go on during working hours.

Neither may interfere with nor threaten the other's exercise of this right. An employees' association can become certified as the sole representative of members in its bargaining unit for the purpose of negotiating a collective agreement for them. Commissioners may be appointed to oversee certifications and a labour court is set up to hear appeals from commissioners' decisions.

Negotiations when begun must be carried on diligently and in good faith; during that time, no changes can be made in the conditions of employment. If negotiations are unsuccessful, first the parties may ask a government officer to conciliate them, and then after a set time is elapsed, viz. ninety days, they may strike or lockout the other respectively, in order to force the other to accept conditions of employment. At no other time may these labour actions be taken. While labour actions last, no new workers may be hired or used to replace those striking or locked out. Provision must be made for maintaining essential services in the case of strikes by employees of public enterprises.

After an agreement has been negotiated, any disputes about it are submitted to an arbitrator for settlement, although most agreements provide for grievance procedures in order to settle disputes internally first. Unions' exclusive representation rights impose upon them a duty to represent members fairly.[40] Discrimination not only on human rights grounds, but also on grounds of different employment or union status, violates this duty.

Despite the *Criminal Code* and *Competition Act* prohibitions against businesses' blocking union activity, there are exceptions. The statutory prohibition on R.C.M.P. officers' forming a union is not unconstitutional, for formation of an employees' union is not part of the freedom of association. The Supreme Court in a 1987 trilogy had found that this freedom did not include the right to strike nor to bargain collectively; and without those rights, there is no relevance to organizing a union.[41]

Once a union is in place, however, reciprocal good faith is required from the participants. Because Royal Oak Mine's management had not bargained in good faith, by refusing to bargain until one dispute over certification and another over rehiring discharged workers had been resolved, the court imposed the last contract which the employer had offered but then had withdrawn, even though imposing nearly a complete collective agreement is usually beyond the labour relations board's reach. Making a reasonable effort to bargain is measured by an objective standard. This "prevents a party from hiding behind an assertion that it is sincerely trying to reach an agreement when, viewed objectively, it can be seen that its proposals are so far from the accepted norms of the industry that they must be unreasonable."[42]

Chapter 7 – Profit

There are several profitmaking activities that are legally wrongful, some of which are found in the *Criminal Code of Canada*.[43] Generally, profitmaking acts which are offences against public order are prohibited. More relevant to business are "fraudulent transactions relating to contracts and trade." Complementary to these are the uniquely commercial remedies by seizing the "proceeds of crime" from "enterprise crime offences" that are more akin to commercial joint ventures.

"Every one who, by deceit, falsehood or other fraudulent means, whether or not it is a false pretence within the meaning of this Act,

defrauds the public or any person, whether ascertained or not, of any property, money or valuable security" is guilty of an offence (sec. 380). This offence of fraud has distinctively commercial occurrences identified for the stockmarket, by mails, or regarding real estate, receipts, advances, bank accounts, fares, mines and minerals. Even more particular to business is fraud falsifying credit statements, employment records, prospectuses, billings or accounts.

Reduction of profitable competition is done by the restrictive trade practices forbidden. Such are refusal to deal, consignment selling and exclusive dealing (restricting supplies to competitors), tied selling (requiring purchase of other products as the condition for supplying the one ordered), freight equalization, fighting brands, pre-emption of scarce facilities, buying up products to keep up prices, product specifications incompatible with any other supplier's products, selling at lower than the acquisition cost to discipline a competitor, and delivered pricing (refusing delivery in a competing region). These acts amount to "abuse of dominant position" and are prohibited when they effect a substantial lessening of competition. Dominant position means that "one or more persons substantially or completely control, throughout Canada or any area thereof, a class or species of business" (sec. 51.(1)(a)).

A requirement for fair competition is to outlaw intimidation, which includes the use of violence or threats of violence "wrongfully and without lawful authority, for the purpose of compelling another person to abstain from doing anything that he has a lawful right to do, or to do anything that he has a lawful right to abstain from doing ..." (sec. 423(1)).

Its unfairness leads society to outlaw both the negative reinforcement of intimidation and the positive inducement of bribery. Under the extended statement of the latter offence when carried out with government officials, at section 121 of the *Code*, the Supreme Court decided that Michel Cogger did not have to know he had received benefits because of his office, but know only that he is an official, that he is receiving a benefit, and that the benefit is for his help in getting business with the government. That is to say, "'[c]orruption' is not a required element." Cogger obtained a loan and received fees from two companies as their lawyer for making representations to several levels of government, both before and after he was appointed to the Senate.[44]

Profit-making is greatly facilitated by incorporation, the creature of law which encourages investment by allowing enterprisers to limit their commercial losses. While "a corporation has the capacity and ... the rights, powers and privileges of a natural person" under section 15 of the *Canada Business Corporations Act*,[45] "[t]he shareholders of a corporation are not, as shareholders, liable for any liability, act or default of the corporation" (sec. 43); nor are directors liable for making good the market value of shares issued below that value, if they dissent from the issue. Directors are liable, however, for six months wages of employees. Shareholders own the corporation, directors set its long-term direction, and managers are employees who run it daily.

Complaints that limited liability (caught in the suffix "Limited" or "Limitée" to corporate names) leads to corporate irresponsibility are captured in the French suffix "Société anonyme." Irresponsibility has been buffered both by holding corporate entities criminally responsible[46] and, as the complementary strategy, by penetrating the "corporate veil" more frequently, namely the artificial legal identity behind which the real entrepreneurs can shield

themselves. Factors which incline toward lifting the veil on misrepresentation and reliance are functional control of the company, and commingling of its assets with officers,' which imply agency on the part of officers.

Statutory prohibition and incorporation are the less humane sources for profitable norms in commercial law, even if the most obvious. Trustworthiness is not only enforced upon business law, but is at home with its own name there. Trusts are those obligations which are sometimes contracted, but now often construed by courts, in order to protect a relation of dependence and vulnerability, entered as the only way to achieve some business profit. Trusts relate traditionally to transactions in real estate, when one party was beholden to the other in a feudal way; and to relations where one puts his welfare into another's hands, as in insurance, warranties and guarantees, and other forms of agency. In addition to these trusts in direct commercial relations, legal relations within the corporation as the commercial agent for "other people's money" are often fiduciary.

Chapter 8 – Uniquely Canadian Issues

The national trust for aboriginal and French cultures is increasingly invoked in figuring their commercial entitlements. The legal trust which the Crown bears for aboriginal peoples, like other commercial fiduciary relations, is directed at developing the culture's distinctiveness, not at infantilising dependency. It is "the two-row wampum," with care that aboriginals' and later residents' cultures remain strong by pursuing their respective paths.

The four thousand pages of the *Report of the Royal Commission on Aboriginal Peoples* in 1996 provides little information on the status of aboriginal businesses, and focuses more upon land claims, self-government, the penal system, and the socio-economic resources to be provided in order to make these work.[47] Specialised texts, instead, focus upon aboriginal enterprise under various statutes: the management and development of communal and individual land and property including its encumbrances, uses for mining, timber, oil and gas, and transactions in products, as well as its taxation regimes.[48]

The courts' decisions have increasingly fostered respect for this commercial trust, in terms of prior enterprises, and newer ones, whether or not centred around the use of land. The *Van der Peet* trilogy is the major recent contribution on traditional commercial activities,[49], as is the *Delgamuukw* decision upon land.[50] In the trilogy, convictions under the B.C. *Fishery Act* were upheld for two Sto:lo fish sellers and overturned in the third case for a Heiltsuk fisher, because their businesses were and were not, respectively, integral to their distinctive cultures.

Dorothy Van de Peet's Sto:lo people's exchanges of fish were only "incidental" to their food fishing, they had no regularized system prior to contact, their later trade was not typical of them, and their lack of specialisation in the fishery meant it was not central to Slo:lo culture. Said Justice McLaughlin in dissent to this,

> "The sale at issue should not be labelled as something other than commerce. One person selling something to another is commerce. The critical question is not whether the sale of the fish is commerce or non-commerce, but whether the sale can be defended as the exercise of a more basic aboriginal right to continue the aboriginal people's historic use of the resource. ... The

right is not the right to trade, but the right to continue to use the resource in the traditional way to provide for traditional needs, albeit in their modern form."

Using this criterion, Howard Pamajewon's high stakes bingo parlour on the Shawanaga reserve was prohibited, since "the evidence presented did not show that gambling every played an important role in the cultures of the Shawanaga ...."[51]

In *Delgamuukw*, however, the Gitksan and Wet'su'wet'en peoples' claim for damages from the province's use of lands on which they claimed aboriginal title was given a new trial, since the trial judge had not allowed evidence from oral histories. In defining what their right to deal with land could be, the court decided, on the one hand that it "incorporates present-day needs. ... [M]ineral rights and lands held pursuant to aboriginal title should be capable of exploitation. Such a use is certainly not a traditional one." On the other hand, "[t]he concept of aboriginal title contains an inherent limit in that lands so held cannot be used in a manner that is irreconcilable with the nature of the claimants' attachment to those lands." That is, the title

> "should not be prevented from continuing into the future. ... Lands held by virtue of aboriginal title may not be alienated because the land has an inherent and unique value in itself, which is enjoyed by the community with aboriginal title to it. The community cannot put the land to uses which would destroy that value. ... If aboriginal peoples wish to use their lands in a way that aboriginal title does not permit, then they must surrender those lands and convert them into non-title lands to do so."

The distinctiveness of French Canadian legal culture in both code and interpretative principles is seen in the distinctive ways of estimating discrimination, labour law, trust property, and exemplary damages. Commercial law may prove the most stable distinctiveness among traditional "creed, code and tongue" when, at least in Québec, the first has been abandoned and the last has become disproportionate.

The narrower distinctiveness in the legal culture of French Canadian business, however, is to be found since 1977 in the requirements under the *Charter of the French Language in Quebec (Bill 101)* that the language of business be French.[52] The "Language of Labour Relations" requires that notices, offers of employment, collective agreements, arbitration awards, and union communications are in French as their official language. Requiring knowledge of any other language for employment is prohibited, as is dismissal for lacking such knowledge.

The chapter on "The Language of Commerce and Business" requires that corporate and commercial firm names be in French only, excepting ones that involve family or ethnic names and non-profit organizations. External signs must be in French only, as must internal signs and business communications, excepting ethnic ones. Catalogues, brochures, and folders must be in French. Labels must be in French, but another language may accompany this if it is given less prominence. Toys and games cannot be sold which require non-French vocabulary, unless a French version is on the market on no less favourable terms. Films are added by regulation; software is being considered. Adhesion contracts must be in French, unless the parties request otherwise.

While these provisions appear to fly in the face of the guarantees for freedom of expression in section 2(b) of the 1982 *Canadian Charter of Rights and Freedoms*,[53] litigation on the language of commercial signs before the Supreme Court resulted in the requirement that unilingual sign laws permit multilingual signs on which the French language is predominant. The reasonableness under law which the Court took to permit this restriction was the threat to the survival of French as a working language in the province, perceived through demographic studies. Remedying that threat cannot become disproportionately restrictive.[54] A 1983 amendment to Bill 101 incorporates this result.

The final sections of Bill 101 that are relevant to business are in the chapter on the "Francization of Business Firms." Francization is a program intended to generalize the use of French at all levels of the business firm, from directors to office staff, at work, on manuals and in ads, internally and with clients, and as a criterion for advancement. The program requires a business firm with fifty or more employees to establish a committee that designs a plan approved by the government's Office de la Langue Française for achieving that goal. That plan entitles a firm to a francization certificate, as does its achievement. The certificate may be withdrawn if use of French declines again. Operating without that certificate is an offence subject to fines up to $5000 per instance. Regulations under the *Act* make provisions for smaller companies, for ads not displayed, and for head offices with more than 50% of their income over the preceding three years from outside Quebec.

Chapter 9 - International Business

The law of contract is of closest relevance to international business. In their contracts, businesspersons create relationships where none existed before, create them to their choice, and create them in order to open up possibilities for action where none existed before. The law of contract codifies the way businesspersons expect others to conduct themselves in freedom and contains the frequent inconsistencies between jurisdictions that one would expect from such spontaneous activity.

Harmonising various jurisdictions' contractual and commercial law can, nonetheless, help merchants. The European Community's 1994 UNIDROIT has recently been found consistent with Québec's new codal provisions of the same year, in making contractual freedom, consensualism and *favor contractus* their starting point, as well as stressing contractual justice by its requirements for public order, good faith, appropriate balance of capacities, and reasonable accommodation.[55] The most famous venture toward harmonisation, the U.S. *Uniform Commercial Code* (UCC), and its predecessors since 1860, has tried to codify local business practice by its "incorporation principle," that in case of silence or insufficiency of the contractual provisions, the UCC's norms are incorporated into the contract, since these are generally known and accepted. That reason has been put in doubt as more fiction than empirical reality.[56] The UCC has been adopted by all states but Louisiana, and is the basis for all provinces' *Sale of Goods Acts* but Québec's. In Canada the Canadian Bar Association since 1918 has sponsored an annual Conference on the Harmonisation of Laws, to suggest model legislation for the provinces. The Canadian government has empowered first the Canada Law Reform Commission and now the Canada Law Commission to do the same for legislation within its own jurisdiction.[57]

The *Canada-U.S. Trade Agreement* in 1987, expanded into the *North American Free Trade Agreement* (NAFTA) several years later, provides typical mechanisms for submission of trade disputes under treaty to a joint commission for resolution.[58] Without a joint hearing, disputes regarding such issues as dumping are heard instead by the importing country's own authorities. Thus the case of *Cars Produced by or on Behalf of Hyundai Motor Company* was decided by the Canadian Import Tribunal (later the Canadian International Trade Tribunal) in 1988.[59] The tribunal acted under the *Special Import Measures Act*.[60] General Motors of Canada and Ford of Canada complained that the South Korean car manufacturer was causing material injury to them by importing its Pony, Stellar, and Excel models into Canada at prices below their normal values in the Korean market. The tribunal found that the average 26.3% margin of dumping for these models had not caused material injury to domestic producers, thus providing an anti-protectionist decision to a protectionist statute, alleged to benefit consumers by enhancing competition.

NAFTA provides also for side agreements on labour and environmental issues, the North American Agreements on Labor Cooperation (NAALC) and on Environmental Cooperation (NAAEC) that took effect in 1994. The former's eleven labour principles reassert domestic principles, adding the prohibition of forced labour and child labour, as well as protection of migrant workers. It does not provide for remedies like certification of unions, nor a tribunal to decide disputes, but makes accessible a flexible forum for transnational action by unions and other groups.

Arbitration and not litigation has been the way in which the internationally adopted "law merchant" of English trade has operated for centuries. The *Commercial Arbitration Act* incorporates the *Model Law on International Commercial Arbitration* for conflict resolution set out by the United Nations.[61] All provinces have also used that name, except Québec which enacts it in the *Civil Code*. Article 7 gives an apt definition of the most usual resolution of commercial claims at law:

> "'Arbitration agreement' is an agreement by the parties to submit to arbitration all or certain disputes which have arisen or which may arise between them in respect of a defined legal relationship, whether contractual or not. An arbitration agreement may be in the form of an arbitration clause in a contract or in the form of a separate agreement."

The World Bank now includes the nurturing of government integrity as part of its development efforts. The Organization for Economic Co-operation and Development has an anti-bribery code that is newly supported by a Canadian law prohibiting the bribery of foreign public officials for commercial gain. Although 'bribery' is the term which has usually been taken to sum up the entirety of business ethics,[62] it remains still only the lay term for this offence. In the *Corruption of Foreign Public Officials Act*, the offence of corruption is committed by one

> "who, in order to obtain or retain an advantage in the course of business, directly or indirectly gives, offers or agrees to give or offer a loan, reward, advantage or benefit of any kind to a foreign public official or to any person for the benefit of a foreign official (a) as consideration for an act or omission by the official in connection with the performance of the official's duties or functions; or (b) to induce the official to use his or her

position to influence any acts or decisions of the foreign state or public international organization for which the official performs duties or functions."[63]

Further subsections of this act recognize the realities of some other countries' practices, however, by exempting such payments when permitted by the foreign laws, or when made to expedite or secure the performance of the official's routine duties.

Chapter 10 –
Business and the Environment

Every jurisdiction has in force environmental legislation which targets the materials and practices of businesses from heavy industry to informational technology.[64] Of course, its sufficiency is disputed, and its impact is subject to avoidance so far as it becomes an obstacle to business practice.

Hydro-Québec dumped PCBs into rivers in early 1990, and was charged with infractions of orders under the federal *Environmental Protection Act*. While the Quebec courts found those orders and sections of the Act invalid as beyond federal heads of power, the Supreme Court barely held them to be a valid exercise of criminal law power. The majority held that protecting the environment is a legitimate public purpose, effected by prohibitions on a limited number of substances, with penalties attached, so as not to invade provincial jurisdiction. A certain amount of imprecision is inevitable with such a wide subject of legislation, and complementary orders are able to specify them without turning the crime into a regulatory scheme. The remaining four justices dissented that, while the purpose was legitimate, there was no prohibition of pollution, but only a regulatory scheme for disposing of some chemicals, which kept these measures from being an exercise of the federal criminal law power. Especially the power of the Minister to issue orders that expand the prohibited list, when of the opinion that the environment is not protected or is inadequately protected from some toxic substance, is inconsistent with exercise of the criminal law power.[65]

The immensity of enforcement being as problematic as that of the subject matter, voluntary settlements by polluters are provided for in many statutes. The usefulness of voluntary settlements, even arbitrated ones, has been brought into doubt. The Canadian firm Cambior Inc. was denounced as immoral and unethical for paying illiterate fishermen in Guyana $150 each to settle all possible legal claims arising from the huge cyanide spill in August 1995 into the Omai River from its gold mine there. This was done while tests on toxicity were still being conducted, when long-term impact on the residents was unknown, and in breach of an agreement to submit its compensation claim to the Guyanese government before settling any citizens' claims, according to reports at the time. Cambior's chief financial officer claimed that the $150 cap on claims was given in order to act as a good corporate citizen, and that this was acceptable and accepted in view of the local economic conditions. "Reasonable people talking to reasonable people established that it was fair compensation."[66]

Chapter 11 – The Medical Business

The range of law applicable to medical businesses is too vast for succinct treatment, so only a selection can be made. The pre-Charter principle of medical experimentation is that "the therapeutical privilege clearly cannot permit information to be hidden on the pretext that the subject must not be disturbed." The inviolability of the person adds that for consent one needs the opportunity to become aware of essential information such as the purpose, means, duration, tests, risks and discomforts, collective benefits, and the right to withdraw. The risk must not be disproportionate to the benefit reasonably hoped for.[67]

The settlement by medical providers of potential claims before they are made, or before the injuries even appear, by filing and settling class action suits for all injuries ("futures settlements") is of increasing concern. While these avoid all the monetary damages going to lawyers, there is no guarantee that the settlement amounts will last long enough to cover future claims, which may take years to develop.

Biotechnology licensing should describe exactly what rights are being granted, e.g., whether the license contains a right to sublicense, whether the licensee participates in any clinical trials which may be required, whether the licensee participates in the regulatory approval process, and whether the licensee receives access to the know-how of the licensor; plus the parties' protection of one another's confidential information and trade secrets, royalties and other forms of payment, product liability and indemnification, use of each other's trademarks, and guarantee of secure supplies.

Patent is more demanding than copyright. Developing a type of mouse that gets cancer easily by injecting its cells with a cancer-prone gene is not an invention under Canadian law, for "they have not invented the mouse. A complex life form does not fit within the current parameters of the *Patent Act* without stretching the meaning of the words to the breaking point."

Only single-cell life forms may be patented. But is Parliament wishes to patent life, it could.[68]

While since 1995 the Criminal Code has had rules of evidence regarding proof by genetic analyses, the federal *Genetic Privacy Act* permits no other person to have in its possession or under its control any identifiable sample of DNA or genetic information about any person. In regulating this, the concept of property is used but is inadequate since this regards human material; the concept of ordinary medical "information" is used. The U.K. suggested but E.C. refused in 1991 that genetic information be considered as the common possession of the persons who share the same genes.

Chapter 12 – Ethical Investing

There are no laws applicable specifically to ethical investing, but those regarding fiduciary obligations, applicable to investment business in general, and those regarding misrepresentation, applicable to advertising in general, would be relevant.

NOTES

1. "The true doctrine is, that there is no confidence as to the disclosure of iniquity" (*Gartside v. Outram* (1856), 26 L.J.Ch. 113, per Sir William Page-Wood V.-C.); or, beyond criminal offences, "It extends to any misconduct of such a nature that it ought in the public interest to be disclosed to others." (*Initial Services Ltd. v. Putterill*, [1967] 3 All E.R. 145 (C.A.) per Lord Denning, M.R.).

2. *Re Ministry of Attorney General, Corrections Branch and British Columbia Government Employees' Union* (1981) L.A.C. (3d) 140.

3. *Canadian Environmental Protection Act*, R.S.C. 1985, c. C-15.3; *Canada Labour Code*, R.S.C. 1985, c. L-2; *Canadian Human Rights Act*, R.S.C. 1985, c. H-6; *Occupational Health and Safety Act*, R.S.O. 1990, c. O.1; *Environmental Bill of Rights*, S.O. 1993, c. 28; *Environmental Protection Act*, R.S.O. 1990, c. E.19; applied in *Marshall v. Varnicolor Chemical Ltd.* (1991), 8 C.E.L.R. 29.

4. *Competition Act*, S.C. 1986, c. C-34; *An act to amend the Competition Act*, S.C. 1999, c. 2.

5. Charles L. Dubin Q.C., John Terry, *Whistleblowing Study*, commissioned by Industry Canada Competition Bureau, 20 August 1997; and *Addendum*, 30 September 1997.

6. *An act to amend the Competition Act*, S.C. 1992, c. 14.

7. R.S.C. 1985, c. C-34, "An Act to Provide for the Investigation of Combines, Monopolies, Trusts and Mergers."

8. *Irwin Toys v. Québec*, (1989) 1 S.C.R. 927.

9. S.C. 1997, c. 13; *An act to amend the Tobacco Act*, S.C. 1998, c. 38.

10. R.S.C. 1985, c. C-38.

11. *R. v. T.Eaton Co.* (1973), 10 C.P.R.(2d) 36 (Ont.Co.Ct.); *R.v. T.Eaton Co.* (1971), 4 C.P.R.(2d) 226 (Ont.Prov.Ct.), respectively.

12. *R. v. K.B.M. Electropedic Adjustable Beds Ltd.* (1983), 75 C.P.R.(2d) 58 (Alta.Q.B.); *R. v. Robin Hood Multifoods Ltd.* (1981), 59 C.P.R.(2d) 57 (Ont.Co.Ct.); *R. v. Irving Oil Ltd.* (1978), 47 C.P.R.(2d) 179 (N.B.Prov.Ct.), respectively.

13. *R. v. Lowe Real Estate Ltd.* (1978), 40 C.C.C.(2d) 529 (Ont.C.A.); *R. v. Reader's Digest Assn. Ltd.* (1974), 17 C.P.R.(2d) 173 (Que.S.C.); *R. v. Cunningham Drug Stores Ltd.* (1973), 13 C.P.R.(2d) 244 (B.C.C.A.), respectively.

14. R.S.C. 1985, c. H-3; R.S.C. 1985, c. W-6; R.S.C. 1985, c. F-27; R.S.O. 1980, c. 376, respectively.

15. One of the most straightforward treatments of commercial contract law remains *The Sale of Goods*, 5 ed., by P.S. Atiyah (Toronto: Pitman, 1975). One of the best introductory collections remains *Cases in Canadian Business Law*, 2 ed., ed. David C. McPhillips, Irwin Davis and Gerald G. Smeltzer (Scarborough ON: Prentice-Hall Canada, 1985). Even broader and more colloquial is *That's Business ... But Is It Legal?* by Claire D. Bernstein (Toronto: Methuen, 1984), taken from her newspaper columns in Québec and common law provinces.

16. *Consumer Protection Act*, R.S.Q. 1994, c. P.40.1; *Consumer Protection Act*, R.S.O.1990, c. C.31; *Consumer Protection Act*, R.S.B.C. 1996, c. C.49. The federal jurisdiction has little to do in this area but oversee interprovincial trade by the *Consumer Packaging and Labelling Act*, S.C. 1993 (R.S.C. 1985), C-38.

17. Ontario Ministry of Consumer and Commercial Relations, *A Consultation Draft of the Consumer and Business Practices Code*, Toronto, 1990.

18. C.C.Q. 1437 and 1623 CCQ, invoked in *Shlush Puppie Montreal Inc. v. 153226 Canada Inc.*, [1994] R.J.Q. 1703.

19. *Consumer Product Warranties Act 1977*, S.S. 1976-77, c. 15; *An Act to Amend the Consumer Product Warrant and Liability Act*, S.M. 1980, c.12.

20. *Bow Valley Husky v. Saint John Shipbuilding*, [1997] 3 S.C.R. 1212 (Nfld.).

21. *An Act Respecting Industrial Accidents and Occupational Diseases*, R.S.Q. 1994, A-3.001; *An Act Respecting Labour Standards*, R.S.Q. 1994, N-1.1; *An Act Respecting Occupational Health and Safety*, R.S.Q. 1994 S-2.1; *Workmen's Compensation Act*, R.S.Q. 1994, A-3; *An Act Respecting Industrial Accidents and Occupational Diseases*, R.S.Q. 1994, c. A-3.001.

22. *Employment Standards Act*, R.S.O. 1990, E.14; *Industrial Standards Act*, R.S.Q. I.6; *Occupational Health and Safety Act*, R.S.O. O.1; *Workplace Safety and Insurance Act*, S.O. 1997, c. 16; *Employment Standards Act*, R.S.B.C. 1996, c. E.11; *Workers Compensation Act*, R.S.B.C. 1996, c. W.492; *Workplace Act*, R.S.B.C. 1996, c. 2.493.

23. *Wallace v. United Grain Growers Ltd.*, [1997] 3 S.C.R. 701 (Man.).

24. *Wallace v. United Grain Growers Ltd.*, [1997] 3 S.C.R. 701 (Man.).

25. *Pearce v. Foster* (1886), 17 Q.B.D. 536 (C.A.); in *B.C. Workers Compensation Bd. v. Compensation Employees' Union* (1997), 64 L.A.C.(4th) 401 (B.C.).

26. *Employment Standards Act*, R.S.O. 1990, c. E.14, ss. 46, 48, 78; *Canada Post Corp. v. C.U.P.W.* (1988), 34 L.A.C.(3d) 392; *Monarch Fine Foods Co. v. Milk & Bread Drivers, Dairy Employees, Caterers & Allied Employees, Local 647* (1978), 20 L.A.C.(2d) 419 (Ont.), respectively.

27. [1990] 2 S.C.R. 489, reversing *Bhinder and Canadian Human Rights Commission v. Canadian National Railway* [1985] 2 S.C.R. 561.

28. *Wiens v. Inco Metals Co.* (1988), 9 C.H.R.R. D/4795; *Heincke v. Emrick Plastics* (1990), 91 C.L.L.C. #17,010.

29. See for citations David Leitch, "Occupational Health and Safety and Human Rights in the Workplace: Not Always a Comfortable Fit," *Canadian Labour Law Journal* 2 (1994), 231 at p. 236.

30. *Canadian National Railway Company v. Canadian Human Rights Commission*, (1985) 62 N.R. 354 (F.C.A.); in Deborah C. Poff and Wilfrid Waluchow, *Business Ethics in Canada*,

2 ed. (Scarborough, Prentice-Hall Canada, 1991), 234.

31. *Battlefords and District Co-operative Ltd. v. Gibbs*, [1996] 3 S.C.R. 566 (Sask.).

32. *Cooper v. Canada (Human Rights Commission)*, [1996] 3 S.C.R. 854.

33. *Isabelle Guimont v. Pietro Turco*, Québec Human Rights Commission, June 1997.

34. For example, *Pay Equity Act*, R.S.Q. 1996, c. E-12.001; *Pay Equity Act*, R.S.O. 1990, c. P.7.

35. *P.S.A.C.(No.3) v. Canada (Treasury Board)* (1998), 32 C.H.R.R. D/349.

36. *Rooke v. Barnard*, [1964] A.C. 1129; approved in *Hill v. Church of Scientology*, [1995] 2 S.C.R. 1130.

37. *Western Grocers v. U.F.C.W., Local 1400* (1993), 32 L.A.C.(4th) 63.

38. *McDonald's Restaurants Canada v. Couture*, Cour supérieure, Montréal 500-05-009527-951, 19 Dec 1995.

39. In Canada, the *Canada Labour Code*, R.S.C. 1985, c. L-2, with the *Fair Wages and Hours of Labour Act*, R.S.C. 1985, c. L-4, the *Public Service Employment Act*, R.S.C. 1985, c. P-33, and the *Public Service Staff Relations Act*, R.S.C. 1985, c. P-35; in Ontario, the *Labour Relations Act*, 1995, S.O. 1995, c. 1, supplemented by the *Rights of Labour Act*, R.S.O. 1990, c. R.33, and the *Employers and Employees Act*, R.S.0. 1990, E.12, as well as statutes for labour relations in particular industries and the public service; in Québec, the *Labour Code*, R.S.Q. 1994, c. C-27, with *An Act Respecting Labour Standards*, R.S.Q., c. N-1.1, and the *Professional Syndicates Act* [R.S.Q., c. S-40]; in British Columbia, the *Labour Relations Code*, R.S.B.C. 1996, c. L.255, and the *Public Sector Labour Relations Act*, R.S.B.C. 1996, c. P.388.

40. *Fisher v. Pemberton* (1970), 8 D.L.R.(3d) 521 (B.C.S.C.).

41. *A.F.P.C. v. Canada*, [1987] 1 S.C.R. 424; *Reference on Public Service Employee Relations Act*, [1987] 1 S.C.R. 313; and *S.D.G.M.R. v. Saskatchewan*, [1987] 1 S.C.R. 460; cited in *Delisle v. Canada*, [1997] R.J.Q. (C.A. Montréal).

42. *Royal Oak Mines v Canada (Labour Relations Board)*, [1996] 1 S.C.R. 369 (Federal Court).

43. *Criminal Code of Canada*, R.S.C. 1985, c. C-46. See *Le Droit de la concurrence au Canada*, by Yves Bériault, Madeleine Renaud, Yves Comtois (Toronto: Carswell, 1999).

44. *R. v. Cogger*, [1997] 2 S.C.R. 845 (Qué.).

45. *Canada Business Corporations Act*, S.C. 1993, C-44 (Office of Supply and Services consolidation of R.S.C. 1985); similarly in the *Ontario Business Corporations Act*, R.S.O. 1970, c. 53; and Québec *Companies Act*, R.S.Q. 1994, C-38.

46. Harry J. Glasbeek, "Criminal Prosecution of Corporate Wrongdoing" (1984), in Poff and Waluchow, 102; and *R. v. Fane Robinson Ltd.*, (1941) 76 C.C.C. 196 (Alta C.A.), *Ibid.* 110.

47. Office of Supply and Services.

48. Such as *Native Law* by Jack Woodward (Carswell, 1994), ch. 9-12.

49. *R. v. Van der Peet*, [1996] 2 S.C.R. 507 (BC); *R. v. N.T.C. Smokehouse Ltd.*, [1996] 2 S.C.R. 672; *R. v. Gladstone*, [1996] 2 S.C.R. 723.

50. *Delgamuukw v. B.C.*, [1997] 3 S.C.R. 1010.

51. *R. v. Pamajewon*, [1996] 2 S.C.R. 821.

52. R.S.Q., c. C-11.

53. Appendix II, no. 44, Annex B, to the *Constitution Act 1982*, in the *Canada Act 1982*, U.K., ch. 11; R.S.Q., c. C-12.

54. *Brown's Shoes Inc., McKenna Inc., Masson Tailors, National Cheese Co., and Valerie Ford v. A.-G.Québec*, [1988] 3 S.C.R.

55. Paul-A.Crépeau, *Les principes d'UNIDROIT et le Code civil du Québec: valeurs partagées?* (Toronto: Carswell, 1998).

56. Lisa Bernstein, "The Questionable Empirical Basis of Article 2's [UCC] Incorporation Strategy: A Preliminary Study," <www.crdp.umontreal.ca/fr/conferences/certitudes>; "Merchant Law in a Merchant Court: Rethinking the Code's Search for Immanent Business Norms," (1996) 144 *U.Penn.L.R.* 1765-1821.

57. See, generally, *Introduction to International Business Law: Legal Transactions in a Global Economy*, sponsored by the American Association of Law Libraries, eds. Gitelle Seer and Maria I. Molka-Day (New York, Oceana Publications, Inc., 1996), with chapters on legislation about the regulation of ventures, antitrust, intellectual property, taxation, labour, and organizations.

58. (1992), 32 I.L.M. 605 (U.S.-Can.-Mex.).

59. CIT-13-87.

60. R.S.C. 1985, c. S-15, implementing 1979 GATT Anti-dumping Code negotiated under the Tokyo Round revisions of the Kennedy Round interpretations of article VI in the *General Agreement on Trade and Tariffs*.

61. S.C. 1986, c. 22, adopting the UNCITRAL Report of the United Nations Commission on International Trade Law, 18th Session, June 3-21, 1985, Supplement no. 17 (A/40/17) of the Official Records of the 40th Session of the General Assembly, United Nations, New York, 1985.

62. Yerachmid Yiegel and Neal P. Cohen's title, *Government Regulation of Business Ethics: U.S. Legislation on International Payoffs* (Dobbs Ferry NY: Oceana, 1978), takes for granted that the breadth of business ethics in law is narrowed to bribery.

63. S.C. 1998, c. C-34. "'Corruptly' ... in the context of secret commissions, means without disclosure ..." *R.v. Kelly*, [1992] 2. S.C.R. 170, Cory J.; in *The Dictionary of Canadian Law*, 2 ed., ed. Daphne A. Dukelow, Betsy Nuse (Carswell, 1995).

64. Besides statutes to preserve particular industries, such as fisheries and agriculture (bees and bulls, butter and cheese, cows and furs, edible oils, and animal health generally), grain and mines, oil and gas, forests and energy, the general statutes include, for example, the following: in Canada, the *Canadian Environmental Protection Act*, S.C. 1988, c. 22, with a replacement now before Parliament, replacing *Environmental Contaminants Act*, R.S.C. 1985, E-12; *Transportation of Dangeorus Goods Act*, S.C. 1992, c. 34, amplifying the act of similar name at R.S.C. 1985, c. T-19, the *Safe Containers Convention*, R.S.C. 1985, c. S-1, and the *Hazardous Products Act*, R.S.C. 1985, c. H-3; *Ocean Dumping Control Act*, R.S.C. 1985, c. O-2; in Quebec, the *Environmental Quality Act*, R.S.Q., c. Q-2; in Ontario, the *Environmental Protection Act*, R.S.O. 1990, c. E.19, the *Environmental Assessment Act*, R.S.O. 1990, c. E.18, and the *Environmental Bill of Rights Act*, 1993, S.O. 1993, c. 28; in British Columbia, the *Environment and Land Use Act*, R.S.B.C. 1996, c. E.117, the *Environmental Management Act*, R.S.B.C. 1996, c. E.118, and the *Environmental Assessment Act*, R.S.B.C., c. E.119.

65. *R. v. Hydro-Québec*, [1997] 3 S.C.R. 213.

66. Problems of compliance were studied also in the Law Reform Commission of Canada's 1986 working paper number 53, on *Workplace Pollution*.

67. *Halushka v University of Saskatchewan*, [1965] 53 DLR 2d 435; *Civil Code of Québec*, S.Q.

1994, sec. s.10-24; *Declaration of Helsinki,* principle 9; *Convention for the protection of human rights and dignity of the human person in applications of biology and medicine,* Council of Europe a.16.

68. *Boutin v Bilodeau,* [1988] 18 C.P.R. (3d) 243; *Harvard University v. Canada (Patent Office),* 22 April 1998, Federal Court.

Notes on the Contributors

SISSELA BOK

Formerly a Professor of Philosophy at Brandeis University, Bok is currently a Distinguished Fellow at the Harvard Center for Population and Development Studies. She has written several books, including *Secrets: On the Ethics of Concealment and Revelation* (1989), *A Strategy for Peace: Human Values and the Threat of War* (1989), *Common Values* (1996), and *Mayhem: Violence as Public Entertainment* (1998).

GRANT A. BROWN

Grant A. Brown could not be located for biographical notes. At the time of publication in *Journal of Business Ethics* (1992), he was a Lecturer in the Faculty of Management, University of Lethbridge, and a D.Phil. candidate in philosophy. His "Critical Notice" of Jan Narveson's *The Libertarian Idea* appeared in the *Canadian Journal of Philosophy* (September 1990).

WESLEY CRAGG

Dr. Cragg is a Professor of Business Ethics at York University, where he is responsible for coordinating research and curriculum development on the ethical dimensions of public, para-public, not-for-profit, and private sector management. He has published widely and his current research includes business and occupa-tional ethics, environmental ethics, moral education, philosophy of law, and philosophy of punishment. He is also President of Transparency International (an international anti-corruption coalition).

PETER DICKEY

With a B.Sc. in Mechanical Engineering from Queen's University in 1966, Peter Dickey worked in a variety of positions in the oil and gas industry and then in 1994 started P.S.Dickey Consultants Ltd., a Canadian company based in Alberta. Areas of focus have included refinery projects, energy conservation, oil sands development, safety and environmental management, issue management (including global climate change, environmental liability assessment, environmental reporting and sustainable development policy implementation), and strategic planning and risk assessment for corporate clients.

SUSAN DIMOCK

Susan Dimock (Ph.D. in Philosophy, Dalhousie University, 1994) is currently an Associate Professor at York University. Professor Dimock's central research interests focus on the philosophy of law and punishment theory, ethics, personal autonomy and political philosophy.

RONALD F. DUSKA

Ronald F. Duska, professor of ethics at The American College, specializes in ethical theory and business ethics. In addition to numerous articles, he has written several books including *Business Ethics, Organizational Behavior in Insurance, Ethics and Corporate Responsibility: Theory, Cases and Dilemmas, Education, Leadership and Business Ethics: A Symposium in Honor of Clarence Walton*, and *The Ethics of Accounting* (in progress). He also has developed a program for senior executives, "Leadership Seminar in Ethics and Market Conduct."

MARY GIBSON

Mary Gibson is Associate Professor of Philosophy at Rutgers University, where she also teaches in the Women's Studies Program. She has served multiple terms as President and as Grievance Chair, among other offices, in the Rutgers Council of AAUP Chapters, part of a national professional association and the collective bargaining agent for Rutgers faculty and teaching and graduate assistants.

ANDERS HAYDEN

Anders Hayden is the Research & Policy Coordinator for 32 Hours: Action for Full Employment, an organization committed to a reduction and redistribution of work time in Canada. With a three-day work week, he has time for the occasional piece of freelance writing. He is the author of *Sharing the Work, Sparing the Planet: Work Time, Consumption and Ecology*, to be published in Autumn 1999 by Between the Lines in Toronto.

MIKE HENDERSON

Mike Henderson (MA, ACIB, DipFS, CertEd) lectures in Financial Services at Sheffield Hallam University and is currently researching into sourcing and inter-firm relationships in the credit card industry. He worked previously for National Westminster Bank for a number of years and has written texts on banking, accountancy and management.

WILLIAM B. IRVINE

William B. Irvine is an Associate Professor of Philosophy at Wright State University in Dayton, Ohio. He is a lifelong investor and has combined his interest in finance with his interest in ethics to write a number of articles on the ethical issues that arise in investing.

ROCKNEY JACOBSEN

Rockney Jacobsen teaches philosophy at Wilfrid Laurier University. His research interests are on topics in the philosophy of mind and language, and theoretical ethics. His recent publications on these topics can be found in *The Philosophical Quarterly, Synthese*, and *Philosophy and Phenomenological Research*.

DALE JAMIESON

As Professor in Human Dimensions of Global Change at Carleton College, Adjunct Scientist in the Environmental and Societal Impacts Group at the National Center for Atmospheric Research, and Adjunct Professor at Sunshine Coast University College in Australia, Dale Jamieson teaches courses in ethics and environmental philosophy. He has published extensively in journals and is currently completing a book on the philosophical dimensions of global environmental change. His homepage is at <http://www.dir.ucar.edu/esig/HP_dale.html>.

FRANKLIN B. KROHN

Franklin B. Krohn, a SUNY Distinguished Service Professor at SUNY/Fredonia, received his PhD from SUNY Buffalo. He is a recipient of the SUNY Chancellor's Award for Excellence in Teaching and the President's Award for Excellence in Teaching. He has published over 50 articles in academic journals.

CHRIS LAKHAN

Dr. Chris Lakhan is a professor in the School of Physical Sciences at the University of Windsor. He is a Fellow of the Royal Geographical Society, and also a Certified Environmental Specialist designated by the Environmental Assessment Association of the United States. He specializes in utilizing geographical information systems and remote sensing techniques to solve environmental and resource problems.

MARY SUE LOVE

Mary Sue Love is a doctoral candidate in management at the University of Missouri, Columbia, Missouri.

STEPHEN MAGUIRE

Dr. Maguire has taught philosophy and business ethics at Queen's University, Wilfrid Laurier University, and Carleton University. He has also taught Organizational Behaviour in the School of Business at Carleton University and in the Department of Management and Policy at the University of Arizona.

LAURA M. MILNER

Laura M. Milner is Professor of Marketing and Director of the Alaska Tourism Institute at the University of Alaska Fairbanks. Her specialities are international marketing and tourism. She has taught in 9 countries and has over 30 publications. Currently Dr. Milner is principle investigator of a grant project designed to foster international tourism to Alaska. Dr. Milner and her marketing students have assisted over 50 Alaskan businesses and organizations with marketing plans and research.

JOHN PALMER

Professor Palmer teaches economics at the University of Western Ontario. He is the president of the Canadian Law and Economics Association and has done a 17-part series on introductory economics which has been shown on educational television networks throughout North America. He has co-authored (with Paul Heyne) the first Canadian edition of an introductory economics textbook, *The Economic Way of Thinking*.

JEAN PASQUERO

Jean Pasquero is Professor of Management at the University of Quebec at Montreal (UQAM). His research focusses on the various dimensions of the business and society interface, including business ethics. He is a Past President of I.A.B.S. (International Association for Business and Society).

KENT PEACOCK

Kent Peacock is an Assistant Professor of Philosophy at the University of Lethbridge. He maintains active research interests in the philosophies of physics, biology, and the environment.

MICHAEL J. PHILLIPS

Michael J. Phillips is Professor of Business Law at Indiana University's Kelley School of Business. He received a B.A. degree from Johns Hopkins University, a J.D. degree from Columbia University, and LL.M. and S.J.D. degrees from George Washington University, and is a former editor-in-chief of the American Business Law Journal.

VAL PLUMWOOD (formerly Routley)

Val Plumwood is ARC Fellow at the University of Sydney, working in feminist, environmental, and social philosophy. Her best known work is *Feminism and the Mastery of Nature* (Routledge 1993).

TOM REGAN

Tom Regan is Professor of Philosophy and University Alumni Distinguished Professor at North Carolina State University. Among his many books are *The Case for Animal Rights* (1983), *Bloomsbury's Prophet: G. E. Moore and the Development of his Moral Philosophy* (1993), and *Ivory Towers Should Not a Prison Make: Animal Rights, Activism, and the Academy* (2000).

H. JOSEPH REITZ

H. Joseph Reitz was instrumental in founding the Center for Ethics and Values at Georgia Institute of Technology and, with Richard DeGeorge, founded the International Center for Ethics in Business at the University of Kansas. In addition to teaching, he has written five books and numerous articles in management, ethics, and human behavior in organizations. Recent publications investigate the relationship between ethics and the principles of entrepreneurial or-

ganizations. Current research interests are in the ethics of negotiations and ethical issues in telecommunications.

DAVID B. RESNIK

David B. Resnik is an Associate Professor of Medical Humanities at East Carolina University. He has published numerous articles in the philosophy of science and ethics, and is the author of *The Ethics of Science: an Introduction* (1998) and a co-author (with Pamela Langer and Holly Steinkrauss) of *Human Germ-line Gene Therapy: Scientific, Moral, and Political Issues* (1999). His research interests include ethical issues in science, biomedical ethics, and the philosophy of biology and medicine.

MARK SCHWARTZ

Mark S. Schwartz is a lawyer in the province of Ontario, who received his M.B.A. and Ph.D. from the Schulich School of Business, York University. He is a Research Fellow for the Center of Business Ethics, Bentley College. His research interests include business ethics and corporate social responsibility.

JAMES R. SIMPSON

James R. Simpson could not be located for biographical notes. At the time of publication in *Journal of Business Ethics* (1982), he was working in the Food and Resource Economics Department at the University of Florida.

JANG B. SINGH

Dr. Jang B. Singh is Professor of Business Administration at the University of Windsor. One of his areas of research is on ethical issues involved in the management process. He is co-author (with Ricky Griffin) of *Management* (Canadian edition, ITP Nelson), which is slated for publication in August 1999.

RICHARD SPINELLO

Dr. Richard A. Spinello is an Associate Research Professor in the Carroll School of Management at Boston College. He has written two books on computer ethics: *Ethical Aspects of Information Technology* and *Case Studies in Information and Computer Ethics*. He has also written numerous papers on business ethics and the ethical issues associated with information technology.

WAYNE STEWART

Wayne Stewart worked with Shell Canada in management of marketing, research and public affairs (integration of environmental concerns with business and development of relationships with stakeholders). He served as Executive Director of The Calgary Foundation, and consulted to the International Institute for Sustainable Development and the Canadian Council for International Cooperation. With Bachelor degrees in engineering, political science, and religious studies, and an MBA, he is now a graduate student in ethics at the University of Calgary.

EUGENE TAN

Eugene Tan graduated from the University of Western Ontario in 1992. At Western, he was active in environmental issues and served as the Environmental Issues Commissioner to the student government. He graduated from the University of New Brunswick Law School in 1995 and currently practises law in Halifax, Nova Scotia.

CHRISTOPHER TUCKER

Christopher Tucker is a Ph.D. Candidate in the philosophy department at the University of Waterloo. His primary interests are social and political philosophy, ethics, and contractarianism.

JAMES A. WALL, JR.

James A. Wall, Jr. is the past president of the International Association of Conflict Management and is a member of the American Psychological Association, Academy of Management, and Society for Conflict Resolution. Current research interests include dynamic bargaining processes, conflict resolution, and mediation. He has published articles in several journals and is the author of two books, *Bosses* and *Negotiation*.

GARY WEDEKING

Gary Wedeking teaches philosophy at the University of British Columbia. His main interests are in metaphysics, including the philosophy of mind, personal identity, and the metaphysical foundation of value. He has published on Locke's theory of personal identity and is co-editor with Andrew Irvine of *Russell and Analytic Philosophy* (University of Toronto, 1993).

from the publisher

A name never says it all, but the word "broadview" expresses a good deal of the philosophy behind our company. We are open to a broad range of academic approaches and political viewpoints. We pay attention to the broad impact book publishing and book printing has in the wider world; we began using recycled stock more than a decade ago, and for some years now we have used 100% recycled paper for most titles. As a Canadian-based company we naturally publish a number of titles with a Canadian emphasis, but our publishing program overall is internationally oriented and broad-ranging. Our individual titles often appeal to a broad readership too; many are of interest as much to general readers as to academics and students.

Founded in 1985, Broadview remains a fully independent company owned by its shareholders—not an imprint or subsidiary of a larger multinational.

If you would like to find out more about Broadview and about the books we publish, please visit us at **www.broadviewpress.com**. And if you'd like to place an order through the site, we'd like to show our appreciation by extending a special discount to you: by entering the code below you will receive a 20% discount on purchases made through the Broadview website.

Discount code: **broadview20%**

Thank you for choosing Broadview.

Please note: this offer applies only to sales of
bound books within the United States or Canada.

LIST
of products used:

5,620 lb(s) of Rolland Enviro100 Print
100% post-consumer

RESULTS
Based on the Cascades products you selected
compared to products in the industry made with
100% virgin fiber, your savings are:

48 trees
3 tennis courts

46,495 gal. US of water
503 days of water consumption

5,877 lbs of waste
54 waste containers

15,278 lbs CO_2
emissions of 2 cars per year

74 MMBTU
362,341 60W light bulbs for one
hour

45 lbs NOX
**emissions of one truck during 64
days**